THE REMOTE INTERPRETER

AN INTERNATIONAL TEXTBOOK

Volume 1

Foundations in Remote Interpreting

Katharine Allen, MA; Marjory A. Bancroft, MA;
Tatiana González-Cestari, PhD, CHI-Spanish; Danielle Meder, RID-NIC;
Caroline Remer, MA; Dieter Runge, MEd; Sarah Stockler-Rex, MA, CHI-Spanish

Contributing authors
Maha El-Metwally, FITI
Analía C. Lang, CHI-Spanish
Lyana Mansour, CHI-Arabic
Gabriella Maldonado, MSc, CMI
Monika McCartney, CoreCHI

With additional contributions from
Sarah Hickey, MA
Rocío Treviño, CHI-Spanish

For further information, contact the publisher.

Culture & Language Press
An imprint of Cross-Cultural Communications, LLC
10015 Old Columbia Road, Suite B-215
Columbia, MD 21046-1865
USA
+1 410-312-5599
info@cultureandlanguage.net
www.cultureandlanguage.net
www.interpretertraining-online.com

Graphic design
Goran Skakic

ISBN: 978-1-7332491-7-1

Suggested citation

Allen, K., Bancroft, M.A., González-Cestari, T., Meder, D., Remer, C., Runge, D., Stockler-Rex, S. (2023). *The Remote Interpreter: An International Textbook, Volume 1, Foundations in Remote Interpreting.* Columbia, Maryland: Culture & Language Press.

When citing information from one of the chapters, please use the following format: [Chapter author(s)]. (2023). [Chapter title]. In *The Remote Interpreter: An International Textbook, Volume 1, Foundations in Remote Interpreting* (pp. [page range]). Columbia, Maryland: Culture & Language Press.

Volume 1

Foundations in Remote Interpreting

Important Advisory

This book takes the perspective that the default role of the interpreter is to enable and support communicative autonomy, that is, the capacity of all parties in an encounter to be responsible for, and in control of, their own communication (García-Beyaert, 2015, p. 363).

The reason for taking this perspective is that the remote interpreting market today is heavily dominated by community (public service), legal and business interpreting, especially medical interpreting. Community interpreting in all its specializations encompasses medical, educational, social and human services, refugee, humanitarian and mental health interpreting, among other areas. Legal interpreting involves not only court interpreting but also interpreting for attorney-client meetings, workers' compensation, legal immigration services, insurance disputes, mediation and arbitration and more. Business interpreting for commercial and financial institutions typically involves customer service, for example, for banks, utilities, insurance, tourism and transportation.

However, if you interpret for other areas of remote interpreting, such as conference interpreting for high-level government or financial meetings (corporate or diplomatic negotiations, for example) or for military and other conflict zone interpreting, the role of the interpreter might shift. Discussions in this book related to transparency, impartiality and other typical ethical requirements might not be relevant for certain specializations. Even in certain areas of business interpreting, corporate requirements sometimes overrule ethical considerations related to communicative autonomy.

Be mindful that any aspect of this book that assumes the interpreter is there to enable communicative autonomy may not apply to you if you perform conference or conflict zone interpreting or any other interpreting that involves higher-level, sensitive negotiations.

Finally, as noted in the text, some of the technology discussed in this book may soon be superseded due to the rapid evolution of the field.

Checklist 1
Prepare for Remote Interpreting

This quick-start guide will help you make sure you have everything in place before your first session.

1. Computer and other equipment

- ❑ A computer (desktop or high-performing laptop)
  - a. **Recommended:** A computer that is ideally less than three years old with as much random access memory (RAM) included as you can afford.
  - b. **Recommended:** A computer system or in some cases, if permitted, a tablet that meets the needs and recommendations of the language services or organizations that you interpret for.
  - c. **Recommended:** A backup computer in case of a computer breakdown.
  - d. **Recommended:** A second monitor or device for accessing resources and/or communicating with a team interpreter.
  - e. **Avoid:** Older computers and low-end computers.

    Do not use a computer or mobile device that is outdated or does not meet minimum requirements.
- ❑ Quality audio
  - a. **Recommended:** A quality universal serial bus (USB) cable headset with a boom (integrated) microphone.

    Note: Expensive headphones with an external USB microphone require a more complicated setup and may not be needed.
  - b. **Recommended:** A second, backup headset.
  - c. **Recommended:** A microphone stand to maintain a separate microphone (if you have one) in a fixed position.
  - d. **Avoid:** Your computer's internal microphone or speakers.
    - i. Default computer speakers generally do not provide adequate audio quality; built-in microphones tend to pick up background noise and other auditory interferences.
    - ii. Sound that may be coming from the computers of other people on the call can create a feedback loop that sounds like an echo chamber.
  - e. **Avoid:** Any microphone embedded on the cord of a headset that physically moves around picking up and creating unwanted noise.
- ❑ Audio equipment management
  - a. **Recommended:** A sound check.

i. Verify how you sound speaking on a remote platform.

ii. Record yourself and play back the recording or get feedback from a colleague listening to you test your audio setup.

b. **Recommended:** A position close to the microphone but not too close.

i. If it is a boom microphone, place the stand at approximately 1-2 feet (30-60 cm).

c. **Avoid:** Speaking close to the microphone.

i. If you are too close to the microphone you cause feedback.

ii. Being too close may also allow others to hear you breathe, make "puff" sounds (plosives) or produce "hiss" sounds (sibilance) that may distract and disturb your listeners.

❑ High-definition web camera (HD webcam)[1]

a. **Recommended:** A quality, external webcam. Select the highest resolution you can find or afford.

i. HD is the minimum and is denoted as 720p at the low end and 1080p at the high end.

ii. Ultra HD or UHD is denoted as 4K and is roughly four times better resolution than HD.

iii. 8K is the highest level of resolution available today.

b. **Recommended:** Checking system settings.

i. Consult with any language services or organizations you interpret for to be sure your webcam meets their standards.

ii. Better still, if you can: check with a technical specialist to determine if your webcam is adequate for VRI, VRS or RSI.

c. **Avoid:** Low-quality or slow webcams.

i. Be careful: webcams built into laptops or desktop computers are often inadequate.

ii. Poor quality webcams may cause color distortions, video lag, and other visual problems. The video image they produce looks unprofessional.

❑ Second monitor or screen

a. **Recommended:** A second monitor or screen as a backup screen or to look up information and resources while you interpret.

i. Some interpreters, when working in a team, use the second screen to see their partner.

ii. A third screen is not usually needed—but some interpreters like them.

[1] Technically a webcam is needed only to perform VRI, VRS or video RSI. However, even if you perform audio-only interpreting, a quality webcam will make you look professional in any video conference meetings with current or potential clients. Look your best!

2. **Computer maintenance**

- ❑ Follow best practices for maintaining your computer.
  - a. **Recommended or required (depending on privacy laws):** Maintaining regular security and essential software and system updates for your computer, tablet or smart device.
  - b. **Recommended:** Consulting with the language services or organizations you interpret for, or with clients, peers or technical specialists, for guidance on best practices for maintaining your computer.
  - c. **Recommended:** Use caution when installing software that might affect your setup; consult a specialist as needed.
  - d. **Recommended:** Computer operating system updates.
    - i. Be aware, however, that these updates may introduce issues with certain software that has not been revised for the update.
    - ii. Check with software vendor frequently asked questions (FAQ) sites for guidance.
    - iii. Speak with any language services or organizations you interpret for, or with knowledgeable colleagues, for suggestions on whether it's safe to update your computer operating system.

3. **Office setup**

- ❑ For VRI/RSI: Keep personal objects and clutter out of sight.
- ❑ For VRI/RSI: Dress professionally.
  - a. **Recommended:** Clothing that is not bright colored (no neon colors) and does not have logos or symbols.

    Note: For signed languages, preferably use colors that contrast with the color of your skin for improved visibility.
  - b. **Recommended:** Adhering to the on-camera dress code of the language services or organizations you interpret for.
  - c. **Recommended:** Keeping a professional jacket nearby for short-notice, on-demand sessions.
  - d. **Avoid:** Clothing with complex designs or striking patterns (such as geometric patterns), which can create disturbing visual effects.
  - e. **Avoid:** T-shirts; big, shiny or dangling jewelry or clothing with holes.
- ❑ Ensure privacy.
  - a. **Required:** Absolute privacy.
    - i. To assure confidentiality and compliance with any relevant data protection and privacy laws, make sure that no one outside of your office door can hear or see you.
    - ii. Exception: Remote interpreting call centers will manage privacy for you.

b. **Required:** A separate room to interpret.

    i. Whether you are in a home office or a work office (except a call center), work inside a separate room and lock the door while you interpret.

    ii. Make sure anyone else located in your house or working in your workspace knows not to disturb you during your work hours.

❑ Silence all noise outside your office.

a. **Required:** Noise management.

    i. If you have young children or infants, animals or other sources of uncontrollable or otherwise random loud noise that can be heard during a call, arrange to have them out of hearing range for all your working hours.

    ii. Be aware that noise-cancelling headphones can help—but they cannot always drown out a crying baby or a loud dog.

b. **Required:** Reduction (as much as possible) of loud street noises (ambulances, traffic horns, construction, etc.) that might be heard during work calls.

c. **Recommended:** Quality noise-cancelling headphones.

    i. Consult language services, interpreters and other colleagues for their suggestions on which headphones to get.

    ii. Purchase the best noise-cancelling headphones you can afford.

d. **Recommended:** Installing inexpensive soundproofing materials (such as foam or even fabric on walls) if your environment might be noisy.[2]

4. Camera presence (for VRI, VRS and video RSI)

❑ Background

a. **Recommended or required:** A neutral, solid-colored background screen, whether it is mounted behind your chair or propped on the floor behind you.

    i. At a minimum, have a blank, neutral-colored wall.

    ii. If needed, hang a solid-colored sheet.

    iii. Determine if virtual backgrounds are acceptable with the language services or organizations you work for and, if so, which types of virtual backgrounds are accepted.

b. **Recommended:** Providing space (a few feet or a meter) between your body and the background.

c. **Avoid:** Leaning against a wall, which looks unprofessional.

d. **Avoid:** A background wall with scuffs, textures, fixtures, visible screws, etc.

e. **Avoid:** A background wall with clutter, photos, pictures or other personal items.

---

2 During professional calls, one language service has heard from the home offices of remote interpreters some startling noises, such as fireworks, roosters—and even street vendors selling onions.

- ☐ Lighting
  a. **Recommended:** Sit facing a window, daylight or a lamp. Otherwise, try to have a window, light or lamp to one side. Natural daylight is recommended when possible.
  b. **Recommended:** Experimenting to see how well-lit you are before every call: natural lighting changes with the weather and the time of day.
  c. **Recommended:** Having three sources of light; one above and slightly in front, and two equal light sources on either side.
     i. Having these is particularly important if you work night shifts or in darkness.
  d. **Avoid:** Sitting with your back to a window or bright light.
     i. Bright light behind you will reduce your video quality in many ways; it is a serious problem.
     ii. Backlight can make you appear fuzzy, seen only in silhouette, or unrecognizably dark.
     iii. Large shadows on screen.
- ☐ Center yourself.
  a. **Recommended:** Face the camera and take a center position in the view field. Sit up straight.
  b. **Recommended:** Look directly into the camera lens so that viewers feel you are addressing them directly.
  c. **Avoid:** Showing a ceiling, window, floor or hall.
  d. **Avoid:** Leaning to one side or looking down at notes in a way that shows the top of your head.
- ☐ Be professional.
  a. **Required:** Finish grooming yourself and eat ahead of time. You may *not* do so while interpreting.
  b. **Required:** Know the greeting script if you work for a language service and be ready to recite it sounding natural and professional. (For example, "Hi, my name is Lin. Kekchi interpreter #654321. How may I help you?")
  c. **Recommended:** Be well-rested so that you're ready to be courteous and kind.

5. Internet and speed

- ☐ Get reliable high-speed internet. You cannot interpret remotely without it.
  a. **Recommended or required:** Meeting the minimum internet speeds required by the language services or organizations you interpret for.
     i. Find out if other people in your household access the internet while you are interpreting.
     ii. If so, test your speed while they access the internet.

iii. If other users slow down your speed, you may need to purchase a plan with higher speeds to account for times when some or several other people are accessing the internet while you interpret.

b. **Recommended or required:** An internet plan that provides as much speed as possible.

i. Your available internet speed options will depend on the physical location where you live or work.

ii. If your speed is too low, you may have to find, and potentially pay for, an office where access to high-speed internet is possible.

❑ Have a hard-wired connection using an Ethernet port on your router.

a. **Recommended or required:** An Ethernet connection.

i. Wi-Fi may not be as secure, consistent or reliable as an Ethernet connection.

ii. Plug your Ethernet cable into your computer's Ethernet port (or use an adapter to connect it).

iii. If you are unsure how to do this, look up the details online or consult a colleague, language service, your workplace or your clients.

b. **Avoid:** Interpreting over Wi-Fi unless an organization you interpret for requires or approves it.

❑ Test your speed! Do *not* assume yours is fast enough for remote interpreting.

a. **Recommended or required:** Daily, or more frequent, speed tests using standard speed test websites. (They are easy to search for online.) Check your upload and download speeds and *write them down.*

i. Make certain your speeds meet the requirements and needs of your language service.

ii. Be ready to report your speeds to language services if they ask for them.

b. **Recommended:** Check your speeds on different days and different times of day.

i. Speed varies by internet service provider and due to many other factors.

ii. Check with your internet service provider to troubleshoot less-than-promised speeds.

❑ Run computer diagnostic tests.

a. **Recommended:** Running diagnostic tests built into your computer.

i. If your computer speed seems too slow on a particular day, try running the diagnostic tests.

ii. Do an internet search to learn how to run these tests on your type of computer.

b. **Recommended:** Do what the diagnostic tests suggest for improving your computer's system performance.

   i. If you still have problems, look up online other diagnostic tools that can help you.
   ii. For example, do a search on "how to speed up my computer."

c. **Recommended:** Get in the habit of regularly running diagnostic tests so that if you need to run one right before you interpret, you can do so quickly.

d. **Avoid:** Interpreting remotely if and when your computer or internet are running slowly.

- [ ] Have an alternate internet connection backup.

   a. **Recommended:** An uninterruptible power supply (UPS).
      i. A UPS is a small battery backup power supply.
      ii. It protects your computer and keeps it running, for example, in case of storms or other electricity outages.
      iii. The battery can maintain power and thus your internet connection for perhaps 30 minutes or more.
      iv. Plug both your computer and router into the UPS.

   b. **Recommended:** A second internet source in case of emergency and if no other source is available.
      i. For example, try tethering the connection to your mobile phone.
      ii. Be aware that alternate internet sources, such as phone tethering, might be too slow for remote interpreting: test them.

6. Resources

- [ ] Gather your best resources.

   a. **Recommended:** Checking with the language services or organizations you interpret for, other interpreters and any staff or colleagues for suggestions about online and print resources to help you interpret, such as glossaries and scripts.

   b. **Recommended:** Deciding in advance if you want to take notes on a notepad, a whiteboard or by typing them on a computer or tablet.
      i. Try out all three methods. Find out which one works best for you.
      ii. Check with the language services or organizations you interpret for to see if they have note-taking requirements.
      iii. Then purchase what you need for note-taking.

   c. **Recommended:** Setting up your printed and online resources in a way that is easy for you to access and use them during calls.

   d. **Recommended:** Use a second screen or second device (if permitted) to organize and access online resources during assignments.

Checklist 2: Setup and Tech Check for Remote Interpreters

Whether you are about to interpret for your first remote call or for the tenth or hundredth time, follow this checklist right before the call to be sure you're ready to interpret.

But first: go through your **Checklist 1: Prepare for Remote Interpreting** to make sure that you have everything you need in place. Then, before you start your interpreting work (or practice) for the day, go through this second checklist.

1. Turn on your computer

❑ Rebooting your computer before you start for the day can help it run faster and more efficiently. Computer speed and efficiency are *essential* for remote interpreting.

a. **Recommended:** Shutting down completely is better than clicking on "Restart." Shutting down helps to completely turn off applications that might slow down or interfere with your computer speed and efficiency.

b. **Recommended:** The older your computer is, especially if it is more than three years old, the more important rebooting your system will become as a matter of habit.

2. Check your speed

❑ Don't assume your internet upload and download speeds are fine today because they were fine yesterday. Test them again.

a. **Recommended:** Use any online speed test to check your speed and see if it meets your language services requirements.

b. **Required:** If your speed is too slow that day, *you can't interpret.*

i. Respect the minimum speed requirements of your language service.

ii. If your computer crashes while interpreting due to slow speed, you may lose all work with that client or language service.

3. Log in

❑ Log in to the remote interpreting web application (app) that you will interpret on.

a. **Recommended:** Use the latest version (download as needed) of the recommended web browsers, such as Chrome or Firefox. Before using a browser, check with the language service or client to know if they wish you to use particular browsers.

i. This platform may be a web-based app or one that is already installed on your computer.

ii. If you interpret directly for an organization, such as a school, hospital or government agency, for VRI or even AOI/OPI, you may be logging in to a webconference platform.

b. **Avoid:** Any browsers that your language service or organization tell you not to use.

i. For example, Apple Safari and/or Microsoft Edge might not be recommended by some language service remote interpreting web-based apps.

- ❑ As needed, verify your camera and microphone web permissions for that browser or app.
  - a. **Recommended:** If you are having trouble with your camera or microphone, do an internet search on "what is a camera [or microphone] web permission" and follow those instructions.

4. Get ready

- ❑ Open what you need.
  - a. **Recommended:** Open the online glossaries and resources relevant for the kind of calls you are about to interpret.
- ❑ Close out what you don't need.
  - a. **Recommended:** Close all unnecessary browsers and other applications and programs.
    - i. They can interfere with your computer's speed and efficiency.
    - ii. They can distract you.
  - b. **Recommended:** Close all applications in the recommended way (search online to learn how to do so: these instructions vary by device and application).
  - c. **Recommended:** Run your computer's task manager or activity monitor application.
    - i. Search online to find out how to do so.
    - ii. Find out which applications are still open and use the most computer resources.
    - iii. Applications that use the most resources can slow down your speed. Close them, if possible.
- ❑ Test your audio (and video) again.
  - a. **Required or recommended:** Make sure the headset you are using is selected for sound input or output, both on your computer settings and on the interpreting platform—and also, as needed, your browser.
  - b. **Recommended:** Ideally, test your audio quality on the same platform used by the language service or client you will interpret for. Adjust as needed.
  - c. **Recommended:** If applicable, test your video and adjust.
- ❑ Arrange your resources.
  - a. **Recommended:** Whenever possible, know in advance what types of calls or sessions you will interpret for and gather the most helpful resources for those calls.
  - b. **Recommended:** Have your note-taking materials (e.g., notepad and pen, a whiteboard or a tablet and keyboard) ready and close to you but not visible on camera.
- ❑ Have your introduction script and briefing instructions ready (may not apply to conference interpreting).
  - a. **Recommended:** Know exactly what to say when you start a session.
  - b. **Recommended:** Memorize that script until you know it perfectly (or know the elements to adjust depending on the situation).

    i. Consider having scripts on laminated cards to read; keep them close to you.
    ii. Having written copies of scripts can be especially important if you work for different agencies with different scripts.

5. Have water at hand

- ☐ You may need to drink during longer interpreted sessions or work shifts.
  a. **Recommended:** If you perform VRI, verify with your language service when and how you may drink water while interpreting, either on camera or by briefly turning the camera off, for example.
  b. **Recommended:** If you need to drink water on camera, have a neutral, transparent container with no logos.
    i. Use a straw.
    ii. Be ready to sip quickly and smoothly at appropriate times.
  c. **Avoid:** Drinking coffee, tea or anything but water on camera.
  d. **Avoid:** Using a nontransparent cup, colorful cup, a cup with logos, or any other attention-getting cup.
  e. **Avoid:** Interrupting any sensitive or important statements to drink water.

6. Be ready to go offline

- ☐ Have your exit script ready.
  a. **Required:** Use the language script provided by the language service (if any).
  b. **Recommended:** Whether you have to leave because someone else has left, or because the session is over, know exactly what to say.
  c. **Recommended:** Memorize that script until you know it perfectly.
- ☐ Whenever you take a break or end your last session of the day, go offline by closing your browser and the application.
  a. **Recommended:** At that time, also close any open applications in the recommended manner.
  b. **Recommended:** Reboot your computer as needed to keep it fast and efficient.

Foreword: How a Global Pandemic Transformed Remote Interpreting

This book is a hands-on guide to remote interpreting. There is an urgent need for such a book. Interpreters need to grasp the different types of technologies involved in remote interpreting, how to use them effectively and how to prepare for challenges in the field.

First, however, let's briefly talk about the event that changed the interpreting market as we knew it: the COVID-19 pandemic.

→ A new virtual world

The year 2020 was unique. Almost overnight, the global COVID-19 pandemic changed life as we knew it. In days, everything pivoted to the virtual world.

This transformation brought many challenges but also triggered innovation. It created opportunities. It led to a significant increase in digitalization on all levels of society and a spike in demand for any kind of technology that helped us all to live and work remotely—including remote interpreting.

Indeed, while it may have felt for many as if "real life" came to a halt, communication carried on. If ever there was a need for global cooperation, it was 2020. Yet cooperation across nations, and within them thanks to migration, can only be successful if it is facilitated by multilingual communication.

Since the onset of the pandemic, governments and international organizations around the globe have come together to discuss the latest findings about the virus and what safety measures should be implemented. Scientists from different countries soon collaborated to develop a vaccine—more swiftly than ever before in human history. Citizens of all language backgrounds frequently needed to receive updates about the pandemic. Healthcare professionals had to communicate with their patients yet reduce the number of in-person visits. Businesses moved to remote work but continued to serve their international clients and work with their global teams.

All of these changes led to a significant spike in demand for remote interpreting.

Although remote solutions had long been making their way into the interpreting market, before March 2020 the majority of interpreting assignments happened in person. Back then, remote interpreting was largely regarded as a solution in search of a problem.

At the onset of the pandemic, remote interpreting came to the rescue of the interpreting market. All at once, face-to-face interpreters in March 2020 lost almost all their work. More than translation, localization or other parts of the language industry, the COVID-19 pandemic had a disastrous impact on interpreting.

However, as a result of the boom in virtual interpreting technology, we have seen new platforms with new features emerge. Interpreting technology has also integrated with major video conferencing platforms, such as Zoom and Webex.

→ Is remote interpreting here to stay?

Let's answer that question right now: yes, remote interpreting is here to stay. Many who resisted remote interpreting before the COVID-19 pandemic have come to embrace it. Now that so many organizations have embraced remote interpreting and are well equipped for it, it is hard to go back in time.

Does this transformation mean the end of face-to-face interpreting? Of course not. There will always be scenarios in which it is preferable to have an interpreter onsite. For example, when dealing with vulnerable clients, in end-of-life cases, in mental health settings or when dealing with children, to name only a few examples, most people who need interpreters would prefer to see them face to face.

It is hard to estimate the market split between face-to-face and remote interpreting at this particular time. One source, Slator, suggests the split is about half and half.[3] In addition, the field is still in rapid evolution, as discussed in Chapters 1 and 2 of this volume. But it is clear that the interpreting market will never go back to the way it was before March 2020.

→ The future of interpreting

In the past, much of the resistance to remote interpreting stemmed from reluctance and fear, both from interpreters and clients who needed their services. Now what has happened cannot be stopped. Too much time and money has been invested in the training of remote interpreters and the development of platforms. Too many untapped markets and opportunities lie ahead.

There will always be a need for face-to-face interpreting, but today clients will be more selective when they evaluate which meetings are worth meeting in person for, to assess when the costs outweigh the benefits.

It is hard to predict what will happen next, but this is what we know.

- Thanks to the boom in remote interpreting, providers in this space are increasingly receiving requests from clients and industry segments that have never used interpreting services before.
- These requests will expand the market for interpreting services and also continue to change the market as new types of meeting requests need to be accommodated.
- Language service providers, tech providers and interpreters who want to succeed in the interpreting market of the future need to be agile and ready to embrace their clients' changing needs.
- The future of interpreting for business meetings, conferences and events will be hybrid—a trend that is already growing in the industry. What this means is that we will see more events that are hosted both onsite and remote, giving participants the option to either travel to the location or join the event from home. For interpreting providers, this means a more complex setup.

---

[3] Retrieved from: https://slator.com/interpreting-services-and-technology-report/

→ Machine interpreting

Machine interpreting is a controversial topic. For a long time, few people in the language industry took machine interpreting seriously. After all, how can algorithms replace interpreters? In machine translation, post-editing by human beings is still almost universally required for professional translations. For interpreting, there is no time for human beings to correct the many mistakes of machine interpreting.

In addition, in sensitive areas, such as medical, legal and business interpreting, the paramount need for both accuracy and human context made machine interpreting unrealistic.

Historically machine interpreting was a misnomer: in other words, the acts performed by machine-interpreting software were really a form of speech-to-text synthesis followed by machine translation followed by text-to-speech rendering. Today, however, technology is improving quickly in the area of actual speech-to-speech machine interpreting. It will be interesting to watch these developments unfold.

Yet even 20 years ago, many people who did not grasp the complexities of interpreting used basic tools of machine translation to replace interpreting. That trend continues. Many easily available tools exist, such as Google Translate.

This trend was and remains risky or even dangerous in certain contexts (such as legal, military or medical interpreting or interpreting for any sensitive meeting). Today, however, enough progress has been made to improve the quality of machine interpreting that these solutions will increasingly enter the market. That is the reality. Some doctors are using it. Teachers are using it. It will not go away.

At first, machine interpreting seems likely to come in for the more low-risk assignments in areas that previously either involved no—or little—interpreting. For instance, machine interpreting is coming into more frequent use at hotel receptions and in cabs and also at the triage stage in a hospital, before the actual interpreter arrives for the consultation. What is certain is that machine interpreting will not replace remote interpreters in the near future.

→ Where next?

Since March 2020, the interpreting industry has engaged in nonstop change. It was stressful; it was scary; it was exciting. Interpreting services changed their business models, added new platforms and features and restructured their operations. They worked on integrations. Demand fueled innovation.

Interpreters adapted to the challenges and the new technology. If they had never worked as remote interpreters, most of them began to do so in 2020.

Coming out of all these changes, language services and interpreters are better set than ever before to meet the increasingly complex demands of their clients. No matter what the future of the interpreting market looks like, what the pandemic has shown us is that remote interpreting is an extremely resilient and agile segment of the language services industry.

Remote interpreting is here to stay and grow. It has transformed the world of interpreting.

Preface

A quote from former U.S. president Theodore Roosevelt has always stayed with me. Roosevelt said, "People don't care how much you know until they know how much you care."

The first thing I need to do is tell you is that this book and training program is a love letter to you, the interpreter.

Let me explain.

This book was planned and designed as a comprehensive, two-volume textbook. It can support training programs and university courses and serve as a multidisciplinary resource guide for the professional development of remote interpreters.

Yet it is also completely a labor of love.

Each author on *The Remote Interpreter* writing team has a passion for interpreter training and professional development. We are all deeply invested in interpreting on a professional and personal level. We were united in the development of this book by a shared calling to create a book and training program to support you—and hopefully inspire you—as you navigate your career in remote interpreting.

It was clear from the outset that a multidimensional book like this would need to draw on a broad spectrum of experience and expertise. The collective experience from each of the authors covers all key domains of interpreting. The authors and contributors have a variety of interdisciplinary backgrounds: some are certified instructional designers and educational technologists; others are certified interpreters, interpreter trainers or interpreting software designers and developers.

This book draws from research and information previously published by Cross-Cultural Communications (under its Culture & Language Press imprint) in community and medical interpreting. The book also addresses new and exciting research and development in this profession across many software platforms and within all specializations of interpreting.

The book includes information, instruction and inspiration distilled from many hours of interviews and discussions with experts and working practitioners from all over the world and in all areas of remote interpreting.

Given the recent explosive growth of the field, due in great part to the COVID-19 pandemic, this book had to carefully ensure that the content was fresh and on point. To say that remote interpreting is a dynamic, rapidly evolving profession would be a huge understatement. The speed of ongoing innovation and evolution in the field made choosing final content for each chapter a constantly moving target.

The writing of this book began shortly before the advent of the COVID-19 pandemic. An unprecedented global human event, the pandemic proved a colossal impetus for the increased demand for remote interpreting and its feverish growth.

The COVID-19 pandemic transformed remote interpreting. Remote interpreting transformed the profession. The world of interpreting will never be the same.

This demand for remote interpreting has put a new spotlight on its global importance. We hope this book will help you grow and succeed in this dynamic, rewarding and important career path. Remote interpreting is accelerating each day in demand and importance. Opportunities are everywhere.

If you've ever had any previous doubts about whether you can make a career in remote interpreting, be sure that you can. Thank you for entering the field! Your services are needed now more than ever.

But who are the book's authors? And how did this book get started?

I am Dieter Runge, a cofounder of Boostlingo, a language technology and software company. It provides a remote interpreting platform available around the world to language services and interpreters.

I was also the first author whom Cross-Cultural Communications (CCC) engaged to write this textbook. In fact, I told CCC we urgently needed a textbook like this one! Here is the backstory.

My career in language technology began in 2005 at Lionbridge Technologies, where I worked as a software localization program manager supporting localization projects at enterprise technology accounts, such as Microsoft and Google and Apple.

Since then, I have worked at several language technology companies, with positions in research, production and development, sales and marketing and strategic business planning and operations. I have worked at some of the largest language companies and small to midsize language services. I've worked at agencies throughout the U.S., in Europe and in the Asia-Pacific region.

I have seen the growing need for remote interpreting. But throughout my career, I also noticed one consistent point at each language organization I've ever worked for: how deeply challenging management of interpreting services seemed to be for everyone—both for agencies and the interpreters who interacted with them.

More important, I noticed the fragmented use of software technology across agencies. No one platform stood out as the standard platform for remote interpreters.

Here was an opportunity for fresh innovation. The goal was to develop a more accessible interpreting software platform. Ideally, all interpreters and the agencies they worked for could use and access that platform together.

My adventures in the language service industry led to forming a startup technology company with other tech entrepreneurs to focus on the technology needs of interpreters and interpreting agencies. That's how Boostlingo was born.

In the process of growing Boostlingo, I began to realize another important gap in the system: the lack of support and training available to interpreters everywhere who wanted to develop their knowledge and skills in remote interpreting. Most of what existed up until recently appeared to be private, proprietary training programs provided by a handful of interpreting companies for their own employees.

Fast-forward a year. It was my good fortune (or destiny, as I'd like to believe) to be introduced to Marjory Bancroft of Cross-Cultural Communications at the 57th annual American Translators Association conference in San Francisco, California, in November 2016. This was the first year of Boostlingo's existence, which had barely begun assembling the Boostlingo Professional Network of Interpreters. Boostlingo was trying to grasp the training and certification options available for remote interpreters.

I was curious how interpreters were learning to adapt their skills to the virtual world. I had been tipped off by Katharine Allen (more about her shortly) that Marjory Bancroft was the best possible source to consult because of her experience and success as a book writer, editor and publisher in the field!

Marjory and I had a quick chat about the state of remote interpreting. We agreed there was a huge gap in available instructional content. We knew of no substantial public training programs, video tutorials, textbooks or training manuals on remote interpreting. This would not do!

I think I said, "Marjory, you know someone really needs to write this book!" And she looked at me…and I looked at her…and she said something to the effect of, "Well, *it sure won't write itself*!"

It became quickly clear how much needed to be researched, developed and written for a book of this scope. It would require a heavy lift from specialists in all areas of remote interpreting. We started putting out inquiries to find our core writing team.

With some good luck, we began to assemble the team. On the Boostlingo side, the choice was clear. I recruited Caroline Remer, who joined Boostlingo in 2017 to take on the language access department, who created our global vendor management programs and became our resident interpreter community champion and liaison. Caroline has been trailblazing since our early days. She has facilitated all Boostlingo remote interpreting webinars, guest presentations and conferences, and her passion for language and interpreting at Boostlingo is a constant inspiration and recharge for me. Today she is the vice president of language access.

Next, Marjory recruited Tatiana González-Cestari and Sarah Stockler-Rex, two seasoned remote interpreters, trainers, language access advocates and senior language service management professionals at the well-known medical interpreting service, My Accessible Real-Time Trusted Interpreter (MARTTI), now part of UpHealth. They were both keenly interested in applying their vast knowledge to building content and curriculum about remote interpreting. Tatiana and Sarah bring unique perspectives to the interpreting world from their respective academic and research backgrounds. Tatiana is a trained pharmacist with a PhD in pharmacology; she is also a researcher, professor and remote interpreter. Sarah holds a master of arts degree in applied linguistics with a specialization in language testing. She has worked as a Spanish medical interpreter in both onsite and remote modalities.

Perfect timing! Tatiana and Sarah write from the real-world perspective of the practitioner. Their hands-on experience resonates throughout this book. So much of what they have written has helped me organize my own thoughts around how technology can more effectively support interpreters, a key theme throughout this book. Their attention to the details of remote interpreting best practices and skills has imbued me with a deeper understanding and appreciation of the unique challenges and requirements for successful remote interpreting.

All of us feel deeply grateful and fortunate that Katharine Allen joined the team. A national thought leader, author, trainer, conference and keynote presenter and curriculum specialist in the field, she is familiar to many. As copresident of InterpretAmerica for a decade, she has also been a tireless advocate for best practices in remote interpreting.

Katharine is a senior interpreter who holds a master's degree in interpreting and translation. She has contributed to several critical books about community, medical and trauma-informed interpreting. Katharine is also the coauthor of a comprehensive training program and manual for indigenous language interpreting.

Another key author, Danielle Meder, came to this team with expertise in highly specialized areas of remote interpreting and in-depth interpreting experience as a sign language interpreter. Danielle is an active, nationally certified American Sign Language interpreter and interpreter trainer. Like Tatiana and Sarah, she is deeply connected to the remote interpreter's daily experience, and that experience constantly informs this textbook.

Danielle came to the team initially from United Language Group, where she oversaw interpreter training and client education programs. Danielle has since joined Tatiana and Sarah at UpHealth as a director of organizational quality. Danielle cares deeply about bringing spoken and sign language interpreters close together to share their wealth of knowledge and experience. Her passion for language access, quality interpreting and expert training makes her a valuable asset to the field. Danielle also spurred on the rest of us. Every book writing team needs someone like Danielle. I don't see how books ever get finished otherwise.

This textbook evolved with additional contributions and important research, data and perspective provided by a number of amazing contributing authors. I would personally like to highlight Maha El-Metwally, a conference interpreter and trainer in the UK, and Sarah Hickey, vice president of research at Nimzdi Insights, for their individual contributions (Volume 2, Chapter 3, on conference remote interpreting in the case of Maha, and timely, in-depth edits and additions in the Foreword, Chapters 1 and 2 from Sarah) as well as their invaluable insights and perspectives.

We are indebted to Rocío Treviño for her help with the Self-Evaluation Tool in Chapter 5 and to Gabriella Maldonado for her work on Chapter 4 of the forthcoming Volume 2. We are also grateful to Lyana Mansour and Monika McCartney for their generous contributions to Volume 1, Chapter 7, and the inimitable, dynamic, inspiring interpreter and trainer, Analía C. Lang, for her significant input in Volume 1, Chapter 8.

You will see quotes, guidance and anecdotes throughout the book from experts and specialists across the field, many of whom generously allowed us to interview them about the state of the remote interpreting field. We are profoundly thankful for their contributions. They have enriched the book immeasurably.

I personally feel blessed to be in a team of such talented, passionate authors. Collaborating on this book was an intense experience. It created a bond fueled by a collective sense of urgency and the goal of providing a rich and meaningful learning experience for you, the interpreter.

We hope our intention shines throughout the two volumes of this book. We were on a mission to make sure that we covered every topic you needed, as clearly as possible. Each of us has taken the time to review, edit and support one another across all chapters in both volumes.

Our greatest concern was always that this book be as clear, comprehensive, complete and up to date as humanly possible. We wanted to deliver a book that had all the important information that the remote interpreter needs to know now and also help keep you vigilant and prepared for the foreseeable future as the field evolves. May this book guide you along your career path, no matter where you may be in your journey as a remote interpreter.

Finally, no gift is ever complete without a dedication. This book was inspired by and written for interpreters everywhere. Interpreting is one of the most critical and universal ways to facilitate access to community services. It provides a pathway to a higher quality of life. Today's tools and technologies are constantly improving and will ensure even greater language access over time. The opportunities for the remote interpreter increase daily as the world embraces remote communication, a way of life that is not possible without you, the remote interpreter.

This book is for and about you!

On behalf of Marjory, Katharine, Caroline, Tatiana, Sarah, Danielle and all the others who have contributed to the creation of this book, I am thrilled to present our gift to you and the field: *The Remote Interpreter*.

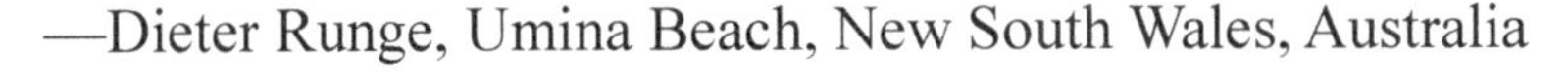

—Dieter Runge, Umina Beach, New South Wales, Australia

Umina Beach, Australia. Credit: Dieter Runge

Acknowledgments

We, the authors, could not have completed this project without the support of our families and close colleagues. Thank you for the unconditional love and patience!

It took an international team of contributors to create *The Remote Interpreter*, Volumes 1 and 2. We would like to extend special thanks and acknowledgment to all who passionately provided "food for thought," content, interviews, editing, feedback, quotes, data, designs and images:

Ken Anders, Piedmont Global Language Solutions
Otisha Ayala-Faya, A Voice
Aimee Benavides, Agro Translator and T.E.A. Language Solutions
Renato Beninatto, Nimdzi Insights
Naomi Bowman, DS-Interpretation
Garrett M. Bradford, Freelance Interpreter
Brian D'Agostino, Boostlingo
Ruth De Jesús, Mano a Mano
Maha El-Metwally, Cultural Bridges
Florian Faes, Slator
Bryan Forrester, Boostlingo
Monica Gallego, Mano a Mano
Olena Hart, Immigrant Platform and UpHealth Inc.
Sarah Hickey, Nimdzi Insights
Tamber Hilton, T.E.A. Language Solutions
Jessica Howard, Certified ASL Interpreter
Amy Jendrek, Freelance Interpreter
Shashiprabha Jinathissa, Freelance Graphic Designer
Nataly Kelly, HubSpot
Katty Kauffman, Conference and Court Interpreter
Analía Lang, Certified Spanish Interpreter and Trainer
Elena Langdon, Interpreter and Training Expert
Sergio Llorian, VoiceBoxer (now BoostEvents)
Daniel Maciel, String & Can
Gabriella Maldonado, UpHealth Inc.
Marina Malkova Mistral, Freelance Interpreter
Lyana Mansour, UpHealth Inc.
Romina Marazzato Sparano, Plain Language Association International
Monika McCartney, UpHealth Inc.
Laura Molinari, Freelance Interpreter

Kerry Moreno, UpHealth Inc.
Michael Nemarich, NAATI
Ernest Niño-Murcia, T.E.A. Language Solutions
Andy Panos, UpHealth Inc.
Melinda Paras, Paras and Associates
Mireya Pérez, Brand the Interpreter
Hélène Pielmeier, CSA Research
Conor Power, Interpreter Intelligence (now Boost | IMS)
Kirsten Riley, UpHealth Inc.
Sal Sferlazza, NinjaOne
Barry Slaughter Olsen, Conference Interpreter and Industry Expert
Andrew Smart, Slator
Sonja Swenson, Freelance Interpreter
Rocío Treviño, Boostlingo
Jesse Tomlinson, Tomlinson Translations
Samuel Williams, Williams Creatives
Simon Williams, Williams Creatives

...and all other colleagues who contributed to this project in one way or another.

Equally important, we would like to thank those who supported the authors' long hours of brainstorming, researching, writing, editing and creating content.

Last, but certainly not least, we extend our immense gratitude to UpHealth Inc., Boostlingo, and Cross-Cultural Communications, who recognized the industry's need for this textbook and spearheaded its creation by providing vital human and financial resources required to make it a reality.

Introduction

→ Purpose of this textbook

The purpose of this textbook is to equip interpreters to perform professional remote interpreting. Whether you are a new or experienced interpreter, and even if you already interpret over the phone or on video, this comprehensive textbook will guide you through what you need to know, learn and practice to become a remote interpreter at a highly professional level.

The two volumes of this book will walk you through the technology, skills, protocols, ethical considerations and best practices in the field and also its most important specializations, including business, conference, educational, legal and medical remote interpreting.

Although most of the authors are based in the United States, this book aims to build a foundation for the education and training of remote interpreters around the world. You will find many practical tips, examples, best practices, suggested scripts, activities and resources.

This book was written by seven specialized and credentialed authors and five highly qualified contributing authors, including two international experts, based on content that is informed by extensive research, data, interviews and communication with specialists around the world.

→ Audience

This book is intended for the training and education of remote interpreters who work anywhere in the world. It will also support trainers of interpreters, educators, language service coordinators, staff and others who work with remote interpreters.

While many examples in this book are drawn from remote interpreting in the U.S., the text as a whole is also intended to support interpreters who work in other countries as well as those who may live and work in one country but provide interpreting services for other countries.

The content of this book spans many specializations. It addresses both spoken and sign language interpreters. It reviews and discusses general and specific requirements for remote interpreting, including relevant laws and best practices that affect or govern remote interpreting services.

The book is also aimed at staff in language services around the world, particularly those who coordinate interpreting services, train interpreters or work in quality assurance. Government agencies, schools, refugee resettlement groups and nonprofit human service organizations that support immigrants and refugees or the Deaf and Hard of Hearing, and any other organizations that work with interpreters, may also find this book useful.

→ The focus of this textbook

This is the first comprehensive textbook that focuses solely on how to interpret remotely. It does not discuss how to perform face-to-face interpreting.

Volume 1 provides general information about how to perform the work. Volume 2 addresses how to work in specific areas of the field, such as remote simultaneous interpreting, various specializations of remote interpreting and relay and team interpreting.

→ How to use this textbook

This textbook is designed for self-study and for use in multiple types of trainings. Its content can support training modules (for example, 1 to 4 hours per module), short-course training programs (for example, 40 to 100 hours) and university and college programs lasting one semester or more. It can be used in several ways.

- As a training manual to support short-course programs.
- As a textbook for reference or class use in universities, colleges and other institutions of higher education.
- To assist language services of any size (from small hospital or school-based interpreter services to multinational interpreter call centers) in training, continuing education and quality assurance programs.
- For self-study.
- For independent interpreter trainers who need a curriculum and textbook for their training programs.
- To support the development of online training for remote interpreters.
- As a source of role plays, activities and exercises to explore and practice remote interpreting.

To earn an online training certificate for the self-paced program based on this book, **The Remote Interpreter Online**, go to www.interpretertraining-online.com.

→ Ethics and standards

It is particularly important to note that, depending on where you work and whom you work for, expectations and ethical requirements for remote interpreters can vary widely. This is especially true if you work in multiple specializations or across national borders.

To address that challenge, this book offers practical guidance in Chapter 6 to help interpreters make decisions about which ethical principles and specific code of ethics to apply to guide their performance in any remote assignment. This guidance is based on an up-to-date review of over 200 codes of ethics from around the world, providing a unique resource to the profession. It also explores how to address ethical concerns or requirements regardless of the country where one works.

→ Sign language interpreters

This textbook is coauthored by a U.S. nationally certified American Sign Language interpreter. It is also based on research and best practices for sign language interpreters worldwide. The authors hope that signed and spoken language interpreters will learn from one another—together, wherever possible—as these two rich fields have much to share with each other. This type of interaction also helps to promote understanding of how our skills and protocols are different or similar so that we can support and collaborate with one another as professionals.

→ Structure and content

This book is divided into two volumes. Each chapter, except Chapter 1 of Volume 1, includes relevant exercises and activities, including some role plays, that address the following content.

Volume 1
Foundations in Remote Interpreting

Important Advisory

Guidance about the limitations of this book.

Two Checklists for Remote Interpreters

Checklist 1: Prepare for Remote Interpreting

Checklist 2: Setup and Tech Check for Remote Interpreters

Foreword:

How a Global Pandemic Transformed Remote Interpreting

Preface

Why and how this book was written.

Introduction

The purpose, focus and structure of this book.

Glossary

A glossary of essential terms in remote interpreting.

Chapter 1 An Overview of Remote Interpreting

An introduction to the field, including OPI, VRI, VRS and RSI.

Chapter 2 Remote Interpreting Technology

A brief history of the recent evolution of relevant technology and what interpreters need to know to function effectively on remote interpreting platforms.

Chapter 3 Set Yourself Up to Perform Remote Interpreting

How interpreters can set up for a career in remote interpreting and for each individual session.

Chapter 4 Essential Protocols and Skills

How to adapt interpreting modes, skills and protocols to remote environments.

Chapter 5 Remote Interpreter Evaluation

An overview of a two-part tool to help remote interpreters evaluate their own performance (self-evaluation) and the performance of their peers and colleagues (through peer feedback).

Chapter 6 A Guide to Ethics in Remote Interpreting

An international review of ethics and standards for interpreters around the world and how to address ethical requirements when interpreting across specializations and national borders.

Chapter 7 Addressing Communication Breakdowns

An international perspective on how remote interpreters may address breakdowns in communication that includes easy-to-use strategies for intervening briefly and effectively.

Chapter 8 Professionalism in Remote Interpreting

How interpreters can demonstrate consummate professional conduct in remote environments.

Chapter 9 Language Access Laws and Language Policies

A brief international perspective on how important laws and legal requirements in some countries have helped to spur the growth of remote interpreting and what remote interpreters need to know about these requirements.

Chapter 10 Portfolios for Remote Interpreters

Strategies for interpreters to obtain relevant credentials to enhance their work opportunities.

Activities Answer Key

Suggested answers (subjective in some cases but provided by the authors) for chapter activities and exercises where an answer key is needed or may be helpful.

Bibliography

The Remote Interpreter Evaluation Tool

A two-part tool to be used in conjunction with the content of Chapter 5 for remote interpreter self-evaluation and peer evaluation, with scorecards.

Volume 2
Specializations and Advanced Skills in Remote Interpreting

Chapter 1 Remote Simultaneous Interpreting (RSI)

An overview of RSI on standard conference interpreting platforms and on videoconference platforms, such as Zoom and Webex.

Chapter 2 RSI Best Practices

Practical guidance on how to perform RSI, particularly outside conference interpreting, with a focus on current trends and makeshift solutions that interpreters have developed for performing RSI in challenging environments.

Chapter 3 Remote Conference Interpreting

A brief history and introduction to the field of RSI in conference interpreting as well as current trends in the field, including the role of international associations, such as AIIC.

Chapter 4 Healthcare Interpreting

How to perform healthcare interpreting remotely, with practical considerations and a focus on the U.S., where healthcare interpreting is an increasingly advanced specialization.

Chapter 5 Legal Interpreting

A glimpse at how legal interpreting is developing differently in remote environments in the U.S. and other countries and some of the challenges that remote court interpreting represents.

Chapter 6 Educational Interpreting

How the COVID-19 pandemic and remote interpreting have transformed the world of educational interpreting in the U.S., with implications for other countries.

Chapter 7 Interpreting for Business

How to interpret remotely for commercial entities, such as insurance, banking, tourism, utilities and customer service, including the importance of nonverbal cues, how to address common power dynamics and business-related confidentiality concerns.

Chapter 8 Team and Relay Interpreting

The special challenges faced by team interpreting, particularly on videoconference platforms, including makeshift solutions, and relay interpreting in remote environments for both spoken and signed languages.

Chapter 9 Self-care for Remote Interpreters

The urgent need for remote interpreters to engage in conscious, ongoing self-care due to additional stressors in the remote environment, the often inadequate breaks for interpreters, particular risks, such as frequent exposure to poor-quality sound, and how to develop effective self-care strategies and wellness plans for remote interpreting.

Bibliography

→ Contact the publisher and the authors

Please contact the publisher with your feedback and questions. We also welcome comments and suggestions for the authors that the publisher will pass on to them.

Culture & Language Press

An imprint of Cross-Cultural Communications, LLC

10015 Old Columbia Road, Suite B-215
Columbia, MD 21046-1846
USA
+1 410-312-5599

clp@cultureandlanguage.net

www.cultureandlanguage.net

www.interpretertraining-online.com

Glossary

Acoustic shock

Symptoms or a set of symptoms arising after exposure to sudden, loud, high-frequency, high-intensity or other disturbing sounds usually delivered through a headset.

Note 1: Symptoms may include headaches, ear pain, nausea, fatigue, vertigo, tinnitus, poor balance and anxiety, among others.

Note 2: Symptoms may arise after short-term or longer-term exposure to these types of noise but may be more intense and sustained after longer or more frequent exposure.

Ad hoc interpreter

Person who speaks or signs in more than one language and is requested to interpret but is not qualified to do so.

Note 1: Some organizations define ad hoc interpreters, for example: "An Interpreter who does not qualify as a professionally qualified interpreter, but who can demonstrate to the satisfaction of the court the ability to interpret court proceedings from English to a designated language and from that language into English, will be classified as a language skilled/*ad hoc* interpreter."[4]

Note 2: Ad hoc interpreters typically have not completed extensive formal interpreter training nor demonstrated interpreting or language skills, except in some courts.

Note 3: Indigenous language speakers or bilingual staff in many organizations will at times act as ad hoc interpreters.

Advocacy

"Taking action or speaking up on behalf of a service user whose safety, health, well-being or human dignity is at risk, with the purpose of preventing harm" (Bancroft et al., 2015, p. vii).

Anticipation

Ability to foresee or predict what will likely be said or signed as a continuation of an utterance.

Note 1: Previous experience or knowledge may enhance the interpreter's ability to anticipate.

Note 2: Anticipation should be used with caution due to the risk of rendering the message inaccurately.

Audio

1. Sound that is transmitted, recorded, received or reproduced.

Note: Audio can also be also defined as sound perceptible to humans (that is, sound transmitted within a certain defined acoustic range).

---

[4] Retrieved from: https://www.uscourts.gov/services-forms/federal-court-interpreters/interpreter-categories

Audio-only interpreting (AOI)

Interpreting conducted via a device or platform using only audio channels when the interpreter or at least one participant is in another location.

Note: Audio-only interpreting may take place using traditional technologies, such as telephone lines.

Authorized interpreter

Interpreter who has met the criteria to be listed on a registry of interpreters.

Note 1: Some public and private organizations, and many courts, have a registry of authorized interpreters.

Note 2: An authorized interpreter might have to complete interpreter training, orientation and language proficiency testing, but such requirements vary by region, organization or court system.

Business interpreting

Interpreting for commercial institutions and their customers or among multiple institutions.

Note 1: The term business interpreting has also been used to denote interpreting for large financial institutions.

Note 2: Most business interpreting that involves customer service, at least in the U.S., is performed by general (nonspecialized) interpreters or by community interpreters.

Note 3: Interpreting between two or more financial institutions for conference calls or high-level meetings is generally considered conference interpreting and may be referred to as financial interpreting.

Certified interpreter

Interpreter who has been assessed as competent in two or more languages by a professional interpreting organization or government entity through a reliable test that has been externally validated and that evaluates both knowledge about interpreting and interpreting skills.

Note 1: Certification exams typically include written and performance components.

Note 2: Interpreters are not usually considered certified by the profession if they are certified only by a language service, school district, hospital or other public or private organization.

Note 3: In the U.S., court interpreters, American Sign Language interpreters and medical interpreters have available certifications. In Canada, community, conference and court interpreters can obtain certification (including sign language interpreters). In Australia, certification is available for interpreting in general but also for healthcare, legal and conference interpreting, in spoken, signed and indigenous languages. The UK offers professional qualification for public service (community) interpreting that many might consider to be equivalent to certification. In various countries in Europe, such as France, Germany, Italy and Spain, and across Latin America, a "sworn" translator or interpreter for the courts is legally accredited and authorized by the government in a process that in many ways parallels certification.

Cognitive load

The relative demand imposed by a particular task, in terms of mental resources required. Also called mental load; mental workload.[5]

Note 1: Mental demands can be fatiguing: "Task and environment factors impose mental load on the interpreter, who then devotes measurable mental efforts to perform the task" (Zhu and Aryadoust, 2022).

Note 2: The cognitive and mental demands of remote interpreting are frequently high due to the complexity and pace of the work in a remote environment.

Colocated

Condition of being physically located in the same place.

Note: This term is often used to refer to participants and interpreters who are located in the same room or building.

Communicative autonomy

"The capacity of each party in an encounter to be responsible for and in control of [their] own communication" (García-Beyaert, 2015, p. 363).

Note: This textbook takes as its most fundamental premise that interpreting supports, to the degree possible and relevant, the communicative autonomy of participants.

Community interpreting

"Interpreting…that enables people to access services available to society as a whole, and which they would otherwise be unable to access owing to a language…barrier" (ISO, 2020, 3.3.2).

"A specialization of interpreting that facilitates access to community services for individuals who do not speak the language of service" (Bancroft et al., 2015, p. viii).

Note 1: Community interpreting may involve a wide array of both private and public services, including healthcare, educational, refugee, faith-based and social services, among others.

Note 2: Community interpreting is sometimes referred to as public service interpreting.

Conference interpreting

"Interpreting…used for multilingual communication at technical, political, scientific and other formal meetings" (ISO, 2022a, 3.2.10).

Consecutive interpreting

"Understanding and reformulating a message in another language after the speaker or signer pauses" (Bancroft et al., 2015, p. viii).

Cultural mediation

Any act or utterance of the interpreter intended to address or clarify a cultural misunderstanding.

---

[5] Retrieved from: *APA Dictionary of Psychology* at https://dictionary.apa.org/cognitive-load

Culturally and linguistically diverse (CLD)

Characteristics of individuals from countries or cultures that may differ significantly from the dominant cultures and languages where they currently live.

Note 1: CLD individuals may need interpreting services to communicate with others.

Example: A monolingual Farsi speaker who moved to the UK from Iran at the age of 50 is considered culturally and linguistically diverse within the context of their new environment.

Note 2: The acronym CALD is also in use, particularly in Australia and New Zealand.

Dialogue interpreting

Rendering spoken or signed conversation between at least two people bidirectionally in at least two languages.

Note 1: Interpreting for a question-and-answer session is an example of dialogue interpreting.

Note 2: The typical mode of dialogue interpreting is consecutive.

Note 3: The term dialogue interpreting has varying definitions. For example, it may refer to community interpreting in some research publications.

Diplomatic interpreting

Interpreting for officials in diplomatic settings, which can include national institutions, international institutions such as the United Nations, UN system agencies, the European Union, and international or inter-regional associations or bodies.

Note 1: Diplomatic interpreting often involves interpreting for interactions with representatives or officials of foreign governments, both privately and at large international meetings.

Note 2: Diplomatic interpreting is considered a subspecialization of conference interpreting.

Direct client

Person or entity that engages a contractor to provide services without the involvement of a third party.

Note: For the interpreter, the entity might be a hospital, school, business or government agency that engages the interpreter without the involvement of a language service.

Distance interpreting

See **remote interpreting.**

Dual team interpreting

1. Act of interpreting for a session in pairs when the language pairs needed are different.

2. Act of working with another interpreter who works in a different language pair from the first interpreter for a session that necessitates both language pairs.

Note: Both interpreters must have the language of service as one of their working languages.

Example: When interpreting a conversation between a nurse who speaks English, a pediatric patient who uses ASL and a mother who speaks Italian, and assuming that a trilingual English/ASL/Italian interpreter is not available, then English<>ASL and English<>Italian interpreters are needed.

Educational interpreting

Subspecialization of community interpreting that facilitates access to primary, secondary and higher education for the purpose of facilitating communication between educational providers and students and their families and guardians who do not speak the language of service.

Note: "Educational interpreter" in the U.S. can refer to a sign language interpreter who provides communication access at school or in higher education for students who are Deaf or Hard of Hearing during classroom instruction, conversations with teachers or professors and other staff, and formal and informal educational activities, including assemblies, field trips and extracurricular activities such as clubs and sports.

Face-to-face interpreting

Modality in which the interpreter is physically present with at least one participant in the same location.

Financial interpreting

Interpreting for representatives and clients of financial institutions. See **business interpreting**.

Note: Financial interpreting may differ from business interpreting in that it is more often performed by conference interpreters and can involve more complex interactions (such as high-level business-to-business transactions and financial conferences) while most business interpreting involves customer service interactions.

Healthcare interpreting

"Interpreting…health-related communication between patients, accompanying persons and treatment providers, or administrators who do not use the same language" (ISO, 2020, 3.3.3).

Note 1: Healthcare interpreting can be performed in a doctor's office, a clinic, a hospital, a home visit or any other medical or healthcare institution, or via telehealth, where every participant is in a different location.

Note 2: Healthcare interpreting is also referred to as medical interpreting.

Hold time

Moments of downtime during remotely interpreted sessions when the interpreter is waiting on an active call.

Note: Many language services that offer on-demand interpreting have guidelines for a maximum time frame for the remote interpreter to wait, and steps to follow while waiting, such as muting the interpreter's microphone and pausing their video while no interpreting is taking place, accepted protocols that may help assure availability of interpreters.

Indirect interpreting

See **relay interpreting.**

Interpretation

Single act or instance of interpreting.

Note: *Interpreting* is used to refer both to the profession of interpreting and the act of interpreting in general. *Interpretation* refers more narrowly and specifically to a single act of interpreting.

Interpreting/interpretation

"Rendering spoken or signed information from a source language to a target language in oral or signed form, conveying both the language register and meaning of the source language content" (ISO, 2022b, 3.1.1).

Interpreting hub

Space that allows remote simultaneous interpreters to work in a team in the same physical location while being located remotely from the event they are interpreting.

Note: A hub provides simultaneous interpreters with an experience similar to working in an onsite interpreting booth when they provide remote simultaneous interpreting.

Language service

Entity that provides services that facilitate multilingual communication, such as interpreting, translation, transcreation and/or localization.

Note: Interpreting services may be delivered remotely or face to face by interpreters who are contracted or employed by the language service.

Language variation

Property of language that results in more than one way of saying the same thing.

Note 1: Users of the same language will use different words or signs, pronunciations and sentence structures.

Note 2: The variation could be a factor of geographic location, social class, gender, age and other demographic and socioeconomic variables (Dawson et al., 2022, p. 429).

Legal interpreting

Interpreting related to legal processes and proceedings, including but not limited to lawyer-client representation, prosecutor-victim/witness interviews, and law enforcement communication (Framer et al., 2010, p. viii).

Note 1: Court interpreting is one part of legal interpreting.

Note 2: Legal interpreting and court interpreting are often confused with each other; a common misperception is that legal interpreting refers only to interpreting that takes place outside the courtroom.

Medical interpreting

See **healthcare interpreting.**

Modality

Means of delivering interpreting services.

Note: Modalities include face-to-face and remote interpreting; submodalities of remote interpreting include audio-only interpreting (AOI), which includes over the phone interpreting (OPI); video remote interpreting (VRI); video relay service (VRS); and remote simultaneous interpreting (RSI).

Mode of interpreting

"Established method for the delivery of spoken language interpreting…and signed language interpreting" (ISO, 2019b, 3.4.11).

Note 1: The three widely accepted modes are consecutive interpreting, simultaneous interpreting and sight translation.

Note 2: The remote interpreter chooses the mode best suited to the encounter and the technology available.

Multimode interpreting

Interpreting in which the source utterance and the target utterance use different forms of oral and written communication.

Note: Multimode interpreting includes, but is not limited to, interpreting from a written text into a spoken target language (sight translation) and interpreting between spoken and signed languages.

Multitasking

Execution of two or more tasks at the same time.

On-demand interpreting

Interpreting that is provided upon immediate request.

Note 1: On-demand remote interpreting is common in community interpreting in the U.S.

Note 2: In on-demand remote interpreting, remote interpreters are logged on to a platform that allows those who need interpreting to connect to a phone number or tap on a screen to obtain the interpreter needed for the corresponding specialization and language pair.

Over the phone interpreting (OPI)

Interpreting conducted over a telephone line when the interpreter or at least one participant is in another location.

Note 1: OPI encounters may have all participants in different locations.

Note 2: The term OPI is commonly (if incorrectly) used to refer to other forms of audio-only interpreting (AOI) that do not involve telephones or telephone lines.

Participant

Any person for whom the interpreter facilitates communication.

Protocol

Accepted or established rule or set of rules to guide procedures and behaviors in any situation.

Qualified interpreter

Interpreter who has been evaluated as competent in two or more languages after meeting established standards for interpreting knowledge and skills but who is not certified.

Note 1: Many interpreters who are considered qualified but who are not certified or tested for language proficiency or interpreting skills may interpret in languages that are not commonly spoken and for which language-specific written or oral interpreting assessments are not available.

Note 2: Public and private organizations may have their own criteria to determine if an interpreter is qualified to interpret.

Note 3: Section 1557 of the U.S. Affordable Care Act of 2010 provides specific minimum requirements for healthcare interpreters to be considered qualified.[6]

Relay interpreting

Practice of interpreting from one language to another through a third language (Shlesinger, 2010, p. 276).

Note 1: Relay interpreting may be necessary if interpreters for certain language pairs are not available.

Example for consecutive interpreting: For a conversation between a teacher who speaks English and a mother who speaks Mixteco, when an English<>Mixteco interpreter is not available, at least one English<>Spanish interpreter and one Spanish<>Mixteco interpreter would be needed if Spanish is a shared language.

Example for simultaneous interpreting: For a German-speaking presenter at a conference, one interpreting team conveys the message from German to English and other interpreters for the conference interpret from English to Japanese, from English to Spanish and from English to Mandarin.

Remote interpreter

An interpreter enabled by communications technology who delivers interpreting services to participants in other locations.

Remote interpreting

Interpreting modality in which the interpreter or at least one participant is in another location.

[6] See Chapter 9 of Volume 1 for details.

Note: Telecommunications technology (such as videophones, telephones or other platforms) is needed to enable remote interpreting.

Remote interpreting platform

Software application that can host scheduled or on-demand interpreting sessions between an interpreter or multiple interpreters and participants requiring interpreting services.

Note: Applications can host audio-only or video-interpreted sessions; the remote interpreting applications may be designed to support remote consecutive interpreting, remote simultaneous interpreting or both.

Remote simultaneous interpreting (RSI)

Simultaneous interpreting provided through technology that permits the interpreter and any or all participants to be in separate remote locations.

Shadow interpreting

Interpreting only as needed while allowing participants to communicate directly with each other or through another interpreter.

Note 1: The term shadow interpreting and shadowing can have different or overlapping meanings in various interpreting specializations and in different parts of the world.

Note 2: The shadow interpreter, when not interpreting, remains actively engaged and ready to interpret whenever needed to assure accuracy.

Example: In U.S. asylum interviews, the person seeking refugee (asylum) status after arrival in the U.S. is required to bring their own interpreter to the interview while a shadow interpreter, known as a monitor interpreter in such hearings, listens in remotely to perform audio-only interpreting as needed, typically to correct errors made by the interviewee's interpreter.

Shadowing

Observing or listening to an experienced interpreter execute an interpreted session in real time in order to learn from the experienced interpreter.

Note 1: Shadowing may involve remote or face-to-face interpreting.

Note 2: In some cases, a shadowing session may be followed by a feedback or mentoring session between the two interpreters.

Note 3: Shadowing may sometimes be called shadow interpreting.

Note 4: Historically in interpreter training, shadowing or parroting often refers to repeating word for word (or sign for sign) in the same language what a speaker says (or signs) while the person is still speaking or signing. However, this book uses the word *parroting* to refer to this activity of repeating a message in the same language in order to avoid confusion with the term shadowing.

Sight translation

Oral or signed rendering of the meaning of a written text.

Skill

Ability or expertise.

Sound

Vibrations through materials, or through a medium, such as gas, a liquid or a solid, that result in acoustic waves perceived and processed by the human brain.

Source language

Language of the original message.

Note: Source and target languages may switch frequently in a conversation as the source language is the one in which the message is being spoken or signed and the target language is the one into which the message is being interpreted. See **target language.**

Speaker

1. Participant in an interpreted session who is speaking or signing.

2. Presenter at a conference or meeting.

3. Output hardware device commonly used to amplify sound (make it louder).

Strategic mediation

Any act or utterance of the interpreter that addresses a communication breakdown.

Note 1: A communication breakdown could be caused by environmental, linguistic, logistical, emotional, cultural, institutional, legal or other factors.

Note 2: The goal of strategic mediation is to restore the communicative autonomy of participants.

Note 3: Strategic mediation is transparent, brief and targeted; it does not violate ethical norms or the interpreter's role.

Summarization

Interpreter coping strategy in which only a condensed version or key points of a message are rendered into the target language.

Note 2: See dual team interpreting and relay interpreting for other forms of team interpreting.

Example: Two sign language interpreters work together while one interprets and the other observes, takes notes and assists as needed. The interpreters switch roles every 15 to 20 minutes.

Target language

Language into which a source message is interpreted.

Note: The source and target languages may switch frequently depending on which language is being spoken or signed (the source language) and which language the utterance is being interpreted into (the target language) at any time. See **source language.**

Team interpreting

Act of working with another interpreter who works in the same language pair in order to provide both interpreting support and linguistic assistance.

Note 1: Team interpreting traditionally refers to having one active interpreter and one or more interpreters in the support role. Interpreters take turns during simultaneous interpreting to avoid fatigue and support each other linguistically and logistically when not actively interpreting.

Therapeutic alliance

"Cooperative working relationship between client and therapist, considered by many to be an essential aspect of successful therapy."[7]

Trilingual interpreter

Interpreter with three working languages who interprets for users of all three languages, sometimes in the same session.

Note: In the U.S., this term typically refers to an interpreter who works in English, American Sign Language (ASL) and Spanish, generally working as either an English<>ASL or an English <>Spanish interpreter.

Turn-taking

Act of speaking or signing one at a time in a conversation or discourse among participants being interpreted consecutively.

Note: The interpreter may need to manage the flow to assure appropriate and timely turn-taking that supports accurate interpreting. For example, if participants speak too fast, do not pause for the interpreter to interpret, speak over each other or otherwise create a flow of communication that impedes interpreting, the interpreter will need to interrupt.

Variation

See **language variation.**

Video relay service (VRS)

Form of telecommunications relay service, funded by the U.S. government and some other governments, for those who are Deaf or Hard of Hearing and use signed language to communicate.

Note 1: Video equipment is used by the person who is Deaf or Hard of Hearing to communicate with voice telephone users.

---

[7] Retrieved from: *APA Dictionary of Psychology* at https://dictionary.apa.org/cognitive-load

Note 2: All participants are in different locations, and VRS can be used only when the person who is Deaf or Hard of Hearing is in a physically separate location from the person they are calling.

Note 3: Even if VRS is government funded, private companies provide the interpreting service and platforms and, in the U.S. model, receive reimbursement for minutes interpreted from the government. The person who is Deaf or Hard of Hearing can sign up with as many providers as they wish; they receive an assigned phone number for each platform and can place calls and receive calls via that phone number and platform.

Video remote interpreting (VRI)

Interpreting conducted over a video platform when the interpreter or at least one participant is in a remote location.

Note: VRI encounters may have all participants in different locations.

Chapter 1

An Overview of Remote Interpreting

Learning Objectives

After completing this chapter, the remote interpreter will be able to:

Learning Objective 1.1: Assess the impact of COVID-19 on remote interpreters.

Learning Objective 1.2: Identify key terms and developments in the history of remote interpreting.

Learning Objective 1.3: Explain general differences between audio-only interpreting (AOI), which includes over-the-phone interpreting, video remote interpreting (VRI) for signed or spoken language interpreting, video relay service (VRS) and remote simultaneous interpreting (RSI).

Learning Objective 1.4: Describe essential technologies and technology skills in remote interpreting.

Learning Objective 1.5: Plan the setup for a first remote interpreting session.

Learning Objective 1.6: Identify essential protocols and skills in remote interpreting.

Learning Objective 1.7: Review and discuss common specializations in remote interpreting.

Introduction

Not long ago, remote interpreting represented a small part of the language industry. For spoken languages, over-the-phone interpreting (OPI) was increasing rapidly. Video remote interpreting (VRI) was expanding more slowly but steadily. For signed languages, video relay service (VRS) was growing widespread.

Then the coronavirus disease 2019 (COVID-19) pandemic began, and the whole world changed.

The professional network LinkedIn reported that in March 2020 only "1 in 67 paid jobs in the U.S. offered remote work." Over a year later, that number was nearly one in six (Kimbrough, 2022). Many countries around the world saw similar increases in remote work.

Remote interpreting, like remote work in general, has expanded exponentially. Few see that trend reversing. It is here to stay.

As a result, remote interpreting today makes up a central part of the language industry. It is a modality used in every interpreting specialization and performed over a wide variety of platforms.

This two-volume textbook covers the field of remote interpreting as comprehensively as possible. By the time you finish reading it, you'll have the information you need to perform remote interpreting in nearly any specialization.

You'll learn about over-the-phone interpreting (OPI), video remote interpreting (VRI), video relay service (VRS) and remote simultaneous interpreting (RSI). You'll explore remote interpreting technology and find out what you need to do and plan for to begin a career as a remote interpreter, including how to set up your workstation at your workplace or at home and how to prepare for each session. If you decide to work at a call center, you'll have a better understanding of the setup there as well.

You'll be introduced to the protocols and essential skills that remote interpreters need to know well to work effectively. You'll have a tool for self-evaluation and evaluation by your peers, which are essential practices for improving your performance. Self-evaluation and seeking feedback are the hallmarks of a true professional.

You'll also learn the ethical requirements, standards and best practices for your work and how to conduct yourself professionally. You'll explore remote interpreting across various specializations, tackle the laws and policies that affect remote interpreting and learn how to build your remote interpreter portfolio of credentials. You'll find out how team interpreting and relay interpreting take place remotely.

Because remote interpreting adds many stressors to the work of the interpreter, you'll also learn why self-care is essential and how to engage in it.

This introductory chapter provides you with a broad overview of the field. It gives a general introduction to the history of remote interpreting and how the pandemic has transformed it, along with general information on OPI, VRI, VRS and RSI.

In short, Chapter 1 will paint a picture for you of the field of remote interpreting as a whole. The textbook will then explore each of these topics in more depth and detail.

Section 1.1 Remote Interpreting in the Time of COVID-19

→ Learning objective 1.1

After completing this section, the remote interpreter will be able to assess the impact of COVID-19 on remote interpreters.

→ Section 1.1 Overview

The COVID pandemic changed how most interpreters worked. The single biggest change was moving from face-to-face interpreting to remote platforms. Starting in March 2020, most face-to-face contracts and interpreting jobs disappeared in the span of a few short weeks. While face-to-face interpreting has recovered to some extent, remote interpreting is now widespread in all areas of the interpreting profession.

During the COVID quarantines, the majority of face-to-face interpreters around the world had to make a swift transition to a remote workplace. Those who already worked remotely saw their workload increase, and the work often grew more stressful.

This section offers you a glimpse into the lives of many remote interpreters in the two years after the pandemic began. This information is partly based on a series of interviews with remote interpreters who work across several interpreting specializations. These stories primarily feature interpreters in healthcare; the rest of this textbook will highlight how the pandemic impacted interpreters who work in other specializations.

Whether you worked remotely already or were new to remote interpreting, the COVID-19 pandemic probably had a huge impact on your work. COVID-19 represents a permanent before-and-after moment for remote interpreting.

→ Section 1.1 Content

Transitioning from face-to-face to remote interpreting

Here is the story of one interpreter who lived through the abrupt disruptions to face-to-face interpreting. She had to make difficult choices between personal safety and the emotional toll it took not to be able to provide services to clients in need.

This interpreter's story illustrates the struggles that arose at the beginning of the pandemic, when many service providers had to find ways to quickly learn how to provide interpreting services remotely. Meanwhile, those who still provided face-to-face interpreting, especially in healthcare, had to learn how to keep interpreters safe.

This story shows why the world of interpreting shifted almost immediately to remote interpreting.

> *I'm a medical interpreter working primarily onsite, and as an independent contractor, I work with several local agencies. And just like with virtually all other jobs, mine has also been affected by COVID-19.*
>
> *My schedule has always been unpredictable. However, starting in mid-March [of 2020], just as the first stay-at-home order was issued in my state, there was nothing but cancellations and no-shows.*
>
> *Then the appointments stopped coming. Although one agency was still sending me requests, they were mostly at the local hospital where all the COVID-19 patients were being taken at the time.*
>
> *Every time I received a request, part of me wanted to take that job—after all, I still needed to make a living, and this might be the only job I'd get that day. I also worried that if nobody was going out there to interpret, patients would be left without adequate language access.*
>
> *On the other hand, I was wondering whether that one-hour fee was worth the risk I was taking coming into the hospital when much was still unknown about the virus and universal mask wearing wasn't yet adopted.*
>
> *This dilemma became even more pressing the following week. An agency called me, asking if I could take a last-minute appointment for an MRI [magnetic resonance imaging] scan at a local hospital. As I arrived at the hospital, I put on a cloth mask a friend had made for me and headed for my destination—which to my utter shock turned out to be the COVID-19 isolation unit.*
>
> *The nursing staff had to wear HAZMAT-style suits and helmets with air pumps to enter the patient's room—and here I was in a handmade flowery cloth mask. In the end, even though a nurse found a face shield and a surgical mask for me, I didn't need them as the procedure was cancelled.*
>
> *This assignment brought up so many questions:*
>
> - *How do I stay safe when I'm working?*
> - *As a freelance interpreter, how do I make sure I have access to PPE [personal protective equipment], such as masks?*
> - *Is it irresponsible for me to keep taking onsite appointments and risk bringing the virus back to my family?*
> - *What will happen if I get sick?*
> - *And if neither I nor my fellow interpreters take that appointment, will the patient still receive interpreting services?*

Those few interpreters who continued to provide services on the ground in hospitals faced a new set of challenges. This same interpreter continues her comments on the next page:

The new reality introduced new challenges:

- *How do you socially distance yourself in a small exam room?*
- *How do you make yourself heard through a mask?*
- *What is a safe way to, for example, take a drink of water while out on assignments?*

There are no ready-made solutions, but luckily, interpreters are nothing if not resourceful and I have every confidence that, whatever life throws at us, we will find a way to keep interpreting!

The story above poses many important questions. Who is responsible for protecting face-to-face interpreters during a pandemic? Many interpreters reported struggling to get access to adequate personal protective equipment (PPE) and to be considered part of the healthcare treatment team. Meantime, many patients who needed interpreters at hospitals had to do without them while overwhelmed healthcare providers struggled to provide basic care.

Though remote healthcare interpreting services has existed for years prior to the pandemic, COVID-19 revealed gaps in healthcare system plans for language access as never before. As a result of these risks, challenges and pain points, not only in healthcare but also in schools, businesses, public services, conference events and more, overnight most of the world shifted to remote interpreting.

The emotional impact of the early pandemic on interpreters

Here is the experience of an interpreter in China who worked both face to face and remotely during the initial COVID-19 outbreak:

Writing at the end of week one of my social distancing period, I think I am finally able to calm myself down to write something about COVID-19. What do I know? What's going on?

The only thing I know [is] it started with a virus outbreak, now it is a pandemic. Governments announced shutdowns. A lot of people started panicking. I am among these people.

This interpreter's previous experience with having been so close to the severe acute respiratory syndrome (SARS) outbreak of 2002 helped her deal with COVID-19 in a specific way.

Early in January of 2020, I heard about people in China catching a kind of acute and contagious pneumonia due to some ferocious virus. I didn't know much about viruses (and I still don't). I didn't even know the difference between a virus and a bacteria.

However, I remember the SARS outbreak (2002–2004) in China. During that time period, I worked as a TEFL [Teaching English as a Foreign Language] teacher at a public high school in a small but affluent town in Guangdong province. We would always perform head counts in the morning and make sure that no one arrived to school sick. The school principal addressed this daily. Put the right measures in the right places. No quarantine was needed in our town. Lucky me, I was not in the epicenter of the outbreak. Before I knew it life went back to normal. I wanted to pat myself on the back—I have survived SARS.

Because this interpreter had survived an epidemic prior to the outbreak of COVID-19, it gave her a unique perspective on how different countries and organizations handle these severe and highly transmissible diseases.

> *Approaching Chinese Lunar New Year, I heard and read more about the contagious pneumonia, from WeChat messages sent by close family and friends living in mainland China. "No worries. Everyone's safe and sound and we don't go out at all."*
>
> *City by city, province by province, the Chinese government imposed lockdown and quarantine. The severity of the situation had surpassed SARS.*
>
> *Toward the end of February, I started reading more about COVID-19 through my volunteer translation work for a nonprofit organization. The health department of the city sent out notices about the disease and recommended self-care preventive measures. I asked, "Is it here yet?"*
>
> *Shortly after, I got to talk with people who were affected by COVID-19 while interpreting remotely. One Saturday I helped a health facility nurse check in on someone in self-isolation. Throughout the call time, no one mentioned COVID-19 or disease or even sickness. They talked about taking temperatures twice a day and the readings. The temperature was normal.*
>
> *Both parties were optimistic about the outcome. "Three more days and I am free," exclaimed the client. The nurse chimed in, "Yes, three more days and you can leave your house." It's quite a relief. I could feel the good spirits. I could even imagine the smiles they were wearing on their face after the call ended.*

The same interpreter goes on to discuss a session during the initial stages of the pandemic in a public university.

> *Another time, a university campus coordinator called in to ask for interpretation assistance. An international student was planning to apply for a special accommodation, which would help ease the emotional burden caused by the COVID-19 situation back home in China. The coordinator was very professional, caring and empathetic.*
>
> *The call lasted for an hour. The wonderful staffer made several calls on behalf of the student to assure the right appointments could be scheduled and good arrangements could be made as soon as possible. The student expressed the anxious feeling but felt grateful that someone who was a stranger a couple of hours before the meeting would go out of the way to help.*
>
> *This call ended but it left me feeling warm and fuzzy in heart. I felt lucky that I talked with warm and kind people.*
>
> *It is March now. The month is going to end soon. COVID-19 has officially landed in North America. The future is full of unpredictable factors. And many challenges are ahead. We may also see the good and the opportunities. We need to believe we are in it together. There is always hope. Hope gives you warmth. Do share the warmth whenever you can. After so much worrying and panicking, you can always do something. That is what I am thinking now.*

Clearly, the COVID-19 pandemic has had a deep impact. Remote interpreters have paid a high emotional toll. They have also offered invaluable support to their clients since the beginning of the pandemic.

Longer-term impacts of the pandemic on interpreters

Interpreters are dedicated, caring professionals. If the COVID-19 pandemic has brought anything positive to the lives of interpreters, it has shed light on the fact that we are all global citizens. We will continue to support one another as the world moves forward.

But what are the costs to individual interpreters? The publisher conducted an informal survey of a small number of remote interpreters in March 2022, asking the question: "How has COVID-19 affected you and your work life?"

The responses were a mix of negative and positive, with many citing financial loss and lower wages on remote platforms, mental and emotional strain, feeling burned out and experiencing vicarious trauma and burnout. On the positive side, interpreters shared feeling useful and valuing the ability to work from home, learn new skills and expand into new areas of the interpreting profession.

You can see from what the interpreters quoted below have to say that many experienced both negative and positive impacts during the pandemic.

- *The pandemic highlighted weaknesses and strengths, forced us to pause and value the normally invisible things.*
- *[It] extended and widened our interpreting capabilities as we transitioned to a new advanced level of interpreting (virtual/phone).*
- *The rate was way too low for remote interpreter in China. I am really regret to choose this career. I couldn't find nice employment because I live in a small town in southwest China. The biggest issue is the exploitation. Chinese agent tend to behave really bad in term of salary exploitation. I have to change my career despite of a hard turn.*
- *The pandemic has affected the usual lifestyle of the whole world in different ways. During the pandemic, I was an essential worker, doing much more, a lot of pressure, big responsibility to take care of others, and risking my own health at the same time, for my regular income, no incentives at all. So the pandemic was not bad at all for me because my duty helped with my family expenses covered.*

  On the other hand, the pandemic gave me an opportunity to find myself more productive and catch new challenges. Something new was born in me! And right now I am doing my last training and taking the final test in order to get my accreditation. In other words, the pandemic brought me an opportunity to continue my education.
- *I've been stuck in front of my computer for literally two years and I'm worn out!*
- *It has changed the entire scope of my position. I now manage a language service provider and fill another role as interpreting is now overseas call centers instead of trained in-person interpreters. I feel like my [onsite] position is becoming obsolete.*
- *I discovered lots of fantastic online resources and took the plunge and transitioned to RSI.*

- *I have a lot less work and often receive lower fees due to the shift to remote. While I enjoy the ability to reach people across the world at the same time, I would like to return to in-person work like conferences and business meetings. However, remote will likely remain in some form and fees will not rebound to what they were, to the detriment of our livelihood.*
- *I noticed that there was more flexibility and more resources than before. Some hospitals integrated microphones to their exam room suites to improve communication, there was a quick evolution to integrate interpretation when it wasn't available onsite.*

Most of these interpreters work in the U.S. Although their experience is anecdotal, their voices give us insight into the huge impact of COVID-19 on the lives of interpreters around the world.

It has been a rough road for many. Yet you can see from these interpreters' reports that their dedication and commitment remain.

You can also see why many interpreters who had never performed remote interpreting chose to switch to the new modality—not only to find work to replace lost face-to-face assignments but also to keep themselves and their families safe.

→ Section 1.1 Review

Each interpreter will have their own experiences resulting from the pandemic. Whether you continued interpreting face to face, began to interpret remotely because of COVID-19 or were already working remotely, you suddenly found yourself helping others during a time of profound crisis when you were experiencing uncertainty and change in your own life.

This section highlighted some of the enormous changes the pandemic brought to the work and lives of interpreters. It also showed the difficult, new and often transformative experiences that many interpreters lived through during this time.

Section 1.2 A Brief History of Remote Interpreting

→ Learning objective 1.2

After completing this section, the remote interpreter will be able to identify key terms and developments in the history of remote interpreting.

→ Section 1.2 Overview

This section introduces you to key terms in remote interpreting. It then provides a brief history of remote interpreting and its submodalities.

The telephone and video technologies that make remote interpreting possible originated in the 1920s and 1930s. Some of the earliest attempts at remote interpreting date from that time. However, modern remote interpreting technology and services really began with OPI in the 1970s, VRI in the 1990s and 2000s and RSI in the 2010s.

The pandemic accelerated the development of all kinds of remote interpreting, which now make up about half of all interpreting services provided.

As a remote interpreter, you will use the most current versions of the software and platforms that make OPI, VRI and RSI possible. Having a basic understanding of what they are and how they developed is important to your work. Read on for some fascinating history.

→ Section 1.2 Content

Key terms

Before diving into the history of remote interpreting, let's first clarify a few key terms.

Every profession has its own lexicon, that is, the vocabulary used to describe key concepts for that profession. Interpreting is a young, fast-growing global profession. Its vocabulary isn't fully established. Terms aren't always used in consistent ways.

As a result, a few important terms need to be defined for this section to avoid confusion. Those terms are *mode, modality, face-to-face interpreting, remote interpreting* and *specialization.*

Two terms that are often confused with each other are *mode* and *modality.* Both are critical to understand. Let's start with *mode.*

What is a mode?

The International Organization for Standardization (ISO) defines mode as an "established method for the delivery of spoken language interpreting...and signed language interpreting" (ISO, 2019b, 3.4.11).

A mode of interpreting is a way to convert or render the interpreted message. In other words, a mode is *how* you transfer the meaning of a message into another language. The main interpreting modes are consecutive, simultaneous and sight translation.[1]

- In consecutive interpreting, you render the message into the target language (the language that you interpret into) after the speaker or signer pauses.
- In simultaneous interpreting, you render the message *while* the speaker or signer is still communicating—with a slight lag.
- Sight translation involves rendering a text into another language, either orally or in signed language.

[1] Some specialists, especially in Europe, do not consider sight translation a mode, but most interpreters do.

What is a modality?

A *modality* is how an interpreting *service* is delivered. It is not about the meaning of the message but how the message is *sent* and *received.* In short, a modality is a means of providing interpreting services.

- Interpreting face to face is one modality.
- Remote interpreting is another modality, with four primary submodalities:
  - Over-the-phone interpreting (OPI)
  - Video remote interpreting (VRI)
  - Video relay service (VRS)
  - Remote simultaneous interpreting (RSI)

For centuries, *face-to-face interpreting,* also called onsite or in-person interpreting, was the only way interpreting was delivered. Interpreters had to be in the same physical location as the people they interpreted for.

The invention of the telephone, and later, real-time video communication, added a new modality: *remote interpreting.* Remote interpreting, which is also called distance interpreting—especially in Europe—involves interpreters who are not in the same physical location as the people they interpret for.[2]

Remote interpreting can be performed over the phone, on video or through a computer connected to the internet. Regardless of the technology, remote interpreting is simply a modality for delivering interpreting services.

Interpreting specializations

Finally, an *interpreting specialization* refers to a specialty of the broader interpreting profession. The primary specializations are conference, business, legal and community interpreting (including medical, social services, educational, refugee and humanitarian interpreting).

Legal interpreting includes court interpreting. In some countries, legal interpreting is considered part of community interpreting and in others it is not. Other specializations include military and escort or liaison interpreting. Any interpreter can work remotely or face to face in any specialization.

Now that these key terms have been defined, let's go on a brief tour of the history of remote interpreting.

---

[2] *Distance interpreting* is the term officially used by the International Association of Conference Interpreters (AIIC) and in European conference settings to refer to remote interpreting. AIIC, however, defines remote interpreting more narrowly in terms of remote interpreting where the interpreter has no direct view of the participants, yet it includes under this umbrella term not only audio remote interpreting but also VRI. The term *remote interpreting* is widely accepted in Europe and is the dominant term used globally. For example, a Google search for "remote interpreting" on June 28, 2022, yielded 232,000 results. A Google search on the same date for "distance interpreting" yielded 6,270 results.

The early evolution of remote interpreting

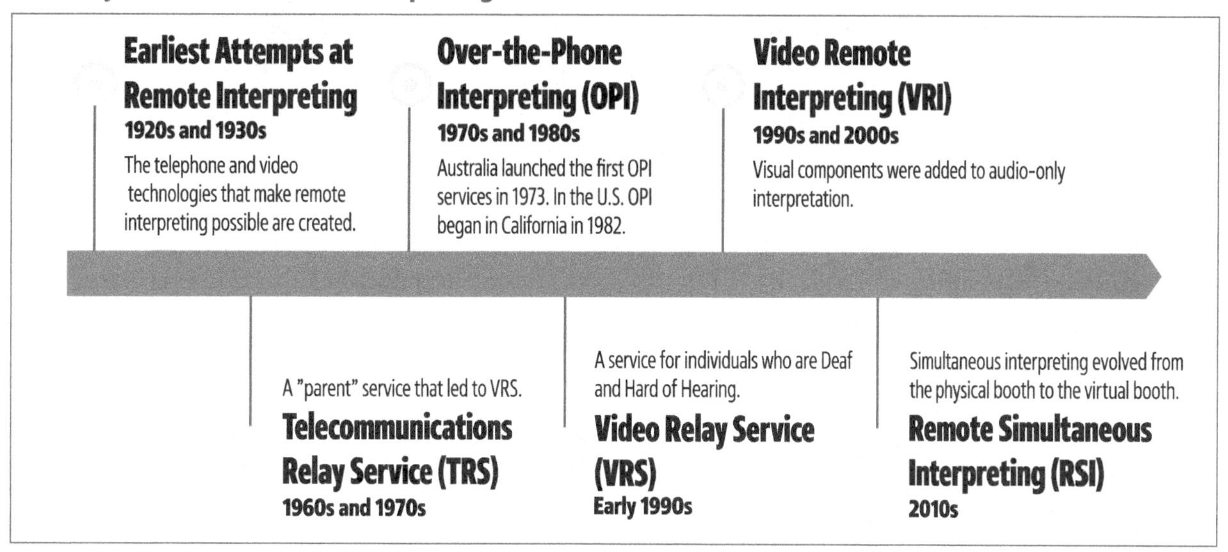

Figure 1.1: Evolution of remote interpreting[3]

Before languages were ever written down, we needed interpreters: that is, individuals who knew more than one language and could help different groups understand each other (Pöchhacker, 2016, p. 9).

However, interpreting was not seen as its own profession until less than a century ago (Gaiba, 1998, p. 19). The modern interpreting profession may be recent, but it is amazing to be part of a long tradition of interpreters that stretches back thousands of years!

Until the 1920s, all interpreting was performed face to face. Then cutting-edge developments based on telephone technology led to the first instances of the interpreter being removed from sitting or standing directly alongside the speakers to being located somewhat at a distance, although still in the same room (Flerov, 2013). Indeed, it was initially referred to as *telephone interpreting* because the first simultaneous interpreting technology was created using telephone equipment available at that time.[4]

This new technology was used only intermittently until the historic Nuremberg trials of Nazi war criminals in 1945 created an urgent demand. The whole world was paying attention. The stakes were high. Accuracy was critical. But the multiple trials needed too many interpreters in too many languages for consecutive interpreting to be effective. Thus, the new technology was adopted to handle the overwhelming multilingual communication requirements at Nuremberg.

How was the technology used? Simultaneous interpreting stations were set up that separated interpreters from the audience, while still being located in the same room. These stations allowed interpreters to speak into microphones, and the audience listened to their language of choice through headsets.

---

[3] Image information sources: Kelly, 2008, p. 5; Braun, 2015, p. 4.

[4] Whispering and the Origin of Simultaneous Interpreting (cont.). *Unprofessional Translation* Blog, December 12, 2012. Retrieved from: https://unprofessionaltranslation.blogspot.com/2012/12/whispering-and-invention-of.html

Today, this setup is considered standard for *on-site* simultaneous interpreting. The stations have evolved into either permanent or temporary booths shared by teams of interpreters. The interpreters are somewhat removed from the main audience, but they are still colocated in the same room and, until recently, usually in view of the speakers and the audience.

Still, the advent of simultaneous interpreting with equipment represents the first step toward developing the technology used in modern remote interpreting. Remote simultaneous interpreting (RSI) now refers to interpreters who are working truly off-site at a greater distance from the participants. The history of modern RSI is discussed in more detail later in this chapter and in Chapters 1 and 3 of Volume 2.

From the telephone to the video screen

Telephonic or over-the-phone interpreting (OPI)

While the first remote interpreting technology technically began with simultaneous interpreting in the early 20th century, the origins of remote interpreting as we know it today came later and were based on the telephone.

Over-the-phone interpreting (OPI) can be defined as follows:

> Interpreting conducted over a telephone line when the interpreter or at least one participant is in a remote location.
>
> **Note 1:** OPI encounters may have all participants in different locations.
>
> **Note 2:** The term *OPI* is also commonly used to refer to other forms of audio-only interpreting (AOI) over the internet that do not involve telephones or telephone lines.

Telephone lines were first considered as a possible way to deliver interpreting services in the 1950s (Pöchhacker & Kelly, 2015, p. 413). However, it wasn't until 1973 that OPI was first introduced in Australia, in response to increased immigration, through a national telephone interpreting service. Initially the service was offered mainly for emergencies but over time its reach expanded. (See Volume 1, Chapter 2, for details.)

In the United States, OPI started in San Jose, California, in 1982 when a police officer experimented with providing interpretation for immigrant community members interacting with law enforcement.[5] Soon, telephonic interpreting expanded into healthcare and other markets.

Two decades later, OPI's structure and the areas it covered evolved:

> *In the 1990s, a handful of other companies began to emerge on the U.S. telephone interpreting scene. Along with the decreased prices in long-distance calls and toll-free access, and the constant immigration trends, the demand for telephone interpreting in the United States began to experience enormous growth* (Kelly, 2008, p. 5).

OPI was adopted in other countries around the world. By 2007, OPI was a USD 2.5 global billion market, with companies in the Netherlands, Sweden, France, the United Kingdom, Canada, among others, listed

[5] Telephone Interpreting Services. *LanguageLine Solutions*. Retrieved from: https://www.languageline.com/s/Phone

as top providers. In general, demand for OPI services was driven by national language policies and immigration.[6] This trend has continued and, once the COVID-19 pandemic arrived, it has accelerated.

OPI is considered by many to be the first true remote interpreting because it was the first technology that allowed the interpreter to work from an entirely different location from the participants.

Audio-only interpreting (AOI)

Nowadays, technology is transforming traditional over-the-phone technology into what is referred to as audio-only interpreting or AOI. AOI is defined here as:

> Interpreting conducted via a device or platform using only audio channels when the interpreter or at least one participant is in a remote location.

Audio-only interpreting may still occur on telephones, but it also takes place through other technologies, such as computer-based platforms that don't require a telephone line at all. For this reason, this book will refer to audio-only interpreting as the all-encompassing term, which includes telephonic/OPI. However, since the term *AOI* is still not commonly used, and OPI is often used in place of AOI, this book will frequently reference OPI even for instances when telephone lines may not be involved.

Video relay service (VRS)

Video relay service, or VRS, is a form of telecommunications relay service that allows individuals with hearing disabilities who use sign language to communicate with voice telephone users through video equipment.[7]

VRS is defined by the authors as follows:

> **A video interpreting service funded by the U.S. government for Deaf and Hard of Hearing people that enables them to make phone calls to any hearing person with the assistance of American Sign Language interpreters.**
>
> **Note 1:** Video equipment is used by those who are Deaf or Hard of Hearing to communicate with voice telephone users.
>
> **Note 2:** All participants are in different locations, and VRS can be used only when the Deaf or Hard of Hearing person is in a physically separate location from the person they are calling,
>
> **Note 3:** Even if VRS is government funded, private companies provide the interpreting service and platforms and, in the U.S. model, receive reimbursement for minutes interpreted from the government. The Deaf or Hard of Hearing person can sign up with as many providers as they wish; they receive an assigned phone number for each platform and can place calls and receive calls via that phone number and platform.

---

6 Global Market for Outsourced Interpreting Services Hit US$2.5 Billion in 2007, New Common Sense Advisory Research Report Reveals. *CSA Research.* Retrieved from: https://csa-research.com/Blogs-Events/CSA-in-the-Media/Press-Releases/-2-5-Billion-Market-for-Outsourced-Interpreting-Services

7 Video Relay Services. *Federal Communications Commission.* Retrieved from: https://www.fcc.gov/consumers/guides/video-relay-services

The origins of VRS are attributed to Ed Bosson of the Texas Public Utilities Commission. More than 10 years before the Federal Communications Commission (FCC) made this service mandatory in the U.S., Bosson envisioned individuals who were Deaf communicating via videophones. Bosson ran trials in collaboration with the telephonic services company Sprint during the last half of the 1990s.[8]

According to GlobalVRS, in the year 2000, VRS became available in the state of Texas. Two years later, it was made available nationwide in the U.S. This marked the second time a country subsidized VRS at the national level, Sweden being the first to do so.[9]

As technology advanced into the 21st century, higher quality video calls became possible. U.S.-based Sorenson Communications and other companies brought VRS videophones to the market in 2003. At the same time, greater access to high-speed internet allowed rapid growth of VRS in the U.S. and beyond.[10]

Telecommunications Relay Service (TRS)

Telecommunications relay service (TRS) is the predecessor of VRS. TRS is a telephone service that allows individuals with hearing or speech disabilities to place and receive calls.

TRS receives and delivers messages on behalf of the person needing TRS via a text input device, such as a teletypewriter, a mobile phone or a computer. For example, a Deaf individual places a "phone call" to deliver a message to a hearing person by typing it. That message is received by a TRS operator, who then reads it aloud to the hearing person that the Deaf person has "called." The hearing person responds verbally and the TRS operator types the message to the Deaf person.

There are many variations of TRS, including one for individuals who are DeafBlind called TeleBraille.[11]

Relay services are found in other countries under other names: for example, in Australia the service is called the National Relay Service,[12] Canada has Message Relay Services[13] (delivered as Canada VRS[14]) and the UK has Relay UK.[15]

VRS, in conjunction with VRI, continues to be an important technology used by Deaf, Hard of Hearing and speech-impaired individuals to communicate with hearing people using signed language.

---

8 Where did VRS Start? *GlobalVRS*. Retrieved from: https://globalvrs.com/help/#q7

9 Where did VRS Start? *GlobalVRS*. Retrieved from: https://globalvrs.com/help/#q7

10 About Us: The Heartbeat of Communication. Sorenson. Retrieved from: https://www.sorenson.com/about/

11 Telecommunications Relay Service TRS. Federal Communications Commission. Retrieved from: https://www.fcc.gov/consumers/guides/telecommunications-relay-service-trs

12 National Relay Service. Healthdirect. Retrieved from: https://www.healthdirect.gov.au/partners/national-relay-service#:~:text=The%20National%20Relay%20Service%20(NRS,is%20an%20Australian%20Government%20initiative

13 Retrieved from: https://crtc.gc.ca/eng/phone/acces/mrsrt.htm

14 Retrieved from: https://srvcanadavrs.ca/en/

15 Relay UK. Relay UK. Retrieved from: https://www.relayuk.bt.com/

Video remote interpreting (VRI)

It is hard to believe, but the first two-way video communication took place back in 1931. The first working video phone was invented in the 1960s and by the early 1980s, the first group video conferencing system was created.[16]

But it wasn't until the 1990s with the spread of the internet and advancements in digital telephony that the earliest versions of modern video remote interpreting developed.

> **Why VRI in Spoken Languages Is Performed Consecutively**
>
> VRI typically refers to interpreting that happens via video in consecutive mode only (with the exception of signed languages).
>
> Though the term video remote interpreting itself is general, the modality is tied to the consecutive mode since it was first applied to interactions performed on platforms that allowed only consecutive interpreting.
>
> Today, dedicated platforms for simultaneous interpreting over video exist, and so do video conference platforms capable of providing simultaneous interpreting, yet the latter are not referred to as VRI platforms. They are called RSI platforms.
>
> As the remote interpreting world constantly transforms itself, and as platforms become more hybridized (meaning that one platform can offer some combination of OPI, VRI, VRS and/or RSI), the terminology surrounding these four submodalities will likely change as well.

In fact, the first documented examples of video remote interpreting took place in Europe as early as the 1970s.

> *The earliest documented experiment was organised by the UNESCO [United Nations Educational, Scientific and Cultural Organization] in 1976 to test the use of the Symphonie satellite. The experiment linked the UNESCO headquarters in Paris with a conference centre in Nairobi and involved three different methods: remote interpreting by telephone, remote interpreting by video link and interpreting in a videoconference between Paris and Nairobi, with the interpreters being situated in Paris* (Braun, 2015, p. 4).

Experiments continued into the 1980s and 1990s with varying results. Early VRI services appear to have been most widely adopted in Europe, and to a lesser degree in the U.S., in the 1990s.

> *Court services and other legal institutions have turned to videoconferencing as a means to make proceedings more efficient, to minimise security concerns arising from the transport of detained persons and to support cross-border judicial co-operation. In many English-speaking countries, videoconference facilities were implemented in courtrooms, prisons, detention centres and police stations in the 1990s to create "virtual courts", i.e. links between court rooms and prisons, for example* (Braun, 2015, p. 7).

---

[16] The History and Evolution of Video Conferencing. TechTarget. Retrieved from: https://www.techtarget.com/whatis/feature/The-history-and-evolution-of-video-conferencing

However, it wasn't until the late 2000s that companies began piloting and then offering VRI to customers for both signed and spoken languages in more settings, especially in U.S. healthcare. Some may ask, why the long delay in developing VRI when OPI has been a viable option and widely available since the 1970s?

The answer: the world had to wait for reliable video connectivity on commercial phones and computers. The first commercially available video-enabled cell phone launched in 1999. Soon after, people were began experimenting more seriously with ways to provide interpreting over a video connection.

Then, in 2011, web real-time communication or WebRTC was released and quickly adopted around the world. This advancement, which made video communication over the internet possible using a wide variety of hardware and software solutions, was a game changer.

Take healthcare as a case study. In the early 2000s a "gradual replacement of telephone-mediated interpreting with video links" began, especially in U.S. healthcare (Amato, Spinolo & González Rodríguez, 2015, p. 112).

One example of early adoption of VRI happened in 2003, when a U.S. hospital system in Ohio was struggling to meet the demand to provide language access to its growing Somali patient population. Leveraging the point-to-point connection potential of emerging telehealth technologies, Andy Panos, founder of Language Access Network (now known as Martti by UpHealth), sat down in a room of doctors and proposed that interpreters join these calls via video using the same telehealth technology (A. Panos, personal communication, December 17, 2020).

Early VRI in Healthcare

Early VRI in Courts

Videoconferencing technology spread rapidly around the world in the 2000s, which made VRI more affordable and increasingly accessible. VRI technology was developed for use in healthcare, legal, financial, business and many other settings.

The use of VRI has always come with controversy and concerns that it does not provide the same quality as face-to-face interpreting. Studies over the past few decades reveal both pros and cons, depending when and how VRI is used.[17]

---

[17] Video-Mediated Interpreting: Bibliography. Home of the AVIDICUS Projects. Retrieved from: http://www.videoconference-interpreting.net/?page_id=29

When it comes to remote interpreting, however, for many participants (and interpreters), VRI offers a far more human element, visual context and even reassurance than OPI. The interpreter's presence is more perceptible. It can also be easier for the interpreter to be more assertive in VRI than OPI when confusion arises and communication breaks down.

While OPI is still more widespread, VRI, especially since the pandemic, is now a widely used and growing modality for delivering interpreting services.

A brief history of international remote simultaneous interpreting (RSI)

Early developments in RSI

Remote simultaneous interpreting (RSI) is exactly what it sounds like: simultaneous interpreting performed remotely. It can be defined as:

> Simultaneous interpreting services provided through technology that permits the interpreter and any or all participants to be in separate remote locations.

As discussed earlier, the Nuremberg trials sped up the development of simultaneous interpreting with the use of equipment, which led to simultaneous performed in onsite booths becoming the dominant mode in conference interpreting.

Eventually it became common practice for interpreters to work in booths in the same *building* as the speakers but not in the same *room*, one of the earliest steps toward modern-day RSI.

Then simultaneous interpreting began to be performed over great distances. One of the first examples was a large multilingual conference in 1976 at the 19th session of the UNESCO General Conference.

Soon after that, international organizations in various countries began to experiment with RSI. The rapid expansion of the European Union led to an increased demand to meet the linguistic needs of an increasing number of languages and countries in international meetings.

Overall, conference interpreters expressed concerns about remote interpreting, citing poor sound and work conditions, inadequate technology and pressure to lower rates. Many refused to perform it. Not only did they feel more stress and negative physical symptoms, such as eye strain, head and neck aches and vocal fatigue; but they also felt their interpreting performance suffered.

Whether interpreting performance is objectively worse in reality can be debated. A 2010 study found that,

> *Whereas the interpreters themselves were significantly less satisfied with their own performance in RI, the objective judgments of a panel of judges (two for each excerpt), based on 1,059 different judgments, point to almost no decline in quality, with a possible acceleration in the rate of decline, compared with the rate in on-site interpreting* (Roziner & Shlesinger, 2010, p. 242).

Keep this research in mind as we fast-forward to the growth of RSI from the mid-2010s to today.

Modern RSI platforms

In the U.S., RSI began in medical interpreting. In the rest of the world, it began with conference interpreting. (See Chapter 2, Section 2.1, of this volume for a history of RSI and Volume 2, Chapters 1 and 2, for a detailed overview of RSI; see Volume 2, Chapter 3, for a history of and perspectives on remote conference interpreting.)

RSI can be performed on platforms with or without video, depending on the setup. Today RSI almost always includes a video component.

Despite initial significant resistance to remote interpreting by both meeting organizers and conference interpreters, the cost of providing onsite interpreting compared to RSI spurred gradual developments in RSI technology.

Soon the hugely lower cost in RSI resulting from not paying interpreters to travel to onsite events led to far more rapid growth. At first, a hybrid model was common, where participants and speakers were all located at one site and only the interpreter was remote.

Eventually, however, interpreters (no longer in physical booths) needed better solutions to help them receive adequate audio and video from an onsite event, a need that led to the rapid development of RSI-dedicated platforms.

> *Early days of remote interpretation faced some resistance within the industry, as there were fears that remote interpretation technologies would dilute the quality and perceived value of interpretation services. The question for the remote interpretation technologies was how to manifest a commitment to interpreters to elevate language professionals and open a world of underserved events to these services. As always, there were visionaries and early adopters, and as exposure and comfort grew, so did acceptance. The pandemic, of course, pushed acceptance into necessity, but the continued focus on the interpreter experience remains and continues to evolve with current needs and technological advances.*[18] —Sergio Llorian, Founder and CEO of VoiceBoxer

ZipDX, VoiceBoxer,[19] Interactio, Interprefy and KUDO were among the early RSI companies that helped build the field of RSI. As the technology developed, resistance to RSI continued.

Then came the COVID-19 pandemic. In short order, simultaneous interpreting services had to be supplied remotely not only to traditional conference interpreting meetings but also to schools, hospitals, small government agencies, nonprofit conferences, government meetings (such as town halls) and training events or online presentations.

In conference interpreting, the dedicated RSI platforms experienced a huge increase in demand, which continues to this day. The original platforms launched in the mid-2010s have now been joined by more than 40 startup companies, all vying to offer a similar service.

However outside of conference interpreting, most organizations couldn't afford the higher fees of dedicated RSI platforms. People are practical. Many organizations found basic but workable solutions to providing RSI on standard video conference solutions.

[18] Taken from an author interview, June 2022.

[19] Acquired by Boostlingo in 2022.

In huge numbers, organizations turned to webconferencing platforms, such as Zoom, Webex, Microsoft Teams, Google Meet, GoTo Meeting and others. Organizations were already familiar with these webconferencing platforms. Many found ways to add the additional audio channels needed to support a simple form of RSI. Some of them added a conference call line, or multiple lines, to provide RSI.

Soon, webconferencing platforms themselves added RSI features,[20] though they were usually only partial solutions lacking the complex technological infrastructure to support simultaneous interpreting that dedicated RSI platforms offer. For example, webconference platforms typically didn't include a way for teams of two or more interpreters to communicate with each other. Though imperfect, these webconference options were far less expensive than RSI platforms.

Because Zoom already had a partial built-in simultaneous interpreting solution at the beginning of the pandemic, it quickly became the most used platform around the world for RSI. Zoom was available and affordable. The hacked solutions that soon developed to address the limitations of the Zoom RSI feature were not easy to use, but functional.

Over time, other big platforms, such as Microsoft Teams, Webex and Google Meet slowly introduced their own simultaneous interpreting functions.

For a brief history of RSI, see Chapter 2, Section 2.1, of this volume. RSI itself is explored in more depth and detail in Chapters 1 and 2 of Volume 2.

RSI and relay interpreting

Finally, as global remote multilingual communications touch an ever-expanding list of encounters, remote interpreting also covers simultaneous relay interpreting.

Relay interpreting can be defined as "the practice of interpreting from one language to another through a third language" (Shlesinger, 2010, p. 276). It becomes necessary when more than two languages are involved in an interpreted event and no single interpreter, or team of interpreters, commands all of the languages (Mikkelson, 1999).

Here's an example. A multilingual panel is discussing vaccination efforts around the world. Most of the presentations are given in English and interpreting is offered in Spanish, French, Portuguese and Mandarin. One panelist presents in Mandarin. In this case, the Mandarin interpreters will interpret into English and the remaining interpreter teams will work off the English interpretation to interpret what the Mandarin speaker says into Spanish, French and Portuguese.

In other words, whether only two languages need simultaneous interpreting or many more, participants *and interpreters* need multiple and separate audio channels to manage the multilingual communication.

As this chapter has discussed, the huge impact of the COVID-19 pandemic forced most interpreters to work remotely, many of them for the first time in their lives. It's worth noting how the pandemic has led to a permanent increase in the use of remote interpreting of all kinds, with VRI and RSI experiencing the greatest jump. Remote interpreting now makes up approximately 50 percent of the interpreting market. The pandemic supercharged its growth, leading to a 30 percent market expansion.

[20] Zoom was the first platform to integrate an RSI solution in fall 2019, a few months before the COVID-19 pandemic began.

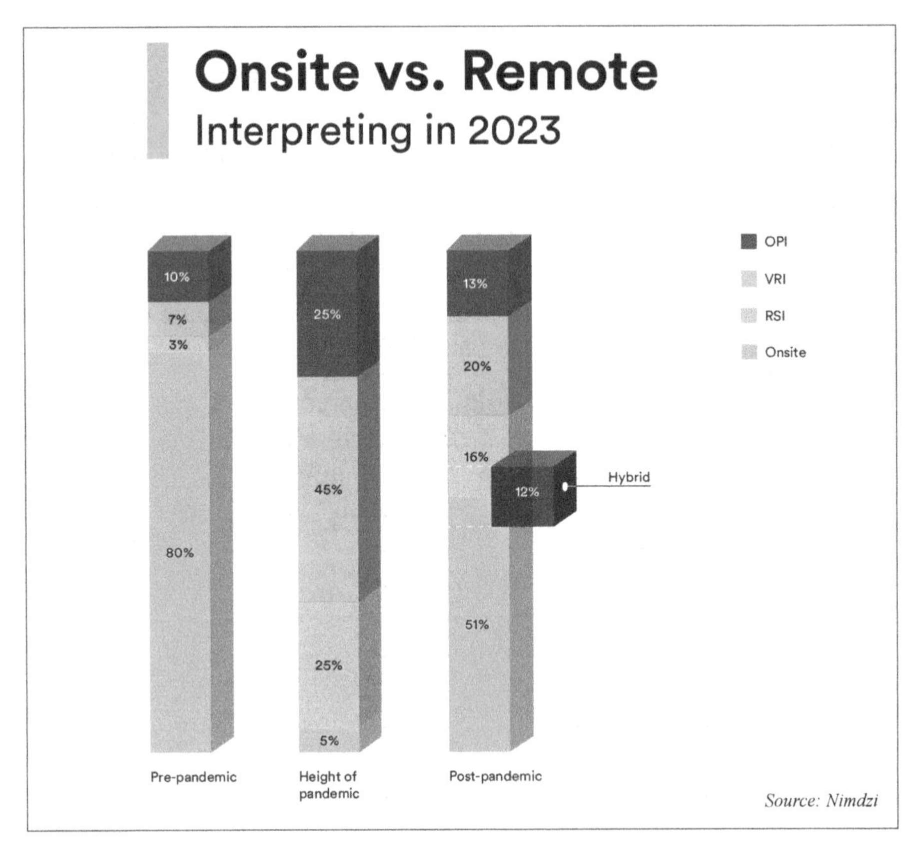

Figure 1.2: **Growth of remote interpreting**

→ Section 1.2 Review

This section briefly reviewed the origins of remote interpreting. The first step toward remote interpreting came into being when technology made simultaneous interpreting in a booth possible after World War II, most famously during the Nuremberg trials. But remote interpreting as we know it today really began with the creation of OPI services in Australia in the 1970s and the United States in the 1980s.

OPI dominated remote interpreting services in the language industry until real-time video communication became possible with technological advances in cellular and internet networks.

Today a growing percentage of OPI is not delivered over phone lines and should more accurately be called AOI: audio-only interpreting. Functionally, however, OPI and other forms of AOI not delivered over phone lines are almost indistinguishable. OPI is still the most widely used term today for this type of audio-only remote interpreting.

VRS and VRI developed slowly at first in the 1990s through the 2000s and picked up speed as 2020 approached. The pandemic pushed both VRS and VRI usage into overdrive. While usage of VRS and VRI differs from country to country, VRS is used only for signed languages while VRI can be used for both spoken and signed languages.

The advantages of visual cues and a greater sense of human connection in VRS or VRI compared to OPI/AOI may continue to result in increased usage over time for VRI. Increased usage of VRS (compared to the older technology, TRS) may depend on multiple factors, such as whether countries enact laws to require language access for the Deaf and Hard of Hearing and also their own preferences within each Deaf community for having face-to-face vs. remote interpreters.

RSI was initially the domain of conference interpreting and for many years faced significant resistance and concerns from the interpreting profession. Despite these obstacles, and especially since the COVID-19 pandemic, dozens of dedicated RSI platforms have emerged.

Since 2020, conference interpreting has pivoted to RSI out of necessity, and RSI has also developed with astonishing swiftness in a broad array of nontraditional simultaneous interpreting settings, from schools to business to local government agencies.

The growth of all areas of remote interpreting has accelerated rapidly around the world at dizzying speed.

Section 1.3 Differences Between AOI/OPI, VRI, RSI and VRS

→ Learning objective 1.3

After completing this section, the remote interpreter will be able to explain general differences between audio-only interpreting (AOI), which includes over-the-phone interpreting, video remote interpreting (VRI) for signed or spoken language interpreting, video relay service (VRS) and remote simultaneous interpreting (RSI).

→ Section 1.3 Overview

Audio-only interpreting (AOI) includes over-the-phone interpreting (OPI). AOI, video remote interpreting (VRI), video relay service (VRS) and remote simultaneous interpreting (RSI) are all remote interpreting, but they are not the same.

This section explores how they differ and why not all platforms work for each kind of remote interpreting. For example, you'll learn why, for some types of encounters, such as a complex end-of-life healthcare session, VRI might be more effective than OPI. VRS may be the best solution for communication between Deaf and hearing individuals. RSI might be necessary for a school board meeting, a health education class or a town hall meeting where government representatives engage with their local communities.

By the end of this section, you will be able to easily distinguish between AOI, VRI, VRS and RSI.

→ Section 1.3 Content

Differences between AOI/OPI, VRI, VRS and RSI

If you're new to remote interpreting, or perhaps you've interpreted only over the phone or by performing VRI, it might be difficult for you to understand how the four types or submodalities of remote interpreting differ and what each option offers. Later in this textbook, across both volumes, we'll explore the differences and similarities in more detail.

This section introduces all four submodalities. Figure 1.3 provides a visual representation of all four.

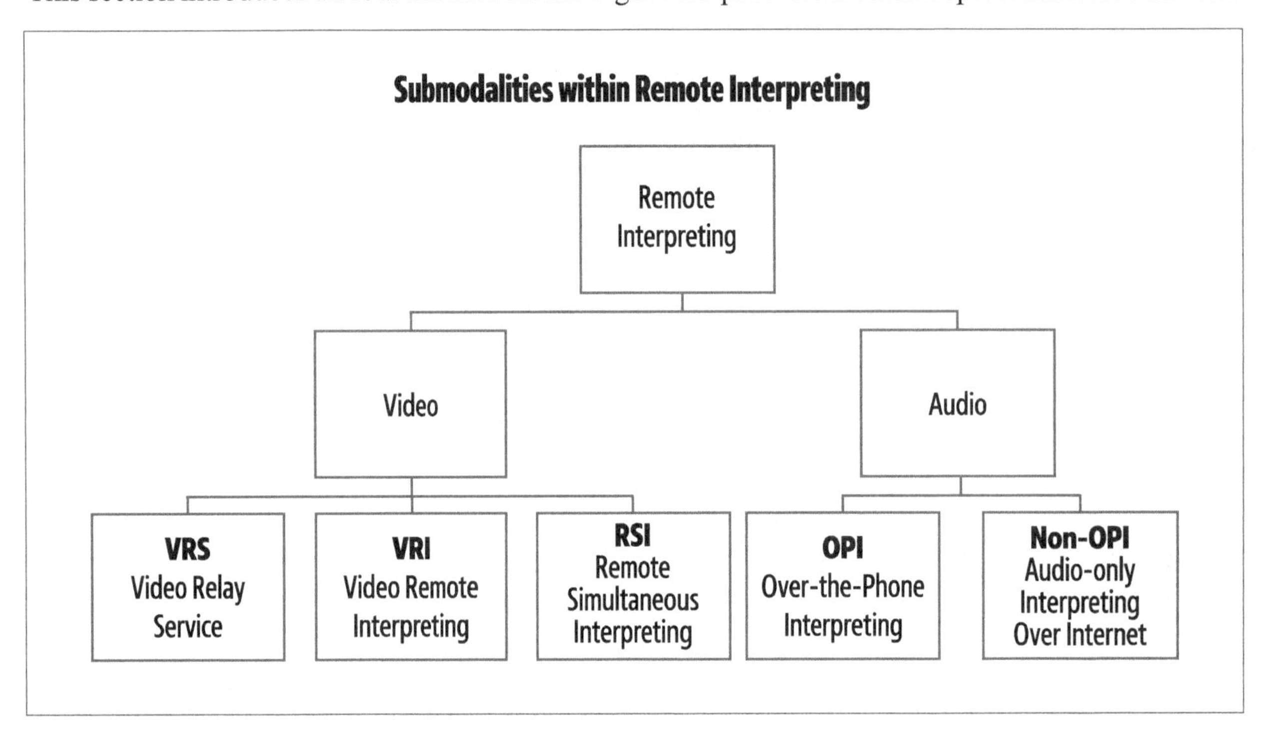

Figure 1.3: Remote interpreting submodalities [21]

Broadly speaking, as defined earlier, remote interpreting is a *modality*, that is, a way of delivering interpreting. (Face-to-face or onsite interpreting is another modality.) In reality, remote interpreting is an umbrella modality that includes four important submodalities: AOI/OPI, VRI, RSI and VRS.

Why, you might ask, are there so many kinds of remote interpreting technologies? Of course, it would be simpler if all kinds of remote interpreting could be delivered using a single platform, but it's simply not possible. Communication between people can be a dialogue, a presentation or a public meeting, for, example, it could involve both spoken and signed interactions; it could take place between a judge and a defendant, a teacher and a student or a town council and its constituents, and among many other possible speakers. At this time, no single remote interpreting platform works for each of these examples—and there are many more.

Figures 1.4 and 1.5 show the key differences among the four remote interpreting submodalities.

[21] RSI can in principle be audio-only, but it typically involves video as well, either for all participants and the interpreter or, at least, for the interpreter.

Three key factors distinguish the four from each other.

1. Whether they are audio only or offer both video and audio.
2. How many audio channels they provide.
3. Whether the encounter is for spoken languages, signed languages or both.

Figure 1.4 shows how the submodalities work for spoken languages, when all parties are hearing. Figure 1.5 shows the same information, but for signed languages.

	Audio Only	Video and Audio	Specialized Technology or Software Required	Consecutive Mode	Simultaneous Mode Can Be Used	Accessible to Deaf and Hard of Hearing	Prep Material May Be Available
AOI/ OPI	✓	✗	✓*	✓	✗	✗	✗
VRI	✗	✓	✓	✓	✗	✓	✓**
RSI	✓	✓	✓	✓	✓	✓	✓

* *The interpreter may or may not need specialized software depending on the platform used.*

** *Not usually available in on-demand VRI.*

Figure 1.4: Remote interpreting submodalities for spoken languages

	Video and Audio	Specialized Technology or Software Required	Consecutive Mode	Simultaneous Mode Can Be Used	Accessible to Hearing and Deaf and Hard of Hearing Individuals	Prep Material May Be Available
VRI	✓	✓	✓	✓	✓	✓*
RSI	✓	✓	✓	✓	✓	✓
VRS	✓	✓	✓	✓	✗	✗

* *Not usually available in on-demand VRI.*

Figure 1.5: Remote interpreting submodalities for signed languages interpreting

Looking at these two figures, you can see that no single remote interpreting modality does everything or has every feature. Just as no single interpreter is ideal for every interpreted session, no single remote solution is perfect for all encounters.

First, notice that not all four submodalities are available for both signed and spoken languages. VRS is for signed languages only. AOI, because it does not have a visual component, works only for spoken languages.

Next, you can see which modes—consecutive or simultaneous—can work in each case. Whether you are a spoken or signed language interpreter can affect the mode as well, as this section will discuss shortly.

All these factors need to be considered when choosing the ideal type of remote interpreting modality for a specific interpreted encounter. For example, for some meetings, such as many types of healthcare appointments, VRI might be more effective than OPI. But if the patient prefers more privacy to discuss a rape or an abortion, or has fears about confidentiality in a small local language community, the patient might ask for a phone interpreter.

And if both a signed language interpreter *and* a spoken language interpreter are needed, video must be used, at least for the signed language interpreter. (For details about this form of interpreting, known as relay interpreting, see Volume 2, Chapter 8.)

The first part of this chapter discussed OPI/AOI, VRI, VRS and RSI and their history. Now let's look at the differences between them, outlined in Figures 1.4 and 1.5, in more detail.

Audio-only interpreting (AOI) and over-the-phone interpreting (OPI)

First, a reminder: when this book references audio-only interpreting, or AOI, the term addresses *spoken interpreting only, with no video component*. AOI is performed in *consecutive* mode, whether over a telephone or via an internet audio connection.

Phone interpreting, or OPI, is *one part* of AOI. Audio only includes audio interpreting performed over any other device that has voice only, not just phones. Today we have several kinds of AOI that don't work over phones and phone lines. AOI is used on computers, tablets, robots and portable machines brought to a patient's bedside and other devices.

In terms of what people actually say, OPI is the term often used to refer to any other kind of audio interpreting because it came first. Think how many people still say, "I accidentally dialed your phone number" when telephones with dials haven't been widely used for several decades.

As OPI technology has moved online, many audio-only interpreted encounters are hybrid in nature. That is, most interpreters today who perform OPI are not working on a phone but over a computer internet connection with a headset and a microphone. However, the OPI *participants*, such as a doctor and a patient, or a teacher and a family member, may be connected using a landline or a mobile phone, or possibly a dual handset phone.

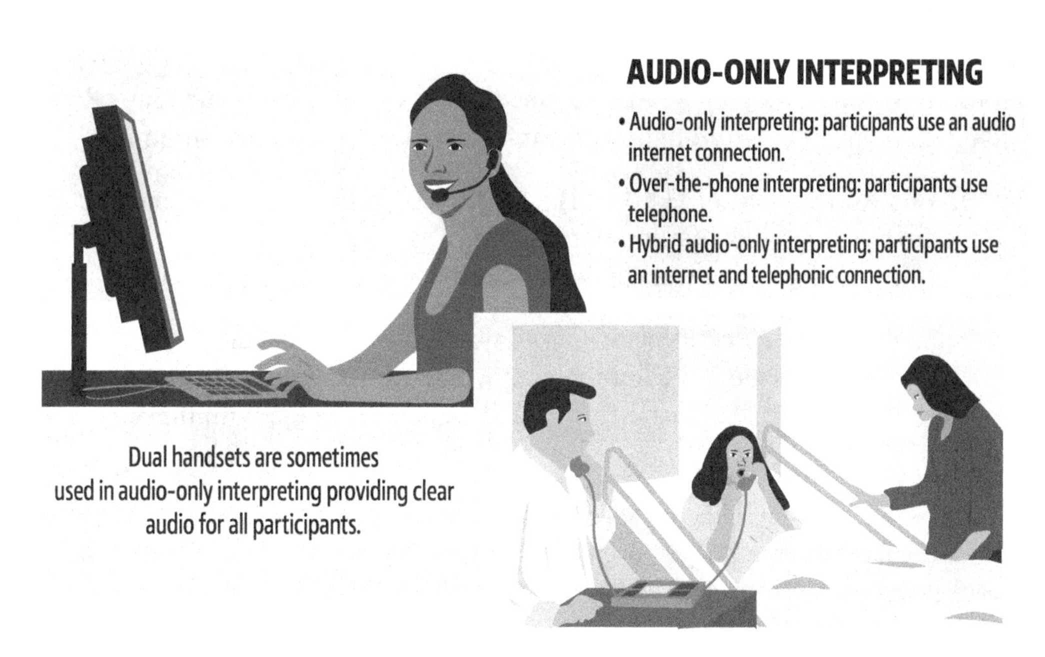

AUDIO-ONLY INTERPRETING
• Audio-only interpreting: participants use an audio internet connection.
• Over-the-phone interpreting: participants use telephone.
• Hybrid audio-only interpreting: participants use an internet and telephonic connection.
Dual handsets are sometimes used in audio-only interpreting providing clear audio for all participants.

Figure 1.6: **Audio-only interpreting**

Don't be confused or get too concerned if you hear OPI when the technology used is AOI. The important thing to remember is that audio only means just that: communication through an audio platform where the participants and interpreters cannot see each other. Even this textbook will sometimes refer to OPI (or AOI/OPI) instead of AOI or hybrid because OPI has become a generic term.

Video remote interpreting (VRI)

Video remote interpreting and video relay service, described earlier in this chapter, both have video and a single audio channel. The video component explains why VRI is increasingly popular, because AOI by definition will never offer a chance for participants to see each other.

VRI can be used for both spoken and signed languages. There is a huge difference in how they are used in each case, however.

In spoken language interpreting, everyone speaks out loud. With only a single audio channel, only one person can speak at a time. As a result, for spoken language interpreting, only consecutive—not simultaneous—interpreting is possible.

However, for signed languages only one person is speaking at a time because someone can be signing while the other person speaks. Signing does not require a second audio channel. This is the reason that, for signed languages, interpreters can perform *either* consecutive or simultaneous VRI interpreting. Most often, VRI sign language interpreters perform simultaneous interpreting.

Video relay service (VRS)

VRS is often confused with VRI, especially since both are used for signed languages. However, the two work differently.

VRS is used *only* for signed languages and how it is used varies by country. VRS was described in the previous section. It is actually a more advanced form of Telecommunications Relay Service (TRS), which is also discussed in Volume 1, Chapter 2, but with a video component.

VRS allows anyone who is Deaf or Hard of Hearing to communicate in a signed language with voice telephone users using video equipment instead of typing text (as they would in TRS). All they need for VRS is a computer, a webcam and a high-speed internet connection.

Using the webcam, the VRS user connects with a communications assistant (CA) who is a qualified interpreter. The VRS user and the CA communicate with each other visually in a signed language. The CA relays the conversation back and forth using signed language with the VRS user, and by voice with the called party.

In some countries, such as the U.S. (where the per-minute rate for VRS is paid by the federal government), VRS has become hugely popular. Using VRS, Deaf or Hard of Hearing users can contact anyone using a standard telephone number.

VRS, like VRI for signed languages, can be performed simultaneously even with only one audio channel. As mentioned above, in signed language interpreting, when the Deaf or Hard of Hearing person signs, the interpreter speaks out loud only for the hearing participants. And when a hearing participant speaks, the interpreter uses sign language. Therefore, only one person is speaking out loud at a time. For this reason, only one audio channel is required for simultaneous interpreting in VRS, and the same is true for VRI with signed languages.

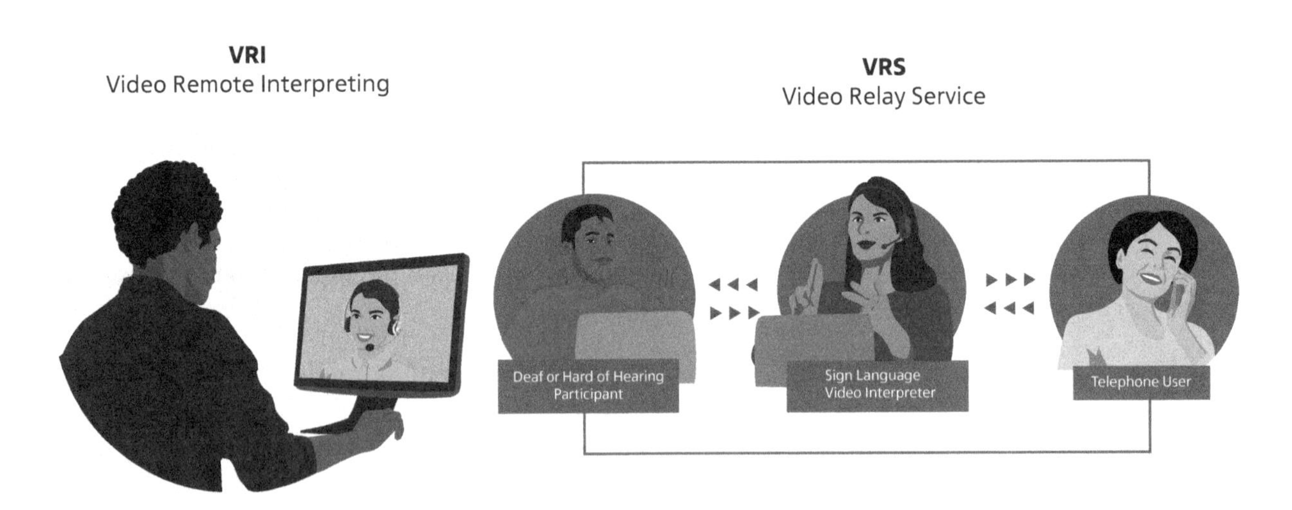

Figure 1.7: **VRI and VRS**[22]

Remote simultaneous interpreting (RSI)

For most audio or video remote interpreting, you need only a single audio channel because only one person is speaking at a time. For RSI, however, you need two or more channels, depending

[22] Second image adapted from California Public Utilities Commission, Deaf and Disabled Telecommunications Program. Retrieved from: https://ddtp.cpuc.ca.gov/default1.aspx?id=1483

how many languages are being interpreted at once, because the simultaneous interpreter is speaking at the same time as the speaker.

Those listening to the RSI interpreter need to hear the interpreter's voice clearly over the speaker's voice. In other words, you'll need at least two separate audio channels to make it possible to hear the interpreter clearly on a remote platform.

For decades, the additional technology required to provide more than one audio channel was a huge challenge for remote interpreting. As a result, before special RSI platforms were developed, most conference interpreting was performed face to face, although some of it was done online using an awkward mix of telephone and video technology.

To make RSI workable, conference interpreters and language service companies developed a few tricks. For example, they might combine a video Skype meeting with a phone call to create two audio channels. Everyone would log on to the video call and those needing interpreting would also call via a phone line to hear the interpreter.

These tricks, which many people call hacks, were complicated, awkward and led to a lot of poor sound quality for interpreters. As this textbook will make clear, poor sound quality is a dangerously unhealthy problem for interpreters—and possibly the biggest complaint of RSI interpreters.

Variations on RSI

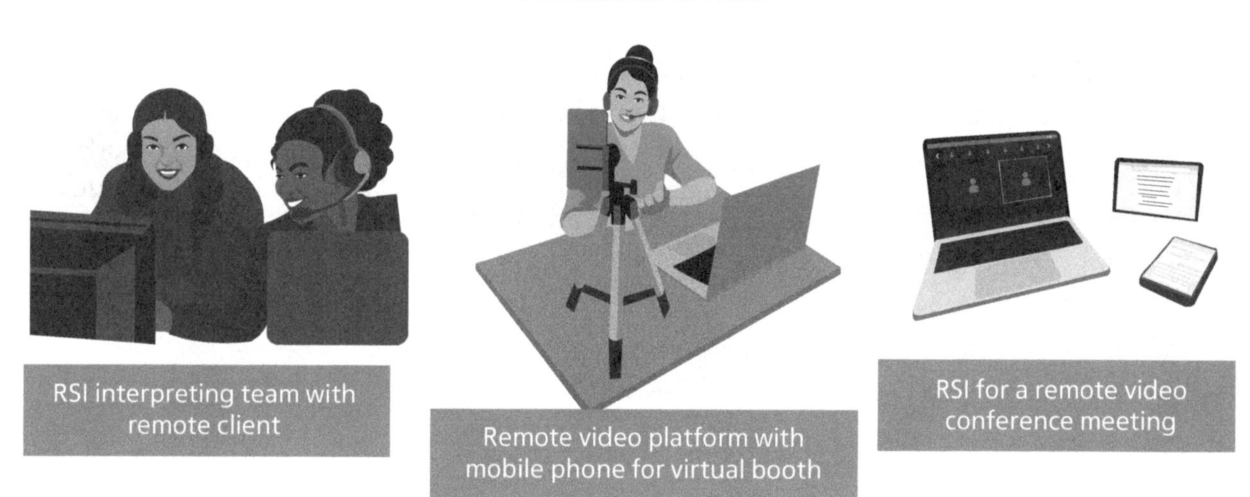

Figure 1.8: **Variations on RSI**

Then the highly specialized RSI platforms described earlier in this chapter came into use. When the pandemic arrived, two parallel developments resulted in RSI. The pandemic supercharged the evolution of RSI technology to improve the dedicated RSI platforms. It also led to the addition of an interpreting function to existing webconference platforms. That second trend, however, has also led to the original hacks of conference interpreters making a return, perhaps especially for educational, local government and business interpreting.

Today the RSI landscape is complex. RSI is explored in depth in Volume 2, Chapters 1 and 2. Of the four remote options, RSI is the one that is delivered over the widest variety of technological platforms and clients.

Where OPI and VRI are usually offered over platforms designed to provide multilingual audio or video *consecutive* interpreting, RSI is performed both on RSI-dedicated platforms and through combining standard video conference platforms with second and sometimes third devices to provide the necessary audio channels.

In addition, sometimes RSI encounters are scheduled through language service companies, but often the work comes directly through governmental institutions or other direct clients, such as school systems and businesses.

This diversity of approaches to scheduling and engaging interpreters can make it hard for interpreters who are new to remote interpreting to get work in RSI or understand how RSI works best in particular settings.

→ Section 1.3 Review

Remote interpreting is a modality, that is, a way to deliver interpreting services. But there is not just one way to interpret remotely.

The four types or submodalities of remote interpreting are audio-only interpreting (AOI)—of which an important part is over-the-phone interpreting (OPI), video remote interpreting (VRI) for signed or spoken languages interpreting, video relay service (VRS), and remote simultaneous interpreting (RSI). This section provided a brief description of all four and compared them, highlighting some of the important differences between the submodalities.

These differences are important to keep in mind as you learn how to interpret remotely, particularly the need for more than one audio channel to perform RSI. The choice of working in OPI, VRI, VRS or RSI will affect many aspects of your work, including which mode you interpret in, the etiquette and protocols you need to follow, and who is engaging you to perform the work.

Section 1.4 Technology and the Remote Interpreter

→ Learning objective 1.4

After completing this section, the remote interpreter will be able to describe essential technologies and technology skills in remote interpreting.

→ Section 1.4 Overview

This section takes a closer look at the technology listed in the previous section.

Technology often alarms or intimidates interpreters who have never performed remote interpreting (or who have briefly tried to do so). The move from traditional face-to-face interpreting to remote interpreting involves getting familiar with a number of technologies and technology-related skillsets. They are not as complicated as they might look at first, yet you will need to acquire an understanding about them and confidence in using new technology in order to be a productive, successful remote interpreter.

This section provides a brief introduction to the different types of technologies you will encounter in the field and what technical areas you will need to become proficient in to prepare well for your first remote calls.

This section also explores why some interpreted sessions are better supported by OPI (AOI) or VRI rather than by RSI.

The purpose of this section is to begin to demystify the technology for you. Chapter 2 of this volume addresses remote interpreting technology in greater detail.

→ Section 1.4 Content

Remote interpreting technologies

If you're new to remote interpreting, you may have no idea how remote interpreting technology works. It is important for you to have at least a basic understanding of that technology, in part so that it doesn't feel so scary, but mainly so that you can work more smoothly and efficiently with it and perform with confidence and skill.

Compared to OPI, video interpreting (whether VRI, VRS or RSI) typically involves a wider variety of software applications. At first it might feel like a challenge to know and understand all the differences among them and understand what each option offers. Don't worry. Over time, the technology will start to feel familiar and become easier to grasp.

In Chapter 2 you'll explore technology differences and similarities in detail. However, for now, let's look at a simple chart in three parts:

- The technologies used.
- The equipment and software required to deliver remote interpreting services.
- The tech checks we recommend you learn how to perform for each type of technology.

Figures 1.9 through 1.12 show key differences among all four types of remote interpreting. As you may notice, VRS is not included in these figures. In the U.S., every VRS company has proprietary technology solutions that differ from company to company. For VRS interpreters, it is best to review the expectations and solutions of the VRS company you're working with.

TECHNOLOGIES USED	OPI	VRI	RSI
Analog telephonic equipment (traditional phones with landlines)	✓	✗	✗
Smartphones and computer tablets	✓	✓	✓
Laptops and desktop computers	✓	✓	✓
Internet connectivity and web browsers	✗	✓	✓

Figure 1.9: **Technologies used in remote interpreting**

It is important to identify some of the skillsets that form the basic minimum ability a remote interpreter should have. We also need to review some skills that can provide additional guidance and will help build your confidence as you work on these platforms.

When Figure 1.9 refers to technologies used, it means that these are the kinds of technologies you will need to learn and feel comfortable using.

Note that Figure 1.9 is simply an overview. *How* you acquire these technical skills will be described, in detail, in several chapters of this volume (Chapters 3, 4 and 7 in particular) and Chapter 2 of the second volume.

EQUIPMENT AND SOFTWARE REQUIRED To Deliver Remote Interpreting Services	AOI/OPI*	VRI	RSI
Analog telephonic equipment (traditional phones with landlines)	✓	✗	✗
Digital telephonic equipment and voice over internet protocol (VoIP) phone systems	✓	✗	✓
iOS (Apple) smartphones, devices (such as tablets) and applications and/or Android smartphones	✓	✓	✓
Web/browser-based software	✓	✓	✓
Webconferencing software	✓	✓	✓
Remote interpreting applications (consecutive interpreting)	✓	✓	✓
Remote interpreting applications (simultaneous interpreting)	✓	✓	✓

* AOI requires an internet connection for calls placed over digital or VoIP phones.

Figure 1.10: **Equipment and software required to deliver remote interpreting**

INTERPRETER TECH CHECKS RECOMMENDED	OPI	VRI	RSI
Review internet connectivity setup and troubleshooting basics.	✓	✓	✓
Go through a tech check checklist before starting work for the day.*	✓	✓	✓
Conduct regular internet speed tests.	✓	✓	✓
Check and adjust your headset sound input and output.	✓	✓	✓
Check for camera presence and lighting.	✗	✓	✓
Exit correctly after the call or your shift, closing browser and applications.	✓	✓	✓

* See Checklist 2: Setup and Tech Check for Remote Interpreters at the beginning of this textbook for a sample checklist; see Chapter 3 for details on how to work with such a checklist.

Figure 1.11: Recommended tech checks for remote interpreters

Knowing the technology alone is not enough, of course. How you adapt your face-to-face interpreting skills when you work on standard remote platforms is just as important. This chart gives you a general sense of the interpreting skills you will need to apply on remote interpreting platforms.

SKILLS TO ADDRESS TECHNICAL CHALLENGES	OPI	VRI	RSI
Developing scripts for what to say during or after technology breakdowns.	✓	✓	✓
Providing, if needed (and appropriate), client or participant education on how to make effective use of technology and equipment, before or during the session.	✓	✓	✓
Managing hold time* if one or more participants leaves the session.	✓	✓	✗
Knowing when and how to work with information technology (IT) staff (if available) for technical difficulties the interpreter can't resolve.	✓	✓	✓
Serving (if needed) as emergency tech support to session participants.	✗	✗	✓

* Hold time is explained in Chapter 4 of this volume.

Figure 1.12: Adapting face-to-face interpreting skills to remote platforms

As you can see, technology and skill requirements are largely the same for all kinds of remote interpreting platforms. Once you familiarize yourself with one kind of remote interpreting, you won't have to learn as much if you then work on other platforms. You will simply be adding to an existing skillset!

→ Section 1.4 Review

The figures in this section outlined some of the key differences in technology that make all types of remote interpreting possible. It also showed you certain skills you will need to have or acquire to work effectively with the technology. Chapters 2 and 3 of this volume will outline all this material in far more detail.

As a remote interpreter, you don't need to be a technology expert. But you do need a general idea of how the technology works, how AOI/OPI, VRI, VRS and RSI technologies differ from each other, and what to do when difficulties arise. Read Chapters 3 and 4 of this volume carefully to become more knowledgeable and proficient on these topics.

Indeed, as you read through this textbook, many other aspects of the technology will become clearer to you. You will feel more relaxed and confident because you will understand the technology far more.

Section 1.5 Prepare for Your First Remote Session

→ Learning objective 1.5

After completing this section, the remote interpreter will be able to plan the setup for a first remote interpreting session.

→ Section 1.5 Overview

This section describes how to prepare for a session as a remote interpreter. For details on setting yourself up for a career in the field and different kinds of remote sessions, see Chapter 3 of this volume.

Consider first where you will work as a remote interpreter. Maybe you plan to work full-time in a language company call center. Perhaps you already perform remote interpreting in a school office, at a hospital or from home. You may be working as an employee or a contract interpreter.

Wherever you work, you'll need to know exactly how to set yourself up for success, including the right equipment to have or purchase if you're at home or an office. Your video background and computer, your seating, positioning, internet speed, having an extra screen and headset and microphone and so on are essential elements of setting yourself up for success.

→ Section 1.5 Content

Step-by-step setup

At this point, you have explored AOI/OPI, VRI, VRS and RSI and their differences. You also explored some of the technology that makes these submodalities possible. Now it's time to go a step further and check out everything you need to set up your personal workspace and begin working as a professional remote interpreter.

To help you prepare, we have provided two setup checklists at the beginning of this textbook that cover everything from which computer or tablet to use to the most effective lighting and your ideal background setup. Take a look. The two checklists are:

Checklist 1: Prepare for Remote Interpreting

Checklist 2: Setup and Tech Check for Remote Interpreters

Let's focus first on phone and video remote interpreting: OPI and VRI. A lot of the information we give you here will be the same if you want to perform RSI, but RSI includes additional equipment that is discussed in more detail in Volume 2, Chapter 3.

Common remote interpreting workplace locations

Imagine you're sitting in your office. It could be your home office, a work office, anywhere. But there you are, sitting at your desk facing your computer—what exactly do you need to have, or do, to take that OPI call and go online to perform a remote interpreting session?

Three common workspace locations for remote interpreters are:

- A language service call center
- A private office at a business, school, hospital or agency
- A home office

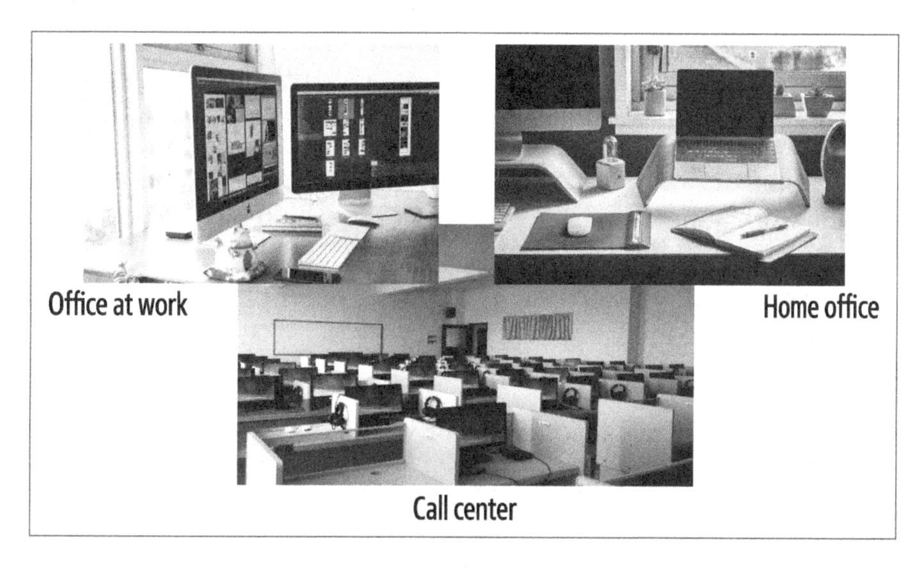

Figure 1.13: Workspace locations

Call centers

More and more remote interpreters in several countries now work at language service call centers, especially if they are employees of the company. A call center usually has large open offices with cubicles or booths for each interpreter. This approach can work because the interpreters work with high-quality noise-cancelling headsets. Each cubicle is equipped with the basic technology setup that remote interpreters need, which is described below.

A big advantage of a call center is that all equipment and privacy requirements can be met by the company in a single location. Also, you, the interpreter, don't have to purchase or worry about your equipment. Problem solved!

Offices inside organizations

A second common workplace location is an office at a business, school or agency. For example, you might be a remote interpreter working for a hospital. You are then likely to be employed by the hospital, which will have a small call center or individual office space set aside for you, and perhaps others, to perform remote interpreting. Like the call center, the hospital will take responsibility for providing the necessary technology and guaranteeing the privacy of the calls.

At a school, a government agency or a lawyer's office, you are probably interpreting from your own office, or an office designated by your workplace for remote interpreting.

Home offices

The third common workplace is the home office. A large percentage of OPI interpreters have historically worked from home. During the pandemic, home also became the most common place for nearly all remote interpreters to work, including RSI conference interpreters.

What are the most common workplaces for remote interpreters?

Around the world, as in the U.S., home appears to be the most common setting for remote interpreters. Such interpreters typically work as independent contractors for one or more language services and possibly for some direct clients as well, such as a hospital, a nonprofit agency or a lawyer who engages you directly (not through a language service) to interpret for them.

However, a growing number of call centers for remote interpreters who work as employees have been built around the world. Some language services work with thousands of remote interpreters. Call centers are essential to their services. Call centers also provide a place to work when a remote interpreter does not have a secure home office to work in.

What you need if you are a contract interpreter

As the interpreter who is an independent contractor working from home, you are responsible for acquiring, setting up and maintaining all the technology you need to perform remote interpreting. You also must maintain all information securely and respect all the privacy laws of your country and/or the specializations you interpret in.

Technology needed for your remote interpreting setup

Regardless of your location, all remote interpreting workspaces require:

- A quiet, private location without interruptions
- A computer (desktop or laptop)
- A quality webcam
- A second monitor or device
- A mobile phone and/or tablet
- A wired, high-speed internet connection
- A noise-cancelling headset with a boom microphone, or a standing microphone with separate headset
- A neutral video background
- Adequate lighting
- The appropriate cables, connectors and other accessories

If you are an employed interpreter, your employer should, in principle, provide you with all the equipment listed above.

If you are an independent contractor, you will usually need to purchase all the equipment yourself, depending on the legal requirements in your country.

Once you get established, you (or your employer) may choose to gradually add items highly recommended by established remote interpreters, such as:

- A second headset
- A backup computer or tablet
- A backup, uninterruptible power supply
- A backup internet connection

In other words, backup equipment and backup plans are important! Technological problems *can and will happen*. Be prepared. To have your system go down when you don't have a backup plan or enough equipment could result not only in one lost session but also potentially losing a valuable client. It is unprofessional not to have backup solutions for emergencies.

The image below shows the setup of a real home office designed for remote interpreting. You can see many of the items on the list above.

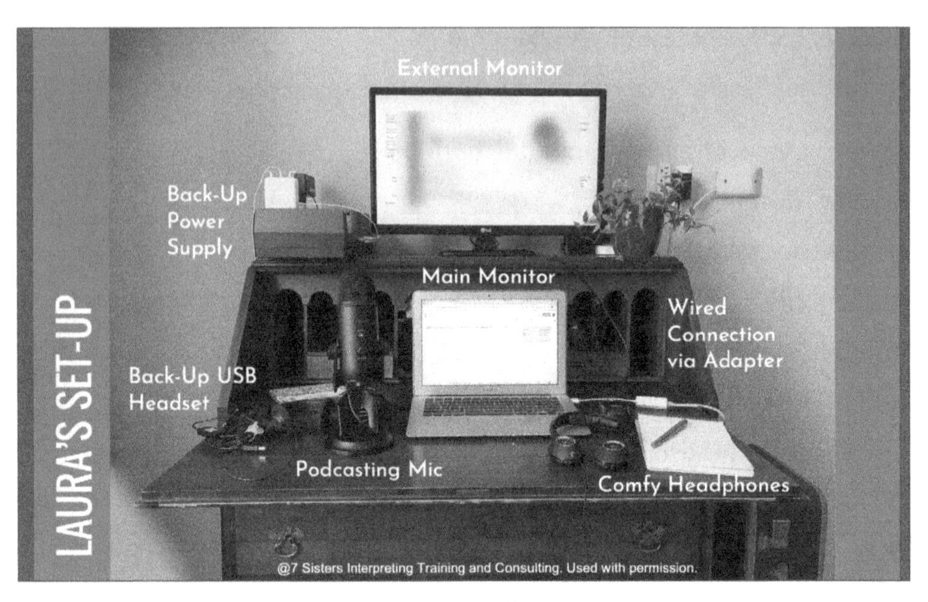

Figure 1.14: **Home office setup**

Each of these workspace elements are explored in detail in Chapter 3 of this volume. If you are new to remote interpreting, the tech setup alone can feel overwhelming at first. Each element requires research and being willing to learn new technology.

The good news is that you don't need to create a workspace that includes every kind of technology or all the latest equipment when you first begin to interpret remotely. Furthermore, if you are starting out as an OPI or VRI interpreter for a language service, that service will probably provide guidance on the minimum requirements for your office setup if you are a contractor.

If you work in a call center, the language service supplies the equipment you need. But if you are working from your home or at a school or a private office, or you have direct clients, keep reading. A school, for example, might not really understand what you need. This section and Chapter 3 will provide you with detailed guidance on how to get started.

Remote interpreting setup resources

Not all your equipment needs to be high tech. Your remote interpreting setup should also include:

- Notepads, pens and paper (optional for sign language interpreters)
- A whiteboard for note-taking (optional)
- Online and print glossaries, dictionaries and subject matter materials
- A way to secure your office space to ensure privacy (lock on the door)
- An ergonomic[23] office chair (optional)

---

[23] Ergonomic furniture is designed for efficiency and comfort—and your health. For example, a good chair can protect your back, improve your posture (which can affect your voice) and reduce fatigue. A quality ergonomic chair might seem expensive, but it is one of the wisest investments in your health and well-being that you might make as a remote interpreter, especially if you interpret for hours a day. (Another wise investment in your health is a quality headset.)

- A standing desk or a standing desktop converter (not necessary, but worth considering if it helps you work comfortably for long periods)
- Adequate lighting

Note that checklists are helpful for identifying everything you need, but how you combine the various elements depends on your own workstyle and needs. For example, as you study the various chapters of this book, you will learn different techniques for taking notes as a remote interpreter. You may decide that you prefer a whiteboard, steno pad or an electronic tablet for taking notes. Your choice will influence what you need to obtain for your personalized setup.

How clients and language service companies address privacy concerns will also influence your setup.

You will need to explore ways to create a space that is quiet, especially if you live in a noisy neighborhood. Your workspace will have to be compliant with all the relevant language service, healthcare and finance industry privacy requirements, including any legal requirements.

In addition, if you spend many hours performing remote interpreting, you will need to exercise self-care, explore how to take care of your body when sitting for long periods and make sure to protect your hearing when working with remote sound—sometimes of poor quality—for hours at a time.

How modalities affect your workplace setup

In the previous section we explored the differences between OPI, VRI, VRS and RSI. Now let's circle back around and see how your physical office setup relates to the technology requirements for each of them.

	Clear Audio Connection	Strong Internet Signal for All Participants	Training on Use of Specialized Platforms	Quiet Environment for All Participants	Video Interpreting Office Setup (Green Screen, Lighting, Etc.)	Interpreter Back Channel Needed for Team Interpreting	Large Enough Screen to See Interpreter and All Parties
OPI	✓	✗	✗	✓	✗	✗	✗
VRI	✓	✓	✓	✓	✓	✗	✓
RSI	✓	✓	✓	✓	✓	✓	✓
VRS	✓	✓	✓	✓	✓	✗	✓

Figure 1.15: Interpreting modalities and tech setup

When you look at Figure 1.15, what do you see? Remote interpreting involves *planning*. Each modality has its own requirements.

While OPI has the shortest list of technical requirements, it is not always the best or most effective modality in all situations. You may have a home desktop or laptop computer, but then you discover that it needs to be updated to handle the technical requirements of video remote platforms. Or you may not be able to provide the highest levels of privacy required for certain kinds of medical, financial or government-related assignments.

To learn in detail how to set yourself up for a remote interpreting session, see Chapter 3, which will walk you through that process from beginning to end.

→ Section 1.5 Review

Setting yourself up for a remote interpreting session may feel complicated at first. But as you read the chapters in this textbook, Figure 1.15 (and other figures in this chapter) will become clearer to you.

Remember, remote interpreting can be performed in many ways. Just as one interpreter is not ideal for all settings, one interpreting modality isn't best for all participants or environments.

It is important to know what you are most comfortable with (for example, phone or video) and whether your work environment supports the technical and other demands of the job. In general, it is easier for most interpreters to start with AOI, VRI or VRS rather than RSI. When you are comfortable with at least AOI and VRI or VRS, then you can try RSI.

This textbook will guide you through many aspects of this process. It will help you prepare for your first remote interpreting assignment and beyond.

Section 1.6 Overview of Modes, Skills and Protocols for Remote Interpreting

→ Learning objective 1.6

After completing this section, the remote interpreter will be able to identify essential protocols and skills in remote interpreting.

→ Section 1.6 Overview

Who is the remote interpreter? Not simply an interpreter who works on a remote platform. Remote interpreting is so much more.

Yes, a remote interpreter is first and foremost a skilled, professional interpreter—and also one who is trained to work in a complex environment, who is comfortable working with technology, who multitasks, is assertive and has learned to handle situations across a wide variety of specializations—often with little context, yet with grace and professionalism.

Remote interpreters make their presence felt without being obtrusive, all while working at a different location from the other participants in an encounter.

Sounds like a lot, doesn't it? And it is. Perhaps you're reading this and you've already had some experience (or many years of experience) interpreting face to face. Now imagine that you're interpreting onsite when someone uses a term you don't understand. You will intervene to ask that person to explain the term so that you can interpret accurately.

Now imagine again: someone teleports you into a box far away and you're still interpreting—but you can only *hear* the participants, not see them. You still need to ask that person to explain the term. All your usual strategies to get everyone's attention with a physical gesture won't work because they can't see you. What do you do instead?

Or imagine that people are calling out to you, the interpreter, trying to communicate with you, to tell you that you're too quiet. They cannot hear you, though you hear them perfectly.

If you interpret for a signed language, imagine that you can see the participant's signs clearly, but they're looking confused and telling you that your video is pixelated, and they don't understand what you're signing.

The people you interpret for may not know how to handle these remote interpreting scenarios, but you will—after you study this book.

→ Section 1.6 Content

Basic skills and protocols in face-to-face vs. remote interpreting

Throughout the various chapters of this two-volume textbook, you will learn how to adapt the skills, protocols and best practices you need for general interpreting to perform successful remote interpreting.

Becoming proficient in these skills and protocols will be helpful whether you interpret remotely for large or small organizations; for language services as a contractor or for government, nonprofit or social service agencies as a bilingual employee; or whether you interpret for healthcare, schools, courts, insurance, banking or almost any other area or specialization.

Remote interpreting is hard work, but it is rewarding when you become skilled in it. This modality of interpreting involves many skills in note-taking, memory, assertiveness, problem-solving and a great deal—we mean a *great deal*—of multitasking.

Points to consider when switching to remote interpreting

While many of the same basic skills are needed in both face-to-face and remote interpreting, they are different in each case. For example:

- My positioning in remote interpreting doesn't matter, right?
  - Or does it?
- Is there time for me, as a remote interpreter, to give an introduction?
  - What do I do if they tell me to skip the introduction? How important is an introduction for remote interpreters anyway?
- Do I always interpret in the first person?
  - Wait. Are there exceptions? Are the exceptions different compared to face-to-face interpreting?
- They think I'm like a machine because they can't see me.
  - How do I make them pause for me to interpret? Or get them to speak, or sign, one person at a time?
- How do I intervene if participants are not looking at me?
  - Why won't they look at me?!
- The participant asked me to wait for a few minutes and never came back.
  - Do I hang up? If so—when? What do I say before I do?
- One of the participants insists on using broken high school Spanish (or primitive sign language), and for every three words or signs they make a mistake.
  - Do I say something? Do I try to interpret instead of this person? Not interpret at all? Leave?

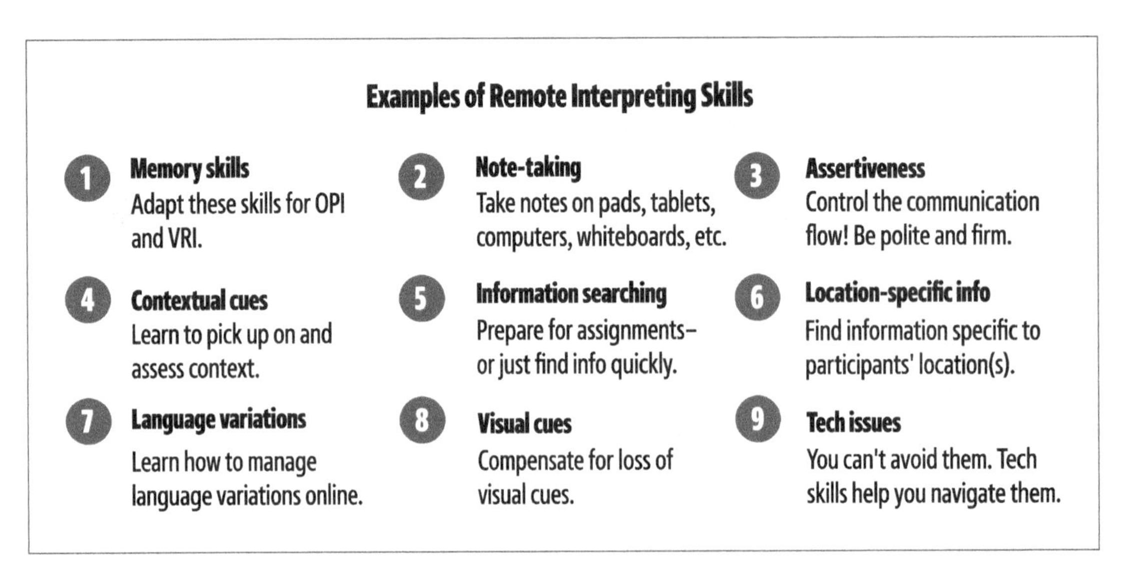

Examples of Remote Interpreting Skills
1
Memory skills
Adapt these skills for OPI and VRI.
2
Note-taking
Take notes on pads, tablets, computers, whiteboards, etc.
3
Assertiveness
Control the communication flow! Be polite and firm.
4
Contextual cues
Learn to pick up on and assess context.
5
Information searching
Prepare for assignments– or just find info quickly.
6
Location-specific info
Find information specific to participants' location(s).
7
Language variations
Learn how to manage language variations online.
8
Visual cues
Compensate for loss of visual cues.
9
Tech issues
You can't avoid them. Tech skills help you navigate them.

Figure 1.16: Remote interpreting skills

This section will help guide anyone with interpreting experience who wants to understand why your interpreting skills and protocols will need to change when you work on remote platforms. Chapter 4 of this volume will guide you in exactly how to make those changes.

Modes in remote interpreting

A mode is a trained technique for the delivery of interpreting. To perform remote interpreting successfully, you will need to know which mode to use, and when. You will also need to understand how technology limits the modes you select (for example, you can perform simultaneously in VRS—which is only for signed languages—and in RSI, but not in AOI/OPI or VRI).

In addition, *how* you perform in each mode will change when you work remotely.

For example, in consecutive interpreting, working face to face you would normally have a notepad and be ready to take notes (at least, in spoken language interpreting). In remote interpreting, perhaps you have a notepad, but many remote interpreters prefer to type their notes or write on a whiteboard, all of which requires adjustments to your note-taking skillset.

In addition, both consecutive and simultaneous are more fatiguing to perform remotely. You will have to plan for that. How will you request breaks? How often? What will you say?

When you work face to face, ideally you may be expected to perform simultaneous interpreting alone for no more than 45 minutes or an hour; otherwise, you would work in a simultaneous team. In remote interpreting, working in the simultaneous mode is even more tiring. If you work alone, your accuracy and focus will go down dangerously. Unfortunately, many interpreters are expected to perform remote simultaneous interpreting for an hour or even two hours without a partner. If you are asked to do this, how can you instead assure that you are working with a team of at least two interpreters for that call or assignment?

Even making decisions about which modes to interpret in may depend on whether you work for:

- A language servic e call center specialized in the needs and requirements of remote interpreting.
- A school, a hospital or a business that often doesn't really understand how remote interpreting works at all.
- A home office, where you, as a contract interpreter, may have to be your own remote interpreting expert!

Interpreting skills

In this textbook, we define professional skills as *learned abilities that lead to competence in one's professional performance.*

Memory skills

In remote interpreting, your short-term memory and analysis skills may be even more essential than when you work face to face, and you may need to practice these skills more often. Again, Chapter 4 will guide you on how to adapt those skills to remote interpreting.

Note-taking

You will have to work on your note-taking skills because note-taking will be different in remote interpreting. For example, instead of using a notepad you might choose to work with a whiteboard and markers, use a tablet with a stylus or type notes on a computer.

Assertiveness

As we saw above, you will also need to be *firm and assertive* when you intervene. Otherwise, participants on the call may ignore you. Assertiveness is a *critical* skill for remote interpreters.

Contextual cues

Lack of context is another challenge. The remote interpreter may be "dropped in" to session after session, and no one bothers to give the interpreter background information to guide them. Where are you? Whom are you interpreting for, and why? What kind of service or event are you interpreting for? Perhaps the participants do not give you enough information even to understand who is in the room or what the meeting is about. Should you do anything about this loss of visual information and context? If so, what?

Due to that lack of context compared to face-to-face interpreting, the tiniest contextual clues can be critical in remote interpreting. For example, in OPI you may have to rely on subtle nuances in tone of voice more often than for face-to-face interpreting (or VRI and VRS).

Information searching

Another vital skill for remote interpreters is the ability to search online for information quickly. Again, that need may come from the lack of visual information and context. Or the problem may simply be that in OPI, VRS and VRI you can move so quickly from one call to the next that you will not be able to prepare adequately for each call. You will then need to develop *information searching skills* that are quick, efficient and to the point.

Location-specific info

Now imagine that you work in one big country and interpret for someone at the far side of that country. Or you live in a big city but interpret for someone in a remote rural area—or even another country! In those cases, sometimes the information you search for during a call needs to be *specific to the location*. There are techniques for how to find that kind of information, and Chapter 4 in this volume will guide you.

Language variations

There is so much more to consider: the huge language variations you might encounter, for example, interpreting across one whole country and perhaps more than one country. Above all, you will need to develop quick problem-solving techniques. They are essential for all remote interpreters.

Visual cues

Another big issue is the lack of visual cues. In OPI, and on conference-call platforms designed specifically for RSI, not seeing participants or the setting is the norm. You hear only the speakers' voices. In VRI, and in RSI with video, poor internet may cause the video to pixelate or freeze—or the camera may be so poorly positioned that you can't see whom you are interpreting for.

Tech issues

Finally, the technology *will* break down. It is inevitable. Tech breakdowns are part of the daily lives of remote interpreters. These challenges involve special problem-solving. If your equipment crashes suddenly—why? How? What will you do about it? If you work from home, will you lose that call, or maybe your job, if the organization thinks your technology or your internet connection is unreliable?

In short, many skills specific to interpreting will need to be either adapted or added to your skillset to perform successful remote interpreting.

Protocols

Interpreting protocols are established procedures and best practices that facilitate a successful interpreted session, whether face to face or remotely. Here are some of the protocols addressed in this textbook, especially in Chapters 4 and 7 in this volume:

Positioning

- How participants and interpreters need to be positioned on technology platforms is vital for a successful session.
  - This is not an issue that face-to-face interpreters need to think about! But positioning of everyone, including you, in relation to the technology is critical.
  - If participants are using a speakerphone but are far away from it, you can't hear them clearly.
  - If you interpret too closely to your own microphone, you can make noises that disturb the participants.
  - If a camera is not well positioned, you may not see all participants or even a demonstration of equipment or a health practice that is then hard to interpret.

Your professional introduction

- What to include in a professional introduction and how to perform it will set the stage for success.
  - Is your introduction to participants the same as when you interpret face to face? No, not necessarily. How will it need to change?
  - Which parts of your introduction might be different depending on the specialization for that session or on whether it is OPI, VRI, VRS or RSI?
  - Do you interpret for a language service that has a particular introduction script you need to use?
  - Do you interpret for several language services or other organizations that each have their own required scripts you are required to remember and say for your introduction?

The remote interpreter
professional introduction includes
technical and logistic instructions.

Figure 1.17: Professional introduction

Direct speech

- The use of direct speech when interpreting, also known as interpreting in first person, is the norm—but there are exceptions to that use.
  - Some of those exceptions will be the same as for face-to-face interpreting.
  - Which ones might be different?

Turn-taking

- Managing the flow of the conversation to avoid people speaking too long or speaking over each other may challenge you.
  - Let's be frank. Managing the flow is often much more difficult in remote interpreting than working face to face. It's easier for participants to ignore the remote interpreter!
  - In addition to being assertive, you will need to develop particular skills to let everyone know that you are speaking up as the interpreter, in your own voice (or signing), and they will need to pay attention to you.

Intervention/mediation

- When and how to intervene or mediate are *critical* skills to learn in remote interpreting—and often much harder to perform well than in face-to-face interpreting.
  - Just as in face-to-face interpreting, you will need scripts in your head for what to say when you intervene, for example, when requesting a pause, a repetition, a clarification, a technical difficulty, the removal of a sound disturbance or a communication breakdown. Those scripts, however, may be different.

- If you work for one language service, they may give you their own scripts for addressing problems that arise in different situations.
- If you work for several language services, you might have to memorize different scripts for each language service!
- If you work for organizations that don't really understand your work as a remote interpreter, you will need to create your own scripts. What will the scripts say?
- How will scripts like these differ from what you say when you intervene in face-to-face interpreting?

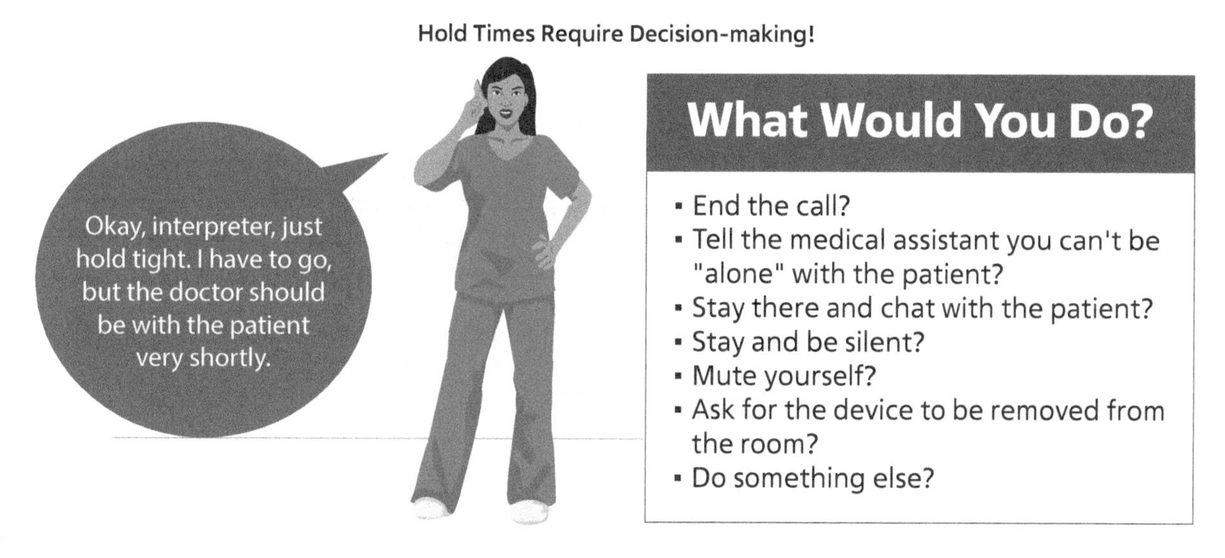

Hold Times Require Decision-making!
Okay, interpreter, just hold tight. I have to go, but the doctor should be with the patient very shortly.
What Would You Do?
▪ End the call?
▪ Tell the medical assistant you can't be "alone" with the patient?
▪ Stay there and chat with the patient?
▪ Stay and be silent?
▪ Mute yourself?
▪ Ask for the device to be removed from the room?
▪ Do something else?

Figure 1.18: Hold times

Hold times

- How to manage hold times is something the remote interpreter needs to know *before* taking calls.
  - Hold times are when someone leaves the session and you are left waiting for the participants to return.
  - In face-to-face interpreting, the hold time is the same as when a provider leaves the room and you are left alone with the patient.
  - For remote interpreting, if one participant leaves the room, you can't step out of the room at the same time. What will you say?
  - How long should you wait for that person to come back?
  - What do you do or say to the other participants while that person is gone?

Shadowing communication

- Knowing when and how to use "shadow" communication, often referred to as shadow interpreting, is another protocol to learn.

- In this context, shadowing[24] communication means that you will wait on standby because the participants may speak fluently enough in a partly shared language to conduct most or all of the encounter without your interpretation. However, as needed, you may have to resume interpreting at any time.
- It's challenging to be the interpreter watching someone who seems to speak enough of the language of service, or a service provider who seems to speak enough of the service user's language when in reality you notice that one or both parties are struggling to either communicate with or understand each other.
- If they only want your assistance "as needed," how do you know when you really should interpret? Who decides? What do you say or do when the need arises?
- What do you do when one person speaking another language is clearly unqualified to do so but still wants you to wait on standby?

The above list is in many ways a preview of Chapter 4 of this volume. Think about any remote interpreting experiences you have had. Specifically, think about what seemed to go right or wrong. What did you do? How did you address those challenges? Did you use any of the interpreting protocols mentioned here? Do you realize you need to sharpen certain skills? Keep these thoughts in mind as you explore this book—and especially Chapter 4.

Support systems in remote interpreting

Who and what supports the interpreter?

Remote interpreting relies on a multilayered system that includes:

- The interpreter.
- The remote platform.
- Participants, such as service users and providers, who may not be familiar with the platforms or their technology.
- Various forms of support, e.g., information technology (IT), quality assurance, mentors, training and professional networking, among others.

For the most part, remote interpreters cannot rely on the participants they interpret for to help out if something goes wrong with the technology. Instead, if the interpreter is lucky, they can rely on specialists who maintain and support remote interpreting platforms—except for remote simultaneous interpreting, when often the interpreter becomes the de facto IT specialist (especially when, instead of a traditional RSI platform, the participants are meeting on a webconference platform, such as Zoom).

Remote interpreters also depend on reliable and secure internet or telephone services as well as agencies, companies or professional networks that help them to find work in remote interpreting.

[24] See the glossary in this textbook for a full explanation of the different uses of the term *shadowing*.

Other key factors

In short, many people in many professions work behind the scenes to make remote interpreting happen. Some of the key factors that support remote interpreting are:

- Technology (development and support of secure remote interpreting platforms).
- Internet and telephony services.
- Leadership, mentoring and support of interpreters.
- Networking.
- Client outreach and client support.
- Forecasting of language needs.
- Quality assurance.
- Interpreter training and client training.
- Interpreter professional development.
- Project management and logistics.

Quality Assurance (QA)

QA is a critically important aspect of remote interpreting that is not commonly seen in face-to-face sessions. It usually means the calls are recorded—and someone in a language service or organization may review the call, either in real time or by reviewing the recording after the session.

Interpreters who have worked mainly face to face and move into careers in remote interpreting may feel insecure or defensive about being evaluated through quality monitoring and coaching. Yes: it can feel scary and disturbing at first to know that someone could be listening in on your call and then later give you feedback on how well you performed.

But as you will see throughout this textbook, and especially in Chapters 5 and 8 in this volume, getting feedback on your performance is essential. Professional feedback will improve your interpreting and can advance your career. It can be exciting and gratifying to know how you are improving over time and to have someone tell you so.

Try to think of QA as a gift. It will help guide you to success.

Consider this example of support systems in VRI for healthcare:

> *VRI may seem simple, but you need more than an interpreter and a camera to ensure quality, compliance, and effective language access. For example, imagine you want to make a movie and all you have is a smart phone to record and your neighbor to act. You could certainly make a movie with these two components alone, but a professional crew, trained cast, high tech equipment, and professional lighting make a huge difference in quality* (Stockler-Rex & Cestari, 2020).

With this book, you will gain the skills and knowledge to go from a low-quality "home video" to a professional level. In other words, you will be able to not only break into the field of remote interpreting but also be able to get ahead.

Those already working as remote interpreters will benefit from this book as well: the knowledge compiled here will boost your career and help you excel.

→ Section 1.6 Review

This section outlined the many reasons why you will need to adapt your use of modes and also adapt your interpreting skills and protocols to perform successfully in remote interpreting.

Selecting the mode appropriate for the platform and the specialization, knowing when and how to take breaks (depending on the mode you interpret in) and being aware of the additional fatigue you experience—again, depending on the mode—caused by interpreting on remote platforms are all critical adaptations to consider for remote interpreting.

Similarly, you will need to greatly adapt your skillsets, such as note-taking, multitasking, positioning and so on. You will even need to develop new skills as well, such as researching information quickly online—including information specific to a remote location—using contextual clues to fill in for missing context, managing hold times and much more.

While Chapter 4 of this volume will show you *how* to make these adaptations, this section showed you why they are important. It also gave you a sense of the particular skills and protocols you will need to learn to become assured and successful in remote interpreting.

Section 1.7 Specializations in Remote Interpreting

→ Learning objective 1.7

After completing this section, the remote interpreter will be able to review and discuss common specializations in remote interpreting.

→ Section 1.7 Overview

It is important for remote interpreters to become familiar with how remote interpreting is delivered across various specializations of interpreting as part of a well-rounded remote interpreting education.

For this reason, Volume 2 of this textbook examines in detail different types of specializations that you may encounter and current trends in the industry. This section also reviews the content of Volume 2 as it relates to interpreting specializations.

Volume 2 begins with two detailed chapters on how RSI is applied across interpreting specializations. Then it addresses how AOI/OPI, VRI and VRS are implemented in the most common specializations in the U.S. and many other countries, including conference, healthcare, legal, educational and business interpreting, with an additional chapter on team and relay interpreting.

Conference interpreting

Chapter 3 of Volume 2 explores conference interpreting for remote interpreters. It addresses common challenges and many of the differences in setups in remote conference interpreting. This chapter also emphasizes, and helps you practice, client education strategies for best outcomes when you work remotely as a conference interpreter.

The chapter, however, doesn't teach you how to perform conference interpreting itself, because that is a specialization for which you are typically expected to have a university degree—or even a graduate degree—in conference interpreting. Rather, the chapter focuses on how conference interpreting works remotely. It can help you decide if this is a specialization of remote interpreting that you want to pursue.

Healthcare interpreting

Chapter 4 of Volume 2 addresses common challenges in remote healthcare interpreting and offers practical, easy-to-implement solutions. Most of the suggestions addressed here are largely accepted best practices. U.S. medical interpreting specialists typically recommend these best practices, and many language services in almost any country would support them too. This chapter focuses on:

1. What to prepare for when you interpret remotely in healthcare.
2. How to acquire specialized medical terminology.
3. Specific common challenges and strategies in remote healthcare interpreting and how to address them.
4. Tips to be assertive in this field.
5. Fields that may intersect with medical interpreting (for example, legal, faith-based and educational interpreting).
6. Differing healthcare systems that often engage remote interpreters.

Legal interpreting

Chapter 5 of Volume 2 discusses legal interpreting and the different kinds of legal remote interpreting performed both inside and out of the courthouse.

In legal interpreting, the types of assignments that a remote interpreter receive can vary greatly. Here you will get a glimpse of how to prepare for remote sessions in legal services, how they may differ from face-to-face sessions, and how to stay up to date with the latest developments in the field.

Court systems and how they work remotely differ hugely from country to country. Because remote interpreting has entered the U.S. courts to a considerable degree, the chapter focuses almost exclusively on the U.S. context. However, the lessons learned in the U.S. are instructive for performing remote interpreting for legal services in other countries.

This chapter reviews the following topics:

1. What it means to be a remote legal interpreter.
2. Court training for remote interpreters.
3. University and college training vs. online training platforms.
4. What to look for in a training program.
5. Legal terminology.
6. Classification of interpreters in the U.S. federal courts.
7. Certified vs. professionally qualified interpreters.
8. Language-skilled vs. ad hoc interpreters.
9. Language access programs by state in the U.S.
10. Remote interpreting in U.S. courtrooms.

The chapter also explores the nuances involved in legal and court remote interpreting, and what to expect from each type of session.

Educational interpreting

Chapter 6 of Volume 2 provides guidance about educational remote interpreting, which prior to the COVID-19 pandemic was rarely provided. Today, this specialization is growing swiftly. For remote interpreters working in education, it is paramount to understand how education is structured in the country or countries for which you provide remote interpreting services.

School systems and districts are a complex puzzle of laws, programs and funding. They vary not only from country to country but also even from state to state (or province to province). Yet remote interpreting in education, like school systems themselves, also has much in common across regional and national borders.

As for the legal chapter, the focus is on U.S. schools. However, the lessons learned about remote interpreting in education, especially since the pandemic began, will be useful for other countries too. Just as legal interpreters can learn the basic structures that make up court proceedings, interpreters in education can learn how the system works overall.

Business interpreting

Chapter 7 of Volume 2 explores interpreting remotely for businesses, such as banking, insurance, workers' compensation, utility companies and tourism.

Working as a remote interpreter for businesses requires interpreters to prepare for the clients and industries they are serving. The interpreter will need to become familiar with industry trends, challenges and specialized terminology, as well as general business practice and norms in the country and region.

Team and relay interpreting

Chapter 8 of Volume 2 discusses multiple forms of team interpreting and how they are performed remotely. Remote interpreters will learn about the special challenges faced when team interpreting, particularly on videoconference platforms, including the necessity for makeshift solutions and the difficulties inherent to relay interpreting in remote environments for both spoken and signed languages.

→ Section 1.7 Content

Remote business interpreting involves a variety of relationship dynamics. This chapter explores business-to-business interpreting as well as business-to-customer interpreting and the modes of interpreting that are most common and effective in each case.

Self-care for remote interpreters

Self-care for remote interpreters is addressed in Chapter 9 of Volume 2, the concluding chapter but it is so important we must mention it here.

While many interpreters often don't prioritize self-care, remote interpreters must do so. If you do not currently have Volume 2 of this textbook, be aware how the toll that remote interpreting takes on interpreters can be serious. Interpreters need proven techniques and guidance for addressing self-care.

Why self-care for remote interpreters is critical

The stressors and challenges that remote interpreters face today range from fatigue to acoustic shocks (and other potential hearing damage) and even vicarious trauma. Vicarious trauma is often caused by quickly moving from call to call, which can include emergencies and tragic situations, often with no respite between calls to seek support.

Remote interpreters are potentially exposed to a greater number of challenging, stressful and even traumatic situations than if they only interpret face to face.

To give you an idea of what to prioritize, Chapter 9 of Volume 2 reviews the following:

1. What types of emotional stressors can occur during remote interpreting sessions.
2. How you can identify emotional stressors in your work.
3. The importance of self-examination.
4. How to define stress, trauma, compassion fatigue and burnout—and avoid burnout.
5. Ten ways to be your best self.
6. What to do before, during and after a remote interpreting session to care for yourself effectively.

That chapter also provides the tools you need to develop a self-care plan for remote interpreters.

What you can do right now for your own self-care

Until you read Volume 2, please try to identify emotional and other stressors that arise during your work as a remote interpreter. Do an internet search on self-care resources for interpreters. Keep in mind that your role often involves acting as a "vessel" to contain the emotions and stories of participants. The impact on interpreters can be huge. Do not underestimate that impact or your own need for support and self-care.

If you work for a language service or any other organization that offers debriefing, counseling or other self-care resources for interpreters, don't be shy: *take advantage of those resources.* They will help your performance. They will help *you.* You will be a better remote interpreter for taking good care of yourself.

We need you. Today, we need more and more qualified, skilled remote interpreters than ever before around the world. Avoid burnout. Take good care of yourself!

→ Section 1.7 Review

The list of specializations in remote interpreting continues to grow. Volume 2 of this textbook focuses on the most common specializations you are likely to find work in as a remote interpreter today, including RSI in general, conference interpreting in particular, and swiftly growing specializations of remote interpreting, such as legal, healthcare, educational and business interpreting. Remember, however, that this field is evolving by the moment.

In addition, this section mentioned that team and relay interpreting have a chapter of their own. This section concluded with a discussion of why remote interpreting can have a stressful impact on interpreters and lead to vicarious trauma. It explored why remote interpreters should immediately explore, and engage in, strategies for self-care, given the immense toll that remote interpreting can take on interpreters' health and well-being.

Chapter Conclusion and Review

This chapter provided an overview of the field of remote interpreting. It began with the personal stories and perspectives of remote interpreters in their own voices, sharing their experiences of how the COVID-19 pandemic has changed their work and its impact on their lives as interpreters. Many interpreters began working remotely for the first time during the pandemic.

The chapter then provided a brief history of remote interpreting and the evolution of AOI/OPI, VRI, VRS and RSI. Remote interpreting has gained even more worldwide importance because of the COVID-19 pandemic. Today remote interpreting is widespread around the globe and will remain so.

This chapter also examined important developments in interpreting technology and platforms. It offered descriptions of the four key submodalities of remote: OPI, VRI, VRS and RSI, comparing the differences between them.

The chapter then turned to introducing the essential requirements needed to prepare interpreters to interpret remotely. It tackled the basic technology used in remote interpreting and tech skills that remote interpreters need to have or develop. The remote interpreter does not need to become expert in all aspects of the technology that makes remote interpreting possible, but a basic familiarity with them prepares the interpreter to manage technical challenges, which are inevitable in remote interpreting.

This chapter also explored why the remote interpreter will need to adapt their use of modes and their interpreting skills and protocols to work remotely (how to do so is addressed in Chapter 4 of this volume). It then listed and described the most important specializations of remote interpreting today, including conference interpreting and medical (or healthcare), legal, educational and business interpreting, which are all covered in Volume 2, in addition to two chapters devoted to RSI.

Remember, however, that remote interpreting has evolved swiftly and continues to do so! By the time you read this book, some information will have changed. The authors believe, however, that the information provided here will greatly assist you on your journey to a successful career as a remote interpreter.

Chapter 2

Dieter Runge, MEd
Katharine Allen, MA

Remote Interpreting Technology

Learning Objectives

After completing this chapter, the remote interpreter will be able to:

Learning Objective 2.1: Discuss the history of remote interpreting technologies.

Learning Objective 2.2: Compare and contrast different types of interpreting software applications.

Learning Objective 2.3: Identify and describe the equipment and software used for OPI, VRI, VRS and RSI.

Learning Objective 2.4: Identify specific technologies required to provide RSI services.

Introduction

Remote interpreting and technology are woven together in both concept and practice. The innovation and advancements in telecommunications and information technology for interpreting are exciting. They help professional interpreters to connect. They support interpreting requests for hundreds of languages. They help the world meet a wide spectrum of needs for multilingual communication.

In short, thanks to technology we are living in a new world where simply pushing a button or two on a phone or computer can instantly connect us to interpreters.

As a result, remote interpreting is a growing and vibrant career option. Today, interpreters will find many exciting new career opportunities. They can participate in the exploding global economy and provide access to critical services in ways that were previously unimaginable. Many logistic and technical challenges have been reduced and even eliminated. Technology hardware and software requirements that for many years were too costly to be widely adopted are now making language access via technology available to most everyone.

All of these rapid developments derive from recent advances in *technology*. In this chapter, you will examine some of the most relevant technologies that spurred the growth of remote interpreting both as an industry and as a profession. You will explore the history, breakthroughs and advances in remote interpreting technology.

This knowledge will help you to become an informed remote interpreter. You will also feel less lost and confused by the technology. It will feel less alien. Even if remote interpreting technology can feel a little scary or overwhelming at first, by becoming informed about it, you will start to feel more at home and at ease with this new world.

The chapter will also provide a broad overview of technology terms and concepts in remote interpreting. The goal is to help you navigate the core technical skills and tools you need to perform successfully and advance your career as a remote interpreter.

Section 2.1 A Timeline of the History of Technology in Remote Interpreting

→ Learning objective 2.1

After completing this section, the remote interpreter will be able to discuss the history of remote interpreting technologies.

→ Section 2.1 Overview

For the majority of interpreters today, remote interpreting is a relatively new career option. Technological advancements in remote interpreting tools and developments in the information technology infrastructure that support remote interpreting have created this new career path for many interpreters.

In addition, the global explosion of internet and wireless mobile telecommunications technology has helped drive remote interpreting to the forefront of language support services around the world. Today, the technology is evolving at a breathtaking pace and advancing the whole profession of interpreting.

The remote interpreter can be described as *an interpreter enabled by communications technology who delivers interpreting services to participants in other locations.* Remote interpreting includes audio and video delivery of interpreting. Its technology supports both spoken and sign languages.

Remote interpreting can even involve sight translation or translation, especially for emergency calls. For example, the remote interpreter may connect a victim who is hiding from an abuser inside a locked bathroom or bedroom who sends direct (text) messages to emergency services. The interpreter then orally relays the victim's written messages to the emergency service dispatch operator and perhaps also to the police. The interpreter then communicates their messages back to the victim by typing messages in the victim's language.

As a remote interpreter, you are more than a language specialist: you are also *an information technology* (IT) *professional*. As an IT professional, you'll have to acquire specific technical knowledge and skills. You'll also need to understand how to use them effectively and appropriately in a wide variety of settings.

This section provides a broad historical overview of the technologies that made remote interpreting possible.

This section also dives into some of the key terms, tools and technologies that you are likely to encounter and need to understand.

→ Section 2.1 Content

The technology roots of remote interpreting

Historically, the first truly functional remote interpreting service and program was TIS: the free Emergency *Telephone Interpreting Service* established by the Australian Department of Immigration in the mid-1970s.[25] TIS exists to this day and was renamed the Translating and Interpreting Service in 1991.

TIS was mandated as a national public service to assist all non-English migrant speakers relocating to Australia. Today it continues as a government support service and provides free public interpreting access throughout Australia.

Programs similar to TIS were eventually implemented in the United States, Canada and Europe. Most are not free. Many of these programs were created in the 1980s and 1990s. In a number of countries, the development of these remote interpreting service programs was largely boosted by civil rights laws that required publicly funded organizations to provide language access and support.

In recent decades, the expansion of healthcare regulation and reform in many countries has also helped to strengthen remote interpreting services. They often include key provisions for those who are Deaf and Hard of Hearing. Such laws offer important assurances for language access both to migrant communities and the Deaf.[26]

During this time, private (for-profit) interpreting agencies grew steadily, and some began offering remote interpreting services—mostly over the phone interpreting (OPI). At the same time, nonprofit, community-based and hospital services still relied largely on face-to-face interpreters.

Multilingual call centers and interpreting service providers began to appear in the early 1980s. Some have since grown into colossal language service companies that today generate millions of dollars in revenue and billions of dollars in market value.

In the mid-1980s, the global interpreting and translation market was tiny in contrast to the world economy. Gradually it grew larger. However, between 2009 and 2021, the global language services industry grew from 23.5 billion to over 56 billion dollars (USD) in market value.[27]

According to a 2021 Nimdzi Insights report, the largest language service provider in the world in the year 2000 (Berlitz GLOBALNET) had revenues of USD 103.9 million.[28] In the 2022 Nimdzi

---

[25] History of TIS National. Australian Government Department of Home Affairs. Retrieved from: https://www.tisnational.gov.au/About-TIS-National/History-of-TIS-National.aspx

[26] It is important to note that individuals who are Deaf and Hard of Hearing may strongly prefer in-person interpreting services. In the U.S., for example, video relay service (VRS) is the next most widely used modality after face-to-face interpreting for sign language interpreting, whereas video remote interpreting (VRI) is used far more slowly. Both are still not well received by many members of the Deaf and Hard of Hearing community. See, for example, American Sign Language Interpreting: The Size and State of the Market. Retrieved from: https://www.nimdzi.com/asl-interpreting/

[27] Market Size of the Global Language Services Industry from 2009 to 2019 with a Projection Until 2022. (2022). *Statista Research Department*. Retrieved from: https://www.statista.com/statistics/257656/size-of-the-global-language-services-market/

[28] Sarah Hickey and Belén Agulló García. (2021). The 2021 Nimdzi 100: The Ranking of the Top 100 Largest Language Service Providers. *Nimdzi Insights*. Retrieved from: https://www.nimdzi.com/nimdzi-100-2021/

Insights report,[29] the largest language service provider in the year 2021 (TransPerfect) had revenues of USD 1.1 billion—about 10 times bigger.

This is astounding growth not only for businesses, but also it has contributed to an exponential increase in opportunities for interpreters, much of it due directly to advances in technology.

> There are many factors that contribute to the growth of the industry. Communication plays a central role in the ever-increasing globalization that continues to generate more demand for people, businesses and governments to interact with one another, across languages and cultures and in many different formats. There is an explosion of content happening right now, with no end in sight. And wherever there is content, wherever there is a need for communication, there is a need for language services.
>
> At Nimdzi, we have long said that our industry is impervious to crises. This is because we don't create anything from scratch, we transform content from all other industries. This makes our industry incredibly resilient. As we like to say at Nimdzi, when times are good, we translate contracts, when times are bad, we translate lawsuits.
>
> —Sarah Hickey, Vice President of Research, Nimdzi Insights

Six defining technologies in the timeline of remote interpreting

Several defining technological events shaped the evolution of remote interpreting. Many of the technologies that resulted are still in use.

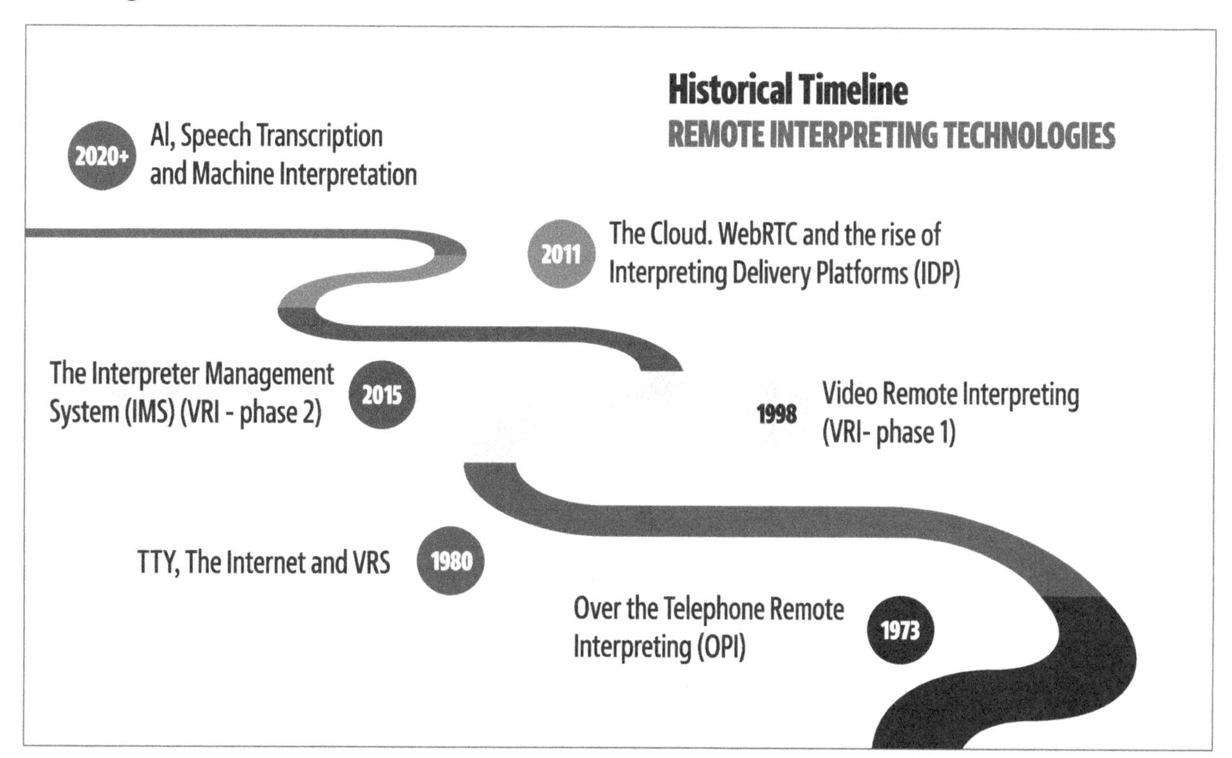

Figure 2.1: Historical timeline of remote interpreting technologies. © Boostlingo

[29] Sarah Hickey. (2022). The 2022 Nimdzi 100: The Ranking of The Top 100 Largest Language Service Providers. Nimdzi Insights. Retrieved from: https://www.nimdzi.com/nimdzi-100-top-lsp/

1970s: Telephony and OPI

The telephonic industry paved the way for the early development of remote interpreting.

The telephone has long been (and largely still is) the easiest and most accessible way to connect people to language support services for spoken languages. Today it remains the most widespread form of remote interpreting technology.

As previously noted, telephonic interpreting was created in Australia in 1973. In the United States, OPI began in 1981 when:

> *A young police officer in San Jose, California, decided to team up with a colleague from the Defense Language Institute in Monterey, California, to form an organization that would help overcome barriers of language, such as those he had encountered in the course of his own work. Language Line Services started off as a charity organization but quickly expanded beyond police clients into the health care market and incorporated as a for-profit organization headquartered in Monterey, California* (Kelly, 2008, p. 5).

This is the historical beginning of LanguageLine Solutions, as the company is known in 2022. As a young company, it began as Communication and Language Line (CALL). It became Language Line Services in 1982. Then in 1990, it was acquired by the U.S. telephone service AT&T, which obtained the company as a strategic business unit.[30] AT&T Language Line Services, as it was renamed, began investing heavily in over the phone technologies and building out what became a modern-day telephonic interpreting system with call centers.

In 1999, Language Line Solutions separated from AT&T and became the largest provider in the world for OPI services. (To this day, at least in the U.S., people still often refer to a "language line" when they refer to any OPI service.)

In 2016, LanguageLine Solutions was acquired by the French customer experience management conglomerate Teleperformance for USD 1.5 billion. At the time of publication, LanguageLine Solutions is one of the world's largest interpreting services company, supporting more than 36 million interpreting calls a year.[31]

Since the 1970s, analog telephone landlines have provided frontline support for OPI services. Even though mobile and wireless technologies and smartphones have made video interpreting accessible, audio-only—including telephonic—interpreting is by far the most widely used type, or submodality, of remote interpreting.

The growth of telephonic interpreting eventually led to the formation of large multilingual call centers and language interpreting super agencies (extremely large language companies).

---

[30] LanguageLine Solutions. Retrieved from: https://en.wikipedia.org/wiki/LanguageLine_Solutions

[31] LanguageLine Solutions. Retrieved from: https://en.wikipedia.org/wiki/LanguageLine_Solutions

CyraCom and dual handsets

CyraCom International, Inc., is another major U.S.-based language service that has had a huge impact in advancing telephonic interpreting. CyraCom developed the first dual-handset telephone prototype in 1995. A simple idea, it caught on quickly because it improved the telephonic interpreting experience.

The dual handset eliminated the need for a speakerphone. Before dual handsets, using speakerphones for OPI was the norm. Of course, this is well before smartphones became widespread. With two or more people in the same room, participants turned on speakerphones instead of just handing the receiver back and forth, which saved time and felt easier for most people.

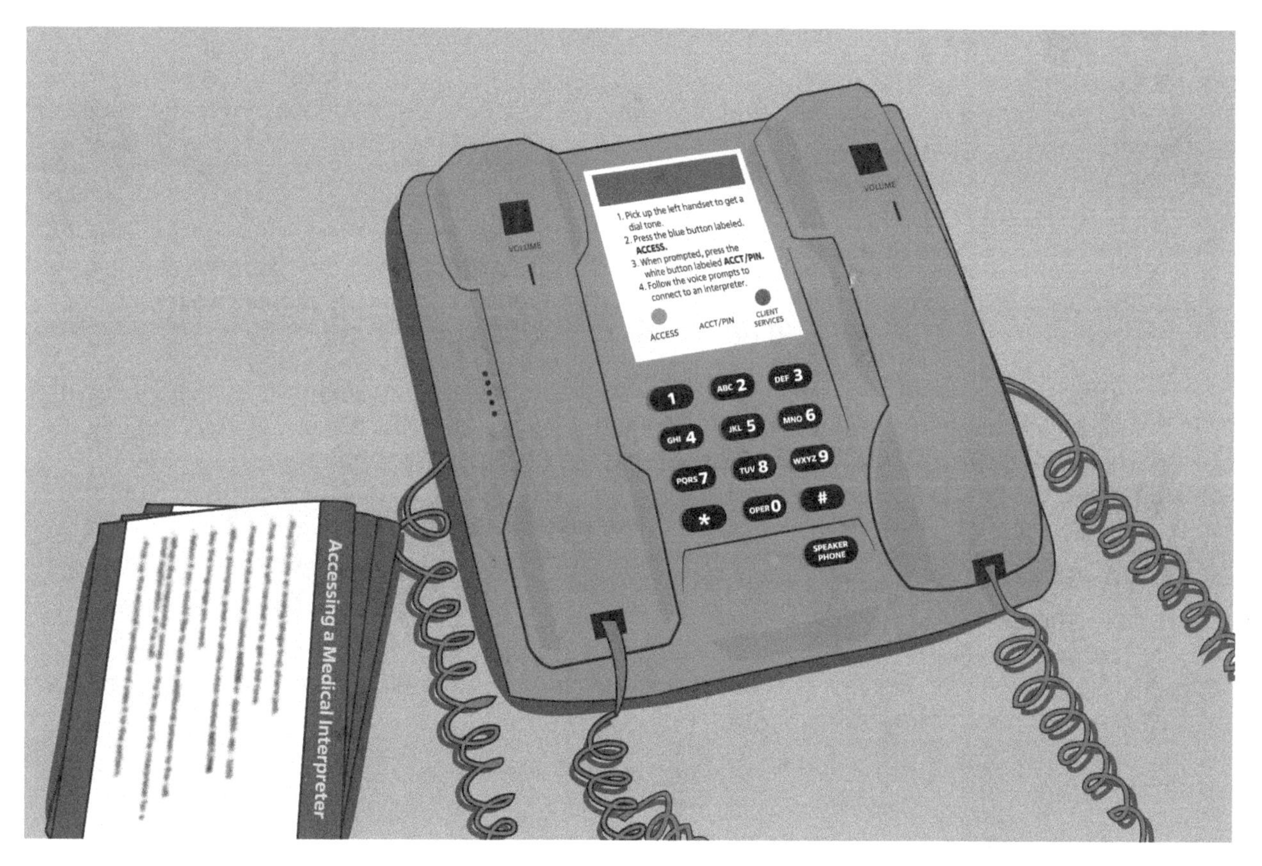

Figure 2.2: **The dual handset phone**

Unfortunately, phones cut off part of the acoustic signal, which is one contributing reason interpreters find it fatiguing to interpret over phones: poor quality sound. Their brains have to work harder to fill in the missing sounds because of what is typically missing from the acoustic signal over any phone line. Speakerphones can often cut out even *more* of that signal than phones alone. As a result, the sound is harder for interpreters to hear, harder for them to understand—and harder to interpret.

Enter the dual-handset phone. It was a simple concept that included two handsets connected to a single phone base. A dual handset allowed two people to connect to an interpreter in a three-way call without having to share a single handset or rely on poor speakerphone quality.

This dual handset may sound somewhat archaic considering today's smartphone devices, which are capable of multiconference communications. But these dual-handset devices are quite common throughout healthcare systems globally and can be found in countless hospitals. Now there are wireless handset and smartphone versions of these devices.

Prior to 1998, there were only a few large-scale over-the-phone interpreting (OPI) service providers. While at that time, AT&T clearly had the largest market share, most providers generally followed a similar strategy with little variation. Typically, the offer was 150 languages, per minute billing, and 24x7 availability. Remote interpreting was facilitated using existing telephony technologies, such as speakerphones and program-dialing capabilities. That is until the introduction of a new and disruptive technology solution developed by a then unknown startup called Kevmark Industries, now known as CyraCom International.

When the dual-handset phone entered the space, offering a more efficient solution with built-in volume controls and other features, the over-the-phone interpreting industry took notice and watched to see what would happen. Never before had a language service provider offered a physical piece of technology as a solution to enhance OPI services.

As the first president and CEO of CyraCom responsible for building the company from the ground up, I recognized that as a startup operation with a small window of opportunity, the strategy needed was to ensure market acceptance and adoptability. Sights were set on healthcare, due to the growing demand for services and the need to protect patient privacy and safety.

Hospitals that had access to over-the-phone interpreters found staff would forget about the service and default to someone who simply spoke the language (bilingual). This created risk to patient safety and placed hospitals in potentially litigious situations. The dual-handset phone would serve as an icon and reminder that interpreter services were just a phone call away. The strategy paid off as healthcare staff and administrators hailed the product as a language access game changer.

Although there were a few bumps along the way (digital [private branch exchange] PBX versus analog issues, inventory control, maintenance and manufacturing), this new method of providing language services propelled CyraCom's success in becoming one of the largest OPI providers on record. Soon other markets opened up, including government and legal support, citing the dual-handset phone as a tangible product for an intangible service.

Although other tools and methods have been created and introduced since that time, no other technology or feature has been able to match the impact of the dual-handset phone. With its unique purpose, this technology forever changed the remote interpreting industry.

—Ken Anders, Language Services Executive

1980s-early 1990s: The advent of TTY, the internet and VRS services

In the mid- to late-1980s, several other new types of telecommunications services were developed, including the telecommunications relay service (TRS). TRS was specifically developed to accommodate the needs of Deaf and Hard of Hearing consumers. These TRS technologies included teletypewriter (TTY) devices and telephone line speech-to-speech relay service (STS).

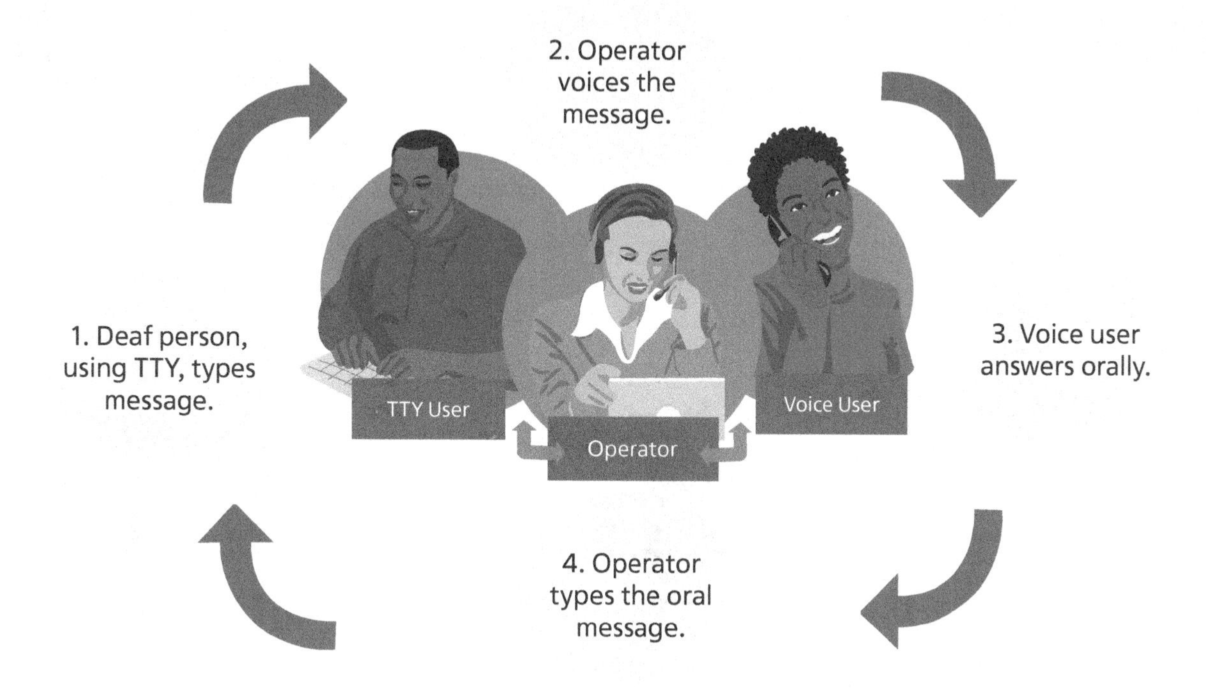
HOW TTY WORKS
2. Operator voices the message.
1. Deaf person, using TTY, types message.
3. Voice user answers orally.
TTY User
Operator
Voice User
4. Operator types the oral message.

Figure 2.3: **Teletypewriter (TTY) service**

TTY

In 1987, California became the first U.S. state to mandate that TTY services be provided to all state residents who are Deaf or Hard of Hearing.

Access to TTY services in the U.S. soon expanded beyond California. In 1990, free access to TTY for the Deaf and Hard of Hearing was written into U.S. federal law under Title IV of the Americans with Disabilities Act (ADA). The ADA legislation expanded access to these programs unilaterally to all 50 states in what became one of the single largest public service laws to support remote interpreting technology. (Chapter 9 of this volume addresses laws and regulations that affect language services.)

At the same time, similar programs emerged in Canada and Europe, but they were not nearly as widespread as in the U.S. at that time.

Video relay service (VRS)

In the early- to mid-1990s, the rise of the internet and eventual creation of the World Wide Web spurred the development of Internet Protocol (IP) Relay Service, and ultimately video relay service (VRS).

VRS was groundbreaking. It introduced the ability for Deaf and Hard of Hearing individuals to access video communications. Now that video interpreting was possible, VRS offered far more robust communications than TTY services by providing the critical visual components necessary for sign language.

VRS was immediately embraced by the Deaf community as a significant leap forward in remote interpreting technology. With VRS, the Deaf person could sign to a relay operator who, in turn, would speak to the hearing individual and then sign back the response to the Deaf individual.

This approach allowed for near simultaneous communication with much better capture of the sign language and a noticeable overall reduction in sign language communication errors.

Figure 2.4: **Video relay service (VRS)**

VRS technology in the U.S. helped pave the way for the design and development of the first video remote interpreting (VRI) systems.

VRS services are regulated by the U.S. Federal Communications Commission and are regularly used throughout the U.S. It may surprise you to learn that VRS services are managed by only a handful of authorized providers. In 2022, there are only four remaining VRS providers in the U.S.[32]

Late 1990s and the 2000s: The first wave of VRI systems

VRI is born

VRS technology systems in the U.S. in part helped pave the way for the eventual design and development of the first video remote interpreting (VRI) systems.

Specifically, new possibilities for delivering interpreting via video became possible through advancements in the satellite and broadcast communications industry along with innovation, development and expansion of new broadband internet technologies, media streaming networks and an expanding server technology industry.

The evolution from OPI to VRI

Video remote interpreting (VRI) was a logical evolution from telephone interpreting. It provided a visual medium that allowed for far more personal engagement for both participants and interpreters. VRI was also available when face-to-face interpreting appointments were not feasible, practical or available.

---

[32] VRS Providers. Federal Communications Commission. Retrieved from: https://www.fcc.gov/vrs-providers. See also https://www.youtube.com/watch?v=WCtWFmkRFvc for a video discussing, explaining and demonstrating VRS.

Soon many of the larger established telephonic language interpreting agencies, particularly in the U.S., added VRI services in addition to their OPI services. The strongest U.S. demand for VRI from the start was in the healthcare sector.

Figure 2.5: **VRI**

These new VRI technologies offered a powerful new platform that quickly expanded language access services. Interpreting sessions could be connected via high-definition broadcast quality video with a visual component that enhanced the quality of the interpreting experience. It could also accommodate both spoken and sign languages, unlike OPI or VRS.

Early challenges for VRI

There were a few key challenges in the early days of VRI. The new wave of video remote technology came at a cost. The ability to build, deploy and support VRI was essentially too expensive for all but the largest interpreting services.

VRI innovation was also achieved largely through private investment. Unlike VRS, the U.S. government did not financially support VRI technology development. Smaller language companies could resell interpreting services using the technology developed by big companies but could not afford to develop the technology themselves.
All these problems slowed the initial growth of VRI. The vast majority of remote interpreting services continued to be provided through less costly OPI, which is still true today to some extent.

2010s: The rise of interpreting delivery platforms (IDPs) and the cloud

The growth in web browser-based applications continued to be transformational for OPI and VRI technology developers. Before cloud-based computing applications and web real-time communications applications, interpreting over the internet was not nearly as easy to plug and play as it is today. Previously, providers and interpreters had to connect over specific hardware.

In other words, to communicate, they needed to have the same kind of phones or computers using the same computer operating systems.

Eventually, several web-based real-time voice and video communications applications became successful, such as Skype, FaceTime, GoToMeeting, and Cisco® Webex. Interpreters and providers could connect with each other regardless of the type of phone, computer or other IT hardware they were using, as long as they were connected to the internet and using the same application.

These applications worked reasonably well. Many are now among the dominant video conferencing platforms used today around the world. They were not built for interpreting and could be problematic for remote interpreters. As a result, many interpreters began finding workaround solutions to compensate for problems they had with these platforms.

However, most of these applications require proprietary plugins that had to be downloaded to a computer to use. Remote interpreters would continually need to update these applications to the latest version. Interpreters would also need to make sure that these application plugins were compatible with the version of the web browser they used and that web browser's security settings.

In many businesses, remote interpreting applications were not always allowed to be installed on company computers. Most corporate IT departments support strong security. They oppose downloading anything on their network that is not approved by the company. Companies followed a general approach to keep things secure. In general, only the largest technology and software vendors were able to accommodate or overcome these barriers to adopting early VRI technology.

The cloud arrives

Then came the "cloud." And the cloud changed *everything*.

A giant disruptive wave of technologies began to sweep across the remote interpreting industry. One of the biggest and most important was cloud communications technology.

"The cloud" is a term that gets used often. But what does it really mean when someone says technology is in the cloud?

What does the cloud mean?

"In the cloud" simply means that a given software application can be accessed primarily on the internet or via mobile networks. The term cloud has been used (and occasionally misused) as a blanket term to describe the internet itself. What it really indicates is that the software you are interacting with resides on a series of networked computer servers located somewhere in a data center, or potentially across multiple data centers, that all reside on the internet.

The key point for you as an interpreter is that *the cloud has eliminated the need to download complex software to your computer*. Now you can simply *interact* with the software you need by using a common web browser.

2015: WebRTC

The cloud helped spread video and audio communication across the internet, but it wasn't until the advent of Web Real-Time Communication (WebRTC) that things really sped up. WebRTC is a free and open Google-devised project that allows for real-time communication on web browsers and mobile applications, using application programming interfaces (APIs).

The WebRTC revolution

A few years after the release of the Google Chrome browser, computer engineers at Google were looking to build a web-based communications solution that could eliminate the need to download software plugins and provide a more secure and easy way to communicate over the internet.

A Chrome WebRTC consortium was created. On June 1, 2011, the components for the first iteration of the WebRTC source code were released to the public for the development of plugin-free internet communications.[33]

This exciting new WebRTC protocol made history! Apple, Google, Microsoft, Mozilla and a few other major technology companies all supported it. This technology provided *an open standard for the development of video, voice and data transmission applications.*

These web application development tools were released to all the major browser providers on the market, that began building innovative new communication applications.

A revolution for remote interpreting

How did WebRTC affect remote interpreting? First, as a direct result, the webconference sector began to grow exponentially. Second, the field of remote interpreting technology expanded too, because it is closely related to webconference systems.

With the new WebRTC software tools in hand, almost overnight, new OPI/VRI software delivery systems began to develop. The progression from OPI to the development of VRI and then remote simultaneous interpreting (RSI) required not only the invention of the internet (step 1) but also the release of WebRTC (step 2).

Healthcare leads the way for OPI and VRI

Much of the early development for new interpreting specific software systems took place in the U.S.—and it was driven by the demand for medical interpreters.

Suddenly there were new VRI platforms available. WebRTC helped create a boom market for multilingual communications devices, applications and platforms. For example, by 2022, Nimdzi Insights was already tracking 140 different virtual interpreting technology solutions in its Language Technology Atlas (Akhulkova et al., 2022).

---

[33] Bruno Couriol. (2021). 10 Years After Inception, WebRTC Becomes an Official Web Standard. Retrieved from: https://www.infoq.com/news/2021/04/webrtc-official-web-standard/

That said, there are now so many platforms and technologies that it's challenging for interpreters (and clients!) to stay up to date with all their functionalities and features—especially contract interpreters who work with several different language services or platforms.

And it doesn't stop there. You'll read more about this massive expansion when we get to the COVID-19 pandemic.

New interpreting platforms lead to integrated services

Scaling interpreter services. As the internet matured, another challenge surfaced
It has always been difficult, even for face-to-face interpreting, to schedule appointments with multiple interpreters speaking or signing many languages. Interpreter scheduling is complex and demanding, even for the largest language service companies that pioneered and developed automated remote interpreter scheduling systems.

After all, around the world, demand for interpreting has grown steadily year after year. It has been an ongoing challenge for interpreting agencies to find local, qualified interpreters and grow their face-to-face interpreting teams to meet the demand. In particular, sudden, large spikes in demand for interpreters have often been a stressful recruiting and support challenge for most interpreter services.

For example, when natural disasters strike, demand for onsite and remote interpreters across multiple languages goes up. When language services cannot locate and schedule enough interpreters to meet the demand, either during an emergency or because of a more gradual increase in need, the term you will often hear is that that the business does not scale.

You can find similar patterns in other language services—even in schools. Think of the start of the school year in areas with a high immigrant population. You need interpreters for parent-teacher conferences, planning services for students with disabilities (special education in the U.S.), public school events and media announcements.

Now think about all the interpreter services the public needs during a migration of refugees, war and crises, or horrific events, such as mass shootings, or during a public health crisis, such as the COVID-19 pandemic.

How do you schedule interpreters? With software, you say. But remote interpreting expanded these challenges *exponentially* because it increased the pool of interpreted sessions from dozens to hundreds to thousands and even millions—per *month.*

Recruiting and training interpreters in all the languages pairs the world needs to meet this demand is an ongoing challenge that is complex and often hard to solve. However, new automated cloud-based solutions have been developed that provide better and more efficient and targeted management of interpreting services.

The solution: An interpreter management system

Cloud-based solutions arrive
New cloud-based remote interpreting software solutions have provided a way to help language services scale up (expand) their interpreting business. For-profit language companies in the U.S. were the early adopters of this technology.

An urgent need to integrate software solutions

OPI and VRI technologies spurred tremendous growth in the availability and flexibility of providing interpreting services. That growth, however, led to new challenges. Language services needed to find appropriate software to better manage the logistics of a growing interpreting business. The software needed to include automated scheduling, invoicing and maintaining an up-to-date database of qualified and available interpreters.

Language services initially struggled to find solutions, often cobbling together makeshift interpreter management systems assembled from different types of off-the-shelf software.

This software was not originally designed to manage interpreting calls or support interpreters.

Language services would try to manage bookings using spreadsheet programs and other desktop office management software programs that didn't work well for interpreting services. Interpreters used whatever communications software their clients were using (because they really had no other options and limited choices).

How could agencies become competitive and manage their services? The answer was the interpreter management system.

2015: The interpreter management system and interpreting delivery platform converge (VRI 2.0)

Enter the interpreter management system (IMS), a software application designed specifically to help language services simplify managing an interpreting business.

The IMS allowed language services to manage face-to-face interpreting schedules intelligently. It automated the scheduling of interpreting sessions. The IMS made it possible to build and run a more sophisticated, growing interpreting business. As a result, it also helped smaller language services compete with larger ones.

> As the market and the demand provide language services grew, so too did the complexity and overhead of managing this service. Providing onsite interpreting services was and still is a regional model, most successfully executed by local agencies that know the local market best, know the interpreters well and can successfully recruit to meet their business needs.
>
> In the early 2000s/2010, software solutions that could meet the complex needs of these organizations were expensive and burdensome to implement and well beyond the budget of the typical regional language service company.
>
> The timing was ripe for the arrival of the IMS. Tailored software for the language services market, integrating scheduling, workforce management, billing and reporting in a single platform at a price point that worked for these regional agencies.
>
> A critical element of being able to fill this gap in the market was the advent of cloud computing, allowing smaller software organizations, such as ours, to build niche software offerings, such as Interpreter Intelligence, on the backbone of cloud services, such as Amazon Web Services in a cost-effective manner.
>
> —Conor Power, Founder, CEO, Interpreter Intelligence

IMS tools

Eventually these new IMS software programs added other business management tools, such as contact management and procurement tools for subcontractor management, billing and invoicing. They also added business analytics and business intelligence data analytics with business reporting capabilities.

Some IMS software platforms added communications capabilities to support on-demand OPI and VRI.

These combined or *unified interpreter management systems* could now effectively support the entire workflow of a busy and growing language service that provided both face-to-face *and* remote interpreting—whether that interpreting was scheduled in advance or provided instantly or on demand.

Face-to-face services as well as on-demand *and* scheduled OPI and VRI services could now be easily managed via one central software application.[34]

Who uses the IMS today?

At first only language companies, and initially only large ones, had the resources for an IMS.

Today, however, IMS solutions assist a growing number of organizations, including smaller local language services, hospitals, school systems, refugee resettlement agencies and other organizations that employ a pool of language services staff and contract interpreters.

If smaller agencies or organizations cannot afford their own IMS, they can simply piggyback onto platforms that offer their IMS to other organizations—a rapidly growing solution for some cost-conscious or resource-lean organizations.

In addition, smaller organizations that contract with a larger IMS platform are able to have their own employee and contract interpreters work remotely—but these smaller organizations can also engage interpreters (for example, for languages they need or at times of peak demand) from the same platform that is offering smaller organizations access to its IMS.

RSI platforms emerge

Let's look at the most recent evolution in of the remote interpreting puzzle the remote simultaneous interpreting platform or RSI platform. OPI and VRI solutions for remote interpreting were the first to gain a foothold in the interpreting market. These solutions, however, only solved encounters where consecutive interpreting was needed for spoken language interpreting.

(**Note:** For sign language, simultaneous is possible over a regular VRI connection, not only VRS, because only one person speaks up at a time, needing only a single audio channel.)

As a result, there was a growing need to create remote solutions for simultaneous interpreting sessions for spoken languages. Parallel to the development of VRI platforms, somewhat less visible work was being done on what eventually became the remote simultaneous interpreting platform.

---

[34] In general, the IMS was not designed for remote simultaneous services.

RSI presents a more difficult technological challenge than OPI/VRI. The interpreter speaks at the same time as the speaker, and their voices have to be separated into distinct channels. RSI can be performed on platforms with or without video, depending on the setup, but more recently it is typically performed with a video component.

The birth of RSI

Let's look at how RSI evolved. Interestingly, it did not launch in the conference interpreting world, where simultaneous interpreting remains dominant today, but in medical interpreting.

In 1972, Bill Wood, a technology pioneer in language services, founded a company called Design Specialists. He obtained what was possibly the first patent in the RSI field for key switching technology and the implementation of remote simultaneous in hospital settings in 1995.[35]

RSI innovation gained momentum, generating national media attention.[36] Research on its effectiveness in patient-provider communication was documented in *Medical Care* (Hornberger et al., 1996).

Yet RSI at the time never gained widespread acceptance in medical interpreting, which instead adopted OPI/VRI for remote interpreting.

RSI arrives in conference interpreting

The next developments in RSI began in the 2010s. This time, they came out of conference interpreting.

Resistance to remote interpreting in conference settings was, and in some areas remains, quite strong. Interpreters and meeting organizers were concerned that having interpreters work remotely would compromise high-quality multilingual communication. Yet the cost of providing face-to-face interpreting could be prohibitive.

Several startup companies began experimenting with hybrid solutions that would allow conference attendees to access face-to-face interpreters through smartphone applications rather than through traditional receivers and earphones. They soon began experimenting with interpreters who worked offsite.

This innovation opened the door to reducing the cost of paying to have interpreters travel to onsite events. There was also no need to rent expensive face-to-face simultaneous booths and equipment. The cost savings were huge.

How RSI developed

In the beginning, efforts focused on a hybrid RSI model where participants and speakers were all onsite together and the interpreter could be remote. But if interpreters were taken out of physical booths, they needed a virtual solution to communicate with each other and receive the audio and video from the onsite event.

Companies quickly started building out platforms to help solve these technical requirements.

---

[35] Who We Are. DS-Interpretation, Inc. Retrieved from: https://www.ds-interpretation.com/who-we-are

[36] SimulTel Client Case Study. Retrieved from: https://web.archive.org/web/20160327070054/http://simultel.com/Solutions_CaseStudy.htm

VoiceBoxer,[37] Interactio, Interprefy, ZipDX and KUDO are several companies that launched platforms dedicated to RSI. At first, each company targeted different communications priorities. For example, VoiceBoxer originally focused on providing interpreting for the explosive growth of webinars.

ZipDX built off the original concept of performing medical simultaneous interpreting over the phone and also developed a platform for international multilingual conference calls.

KUDO became one of the first full-service webconference platforms, similar to Zoom and Webex, created specifically for RSI, with technology that allowed interpreters to work in virtual booths.

For more information about the evolution of RSI in conference interpreting, see Chapter 3 of Volume 2.

THE Zoom boom and rapid growth of RSI

Since the mid-2010s, two developments swiftly advanced the development of dedicated RSI platforms. As previously noted, WebRTC was a significant change for all kinds of real-time video communication and has fueled the huge expansion of social media, video call software and webconference platforms around the world.

This same technology gave RSI companies the tools they needed to integrate multiple audio and video channels to facilitate multilingual communication.

Another development to transform RSI was the COVID-19 pandemic. Let's first understand how the pandemic impacted remote interpreting in general, and then we'll come back to how it impacted RSI technology, which was then in its infancy.

2020: The arrival of COVID-19

COVID-19 as a super-accelerator for remote interpreting technology

One historical event, discussed in Chapter 1 and the Foreword of this book, has also been responsible for the most unprecedented, explosive growth in remote interpreting technology—and as a result, interpreting services.

This event is of course the global pandemic (COVID-19), which had a profoundly transformational effect on the industry.

The COVID-19 pandemic further accelerated the growth of webconference tools starting in 2020, as both private businesses and government agencies were forced to operate virtually and use webconference services to communicate with remote teams and clients. While estimates vary, most market experts believe that the market for video conferencing software reached USD 9.2 billion in 2021 and is expected to reach and surpass USD 22.5 billion by 2026.

Some of the key participants in the webconference industry include Zoom, Microsoft, Google, Facebook, Cisco, IBM, Adobe and GoTo.

---

[37] Acquired by Boostlingo in 2022.

As it turns out, the almost universal dependence on webconference platforms for global communication during the pandemic brought big changes to remote interpreting. Where many had resisted remote interpreting, and RSI in particular, the sudden shift to virtual communication around the globe eroded resistance. The pandemic led to the rapid adoption not only of OPI, VRS and VRI but also of RSI.

Remote interpreting was now widely seen as viable—and a critical solution for urgent language access.

When the COVID-19 pandemic first hit

The impact that COVID-19 had on the global demand for remote interpreting happened on such a colossal scale that it brought in a new age for the industry.

Many onsite interpreting programs were quickly shut down in response to the rapidly spreading pandemic. Most organizations with face-to-face interpreting programs that could shift to remote interpreting made that transition: they needed to continue providing language access to all their participants who needed interpreters.

The sudden change affected a wide spectrum of both public and private organizations.

Webconference platforms drive big changes

Of course, this overnight shift in demand also had an immense impact on the technology that makes remote interpreting possible. In short order, web communications platforms became vital business. Webconferencing and web meeting software companies experienced unprecedented triple-digit growth almost overnight.

For example, in the second quarter of 2020, Zoom's share prices rose by over 40 percent.[38] Zoom's number of daily meeting participants increased from 10 million to 300 million.[39] Video calls at large enterprises increased nearly five times between the start of the year 2020 and the early days of the pandemic.

> The language industry has shown great resilience—2020 provided conclusive proof that language services are not discretionary spending but essential.
>
> —Florian Faes, Slator Managing Director

This dramatic growth increased demand for language support, which established remote interpreting as an essential service around the planet.

---

[38] Sergei Klebnikov. (2020). Zoom Stock Skyrockets Over 40% After Blowout Quarter, and It Expects to Keep Rising. *Forbes*. Retrieved from: https://www.forbes.com/sites/sergeiklebnikov/2020/09/01/zoom-stock-skyrockets-over-40-after-blowout-quarter-and-it-expects-to-keep-rising/?sh=632af37069f1

[39] Tom Warren. (2020). Zoom Grows to 300 Million Meeting Participants Despite Security Backlash. *The Verge*. Retrieved from: https://www.theverge.com/2020/4/23/21232401/zoom-300-million-users-growth-coronavirus-pandemic-security-privacy-concerns-response

Remote interpreting swiftly takes over from face-to-face interpreting

To put this rapid change into sharp perspective, Figure 2.5 maps how abruptly the interpreting business changed in parallel with the emergence of the COVID-19 pandemic.

In February 2020, remote interpreting, for example, was approximately 20 percent of global interpreting services. Face-to-face interpreting was still the primary—and preferred—interpreting delivery method.[40]

Then, during the last two weeks of March 2020, COVID-19 brought most face-to-face interpreting services to a dramatic and abrupt halt throughout the U.S.

For most interpreters, especially those not already performing at least some remote interpreting, the disruption was *immediate*. Most saw their face-to-face assignments put on hold or canceled until further notice. In many cases, some of these jobs have recently since returned; but in many others, the jobs have simply not returned and likely never will.

In large healthcare systems in 2022, many of the face-to-face interpreting programs that were replaced by remote interpreting programs have yet to return.

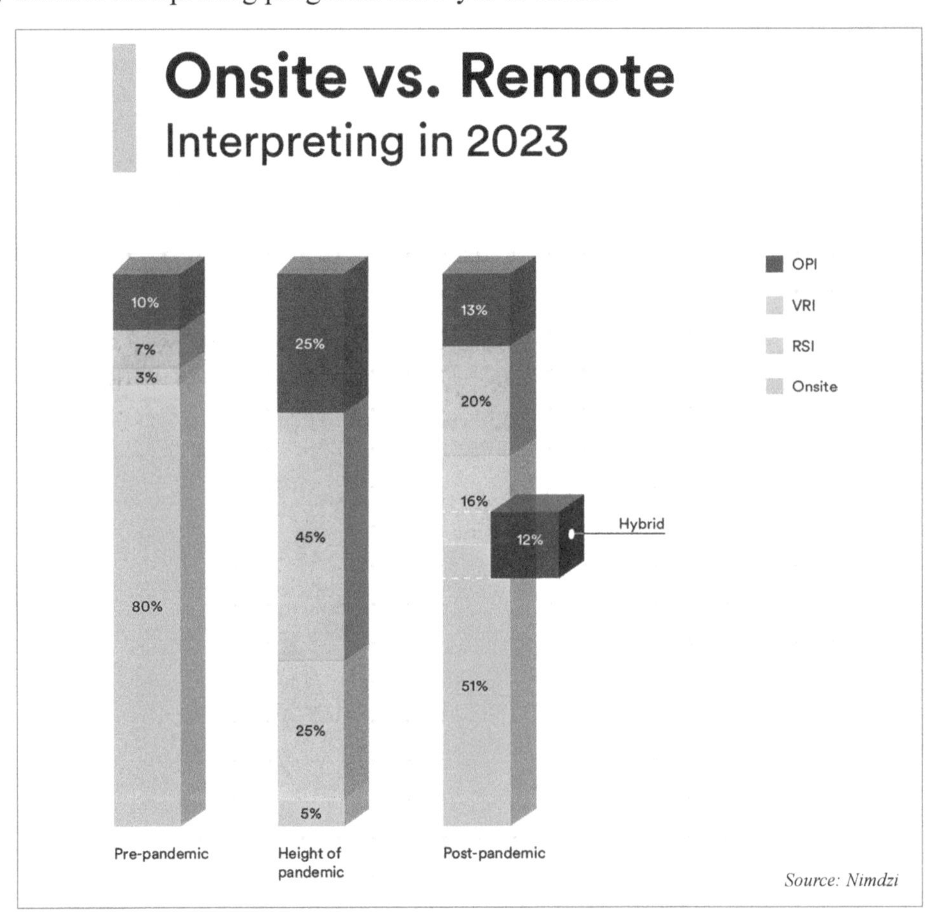

Figure 2.6: Remote interpreting is here to stay. Source: Nimdzi Insights (Hickey, 2021).

[40] Sarah Hickey. (2021). The 2021 Nimdzi Interpreting Index. Nimdzi Insights. Retrieved from: https://www.nimdzi.com/interpreting-index-top-interpreting-companies/#Remote-interpreting-is-here-to-stay

Was the shift permanent?

Only time will tell if there is a full return to prepandemic levels of face-to-face interpreting services. Current indicators are that it is unlikely because society has become far more comfortable with remote media interactions in all facets of life.

In addition, countless companies and clients have taken advantages of the cost savings and efficiencies in remote interpreting. They are not eager to go back to a more costly alternative.

A global evolution. Other countries, at slightly different points in time, saw the same effect and changes as a result of the pandemic. By June 2020, face-to-face interpreting around the world had come to a near complete halt except for a few intrepid interpreters, mostly in hospitals, who donned personal protection equipment (PPE) to provide urgent frontline language support in healthcare.

Many language services whose revenue was largely dependent on providing face-to-face language services struggled. Those businesses that could not pivot quickly to a remote model floundered with a dramatic drop in interpreting requests. They cut down staffing hours, reduced offerings and scaled down and restructured their contracts with both employed and contract interpreters.

Some language companies simply shut down interpreting services and focused solely on translation and localization.

The language services that provided remote interpreting had the opposite experience. The sudden surge in demand for remote interpreting grew overwhelming. Requests for service often eclipsed the number of available remote interpreters.

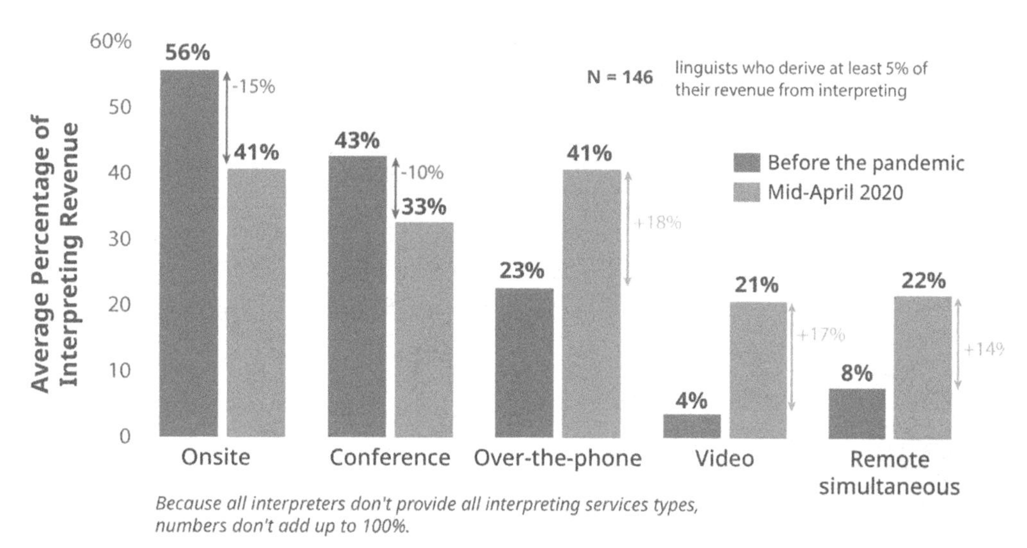

Figure 2.7: The early impact of COVID-19 on interpreter revenue (based on freelance interpreter revenue)[41]

[41] Note: *Freelancers* refers to self-employed interpreters; *onsite* refers to face-to-face interpreting.

A career change for many interpreters.
For the interpreters employed or engaged by remote interpreting services, the influx of requests for on-demand interpreting[42] was staggering. Many face-to-face interpreters had to switch to remote interpreting overnight to make a living. For many, it was an eye-opening introduction to a broad spectrum of remote platforms they might have never experienced before and which they often had to learn how to navigate at a moment's notice.

Remote interpreting is now a far bigger percentage of interpreting services than it was before the pandemic. There is new global awareness and appreciation for professional remote interpreting. It is fair to say that following the global pandemic the age of the professional remote interpreter has arrived—and it is here to stay.

The pandemic and RSI

But how did the pandemic impact remote simultaneous interpreting?

After all, these technology platforms were just gaining ground before the pandemic. When global travel shut down for an extended period of time in the spring of 2020, the business of diplomacy and international relations had to continue. The pandemic, by necessity, overcame the resistance against widespread adoption of RSI solutions in conference interpreting.

Without RSI, there was no work for conference interpreters.

How RSI met the pandemic demand
The pandemic-fueled demand for RSI has been filled in three creative ways:

- New RSI services (that may also provide consecutive interpreting).
- Webconference platforms with interpreting functions built in (such as Zoom and Webex).
- Hybrid phoneline/web platform combinations.

New RSI services
First, the existing companies with dedicated RSI solutions experienced tremendous growth; their new RSI solutions were constantly evolving and improving. At the time of publication of this book, more than 40 new RSI services were on the market.

However, dedicated RSI platforms remain limited primarily to the international government and large business space. They have remained mostly in the conference interpreting market.

---

[42] Most face-to-face interpreting is scheduled ahead of time or prescheduled. Remote interpreting can also be prescheduled, but it relies heavily on on-demand services, where individuals in a variety of organizations and services (such as hospitals, schools, law enforcement, business, tourism and social services) simply call into a remote interpreting platform to request immediate connection to an interpreter.

> Early days of remote interpretation faced some resistance within the industry, as there were fears that remote interpretation technologies would dilute the quality and perceived value of interpretation services. The question for the remote interpretation technologies was how to manifest a commitment to interpreters to elevate language professionals and open a world of underserved events to these services. As always, there were visionaries and early adopters, and as exposure and comfort grew, so did acceptance. The pandemic, of course, pushed acceptance into necessity, but the continued focus on the interpreter experience remains and continues to evolve with current needs and technological advances.
>
> Though the threat from the traditionally monolingual solutions with big pockets is real, the full-service technology solutions that specifically serve the language services industry offer diverse and flexible solutions that serve language services professionals as well as they serve the end users.
>
> —Sergio Llorian, Founder & CEO, VoiceBoxer

How standard webconference platforms hacked RSI solutions

Even though dedicated RSI solutions existed when the pandemic hit, they were not widely available outside of the conference interpreting market, partially due to cost. Overall, the rest of the world turned to two more inexpensive and accessible solutions to provide RSI: webconference platforms such as Zoom and Webex, and hybrid phoneline/web platform combinations.

At the beginning of the pandemic, Zoom was the only one of the big webconferencing platforms to have a simultaneous interpreting functionality. Despite the imperfect design (when compared to dedicated RSI platforms), Zoom, nonetheless, quickly became the most used platform around the world for RSI because of its availability and affordability.

Then other big platforms, such as Microsoft Teams, Webex and Google Meet started to introduce their own functions. However, it has taken other platforms months or years to catch up to Zoom, which continues to dominate the market.

Hybrid phoneline/web platform combinations

When using webconference platforms without a simultaneous interpreting feature built in, clients, buyers and interpreters have worked out a variety of phone solutions. These solutions add phone lines for the audio channels that interpreters need to perform simultaneously over a video conference platform.

For example, a U.S. school might hold a back-to-school night (an event where parents go to school to learn details about their child's upcoming school year) over a platform such as Google Meet. Parents and families who need interpreting will then call into a conference call line to hear the interpreting while they are logged in to Google Meet on another device.

Such a solution is imperfect, to say the least, but it is affordable for many all the same. Many U.S. schools and other organizations have embraced similar workarounds.

For more information about RSI, how it works and what interpreters need to know to perform it, see Chapters 1 and 2 of Volume 2.

2020 and beyond: AI, speech transcription and machine interpreting

Beyond the staggering impact that the pandemic has had on interpreting technology, other new innovations and language technology developments in the past decade are also shaping the remote interpreting profession.

For example, the boom in artificial intelligence (AI) for language technologies has driven innovation and software development. It has also had a huge and deep impact on language services.

Artificial intelligence simulates human intelligence using machines, typically computers with AI software. It is a branch of computer science—often a controversial one. Today, AI essentially refers to computer programming that simulates human characteristics, particularly about learning, often called machine learning.

AI is based on computer code designed to mimic human behavior and characteristics, especially how humans learn and problem-solve. You can think of AI as computer code that gets smarter over time and begins to take on human-like traits.

Innovation in machine learning in language technology research has led to what is now known as machine translation. Developments in machine translation have focused on trying to achieve human parity, that is, translation by machines that is just as good (if not better) than what a human translator can produce.

The past few years have brought huge progress in reaching the goal of human parity, but we are not there yet—if that goal is truly possible. (Many believe that it is not, but we also say never say never.)

Today, machine translation in several of the world's top languages has achieved remarkable quality for clear and simple texts. That said, to this day machine translation struggles for accuracy with complex texts, and in most languages, due to the inability of AI code to understand and incorporate context, including human culture, life experience, socialization and much more.

It was, of course, only a matter of time before developers in the machine learning and machine translation labs decided to pivot interpreting to see what AI could accomplish there. Could computer data learn how to interpret? Let's explore this question.

How machine interpreting works

Machine interpreting, also called speech-to-speech translation, is a multiple-step computing process that involves several distinct types of technology. It begins with speech and ends with speech. Here are the technologies involved, in order:

- Speech recognition.
- Text transcription of the audio data.
- Text machine translation of that transcribed data into the target language. (This step is quickly becoming optional through the rapid evolution of this technology.)
- Conversion of the text data into audio files or "speech."

The year 2019 marked the debut of speech-to-speech machine interpreting (which is working toward eliminating the intermediate step of text translation).[43] Since its debut, the technology has developed quickly. In June 2022, Meta announced it was developing the first speech-to-speech machine interpreting to be trained on mega speech samples available in "publicly available real-world data on multiple languages."[44]

By October 2022, Meta announced the successful speech-to-speech machine interpretation Hokkien, a primarily spoken language, although it still relied on translating English and Hokkien into Mandarin as a way to bridge the lack of a Hokkien written form.

At the core of all these is the *translation* of speech input (converted to text) to speech output (converting text back to speech).

Speech-to-text-to-speech machine interpreting is well advanced. We will refer to both types here as speech-to-speech translation or machine interpreting.[45]

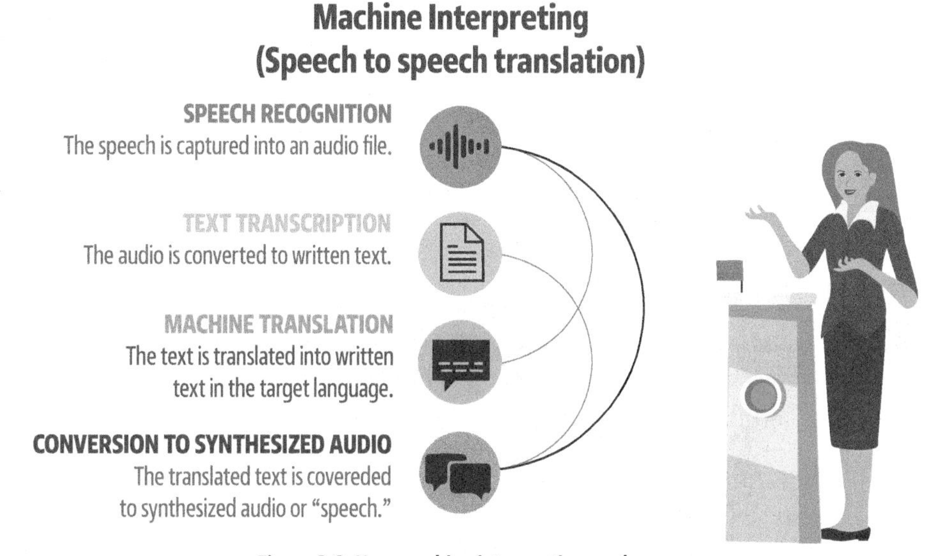

Machine Interpreting
(Speech to speech translation)
SPEECH RECOGNITION
The speech is captured into an audio file.
TEXT TRANSCRIPTION
The audio is converted to written text.
MACHINE TRANSLATION
The text is translated into written text in the target language.
CONVERSION TO SYNTHESIZED AUDIO
The translated text is covereded to synthesized audio or "speech."

Figure 2.8: How machine interpreting works

How well machine interpreting works

Today, most speech-to-speech translations programs tend to be fairly literal. Will they become more context aware and capable over time? Will AI be able to deal with many or most of the unique language idiosyncrasies that interpreters face every day on the job? There is no widespread agreement on this question. Only time will tell.

---

[43] Ye Jia and Ron Weiss. (2019). Introducing Translatotron: An End-to-End Speech-to-Speech Translation Model. Retrieved from: https://ai.googleblog.com/2019/05/introducing-translatotron-end-to-end.html

[44] Rocío Txabarriaga. (2022). Meta Doubles Down on Direct Speech-to-Speech Translation. Retrieved from: https://slator.com/meta-doubles-down-on-direct-speech-to-speech-translation/

[45] Meta's New AI-Powered Speech Translation System for Hokkien Pioneers a New Approach for an Unwritten Language. (2022). *Meta AI*. Retrieved from: https://ai.facebook.com/blog/ai-translation-hokkien/

Machine interpreting and interpreters

Here is another big question. As a remote interpreter, should you be concerned about being replaced by some future speech-to-speech translation technology? This question often comes up at language industry conferences. It can trigger fear and insecurity among interpreters and language services. (It also provides some entertaining and lively debates.)

It is important to keep in mind that machine translation never eliminated the need for human translators. Yet in many ways, translators' jobs *evolved* once machine translation became widespread.

A similar scenario may occur for remote interpreters. Just as translators need to learn about machine translation and become proficient with relevant software, tools, processes and procedures, so over time interpreters will need to adapt to advances and trends in machine interpreting.

For example, in the future you may need to know when machine interpreting is *not* appropriate. Perhaps one day, in the not-too-distant future, machine interpreting will be able to help schedule or confirm appointments, interpret basic instructions or navigate simple interpreted sessions.

But no matter how accurate AI and machine interpreting may become, they will not—or at least should not—be used in high-stakes encounters. For example, if you were a patient, would you want machine interpreting to inform you that a loved one has a terminal health condition? Would you want RSI machine interpreting for a politically sensitive conference?

What about mental health and therapy, military interpreting in the field, high-stakes meetings between CEOs of large companies or between leaders of government agencies?

Will machine interpreting replace interpreters?

AI is generating fear in many professions that jobs will be replaced by technology. Will machine interpreting replace interpreters? This question has been asked in interpreting and translation circles for several decades, and the short answer is no.

It is hard to predict how quickly any one technology may move forward. And whatever happens may affect the kind of work interpreters do. But based on how technology has affected the translation and interpreting professions up to now, it's more likely that AI will change and expand opportunities in interpreting rather than replace humans altogether.

> It is not about competition. AI is rather about new use cases and bringing interpreting to places and clients that previously had none. For example, many solutions AI solutions are currently aimed at individuals, tourists, cab drivers, in other words, clients with a smaller budget. AI can also help in the triage phase in hospital admissions and the emergency room until the interpreter arrives. If anything, it is likely that AI will expand the interpreting market and create more opportunities.
>
> —Sarah Hickey, Vice President of Research, Nimdzi Insights

AI in language and interpreting research will continue to improve. For example, webconference interpreting platforms are starting to create AI-generated multilingual captioning and subtitling. Captions are simply the written version on screen of what is being said. Closed captions also include paralinguistic and sound information on top of the dialogue. Subtitles are translations of what is being said on the screen. Captions are geared primarily for the Deaf and Hard of Hearing, and subtitles are for hearing people who don't speak the language of the original video.

In late 2022, the reliability of AI-generated captioning and subtitling varied across languages, but their accuracy is likely to evolve quickly, and they are certainly in use. (Some RSI interpreters use live captioning in English on Zoom to assist them with their interpreting.)

For now, however, machine interpreting technologies continue to struggle with speech that only professional interpreters can manage with accuracy. Those challenges include accurately detecting context and meaning, pronunciation, regionalisms, other language variations and many other aspects of language that we often take for granted and interpret instinctively.

Machine interpreting, on the other hand, has become impressively accurate with topics that are more technical in nature, or that are simple and straightforward, requiring less nuance. Machine interpreting continues to struggle with conveying emotion, irony, culturally specific references, gender and so on; all elements of language that are intrinsically part of a human's ability to interpret, which computers find difficult. These challenges for AI development likely mean that interpreters' jobs are safe for now—at least where creativity, context and critical accuracy matter.

One other reason we probably do not need to worry for now about machine interpreting replacing interpreters is that most machine interpreting solutions are focused on encounters or services that previously have not included hiring interpreters. While the future is by no means certain, machine interpreting may become more about enabling or determining straightforward or initial forms of language access than about replacing interpreters altogether. For example, machine interpreting might help determine if someone needs an interpreter, or to assist in the scheduling of an interpreter.

A real-life example of the perils of using machine interpreting where human interpreters belong occurred in 2018. Here's what happened to a major internet company in Asia, during a high-profile conference.

> *[It] used its AI engine to power the live translation and broadcast of some of the side conferences to screens next to the stage and for followers of the event within [a messaging app]...the engine frequently went haywire and generated certain words needlessly and repeatedly, as well as getting confused when some speakers spoke in an unstructured manner or used certain terminology wrongly.*[46]

Language is complex. It holds meaning. Interpreters have a human advantage that machines do not. Interpreters interpret meaning and machines do not. Machines may try to interpret, but they often struggle and fail (and sometimes sound ridiculous in the process).

History, however, has also shown us that we learn to never say never when it comes to betting against human ingenuity and innovation in technology. Today, and at least for now, the chances of machines being able to interpret complex speech with the same level as human accuracy and human sensitivity to meaning anytime in the near future are extremely low.

---

[46] Lance Ng. (2018). AI Interpreter Fail at China Summit Sparks Debate about Future of Profession. *Slator*. Retrieved from: https://slator.com/ai-interpreter-fail-at-china-summit-sparks-debate-about-future-of-profession/

→ Section 2.1 Review

This section introduced the history of the technology that makes remote interpreting possible. It began with the introduction of a national OPI service in Australia and explored how OPI spread to other countries during the 1970s and the special role of dual handset phones in OPI. It discussed how later in the 20th century, TTY technology evolved into VRS services for individuals who are Deaf and Hard of Hearing. Soon after came the birth, expansion and later rapid growth of VRI (especially after the pandemic began).

This section also examined the special role of Web Real-Time Communication (WebRTC) technology, which made webconferences truly feasible and thus, by extension, greatly expanded remote interpreting. The birth of cloud services and the rise of interpreting delivery platforms (IDPs) in the 2010s spurred additional advances culminating about 2015 in the development of interpreter management systems and another phase in the development of VRI. This section then explored how RSI works and how it expanded exponentially during the COVID-19 pandemic, going far beyond its conference interpreting historical roots. This section concluded with an overview of the role of AI and machine interpreting in the historical evolution of remote interpreting.

Section 2.2 The Remote Interpreting Software Platform

→ Learning objective 2.2

After completing this section, the remote interpreter will be able to compare and contrast different types of interpreting software applications.

→ Section 2.2 Overview

In the previous section, we traced the history of remote interpreting technologies that led to the systems we have today. Now let's take a closer look at components that make up a typical remote interpreting system and some of the differences between systems.

Different platforms and software systems have their own ways of serving the needs of language services and the interpreters who work for them. As a remote interpreter, you will probably encounter several different software systems in your career. This section looks at some of the features and configurations of remote interpreting systems used today.

→ Section 2.2 Content

The technology landscape today

The size and diversity of related interpreter technology growth and innovation may surprise the uninitiated and new remote interpreter.

The *Nimdzi Language Technology Atlas* (Akhulkova, Hickey & Hynes, 2022), compiled and updated each year by Nimdzi Insights, does an excellent job capturing various sectors of interpreting technology, including many fields of innovation.

Let's take a look at some technologies included in the report.

- Translation management systems.
    - These systems provide modules for translation, editing and project management, including translation memory, term bases and quality assurance.
- Translation business management systems.
    - These address the business *operations aspects of translation services.*
- Audiovisual translation tools.
- Machine translation.
- Integrators.
    - These are systems to help systems integrate with each other.
- Marketplaces and platforms.
    - In marketplaces, language services can post job advertisements, then hire or engage the successful candidates directly onto their platforms.
    - The platforms can also manage much more.
- Interpreting systems.
    - These include both the topics of this section and AI solutions.
- Quality management.
    - These tools focus on translation: quality assurance, review and evaluation and terminology management.
- Speech recognition solutions.
    - Automated transcription and captioning.

And the atlas includes still other interpreter technologies.

As a remote interpreting professional, pay attention: tune into developments in this industry when you can. This is your world. This is the technology landscape of language services today, and the environment you may work in. Try not to be afraid of it. Think of it as an exciting new world of opportunity.

Remote interpreting software platforms

Providing language solutions is complicated. Hospitals and courts, for example, generally fill their interpreting needs through a mix of face-to-face and remote interpreters. They have to find the right interpreter for a certain language at a particular time and place.

The scheduling of qualified interpreters, while managing language demand, all has to come together in a seamless flow.

You will likely encounter four kinds of remote interpreting software applications used to make interpreting services more effective and efficient. Whichever system you work with, you will be expected to have a basic understanding of how to use them.

The four kinds of remote interpreting systems are:

- Interpreter management systems (IMS).
- Over the phone (OPI) and video remote interpreting (VRI) platforms.
- Unified remote interpreting platforms with an integrated IMS.
- Remote simultaneous interpreting (RSI) platforms.

The interpreter management system (IMS)

The interpreter management system on its own is essentially a sophisticated scheduling system that has traditionally focused on face-to-face interpreting and OPI and VRI but recently has expanded to include RSI.

Some IMS systems are built solely to manage and coordinate face-to face interpreting and face-to face interpreters. These systems do not on their own possess remote interpreting functionality, nor do they have any audio or video communications delivery capabilities.

Although they are not considered remote interpreting platforms, it is important to include these systems here. The scheduling functions of IMS systems are generally also a key component for most remote interpreting platforms, especially when OPI and VRI services need to be scheduled ahead of time.

IMS systems are more than just sophisticated calendars. Many of them allow clients to schedule interpreters across organizations, provide a payment portal, track language demand across services and much more. They produce the data that organizations need to understand their language access needs in detail.

Examples of such data include how many sessions of interpreting have been provided in that month, by language; total number of minutes of interpreting provided, by language; how many interpreters were engaged and much more.

As remote interpreting matures, we are likely to see the push for integration expand.

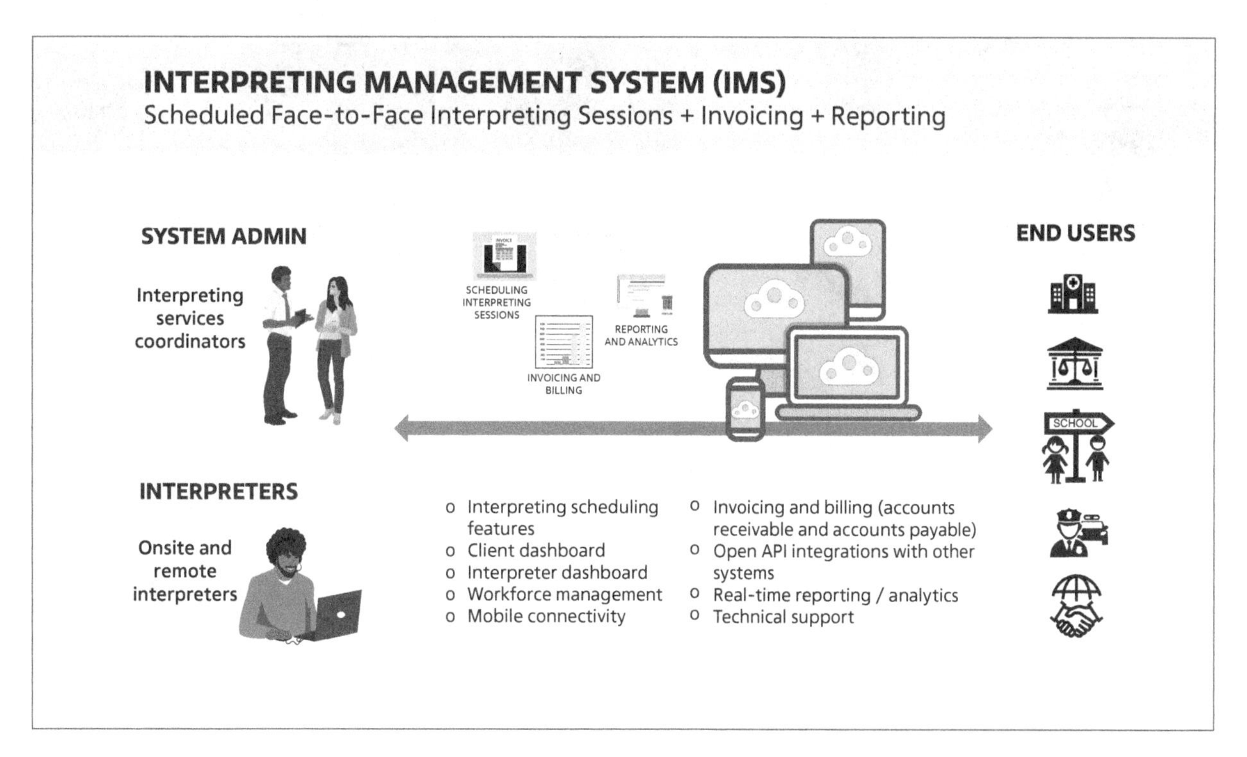

Figure 2.9: **Interpreter management system (IMS)**

The interpreting delivery platform (IDP) for consecutive interpreting

Interpreting delivery platforms are dedicated remote interpreting platforms. IDPs facilitate telephone (and other audio) and video interpreting between interpreters and participants. Their primary use is for on-demand OPI and VRI consecutive interpreting.

These platforms use web communications software and internet infrastructure to connect the remote interpreter directly with the participants who need interpreting.

You, the remote interpreter, may be at home, in an office or at a call center. The participants may be located anywhere in the world (see Figure 2.9).

Many IDPs integrate multiple administrative elements, such as monitoring and reporting features that evaluate interpreter performance, customer service and productivity as well as supporting interpreters.

IDPs are used across many market segments, particularly in medical interpreting, community interpreting, legal interpreting, court interpreting, financial interpreting, educational interpreting and travel or tourism interpreting.

For example, in medical settings, the basic interpreting delivery platform might be used for a Russian-speaking patient who arrives at the emergency room and needs an interpreter. There are no Russian interpreters on staff, so the nurse brings a VRI console into the room and dials the language service to request an on-demand Russian medical interpreter.

Within a few seconds, the interpreter receives the request to interpret and joins the call (whether from home, a call center or an office).

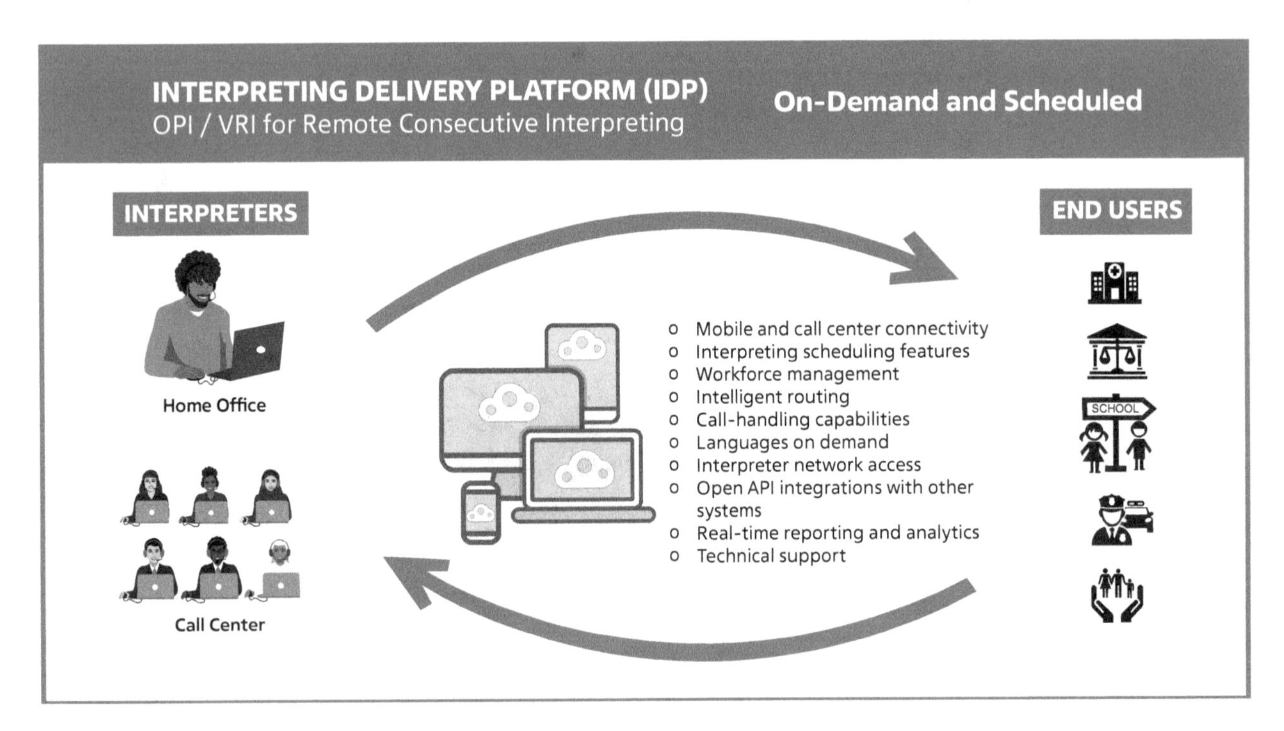

Figure 2.10: Basic remote interpreting delivery platform for consecutive interpreting

Figure 2.10 shows the typical set up for OPI and VRI system most often used in dedicated remote conference interpreting situations for scheduled simultaneous OPI or VRI sessions.

Unified remote interpreting platform for consecutive interpreting: IDP and IMS

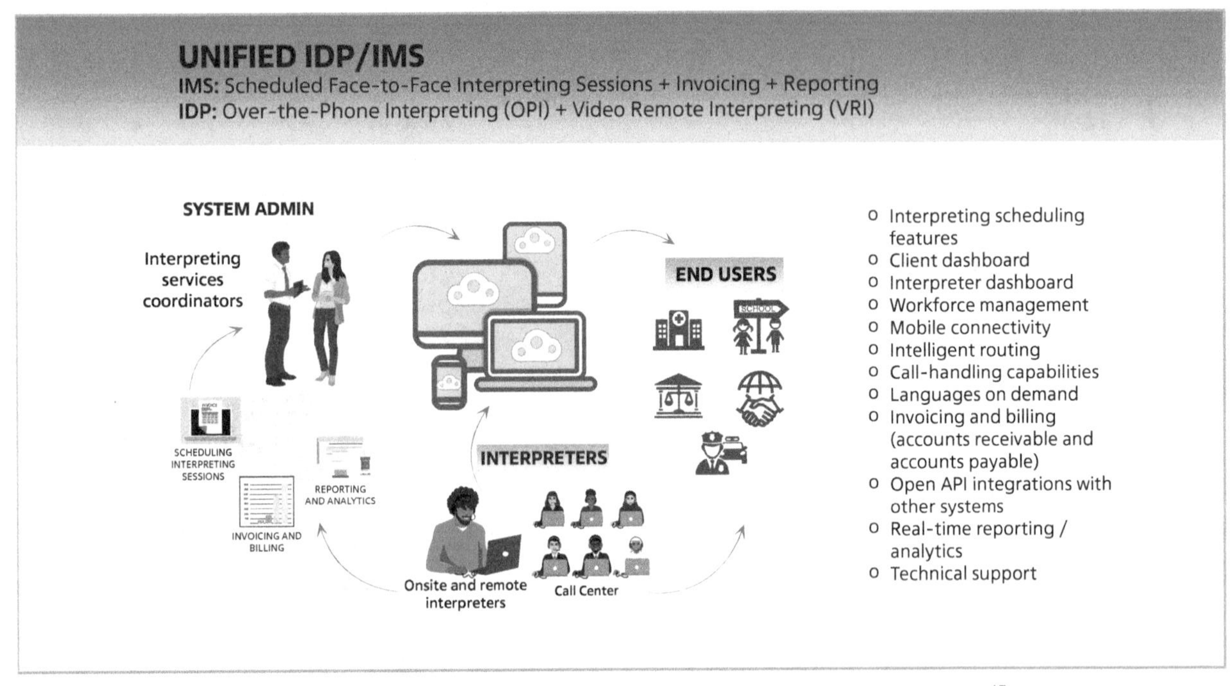

Figure 2.11: Unified remote interpreting delivery platform for consecutive interpreting[47]

[47] Note: OSI is a U.S. acronym that refers to onsite [face-to-face] interpreting.

The unified remote interpretation platform combines the main components of an IDP but includes the ability to schedule appointments ahead of time. It can manage OPI or VRI. It is used to support both on-demand delivery and scheduled sessions, whether face-to-face, OPI or VRI.

The unified platform is configured to handle all the interpretation workflow management tasks. Its core functions are scheduling and managing interpreting assignments and supporting the delivery of interpreting, both audio and video.

In addition, the IDP handles the logistics and routing of incoming interpreting requests in real time. It connects participants to qualified interpreters who are active in the network or logged on and ready to interpret.

Scheduled OPI and VRI calls are handled much as live onsite appointments are, except that the interpreter and the participants meet in a virtual meeting space.

The unified interpreting platform is used frequently in medical interpreting, community interpreting, legal (including court) interpreting, business and financial interpreting, educational interpreting and travel or tourism interpreting.

Remote simultaneous interpreting delivery platforms

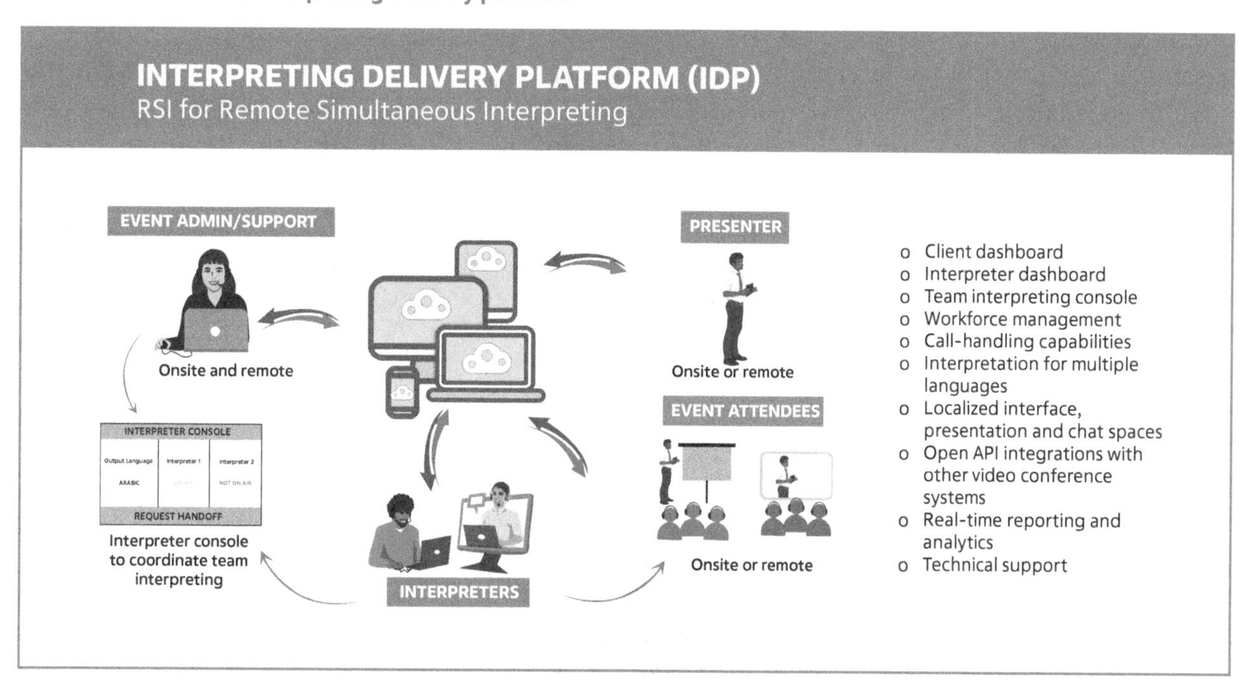

Figure 2.12: **Basic remote interpreting delivery platform for simultaneous interpreting**

The RSI IDP platform contains many of the general features and functionality found in a consecutive interpreting IDP OPI/VRI system, but it also has some fundamental differences and additional features necessary for RSI management and delivery. It supports the interpreter performing simultaneous interpreting (who speaks at the same time as the speaker) by adding a way for the interpreter's audio to be isolated from the speaker's audio. It also lets participants choose which audio feed or "channel" they would like to listen to.

The primary use of RSI IDPs is for delivery of remote audio or video *simultaneous* interpreting.

These RSI IDPs also accommodate team interpreting, where two or more interpreters work together and take turns interpreting. (Team interpreting is the subject of Chapter 8 in Volume 2). The interpreters in the team who take turns interpreting simultaneously need to interact privately on the platform while the meeting is taking place. For example, they need to alert each other about when to switch roles (from monitoring the other interpreter to interpreting).

Unlike standard webconferencing platforms, such as Zoom, Webex or MS Teams, RSI IDPs have all the necessary features required to provide RSI integrated into a single platform. There is no need for interpreters to use additional devices to connect outside the platform to communicate with their partner.

Full-service RSI IDPs are used mostly in conference, diplomatic, business and financial interpreting. At the time of publication, that situation was beginning to change as these platforms are expanding into community and legal interpreting.

Chapter 1 of Volume 2 examines RSI delivery in more detail.

Which technologies are used more?

Research conducted at the beginning of the pandemic captured the growing diversification and adoption of remote interpreting technologies. Figure 2.13 shows the continued importance of OPI and VRI platforms, but other technologies, including machine interpreting, were gaining ground (Pielmeier & O'Mara, 2020, p. 47).

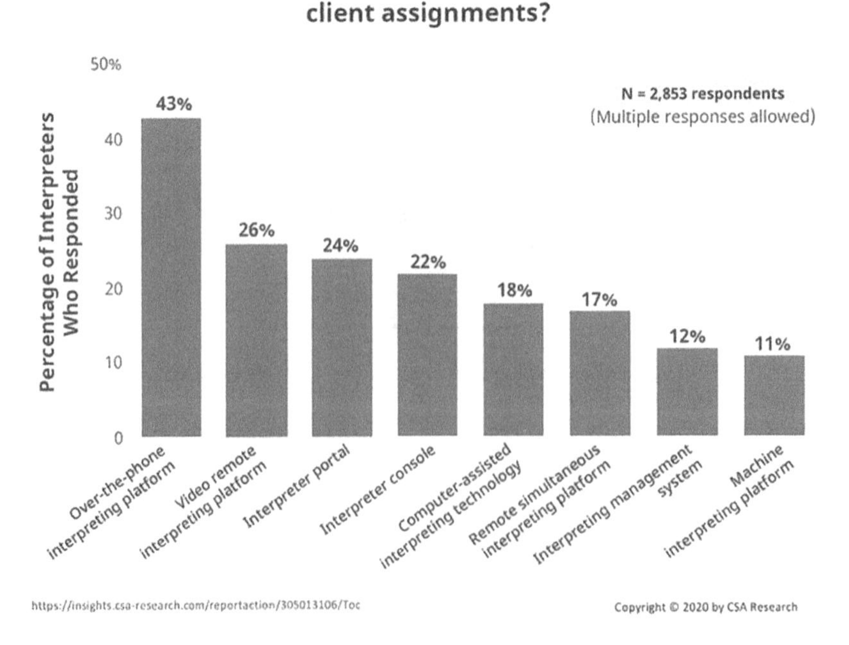

Figure 2.13: The state of the linguist supply chain

All this change and growth can be confusing. As an individual remote interpreter, tracking every detail is not what's important. But it is a good idea to pay attention to general developments in remote interpreting. Follow interpreting research in the news or read professional association newsletters. Don't assume that what you knew about remote interpreting technology a year ago is the same now. It's probably already changed.

→ Section 2.2 Review

This section has explored the four most common software applications used to coordinate and deliver interpreting services. Delivering remote interpreters to the many locations they interpret for is a complicated, technological challenge. The interpreter management system (IMS), together with OPI, VRI and RSI platforms, meets that challenge. By the time you read this chapter, new applications will be on the market and current ones will have evolved.

Section 2.3 The Remote Interpreter's Toolkit

→ Learning objective 2.3

After completing this section, the remote interpreter will be able to identify and describe the equipment and software used for OPI, VRI, VRS and RSI.

→ Section 2.3 Overview

In the last section, we discussed the platforms and software systems used by language services to deliver interpreting. The same platforms and systems are used by interpreters: both employee and self-employed interpreters. Today, these software applications are accessed by interpreters almost anywhere in the world.

In this section, we'll look more closely at the technology you will use to build your own workstation—or at least you'll understand the interpreter's workstation and equipment you may be given or required to use (for example, in a call center) and how it works.

As a self-employed remote interpreter, or one who ends up working for several different language service companies, you may encounter several of the remote interpreting platforms described in the previous section. You will need to become familiar with how each one you work on operates and how these platforms differ from each other.

If you work from home, or in an office of an organization that is not a language company, you will also need to set up and organize your own office work area with the right equipment. This section also examines the different types of equipment and technologies that will be important for you to understand to do your job well.

Remote interpreters need to keep up with constant changes in technology. It is possible that some of the equipment and technology discussed in this book could potentially be outdated by the time you read about it here. And that's all right: having a general understanding of the remote interpreting technologies and equipment discussed here will still be useful to your professional journey. The confidence that understanding this technology will provide when you get hands-on experience, will help you become a more competent and polished professional.

Interpreting technology may be ever-evolving, but your gradual exposure to it, and continual use, will ensure that it remains familiar—and is never overwhelming.

→ Section 2.3 Content

Evolving technology

Technology evolution means that as a remote interpreter, you need to regularly update and replace your equipment for as long as you work in this profession.

Gordon Moore, the cofounder and former chair of Intel Corporation, predicted in 1965 that the number of components in integrated circuits (the microchips that provide power and speed for computing) would double about every year because developers were continuing to improve them (Moore, 1965, p. 8). Known as Moore's Law, so far this prediction on the pace of change has held mostly true.

Each year, technology specialists, pundits, futurists and tech industry writers have declared Moore's Law to be dying, but each year new waves in technology breakthrough have helped to keep his principle more or less valid.

The good news for interpreters, especially self-employed interpreters, is that the consumer electronics industry has also done a good job of keeping pace with the ever-increasing need for more processing power and capacity while keeping the costs fairly steady and even trending down for some technologies year over year.

That said, whether you pay for it yourself or your organization pays for it—as a remote interpreter you will absolutely need to work with the most up-to-date equipment and technology that you can.

Updating your technology

For a remote interpreter, the technology and devices that you will need are in general readily available, at least in most of the major urban areas of the world. In other areas, there may be online ordering options.

However, depending on your own budget or your employer's, it may be difficult to replace the technology you need as often as recommended. When you read through this section, take note of which technologies will be top priority for you to upgrade often. But don't worry. You don't have to replace everything every year!

As you set up or upgrade your remote interpreting home office or official workspace, the choices you have to make might seem overwhelming at times. That said, you do *not need to be an information technology expert to make good, sensible decisions.*

This section breaks down the technology into manageable basics. Any interpreter with any level of information technology (IT) experience and comfort can make informed decisions with confidence. After you read this section, you will know which technologies and devices will satisfy your work needs. If you work for an organization that isn't a language service, you may be able to inform them about the need to upgrade and know how to justify that expense.

This section also provides you with requisite hardware and software vocabulary as well as definitions for the products and technology that you may need to purchase or have available.

Let's get started. Let's find out what, exactly, is in the modern remote interpreter's toolkit.

The remote interpreter's toolkit

Laptop or desktop computer

Here is your first and most important priority: as a remote IT specialist (because yes: that's what you are), you will need a desktop or laptop computer that is ideally no older than three years.

As a language professional and a remote interpreter, try to make this your personal goal: avoid becoming the weakest link in the technology chain. If you get a reputation for being technology challenged about or fearful or nervous while using remote interpreting technology, you can damage your good name and your career before it even starts. Don't risk it.

Unless you work for a multilingual support call center, or you are directly employed by an interpreting service, the interpreting computer hardware and equipment decisions will fall on your shoulders. An ongoing investment in new computer technology at least every 4-5 years will help ensure that you stay current and reduce some of the inevitable challenges that accompany dated or underperforming equipment and software.

The hours spent troubleshooting an outdated computer system and the problems and the fatigue you feel when you deal with aging equipment are just not worth the stress. It is generally a waste of time, money and space to hold on to out-of-date equipment.

If you find you often have problems on the job that come from your technology setup, those problems can hurt your business and reputation. If you're a self-employed interpreter, your business software and computer hardware purchases are an investment in your future and your career.

On a positive note, if you are self-employed, your yearly technology purchases may be tax deductible as work expenses, which is generally the case in most countries. If you're not sure, check with your personal accountant or local tax office.

Mobile devices

The next set of tools in your remote interpreting toolkit are your mobile or wireless communications devices. You may need to provide remote interpreting services relying on wireless fidelity (Wi-Fi) or mobile network connectivity if you are providing services outside your office (but *only* if it is requested or allowed by the organization you interpret for).

As a general practice, do not use your mobile or wireless devices to interpret unless absolutely necessary or if you are required to do so. As you will see in this section, telephone technology is often not adequate for most remote interpreting requirements. When you use mobile or wireless technologies, the risk always exists that you might be disconnected, experience poor audio quality or deal with an ongoing bad connection.

There are also privacy laws and concerns that make interpreting by mobile or wireless devices risky or illegal. Chapter 9 of this volume discusses data security and data privacy compliance for remote interpreters.

If, however, you are required to interpret over a mobile device, including smartphones, mobile pads or tablets, make sure that device is up to date. You may also need a phone for other reasons, for example, to communicate with your partner if you perform team interpreting for RSI. In addition, many interpreters use mobile pads or tablets to take notes, look up terminology in glossaries, access resources, search for session-specific information on the internet and for other job-related reasons.

While some interpreters today may choose to use tablets to interpret, we would caution you to avoid doing so unless you are a highly qualified, seasoned remote interpreter and you are certain that you have the right tablet for the work. Also, verify first with the organizations and services that you interpret for to make certain that interpreting with your tablet is acceptable to them.

Just as with computer equipment, these devices should be replaced every 3-4 years to keep up with software and network connectivity demands. This area of remote interpreting hardware may become more widespread. Mobile networks are continuously improving, and mobile devices are evolving too. Some higher-end mobile devices have processing power and features that are comparable to laptops and desktop computers in terms of their functionality and performance.

Connectivity

Internet connectivity can be both the remote interpreter's best friend and worst enemy. To interpret remotely, you *must* have consistent access to secure, stable, strong internet services with as much bandwidth as you can possibly attain.

It is worth repeating: *You will always* ***need*** *access to a* ***strong, stable*** *internet connection or you cannot work effectively as a remote interpreter.*

The network demand for video and VRI is also significantly higher than it is for telephonic and audio only interpreting (AOI, including OPI). The demand for trouble-free connections is increasing at exponential rates around the world, not only due to interpreting needs, but also because in general the demand for quality high-definition video transmission is growing everywhere.

At some point in the future, it is possible that the technology minimum specification or the technology requirement checklist may become a thing of the past—but we're not there yet. Personal computing and mobile devices are rapidly approaching a level of power and technical sophistication to handle almost any processing requirement. There will be a time soon where nearly any device that you buy for your work will be configured with more than enough technology to seamlessly handle the day-to-day needs of a remote interpreter.

For now, let's look at some best practices and guidelines for the devices and technologies you need to do your job.

Best practices and guidelines for remote interpreting technology and devices

Technology minimum requirements for remote interpreters

The minimum recommended technical requirements for the software and hardware you need as a remote interpreter change all the time. They evolve almost as soon as technology devices are upgraded and updated. Technology specifications are dynamic.

Plan for change. Expect it. Many of the minimum specifications (or specs) that this book may recommend for you will invariably change, some even before you read them here.

The best practice is to continuously figure them out yourself. What specs do you need? Consult the language services (or any other organizations) that you interpret for. Find out now. Get their specific guidelines and recommendations. Then act on them.[48]

But what if you're not a contractor? If you work for a language service, it may provide you with guidelines, or it may look to you for guidance. But if you work as an employee for an organization, such as a school, a nonprofit agency or a government office, they may not understand what technology you need. Again, it will be your responsibility to determine the technologies you need.

In that case, you may need to find a colleague or consultant who is an IT expert. Write down what they recommend. Then make your case to your employer—and try to have the organization purchase the technology you need. You may encounter initial resistance. In that case, consider reading to them from this section for motivation!

If your employer wants you to interpret remotely, they need to ensure you are working with *adequate, up-to-date interpreting technology*.

Core technology requirements

Technical terms and acronyms are inevitable when you talk about technology. But don't worry: this section will cover only the most important concepts for computer hardware requirements and the most relevant technical terms associated with them.

Let's start with CPU and RAM. You need to know both these terms.

---

[48] If they have any guidelines: language services generally will, but if you interpret as a contractor for a school system, a hospital, a social services nonprofit or other organization, they may know little about remote interpreting and may not have guidelines for you.

CPU and RAM

CPU stands for *central processing unit*, and you can think of it as the heart of your computer system. It typically runs the programs on your computer and performs other calculations and actions.

RAM is an acronym for *random access memory*. It refers to the short-term storage capacity your computer has available. This storage can quickly access the data (applications) that you use the most.

The CPU and your RAM capacity are initially the two most *critical computing factors* that affect your work. They represent your computer's overall ability to support your interpreting software and process your audio and video needs, which are key factors that can mean success or failure your interpreting session.

From an IT readiness perspective, you need to know how fast your CPU is and how much RAM you have installed and available to you.

Both matter.

Both will affect your work. *A lot.*

If you don't have enough RAM, or your computer's CPU is slow or overloaded, then these problems will affect your session. If your computer processes audio and video too slowly, your session can break down.

In general, the older your computer system is, the less likely it is to have optimal performance for remote interpreting.

Other factors, like the type of hard disk (your computer's long-term memory and data retrieval abilities) and disk drive speed (how fast your computer is able to access the information on your computer), are also important. We will look at these IT considerations next.

Power, speed, memory and storage

All right. Let's say you need to purchase new technology, or upgrade what you have. Where next?

Without getting too detailed about technical specs, there are four important measurable elements to guide you in your selection process. When the time comes to invest or reinvest in your computer system, and you ask, "What computer do I need?" whether you buy a desktop or laptop, *focus on buying the* ***maximum*** *amount of the following four attributes based on your current budget*:

- Power
- Speed
- Memory
- Storage

Power

It's important to ensure that your central processing unit (CPU) is new enough to handle today's remote interpreting applications. Remember, the CPU is the core piece of hardware inside your computer that allows your computer to interact with all the applications and programs you need to interpret.

The processor interprets the software program's instructions. It creates the output that you interact with when you are using a computer. If your computer or CPU is less than 3-4 years old, it can *probably* keep up with what you need to interpret.

Speed

Many factors affect computer performance. Processor speed is one of the most important.

The CPU is generally regarded as your computer's brain. You want to make sure it can "think" really fast. This is a basic requirement for remote interpreting. It's essential.

The clock speed of your CPU decides how quickly your system can access and execute software instructions. That speed affects how quickly your computer can support different tasks.

In the processor world, speed is measured in gigahertz (GHz). *The larger the GHz value, the faster your system is*. When it comes to processing speed, *choose the fastest speed that you can afford.*

You won't regret it.

Memory

Basic rule: you can never have too much RAM (random access memory)!

RAM controls a computer's short-term memory. All the ways you use your computer require RAM. The more RAM you have, the more things you can do on your computer at the same time. RAM is *active* computer memory.

Again, get as much RAM as you can afford, because remote interpreting applications require *plenty* of it. You will be happy if you buy lots and lots of RAM!

Storage

Most systems today come with more than enough storage to support your interpreting needs. There is one performance consideration you may want to pay attention to: the type of storage disk drive included in your setup.

Disk drives these days tend to be hard disk drives (HDD) or solid-state drives (SSD). The trend in technology is moving more toward SSD because it is faster and more stable technology, but SSD costs more.

Additional hardware requirements

Second computer monitor

A second computer monitor is not always required for all remote interpreting platforms.

But it can make your life *so much* easier.

Nowadays, some language services actually require that interpreters deploy two monitors, because the interpretation platform they use is designed to run on two screens. Whether or not a second monitor is required, our recommendation is just try it, if you can. If you happen to work with several different remote interpreting applications and related software, you will be even happier to have that extra monitor.

Research has shown that additional screens may provide a more efficient workplace. They can make you more efficient too (Burruss et al., 2021). They can certainly make it much easier for you to move between all the different windows you may have to keep open while you interpret.

That said, the correct approach to how many work monitors you need is to choose the number that work best for *you*. Some interpreters prefer everything on one screen, even if that reduces the size of individual programs you are running. Others set up *three* monitors to interpreter remotely. It's your work environment; it's your choice.

Professional headphones and headsets

The headphone, microphone or audio headset you use for interpreting is one of the most critical and important investments you can make.

Even if you have to pay for it yourself, think of it as a necessary cost of doing business. For an interpreter, your ability to hear and to be heard clearly are vital to your job.

When you interpret without a headset and rely instead on your computer's built-in microphone, both your ability to hear and the ability of those who listen to you can be negatively impacted. Without a headset or headphones, you can't control how loudly or quietly the person is speaking. Any kind of background noise will be heard by the participants, and your volume may be too low.

In addition, using the computer's built-in microphone can create echoes and feedback loops that are frustrating to those who listen to you on the other end.

For these reasons, and others, it is *essential* to provide the best possible sound you can.

Over time you will find out that not all headsets and headphones are equal, so let's get our terms straight.

Figure 2.14: **Headset with boom microphone (boom mic)**

Headset with boom mic vs. headphones

A headset generally has an attached microphone—or boom mic—that you speak into. This type of attached microphone is ideal for communicating over audio-only and video conference platforms. Here is the reason: the microphone prioritizes capturing your voice when you talk and the headset captures the incoming voices of participants.

Headphones are earphones that do not have an integrated boom mic that is attached. Instead, you need to pair headphones with a separate, external microphone (discussed shortly).

Why boom mics are important for remote interpreting

Let's focus on headsets with boom mics first. Most remote interpreters rely on them. They are the recommended piece of equipment for most OPI and VRI software applications.

Be careful what you buy. Most headsets will not meet your needs. They may be adequate on short notice: they get the job done when you have no other choice. But a professional-grade headset will make a big difference. Professional-grade headsets do tend to be more expensive than your average consumer-level headsets, but cheap headsets are a false economy when it comes to doing your job. Comfort and audio clarity are critical for your work.

The bottom line is that pro-level headsets are a mandatory core piece of equipment for the remote interpreter.

When you select your headset, look for dynamic, closed-back headphones that fit securely around your ears or alternately on-ear headsets that sit more superficially over your ears. Both of these types of headsets can deliver higher-quality audio and tend to be more comfortable for long-term use.

Buying a headset

It's always a good idea to test any headset that you intend to buy, if you can. Make sure it fits comfortably. Leave it on for a while to see how it feels over time. Check to be sure it has noise-control features and can effectively reduce or eliminate ambient (surrounding) noises. To the best of your ability and with technology support you will want to control and contain any audio interference. Interference is distracting, and your participants will dislike it and may complain.

Look for a high-sensitivity and low-impedance rated headset. It will help you be sure that what you hear is loud enough and is also crisp and clear. The high-sensitivity and low-impedance specifications are usually clearly indicated on the product box or in the product specification sheet if you order online.

You don't need to have a deep understanding about audio sensitivity, frequency or impedance, but you can be sure that asking for high-sensitivity and low-impedance headsets at your local electronics outlet will make you sound really cool the next time you shop for a new interpreting headset. The important point here is to ensure you look for headsets that can achieve a clean, clear, loud-enough sound. That level of clarity should be audible across all the frequency ranges the human ear can detect.

Figure 2.15: Ensuring clean sound and adjustable volume is key to avoid acoustic shock syndrome

One more point: make sure the headset does not require additional power to achieve this level of clarity.

Headphone paired with an external microphone

If your budget can afford it, and once you understand your computer's audio settings reasonably well, you might consider headphones.

A headphone needs an external, or standalone, microphone. In other words, the microphone is separate from the headset and connected directly to your laptop or desktop system. Typically it stands on your desk. (But check with your language service first, if you interpret for one, as they may still prefer that you work with a headset and boom mic.)

This headphone setup is really only feasible if you have the ability to maintain and manage a relatively soundproof home office environment. Otherwise you will need to take additional steps to physically soundproof your interpreting studio. The reason is that standalone microphones are so sensitive they can pick up many other sounds besides your voice.

In this type of setup, your selection of microphone is just as critical as your headphones. The standalone microphone is your interpreting output capture and processing device. Translation: the microphone is responsible for capturing and delivering your speaking voice as clearly as possible.

Figure 2.16: **Headphone with an external microphone**

Your configuration

Many full-time remote interpreters experiment with headsets and then headphones and an external microphone. They want to find out which configuration, or audio setup, they prefer.

Both a headset with built-in mic and a headphone with a standalone mic will allow you to set up and control your audio. For example, you can easily mix the volume levels and quality of sound of the speaker and your own voice while you interpret.

We recommend that you start with a headset with a boom mic, because many of the audio settings are built in. They are plug and play.

When you switch to a headphone with a separate mic, you have to know how to manipulate the audio settings on your computer and the mic. That process can initially be tricky.

Both setups, either headsets or headphones, can work well. Just be sure you have the technical know-how for the option you choose.[49]

A brief word about acoustic shock syndrome

Some headsets now come with the ability to monitor for and reduce the risk of *acoustic shock syndrome*.

No section on headsets for remote interpreting can be complete without discussing acoustic shock syndrome. This is a real and potentially dangerous condition that can arise after you are exposed to sudden high decibel spikes in audio volume. It can also occur if you suffer prolonged exposure to loud sounds for extended periods of time (Noreña et al., 2018, p. 1).

---

[49] An excellent source of more detailed technical information on sound and video for interpreters is *The Interpreter's Guide to Audio and Video* by Josh Goldsmith and Naomi Bowman, available at https://techforword.com/p/interpreters-guide-audio-video

For example, in a study of conference interpreters,[50] 59 percent of surveyed interpreters in Canada reported suffering symptoms of acoustic shock—and *96* percent of interpreters in Brazil. This problem is so serious that in April 2022, one-sixth of federal conference interpreters in the Canadian Parliament could not perform their work due to acoustic shock that was apparently caused by poor audio quality in remote interpreting.[51] In October 2022, despite attention being given to this issue, a freelance interpreter working during a Canadian Senate hearing collapsed and was taken to the hospital after experiencing an acoustic shock.[52]

Acoustic shock syndrome is real, and it is serious. Let's be clear. It can happen to any remote interpreter.

Symptoms of acoustic shock syndrome

The symptoms associated with acoustic shock syndrome occur due to the muscle contractions in the middle ear after exposure to loud traumatic sounds. They can also be caused by prolonged exposure to repetitive destructive sounds.

People who experience acoustic shock syndrome often report symptoms like headaches, tinnitus (a ringing sound in the ears), ear pain, nausea, jaw and neck pain, fluttering noises in the ear, poor balance, hypersensitivity and fatigue (Noreña et al., 2018). If you know any RSI interpreters, headache is a word you will probably hear them say often!

The experience of acoustic shock syndrome has also been described as "electrocution in the ear." It can lead to extended ear health problems. These include short-term, long-term or even permanent loss of hearing.

This syndrome can also contribute to additional psychological effects like anxiety, depression, and even post-traumatic stress disorder.

Research on acoustic shock syndrome in remote interpreters is in the early stages. During the pandemic, conference interpreters at international organizations reported significant health issues related to remote simultaneous interpreting. This problem launched research on this issue. Such research is ongoing.

Previous research on acoustic shock injuries indicates that nearly 13 percent of all call workers are affected (John et al., 2015). Remote interpreters almost certainly suffer similar—if not higher—levels of injury.

---

[50] Canada Among the Most Dangerous Places for Language Interpreters. (2020). Speech-Language Audiology Canada (SAC). The study was conducted by the International Association of Conference Interpreters, who surveyed more than 1,000 interpreters. Nearly half (47 percent) reported symptoms. Retrieved from: https://www.sac-oac.ca/news-events/news/canada-among-most-dangerous-places-language-interpreters

[51] Hearing-related Injuries Cause Interpreter Shortage in Canada. (2022). *MultiLingual.* Retrieved from: https://multilingual.com/hearing-injuries-canadian-interpreters/

[52] Marion Marking. (2022). Canadian Translation Bureau Investigates Interpreter Collapse at Senate Hearing. (2022). *Slator.* Retrieved from: https://slator.com/canadian-translation-bureau-investigates-interpreter-collapse-senate-hearing/

Protecting yourself against acoustic shock syndrome

Individuals who get exposed to noise levels repeatedly over 85 decibels (dB) will be at high risk for acoustic shock syndrome.

If you wear headphones for any extended period of time, be careful. Buy quality. Today there are many high-quality headsets on the market with built-in amplifiers. They can give you some degree of protection from loud or sudden noise. They are also engineered to lower the sound automatically whenever high-pitched tones are detected.

Acoustic shock syndrome in interpreters may be caused by the long-term impact on inner ear health during remote interpreting. Protecting your ears means protecting your health—and your job. Quality should be an important consideration when you purchase headphones and headsets.

Buyer beware! Those bargain-priced headphones on sale are probably a dangerous idea for you. For a remote interpreter, perhaps nothing will be more important than protecting your hearing health.

A detailed look at headsets and headphones recommended for remote interpreting

If you spend hours a day interpreting remotely, you will need to carefully consider all the features of the headset you should buy. Whether you choose a headset with a boom mic or headphones, consider your selection with the following components in mind.

Circumaural (around the ear) or supra-aural (on the ear) closed-back headsets and headphones

This type of headset or headphone is designed to provide maximum sound isolation. It will not permit much, if any, ambient (surrounding) noise feedthrough. This headphone also prevents the sound you hear online from "bleeding" out into the room that you work in for added privacy and reduced distraction.

Full frequency range

Look for headsets and headphones that are rated to capture the complete range at which the human ear can hear sounds. This information is listed on the headphone product packaging and indicates the range coverage.

Look for support within a frequency of **20 Hz** (hertz) and **20 kHz** (kilohertz).

High sensitivity/sound pressure level (SPL)

High-sensitivity headsets and headphones do a better job of delivering acoustical sounds than lower-sensitivity headphones. This sound quality can help protect your hearing.

The level of sensitivity indicates how loud the headset earphones can get. Look for headphones that have a sensitivity in the range of **80 to 125 dB SPL/mW** (sound pressure level per milliwatt).

Low impedance

Low-impedance headphones require less power to deliver acceptable audio levels. Look for headphones that provide audio monitoring within 32 to 80 ohms (electrical resistance). Headphones with higher impedance often require additional amplification.

Noise-cancelling headphones

This type of headphone uses internal audio processing technologies to remove and filter out unwanted external or outside noise. This can be an important feature if you work from home or a call center—it can reduce or eliminate sounds from your environment, such as traffic outside your window and sounds from family members, pets or coworkers.

But a warning: sometimes this feature can also reduce sound that you need to hear. It may also give you an inaccurate representation of what you hear.

Be sure to look for headsets or headphones that have the option to turn noise cancellation on or off. RSI interpreters tend to use headsets with this option. Some RSI interpreters avoid noise cancellation altogether.

Open-back headphones

These types of headphones, as the name suggests, have an open back that allows sound to escape or "leak." These leaked sounds can in turn be picked up by your microphone. Avoid them.

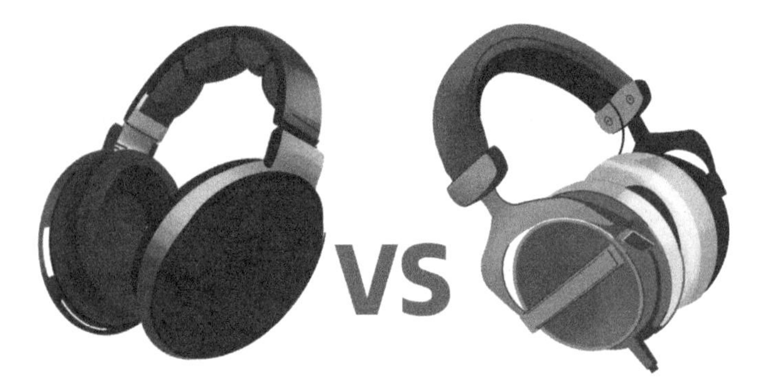

Figure 2.17: **Open-back vs. closed-back headphones**

Bluetooth wireless headsets and headphones

Bluetooth headphones are not always reliable; they are highly susceptible to interference.

Other devices can cause problems with your Bluetooth connection, such as microwaves, Wi-Fi routers, wireless speakers and even baby monitors. Bluetooth headphones also need to be regularly charged to function reliably.

Don't be that interpreter whose Bluetooth headset charge dies mid-sentence.

DECT wireless headsets and headphones.

A more stable wireless option for interpreters is DECT, which stands for digital enhanced cordless telecommunications. DECT provides an alternative or sometimes complementary option with Bluetooth connectivity.

DECT is currently a universal standard in Europe, Australia, Asia and South America. The adoption of DECT in the U.S. was delayed due to ongoing disputes about frequency utilization. The U.S. uses a standard called DECT 6.0, which unfortunately is not compatible with DECT in other countries at this time.

There are some headsets available that provide both technologies and give the ability to connect either way. Depending what countries your participants are located in, those headsets could be helpful.

DECT vs. Bluetooth

vs.

DECT differs from Bluetooth in four important ways:

Dedicated connectivity: DECT headsets connect to a base station, which then connects to an internet connection, typically through your computer.

Great stability: Although interference can be a problem, you will likely have far less interference with DECT than Bluetooth.

Extra security: Although both DECT and Bluetooth have encryption for data security, the DECT headset can provide an extra level of security. If you perform legal or medical interpreting, that extra security might be important.

Longer range: The DECT headset connects to its base. That base has a far greater range than Bluetooth. For example, at the time of publication, where the Bluetooth range is 30 to 80 meters (about 100 to 260 feet). The DECT range is 100 to 200 meters (about 330 to 660 feet).

Earbuds

Everybody uses them. Earbuds are everywhere.

They are small, convenient, wired and wireless, easily transportable and not bulky. However, earbuds are *not* ideal for remote interpreting. The sound they produce when connected to computers is generally inferior to the audio reproduction capabilities of headsets and headphones.

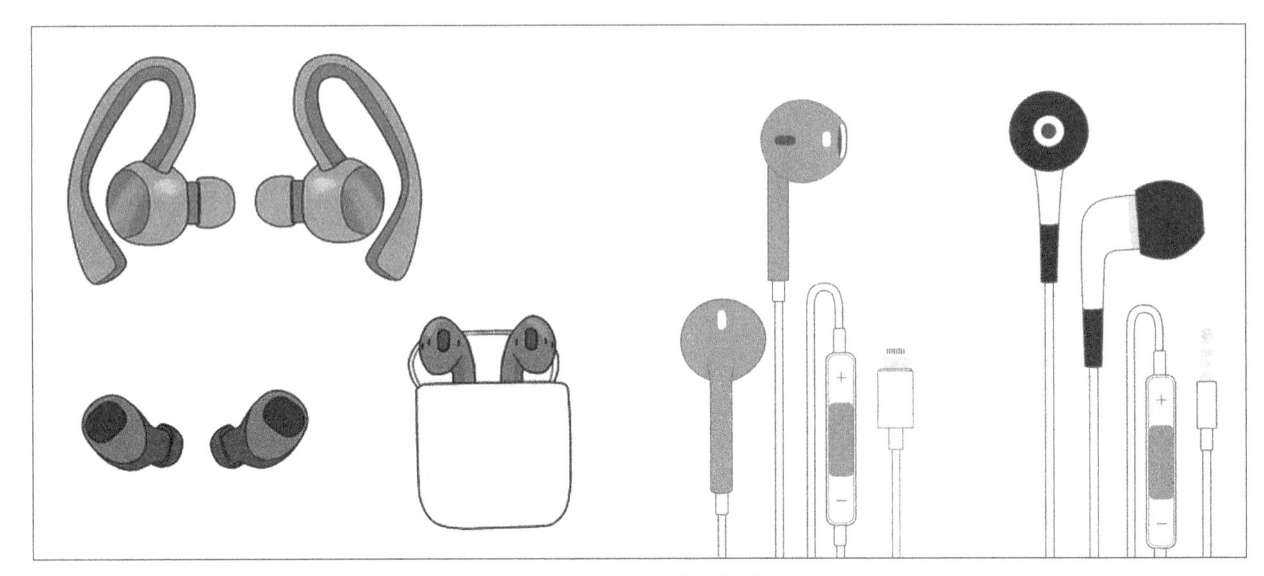

Figure 2.18: **Types of earbuds**

A final note on headsets

In late 2022, the International Organization for Standardization (ISO),[53] approved ISO Standard 24019 for simultaneous interpreting delivery platforms (ISO, 2022b). This standard outlined formal requirements for headsets used on RSI platforms. If you are a conference interpreter, pay attention to these requirements. Companies that provide services over dedicated RSI platforms may require interpreters to use ISO-compliant headsets.[54]

Volume 2, Chapter 1, explores sound, audio and RSI in more depth.

Webcams

Most laptops and smart devices these days come equipped with an adequate built-in webcam and video capture capabilities.

Some desktop systems also come with webcams built into their monitors. However, even if your desktop computer has a webcam, you may still need to buy an additional (external) USB webcam. The exception may be all-in-one computers, where the computer and monitor are one piece of equipment.

At this time, many of the built-in webcam systems in computers still utilize lower-resolution webcams. As a result, you may still need to upgrade to higher-quality video resolution webcam.

When you open your computer's system specifications, you can check for your built-in webcam specifications in your computer's system settings. At the time of publication, for example, your webcam should be capable of a resolution of high definition 1080p (pixels) or ultrahigh definition 4K (4,000 pixels). If not, purchase an adequate USB webcam.

[53] ISO is the leading world organization for international standards in general and standards for interpreting and translation in particular. ISO has several standards that address simultaneous interpreting equipment.

[54] New headsets come on the market on a regular basis. Research "ISO-compliant headsets" online to determine which headset is best for you.

You would typically plug the USB webcam into your computer, download any software (if needed) and then follow the instructions to install the webcam and adjust the settings.

Do not purchase or install a wireless webcam that connects over Wi-Fi. You want to buy a USB webcam.

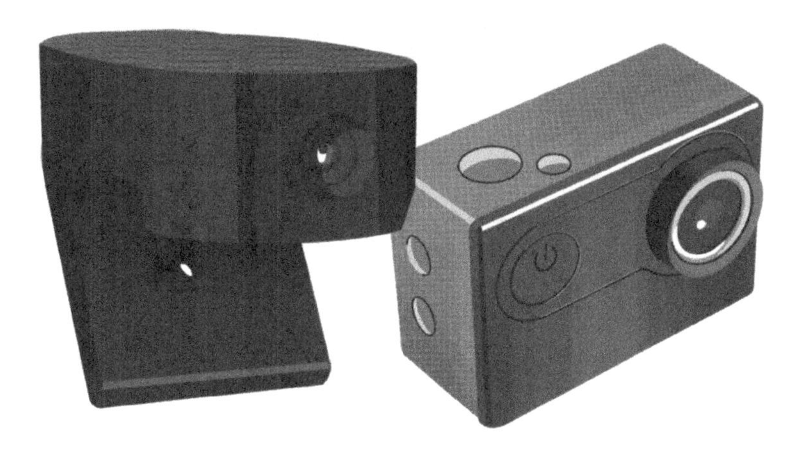

Figure 2.19: **Jabra PanaCast 20 webcam**

Figure 2.20: **Jabra PanaCast 180 webcam**

VRI and VRS interpreters, and most RSI interpreters, need high-quality video to do their job. If your camera is producing pixelated, blurry or poor images, it may be time for an upgrade.

Sign language interpreters especially need high-quality video. Without it, the Deaf and Hard of Hearing consumers are not able to properly understand what is being signed. Remote interpreting companies regularly audit interpreters to make sure their cameras are producing clean, crisp video. Your camera is an essential part of your remote interpreter setup.

Mobile network bandwidth

The need for speed

What speed will you need from your internet service provider? This is one of the most important questions you will need to answer as a remote interpreter! Poor internet connectivity and data upload and download speeds can destroy your career before it even begins.

See Chapter 3 of this volume for additional detail and information about connectivity and also upload and download speeds: both what these speeds are and why they matter for remote interpreters. (Chapter 3 shows you how to set up for your career as a remote interpreter and for each interpreting session.)

There are two important points worth mentioning here. First, *ensure* you can connect to the internet via the best speed you can purchase—even if it means setting up a separate office. For example, perhaps you live in a rural area. You can't get access to strong internet connections. In that case, you may have to rent an office in a town and interpret from there.

How much speed do you need?

Second, computer speed is constantly evolving. So are remote interpreting platforms. As upload and download speeds increase, so does the need for higher speed.

For example, right now for video (VRI, VRS and RSI) 2 megabits per second (Mbps) is considered to be the minimum to perform remote interpreting successfully. For OPI and audio-only interpreting in general, a minimum of 400 kilobits (Kb) per second is said to be sufficient.

Again, these are minimum specifications that do not factor in many other things that can impact internet connectivity, bandwidth and stability. A good guideline is to try to double and even triple your available network data rates based on any minimum specification you are given.

And be careful! The speeds we mention could already be outdated by the time this book is published! Yes. That is how quickly the technology evolves.

You should always be familiar with your minimum upload and download speeds at the location you interpret from. You should also know what those speeds should ideally be in order to safely ensure a stable connection. Just ask at your workplace, or ask an IT expert if you are a contractor. Invest in whatever they require or recommend.

Upload and download speeds

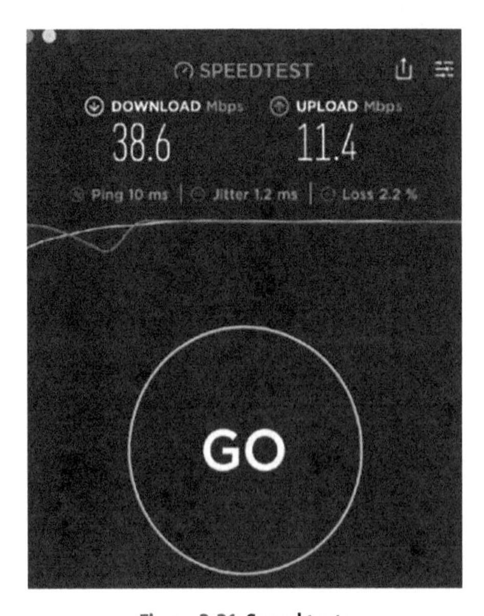

Figure 2.21: Speed tests

Figure 2.21 shows the results of a typical speed test. Many websites run speed tests: you can do a quick search online to find them. Search for "test my internet speed," for example.

The download speed represents how quickly your computer receives data from the internet.

The upload speed shows how quickly your system can send data to the internet.

Speed tests will be discussed in more detail in Chapter 3. Until you read that chapter, you can prepare by teaching yourself how to run a speed test. It's easy!

Now let's talk about mobile networks—and how they have evolved. They vary around the world.

5G mobile network

5G (fifth generation) mobile technology connections have been deployed since 2019. Some countries have been faster than others at deploying it, but in industrialized countries, 5G is expected to take over from 4G cellular networks over the next decade.

The 5G network has significantly greater bandwidth with faster download speeds of up to 10 gigabits per second (Gbps). 5G provides more than enough speed and connectivity for a stable, high-definition remote interpreting.

As the world transitions from 4G to 5G networks, 4G technology will not be able to take advantage of the new 5G networks. Therefore, only new hybrid 4G/5G capable devices will cover the eventual transition.

If you are using a 4G device and believe it is also 5G enabled, consult your local mobile services provider. Ask them how and when your network will transition fully to 5G. Make sure your current device is 5G enabled and ready for the change.

Fully 5G-dedicated devices will become the standard. They will be able to take full advantage of the new data transmission gains that 5G makes possible. No matter where you live, unless everything is now 5G, you should stay informed about this critical transition.

4G LTE mobile network

4G long-term evolution (LTE) connections or mobile hotspots are adequate for most remote interpreting if you also have an adequate connection to your LTE service provider.

However, LTE quality is heavily influenced by your location. It is also greatly affected by the number of users connected to the same cell phone tower as you are at the same time. That number varies hugely. As a result—and this is a big problem—the quality of your connection can be highly unpredictable.

Interpreters should *always prioritize having a wired connection* where possible. What is a wired connection? It is when your internet is connecting directly to your computer through an Ethernet cable. In other words, that connection is hardwired. You are not connected to the internet over Wi-Fi.

(Don't worry. How to hardwire your internet connection is a detailed discussion coming in the next chapter. *Read it carefully.*)

3G mobile network

3G connections/mobile hotspots are not recommended. They might be enough for two-party calls when the 3G connection is not in use by other internet applications—and if you have a strong connection to your 3G service provider. Our recommendation is to avoid 3G wherever possible.

→ Section 2.3 Review

This section provided general information on remote interpreting technologies for the remote interpreter. You were introduced to the kinds of computers, headsets, webcams, mobile network and other kinds of technologies you need to perform remote interpreting.

However, this is an international field. Products and solutions evolve by the moment. While you were reading this section, someone, somewhere, just improved or invented a process or a technology that you will use for remote interpreting someday soon.

It is your responsibility and duty to keep up with these exciting changes and developments. They impact your work and the field. At the top of your work to-do list, keep this item:

"Stay on top of changes in the technology that I use to do my job!"

Section 2.4 Technology Considerations for Home-based RSI

→ Learning objective 2.4

After completing this section, the remote interpreter will be able to identify specific technologies required to provide RSI services.

→ Section 2.4 Overview

The workspace requirements for the remote simultaneous interpreter—whether in a home, an office building or at an RSI agency location—can be similar to what professional video remote interpreters use to support consecutive interpreting today. However, here are additional important differences and considerations.

If you work directly with a language service offering RSI, they will most likely provide or at least at a minimum will inform you about the technology that you're expected to use.[55]

[55] After the COVID-19 pandemic began, language services that were not familiar with RSI, in addition to school systems, government services and other entities, began offering RSI without becoming experts in what is needed to deliver RSI effectively. See Chapters 1 and 2 of the second volume of this textbook for details about RSI and how to work effectively in challenging RSI situations. See Chapter 3 of Volume 2 for details about RSI in conference interpreting.

However, if you perform RSI as an employee for another type of organization (such as a school system, a government office or a hospital), that organization may not be equipped nor know how best to set up your RSI station.

And of course, if you work as an independent contractor, you will need to set up your own office.

In this section, we will look at the main hardware and software you need to consider for supporting RSI from your own home or another workspace. We will examine some standard home studio and office setups with specifications and recommendations from simultaneous interpreting associations and stakeholders.

→ Section 2.4 Content

AIIC recommendations for RSI

The Association Internationale des Interprètes de Conférence is also known as the International Association of Conference Interpreters, or AIIC (which is pronounced "eye-eek"). AIIC is the leading international authority on conference simultaneous interpreting and, more recently, on remote simultaneous interpreting.[56]

AIIC set itself a mandate to evaluate and set definitions and specifications for its RSI practitioners. AIIC has also worked to establish requirements and best practices for RSI. (See Chapter 3 of Volume 2 of this textbook for an overview of remote conference interpreting that follows AIIC requirements.)

In 2020, AIIC defined RSI to be simultaneous interpreting that can be performed either from the home or from an interpreting hub. For AIIC, the home is considered a fully decentralized model: in other words, in a decentralized model the interpreters are not physically located near one another.

An RSI hub, on the other hand, is defined as a remote location properly equipped with ISO-compliant mobile or permanent interpreting booths.[57]

RSI hubs

In a hub, the interpreters are not physically located directly where the participants are located but they interpret together in the same physical place. You can think of a hub as an RSI call center or centralized workspace with highly specialized, high-end equipment.

A standard office conference room can be used for RSI and technically can be an RSI hub if interpreters perform their interpreting together there while the participants are located remotely.

---

[56] Like many organizations in Europe, AIIC usually refers to distance interpreting rather than remote interpreting. Although remote interpreting is the more common international term, this textbook uses both terms more or less interchangeably.

[57] ISO is the International Organization for Standards—the world's leading organization for international standards—and AIIC supports both equipment and practices that meet ISO international standards for interpreting and interpreting services.

However, if an interpreter works alone in an office in their workplace, that setting will likely be more similar to what AIIC considers a home environment. Most hubs are built to be high-tech RSI-specialized workplaces.

Recently, it is a more common practice since the COVID-19 pandemic began for U.S. schools, hospitals, community and government services to provide RSI services by setting up RSI hubs for certain events. Before the pandemic, these services had not previously provided RSI. Often, even now, they may not know how to equip the interpreter's office for successful RSI. That lack of knowledge is a serious problem if you are the interpreter performing RSI there. *You* may need to take action to ensure the office is correctly set up for RSI.

What do you need in place to perform RSI?

Home and hub environments should include:

- Secure, stable, *wired* internet access.[58]
- Traditional or soft (i.e., computer-based) CGI simultaneous interpreting consoles.
    - **Note 1:** CGI refers to common gateway interface; it is the RSI interpreting platform's proprietary software.
    - **Note 2:** This requirement is realistic only for conference interpreting hubs.
- Up-to-date internet browsers.
- A quiet zone appropriate for interpreting needs and privacy requirements.
- Headsets with built-in mics, or (ideally) headphones and standalone microphones.
- Hearing protection devices or other hearing protection built into the system, platform or headphones.
- ISO standards in place—ideally ISO/PAS 24019:2020, ISO 22259:2019, ISO 20108:2017, ISO 2603:2016, ISO 4043:2016 and ISO 20109:2016.

If you do not understand these requirements, you may need to work with an expert who does. (The expert could be an experienced RSI conference interpreter, for example, especially one who is a member of AIIC.) Consult that expert before you set up a home office for RSI. Otherwise, you may need to restrict your work to OPI, VRI and/or VRS until you feel able to set your office environment up for RSI support.

AIIC 2020 reference guide for RSI

The point here is not to overwhelm you with technical details but to demonstrate that RSI is not the same as providing consecutive interpreting over OPI, VRI or VRS platforms, particularly when you provide services from your home office.

---

[58] As mentioned in Section 2.3, having a wired (or hardwired) connection means that you have cables, called Ethernet cables, that connect your computer and other devices to the internet (instead of having a Wi-Fi connection). A wired connection is always preferable to Wi-Fi in remote interpreting because it provides a faster, more secure and more reliable connection. Wired connections are discussed in detail in the next chapter.

Consecutive remote interpreting is different. There, the interpreter interacts with the platform in the same way as all the other participants connected to the system. Everyone accesses a single audio channel and communicates by speaking one at a time.

For RSI, layering on the ability for some or all participants to hear the interpreter *at the same time* as the speaker—remotely!—is a lot more complicated. You either need a specially designed platform to handle more than one audio channel or create what is often called a mashup or hybrid solution—in other words, a workaround solution.

In either situation, the interpreter will need to manipulate many more elements to provide the interpreting service.

These extra elements add additional cognitive stress compared to performing OPI, VRI or VRS—even when you have excellent remote interpreting equipment.

Setting up your home studio for RSI

Think of your RSI home office as an audio production studio. It may take you some time to create the ideal home studio, especially one designed as an RSI studio.

Here are some key considerations. They will help you get ready quickly for RSI.

First, you really don't need to spend a huge amount of money to get started. It's important not to be obsessed with acquiring the latest and greatest equipment. Generally you can create a suitable RSI studio without having to invest in expensive high-end equipment.

This point also applies if you work for an office where staff do not understand RSI well and do not want to spend a great deal of money on supporting the equipment you require.

Let's take a closer look at some of the components in the home office RSI studio that can also apply if you work in a school, hospital or other office that is not an RSI hub (and would still be considered a home environment by AIIC). You'll also see some of the things your workstation needs in place before you perform RSI.

Figure 2.22: **RSI home (i.e., non-hub) laptop setup**

Figure 2.23: **Budget-friendly, minimal setup for RSI home environment**

Figure 2.24: **Homebuilt, customized, three-monitor RSI home environment**

Figure 2.25: **Improvised RSI home environment**

Setting up a booth

As a remote interpreter, try to set yourself the goal to recreate, to the best of your ability, the standard RSI hub environment with soundproof booths.

These are also the booths that simultaneous interpreters use at live events and conferences, not only in RSI hubs.

To do this, you will need to achieve some control over the acoustics in your office or home studio. You may decide to install or build your own sound enclosure, or simply soundproof your office the best you can to reduce any external and ambient (surrounding) noise.

Figure 2.26: **Soundproofed RSI home environment**

Eliminate noise and interruptions

You also need to reduce and ideally eliminate potential interruptions or disruptions. Do you have pets in the house that make noise? Babies or children? Teens who like to play loud music? A neighbor who practices drums?

In that case, it is on you to make the appropriate provisions and adjustments to prevent them from making noise and interrupting while you work.

If you live near a railroad, an airport or on a major street where ambulances and police cars pass with sirens, noise abatement will need to be your mission.

Let's be completely realistic: you will need to plan for noise. You will also need to make sure you can eliminate it with quality equipment when you interpret.

What about deliveries? Some interpreters put a sign on the door saying, "Please do not knock or ring the bell from [time X to time Y]. Recording in progress." (or a similar notice). Plan for people who might arrive at your door or the office where you work while you are performing RSI.

See Chapter 3 (the next chapter in this volume) for details about the problems of surrounding noise and how to eliminate or at least significantly reduce them in your home office.

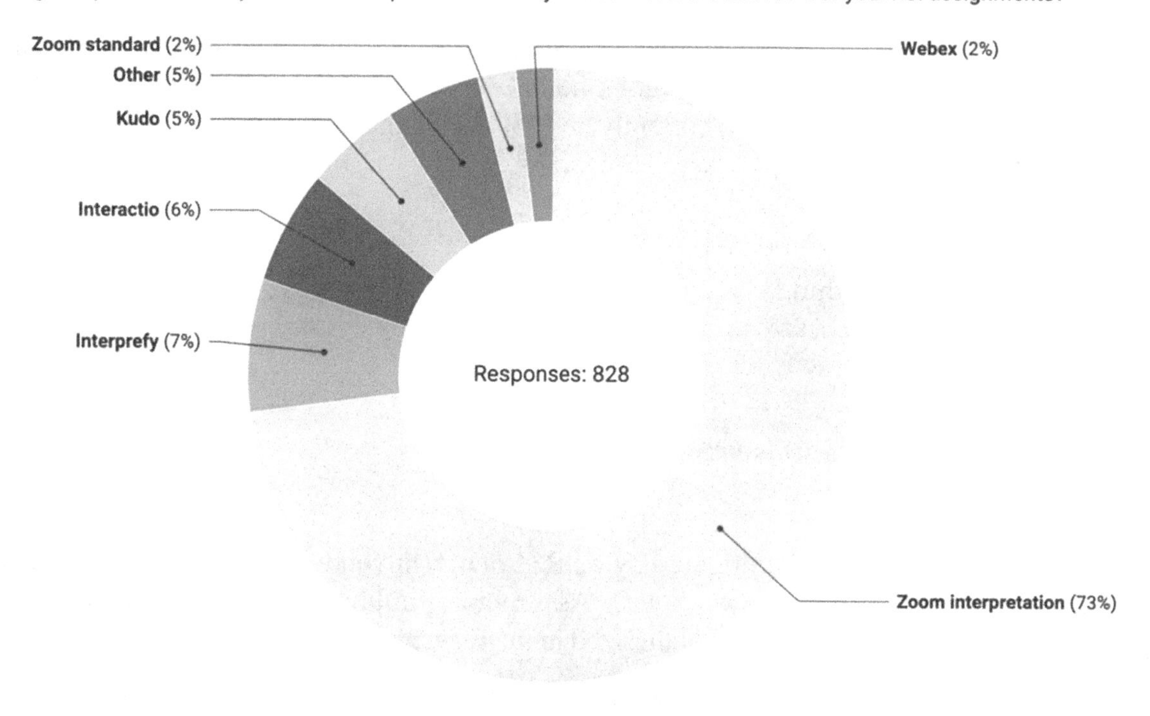
Which platform have you used for more than 50% of your RSI assignments?
Percentage responses to the question: which platforms have you used for more than 50% of your RSI assignments?
Zoom standard (2%)
Other (5%)
Kudo (5%)
Interactio (6%)
Interprefy (7%)
Webex (2%)
Responses: 828
Zoom interpretation (73%)
The sample size is 828 as some participants were not able to give an answer. "Other" includes IBridge People, Teams, VoiceBoxer, Olyusei, Pexip, QuaQua, WhatsApp, Streamyard, Skype, and Jitsi Meet.
Chart: Slator • Source: ESIT • Get the data • Created with Datawrapper

Figure 2.27: Interpreters' use of RSI platforms

Typical RSI hub and home office setup

Software requirements

Currently supported web browsers

Chrome, Firefox, Edge, Chromium

Access to an RSI software platform (browser based)

It is strongly recommended that your RSI studio be connected via a wired Ethernet connection. (Getting a wired connection to the internet was mentioned in both the previous sections; it is discussed in more detail in the next chapter.)

Why you need a wired connection for RSI—whenever possible
Why do you need to be hardwired to perform RSI?

Technically Wi-Fi connectivity may also be used, but network stability issues are always a concern. In addition, a Wi-Fi connection is more vulnerable to hackers than a wired one.

You do not want to have your system suddenly cut out or start to destabilize while you interpret.

Continual issues with network connectivity and network stability will make a poor impression on employers and contracting agencies. You could potentially jeopardize and even lose contracts due to this problem.

That said, if an Ethernet connection is not an option, Wi-Fi has improved a great deal over the past few years. If you invest in a business (not a home) wireless router and modem, you might have an adequate connection. However, currently an Ethernet connection to the modem is still the best way to reduce the risk of internet disruption.

In short, internet speed and stability are *essential* for your work.

You need to hear everything—and (for video RSI) you also need to see as much as possible. Participants also need to hear you (and often see you). Having a strong internet connection makes that stability possible.

RSI studio and setup requirements and best practices

Hub

The hub studio is generally configured by an RSI platform vendor and either their client or the language services provider they work with. As a remote simultaneous interpreter, you will most likely be expected to be trained and authorized in the use of the specific RSI software they require.

If you work in a hub, the only interpreting hardware that you will probably be required to bring are your own personal headphones or headset and perhaps your own laptop. Isolation booths or soundproofing of the hub is handled by the agency and the RSI software vendor. So are the computer hardware, software and networking. Easy for you!

For more information about hubs, see Volume 2, Chapters 1, 2 and 3, on RSI and conference interpreting.

Figure 2.28: **Hub**

→ Section 2.4 Review

This section provided a brief description of the additional technology needs, requirements and recommendations for RSI. Most of these are in *addition* to the ones discussed in the three previous sections for OPI, VRI or VRS.

Though similar to the setups for OPI, VRI and VRS home studios, the standards for RSI home setups as outlined by the International Association of Conference Interpreters (AIIC) are important guidelines to follow. While AIIC's standards may be enforced more frequently in Europe, and more realistically achieved for conference interpreting encounters than in the United States, they are still hugely important if you perform RSI and shouldn't be ignored.

Remember the troubling health problems experienced by many conference interpreters who have performed RSI since the pandemic began. The best sound and working conditions need to be a high priority for both you and any organizations that work with you—especially for RSI.

→ Chapter Activities

Activity 2.1 (a): A remote interpreting technology quiz

Instructions

For each statement, write down whether you consider that statement true or false.

1. VRS technology developed after VRI technology. ______
2. The cloud (cloud-based computing) made remote interpreting easier. ______
3. IMS stands for interpreter manager services. ______
4. AI (artificial intelligence) in interpreting will soon replace interpreters. ______
5. IDP refers to interpreting delivery platform. ______
6. Sign language interpreters can work on both VRI and VRS platforms. ______
7. Machine interpreting isn't really interpreting because it's text-based. ______

Activity 2.1 (b): The evolution of RSI

Instructions

For each of the three parts of this exercise, use the list of words at the bottom to fill in the blanks for each missing word or phrase in the text.

RSI evolution, part 1

When did RSI launch? It started in medical services in the mid-1990s in New York City. But there was a long gap before real RSI platforms were __________ after 2010. Yet even before special platforms existed, interpreters figured out the real problem. To perform simultaneous interpreting __________, you need *more than one audio channel*!

More and more interpreters figured out how to hack consecutive interpreting __________ platforms by adding a second phone line. But these were the "bad old days." Then came new special __________ that *combined* a video platform with the ability to provide __________ interpreting. How? By adding: (a) multiple __________ channels; and (b) a back end for interpreters to __________ with each other.

simultaneous, coordinate, audio, developed, remotely, RSI platforms, video

RSI evolution, part 2

By the mid-2010s, RSI was just beginning to be performed on what we call __________ RSI platforms. These are videoconferencing platforms that add __________ channels and a __________ where two remote simultaneous interpreters can take turns interpreting and communicate to say whose turn it is, or other information.

But dedicated RSI platforms are ___________. So far, mostly conference interpreters work on them. Then the pandemic hit. Overnight, community and business services, schools, courts and healthcare often wanted interpreters to interpret ___________ on standard ___________ platforms that didn't have ___________ audio channels or a back end. Community services and interpreters worked hard to create hybrid solutions.

expensive, back end, audio, simultaneously, videoconference, dedicated, multiple

RSI evolution, part 3

What are hybrid ___________? They are newer versions of the hacks (workaround methods) that add _______ channels to videoconference ___________ such as Webex to perform simultaneous ___________. Today, as a result of the COVID-19 pandemic, many services provide ___________ over videoconference platforms such as Zoom, Microsoft Teams, Google Meet, GoToMeeting and Webex.

At the beginning of the pandemic, Zoom was the only one with a built-in simultaneous interpreting ___________ by adding audio ___________. This RSI feature is still not fully developed. However, Zoom is big in RSI now—and not only for community services. A 2021 study from CSA Research showed Zoom is used 60 percent of the time for RSI, which means that many conference interpreters use it too!

interpreting, platforms, solutions, feature, channels, RSI, audio

Activity 2.2: Remote interpreting scenarios

Instructions

Match the scenario to the best remote interpreting technology by writing down, in the blank right column, the platform that best matches each scenario on the left.

OPI/VRI platform IMS RSI platform Unified IDP and IMS

Scenario	Technology Platforms
A public health department holds a monthly community meeting at rotating locations. Three times a year, the meeting is held remotely. They need simultaneous interpreting in Spanish, Hmong and Russian.	
A school district needs to schedule half hour parent-teacher conferences for seven schools in six languages. The meetings will all take place onsite.	
A hospital needs on-demand interpreting services for weekend and evenings.	
A small, rural clinic has three face-to-face Spanish-English interpreters who cover 90 percent of interpreting services requested, but it occasionally needs on-demand interpreters for emergencies and languages other than Spanish.	

Activity 2.3: Get ready for remote interpreting

Instructions

1. Before you perform remote interpreting, do a readiness evaluation of your system setup and technology. In the blank middle column, note your answer to the questions in the first column.
2. Next, review Section 2.3 to determine if you think your answer means that the equipment or technology you are using is adequate for remote interpreting.
3. If you do not know the answers, *find them.* Consult with a language service, interpreter colleague, IT specialist in remote interpreting or any other specialist who can help you answer the questions.
4. Review the "No" answers.
5. Answer the question below the table by writing on the lines.

Assess Your Technology		
Question	**Your answer**	**Is your technology adequate for remote interpreting? (Yes or No)**
1. How fast is your CPU?		
2. How much RAM does your computer have?		
3. How much storage does your computer have?		
4. What kind of headset are you using? Is it noise-cancelling?		
5. Run a speed test on your computer and write down your download and upload speeds.		
6. Is your camera built-in or external?		
7. Do you have a wired or a Wi-Fi connection?		
8. What is your local cellular phone network? 5G, 4G, 3G?		

Based on your "No" answers above, what technology or equipment will you need to buy or procure to perform remote interpreting?

Activity 2.4: Experience RSI

The biggest difference between OPI/VRI and RSI for spoken language interpreters is how you experience sound. In consecutive, only one person speaks at a time. In simultaneous, the interpreter has to speak while also hearing the speaker.

Instructions

1. Have someone record the Audio Transcript below for you at a reasonable speed.
2. Interpret the brief audio recording consecutively.
3. Record it while you interpret.
4. Pause the audio as needed to interpret.
5. Next, interpret the same file simultaneously *twice*.
   a. First, interpret the file without a headset.
   b. Next, interpret the file with a headset on.
6. Record your interpreting each time.
7. Now, using the transcript of the audio file, listen back to all three recordings and answer the following.
   a. Which recording is the most accurate rendition of the audio file?
   b. Note any differences in your simultaneous recordings.
   c. Describe the difference between interpreting with and without a headset on.

Audio Transcript

I love coffee. I drink it every day. Some people say caffeine is bad. I'm here to tell you about why coffee is healthier than you think. First of all, coffee gives us energy. The caffeine in coffee boosts our energy. It can also improve our physical performance. And some people say it can even help them lose weight. Coffee also lowers our risk of certain diseases. It's good for the liver, can lower the risk of cancer and diabetes and it helps clean out the stomach. It can even reduce depression. But the best thing about coffee is how it makes me feel every morning when I wake up. Nothing is better than that first cup of coffee to get the day off to a great start!

Chapter Conclusion and Review

Remote interpreting cannot be separated from the technology that makes it possible. As a remote interpreter, you are also a technical specialist. You will need to understand and be familiar with the relevant technology.

This chapter explored remote interpreting technology from when it began to what it is today. Soon many more developments will take place that are not mentioned here: remote interpreting technology is constantly evolving and improving. Stay up to date with changes and innovations in this industry.

The history of remote interpreting is a reminder of how recent remote interpreting became widespread. While the first examples of remote interpreting technology occurred decades ago, remote interpreting really began escalating at the end of the 20th century.

OPI and VRI/VRS came first, followed by dedicated RSI platforms. Each kind of remote interpreting requires its own technology platforms and processes. Today, interpreters work on many different kinds of remote interpreting platforms.

Remote interpreters don't need to be technology experts. They do need to have a general understanding of the technology that makes remote interpreting possible to work with it smoothly and effectively (and not be afraid of it!). In addition, remote interpreters need to stay up to date with how remote platforms change over time.

While technology companies work to provide ever-improved platforms, interpreters are responsible for setting up their home or call center offices to work on the platforms. This chapter offered information on how to do so, exploring the basic technology and equipment that remote interpreters need, including computers, webcams, headsets, internet connections and more.

It's true that remote interpreting technology can seem overwhelming at first. Still, thousands of remote interpreters log in to platforms every day and manage all the hardware, software and equipment with incredible ease and speed. It's impressive and exciting—and urgently needed.

Once you have completed your basic setup, soon all the technology in your office will seem as easy to manage as taking a bottle of water to onsite encounters.

Be patient. The time will come when the technology of remote interpreting starts to feel comfortable and easy—and simply an important part of your work.

Chapter 3

Caroline Remer, MA

Set Yourself Up to Perform Remote Interpreting

Learning Objectives

After completing this chapter, the remote interpreter will be able to:

Learning Objective 3.1: Use a step-by-step process to prepare to interpret on standard OPI, VRI and VRS platforms.

Learning Objective 3.2: Set up for a typical OPI, VRI or VRS session on standard platforms.

Learning Objective 3.3: List common potential technical and logistic problems in remote interpreting and review practical solutions.

Learning Objective 3.4: Practice interpreting on standard platforms for OPI, VRI and VRS.

Introduction

It's time to set up. Prepare for your work as a remote interpreter!

Do you feel confident that you have everything in place that you need to perform excellent work? Are you sure you know exactly what to do before for each session?

Not to worry! This chapter will guide you. It will provide you with the tools and information you need to establish yourself as a remote interpreter. It will also walk you through how to prepare for each session and troubleshoot common technical problems you may face.

Yes, it can feel a little intimidating at first to get on the phone to interpret or see your face on a computer screen while you're interpreting. But after you've read this chapter, it won't seem alarming. Simply follow the guidelines to prepare yourself for successful remote interpreting.

Go through this chapter step by step. Some of the steps might surprise you at first, or seem a little overwhelming, but this guidance comes from experts. Taking these steps will also help protect your computer from crashing (shutting down) in the middle of a session. They will build your confidence and show everyone how professional you are.

Section 3.1 Preparing to Work on OPI, VRI and VRS Platforms

→ **Learning objective 3.1**

After completing this section, the remote interpreter will be able to use a step-by-step process to prepare to interpret on standard OPI, VRI and VRS platforms

→ Section 3.1 Overview

This section focuses primarily on audio-only interpreting (AOI)—which includes over-the-phone interpreting (OPI)—and video-remote interpreting (VRI) or video relay service (VRS) sessions. Note that more and more former OPI services are shifting to the internet rather than being performed over phone lines. However, some language services and other organizations may continue to ask interpreters to work over a landline phone to perform traditional OPI.

Much of the guidance here, however, will also be useful for remote simultaneous interpreting (RSI) performed in a home office.

For details about setting up for sessions performed on RSI platforms, and how to work effectively on those platforms, see Chapters 1 and 2 of the second volume. See Chapter 3 of the second volume if you perform remote conference interpreting.

→ Section 3.1 Content

Let's go step by step to get you fully prepared to begin a remote interpreting session.

Before you do, you will need to have the right equipment in place and make sure that it's up to date and can adequately meet the technical requirements for this work.

Imagine you are in your home office, sitting at your desk, your computer in front of you—what do you need to have before logging in to do a remote interpreting session? What will prepare you best?

Here is a checklist that shows what you should always have before going online. Take a quick look at it. Then we'll discuss the items on the checklist in more detail.

Remote interpreting setup

As you saw in the previous chapter, it's extremely important to make sure you have the right technology setup and equipment for this work. What does the right setup mean exactly? Take a look at this checklist.

Checklist 1
Prepare for Remote Interpreting

This quick-start guide will help you make sure you have everything in place before your first session.

1. Computer and other equipment

❑ A computer (desktop or high-performing laptop)

a. **Recommended:** A computer that is ideally less than three years old with as much random access memory (RAM) included as you can afford.

b. **Recommended:** A computer system or in some cases, if permitted, a tablet that meets the needs and recommendations of the language services or organizations that you interpret for.

c. **Recommended:** A backup computer in case of a computer breakdown.

d. **Recommended:** A second monitor or device for accessing resources and/or communicating with a team interpreter.

e. **Avoid:** Older computers and low-end computers.

Do not use a computer or mobile device that is outdated or does not meet minimum requirements.

❑ Quality audio

a. **Recommended:** A quality universal serial bus (USB) cable headset with a boom (integrated) microphone.

Note: Expensive headphones with an external USB microphone require a more complicated setup and may not be needed.

b. **Recommended:** A second, backup headset.

c. **Recommended:** A microphone stand to maintain a separate microphone (if you have one) in a fixed position.

d. **Avoid:** Your computer's internal microphone or speakers.

i. Default computer speakers generally do not provide adequate audio quality; built-in microphones tend to pick up background noise and other auditory interferences.

ii. Sound that may be coming from the computers of other people on the call can create a feedback loop that sounds like an echo chamber.

e. **Avoid:** Any microphone embedded on the cord of a headset that physically moves around picking up and creating unwanted noise.

❑ Audio equipment management

a. **Recommended:** A sound check.

i. Verify how you sound speaking on a remote platform.

ii. Record yourself and play back the recording or get feedback from a colleague listening to you test your audio setup.

b. **Recommended:** A position close to the microphone but not too close.

i. If it is a boom microphone, place the stand at approximately 1-2 feet (30-60 cm).

c. **Avoid:** Speaking close to the microphone.

i. If you are too close to the microphone you cause feedback.

ii. Being too close may also allow others to hear you breathe, make "puff" sounds (plosives) or produce "hiss" sounds (sibilance) that may distract and disturb your listeners.

❑ High-definition web camera (HD webcam)[59]

a. **Recommended:** A quality, external webcam. Select the highest resolution you can find or afford.

i. HD is the minimum and is denoted as 720p at the low end and 1080p at the high end.

ii. Ultra HD or UHD is denoted as 4K and is roughly four times better resolution than HD.

iii. 8K is the highest level of resolution available today.

b. **Recommended:** Checking system settings.

i. Consult with any language services or organizations you interpret for to be sure your webcam meets their standards.

ii. Better still, if you can: check with a technical specialist to determine if your webcam is adequate for VRI, VRS or RSI.

c. **Avoid:** Low-quality or slow webcams.

i. Be careful: webcams built into laptops or desktop computers are often inadequate.

ii. Poor quality webcams may cause color distortions, video lag, and other visual problems. The video image they produce looks unprofessional.

❑ Second monitor or screen

a. **Recommended:** A second monitor or screen as a backup screen or to look up information and resources while you interpret.

i. Some interpreters, when working in a team, use the second screen to see their partner.

ii. A third screen is not usually needed—but some interpreters like them.

---

[59] Technically a webcam is needed only to perform VRI, VRS or video RSI. However, even if you perform audio-only interpreting, a quality webcam will make you look professional in any video conference meetings with current or potential clients. Look your best!

2. **Computer maintenance**

- ❑ Follow best practices for maintaining your computer.

  a. **Recommended or required (depending on privacy laws):** Maintaining regular security and essential software and system updates for your computer, tablet or smart device.

  b. **Recommended:** Consulting with the language services or organizations you interpret for, or with clients, peers or technical specialists, for guidance on best practices for maintaining your computer.

  c. **Recommended:** Use caution when installing software that might affect your setup; consult a specialist as needed.

  d. **Recommended:** Computer operating system updates.

    i. Be aware, however, that these updates may introduce issues with certain software that has not been revised for the update.

    ii. Check with software vendor frequently asked questions (FAQ) sites for guidance.

    iii. Speak with any language services or organizations you interpret for, or with knowledgeable colleagues, for suggestions on whether it's safe to update your computer operating system.

3. **Office setup**

- ❑ For VRI/RSI: Keep personal objects and clutter out of sight.

- ❑ For VRI/RSI: Dress professionally.

  a. **Recommended:** Clothing that is not bright colored (no neon colors) and does not have logos or symbols.

     Note: For signed languages, preferably use colors that contrast with the color of your skin for improved visibility.

  b. **Recommended:** Adhering to the on-camera dress code of the language services or organizations you interpret for.

  c. **Recommended:** Keeping a professional jacket nearby for short-notice, on-demand sessions.

  d. **Avoid:** Clothing with complex designs or striking patterns (such as geometric patterns), which can create disturbing visual effects.

  e. **Avoid:** T-shirts; big, shiny or dangling jewelry or clothing with holes.

- ❑ Ensure privacy.

  a. **Required:** Absolute privacy.

    i. To assure confidentiality and compliance with any relevant data protection and privacy laws, make sure that no one outside of your office door can hear or see you.

    ii. Exception: Remote interpreting call centers will manage privacy for you.

b. **Required:** A separate room to interpret.

   i. Whether you are in a home office or a work office (except a call center), work inside a separate room and lock the door while you interpret.

   ii. Make sure anyone else located in your house or working in your workspace knows not to disturb you during your work hours.

- [ ] Silence all noise outside your office.

   a. **Required:** Noise management.

      i. If you have young children or infants, animals or other sources of uncontrollable or otherwise random loud noise that can be heard during a call, arrange to have them out of hearing range for all your working hours.

      ii. Be aware that noise-cancelling headphones can help—but they cannot always drown out a crying baby or a loud dog.

   b. **Required:** Reduction (as much as possible) of loud street noises (ambulances, traffic horns, construction, etc.) that might be heard during work calls.

   c. **Recommended:** Quality noise-cancelling headphones.

      i. Consult language services, interpreters and other colleagues for their suggestions on which headphones to get.

      ii. Purchase the best noise-cancelling headphones you can afford.

   d. **Recommended:** Installing inexpensive soundproofing materials (such as foam or even fabric on walls) if your environment might be noisy.[60]

4. Camera presence (for VRI, VRS and video RSI)

- [ ] Background

   a. **Recommended or required:** A neutral, solid-colored background screen, whether it is mounted behind your chair or propped on the floor behind you.

      i. At a minimum, have a blank, neutral-colored wall.

      ii. If needed, hang a solid-colored sheet.

      iii. Determine if virtual backgrounds are acceptable with the language services or organizations you work for and, if so, which types of virtual backgrounds are accepted.

   b. **Recommended:** Providing space (a few feet or a meter) between your body and the background.

   c. **Avoid:** Leaning against a wall, which looks unprofessional.

   d. **Avoid:** A background wall with scuffs, textures, fixtures, visible screws, etc.

   e. **Avoid:** A background wall with clutter, photos, pictures or other personal items.

---

[60] During professional calls, one language service has heard from the home offices of remote interpreters some startling noises, such as fireworks, roosters—and even street vendors selling onions.

- [ ] Lighting
  a. **Recommended:** Sit facing a window, daylight or a lamp. Otherwise, try to have a window, light or lamp to one side. Natural daylight is recommended when possible.
  b. **Recommended:** Experimenting to see how well-lit you are before every call: natural lighting changes with the weather and the time of day.
  c. **Recommended:** Having three sources of light; one above and slightly in front, and two equal light sources on either side.
     i. Having these is particularly important if you work night shifts or in darkness.
  d. **Avoid:** Sitting with your back to a window or bright light.
     i. Bright light behind you will reduce your video quality in many ways; it is a serious problem.
     ii. Backlight can make you appear fuzzy, seen only in silhouette, or unrecognizably dark.
     iii. Large shadows on screen.
- [ ] Center yourself.
  a. **Recommended:** Face the camera and take a center position in the view field. Sit up straight.
  b. **Recommended:** Look directly into the camera lens so that viewers feel you are addressing them directly.
  c. **Avoid:** Showing a ceiling, window, floor or hall.
  d. **Avoid:** Leaning to one side or looking down at notes in a way that shows the top of your head.
- [ ] Be professional.
  a. **Required:** Finish grooming yourself and eat ahead of time. You may *not* do so while interpreting.
  b. **Required:** Know the greeting script if you work for a language service and be ready to recite it sounding natural and professional. (For example, "Hi, my name is Lin. Kekchi interpreter #654321. How may I help you?")
  c. **Recommended:** Be well-rested so that you're ready to be courteous and kind.

5. Internet and speed

- [ ] Get reliable high-speed internet. You cannot interpret remotely without it.
  a. **Recommended or required:** Meeting the minimum internet speeds required by the language services or organizations you interpret for.
     i. Find out if other people in your household access the internet while you are interpreting.
     ii. If so, test your speed while they access the internet.

iii. If other users slow down your speed, you may need to purchase a plan with higher speeds to account for times when some or several other people are accessing the internet while you interpret.

b. **Recommended or required:** An internet plan that provides as much speed as possible.

i. Your available internet speed options will depend on the physical location where you live or work.

ii. If your speed is too low, you may have to find, and potentially pay for, an office where access to high-speed internet is possible.

❑ Have a hard-wired connection using an Ethernet port on your router.

a. **Recommended or required:** An Ethernet connection.

i. Wi-Fi may not be as secure, consistent or reliable as an Ethernet connection.

ii. Plug your Ethernet cable into your computer's Ethernet port (or use an adapter to connect it).

iii. If you are unsure how to do this, look up the details online or consult a colleague, language service, your workplace or your clients.

b. **Avoid:** Interpreting over Wi-Fi unless an organization you interpret for requires or approves it.

❑ Test your speed! Do *not* assume yours is fast enough for remote interpreting.

a. **Recommended or required:** Daily, or more frequent, speed tests using standard speed test websites. (They are easy to search for online.) Check your upload and download speeds and *write them down.*

i. Make certain your speeds meet the requirements and needs of your language service.

ii. Be ready to report your speeds to language services if they ask for them.

b. **Recommended:** Check your speeds on different days and different times of day.

i. Speed varies by internet service provider and due to many other factors.

ii. Check with your internet service provider to troubleshoot less-than-promised speeds.

❑ Run computer diagnostic tests.

a. **Recommended:** Running diagnostic tests built into your computer.

i. If your computer speed seems too slow on a particular day, try running the diagnostic tests.

ii. Do an internet search to learn how to run these tests on your type of computer.

b. **Recommended:** Do what the diagnostic tests suggest for improving your computer's system performance.

i. If you still have problems, look up online other diagnostic tools that can help you.

ii. For example, do a search on "how to speed up my computer."

c. **Recommended:** Get in the habit of regularly running diagnostic tests so that if you need to run one right before you interpret, you can do so quickly.

d. **Avoid:** Interpreting remotely if and when your computer or internet are running slowly.

❑ Have an alternate internet connection backup.

a. **Recommended:** An uninterruptible power supply (UPS).

i. A UPS is a small battery backup power supply.

ii. It protects your computer and keeps it running, for example, in case of storms or other electricity outages.

iii. The battery can maintain power and thus your internet connection for perhaps 30 minutes or more.

iv. Plug both your computer and router into the UPS.

b. **Recommended:** A second internet source in case of emergency and if no other source is available.

i. For example, try tethering the connection to your mobile phone.

ii. Be aware that alternate internet sources, such as phone tethering, might be too slow for remote interpreting: test them.

6. Resources

❑ Gather your best resources.

a. **Recommended:** Checking with the language services or organizations you interpret for, other interpreters and any staff or colleagues for suggestions about online and print resources to help you interpret, such as glossaries and scripts.

b. **Recommended:** Deciding in advance if you want to take notes on a notepad, a whiteboard or by typing them on a computer or tablet.

i. Try out all three methods. Find out which one works best for you.

ii. Check with the language services or organizations you interpret for to see if they have note-taking requirements.

iii. Then purchase what you need for note-taking.

c. **Recommended:** Setting up your printed and online resources in a way that is easy for you to access and use them during calls.

d. **Recommended:** Use a second screen or second device (if permitted) to organize and access online resources during assignments.

Understand the checklist

Did any of these items confuse you? Don't worry. We'll come back to them. For now, let's focus on the big picture: what will you need to think about first if you are planning to provide remote interpreting?

How to set up your home office

The first big question is—where will you interpret? For many interpreters the answer today is "at home."

If you do not work in a remote interpreting call center or another office, plan ahead. You will need a professional setting to interpret.

If you perform VRI, VRS or RSI with video (most RSI involves video), it's critical that you have a neutral background so that your clients are not seeing pictures of your dog or children during a session. It may seem extreme to worry about someone seeing a poster or piece of art in the background while you interpret, but it's a key part of keeping a private and professional setting.

A neutral background also helps keep you comfortable. For example, if you are called to do a VRI session for an inmate at a correctional facility, and the first thing they see is a picture of you and your baby, it may stir up psychological issues for the inmate and cause discomfort for them and you.

In addition, you want to protect the privacy of your home. It's best to keep your personal effects safe and away from view. Keep clutter and clothes out of sight as well.

Also, remember to dress professionally. You may think that working remotely means you get to work in pajamas every day, but if you're on video even some of the time, you'll have to dress the part. Some language services, for example, might require formal business dress. Other organizations may let you wear business casual clothing, which is somewhat less formal but still what you might wear to work in an office.

Here are some easy tips from remote interpreters for how to dress for online sessions:

- ❑ Keep a professional jacket on the back of your work chair to throw on when you start a video session.
- ❑ Wear colored tops without bright colors, logos or holes.
- ❑ Wear clothes that won't offend others or bring up any controversy.

Apart from the way your home office looks to the client on a screen, it's also important to make sure that no outside noises disturb your sessions. We will repeat this point *many times* because it is the source of *many, many complaints* about remote interpreters. The noise-cancelling headphones will help, but if you work from home and there is a crying baby or a loud dog barking in the next room, you will need to find another location to interpret.

As you saw from the checklist, always ensure that your home office is locked while you interpret so that nobody can walk in and violate the privacy of the session. Tell your roommates or family members in your home that you are working and you need them to stay out of the room and be as quiet as possible.

Keep yourself comfortable

It may seem obvious that you need to keep yourself comfortable and ready, but here are some additional tips to remember before answering the phone or accepting a video call so that you are not shuffling to get water or a pen.

Desk and chair

You will need a desk that is big enough for:

- Your computer setup and related equipment, such as headset and perhaps a separate microphone.
- Your interpreting resources, such as glossaries, scripts and other printed materials.
- A second screen or tablet.
- Note-taking materials.
- Water to hydrate yourself.
- Anything else you may need to interpret.

You may also want pictures no one else can see that make you happy and relaxed, such as family, friends or pets.

As for a chair—you want to buy the best ergonomic chair you can afford. An ergonomic chair is scientifically designed for your comfort. Sitting for long hours at a stretch can be bad for your back and your health. A good chair can make all the difference!

If you can, try out different chairs before you buy. Every human body is different. Find the chair that is right for you. You will be glad you did!

Pens, pencils and notepads

Keep a notepad and pen or pencil available on your desk. You'll need a way to easily jot down notes during the session to help you remember or to go back to later to look something up that you were not familiar with.

If you prefer, however, have a whiteboard and markers—some interpreters prefer them, and a language service might even require it. Other interpreters prefer to type their notes, often on another device, such as a separate laptop or tablet. Check with the language service or any other organizations you interpret for in case they have note-taking requirements or recommendations.

Destroy your notes!

Do not forget to destroy these notes after your sessions. Do not leave the personal data of *anyone* that you have interpreted lying out for your child, partner or roommate to accidentally see.

Take frequent breaks

Stay hydrated. Sure, you're at home, and you may say, "Oh, I can just go get water when I need to." But it's easy to forget to stop and take a break, to drink water, stretch your legs or use the bathroom.

Remote work can be rewarding, but don't forget to get up and get some fresh air and water from time to time so you are not burnt out and your mouth dries out from speaking so much.

For sign language interpreters, the physical demands of remote interpreting for hours on end can be high. It's especially important to remember to take breaks frequently, stretch your hands and fingers and close your eyes for a few minutes when you can.

Setup checklist

Now let's walk you through the step-by-step setup checklist you just saw that will help you feel ready for your work as a remote interpreter.

Then we'll go through each step to explain them all.

Step 1: Check your computer and other equipment.

Step 2: Maintain your computer: Follow best practices.

Step 3: Get your office setup right.

Step 4: Check your video background and lighting if you perform video interpreting.

Step 5: Check your internet and speed.

Step 6: Gather your resources.

Step 7: Check your camera presence (for video interpreting)

And after each assignment, even if it's a few hours later, try to evaluate how well your planning went. It's essential.

(Chapter 5 of this volume will talk about how to evaluate your interpreting—that is important too!)

Step 1: Check your computer and other equipment

Your computer setup

As you know from the checklist, it's critically important to make sure you have the correct technology setup for the job. So let's start there. What does the right computer setup mean for *you*? Let's go over the basics.

To begin with, your setup depends on the kinds of remote interpreting you do, and the kind of organization or organizations you interpret for.

For example, if you work for a language service call center, you're already set up: you will have all the equipment you need at your call center workstation or cubicle. But if you work from home for several different language companies, then each company could have its own platform and its own setup recommendations or requirements.

Or perhaps you interpret from home for a language service, three schools, two hospitals and a couple of government agencies. Then you will need a setup that meets all their needs and requirements.

What should you get?

Ideally you will have a computer that is *no more than three years old*. Your computer can be a personal computer (PC) or a Macintosh (Mac) sold by Apple, Inc. A desktop or a laptop. But avoid low-end computers—in other words, don't buy something that is too inexpensive. Invest in a good computer.

If you interpret on the job as a staff interpreter or bilingual employee at a workplace, such as a school or health department, where you interpret remotely part-time—then ask your employer to invest in a good computer for you. Be prepared to explain why you need an up-to-date and fast computer. (This chapter will help you explain why!)

Also to consider: getting a second computer as a backup. Computers do break down. Eventually, all of them do. Don't lose work or risk your reputation because your computer broke down at the worst possible time!

Finally, do *not* use a telephone to interpret remotely unless your job specifically requires you to do so.

Is It All Right to Interpret Remotely on a Tablet?

The answer to this question is: "Maybe."

A tablet has limitations. Before trying to perform remote interpreting on a tablet, first make sure you have permission from any organizations you interpret for to do so, and then make sure the tablet itself meets the required specifications.

What we can say today is that technology will continue to advance to a point where a remote interpreter may not need a desktop or laptop computer at all to interpret. At the current time, however, while some mobile technologies have been developed that are impressive, they are certainly not yet as reliable as a desktop or laptop computer for interpreting.

In addition, what is available for you to buy or is affordable to you will vary by country and region.

However, even if you don't interpret on them, tablets can be helpful to look up words or other information while you're on the job—or take notes!

Make sure you have all your other equipment and supplies

What else will you need? Take a look. Again, if you work for a language service call center, you won't usually have to worry about these items.

Audio equipment

- A good headset with boom (built-in) mic
    - You *must* have a good headset! It does not need to be too expensive, but it must be adequate quality. Do your research. Invest wisely.
    - Yes, you can buy a separate microphone and headset—but that complicates your setup and it isn't really necessary at the start. (A possible exception is conference interpreting.)
    - A good quality headset can protect your hearing and your health, especially if you perform remote interpreting for hours a day.

  - Don't assume you have a good microphone. Test it. Find out how you really sound.
    - Test your positioning for best results.
    - Record yourself interpreting on a practice platform and listen.
    - Ask another interpreter or a colleague to listen to you and give feedback.
- A second headset
  - A second headset is essential in case the first one stops working.
  - It needn't be too expensive but should be of adequate quality.

Video equipment

- Quality webcam
  - If you perform VRI, VRS or RSI, you will absolutely need a high-quality webcam.
  - The webcam that comes built into your computer may not be adequate.
  - Check with the experts; also test your webcam to make sure you look crisp and clear.
  - Even if you perform only-audio interpreting, such as OPI or audio-only RSI, you might need a good webcam to look professional at work-related online meetings.
- A second monitor or screen is *highly* recommended.
  - You can use your second screen to look up terms and other information.
  - Some interpreters who work in teams like to use the second monitor to see their partner visually.
  - A third screen is certainly not required—but many interpreters (especially if they perform RSI) find them useful.

Equipment to consider

Here is other possible equipment to consider when you are ready to invest further.

- A second computer
  - It is ideal to have a backup computer in case your main computer breaks down. Someday that second computer could rescue you from a disaster.
  - A second computer can also be useful for research or other purposes.
- A separate, stand-alone microphone
  - A high-quality stand-alone microphone with adjustable audio settings is an option over a headset with a boom mic. Many RSI interpreters prefer these mics for better quality sound and sound control.
- A standing desk
  - Remote interpreting involves long hours sitting down, which can put a strain on you and lead to lower back injuries. Some interpreters love working from a standing desk instead.

Step 2: Maintain your computer: Follow best practices

This step is easy: Follow Section 3 of your checklist.

What if you don't understand the steps? Find a specialist to guide you! Don't just omit the maintenance.

Who can you ask? If you work for a language service, or an organization with technical specialists, start there. If not, ask other interpreters or colleagues, or anyone you know who is tech-savvy with computers—a family member, friend or your favorite computer geek. Show them this part of the checklist and ask questions.

Step 3: Get your office setup right

Take a look at Figure 3.1. A remote interpreter is interpreting for attendees of an online training. Look how they have arranged the computer, the second monitor, the tablet, lighting and so forth (even water and a box of tissue).

The interpreter's goal with this setup was to make sure they have everything they need to interpret for several hours.

Plan carefully how you will organize all the equipment and resources you need. When it comes to terminology, scripts, glossaries and the ability just to check something online—and more—you'll need excellent resources on the job. Organize them well!

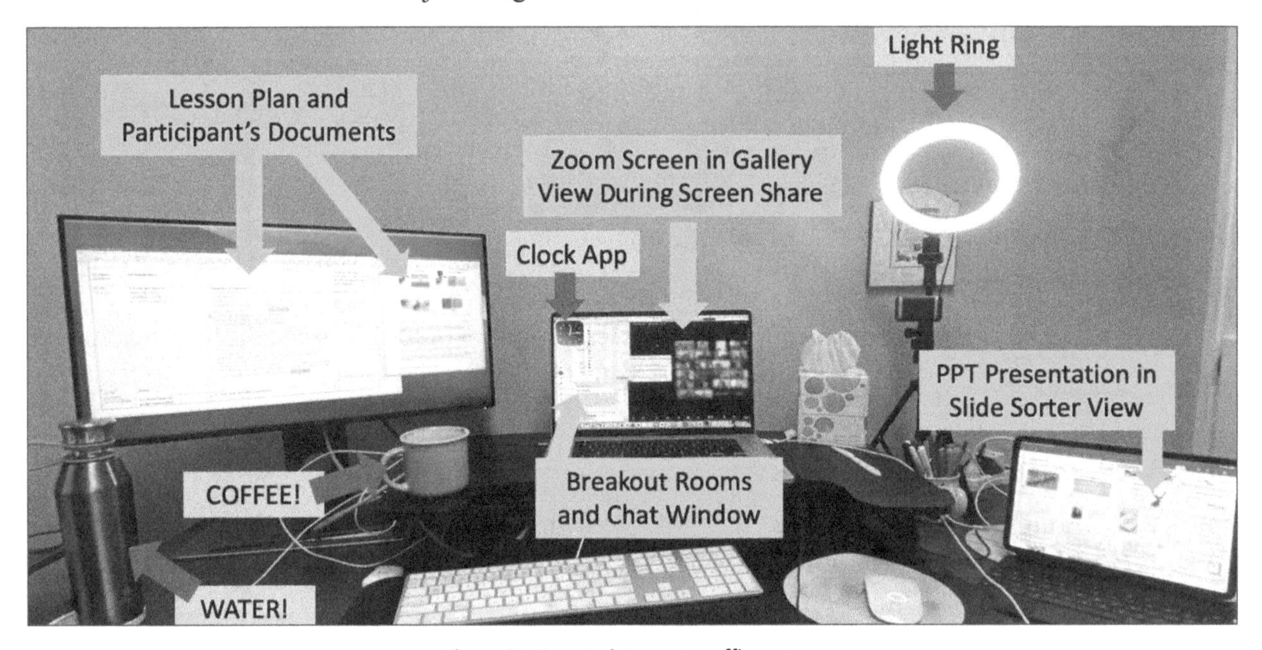

Figure 3.1: Remote interpreter office setup

Check your space

Do you have a confidential, clean environment? Is your office truly private?

If your employer isn't a language service, but perhaps a government office or school or human services organization, make sure that your supervisor and colleagues understand why you need a *private* office to interpret.

There are many reasons to protect privacy. To start with, many and perhaps most countries have privacy laws. In the U.S., for example, if you perform healthcare interpreting, you *must* be compliant with the Health Insurance Portability and Accountability Act, called **HIPAA** (pronounced *hip*-uh) for short. HIPAA protects sensitive patient data. Companies that deal with protected health information (PHI), are required to have physical, network and process security measures in place and follow them for HIPAA compliance. As an example, if someone can burst into your room because the door doesn't lock, you mustn't interpret in that room.

Beyond privacy laws, imagine the discomfort that participants on a call could feel if you are interrupted by a child bursting in or someone knocking at your door. Such disruptions can derail a session.

The ideal workspace

Interpret in a separate room with a closed door that can be locked. It should be free of background noise and disturbance. *No one outside the session should be able to hear any confidential information while you interpret.*

Step 4: Check your video background and lighting if you perform video interpreting

Plan for a plain video background

You would be amazed how many complaints the authors of this book have heard about poor lighting and other background problems in remote interpreting.

Obviously, as mentioned earlier, the guidance here does not apply to interpreters who work in call centers. But if you work in a home office, or an office inside any workplace that is not a professional language service, please pay attention.

First: if possible, buy a *plain backdrop without bright color*, a type of screen with different names, such as "collapsible backdrop" or "popup backdrop."

A collapsible or portable chair backdrop can attach to the back of your chair. A popup or collapsible backdrop goes on the floor behind your chair.

Ideally your backdrop will be a solid color, not too dark. If appropriate, ask for guidance from any language services or other organizations you interpret for.

Virtual backdrops

These days, however, the language service or organization you work for might have a virtual backdrop they want you to use. If several have their own backdrops, make sure to prepare yourself and practice using them.

However, the service or organization might not permit you to use a virtual backdrop of your own choosing. Don't assume it's all right to do so. Ask.

Avoid blurred backgrounds

Perhaps you know how to blur your background or create an electronically generated alternative background if you interpret on a videoconference platform, such as Zoom. Be careful. First, maybe you assume you can blur your background but the video platform you log in to doesn't have that option. Suddenly, everyone sees your bedroom, or a spare room stacked with storage items, and there is no time to fix the problem!

Note that for signed languages, an electronic or blurred background can be problematic and frequently cause the interpreter's body parts to blink in and out of view as they sign.

At this point in time, blurred backgrounds are not advisable because for some (and perhaps many) language services, they are not acceptable. However, this situation may change over time. Stay informed and up to date. The profession of remote interpreting seems to evolve by the minute!

Remove personal items from your background

Next, as your checklist noted, make sure that your background excludes any personal items, such as a bookshelf, vase or painting. That may sound extreme but you need a setting that is both private and professional.

Also, a clean background is less distracting for the people who watch the interpreter. That is important for all remote interpreting but it's especially critical for signed languages.

Optimal lighting

You will need excellent lighting for VRI, VRS or RSI with video. You may not need to purchase special lighting or equipment, however, as long as your lighting shows you clearly, without halos or shadows.

Strategically place your workstation, if at all possible, facing a window, or by standing lamps to have good light. If your light is too low or dim, consider ordering a ring light.

For optimal lighting, do you know if your window or lamp or other source of light should be behind you, in front of you or beside you? The answer, in most cases, is to have the source of light *in front of you.*

However, you can also position your lighting to be beside you (especially on both sides), but not behind you. Why not? Light coming from behind you can make you appear too pale. It doesn't matter whether it is daylight from a window or lamplight: if your light is behind you, other people may not see you clearly. In fact, they might see just a haze or glow—or you might be completely in shadow.

Position yourself for effective lighting

Turn your equipment around so that you're frontlit or sidelit and ideally showing up in natural light. If you are sidelit because of light from a window, consider adding a desk lamp on the other side to balance your light sources.

Lighting is serious. Low light can degrade your camera's performance. You might lose work if your lighting is poor.

Step 5: Check your internet and speed

Here is the simple fact. You *can't interpret remotely without high-speed internet.*

Make sure your internet is adequate. Follow the instructions in the checklist carefully. If you do not follow those checklist items, you may end up looking so unprofessional that no one wants to have you interpret remotely.

High-speed internet

First, make sure you have *reliable* ***high-speed*** *internet*, whether you're working at an office or at home. Remote interpreting call centers have high-speed internet, of course, and depending on the country where you live, most workplaces probably have it too.

But does your homes office have adequate internet speeds? If not, you may need to rent office space for your interpreting work.

Get a hardwired connection

Ideally, as the previous chapter mentioned, you will also need a *wired* Ethernet connection, because wireless internet isn't as reliable as a wired connection.

Do your research. Do you know how your router works? What an Ethernet port is? How that port can be connected to your computer with the right kind of cable?

If not, you'll need to find out. Now. That's basic computer literacy, and it's hugely important for remote interpreters. Ethernet is simply much faster, and much more reliable, than Wi-Fi access.

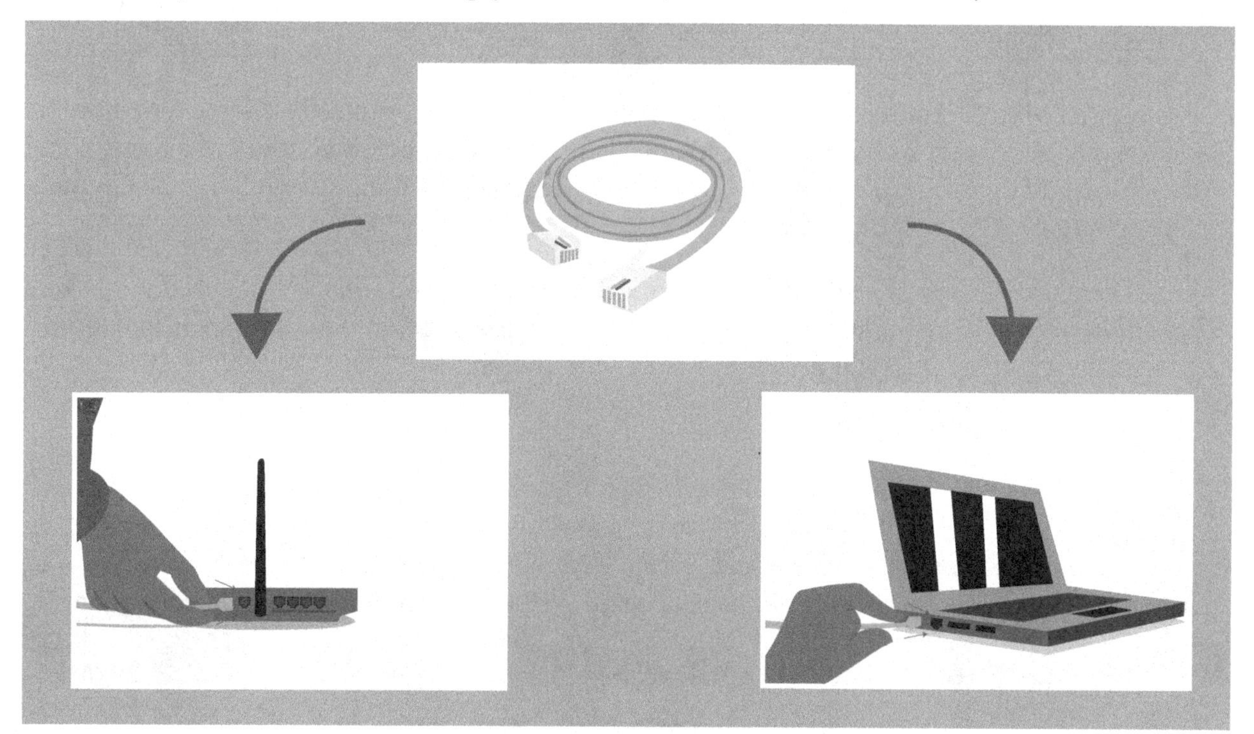

Figure 3.2: **Plugging an Ethernet cable into a computer**

If you don't know how to set up a wired connection, simply perform a search online on how to get a hardwired Ethernet connection. Once you find out, plug your Ethernet cable into your computer's Ethernet port (you might need to buy an adapter) and *interpret using this direct, hardwired Ethernet connection and not Wi-Fi* whenever possible.

Also, be absolutely sure that your internet connection is *private and secure*.

What does speed mean?

Adequate speed means *professionalism* for remote interpreting. If your internet connection is slow, no one will want to work with you. If you are a freelancer, you could lose contract after contract.

What does internet speed mean exactly? First, internet broadband speed is measured in megabits per second (Mbps), the standard measure that assesses the speed at which packets of information are downloaded from, or uploaded to, the internet.

Second, speed changes constantly—both the speed that you or your employer can receive through an internet service provider (ISP) *and* the speed that you need to interpret remotely. You'll have to stay up to date on the speeds required and the speeds available. Ask a language service what they recommend. Typically, a language service will know best.

Periodically ask your ISP if its services have changed and the provider now offers a monthly service with higher speeds.

Do not assume your speed is good enough!

A big mistake that many remote interpreters make who work from home is to say, "Well, my ISP says I get such-and-such download and upload speeds so everything is fine." That is a false assumption.

Let's say that you interpret as a freelancer. You pay your ISP a monthly charge that may be higher than it charges for its basic service to get adequate speed—but to your astonishment, some organizations that you interpret for tell you it is not adequate, even though you may be paying a lot of money to get the speed you wanted.

This problem arises because, no matter what your ISP may tell you, *your actual speed varies day to day, hour to hour, even minute to minute*. Please do not assume that your internet is high-speed on any given day or hour. *Test it before you start interpreting.*

Otherwise, right in the middle of a session your connection could freeze, pixilate or crash.

Pay for good speed—but test it—and test it often

Buy the fastest internet access you can get. Test it. Test it again, at different times of day. Test your speed when other family or household members are on the internet at the same time as you are.

And if the speed you get isn't what you're paying for—call the service provider!

How to test your speed

Here is the good news. Testing your speed is easy.

First, ask the language services or organizations you work for—or a qualified interpreter—which speed is currently required. Make sure that you get both the *upload and download speeds*. Also, ask about speeds for OPI, VRI, VRS or RSI assignments, because they might be different.

Then simply go to any online speed test (such as Speedtest.net) and check to see if you have sufficient upload and download speeds. Run the test. See if your speed is adequate. Yes, it's that simple.

But let's say you do a speed test, and your internet connection is too slow. What should you do then? The answer is: consider running a diagnostic test.

Run a computer diagnostic test

Is your connection slow? Or is your computer slow? You might need to run a diagnostic test to find out.

Knowing how to run a diagnostic test is another part of basic computer literacy. If you don't know where that program or application on your computer is—do an internet search to find out. Then run it. Maybe you'll learn how to improve the speed of your computer.

If your internet connection is too slow one day, and you need to run a computer diagnostic test, be aware this test is quite different from a speed test. A diagnostic test helps you to test the overall *performance* of your computer, which can affect speed. The results of that test could show you how you can boost your computer performance, which could speed up your computer and perhaps get you a faster internet connection.

A diagnostic tool doesn't cost money or take too long. Again, just do an internet search on how to do a performance test for your particular computer, or use the diagnostic tools that comes with your computer. Then follow the instructions. You'd be surprised what these tools can find.

A backup power supply

Buy a UPS
No, we are not telling you to buy a big company called United Parcel Service. UPS also means an *uninterruptible power supply.* Basically it's a backup power supply.

Let's say you're interpreting during a storm—and suddenly you lose electricity. That UPS will keep your computer running *and* protect your internet access for a certain period of time—perhaps for half an hour or longer.

How does a UPS work?
A backup power supply, such as a UPS, is an external battery that you plug into the computer. It has its own power cord. If your power goes off, and your computer shuts down even briefly, you could lose your connection to the session. A backup power supply might only last a few minutes or half an hour, but it maintains your connection to the session.

That could mean you can keep interpreting—and maybe the power will come back before the battery runs out.

By the way, a backup power supply can also be a powerful surge protector that protects your computer from getting destroyed by lightning, outages and power surges.

A backup connection to the internet

Plan for losing internet access.

If your internet service provider goes down, how will you continue interpreting for that call? Have another plan for internet access ready.

In an emergency, if you lose your internet connection, you may be able to tether your computer to your smartphone. Some interpreters with a good phone plan do tether their phone: that is, they use their phone as a hot spot or modem to connect another device—in this case, their computer—to the internet.

No, that is not ideal. To be frank, the connection might not be powerful (and you might have to turn off video and interpret in audio only). But if your internet service breaks down for any reason, tethering could be an emergency option.

And if tethering to your phone gets you through the call, participants may forgive a fuzzy image or less-than-high-quality sound.

Research your smartphone and your phone service to find out if you can tether your phone to connect your computer to the internet and how to do so. Test your tethering capability before you use it for a real remote interpreting assignment.

Step 6: Gather your resources

Have you ever been asked to interpret a word or phrase you've never heard before? Of course you have. Be prepared!

Perhaps the language services or other organizations you interpret for, such as a school system or hospital, have special glossaries for your language. You probably have your favorite resources.

In addition, many language services have special scripts for you to use when you request a pause, a clarification or time to interpret.

Remote interpreters (unlike most face-to-face interpreters) can also look up resources online *while* they interpret. (We are not saying that is easy!) Have your best online resources bookmarked and ready or open. If possible use another device, such as a second laptop or tablet to look up valuable information you might need.

If you have a team, you can also help your partner by looking up information to help them interpret while you are not interpreting.

Note-taking materials

Of course, you may need to take notes if you perform consecutive interpreting. Do you prefer old-fashioned paper and pen, a whiteboard, or typing notes on a computer or tablet? Find out first if the language services or other organizations you interpret for have a preference. If not, try out the three methods, decide what works best for you and have your resources available.

Make sure your desk is tidy and your note-taking materials are easy to access.

Step 7: Check your camera presence (for video interpreting)

Camera presence is how you come across professionally on video while you interpret.

For OPI, your audio matters. It should be clear enough that your voice is easy to follow and understand, with a good pace and rhythm and no distracting static, hum, hissing or puffing.

But for VRI, VRS and RSI, you have to think about camera presence too.

Here is a story from one of the authors of the book.

> *A remote VRI interpreter, a young man, decided it was fine to show up for the session wearing no shirt! In fact, he wore nothing at all for that session, from the waist up. Yet it never occurred to him that this was a problem.*
>
> *(He was quite surprised when he stopped getting interpreting assignments from that language service!)*

For a professional camera presence, pay attention to every one of the elements below.

Dress

Dress professionally and appropriately for that session. For example, if you work for a language service, know the dress code and follow it. Be prepared to adapt your clothing as needed. Many court interpreters wear formal business attire. Interpreting for tourism could involve business-casual clothing.

Camera view

Make sure you are centered in the camera view. That view should not show a ceiling, floor or hallway. Sit up straight, with good posture. Avoid leaning back or to one side. If you are not using a backdrop screen, make sure that your workspace is clean. No one should see any mess, or even other equipment.

And when you interpret from your notes, be sure to look up at the camera as much as possible.

Background/light

See the guidance in step 4. Test your lighting.

Voice

A good headset should help your voice sound clear. Speak at a pace that is not too fast or slow. Make your voice easy to hear and understand. For consecutive interpreting even when the person that you're interpreting for speaks or signs quickly or slowly, you can interpret at a moderate pace.

Courtesy

Be polite, especially during your introduction and closing. Pay attention to the participants. Listen carefully to any information and instructions you receive. If someone believes you are rude because you have interpreted rude language accurately, clarify that you are simply interpreting.

Conduct

Behave like the interpreter you'd want to have for yourself. Focus on doing the best job possible. Be aware. Don't move around a lot or fidget. Try to avoid letting your gaze wander. Look focused and intent.

Also, pay attention to how your movements look to others. If you roll your eyes, it will be visible on video! If you bend down to glance at your notes, participants will see the top of your head. If you get frustrated, your body language can be more obvious on a video call than you realize: try hard not to show frustration. (Even in OPI, participants can often hear frustration in an interpreter's voice!)

Drinking and eating

Don't eat while you interpret. Don't drink—except water. Interpreters do need to stay hydrated: if you need to drink while you interpret, try to have a neutral water container with no logo. Use a straw.

Some language services or clients will let you quickly turn off the video to sip water. But get permission to do so, and if you ever do turn off the video, be quick. If you drink water on video, try to look as professional as possible.

For longer sessions, you might wish to alert your client beforehand that you will occasionally need to drink water while interpreting to refresh and protect your voice. You can explain that interpreters need water at hand in the same way they need to have note-taking materials or equipment, as part of their work.

Be professional on camera

The authors of this book hear many stories. Interpreters who put on lipstick during a VRI session. Interpreters who eat or drink coffee on camera. Interpreters who wear big, shiny or noisy jewelry. Use your common sense. Look professional for video interpreting.

→ Section 3.1 Review

In this section we walked you through the steps of a checklist on how to set up for remote interpreting. Do you feel ready? Let's review!

Step 1: Check your computer and other equipment.
Step 2: Maintain your computer: Follow best practices.
Step 3: Get your office setup right.
Step 4: Check your video background and light if you perform video interpreting.
Step 5: Check your internet speed.
Step 6: Gather your resources.
Step 7: Check your camera presence (for video interpreting).

After each assignment, even if it's a few hours later, try to do some self-evaluation. It's essential.

Also remember to review and keep reviewing Checklist 1: Prepare for Remote Interpreting. It summarizes much of the content of this section.

Section 3.2 Set Up for OPI, VRI and VRS Platforms

→ Learning objective 3.2

After completing this section, the remote interpreter will be able to set up for a typical OPI, VRI or VRS session on standard platforms.

→ Section 3.2 Overview

The previous section of this chapter walked you through how to set up for work as a remote interpreter. This next section focuses on a narrower window: what to do to prepare for each session of OPI, VRI or VRS.

As with the previous section, much of the guidance will also apply to RSI. However, see Chapters 1 and 2 of Volume 2 for more detail about setting up for and performing RSI.

This section will also help you manage the common technical and logistic problems that you will run into. Some of the best ways to prevent those problems is to set up for a session correctly, but we'll also discuss what to do if technical breakdowns and other challenges happen anyway.

Do you want to set up your session for success? This section will show you how.

→ Section 3.2 Content

The first rule of remote interpreting: Do not panic

Technical problems. Let's face it. Remote interpreting has its ups and downs, like any job. In remote interpreting, many of the biggest challenges you'll face are technical.

Let's start with the most basic fact of all. *You are going to have technical problems.* It's just the nature of this work. Don't worry about it. Take it for granted that things will go wrong and sometimes everything will break down.

Many if not most of the things that go wrong are related to technology. Simply accept that technical challenges are a way of life in this job and a key part of the work that you do will be to deal with them effectively.

All right. Then how do you handle tech problems? The first rule is simple. Since computers and the internet have problems—lots of problems, they just do—the most important thing to remember when you have a technical problem is:

Do.

Not.

Panic.

That's right. Accept that dealing with technical issues is not your fault but it is still your responsibility to try and fix. To repeat: addressing technical problems is not a big concern; it is simply part of your job. So again, if things break down:

Do.

Not.

Panic!

Instead, relax. This section will help you set up for a trouble-free session—or at least, as trouble free as possible. Simply having a few simple setup and troubleshooting techniques will make you feel calmer and more in control. Then you can perform a remote interpreting session smoothly. You will look—and feel—professional.

All that said, the best time to troubleshoot is before you start. No, you can't prevent *all* the technical difficulties in remote interpreting. But good planning and the correct setup can help you avoid *many* problems.

Your checklist for setup and tech check

At the beginning of this chapter, you read Checklist 1: Prepare for Remote Interpreting, which provides a summary of most of the points discussed in the previous section.

Now let's turn to Checklist 2: Setup and Tech Check for Remote Interpreters. Here is the checklist itself. We hope you find it clear and self-explanatory.

Checklist 2: Setup and Tech Check for Remote Interpreters

Whether you are about to interpret for your first remote call or for the tenth or hundredth time, follow this checklist right before the call to be sure you're ready to interpret.

But first: go through your **Checklist 1: Prepare for Remote Interpreting** to make sure that you have everything you need in place. Then, before you start your interpreting work (or practice) for the day, go through this second checklist.

1. Turn on your computer

- ❑ Rebooting your computer before you start for the day can help it run faster and more efficiently. Computer speed and efficiency are *essential* for remote interpreting.
  a. **Recommended:** Shutting down completely is better than clicking on "Restart." Shutting down helps to completely turn off applications that might slow down or interfere with your computer speed and efficiency.
  b. **Recommended:** The older your computer is, especially if it is more than three years old, the more important rebooting your system will become as a matter of habit.

2. Check your speed

- ❑ Don't assume your internet upload and download speeds are fine today because they were fine yesterday. Test them again.
  a. **Recommended:** Use any online speed test to check your speed and see if it meets your language services requirements.
  b. **Required:** If your speed is too slow that day, *you can't interpret.*
     i. Respect the minimum speed requirements of your language service.
     ii. If your computer crashes while interpreting due to slow speed, you may lose all work with that client or language service.

3. Log in

- ❑ Log in to the remote interpreting web application (app) that you will interpret on.
  a. **Recommended:** Use the latest version (download as needed) of the recommended web browsers, such as Chrome or Firefox. Before using a browser, check with the language service or client to know if they wish you to use particular browsers.
     i. This platform may be a web-based app or one that is already installed on your computer.
     ii. If you interpret directly for an organization, such as a school, hospital or government agency, for VRI or even AOI/OPI, you may be logging in to a webconference platform.
  b. **Avoid:** Any browsers that your language service or organization tell you not to use.
     i. For example, Apple Safari and/or Microsoft Edge might not be recommended by some language service remote interpreting web-based apps.

- [ ] As needed, verify your camera and microphone web permissions for that browser or app.
    a. **Recommended:** If you are having trouble with your camera or microphone, do an internet search on "what is a camera [or microphone] web permission" and follow those instructions.

4. Get ready

- [ ] Open what you need.
    a. **Recommended:** Open the online glossaries and resources relevant for the kind of calls you are about to interpret.
- [ ] Close out what you don't need.
    a. **Recommended:** Close all unnecessary browsers and other applications and programs.
        i. They can interfere with your computer's speed and efficiency.
        ii. They can distract you.
    b. **Recommended:** Close all applications in the recommended way (search online to learn how to do so: these instructions vary by device and application).
    c. **Recommended:** Run your computer's task manager or activity monitor application.
        i. Search online to find out how to do so.
        ii. Find out which applications are still open and use the most computer resources.
        iii. Applications that use the most resources can slow down your speed. Close them, if possible.
- [ ] Test your audio (and video) again.
    a. **Required or recommended:** Make sure the headset you are using is selected for sound input or output, both on your computer settings and on the interpreting platform—and also, as needed, your browser.
    b. **Recommended:** Ideally, test your audio quality on the same platform used by the language service or client you will interpret for. Adjust as needed.
    c. **Recommended:** If applicable, test your video and adjust.
- [ ] Arrange your resources.
    a. **Recommended:** Whenever possible, know in advance what types of calls or sessions you will interpret for and gather the most helpful resources for those calls.
    b. **Recommended:** Have your note-taking materials (e.g., notepad and pen, a whiteboard or a tablet and keyboard) ready and close to you but not visible on camera.
- [ ] Have your introduction script and briefing instructions ready (may not apply to conference interpreting).
    a. **Recommended:** Know exactly what to say when you start a session.
    b. **Recommended:** Memorize that script until you know it perfectly (or know the elements to adjust depending on the situation).

i. Consider having scripts on laminated cards to read; keep them close to you.

ii. Having written copies of scripts can be especially important if you work for different agencies with different scripts.

5. Have water at hand

- ❑ You may need to drink during longer interpreted sessions or work shifts.
  a. **Recommended:** If you perform VRI, verify with your language service when and how you may drink water while interpreting, either on camera or by briefly turning the camera off, for example.
  b. **Recommended:** If you need to drink water on camera, have a neutral, transparent container with no logos.
     i. Use a straw.
     ii. Be ready to sip quickly and smoothly at appropriate times.
  c. **Avoid:** Drinking coffee, tea or anything but water on camera.
  d. **Avoid:** Using a nontransparent cup, colorful cup, a cup with logos, or any other attention-getting cup.
  e. **Avoid:** Interrupting any sensitive or important statements to drink water.

6. Be ready to go offline

- ❑ Have your exit script ready.
  a. **Required:** Use the language script provided by the language service (if any).
  b. **Recommended:** Whether you have to leave because someone else has left, or because the session is over, know exactly what to say.
  c. **Recommended:** Memorize that script until you know it perfectly.
- ❑ Whenever you take a break or end your last session of the day, go offline by closing your browser and the application.
  a. **Recommended:** At that time, also close any open applications in the recommended manner.
  b. **Recommended:** Reboot your computer as needed to keep it fast and efficient.

A few other points

Checklist 2 is helpful, but in order to be prepared for your first session of the day, see If you can also get a formal tech check on the actual language service interpreting platform that you're going to interpret on that day.

If, instead, you will be interpreting not for a language service but (for example) over a webconference platform, such as Zoom, then at least get on the platform early enough to check your headset connection and audio, and also check your video if you're doing video interpreting. Even if your connections worked perfectly the day before, unexpected problems connecting to your audio and video are common. Fix them before you start.

Observe yourself for video interpreting. For example, are you leaning to one side against a wall? How does your background look? Examine your posture and appearance carefully.

Call readiness

Call readiness is simply a term that means the remote interpreter is truly ready to begin. First, position yourself. Keep both feet flat on the floor if you can. Keep your back straight. (Yes, even for OPI. Good posture affects the quality of your voice.)

For video calls, make sure that the camera clearly captures your head and shoulders and look directly at the *camera*. Focus your vision on the screen. Check that there is at least some space just above your head.

Also, the camera should face you directly, not at an angle. In other words, the camera shouldn't point up or down. Make sure that all participants on a video call are able to see all of your head and all of your face.

Check your video surroundings

For video calls, check your surroundings. Your background should be well-lit. No one should see big shadows. Angle your camera to show only you. And of course, for signed language, it should clearly show your signing space.

The camera view should not include any of the ceiling or floor, the hallway, a door, a window or any personal items. In fact, your background should really show no objects at all, which is why it is recommended that you use a plain color backdrop.

Your greeting

Have a greeting prepared. If you interpret for any language services, each one will probably have its own greeting and will give you an ID number too. If so, use the greeting and number they give you.

But if you work freelance or you interpret for a workplace, a fairly standard greeting would be, "Hi, my name is so-and-so, ID #123456 [if you have an ID number], Spanish interpreter. How may I help you today?"

By the way, mentioning your language is important because often remote interpreters are sent to calls for the wrong language!

Your greeting vs. your introduction

A greeting is not the same as a professional introduction. You say a greeting when you first come onto a call when perhaps not everyone is present yet. In fact, some interpreters ask, "Is everyone present?" before they begin.

Also, when you say your language, you might determine there is a problem and they need another interpreter. In that case, you leave.

Your introduction, on the other hand, is more than a greeting because it includes certain elements that everyone needs to hear before you begin. It will vary from organization to organization or you may have to write one yourself. At a minimum it should include your first name and the fact that you will interpret everything and keep the session confidential. Many interpreters add other elements if they have time, for example, requesting the participants to speak to each other and not the interpreter and that you may ask them to pause (in consecutive) for the interpreter to interpret.

Of course, in some cases you can simply combine your greeting with your introduction, where appropriate. But make sure you know what introduction you are using and memorize it. (See Chapter 4 of this volume for details about introductions and sample scripts.)

→ Section 3.2 Review

This section examined a second checklist called Setup and Tech Check for Remote Interpreters. That checklist helps you prepare to interpret your first session of the day, whether audio only or also on video.

The checklist addresses many aspects of preparing for the session in detail, from rebooting your computer (how and why), the importance of testing your speed before you interpret, how to log in, call readiness, why you will need water ready (and how to prepare and also drink it) and procedures for going offline.

This section also addressed your video surroundings and the difference between your greeting and your interpreter introduction.

Section 3.3 Troubleshoot on OPI, VRI and VRS Platforms

→ Learning objective 3.3

After completing this section, the remote interpreter will be able to list common potential technical and logistic problems in remote interpreting and review practical solutions.

→ Section 3.3 Overview

The interpreting field has its ups and downs, just like any other job. However, technological problems are a common challenge for many remote interpreters and their clientele.

Don't worry: this section describes many of the most common challenges and how to troubleshoot them.

Having a few simple troubleshooting strategies can make or break a remote interpreting session. In this section, we will address the most common technical and logistic problems remote interpreters are likely to encounter and what to do about them.

→ Section 3.3 Content

Basic technical problems

While computers are not prone to having emotional meltdowns or saying the wrong thing, they do have glitches here and there, and the most important thing to remember when they do occur is: Do. Not. Panic!

These things happen with or without our control and are inevitable. There isn't much you can do to stop it.

Scary? Again: Do. Not. Panic! Here we will go over some of the most common technical problems that may occur and how you can address them. Maintaining your devices and following this handy tip may potentially prevent them from occurring in the first place.

Why do tech problems happen? Sometimes we know exactly why, while other times they just occur and they can be difficult to diagnose. Let's go through some of the more typical tech problems to see what the root causes are and how we can solve them each time.

The remote interpreter: A tech specialist

Before we go any further, we want to invite you to think of yourself in a new way. Yes, you're still an interpreter. But in remote interpreting, you're also your own tech specialist.

At the least, you are a tech specialist for your own setup. But the reality is that participants in the session—and sometimes even the people who organize the session—will often turn to *you,* the remote interpreter, for technical guidance.

No, that doesn't mean it's your job to manage or solve the tech issues for everyone else on the call. And if you work for a large language service, it will usually have tech specialists ready to assist.

But if you don't work for a language service, participants in the session may simply assume that *you* are the person to help them. And sometimes you will need to do so.

That said, if you're a freelance interpreter, before you take the job, try to make sure that everyone has the same expectations about the services you are providing. Wherever appropriate, you may need to charge separately for those services. After all, think about it: tech support itself is not interpreting!

But being realistic, things will go wrong during a call and you may need to step in to help fix technical problems. So let's be clear: you're a tech specialist *only for the tech that helps you interpret.*

Don't be afraid of this new identity. Embrace it. Think of being a tech specialist as part of who you are as a remote interpreter.

Before we jump into the common tech problems, let's talk about the equipment needed for the best remote interpreting experience. This is review from the previous chapter and also the previous section in this chapter, but it's really, *really* important information, so we're going to repeat a few things. (Be patient with us in this book. If we repeat certain information, trust that we have good reasons!)

Good equipment helps you prevent tech and other problems before they start.

A quick review of your equipment and connections from Section 3.1

1. First, have a working computer. We recommend a desktop or laptop, even though some interpreters have a powerful stationary tablet instead. Ideally your computer should not be older than three years.
2. We keep saying this. We'll say it again. Unless you work in a call center, you need to have a hardwired, high-speed connection to the internet. (See Section 3.1.)
3. Have a quality high-definition (HD) webcam. We mentioned that often the webcam that comes built into your computer or laptop isn't sharp enough. But it may also not have the speed or quality you need for video interpreting. Check with a colleague or expert.
4. Make sure you have a decent headset (or external mic) with good sound.
5. Have a backup headset—and ideally a backup computer or quality tablet—in case something goes wrong. Because sooner or later, it will!
6. Have a phone or some other way to communicate if something really serious breaks down—including your internet connection.
7. If possible, have a second monitor or screen. It will help you in many ways, for example, to look up terms on your computer glossaries or information online during the session.
8. Finally, storms happen, electrical surges happen, accidents happen, and so on. We recommend you buy that special backup for your battery we mentioned called an uninterruptible power supply (UPS). Your UPS can save you by not interrupting the call if you have a brief loss of electricity.

How to avoid technical problems before they start: Have good equipment

To repeat, avoid older computers, low-end computers and older webcams. You need quality audio and video—and excellent speed.

For example, let's say you have a VRI call that has poor quality, and you notice that your self-view window—that's the image you see of yourself—doesn't show a smooth video feed. As a result, you look pixelated and unclear. This probably means that your computer is struggling to keep up with your webcam's video processing demands—and it's time to get a new one.

Maybe your computer is too old, or its graphics processor is. Using a computer with better graphics and processing—in other words, a more up-to-date and powerful computer—can help you solve a *lot* of technical problems before they start.

Also, unless you have a lot of light in the room where you interpret, some of the cheaper webcams or the ones that come built into laptops and some desktops might not have the speed or quality you need. You may see video trailing, or splotches and yellowing of people or other odd colors and many other quality issues.

Finally, please, *please* don't use your computer's audio without a headset! It's just not adequate for professional interpreting. The built-in audio of your computer cuts out too much of the sound signal, it's hard for other people to hear well and the poor sound will fatigue them (and you) as well as making you look unprofessional.

In addition, if you don't have a headset or headphones, your computer microphone can pick up the other person's voice from the speakers and create a feedback loop, which sounds truly terrible—it's painful to listen to.

Finally, if you are taking notes for consecutive interpreting without a headset and you flip the pages, that sound can be loud. Using a headset is essential to reduce speaker feedback and other background noise. Make sure you have a decent quality headset!

Check your own tech—record yourself

Do you think your equipment is adequate? To be sure, record yourself. Otherwise, you won't really know what your audio and video sound and look like to others.

You'd be amazed how many interpreters believe they sound and look fine online when in reality they do not. Remember to record yourself on any webconference platform, such as Zoom, for audio and video, even briefly as Checklist 1 recommends. Then watch and listen to the recording carefully. You will learn a lot. (And not only about the quality of your equipment.)

A language service checklist

Let's say you work for a specific language service. It may not have the checklists we showed you in this chapter: the service may have its own checklist.

Always pay attention to a language service's requirements. The service will often give you a list of the things that you will need to do *right before* you log in to its platform.

It's true that another checklist can add up to a lot of tasks to do before every session. It might also seem like a lot for you to remember at first. But please trust that if a language service asks you to do something specific to set up, *it's because it sees the problems with interpreters who do not follow the requirements.*

Each remote interpreting platform is different. Follow the requirements for that platform.

That said, many of the sample setup items in the next few paragraphs would be helpful for any remote interpreting platform. Besides, before you know it, simply doing these things every time you prepare for a session or a day's work will soon become an automatic habit. You won't even need to think about them.

Log on

Many language services ask you to use Google Chrome or Mozilla Firefox. Other browsers, such as Apple Safari and Microsoft Edge, might not work well for their platform.

Browser permission

Make sure that you select your headset and webcam for audio and video on your computer settings. *The browser might have to give you permissions for those selections first.*

How do you get browser permissions? Let's take Chrome as an example, because it's a common browser used in remote interpreting. At the time of publication, in Windows, you would open Chrome and look at the top of the browser to the left of the URL for the website. To the right of the refresh button, if you see a lock icon, click on that. Then you can change or confirm that camera and microphone both say "Allow."

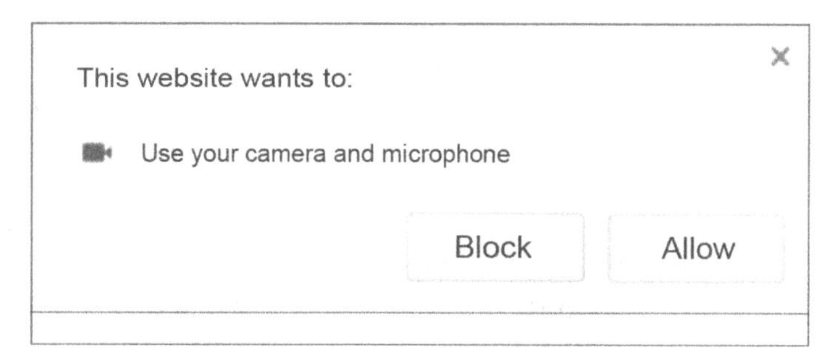

Figure 3.3: **Browser permission**

(Please note that technology changes all the time so this guidance could be outdated when you read this.)

If your audio or camera still aren't working, then make sure your computer's audio and video settings are correct. You can do this by opening Settings (in Windows) or System Preferences (in Macs) to make sure you have selected your headset for audio and the correct video input (such as an external webcam) so you are not relying on the computer microphone and speakers—or the computer webcam, if it is inadequate.

Close out

You don't want anything running on your computer that could slow you down. All those open programs and tabs can cause serious tech problems for you.

To prevent that problem, exit from *anything*—browsers, programs or apps—that you have open but you don't need for the assignment, including any unneeded browser tabs, which can drain energy. Keep open only the tabs or windows necessary for interpreting (for example, online dictionaries or glossaries).

Run task manager

The special utility monitor called a task manager or activity monitor logs all your computer activity. Check it to find out which programs and apps are still running. If you just closed out of everything that you don't need, although you might not know it, other applications might still be running—and they can slow you down.

If you see any application in the task manager that *shouldn't* be running, close it!

Take a screenshot

When only the browsers, programs and apps that you need to *interpret* are open, you might be asked by a language service to take a screenshot of your task manager or activity monitor. (We'll explain why in a moment.)

Test the network

Make sure that everything is running smoothly.

Save screenshot

You might then be required by a language service to save the screenshot. Why? Well, if anything goes wrong, that screenshot is proof that you set yourself up the way the company asked you to.

Go online

The next step is to log in to the platform where you will interpret and check out everything there—audio, video, the interface, everything. Make sure it's working well today, even if it went well yesterday.

Start your session

You are now ready to interpret!

Additional setup guidelines

Now that you know how to set up for each session, let's look at a few additional guidelines for setup.

Go offline when you're done

Whenever you take a break or end your shift, close out of your applications and log off the platform. Close the browser or application. Please note that failure to hang up or log off of an application can result in call dragging (the caller continues to log the time of the call even without any interpretation occurring).

Another potential issue that arises with not logging off or hanging up after your shift could be that you will show as online, which can cause the routing algorithm to route to you even if you are not actively waiting for a call, which will increase hold times for the client.

Close out completely and correctly

Also, when you close out any app or program, *do it correctly*. For example, don't just click on a little X. Exit the program the way you are supposed to by quitting it completely.

Check with a language service before you install new software

If you work for a language service (or several), before you install new software—even standard antivirus software, for example—make sure you consult first with the language service, who may advise you on how to do so safely. That way, the installation doesn't affect your online performance over their platform when you interpret.

Stay up to date

Keep updating your operating system. It's important to stay up to date in general, but especially for security updates.

Reboot often

Reboot before you start work. Reboot again once a day or several times a day. It won't hurt. It can often help, depending in part on the age and specifications of your computer.

Simply rebooting before you start your workday or your first call of the day can help your computer to maintain speed and efficiency. Rebooting may include closing out all of your open applications if your computer doesn't automatically do this. In remote interpreting, to avoid technical difficulties, you want lots of speed and efficiency.

Restarting from time to time during your workday can be helpful. But be careful too: only reboot when you are sure you have enough time to reopen the apps and programs that you need to interpret!

Make setup for the session a routine

Yes, all this setup work for each workday or session seems like a lot to remember. But if you do it regularly, it will soon become a habit and won't take much time at all.

Managing typical technical problems

Now let's turn to the aspect of remote interpreting that often frightens new interpreters: tech challenges.

The reality is that if you prepare for a few of the most common technical problems and learn to fix them, you'll become calmer and more confident in no time. That way, when you have a new technical problem that you haven't seen before, it will be easier for you to use your previous knowledge to provide good customer service and come up with solutions.

Let's examine a few of these common technical problems one by one.

Typical tech problem #1: The call is not connecting

One of the most common problems you'll have on a language service platform is that the call just won't connect.

Maybe after you answer an incoming call, you see something like a button that says "Connecting" but the call never connects. You have nothing to interpret. What do you *do?*

Solutions for tech problem #1

The first thing to do is remember not to panic! Here are six possible solutions.

Solution #1
Use the supported hardware, the correct software and the organization's recommended web browser. Make sure that participants are using them too.

Solution #2
Check your speed. Inadequate speed is a highly common problem. Your speed can change from moment to moment. Go to any standard speed test, such as Speedtest.net, to verify your upload and download speeds.

Also be aware that participant speed may be slow and may be causing problems.

Solution #3
Use the recommend browser and apps. Each organization or language service will typically give you a recommended browser or two for their platform, for example, Chrome or Firefox. A language company may also ask you to download an app onto your computer for you to interpret using that app.

Solution #4
Update all apps. If you are using a mobile application, make sure it is up to date. If you're not sure how to do so, ask the language services or other organizations that you interpret for, or a colleague. Believe it or not, some apps are updated several times a month. For remote interpreting, try to check once a week at least to make sure that all your apps are up to date.

Solution #5
Allow browser access to your camera and microphone. If you forgot to do so before the session, you may now need to allow microphone and camera access. The first time you use a remote interpreting app in a web browser or on a mobile device, you may get a prompt asking you to allow the application access to your camera and microphone. If you are using a Mac, you may have to go through additional security steps to authorize the use of the app as well. Please remember that you won't be connected until you click "Allow" or "Share" or whatever that browser or device asks for. Again, if you're not sure how to do it, ask for help.

Solution #6
Refresh your browser page—or force quit the application. Sometimes a refresh will do the trick. (Do an internet search on "how to refresh my browser" if you don't know how.) If your problem

is a temporary connectivity issue, which often happens, fix it by refreshing your browser page. Or, if you interpret for a language company, force quit the company's app and reopen it. Yes, if you close the app and reopen it, then the call will be interrupted, but depending on the language service or organization you interpret for, the call may still be reconnected to the same interpreter (you).

Typical tech problem #2: A lag (delay) in your connection

Here's another extremely common problem: you have a significant lag in your connection. This is why it is so important to test yourself on the remote interpreting platform before your first call or assignment. Whether the lag is audio only, or audio and video, that lag makes it extremely hard for you to interpret—if you can interpret effectively at all.

Sometimes the problem fixes itself quickly. Sometimes it doesn't.

Solutions for tech problem #2

No Wi-Fi!

Make sure you are correctly connected to the internet directly and not through Wi-Fi. We have already mentioned that except for emergency situations, you need to be hardwired. That means you'll need to plug your Ethernet cable into your computer's Ethernet port or adapter, which is the only way to connect directly to the internet.

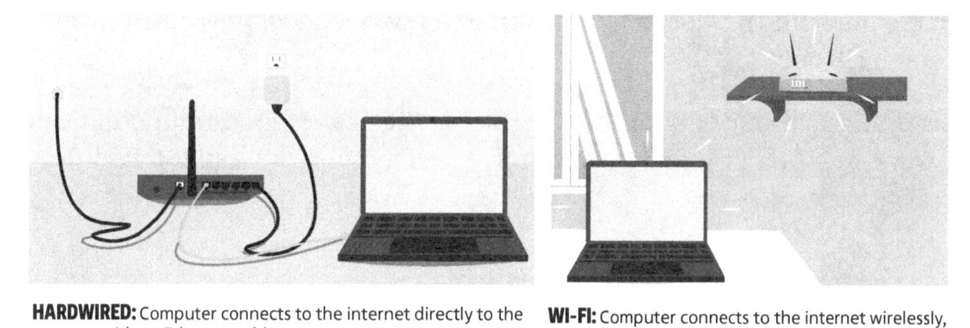

HARDWIRED: Computer connects to the internet directly to the router with an Ethernet cable.

WI-FI: Computer connects to the internet wirelessly, without a cable.

Figure 3.4: **Ethernet cable connection compared to Wi-Fi**

People sometimes get confused and think that Wi-Fi is the same thing as the internet. The hardwired Ethernet cable and Wi-Fi are what connect you to the internet. To interpret you should be hardwired to the internet. Wi-Fi is often slower and not nearly as reliable as a wired connection.

At the risk of sounding repetitive, to work as a remote interpreter, *you have to have a reliable connection to the internet.* A direct internet connection definitely reduces lag if you have high-speed internet. Plug that Ethernet cable in!

Clear your cache

Especially if this is a test call and you're not interpreting yet, clear your cache on your browser.

Cache simply means a file where your computer memory stores information for easy retrieval. These files can interfere with browser-based applications.

Sometimes by opening your account in more than one browser tab, or logging in to a different account in the same browser, you can lead an application to do unexpected things. If you refresh the browser page and that doesn't work, you may have to clear your history and cookies.

If you're not sure how to clear your cache, or your history and cookies, don't worry. It's easy to do an internet search on how to do these things. Be sure to do a search that is relevant for your computer—a PC vs. a Mac—as the instructions can be different.

Check your modem and router

If your lag is coming from slow internet speeds, reboot your modem and your router. The modem brings the internet to your office or home. The router is what brings the internet to your device. Restart your modem and your router at least once a week.

Troubleshoot slow internet speed. Rebooting your modem and router is easy to do—except while you're interpreting, unfortunately. But if you notice the problem during your tech check time *before the call*, try rebooting. Rebooting your modem and router just means turning them off and on.

To reboot them, unplug the power and Ethernet cables from the modem and turn off and unplug the router. Wait at least 30 seconds to let everything fully cycle down and clear its memory and also to let your computer know what is happening.

Then plug in the modem. If it doesn't power on in a few seconds, press the power button. Then turn your router back on.

While you're doing that, make sure that all your cables have good tight connections and the ports are all working. If all else fails, you can try even moving the router to a different position. Whatever works!

Typical tech problem #3: My microphone and/or camera are not working

Here's another highly common problem: you log on and find out that your camera and microphone don't work. Of course, we hope you find this out *before* the call.

Solutions for tech problem #3

Make sure your microphone and camera access are enabled

As this chapter mentioned earlier, when you use common remote interpreting applications for the web, you will need to allow microphone and camera access for each individual browser. If that didn't happen, or there was a problem, you may have to do it now.

Each browser requests access in different ways. When you take your first call, you could see a prompt like one of these two below.

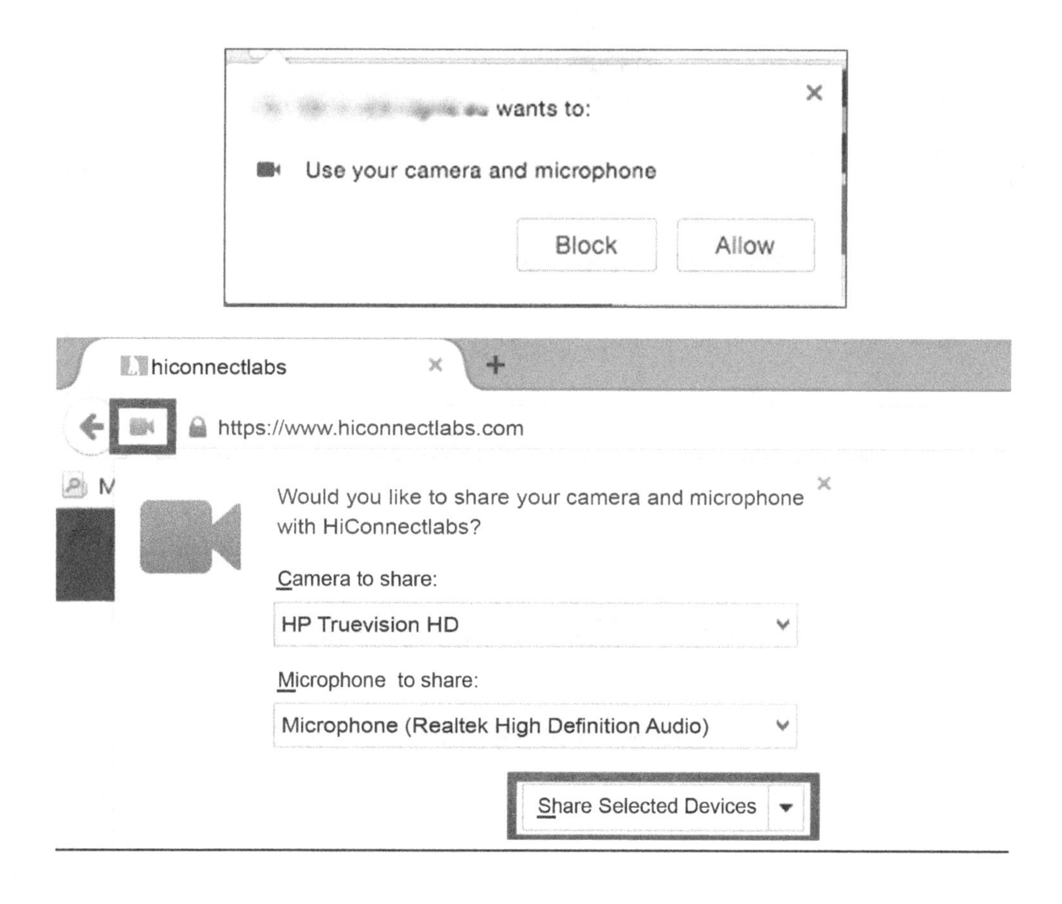

Figure 3.5: **Computer prompt**

In fact, a number of current remote interpreting platforms may remind you to do all this checking before you start.

Make sure you have selected the correct audio and video

Did you select the correct audio and video? Verify that you did so. Go to the platform's settings or preferences and find the audio and video settings. Next, select your headset and correct webcam there for input and output.

If that doesn't work, go into Settings (for Windows) or System Preferences (for Mac), and go into "Sound." Select your headset for input and output. And while you're at it, make sure your webcam cable is plugged in tightly if your webcam is external.

Typical tech problem #4: I look awful...sound awful...or they say I do!

Sometimes you can see that you don't look right in your video feed. Or perhaps someone tells you they have a hard time hearing you well or seeing you clearly. These are serious problems. Fix them.

Solutions for tech problem #4

First, to solve an audio or video problem, make sure that you performed all the setup steps we showed you in this chapter.

Next, try the troubleshooting strategies you just learned for slow internet connections. Slow internet can be destructive for both audio and video.

Finally, if this is a test call, check to see if anyone else has the same problem hearing or seeing you. If none of these setup approaches work, try these strategies.

Check your lighting

Remember what we said earlier in this chapter: *avoid having a bright light directly behind you.*

Do have adequate light, daylight if possible, or at least good-quality lighting. It should ideally come from in front of you or beside you. If it comes from beside you, you may need to have it come equally from both sides, depending on the lighting.

Check your headset and your environment

If the complaint is that you sound as if you are hissing, or certain sounds you make (such as "p") pop or sound puffy, and so on, these noises can be disturbing to participants and distract them. Immediately check the boom microphone on your headset and adjust it. Lower it a little, or otherwise change the position, so that it is not too close to your mouth. Doing so should fix the problem.

If the complaint is about background noise, remember that a good quality headset with a built-in microphone will filter out a lot of background noise. Do you have a reasonably good headset? Did you *select* your headset audio, or are participants hearing you through your computer, even though your headset is plugged in? Remember that your built-in computer audio is *not* adequate for remote interpreting.

Next, check the room where you interpret: is your door tightly closed, with a sign on it to alert anyone around that you are interpreting? Is noise coming from the street? If the other parties on the call tell you that they can hear your background noise, change the room or consider soundproofing it.

Search online to find out how to soundproof a room. It's simpler than you might expect, and there are affordable options. You might need to buy sound blankets for your walls, vinyl strip door kits, sound sponges, sound barriers and more! However, again, check your headset. A better quality headset with a headset microphone may fix the problem.

Your background noise is your *responsibility*

Maybe you don't hear your own background noise because you're used to it. However, language services report hearing fireworks, dogs, babies, police sirens and much more from remote interpreters' environments. That's *not* a tech problem. That's just background noise, and it's your responsibility.

Remember, background noise is not only unprofessional, but it also means you may be in violation of privacy laws and, most especially, that people can't hear you well when you interpret.

Dress the part

If the complaint is about how you *look* on camera, remember to dress professionally with no T-shirts, dangling earrings (which can get caught on your headset or make noise) or extremely bright clothing. Let no clutter or personal objects appear on your desk or behind you, not even books.

That said, "professional" does not mean "Western culture." It might be perfectly appropriate to wear traditional clothing while you interpret. Simply check with the language services or other organizations that you interpret for as they may help guide you in ways to wear traditional clothing on camera that still adhere to their dress code (if any).

→ Section 3.3 Review

The previous section showed you how to set up for your work as a remote interpreter. This section showed you the technical setup for each session to help you prevent problems.

In particular, since technical problems are common in remote interpreting, and the interpreter is often expected to manage them, this section explored some of the most common technical challenges or breakdowns and potential solutions for each of these problems.

Remember the big lesson: don't panic. After all, tech problems happen to *everyone* in this work. Try to remember to go through Checklist 2: Setup and Tech Check for Remote Interpreters before every call until everything on that list becomes automatic. Remember above all that the *best* way to troubleshoot in remote interpreting is to prevent tech problems from happening in the first place.

The goal of this section was to help you prepare mentally as well as logistically so that you can stay calm and composed whenever technical difficulties arise during a session and be prepared how to handle them calmly and professionally.

Section 3.4 Practice Interpreting on OPI, VRI and VRS Platforms

→ Learning objective 3.4

After completing this section, the remote interpreter will be able to practice interpreting on standard platforms for OPI, VRI and VRS.

→ Section 3.4 Overview

At this point, you may still feel a little overwhelmed by everything it takes to perform remote interpreting. Practice will take away much of your anxiety or nervousness.

This section will show you how to practice remote interpreting in a way that nobody gets hurt or humiliated. It will be fun!

Try to practice interpreting a few times on the same platform you'll be working on *before* you actually take a call for that service or organization. Practicing on the platform will help to reduce any tech anxiety you might feel. It will also build your confidence.

Practicing on the same platform where you are going to interpret may be your single best strategy to reduce tech stress. This section will guide you and show you how to practice remote interpreting and also how to benefit most from that practice.

→ Section 3.4 Content

Setting up to practice

If you work for one or more language services, chances are you will interpret over one or more of the main VRI/OPI platforms on the market. It's important to meet with a platform provider ahead of time to get yourself set up to practice before going online.

Some VRI/OPI platforms offer the built-in capacity for interpreters to practice on their own. This may mean that you can log in and practice on the platform by yourself, or that the platform's support team can help you do so. Be sure to ask when you start working with a new company.

Before you practice online

We highly recommend that you look at Sections 1 and 2 of this chapter and follow all the steps to prepare to interpret before you start any practice sessions. Each platform varies, but we recommend that before you log in, make sure you are prepared and know the basics of the platform.

If you work with a language service, when you are onboarded[61] for the first time to their platform, the language service will log you in, get you ready, and do camera and microphone checks with you. They may do many or most of the steps you've just studied in this chapter.

How to practice if you don't interpret for a language service

If the platform doesn't have a practice feature, or you don't interpret for language service companies, you can practice anyway.

Go to a video conference platform, such as Zoom, Google Meet or Teams, and use their in-app video recording software. Then practice interpreting online. For example, you can get friends to record the participant text for any role plays in this chapter or this textbook. Interpret what they record. If necessary, record yourself speaking the role play scripts. Then interpret whatever you said in that recording. Yes, doing this will still be good practice!

---

[61] Onboarding is an orientation session that you may receive when you are first hired or engaged by a language service (especially a large one) to interpret on their platform.

Make your practice real

To practice well, first set up your audio and equipment as if you were truly going to interpret. Start by going through Checklist 2: Setup and Tech Check for Remote Interpreters.

Once you start practicing and self-recording, don't stop. Just keep going no matter what happens (short of an emergency). It's important to hear how you sound and see how you look naturally.

Keep in mind that in an actual session, you will not be able to stop and correct yourself anyway, or not often. Let yourself continue fluidly and then review your recording afterward to catch and correct any mistakes you may have made.

Slow down

Feeling nervous can make you interpret too quickly. Slow down! It won't help if your audio and video are great but you rush through a session and nobody can understand you. Slowing down also helps you process better what you have heard so you can give a better delivery at an even, moderate pace.

Take a deep breath and focus on the job—not on whether your hair is a mess or your sweater looks wrinkled.

Rushing usually comes from nervousness. With practice, you will soon become comfortable seeing yourself on camera and won't focus so much on your self-view.

Record your practice sessions

Some remote interpreting platforms have in-app practice tools to let you record yourself while you interpret on their platform. They may even have recorded sessions for you to interpret as practice.

These tools are different on each platform. Check with the platform provider on whether they have practice tools available, and, if so, how to record yourself and access your practice recordings.

Practice makes perfect, so don't worry if you notice yourself getting nervous about being recorded or hearing or watching yourself afterward. You are not the only nervous remote interpreter, and every interpreter has their own strengths and weaknesses. Keep note of what those strengths and weaknesses might be for you and monitor your progress over time so you can applaud your own improvements. Work to improve your skills but also give yourself credit for those improvements because doing so will help build your confidence and actually help you look—not only feel—professional.

If the remote interpreting platform does not have the in-app practicing feature, use video recording software to practice interpreting online.

Review your practice recordings

When you are able to access your recordings, review them yourself but also have a colleague or mentor listen to your practice session and give you feedback.

Use the tools in Chapter 5 (which is about self- and peer evaluation) to help you assess your performance.

If you work for a particular language service, contact the service to see if and how you can both practice and record your practice. Afterward, don't put off reviewing your practice recordings. If you work for several language services, at least one of them will probably have practice and recording opportunities for you.

Whenever you practice, *wear the same headset you will use for interpreting*. Try to make sure that your voice is clear and easy to understand. Have a mentor or colleague either watch you practice or listen to your recording and give you feedback.

Review your recording carefully

As you review your recording, be observant. How was the audio? For VRI, how was the lighting? Did you hear background noise? For signed language interpreters, how were your visual cues and the visibility of your signing?

Again, be kind to yourself. It may feel strange to review your own recordings if you haven't already done so, but you'll get used to it.

As we said, keep noting your strengths, not just your weaknesses. Build on your strengths and work to improve your skills. You'll learn much more about how to perform self-evaluation in Chapter 5 of this volume.

Platform requirements

Choose the right browser

Always write down and remember which browser you're supposed to use on a particular platform. Different language services and other organizations have different requirements. Even a school system or a private office might have a specific preference. If not, then you're usually safe if you choose Chrome or Firefox for remote interpreting.

Even when you practice, make sure you are using the appropriate browser.

Click the right buttons

If you work for a language service, you may need to remember to click on the correct button for audio or video, depending on whether that call is for OPI or VRI. But it's better to get these habits in place during practice than to make mistakes during a live call.

Allow browser audio and camera permissions

Always try to remember that many language services require you to allow audio or camera permissions—but if you answer the call or take the assignment first and *then* allow your audio or camera permissions, you *will not connect to the call* in most cases.

Be careful. Make sure you remember to allow your audio or camera permissions *before* you interpret.

If you want to mute yourself for any reason, turning off your audio and video are two separate buttons. Wouldn't it be embarrassing if you turned off your video but not the audio, and then everyone heard you talk to your spouse or go to the bathroom—or worse?

Again, practice is the perfect time to get these good habits in place!

Practice often–on every platform

Every platform is different. Each one will be similar in how it functions, but the buttons to push and the steps to follow will vary. All this variation can make us afraid of technology. In that case, the solution is to *practice* so often on each platform that you start to feel at home and relaxed there.

The quicker you get using the technology, the more brain power you have left for interpreting!

Tips for practicing effectively

Use those two checklists

Set up your environment and technology as if you were going to perform a live session. Go through the two checklists in this chapter. Take notes if you find you are nervous about certain parts of the session and afterward review the terminology you weren't sure of. Look up answers to your own questions.

Ask a colleague to watch you

Ask a colleague to monitor your practice session, or at least review the recording, and give you feedback. We cannot stress enough the importance of peer feedback. Often we forget the smallest things we do (or forget to do) without realizing it when we interpret remotely, but those small things can have a big impact.

Having someone to take notes on your performance and give you tips and pointers is invaluable.

Evaluate yourself

Self-evaluation and reflective practice are the hallmark of a professional interpreter.

Of course if you interpret many calls in a day, one after the other, you can't engage in self-evaluation after each and every call. But you can still evaluate your own performance later.

Chapter 5 of this volume will give you all the information you need to evaluate yourself. Quickly, though, here are a few tips for reviewing yourself. Try to note:

- What can you be doing better?
- How was the lighting?
- Did you hear any background noise?
- How were your visual cues and visibility of your hands (for signed language remote interpreting)?

When you practice–don't pause

Don't stop yourself mid-practice session. It's always good to hear what you would sound like and see what you would look like naturally, without pausing. In an actual session, you will not be able to stop and correct yourself every five seconds. Keep interpreting and then review your recording afterward to correct any mistakes you may have made.

Just because you are remote doesn't mean you aren't human! We all make mistakes, so don't judge yourself too harshly and keep going until you feel confident about your performance.

→ Section 3.4 Review

This short section showed you how to practice remote interpreting. Practice will make you a more confident interpreter. If you can work on more than one platform, you can familiarize yourself with the similarities and differences among platforms.

This content addressed what to do to practice effectively before, during and after the practice session. Chapter 5 will be important for that practice too, because it shows you, in detail, how to evaluate your own remote interpreting performance, whether in practice or after a live call.

→ Chapter Activities

Activity 3.1: Review Your Checklist 1: Prepare for Remote Interpreting

Instructions

1. Go through Checklist 1 as if you were preparing to work as a remote interpreter. Consult the detailed guidance in this section as needed.
2. Write down any items you are *not* able to do.
3. Write down the reasons you are not able to do them.
4. Write down your plan to either purchase what you need, or any action you need to take, to be able to carry out each step on the list.

Activity 3.2: Compare the checklists

Instructions

1. Study both checklists in this chapter. Checklist 1 is Prepare for Remote Interpreting. Checklist 2 is Setup and Tech Check for Remote Interpreters.
2. Compare the two documents.
3. For each statement below, write #1 or #2 in the blank space to indicate which checklist that statement applies to. If the statement applies to both checklists, write #1 and #2.
    1. Use *this* checklist to prepare yourself for your remote interpreting career.___
    2. Use *this* checklist if you are preparing for a session right now.___
    3. Use *this* checklist to help you decide what computer to buy.___

4. Use *this* checklist to help assess your audio and video.___
5. Use *this* checklist to remember to reboot your computer before starting.___
6. Use *this* checklist to assess what kind of headset and microphone to use.___

Activity 3.3 (a): Solve the Technical Difficulties

Instructions

For each technical challenge below, identify the appropriate solution.

1. Your webcam is working, but no one can see you because your image is too bright and hazy. What should you have done before the call? Choose one answer.
   a. Turn the video off and interpret without video.
   b. Change the lighting so it comes from behind you.
   c. Check how you appear and change the lighting from behind you to in front of you or on both sides before accepting calls.
   d. Turn off all artificial lighting.
   e. All of the above.
   f. None of the above.
2. Your webcam isn't working properly. You aren't visible. What do you do? Choose one answer.
   a. Check to see if you gave video permissions to the browser/app.
   b. Pause/resume the video.
   c. Check to see if your external webcam has a tight connection and is well seated.
   d. All of the above.
   e. None of the above.
3. You have an audio problem: participants hear hissing sounds when you speak. What do you do? Choose one answer.
   a. Turn the audio off and then back on.
   b. Adjust your microphone so that it is just a little lower—not too close to your mouth.
   c. Adjust your microphone so that it is just a little higher—not too close to your mouth.
   d. Lower your volume.
   e. All of the above.
   f. None of the above.
4. Your webcam is working, but you're washed out and look pale. What should you have done before the call? Choose one answer.
   a. Turn the video off and interpret without video.
   b. Change the lighting so it comes from behind you.

c. Check how you appear and change the lighting from behind you to in front of you or on both sides before accepting calls.
d. Turn off all artificial lighting.
e. All of the above.
f. None of the above.

5. During a VRI or VRS call, participants tell you that you are pixilating and they can't see you anymore. This is a serious video problem. You know it is *your* problem because both the participants are pixelating for you too. What do you do? Choose all the answers that could apply here.
   a. Run a quick speed test.
   b. Clear your cache, if you can.
   c. Reposition your router.
   d. If your speed test shows slow speeds, inform both parties that you are turning off your video to improve internet connection, then pause/resume video.
   e. None of the above.

Activity 3.3 (b): OPI or VRI role play

Classroom instructions

1. In class, act out this role play according to the directions given by your trainer or instructor.
2. Do not allow the interpreter to see the script.
3. If the people playing the interpreter and the worker share the same language, have the worker sight translate the text into the other language so that the interpreter can interpret in the usual way.
4. If the people playing the interpreter and the worker do *not* share the same language, let the two playing the investigator and the worker read the text out loud in English while the interpreter interprets everything into their other working language.

Instructions for self-study

1. If you are doing this role play for self-study, see if you can get two family members, friends or colleagues to record themselves playing these roles and then interpret what you hear.
2. Record your performance, whether by audio only or (ideally) by video as well. (Video recording will be necessary for sign language interpreters.)

Workers' Comp Investigation

Investigator and worker in separate locations

INVESTIGATOR: First, I'm sorry we can't meet in person. But now that we're here, can you describe the accident?

WORKER: Oh, my goodness, it's so embarrassing. All I did was trip and fall down. And look at the big mess, and all the trouble it's caused! I'm really sorry about it all. I never want to cause trouble.

INVESTIGATOR: Interpreter, I hear you, but I can't see you.

INVESTIGATOR: But can you tell me what happened? You say you tripped and fell. Where did the fall take place?

INVESTIGATOR: Interpreter, I can see you now, but not very well. You're all bright and kind of washed out.

WORKER: It was a—whatever I tripped on, they call it something, I can't remember what. Near the entrance. So there's the first entrance to my part of the warehouse and one door to come inside, and then a second door inside.

INVESTIGATOR: (*impatient*) It wasn't the main entrance where you came in?

WORKER: No, no, we have several entrances. This is the one closest to where I work. And when you come inside, it's like this little shelter and then there is that second glass door and right there it's—it's a little, flat hump in the floor, sort of like a speed bump in the road, and that's what I tripped on.

INVESTIGATOR: So you hadn't started work.

WORKER: No, no.

INVESTIGATOR: Has anyone else there tripped at that second entrance?

WORKER: I don't think so. I almost did once myself. They replaced that door a couple of months ago. But you know, I am a very clumsy person and always thinking of other things and not paying attention. It's a bad habit of mine.

INVESTIGATOR: So you came in the entrance of the building closest to your workspace through one door. And as you were coming in through an interior door, you tripped on a door threshold or something—do you have a picture you can send me? I didn't see a picture of that in the FROI.

WORKER: In *what*?

INVESTIGATOR: Sorry. The first report of injury. There should have been a photo if that's how you fell. I need one.

WORKER: I thought they sent you a photo. You're right, that's very surprising. I will make sure. I can even text you a photo.

INVESTIGATOR: We'll see about that later. Right now, tell me how you fell. Straight forward?

WORKER: Oh, yes, like a rocket. But I went down instead of up! And it's a narrow hallway. And there was a metal storage case right there, because we have no room for everything you know, and that's what they said I hit my head on. Going down.

INVESTIGATOR: You mean you don't remember?

WORKER: No.

INVESTIGATOR: Interpreter, we hear you, but you are making these puffing sounds and lots of sssssss sounds, and it is making it hard for me to concentrate. Can you adjust your sound, please?

INVESTIGATOR: You say you hit your head on a metal storage case. Was there anything else in the hallway?

WORKER: No, just the floor.

(*Video pixilation is now so extreme that the images of the investigator and the worker are both hard to see.*)

INVESTIGATOR: What kind of floor?

WORKER: Concrete.

INVESTIGATOR: Was it wet? Was there any liquid on the floor?

WORKER: No, nothing.

INVESTIGATOR: No garbage, no litter?

WORKER: No, just the big metal thing.

INVESTIGATOR: Did anyone see it happen?

WORKER: No, they told me I kind of shouted on the way down, I don't remember. So they came out to see.

INVESTIGATOR: What happened then?

WORKER: I must have passed out. Because when I woke up, I was looking at this circle of angels. Just all these faces in a big oval looking down like from the sky, it was the strangest thing, I tell you. In all my life, I never saw such a strange thing. I thought I died and went to heaven. But they were saying, "Are you OK, are you OK?" And in my mind I'm thinking, *I don't think if I am in heaven everyone is asking if I am OK!*

INVESTIGATOR: How long were you unconscious?

WORKER: I don't know. They told me it was just a minute or two.

INVESTIGATOR: And then what happened?

WORKER: Oh, I was so nauseous! I had to curl up like a little mouse. It was awful. But they knew someone in the building who used to be a nurse and they brought her over while the ambulance was coming. And she told them, "I can't get a pulse." I remember that. Isn't that strange? And she asked me the same questions over and over. What is your name? What is your address? Where do you work? Why did she keep asking me those questions over and over? I keep meaning to go find where she works and ask her that. And I tried to answer all her silly questions, every single time, but I was so nauseous. And my head hurt, where I hit it. On the right side.

INVESTIGATOR: What happened next?

WORKER: The ambulance came, and they took me to the hospital and called my family, and they did so many tests, and my supervisor came to see me. I had a little bleeding, but I didn't need stitches, and then tests, I don't even know how many tests. I was there for hours doing tests. And then they let me go home but they said I had to watch out for certain symptoms at home in case something serious happened.

INVESTIGATOR: And something did happen?

WORKER: Oh, yes, that night I had a bit of trouble walking when I went to bed. And I felt horribly tired. But you know, at my age, you don't think too much about those things. But the next morning, my family said I was talking all funny, and not very clearly. I was messing up my words. I had a terrible headache, and you know, I'm a hard worker and I was so tired I could barely even think about going to work. And my family made me go back to the hospital, because they never saw me so weak before. And it scared them.

INVESTIGATOR: What happened at the hospital?

WORKER: They gave me another CT scan and then an MRI and they said I had something called a subdural hematoma, maybe partly because I take a blood thinner medication called warfarin. And that's when I knew it was serious.

INVESTIGATOR: What other symptoms have you been experiencing?

WORKER: The medication makes me feel a bit strange, but no pain anymore, and my speech is normal again. I just feel a little weak and scared, to be honest. Scared I won't be able to work again. The doctor was so strict, he said I had to do everything they say and not go to work. And I said, but I have to work, I have to support my family and they said no, not yet, or I could kill myself. So that was a week ago, and now they say I can go back but I can't lift anything heavy or do hard work. And that's my job! So my supervisor is trying to figure out what I can do instead.

INVESTIGATOR: Have they found something for you to do?

WORKER: He's trying hard, yes. That's all I know so far. I'm happy to do anything they want me to do as long as it doesn't make the doctor angry with me. That doctor, he is really something. *So* strict. He said two, maybe three times, I could die if I'm not careful. All because I tripped. Why didn't I pay attention?

INVESTIGATOR: Have they done anything about that threshold where you tripped?

WORKER: For now they put up a big sign to be careful, but they're going to change the entrance somehow to make it safer. At least, that's what I heard.

INVESTIGATOR: What about that metal case in the hallway?

WORKER: My buddy Piotr says it's gone.

INVESTIGATOR: And my records say you haven't applied for workers' compensation benefits before, is that correct?

WORKER: Yes, yes, I have never had an accident on the job. I wasn't even working yet that day. All I did was come inside!

INVESTIGATOR: And right now, except feeling a little weak and the effects of the medication, you feel mostly normal.

WORKER: Yes, yes, I want to work.

INVESTIGATOR: Look, I have to go now, but is this still the best number to reach you if I have more questions?

WORKER: Yes, yes, it's my cell phone. I will answer anytime I can.

INVESTIGATOR: Thanks for your time, have a good day.

WORKER: You too, thanks. Have a blessed day!

Activity 3.4: OPI or VRI role play

Classroom instructions

1. In class, act out this role play according to the directions given by your trainer or instructor.
2. Do not allow the interpreter to see the script.
3. If the people playing the interpreter and the parent share the same language, have the parent sight translate the text into the other language so that the interpreter can interpret in the usual way.
4. If the people playing the interpreter and the parent do *not* share the same language, let the two playing the teacher and the parent read the text out loud in English while the interpreter interprets everything into their other working language.

Instructions for self-study

1. If you are doing this role play for self-study, see if you can get two family members, friends or colleagues to record themselves playing these roles and then interpret what you hear.
2. Record your performance, whether by audio only or (ideally) by video as well. (Video recording will be necessary for sign language interpreters.)

OPI or VRI Role Play
The Teacher Calls Home

TEACHER: Hi, this is Ms. Weisner, Mori's teacher.

PARENT: Oh, hi. Thank you.

TEACHER: Am I speaking to Mori's parent?

PARENT: Yes, speaking.

TEACHER: Have I caught you at a good time? Do you have some time to chat about Mori?

PARENT: Uh, yeah, sure.

TEACHER: First, I just wanted to mention that Mori did an amazing job today in math on some really tough problems that other students were struggling with.

PARENT: Yeah, Mori has a math brain. I wish I had that kind of brain!

TEACHER: Yes, and Mori can also be really good at helping other kids with some of those problems. But I just wanted to alert you that often Mori's homework isn't arriving. Or it's incomplete.

PARENT: What? Really? I had no idea.

TEACHER: Yes, and homework is really important. It really helps students maximize their time in class, and it helps them make progress. I encourage all my students to get their homework done before class, and I've talked to Mori to help him understand this and develop some strategies for getting his homework done on time.

PARENT: I don't get it. I thought Mori got all the assignments in. Whenever I ask, that's what I hear.

TEACHER: (*laughing*) Well, that's not an unusual problem, I can assure you. But here's how you could help. If you could ask Mori to show you the daily assignments and give some reminders about them, that could help a lot.

PARENT: Daily? Mori has homework every day?

TEACHER: Yes, every day.

PARENT: That really concerns me.

TEACHER: You could also ask Mori to show you all the good things, the accomplishments, and especially in math. Mori likes to talk about those accomplishments, and they're very meaningful ones. I see a lot of gifts in Mori. What do you think?

PARENT: Well, yes, I know Mori's really smart, but when it comes to chores and things like that, well—any kid can be a bit lazy, right?

TEACHER: Yes, but have you found anything that motivates Mori to finish assignments and schoolwork?

PARENT: More time for video games. Trips to the mall. Things like that, normal things.

TEACHER: Do you think there's anything I could do to help?

PARENT: Well, Mori has a high opinion of you. If you would send a note about those math accomplishments from time to time, things like that in writing that I could read out loud to Mori—that would mean the world. Just the whole world, I promise.

TEACHER: I'd be happy to do that! Honestly, I think anything you and I can do to support Mori will lead to success. If you watch out for schoolwork at home, I'll check in about once a month and I can get you a list of assignments. They're also available at my home page, I don't know if you've been there?

PARENT: Yes, yes, but I work two jobs and, to be honest, I'm not so good at computers.

TEACHER: Not to worry, I can email all this to you every week so you know what the assignments are and you can ask Mori about them.

PARENT: Yes, I'll do that.

TEACHER: And on my end, I can check with Mori to see if the directions are clear and easy to follow or if there's any confusion. And then I'm always more than happy to help.

PARENT: Great, thanks.

TEACHER: And I'd love to keep in touch, if that's all right with you. What would work best—phone calls or email or texting?

PARENT: This phone call was really nice.

TEACHER: Sure. Say, about once a month, until Mori is regular with assignments?

PARENT: Yes, that would be perfect, thank you, thank you so much.

TEACHER: And is this the best number to reach you?

PARENT: Yes, definitely it's the best, and I'm really honored and grateful you called me today.

TEACHER: Look, I love Mori's intellectual curiosity and that vibrant approach in all Mori's questions. It adds a lot to our classroom life, I can tell you. I just know Mori's going to have a great and successful year, and if you ever have any questions, please don't hesitate to give me a shout.

PARENT: I'll be happy to do that.

TEACHER: Thanks for your time, and take good care!

PARENT: Thank you again, bye!

Chapter Conclusion and Review

This chapter showed you how to prepare for your work as a remote interpreter and set up for success.

Section 3.1 showed you what you need to purchase or have in place at your workstation, whether you work in a call center, a private office in a workplace (where you might be either a staff interpreter or a bilingual employee who interprets part-time) or in a home office because you work as a freelance contract interpreter. It also gave you a simple list of steps to follow to set up for your work in remote interpreting and explained each step.

Section 3.2 provided you with a technical checklist to help you set up for success and prepare for each remote interpreting session or a day's work. Following those steps might seem complicated or too detailed at first, but doing so will prevent many problems and highlight your professionalism.

Section 3.3 showed how you, the remote interpreter, are actually also a tech specialist. You will need to be ready to manage some common technical difficulties in remote interpreting. You explored a list of common technical challenges and breakdowns and many solutions to try out to address them. Working on this technical aspect will demystify it and take away a lot of the fear or anxiety that many interpreters have of remote interpreting.

Section 3.4 showed you the importance of practicing ahead of time on the actual platforms where you will be interpreting and showed you how that practice works. It gave you some tips for practice and emphasized the importance of recording your performance, reviewing it and getting feedback on your practice or your recordings from colleagues and mentors.

This chapter as a whole provides valuable guidance, but only you can actually follow the recommendations. If you do, you'll see technology is just a part of life in remote interpreting, including technical breakdowns.

And remember perhaps the single most important lesson of this chapter—do not panic! Instead, decide to be a tech specialist, because you are. Follow the steps in this chapter. Enjoy the freedom this knowledge gives you to focus on your real work—interpreting!

Chapter 4

Tatiana González-Cestari, PhD, CHI-Spanish
Sarah Stockler-Rex, MA, CHI-Spanish

Essential Protocols and Skills

Learning Objectives

After completing this chapter, the remote interpreter will be able to:

Learning Objective 4.1: Distinguish the use of two primary modes, consecutive and simultaneous, in remote interpreting, and decide when and how sight translation and summarization should be performed when the interpreter is remote.

Learning Objective 4.2: Develop the following skill sets as they apply to remote interpreting: message transfer, session preparation, assertiveness and problem-solving.

Learning Objective 4.3: Explain and practice protocols specific to remote interpreting.

Introduction

Now that you have a general sense of the field of remote interpreting and its technology, and you know how to prepare both for your career and your first session as a remote interpreter, it is time to focus on the essential protocols and skills that you need for professional performance.

This chapter will guide you through the modes of interpreting and the skills and protocols that a remote interpreter will need for over the phone interpreting (OPI), video remote interpreting (VRI) for spoken and signed languages, with some attention to remote simultaneous interpreting (RSI) and video relay service (VRS).

In general, this chapter focuses on those skills and behaviors that apply to remote interpreters working from a call center or from home, though it also mentions a few other situations.

With an approach that is both theoretical and practical, this chapter covers the required general skill set and best practice protocols for interpreting that are specific to remote interpreting. These skills and protocols will be helpful whether you interpret remotely for large or small organizations, government agencies, schools, businesses, social services or healthcare, among other entities and organizations.

In this context, a *skill* refers to expertise or an ability, whereas a *protocol* is defined as an accepted or established set of rules that guides procedures and behaviors in work settings.

By the end of this chapter, the interpreter will have studied and practiced basic scenarios in remote interpreting and be prepared to continue with the more advanced and challenging situations that follow in the next chapters.

Section 4.1 Modes of Remote Interpreting

→ Learning objective 4.1

After completing this section, the remote interpreter will be able to distinguish the use of two primary modes, consecutive and simultaneous, in remote interpreting, and decide when and how sight translation and summarization should be performed when the interpreter is remote.

→ Section 4.1 Overview

Interpreting involves communicating an oral or signed message between speakers of different languages from a source language into a target language.

A *mode* is a technique for the delivery of interpreting. Whenever you interpret, you will have to select the correct mode for the session.

This section will focus on performing accurate message transfer in remote consecutive and simultaneous interpreting.

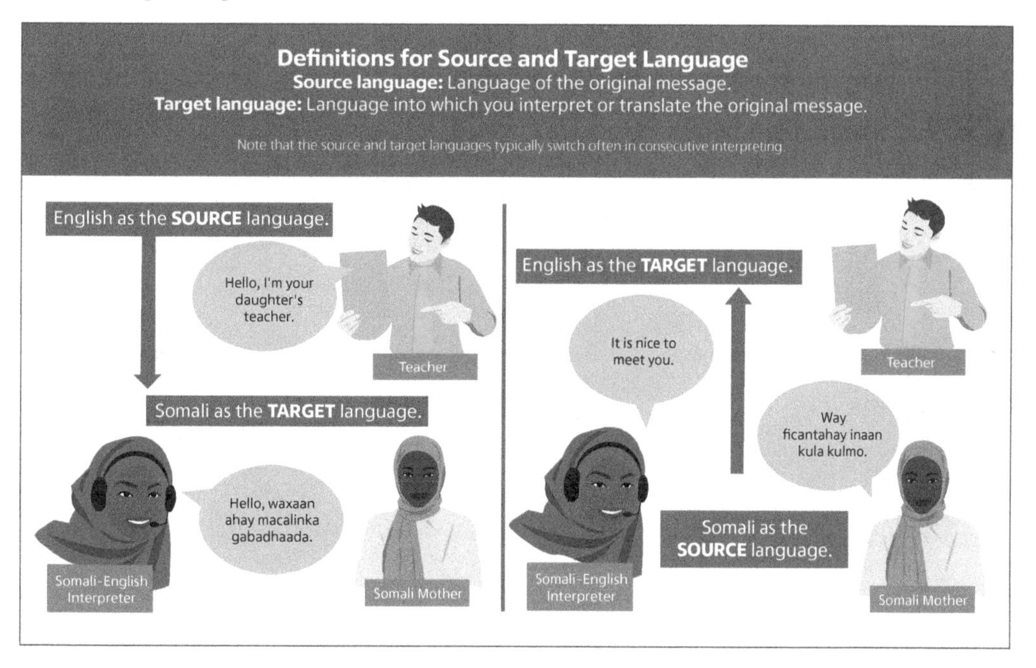

The two primary modes of interpreting are consecutive and simultaneous, and they are the focus of this section. Since sight translation, another mode, is rarely something that is performed remotely, this chapter will only briefly mention sight translation.

This section also reviews summarization, which is used as a last resort in either face-to-face or remote interpreting. Yet summarization is often needed in community interpreting, and a great deal of remote interpreting involves community interpreting.

→ Section 4.1 Content

Modes of interpreting

Let's define modes of interpreting. A mode is a skilled technique for the delivery of interpreting by professional interpreters. The two main modes used by most interpreters around the world are consecutive and simultaneous.

> **ISO Definition of Mode**
>
> The International Organization for Standardization (ISO) is the leading entity that publishes international standards, including standards for interpreting, translation and interpreting equipment.
>
> ISO defines a mode of interpreting as:
>
> *Established method for the delivery of spoken language interpreting...and signed language interpreting* (ISO, 2019b, 3.4.11).

Consecutive interpreting

Consecutive interpreting is "understanding and reformulating a message in another language after the speaker or signer pauses" (Bancroft et. al., 2015, p. viii). For example, in a parent-teacher conference, consecutive interpreting would go like this:

1. Teacher speaks, then pauses.
2. Interpreter interprets, then pauses.
3. Parent speaks, then pauses.
4. Interpreter interprets, then pauses...and so on.

This is a sample figure for reference.

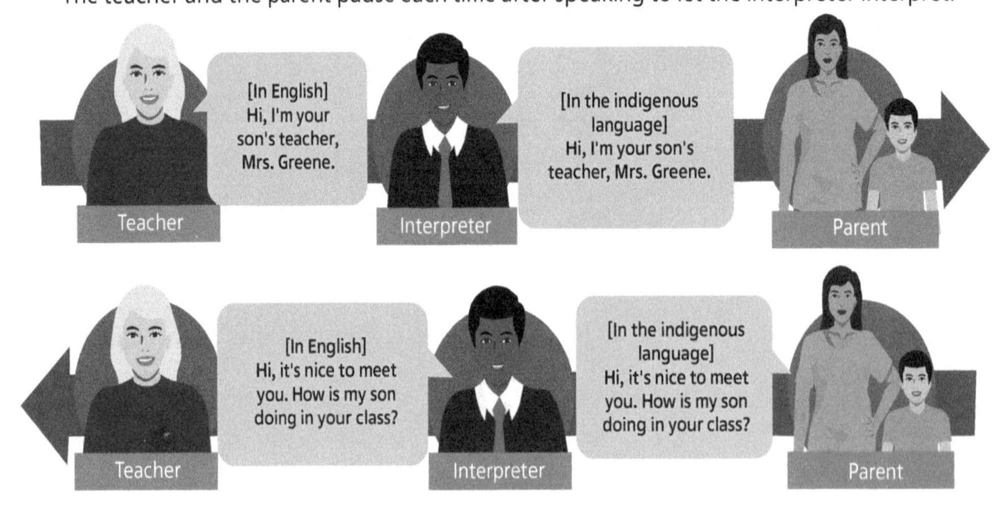

Figure 4.1: Consecutive interpreting

No one should be communicating while someone else is speaking or signing. If that situation occurs, the interpreter will need to manage it—which is more challenging for remote interpreters than face-to-face interpreters. Section 4.2 will discuss that challenge.

Consecutive mode is the most common mode for spoken language interpreting. It is often considered the default mode in dialogue interpreting (such as community—including medical—legal and business interpreting) whether it is performed remotely or face to face. Dialogue interpreting is interpreting that involves a conversation, often in question-and-answer format, such as a medical appointment or an interview with a lawyer. Dialogue interpreting is bidirectional in nature, or the interpreting is performed back and forth between one language and another, in either direction.

If you work in OPI or VRI, you will probably interpret consecutively. In many or most cases, you will perform dialogue interpreting.

Interpreter fatigue in consecutive interpreting

Fatigue can happen in remote or face-to-face interpreting. Though some interpreters have the capacity to interpret in consecutive mode accurately for a long period of time, interpreters are still human. Sooner or later, they need a break!

Many times, rest comes naturally between sessions or with scheduled breaks—but not always.

A remote interpreter could remain in one long session, such as labor and delivery in a hospital or a court case, and grow fatigued.

Research on the topic of whether remote interpreting is more or less fatiguing than face-to-face interpreting is preliminary and even contradictory. However, anecdotal evidence and the experience of the authors suggest strongly that remote interpreters can suffer intense and even debilitating fatigue if they are not careful.

Signs of interpreter fatigue

Common signs of fatigue that remote interpreters need to watch for include (among others):

- The need to drink more water or use the restroom more often.
- Making more frequent requests for repetitions and clarifications.
- Taking longer to find appropriate translations for certain terms or phrases.
- Eyestrain.
- Headaches.

Chapter 9 of Volume 2 addresses self-care for remote interpreters.

How to take a break in remote consecutive interpreting

Be sure you know how to get a break when you need one. It will typically be easier to do so if you work for a language service.

Because most sign language interpreters work in teams (since they mostly interpret simultaneously), and because RSI interpreters also interpret simultaneously, sign language and RSI interpreters working in a team can ask their partners to step in earlier than planned if they need a break.

Remote Sign Language Interpreters and Breaks

In the U.S. and many other countries, it is common practice to schedule two face-to-face sign language interpreters for community work if the assignment is for 1.5 hours or more since they interpret simultaneously. Team interpreting may also be common for sign language interpreters who work remotely.

Note that the amount of assignment time that requires a second interpreter depends on the subject to be interpreted, the setting, the language service or the region or country where the interpreter works.

In general, team interpreting for sign language for an assignment of any serious length is a best practice—but not always the reality.

However, taking a break in *consecutive* interpreting requires more planning. That is because most spoken-language remote interpreters in OPI and VRI do not work with a partner.

Replace the interpreter!

Perhaps the most common way for an interpreter to take a break in remote consecutive interpreting is to replace the working interpreter with a new one. Most large language services today, at least in the U.S., have a process in place to do so. In many ways, switching out interpreters at short notice is easier to do remotely than face to face.

A face-to-face interpreter may have to stop the session completely to step out and communicate with the appropriate person to send a replacement. There will then be a wait time for the replacement to arrive. Requesting a replacement face-to-face interpreter, unless you are deeply exhausted, is an important and challenging decision for the interpreter.

But switching out a remote interpreter might be a matter of a few seconds! A remote interpreter working for a language service might simply need to ask the participants to call back for another interpreter for which a wait should be minimal (or shorter than waiting for a face-to-face replacement to arrive).

In other cases, the remote interpreter may be able to facilitate the switch independently by pushing a button! A great deal depends on the language service's platform policies, protocols and features. Make sure you know them.

Interpreters for Less Common Languages

Interpreters of hard-to-find languages may not be able to ask for a new interpreter.

In such a case, or any time you have no replacement, if possible request a short break. When pausing the session is not possible, you may need to address your fatigue by pausing your video, closing your eyes, taking a sip of water, stretching and so on. Experiment with fatigue-reducing techniques that work well for you.

When to replace fatigued interpreters

No matter how the switch is carried out technically, it is critical to first identify the best moment to withdraw without disrupting the flow and experience for the participants. But remember: while it won't be ideal for the next interpreter to jump in mid-conversation, it might be riskier for accuracy and your overall competence to stay when you're starting to feel fatigued.

Certain sessions may take several hours, such as a clinical trial informed consent, and you may have to prioritize accuracy by switching out interpreters rather than trying to power through.

Scripts for taking a break or switching out interpreters

As always, keep your language service's procedures in mind and be prepared with a plan and scripting for different circumstances. Below are some helpful sample scripts for interpreter fatigue scenarios:

- "Interpreter speaking. To ensure accuracy in the communication, we've reached a good moment in the conversation to switch out interpreters. Please call back, and another interpreter will gladly pick up where we've left off."
- "This is the interpreter. Due to the lengthy and complicated nature of this session, the interpreter would like to inquire how much longer you believe this session may last? This will ensure accuracy in the interpretation. Thank you."

In sensitive situations, ask yourself if it would do more harm than good to switch out interpreters.

- If the answer is yes, consider asking the participants about a time frame for when the session may be complete. (Of course, if it's labor and delivery in a hospital, only the baby will provide the answer to that question!)
    - You may also mention at the start that you may be able to stay only for a specific period of time before you will need to be replaced.
- If the answer is no, and the session will be lengthy, proceed with suggesting switching out interpreters.

Simultaneous interpreting

Simultaneous interpreting involves interpreting while someone is still speaking or signing but with a slight delay (also called *décalage*).

For example, in a parent-teacher conference, the English-speaking student might start a direct conversation with the teacher and forget to pause for the interpreter to interpret for their parents. In this case, the interpreter uses simultaneous mode to capture everything the student is saying.

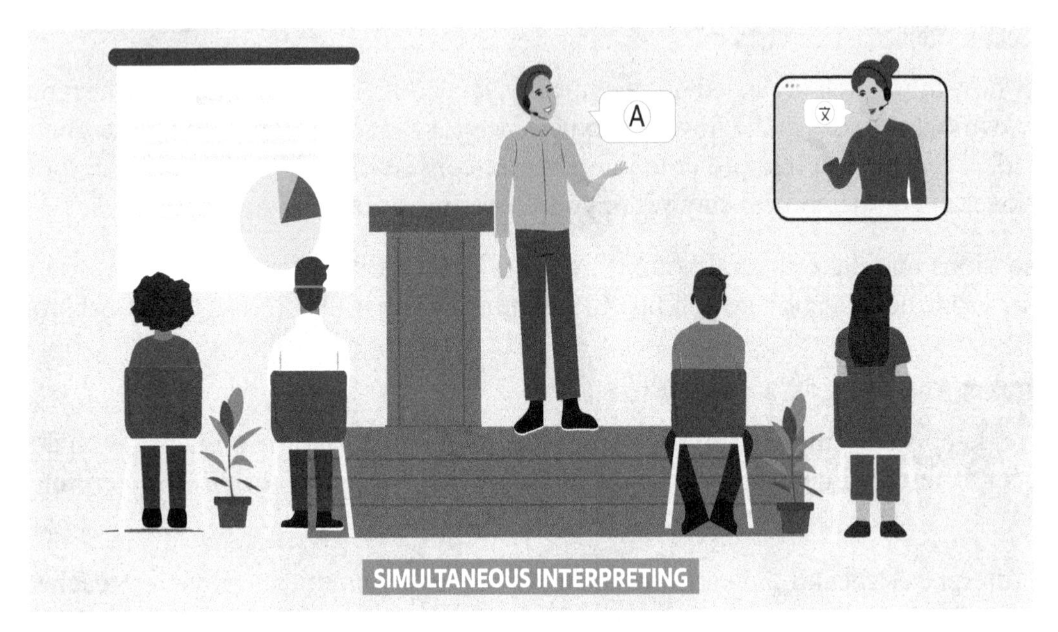

Figure 4.2: Simultaneous mode

Mode-switching: A challenge in remote interpreting

In remote interpreting, performing in simultaneous mode is only possible when using an RSI platform or a webconference or similar platform that has been adapted for RSI (in basic ways). If you are interpreting over an OPI or VRI platform performing consecutive interpreting, you will not be able to make a sudden switch to simultaneous. There is only one audio channel on OPI and VRI platforms. If two people speak at once, neither person's voice will come through clearly. The mode to be used during the session has to be determined ahead of time as that decision dictates what kind of remote interpreting platform is appropriate.

Simultaneous mode is more common in remote interpreting for signed languages and certain types of events that require simultaneous interpreting: for example, conferences, meetings and presentations, such as webinars.

Why simultaneous interpreting feels challenging at first

To process two languages simultaneously requires a high level of expertise of register, general and technical vocabulary and a wide knowledge of regional variations. You have no time to reflect: you have to interpret on the spot.

While this immediacy reduces pressure on your memory skills, it increases the demand for other cognitive skills. Developing these skills requires energy; specialized, intensive, long-term training and a great deal of practice, even for face-to-face interpreting. These challenges can be even harder in remote interpreting. (See Volume 2, Chapters 1 and 2 on RSI.)

Don't worry. If you want to perform simultaneous remote interpreting, and you continue to practice it, one day simultaneous will probably feel much easier to you than consecutive interpreting! Still, getting to that point takes time and practice.

While many OPI/VRI platforms are still limited in their ability to accommodate simultaneous interpreting, the demand for RSI capability is growing. Simultaneous mode is typically the default for signed language interpreters on any kind of VRI or RSI platform. How so? Spoken language interpreters cannot interpret simultaneously on VRI platforms.

However, simultaneous interpreting is possible for *sign language interpreters* over VRI because only one language is spoken out loud.

For more information on RSI for spoken languages, see Chapters 1 and 2 of Volume 2. In addition to conference interpreting, here are some examples of when RSI would be an ideal choice (technology permitting):

- Workshops or seminars
- Group therapy
- Courtrooms
- Public speaking

One step at a time

Simultaneous interpreting is considered a higher-level skill due to the many cognitive demands it places on you. When you interpret simultaneously, the component interpreting skills that you perform one at a time during consecutive sessions—such as listening to the message, analyzing it for meaning and *then* delivering— will need to be performed together *at the same time*.

Because of this, it is usually better to work on simultaneous interpreting after learning the basics of consecutive interpreting. We will discuss component interpreting skills in detail in the next section.

Unimodal vs. bimodal

Fran Whiteside is an ASL<>English VRI interpreter. In an article titled "Why American Sign Language Interpreters [ASL] are Bilingual, Bicultural, and Bimodal" (Whiteside, 2019), she comments on some of the dynamics that signed language interpreters have to learn. She also explains how sign language interpreters differ from spoken language interpreters in part due to the modes they perform in (at least in dialogue interpreting). In doing so, she highlights the complexity of modes of communication in general and for sign language interpreting in particular.

> *Unimodal interpreters hear one language and speak another, therefore using two spoken languages. Bimodal interpreters are also spoken language interpreters, speaking in English, but they have the added change in mode from understanding not only speech but also sign language.*
>
> *How does bimodal differ from unimodal? Bimodal…interpreters use spoken language that is perceived by the ears and produced by the vocal tract and also sign language which is perceived by the eyes…So let's look at this definition—Visual language interpreting is the practice of deciphering communication in sign languages, which use gestures, body language, and facial expressions to convey meaning. But using visual cues for the process of interpretation is still bimodal using two different forms of processing.*

> *There are other ways that ASL interpreters process communication. It might be from a written document that is not understandable to the Deaf client. It may be through tactile interpreting (hand over hand) for a DeafBlind client. Regardless of how it is done, ASL interpreters are still considered bimodal.*
>
> —Whiteside, 2019

For information, practice and activities for remote simultaneous interpreting, see Volume 2, Chapters 1 and 2.

Sight translation

One of the first things you learn when you become an interpreter is that "interpreting" refers to converting oral or signed messages from one language into another and "translating" refers to rendering written text into another language. Sight translation is a combination of both, an oral or signed rendering of the meaning of a written text.

As you may have guessed, interpreters do not typically sight translate in remote interpreting. Even when there is video, most platforms do not have the technology needed to consistently share documents with high-enough quality and resolution that the interpreter can sight translate them. For this reason, it is not currently commonplace to sight translate remotely, even via video.[62]

Formal Guidance on Sight Translation

Depending on the country and specialization for which you interpret, try to find out if written guidelines are available.

For example, for healthcare interpreting in the U.S., you can refer to the *Sight Translation and Written Translation: Guidelines for Healthcare Interpreters* published by the National Council on Interpreting in Health Care (NCIHC, 2009).

For court interpreting in Australia, look for the Judicial Council on Cultural Diversity, *Recommended National Standards for Working with Interpreters in Courts and Tribunals* (JCCD, 2022).

In certain cases, participants may share internal documents electronically with interpreters who work remotely to facilitate sight translation during a session. For example, a hospital staff interpreter who works remotely might have access to an internal intranet of documents to sight translate.

Sight translation is a special case whether you're interpreting face to face or remotely. Whether or not to perform it depends on multiple factors, such as the length and complexity of the document, participants' institutional policies, etc. Request the guidelines for sight translation from the language service or client or organization—and for the specializations—that you interpret for, so you can prepare yourself.

---

[62] Speed sight translation, which some simultaneous interpreters perform, is a part of the overall simultaneous skill set that interpreters use when they are given speeches or presentations ahead of time to prepare. This is not sight translation as used in OPI and VRI.

Practical Guidance to Address Documents in Remote Interpreting

Sight translation isn't always feasible, or even possible, in remote interpreting.

If you interpret remotely in healthcare, education, social services, business or other areas and documents are involved in a service being provided, often the best strategy may be a simple one. Ask the relevant participant to read the document aloud—or summarize or explain it—while you interpret.

This simple approach might be a highly effective solution!

But what could you say in such situations? First, if you interpret for a language service or a large organization, find out if they have a script that they want you to use. If not—develop one! For example:

> "I would love to help you with that document—unfortunately I can't read it well through the camera. But I'd be happy to interpret while you explain [or summarize, or discuss] the document for the patient."

Summarization

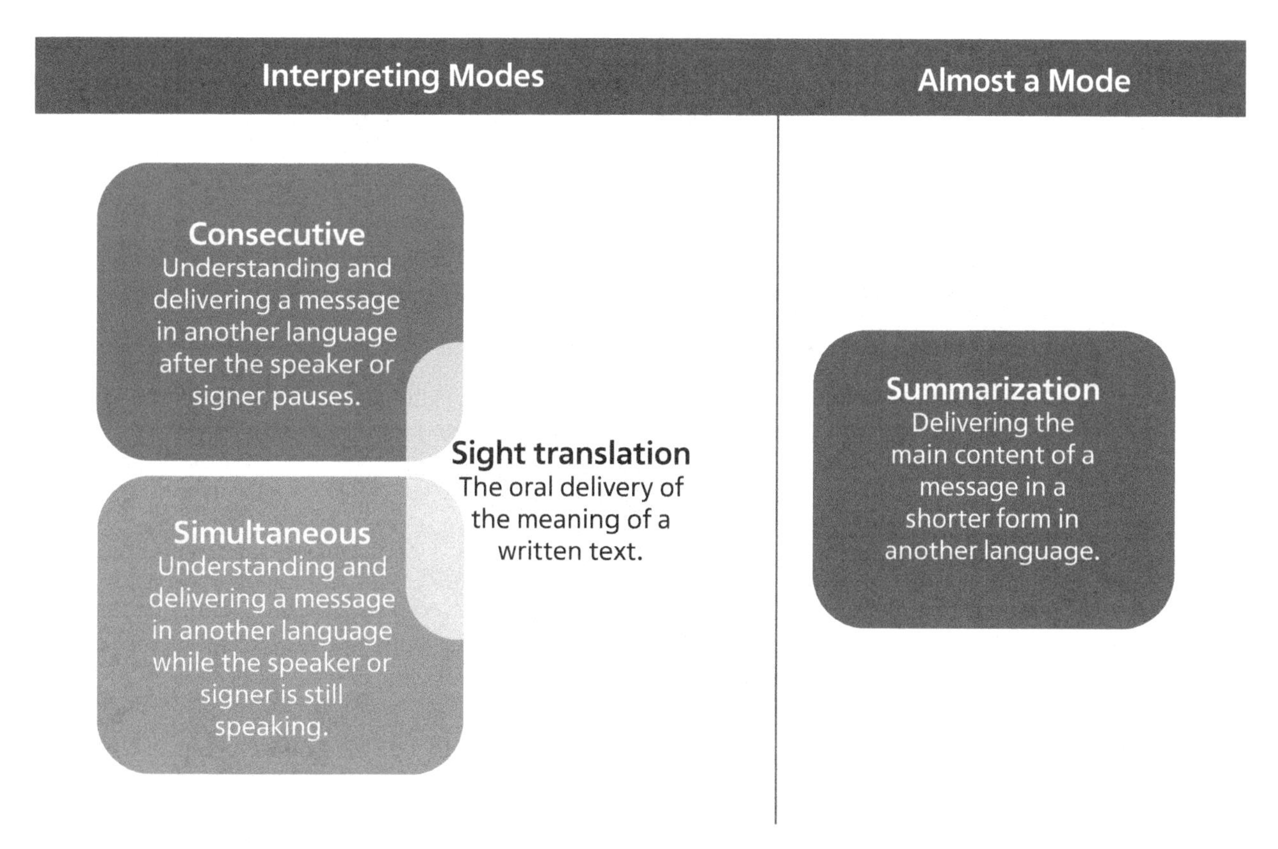

Figure 4.3: **Modes**

When you will need to summarize

Summarization, as you know, is a last resort. It is not a formal mode—think of it as a coping strategy. In other words, summarization is something you'll probably have to do, but only in out-of-control situations.

For example, you might have to summarize for:

- Emergencies.
- Fast-paced events.
- Audio recordings (unless you can pause them).
- Young children.
- Participants who may be incoherent, due to:
  - Mental illness.
  - Neurological disorders or other illness.
  - Substance abuse issues.
  - Dementia.
- Participants who will not pause or slow down for the interpreter (including public speakers).
- Participants who will not speak one at a time.

How summarization works

Summarization means the interpreter is reformulating the primary content of a message in a shorter form. It is "almost a mode" because it is another way of delivering a message—but not a complete one, so it is generally not considered to be interpreting.

As a result, interpreters often think summarization is easier than the three official modes. Be careful. When you summarize, you still have to engage in active listening, short-term memory, message analysis, and converting the message.

The great challenge of summarization is that you have to choose what to leave in and what to leave out, which can be quite difficult. What matters most? Which content is significant? Summarization takes skills and practice!

Interpreters do not summarize unless they must

Interpreters who have not had adequate training often summarize because they can't remember a full message, or they are too shy to ask participants to pause or slow down. Interpreters with professional skills do not summarize unless they truly have no choice.

Remember: accurately interpreting everything in the session or call sets you apart as a professional.

Be prepared to summarize

Why discuss summarization? Though controversy surrounds it, the truth is that *many* interpreters find summarization necessary in extreme situations.

Here are our recommendations:

- Use summarization with caution.
- Disclose as soon as possible that you have summarized.
- Reserve summarization for situations when it's *absolutely necessary.*

Though it's never ideal to summarize, having an intentional and practiced strategy for handling situations when summarization is inevitable is part of being professional.

Also, have a script ready. For example:

> "Interpreter speaking, the participant is unable to slow down their speech. Here is a summary of what they said…"

The interpreter should be transparent, giving the same information to all parties after every summarization.

Consecutive vs. simultaneous interpreting

Consecutive interpreting has several advantages: it promotes direct communication, is less distracting, allows for note-taking and can enhance accuracy. In addition, its slower pace gives the interpreter time to find more precise equivalencies as well as make decisions on whether or not to intervene.

Consecutive is also less exhausting than simultaneous, which means it can be performed for longer periods (without a break) with more accuracy. For the participants, there is often less potential confusion and distraction with only one person speaking at a time and with more time to process, clarify and understand the message.

The main drawback to consecutive interpreting, as you may have guessed, is time: by definition, consecutive takes longer than simultaneous.

Choosing between consecutive and simultaneous interpreting

You might have no choice between consecutive or simultaneous. If you perform OPI or VRI, you will interpret consecutively. If you perform VRI or VRS for sign language, or RSI for public speakers, almost certainly you will be expected and need to interpret simultaneously.

That said, depending on the specialization or the equipment used to deliver the message, the session may need to be planned in advance to prioritize one mode over the other. You will find some examples of the reasons to choose a particular mode in Figure 4.4.

Remote interpretation for...	Mode	Main reasons for the mode selection
Business (with clients)	Consecutive	Dialogue.
Business (with other businesses)	Simultaneous	Multiple people talking at the same time, presentation-style meetings with time constraints.
Conference	Simultaneous	Time constraints, fast-paced environment, mostly monologue.
Court	Simultaneous/consecutive	Time constraints, fast-paced environment, set proceedings, public statements (monologues). Consecutive used, for example, when a lawyer is consulting with the defendant and for witness interviews. Simultaneous for public statements and when an interpreter is interpreting the proceedings for a defendant.
Higher education/seminars/ presentations	Simultaneous	Time constraints, fast-paced environment, mostly monologue.
Educational in schools (meetings with parents)	Consecutive	Less formal environment, dialogue, communicating information about a child.
Educational (public meetings, such as school board meetings)	Simultaneous/consecutive	Simultaneous for public speaking where only one part of the larger group needs interpreters. Consecutive when switching to question-and-answer discussions.
Healthcare	Consecutive	Most appointments are dialogue (question-and-answer format); accuracy is essential for patient safety.
Healthcare (group therapy, health education or emergencies)	Simultaneous	Time constraints, quick-paced environments (for emergencies), multiple people talking at the same time (therapy), or health education that is mostly monologic speech.

Figure 4.4: **Modes of remote interpreting based on specializations**

Both consecutive and simultaneous interpreting can be performed remotely during the same call *only* if the platform used allows it. See Chapter 2 of this volume for details.

Participants Need Headsets for Simultaneous Calls or Meetings

In many cases, participants who act as public speakers during a session need to use a headset with a good microphone for optimal sound quality.

Participants who are only listening to simultaneous interpreting can choose to use a headset or switch audio channels so that they only hear the interpretation in their language, not the speaker or the other interpreters. But they too will need good equipment for optimal sound quality.

→ Section 4.1 Review

This section explored the two primary interpreting modes and the differences between them:

- Consecutive mode: where each speaker pauses to allow the interpreter to interpret, with one person speaking/signing at a time.
- Simultaneous: where the interpreter renders the message in real time with the speaker/signer, with a slight delay of a few seconds.

You'll need to focus on accurate message transfer no matter what mode is used, but we recommend that you learn consecutive interpreting before moving on to simultaneous.

This section also briefly introduced a third mode, sight translation, as well as summarization, which is a coping strategy. Both are less frequently utilized in remote interpreting than the two primary modes, but they may still be needed at times.

- Sight translation (a mode): Converting the meaning of a written text into an oral or signed message.
- Summarization (a coping strategy): Condensing key points of a message. Use with caution and only when absolutely necessary, in out-of-control situations, such as emergencies or speakers who refuse to pause.

Section 4.2 Skills for Remote Interpreting

→ Learning objective 4.2

After completing this section, the remote interpreter will be able to develop the following skill sets as they apply to remote interpreting: message transfer, session preparation, assertiveness and problem-solving.

→ Section 4.2 Overview

As you already know, interpreting requires many skills, some of which are shared across all modalities and settings. However, when we look closely, we notice that the use of some skills in remote and face-to-face interpreting vary in timing, priority ranking, frequency of use and other aspects.

The skill sets needed in remote interpreting include a group of abilities that range from message transfer skills to quick problem assessment, assertiveness and decision-making expertise. The environment of a remote interpreter tends to be faster-paced compared to face-to-face interpreting. However, having face-to-face experience means that you have already learned some of the needed skills.

This section will address how to work on and develop certain skills and skill sets and prioritize them. You will notice that interpreting skills happen differently depending on the submodality (OPI and other AOI vs. VRS or VRI or RSI), and whether the interpreter is working in signed language, spoken language, both or in relay or team interpreting.

It is critical that you work on enhancing your message transfer and problem-solving skills as well as being assertive. However, there are many ways to prepare for sessions and problem-solve that are specific to certain environments.

Let's identify which specific skill sets in problem-solving you should work on first (and which skill sets are the hardest for you). Then, you will be able to develop a personal prioritized list of what to target first to improve, depending on which modality/modalities you work in most often.

→ Section 4.2 Content

Message transfer skills

Message transfer skills are those you utilize the most as an interpreter. Transferring a message as accurately as possible from one language to another is not an easy task. Message transfer skills are made up of component skills, which help you through every step of the interpreting process.

But before we talk about component skills, let's focus on accuracy for a moment.

No matter which mode is involved, every interpreter's goal is accuracy. Accuracy can be defined as "convert[ing] messages rendered in one language into another without losing the essence of the meaning that is being conveyed and including all aspects of the message without making judgments as to what is relevant, important, or acceptable" (NCIHC, 2004, p. 13).

Accuracy is the main ingredient in every interpreting "recipe" (session). You will focus on and practice ways to enhance this skill for the rest of your interpreting career.

Also, you want the main ingredient of your "recipe" to be of the highest quality. For this, you need to enhance accuracy by focusing on message transfer skills.

As with any multilayered skill set, core concepts start to intertwine. To interpret accurately, you need to learn the components skills. Once you've obtained the component skills, your ability to accurately and completely transfer the meaning (message) of what speakers say becomes possible.

Component skills for message transfer

But just what do we mean by component skills? Essentially, they are subskills you need to master to be able to interpret. Component skills are to accuracy what reading and analyzing music, breathing and fingering are to playing a musical instrument. Before you can play the violin, you usually need to be able to read music, and your fingers need to know where and how to touch the strings. Musicians practice these "component" skills over and over to be able to play.

Component skills in interpreting are similar. Time and effort need to be given to the individual components of message transfer before you can actually interpret at a professional level.

For example, as the interpreter, you need to express the *equivalent* of the original message a teacher explains in a parent-teacher conference in the parents' language.

These are the critical component skills you need to achieve this:

1. Listen to the message with focused attention, using your short-term memory to remember it.
2. Analyze the message and extract (determine) the meaning.
3. Convert the meaning by finding equivalent concepts in the target language.
4. Deliver the reformulated message.[63]

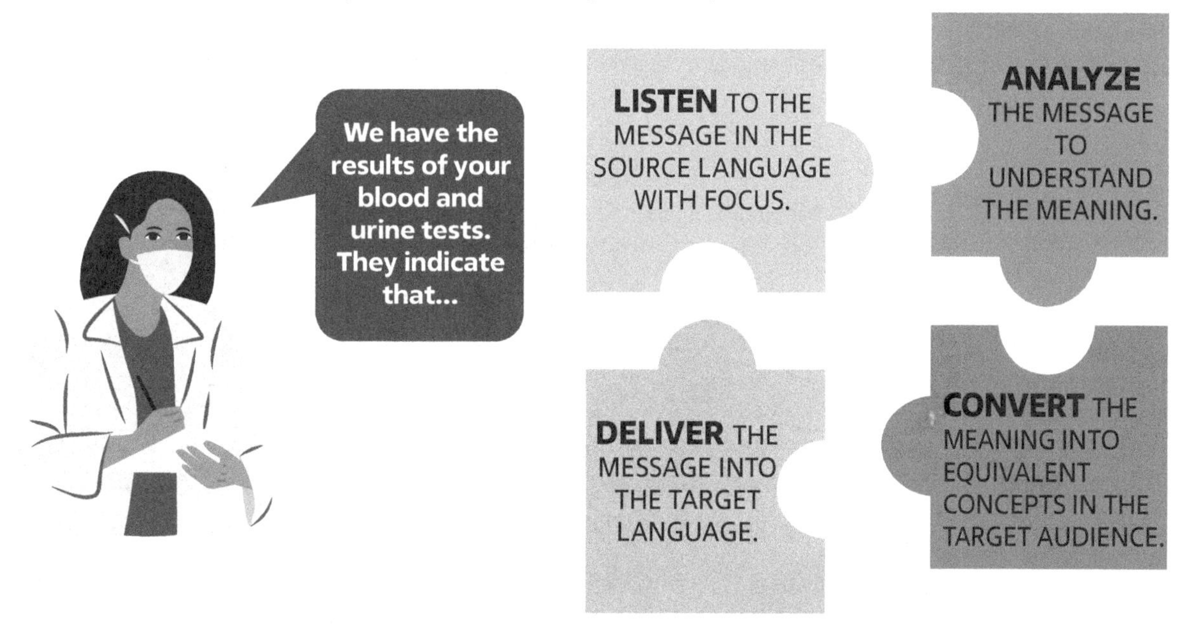

Figure 4.5: Critical component skills

[63] These four skills are adapted from those discussed throughout Bancroft et al., 2015.

In other words, if the teacher says, "Your child is just a delight to have in class," you first need to understand that the teacher is saying, "It's a pleasure to have your child in class" and then find the most natural sounding way to say that in the parents' language. You do not simply repeat each word in the parents' language: you express the *meaning.*

And you don't have much time! You will have to perform these actions almost instantaneously. How do you improve your message transfer skills? You target the various components that promote accurate message transfer.

Let's review three key exercises that will help you develop your component skills: anticipating, parroting and paraphrasing. However, there are many other strategies to develop message transfer skills. These are only examples.

And practice, practice, practice! You will soon see the rewards.

Anticipating

Defining Anticipation

Anticipation

The ability to foresee or predict what will likely be said or signed as a continuation of an utterance.

Note 1: Previous experience or knowledge may enhance the interpreter's ability to anticipate.

Note 2: Anticipation should be used with caution due to the risk of rendering the message inaccurately.

Note 3: Anticipation is a critical skill in simultaneous interpreting.

Imagine that you are interpreting while a doctor explains the risks of a surgical procedure to the patient. Since the surgery includes an incision, you know from experience that the doctor is going to at least mention infection, bleeding and damage to tissues.

Predicting what the doctor might say, and preparing yourself to render that message, can help you be more accurate. In addition, it can help you to improve your focus, interpret quickly, remember concepts and be smooth in your delivery. It can even make it easier and less tiring to interpret!

Be careful, though, as becoming overconfident and not paying attention to slight changes in the message could lead to mistakes. One error could lead to a patient showing up for surgery on the wrong day!

Anticipation is much easier if you know something about the subject you are going to interpret. If you've scrambled eggs every morning for several years, you have a personal understanding of all the ingredients and steps to scrambling the perfect egg.

But if you've never cooked eggs on a stove before, it will be much harder to imagine turning on the burner, selecting the pan, adding butter, mixing the eggs and maybe sprinkling them with spices. You get the idea.

First and foremost, the best way to make the most of anticipation exercises is to learn a bit about the subject you are focused on.

You can start to practice anticipating what you may hear during interpreting sessions by trying to notice and predict common patterns like these:

- Words that are often joined (for example, advance directive, progress report, customer service).
- Idiomatic expressions (such as "It's a piece of cake" in English, which means "It's easy").
- Two-part verbs, i.e., phrasal verbs with a verb and an adverb or preposition attached (for example, find out, fill out or give up).
- Place names (such as the names of local ports, airports, stations, etc.).
- Dates.

Still, even if you are interpreting for a topic that is new to you, chances are you can brainstorm some of the elements that might be discussed. Anticipation allows you to prepare terminology and "activate" your existing knowledge about a subject, which gives you a better chance of understanding what the speakers say during the session.

Parroting

To parrot, simply repeat word for word (or sign for sign) what a speaker says. Do so *in the same language* and while that person is speaking or signing.

(Historically in conference interpreting, parroting has also been called shadowing. However, this book refers to this activity as parroting to avoid confusion with other meanings of shadowing that have developed over time in community interpreting settings.)

How to Practice Parroting

Parroting is a wonderful exercise to practice; it speeds up your thinking and improves your word choice. It can help you to develop the skills to listen, understand, speak clearly and monitor yourself. It will almost certainly increase your speed and improve your fluency.

Start with your most fluent language and simple speeches. Use a recorded speech, for example, from a radio or television program or a speech downloaded from the internet. When you get smoother at it, move on to harder ones.
When you are ready:

- Select three speeches, each about two minutes long, all in your strongest language.
- One of them should be a relatively slow recording, one of them a slightly faster recording and the third one should be a rapid recording.
- Start with the slowest speech.
- Parrot the whole recording in the same language while the speaker is speaking.
- DO NOT INTERPRET: repeat every word in the same language.
- While parroting, try to capture the tone and expression of the speaker, not just the words.
- Select the medium-paced speech and repeat the exercise.
- Now play the most rapid speech and do the same.

Once you have parroted for about six minutes with a slow, medium and rapid recording, repeat the same three-stage process with your second-strongest language. Then, if you know any other languages, try the same exercise in those languages too (Socarrás-Estrada, 2016, p. 104).

Paraphrasing

Paraphrasing is simply finding different words to express the same words, phrases or longer passages *in the same language*.

Why paraphrasing is helpful

In paraphrasing, you reformulate words, phrases or statements but keep the same basic meaning. Change the word order, use synonyms and find equivalents—all wonderful exercises for interpreters. You may remember the written paraphrasing activities you probably had to do in school as a child. Those are helpful for interpreting, but it's even better if you practice paraphrasing orally. Listen to increasing longer statements and practice paraphrasing them *out loud.*

By paraphrasing often, and out loud, you increase the number of word choices that spring to your mind quickly when you interpret—an incredibly valuable ability. Mental agility is an essential skill for interpreters.

Why paraphrase into the same language? Doing so actually helps to shorten your reaction time when you interpret into another language. You will be able to interpret more efficiently.

How to paraphrase

Develop or find a list of words or phrases, such as idioms, adjectives or types of activities. (The content doesn't matter.) Paraphrase them yourself, then later ask someone to read the lists out loud for you at random and paraphrase what you hear (or see, for signing) either out loud or by signing.

Once you have practiced paraphrasing words and short phrases, you can move on to longer expressions and even sentences. When you are comfortable with those, working in your *stronger language*, record slow speeches or find them online (you can even find websites where interpreters share speeches). If possible, use simple speeches with short sentences. Rephrase each sentence. If you are able, paraphrase *while* the speaker is still speaking.

Remember: paraphrase in the same language. Do not interpret! You can record yourself and then compare your paraphrasing to the original.

As you become more skilled, you will be able to find paraphrasing activities for interpreters online and in books and other resources. Have fun with them!

Memory skills

Good memory is important for all types of interpreting, and memory is a "muscle" we can exercise. Regarding modes, when interpreting simultaneously, you rely more on short-term memory of partially digested content. In contrast, when interpreting consecutively, you need to retain and focus for a little longer or much longer (here is where good note-taking comes in handy). Develop some tricks to enhance your memory skills; you will use those skills in every session.

Why do your short-term memory and analysis skills matter so much in remote interpreting? The short answer is—accuracy and completeness.

Memory and analysis skills are critical no matter what kind of interpreting you perform. But remote interpreting can be especially stressful. It is also often fast-paced. Unless you develop strong short-term memory skills and can quickly understand what you hear, stress can overload your ability to interpret parts of statements that are critically important for capturing the full meaning of what people say.

For example, it's incredibly easy to forget to interpret qualifiers, which are the words that describe an adjective or adverb. You can also interpret them inaccurately. For example, you might interpret "he was extremely tired" as "he was tired." Or you might interpret "very" instead of "extremely." For a doctor, the difference between "extremely tired" and "tired" could be significant in making an accurate diagnosis. In business, the difference between a "good" deal and an "excellent" deal can be critical.

Interpreters who have trouble with their short-term memory and analysis skills can also forget to interpret whole clauses. Clauses can hold a lot of meaning. Consider this example:

> "The woman, whom he briefly saw, was not the accident victim but another witness."

Figure 4.6: **Interpret everything**

Now if the interpreter forgets to say, "whom he briefly saw," the whole meaning of the sentence changes. What are the consequences? Imagine if this statement came up in a court case.

To enhance your memory and analysis skills, get training in these and other component skills. If you do a search online, you may find exercises that can help you interpret longer and longer segments. Most of these techniques will help you not only with your short-term memory but also your listening and analysis skills.

Three techniques to enhance memory and analysis skills

Two essential memory and analysis exercises that interpreters study are chunking and paraphrasing. You've just looked at paraphrasing. Let's examine chunking.

Chunking

Chunking means to break something into smaller parts. For interpreters, when you chunk a message you divide it into smaller parts, often called units of meaning. Chunking helps you remember the parts. You can also analyze them efficiently because chunking acts as a *bridge between listening and memory.*

It's easier to understand individual ideas as chunks, and then anchor each chunk into your memory, to interpret what you've just heard. Consider this example of a statement by an interpreter about her experiences during the COVID-19 pandemic included in Chapter 1:

> *Starting in mid-March [of 2020], just as the first stay-at-home order was issued in my state, there were nothing but cancellations and no-shows. Then the appointments stopped coming. Although one agency was still sending me requests, they were mostly at the local hospital where all the COVID-19 patients were being taken at the time.*

How many chunks or parts or units of meaning can you find? There's no one correct answer, because we listen and group ideas differently, but here is one way to chunk the information:

Idea 1: Starting in mid-March [of 2020],

Idea 2: just as the first stay-at-home order was issued in my state,

Idea 3: there were nothing but cancellations and no-shows,

Idea 4: Then the appointments stopped coming,

Idea 5: Although one agency was still sending me requests,

Idea 6: they were mostly at the local hospital where all the COVID-19 patients were being taken at the time.

Some "chunks" or "units of meaning" are short. Sometimes they might be just one word. Other chunks are quite long. Chunking not only helps you organize what you've heard, but also helps you focus on the meaning instead of all the individual words. This passage has almost 60 words, but really there are only six or seven ideas expressed.

When you interpret, you are focusing on the ideas, not the words. Chunking helps you do that!

Note-taking for consecutive interpreting

Consecutive note-taking is not considered a component skill, but it is a critical message transfer skill because it supports accuracy. Indeed, when done correctly, consecutive note-taking helps support component skills.

Let's look at note-taking in detail as it applies to remote interpreting.

Face-to-face vs. remote note-taking

The main techniques for consecutive note-taking are the same whether you interpret face-to-face or remotely. You actively listen to the message and analyze it, while you note down key ideas. You use a technique specific to consecutive interpreting that serves to jog your memory and helps you to deliver a complete and accurate interpretation of the message you have just listened to.

However, when you are interpreting remotely and need to take notes, certain things change from interpreting face to face. These changes are mainly logistical. For example, in face-to-face interpreting, having a spiral notebook with a sturdy cover that is easy to keep stable while you stand and that has easy-to-flip pages might be the best choice. But a remote interpreter might need a pad with smaller pages, or a small whiteboard that fits on their desk in front of their keyboard.

The point here is to have easy—and quiet—access to your note-taking materials or equipment at any time when you interpret remotely.

Some remote interpreters even choose to type notes. They say it helps them to keep their focus on the screen at all times. They find it easier to toggle between screens or programs than to write down notes on a pad or markerboard.

Every remote interpreter finds what works best for them. Let's look at benefits of both handwritten and typed note-taking to help you decide which method and setup will work best for you as a remote interpreter.

Why take notes?

Note-taking is an essential skill if you perform consecutive interpreting. Strong memory skills are not enough! Even interpreters with excellent short-term memories can misremember numbers, dates, dosages, addresses and more. Short statements with a complex message or a list can also lead to dangerous errors. Don't take risks. Take notes.

Note-taking has other benefits. For example:

- It can help you focus on the message.
- Strong note-taking skills help you pay attention to the meaning, not the words, precisely because there is no time to write down all the words and you are forced to analyze meaning instead.
- With note-taking, you rely less on your short-term memory, which means you can interpret longer messages and feel less tired.
- When you don't interrupt often, speakers have a more natural conversation that can help them build rapport.

The Rozan method

In 1956, Jean-François Rozan published his famous book, *Note-taking in Consecutive Interpreting*. It outlined a seven-step method. Most note-taking courses rely on this method, which is still the main method that conference (and many legal) interpreters use today.

Rozan's method involves writing notes by hand, not typing them—but a whiteboard or tablet can work too. This method relies on developing a system of symbols and abbreviations. The goal here is to note down as little information as possible while visually capturing the meaning of whole ideas and how they are connected.

The Rozan method is language neutral. It is also a symbols-based, visual and spatial method (meaning it uses space on the page deliberately). Its success is because it captures meaning efficiently, using the minimum number of penstrokes possible.

Seven Elements of the Rozan Method

Rozan laid out seven core elements for note-taking during consecutive interpreting.

1. Noting the idea, rather than the words
Look for units of meaning and learn to represent them with a brief note. "Increase" may be represented as ^ or "heart" may be written as ❤. More complex units of meaning such as "the age-old question" may be more difficult at first but are key to this method.

2. The rules of abbreviation
Abbreviation is not always possible, depending on the language. For example, symbols-based languages, such as Japanese or Korean, do not lend themselves to abbreviation. For romance languages, the key is to note down key letters in the beginning, middle and end of the word. In English, this usually means cutting out vowels and capturing the syllables. So instead of writing "gov" for "government" you would write "gvt." In Spanish, instead of writing "gob" for "gobierno" you would write "gbo." If your non-English language is possible to abbreviate, develop a system that works for that language's structure.

3. Links
Links are symbols or abbreviations that show relationships (cause and effect, before and after, etc.). They are especially critical for long consecutive interpreting needed in conferences and courtrooms or to capture long victim or parent statements.

4. Negation
Deciding how to express negation in your notes is important (for example, "I will not accept blood transfusions"). This can be done with a line through the concept (the previous example becomes bld trns) or other symbols such as X or Ø.

5. Emphasis
Assign a symbol to represent emphasis such as "!!" You could also use underlines to indicate emphasis and multiple underlines to mean "many."

6. Verticality
Write notes up and down rather than left to right as you normally would. The white space on the page and vertical writing actually make it easier for your eyes to scan, follow and absorb the information.

7. Shift (using the space on the page to represent meaning)
Similar to verticality, "shift" utilizes the space on the page to show meaning. Conference interpreters are trained to capture the subject (S), verb (V) and object (O) by writing diagonally from left to right at a downward slant. The focus on sentence-level structure is needed because they interpret a lot of structured, written speech. In medical/community settings, interpreters can use diagonalization by capturing the beginning, middle and end of ideas expressed instead of trying to focus on sentence-level statements.

—Adapted from Allen, 2015, pp. 179-181

Hand-written vs. typed notes

We've said it before, and we'll say it again: find the note-taking tools that work for you!

Some remote interpreters prefer to type notes on a keyboard. Good news: the essential elements of the Rozan method can still be applied. Yes, you *can* take notes electronically (either by typing them or by using a tablet with a stylus). You don't have to rely on handwritten notes with pen and paper if they don't work for you.

Figure 4.7 provides ideas and examples on how each of Rozan's seven core elements can be adapted to typed notes:

Core element	Typed representation
1. Noting idea rather than words	✓ Use keyboard symbols, such as #, @, %.
2. Rules of abbreviation	✓ The same Rozan guidance on abbreviations applies to typing them. You might need to download a special keyboard to be able to type in your non-English language. The feasibility of doing so will depend on whether you use your own computer while interpreting and which keyboards are available for your language.
3. Links	✓ Useful keyboard symbols to show links could be < (less than), > (greater than), = (equals), + (in addition to).
4. Negation	✓ The program you use to take notes electronically may have hot keys (keyboard shortcuts) to ~~strike through~~ text. A capital "X" will work as well.
5. Emphasis	✓ !! may be used as well as hot keys to bold or underline text in notes.
6. Verticality	✓ Hit enter after each idea/thought in your notes to keep the flow vertical. Your eyes will thank you!
7. Shift	✓ This is perhaps the one element that cannot always be achieved with typed notes. Some programs allow you to utilize tab and return keys to employ shift; however, this approach will vary by program. The time and effort it would take to arrange typed notes diagonally may slow you down too much to be able to take notes effectively while interpreting.

Figure 4.7: **How the core elements of the Rozan method can be typed***

*Some of these typed representations may only apply to English and certain Romance languages. Languages with a different script, such as Arabic or Mandarin, may require different strategies to abbreviate, link, etc.

However, taking notes by typing will limit your ability to apply the full Rozan method. The full method, with practice, lets you capture with a minimum number of pen strokes all the content of what a speaker says, including how information is linked together and smaller, hard-to-remember details. Here are some of the pros and cons of writing notes by hand vs. typing them.

Pros and cons of handwritten notes

Pros

You can:

- Write and draw symbols freely, without the restrictions of a keyboard.
- Utilize all seven elements of the Rozan method.
- Capture ideas and the links between them more efficiently with less writing (for example, you can return to a note several lines above and quickly write out a connecting arrow if the speaker connects previous ideas to the current one being expressed).
- Lower your risk of a cybersecurity breach.[64]

Cons

You may:

- Feel physical fatigue from writing.
- Have trouble reading your own handwriting.
- Find it hard to switch visually back and forth between the screen and your notepad.
- Pay for note-taking supplies, such as pens and paper or notepads.
- Need backup supplies to avoid running out of them.

Pros and cons of typed notes

Pros

You can:

- Maintain eye contact with participants and a more professional camera presence when typing during video sessions. (For more on eye contact, see Chapter 8 of this volume.)
- Toggle more easily between notes and online resources, such as dictionaries.
- Be more environmentally friendly.
- Take notes for free—no purchases required.

Cons

You cannot easily:

- Take full advantage of symbols that you can create and use when writing by hand.
- Avoid confusion from toggling between programs and possibly "losing" your notes below another program.
- Fully employ the Rozan technique of shift.
- Avoid physical fatigue from typing.
- Prevent the risk of a cybersecurity breach (but at least don't save your notes)!
- Avoid making noise: certain keyboards/typists create unwanted—and possibly distracting—background noise.

---

[64] In other words, there is no risk of someone inside or outside the organization hacking your account and reading your private notes if you write them by hand. If you shred your notes immediately after the session, the risk of a security breach is almost zero.

Other considerations when choosing a note-taking method

Handwritten and typewritten electronic notes are not always mutually exclusive. It's worth mentioning that more and more interpreters (remote and face-to-face) are using tablet-based programs to combine the two.

These apps function in a way similar to a whiteboard. Using your finger or a stylus, you have the freedom to write as you would with pen and paper, plus the benefits of an electronic system. Just be sure you can charge your device or have backup pen and paper.

Check your language service's policy before buying anything. Some organizations may not want you using external devices even for note-taking.

Also consider your typing and writing skills. For example, if you write quickly but type slowly, typed notes may not be for you. If you can't read your own handwriting and get confused by your own notes, electronic note-taking may be worth trying.

Also, if you decide to type your notes, try a test call with a trusted colleague or friend to see if they can hear background noise. If it is distracting, consider going with pen and paper or purchasing a quieter keyboard.

Assertiveness

Assertiveness for interpreters

Let's look at another key skill set for remote interpreters, one that you might not have thought about, even though it is critically important: assertiveness.

According to the Merriam-Webster dictionary, assertive means "disposed to or characterized by bold or confident statements and behavior."[65] As applied to interpreting, being assertive means acting and expressing yourself *firmly* in a calm, direct and professional manner.

Assertiveness is an absolutely necessary skill for interpreters in general, but perhaps especially for those who work remotely. Let's look at some examples.

You may need assertiveness skills when:

- Participants speak in lengthy utterances without pausing.
- You ask for a repetition.
- Participants ask you to stay on the line even after you notify them that you have to withdraw due to audio or video issues, conflict of interest or any other important reason.
- Participants instruct you to act outside your interpreter role ("I'll just step out for a moment, interpreter—go ahead and chat with the client while I'm gone").
- You notice inconsistencies in the message and have to correct them (whether from your own mistake or that of someone else).
- A linguistic or cultural barrier arises and you need to intervene.

---

65 "Assertive." Merriam-Webster. Retrieved from: https://www.merriam-webster.com/dictionary/assertive

As you can see, this list covers many situations ranging from rare to common, but the point is this: when you interpret remotely, you have to learn to be more assertive than when you interpret face-to-face. You need to do so both to ensure clear communication and to adhere to your code of ethics (more on ethics in Chapter 6 of this volume).

Assertiveness is a key skill that helps interpreters manage many elements of communication they are responsible for, such as managing the flow, ensuring accuracy and upholding communicative autonomy. Communicative autonomy is the capacity of each participant in a session to be responsible for and in control of their own communication (García-Beyaert, 2015, p. 363). In other words, the people having the conversation should be in full control of what they say and how they say it, even if a linguistic barrier exists. We will talk more about communicative autonomy in the Chapter 5 and throughout this textbook.

How assertiveness makes a difference

So why is it especially important to be assertive in remote interpreting, and why does this skill in particular make a difference? To answer this question, let's look at an example handled in a few different ways :

> **You are interpreting for a customer service interaction for a bill dispute. The female representative needs to place the caller on hold, and instructs you, the interpreter, to explain why the charges can't be removed in the meantime:**
>
> **Passive approach:** You say, "All right" but refrain from re-explaining anything to one participant while the other is away. You don't want to tell her it's not your job and make her upset, so this way everyone stays happy.
>
> **Issue with the passive approach:** By agreeing to carry out the rep's wishes, even though you won't actually step out of your role, you've created false expectations for future interactions with interpreters. Additionally, you may get stuck. What if the representative comes back on the line and asks you if the caller understands now?
>
> **Aggressive approach:** You tell the representative firmly that **no**, you will not do this as it is **not** your job. If she wants anything explained to the other participant, she will have to explain it herself, and you will interpret the explanation.
>
> **Issue with the aggressive approach:** Interpreters sometimes misunderstand the need to be assertive and may cross the line into aggressive. This will certainly be heard in a difference in tone between the two. While it can be frustrating when participants don't seem to understand the basics of the interpreter role, we have to remember that working with an interpreter may be rare for them.

Now let's look at how to handle this situation assertively and professionally.

> **Assertive approach:** This is the interpreter speaking. If you can go ahead and speak directly to the caller, I would be happy to interpret for you. Otherwise, I'll stand by until you're back on the line and I'll inform the caller what was just said. Thank you.

As you can see, being assertive allows you the firmness you need to explain your role in the session in a quick, concise and convincing way. You provide options and manage to say no without being overly aggressive or even using the word "no." You do what you need to do but maintain respect, manners and even provide some quick education on how interpreting sessions should work.

The SAY NO model

This example of an assertive approach follows the first two steps of the SAY NO model (Bancroft et al., 2015, pp. 100-103). The SAY NO model is a way to decline inappropriate requests while still offering possible solutions. The three steps of the updated model are:

1. Be gracious (validate the request).
2. Offer 2-3 choices (solutions).
3. Give reasons (to decline the request).

The third step was not added in this example due to the fast-paced environment, so common in remote interpreting. However, if the participant had resisted or pushed back, you could add the third step by giving reasons. For more on the SAY NO model, see Chapter 7 of this volume.

Being assertive allows you to state things confidently. This is especially important when you ask for clarification of any unknown terms or concepts. There is a *major* difference between the passive interpreter who timidly asks for the spelling of a term versus the interpreter who asks for it assertively and confidently.

After all, we want the participants to have confidence in our ability to interpret. Though we do not know everything, we have the tools to find what we need to know.

Session preparation

Most often you will have no time before or between calls to prepare for each session.

However, there is still a lot you can do to prepare for calls in general—and for a career in remote interpreting.

Information search

Depending on the content of any specializations you interpret for and their complexity, you may have to search for information during the session.

As a remote interpreter, you will most likely rely on online resources. Have a pool of trusted resources and websites ahead of time so that you can familiarize yourself with them. Using them will speed you up immensely during the session.

In addition, it helps to practice your internet search skills so you can find what you're looking for fast. Let's look at how you can develop such skills.

Developing online search skills

The remote interpreter will need to become familiar with reliable search engines and websites that explain specialized terminology in more detail. After all, unlike face-to-face interpreters, you may often be looking up information *during* the call.

To be efficient, familiarize yourself with bilingual dictionary websites, such as WordReference, and search engines, such as Google, to become efficient at quickly finding a specific term.

Google can be used to find specific jargon you may not be familiar with in any of your languages, such as insurance terminology, human resources vocabulary, legal phrases, names of medications or medical conditions, etc. For example, in the search bar, you can type "insurance deductible in italiano" (or in "Arabic MSA" etc.) or "deducible en inglés" and a list of websites with the requested information may come up.

One of the main advantages of using search engines, such as Google, when an unknown term comes up is that it will give you suggested alternate spellings (if you are close enough to the original spelling). For example, the remote interpreter hears the word "Kool-Aid" and is not familiar with this flavored drink commonly given to children in the U.S. The interpreter googles "cool aid" and the search engine might ask, "Did you mean Kool-Aid?" From the related results, the interpreter quickly sees and confirms that Kool-Aid is a brand name drink and is rendered the same in the working language.

Figure 4.8 lists a few examples of keyboard shortcuts you can use when you search online for words or concepts. Please note that these shortcuts will vary depending on the search engine you use. Also, some search engines allow you to create custom shortcuts.

Keyboard shortcuts	How to use it while interpreting
" "	To search for exact wording.
Ctrl f or Command f	To find a specific word or phrase quickly in a large body of text.
+	To give context to your search by ensuring it contains a specific word. For example, add "+ medication" to only get medication results.
-	To exclude unwanted information.
~	To search for a keyword and its synonyms.

Figure 4.8: **Examples of online search keyboard shortcuts**

There are many additional quick and easy tips for making targeted searches online. They are easy to learn. Just search online for "tips for online searching" or "best online search strategies." The results will include many resources you can use to become expert at online searches.

Internal resources

Many language services and other organizations that you may interpret for have internal chat features where you can quickly ask a team of colleagues how to say a term. This is another speedy way to find help.

If you're a self-employed interpreter, you may still have chats with colleagues, or you can access online forums and social media pages that can serve the same purpose.

> **Remember: Respect Privacy and Confidentiality!**
>
> If you're using chats, forums or social media to communicate about terminology while on a call, be sure that communication follows all privacy guidelines. Use this as a quick lifeline to interpret accurately, but never let these features distract you from your focus on the interpretation.

Build your glossaries

Making glossaries

Glossaries created by the interpreter for the specific specializations and types of sessions they interpret are *invaluable.* No book or online resource will be as specific as your own experience.

Here are some steps you can follow before the session to build your own glossaries based on the topic and need:

1. Go to Google.com.
2. Search a key term or phrase to build your glossary based on the topic.
3. Click on "Settings" and select "Advanced search."
4. Modify your search parameters in the "Find pages with..." section as desired.
5. Go to "Then narrow your results by..." and specify the language and regions you would like results from.
6. Using the results, build a glossary of key terms you notice come up often.[66]

As with the component skill of anticipation, glossaries are much more helpful when you do enough research to understand the basic ideas the search terms refer to. For example, many insurance policies are based on health maintenance organization (HMO) services or preferred provider organization (PPO) services. They require patient deductibles, copays and may pay out secondary to Medicare benefits. If you don't understand the previous sentence, but you try to build a glossary out of the unknown terms without first understanding the basic insurance concepts expressed in it, then your terms will not really help you in the moment of interpreting.

Using glossaries

Now that you've created your glossary, make a plan for how you will quickly access and search it during a session.

---

[66] Note that due to ever-evolving browser interfaces and technology, these advanced searches features may need to be researched first; the sample instructions should be adjusted accordingly as needed.

Strategically organizing the information in digital folders is key when you need to find details. For example, if your glossary is about medical terminology, you may have a folder for each medical specialization, subfolders for subspecializations, and each subfolder may contain glossaries of treatments and procedures. Routinely revisit these glossaries to refresh what you've learned and make additions.

Location-specific information

Glossaries are not enough in remote interpreting. Another common problem that remote interpreters routinely deal with (and face-to-face interpreters usually don't) is a combination of unfamiliar information and lack of context. Remote interpreters often need *location-specific information.*

For example, a service provider refers a customer or client to a specific service—such as a homeless shelter, adult education program, mortgage program, clinic or government agency—and you don't even understand what it is because the name is unfamiliar—or you mishear it and interpret it incorrectly—or perhaps you simply don't interpret it at all (according to complaints by some service providers).

Think about this: when you go out and about in your own community, you have a vast treasure of resources that you may not even think about. Even if you don't personally go everywhere locally, you are aware of banks, insurance companies, pharmacy names, transit systems, the populations you likely encounter day-to-day and maybe even some government programs.

You will soon realize that learning these variables for the communities where your participants are located can help you tremendously in a remote interpreting session. Building up this kind of resource knowledge may enhance your ability to effectively anticipate what will be said.

The value of location-specific resources

Let's look at some examples of why location-specific resources are so beneficial:

> Which subway?
>
> You're interpreting and everything is going smoothly. Participant A starts giving participant B directions to arrive at the store they need to find.
>
> "At Brown Street you'll turn right. Then you should see a subway on your left."
>
> At the mention of the word "metro" in Spanish by the interpreter, participant A laughs and quickly tells the interpreter, "There's no 'metro' here!"
>
> If only we could hear capitalization, because participant A actually meant "you should see a Subway (the *restaurant*) on your left."

Unless you are familiar enough with the U.S. city where the participants are located and know that Subway is a common chain of sandwich fast-food restaurants there, and you grasp the context easily, you (or any other interpreter) could easily make the same mistake.

Yes, you likely will make these kinds of errors! That's all right. Sometimes we just have to laugh, correct ourselves, and move on.

Harvest Clinic vs. Clínica La Cosecha

Here's one trick you may have figured out on your own already, but maybe not.

Most names (proper nouns) will not change when rendering them into the target language. For example, imagine an English-speaking nurse who tells a Spanish-speaking patient to use the pharmacy "Quick Aid" on Main Street. The interpreter does not need to literally interpret the meaning of this pharmacy's name into the other language, as it will only serve to confuse the patient. (See Figure 4.9.)

Figure 4.9: **Directions to the Quick Aid Pharmacy**

However, be careful. Some communities have started to translate certain program or organization names into common participant languages where it seems helpful to do so. For example, Harvest Clinic in North Carolina, USA, is also referred to as *Clínica La Cosecha* (a literal translation into Spanish).

You probably won't know about these special cases until you have to interpret them, and that's all right. The good news is that remote interpreters are still human, and you are not expected to know *everything*—though it can certainly seem that way at first. The more sessions you interpret, the more familiar you'll become with these different details. Even then, information searching and asking for clarifications are trusty tools.

Problem-solving skills

Thinking fast vs. thinking slow

Interpreters frequently problem-solve on the job. Remote interpreting is no exception.

Given that remote interpreting is a fast-paced environment, you often have situations that require "thinking on your feet"—in other words, thinking quickly. This approach is often referred to as "System 1 thinking," as described by Daniel Kahneman (2011).

When problems are routine and you're under a time constraint, without much conscious effort you make a quick decision based on similar past situations. When, however, you face a new problem, System 1 thinking can fail you. You may need to quickly make a difficult decision and realize later that you could have taken a different approach.

This is where System 2 thinking comes in. System 2 thinking is more analytical, deliberate and rational (Kahneman, 2011). It allows us to think through a problem and plan out a good solution or set of actions to use when it arises. In an ideal world, we would always have time to employ our System 2 thinking. However, as proficiency and skill are acquired, some decisions that may once have required slow deliberation can become automated and move to your "System 1" (Tay, Ryan & Ryan, 2018).

In this next section, you will look at common problems in remote interpreting and information to help you be prepared to solve them.

Common problems to solve in remote interpreting

1. Tech issues

Without technology, remote interpreting would not exist. As Chapters 2 and 3 of this volume made clear, while technology makes remote communication possible, like everything else in life, it may have its failures from time to time and need maintenance.

Here are some ways to manage situations when technology has some challenges or fails completely:

- The most important thing (remember Chapter 3!) is to remain calm.
- Always proceed as if the participants can still see or hear you, even if it seems that they cannot.
- For poor audio or video quality, ask participants to move the device or change the positioning. They may try moving to an area closer to an internet access point.
- For echoes, ask participants to lower their volume to avoid sound reverberation.
- For video connectivity issues, pause the video then resume it.
- If these steps are not successful, you may need to transfer the call (when applicable), switch with your teammate (when applicable), have the participants call back or log back in. Never try to interpret if technology is hindering your ability to remain accurate!

(For other strategies to address technical issues, see Chapter 3 of this volume. For managing tech difficulties in RSI, see Chapter 2 of Volume 2.)

At other times you may need to walk the participants through technical failures or basic platform functions. As a remote interpreter, you may find that you act as basic tech support. Not only do you need to know how to navigate the platform yourself, but you also may need to briefly explain functions, such as mute, volume, video settings, etc. (See Chapters 2 and 3 in Volume 2 for more information on client and participant education.)

Your language service may have other steps or policies in place for these situations. For example, some remote interpreters may have a tech support number, which they can provide to participants experiencing technical issues.

2. Lack of context

Context is essential for interpreters. Context is inherent in the circumstances that surround an event, statement or idea. Knowing these circumstances helps to fully understand and assess the situation.

Without context, we often can't follow a conversation or grasp its meaning, even if we understand all the individual words. *In remote interpreting, lack of context is a chronic and unavoidable part of the job.*

The Remote Interpreter "Parachutes" In

We can think of remote interpreting, in many cases, as "parachuting" virtually into conversations all over the world. This is pretty amazing!

The downside of a sudden virtual arrival is coming in without any context, and in some cases via audio only, into a room or space where the participants present see a great deal more than you do and are far more familiar with the context.

Look for contextual information

For better problem-solving skills, refine your ability to pay close attention to any and all contextual information. Let's look at an example.

> Francisco is a Spanish video interpreter who frequently interprets for healthcare settings. He answers a call and sees a woman in scrubs on video. As he's collecting the required information from the medical provider, he notices the woman answering his questions is not the woman before him in the scrubs, but someone off-screen.
>
> Context clue #1: The woman on camera may be another healthcare provider present for the session or she may be the patient or accompanying the patient.
>
> Francisco continues to collect the required data and asks for the patient's name and date of birth. The off-screen person tells him, "Stephanie Ortega. October 12, 2013."
>
> Context clue #2: The patient is likely female. At the time of the session, she was only nine years old. The woman in the camera view is likely the patient's mother.

A common mistake that new remote interpreters make is disregarding these context clues. When the medical provider's first question is "Did the doctor explain the child's discharge plan to you?" Francisco should know to use the feminine "*niña*" for child rather than masculine "*niño*."

> The provider goes on to explain medication instructions:
>
> "She needs to take 15 milliliters, once a day, for four days."

Rather than remembering this patient is nine years old and he is interpreting for the mother, the interpreter assumes the provider is referring to an adult patient indirectly (using third person). He goes on to interpret:

> "You need to take 15 milliliters, once a day, for four days."

Of course, not every session will provide this context naturally. In addition to picking up on these cues, you need to gain confidence to be able to clarify up front. Francisco could have avoided confusion by simply asking from the start:

> "Provider, can you clarify for the interpreter, will I be interpreting for the patient or a family member? Who is in the room with us? Is the patient male or female?"

Don't be shy about asking for information you need in order to competently perform your job!

3. Unfamiliar information

Interpreters working in any modality will come across unfamiliar information, but remote interpreters often have the advantage of having the internet at their fingertips.

You will need to acquire various resources and information from your consumers. They may be collected throughout your interpreting sessions (that you keep as a general set of resources) or during research you do before or during the session. Some of them may be provided by the language services or organizations that you interpret for. See "Session preparation" in this section for details.

Scripts for unknown terms
If you encounter an unfamiliar term and don't have the right glossary at hand, and you can't find the information quickly online, you will need to request a clarification.

Some language services have scripts they want you to use to request clarification. If not, you will need to develop your own. Here are a few examples from the authors.

Example 1: This is the interpreter speaking. Would you please clarify what you mean by "homeroom" so I may describe it in Vietnamese to the parents?

Example 2: Excuse me, this is the interpreter speaking—I'm not aware of an equivalent in [my other language] for "charter school." Would you please explain the term so I can interpret your explanation?

Example 3: Doctor, this is the interpreter speaking. Can you explain what you mean by "Medi-Cal"? (Medi-Cal is the state of California's Medicaid healthcare program.)

Example 4: Excuse me, this is the interpreter speaking. What does LOA mean?
(This term came up in a human resources context; it refers to leave of absence, an authorized time off from the employer).

Notice that none of these scripts contain apologies or the words "I'm sorry." Interpreters do not need to apologize for doing their job.

Write It Down

Just because you looked up a term or phrase during a call, or asked someone to clarify it, does not mean you will remember it! Especially if you looked it up or requested clarification during a long or intense call, or if you quickly transfer from call to call.

Go ahead and note down that term as soon as you can. Then. make sure to review it later and add it to your personal glossary so that you remember it for next time.

4. Loss of visual cues

Perhaps one of the biggest differences you will find when interpreting remotely rather than face to face is the loss of visual cues. This could involve a complete loss of visual information (in AOI, including OPI) or partial loss (in VRI, VRS or video RSI).

It is true that remote interpreters lack access to some, or all, visual communication. However, it is also important to note that nonverbal communication is powerful—and often perceptible.

Nonverbal communication includes hesitations, inflections, tone of voice, emotional coloring, breath sounds (such as gasping, wheezing, accelerated breathing) and vocal volume. Remote interpreters often develop excellent listening skills to help compensate for the absence of visual cues (Kelly, 2008, p. 83).

Setting up the session

Many of the issues that stem from lack of visual cues can be addressed at the start of the remote interpreting session. For example, all participants are in the same location but the interpreter is unsure if there are additional participants present who have not spoken. The interpreter can say before providing the full introduction, "Who all do we have in the room with us today?" That is, if it's an appropriate question to ask (you wouldn't ask if you're interpreting for a courtroom full of people including audience members, for example).

The answer to that question helps you know what to expect and mentally prepare for it. Now you know there are several family members present, you won't be surprised when a new voice speaks up. If you know one of the participants is bilingual, you will be prepared if they switch from one language to another and also know that you must continue interpreting for others in the session.

Additional steps

Video interpreters learn to request appropriate positioning of the relevant device to provide clear video footage of participants and any visual aids used in a session. Interpreters may at times need to prioritize visualization of one element over another.

In a signed language session, for example, the interpreter will definitely need to see the entire signing space of the signing participants but may need less visual information from hearing participants who use spoken language.

Examples of Interpreter Requests to Obtain Better Visual Information

Example 1: A lawyer is describing photographic evidence of a crime scene where the video interpreter cannot fully see the image.

The interpreter can ask for the device to be repositioned in order to see the photo.

Note: In situations like this, telephonic interpreters can sometimes use resources, such as online image searches, to aid in visualizing what is being discussed. Having these visuals helps to interpret the discussion accurately. Here is a specific example.

Example 2: A customer calls a business about malfunctioning equipment, which the telephonic interpreter is not familiar with.

The interpreter does an online search for the brand and model number to find a visual image of the equipment in order to easily follow along with the various parts and functions.

Otherwise, share with the participants that you are having difficulty interpreting because you cannot see the equipment, and that will alert them to describe what they are doing more clearly—which can help the other participants, not only you!

When in doubt, clarify!

Of course, there are times when something ambiguous springs up in conversation and you cannot see the visual context. For example:

- A participant refers to "you" and you don't know if "you" is singular or plural.
- A participant is talking to two females or two males and keeps saying she or he to both, so you don't know which one the participant is referring to.
- A participant refers to "we" but does not specify if it includes the person receiving the message or not (inclusive vs. exclusive—in some languages, this is an important distinction)!
- A participant refers to a person based on a profession that may not be gendered in one source language but is in the target language (nurse, doctor, teacher, lawyer, social worker).

If you are able to request a clarification to be more accurate and have a better communication flow, then do so as soon as possible!

5. Language variation

Variation is a characteristic of language: in every language, there is more than one way of saying the same thing. Speakers of the same language use different words, pronunciations, and even sentence structure (Dawson et al., 2022, p. 429). This can be true even for people who have always lived in the same city or rural area—even if they live close to each other.

Regional variation

However, regional variation can often cause challenges for remote interpreters who serve participants from different states and countries. They serve a highly diverse, spread-out group of consumers. Because of this challenge, they face regional terms, signs and expressions, often with a high number of daily sessions (because they don't have to travel from session to session).

You'll need to be ready for this scenario by learning and understanding regionalisms. For example, if you work in the U.S. and one of the languages you interpret is English, you will notice words, such as tennis shoes or gym shoes from a person who lives in the northeastern U.S. whereas an English speaker originally from England may call them trainers.

Figure 4.10: **Different ways to sign the same word**

Other factors in variation

Geography is not the only factor that influences variation. Age, gender, education background, ethnicity and contact from other languages also affect variation (Dawson et al., 2022, p. 429). This may pose challenges for remote interpreters if they have not been exposed to English speakers from India, for example, or someone who learned English as a foreign language.

Rather than get frustrated with this, it's important to use it as an opportunity to improve your listening skills! Listen for patterns in the pronunciation. If a participant pronounces the word "bit" like "beat," then you know that if you hear an "eee" sound, it may actually be an "ih" sound in any given word. Try to spot these patterns. You will become better at this with practice (N. Kelly & B. Treumann, personal communication, August 1, 2019).

One helpful thing to remember when you deal with variation across speakers is that interpreters are already expected to request clarification. *Never guess at what is said!* If an unfamiliar pronunciation pattern is causing you problems, ask for the participant to speak at a higher volume (or use a larger signing space). When people speak louder, speakers automatically use more breath, may slow down and tend to articulate better, which may result in better enunciation. When signers sign in a larger space, they tend to slow down. When they slow down, it is easier to see the sign elements. When finger-spelled words are slowed down, it is easier to identify the spelled word.

Ask for repetition when you need it, but be specific. To avoid someone repeating a whole long statement, which might irritate the speaker, focus on the specific word or phrase that's giving you trouble: "Interpreter speaking—you said to call the bank directly and provide *what*?"

Whatever you do, avoid saying things like "I can't understand your accent," or "I'm having trouble understanding you." Comments like these may cause the speaker to become frustrated and self-conscious. As interpreters, we know better than anyone what it takes to learn another language, so try to handle these cases with patience and grace.

6. Multitasking

You may have already noticed that interpreting requires the execution of multiple tasks at the same time (multitasking). Yes. Multitasking is a challenge. (Isn't interpreting hard enough?)

Multitasking is a skill that is especially important for remote interpreters who have to work with multiple programs and computer windows (for online dictionaries, online search engines, chats, etc.) and more than one computer screen while also interpreting, making decisions, taking notes and searching online (or paying attention to a teammate when partnering with another remote interpreter).

In addition, your component skills (active listening, message analysis, message conversion and delivery—and often note-taking) mean that interpreting *by itself* is multitasking, but you may also be dealing with technical challenges, requesting a clarification, toggling between screens, intervening to address a complex cultural misunderstanding, asking someone to reposition a device or visual aid and so much more.

It sounds exhausting…and it can be. This is one reason why self-care is vital for remote interpreters. (See Chapter 9 of Volume 2.) But don't worry: practice will help you excel in multitasking. Here are some tips to boost your remote interpreting multitasking skills:[67]

- Accept your limits: your (work) day has a limited number of hours. Your resources in the moment are what they are.
- Learn to concentrate: taking notes (for spoken language interpreters) could help with concentration. Often, not having visual cues (which are absent in AOI/OPI) helps you focus more on what you are hearing.
- Avoid distractions: make sure to reduce distractions in your workplace. When interpreting remotely, turn off notifications from your electronic devices, for example.
- Plan ahead: have your resources available before your work shift.
- Take breaks: moments of rest help you stay sharp and ready to multitask when needed.

---

67 Michelle Griffin. (2021). "12 Tips to Boost Your Multitasking Skills." Cirkus. Retrieved from: https://cirkus.com/blog/multitasking-skills/

Build a toolkit

What do you need to work on?

Message transfer, assertiveness, session preparation and problem-solving are not only vital skill sets, but they are also foundational tools for your professional interpreting practice.

We will now look at building a toolkit to help you address all these skill sets.

Some of these tools may be more valuable to you based on the kind of remote interpreting sessions you encounter. Note-taking is essential, for example, if you perform consecutive interpreting for spoken languages or need to take notes in a simultaneous team.

In addition, interpreter assertiveness is critical for almost any remote interpreting session to run smoothly.

Problem-solving is another skill that you need in almost every interpreted session and…in any aspect of your life! Now, *how* you problem-solve depends on the scenario you are interpreting for.

An additional factor is timing: the faster the pace of the environment you interpret in (whether for the mode, modality or setting), the faster you need to problem-solve. You will likely problem-solve more quickly for a patient in the emergency room than for someone calling in to pay their electric bill, for example. Like memory, problem-solving is a skill you can develop with practice and by building your library of tools and strategies.

Where to start

Now that we've reviewed common skills sets you'll need in remote interpreting, let's prioritize which areas to focus on first. That priority list is based on your strengths; needs; the mode, modality, and field in which you will be performing.

Ask yourself...	If yes, work on...
Do I interrupt often to request a pause to interpret?	Memory skills Note-taking
Do I often have to request repetitions?	Assertiveness Addressing tech issues
Do I struggle with complex statements?	Note-taking
Will I be interpreting for many different subject areas?	Information search Ability to pick up on context
Do I have a specific focus (for example, legal, medical, etc.)?	Information search
For my interpretations, will the policies and procedures vary (for example, from state to state) for the participants?	Information search Handling location-specific information
Will I interpret for a diverse pool of participants?	Improving knowledge of language variation Information search

Ask yourself...	If yes, work on...
Am I slow in typing, internet searches, or multitasking?	Information search
Have I identified a lack of knowledge about the participants' locations?	Information search Handling location-specific information
Are there a variety of location-specific names (such as pharmacies, transit systems, government programs) relevant to the sessions?	Handling location-specific information Information search
Are there differing privacy laws and requirements based on the location of the participants?	Handling location-specific information
Do I lack knowledge about the language backgrounds of the participants for my working languages? For example, where the participants learned the language or if they are native/nonnative speakers.	Improving knowledge of language variation
Do I struggle with many different accents, pronunciations, and word choices in general? Or variation in signs among signed language users?	Improving knowledge of language variation
Do participants often get confused with my word/sign choices? For example, when using region specific terms.	Improving knowledge of language variation
Will I interpret for subject areas that teach with visual aids frequently (such as education or medical device teachings)?	Coping with loss of visual cues
Will I frequently interpret for movement-based therapies, such as physical therapy or occupational therapy?	Coping with loss of visual cues
Do I struggle with paying attention to context clues even when it's just a word or two?	Ability to pick up on context
Do I process information best visually?	Coping with loss of visual cues
Do I get nervous when technology fails or is not functioning the way it should?	Addressing tech issues
Do I struggle with the protocols I should follow when there are tech issues?	Addressing tech issues

Figure 4.11: **Identifying needed skills and skill sets: Practical examples**

How to develop the skill sets

Once you have identified the skills you need to learn to problem-solve by answering the questions in Figure 4.11, you will be able to plan which problem-solving skills to target.

By the way, it's all right if you did not have answers to all or most of the questions in Figure 4.11. In that case, you can start developing *any* of those skills in no specific order; work on whatever draws you the most first.

A way to prioritize which skill set to work on first would be to identify the skill sets that correspond to the questions that apply to you the most (that is, the questions to which you answered "yes").

For example, if you answered "yes" to all the questions that involve technical issues but only answered "yes" to one question about coping with loss of visual cues, start with working on your technical skills first.

Now go to Figure 4.12 to obtain ideas on how to work on the corresponding problem-solving skills.

Skill sets	How to work on them
Memory skills	• Practice active listening. • Work on chunking. • Engage in paraphrasing activities and exercises. • Take courses or programs on note-taking.
Note-taking	• Study and practice the Rozan method. • Find a partner to practice note-taking with. • Work on symbols you find useful and easy to remember.
Assertiveness	• Develop scripts for intervening and say them out loud. • Record them, listen to them and try again. • Practice your scripts with friends, family or colleagues and ask them if they find your delivery calm, clear, firm and professional.
Ability to pick up on context	• This is a skill that takes extensive practice. • While working on practice exercises, ask anyone evaluating you (quality assurance, team leads, etc.) to listen for examples of this. • When interpreting your first sessions, have the evaluator listen for this as well. Real life has more context than practice exercises!
Information search	• Gather a list of online resources you plan to use while interpreting and bookmark them. • First try this while working on interpreting practice scenarios. Try quickly searching something you don't know without pausing the exercise or taking too much time.
Handling location-specific information	• Make a list of your participants' locations. You may reach out to your language service or the organization for which you will be interpreting to obtain the locations if you don't know them. • List location-specific topics that do or may come up in your interpreting sessions. • If possible, connect with a colleague in that location to exchange information on location-specific resources (this could be a colleague who also works for your language service or someone you find through professional forums or memberships).

Skill sets	How to work on them
Improving knowledge of language variation	• Make a list of the language variations you find most difficult to understand and try to identify what aspects of them are hard for you to interpret. • If finding word choices gives you difficulty, start by researching that variation's vocabulary (for example, try searching "New Zealand English terms"). • If you find the signs or pronunciations hard to understand, find examples in videos. These videos do not have to be related to interpreting! They are merely to train your eyes or ears to that language variation.
Coping with loss of visual cues	• Turn on a TV program but close your eyes while it plays. • Pay attention to anything you may not understand that makes you want to open your eyes. • Think about how you might ask for clarification of the ambiguity if you were interpreting.
Addressing tech issues	• Grow familiar with the platforms you will be interpreting on. • Acquire a list of recommended tech problem-solving steps from your language services or other organizations you will interpret for if they have any. • Use such lists whenever tech problems come up in your sessions. Remember to note down which steps are difficult for you. For example, if you have to describe for participants where the volume controls are on a device that you've never seen, you may want to request images, videos or training materials on their devices so that you can better understand what you're describing to the participant.

Figure 4.12: **Ideas on how to work on problem-solving skills**

Explore specialized skill sets

There is a specialized set of skills needed in remote interpreting covered elsewhere in this textbook for situations, such as:

- How to address a communication barrier when communication breaks down: see Chapter 7 of this volume.
- How to perform RSI: see Volume 2, Chapters 1 and 2.
- Performing team and relay interpreting: see Volume 2, Chapter 8.

→ Section 4.2 Review

This section reviewed four key interpreting skill sets that are particularly important for remote interpreters and explored how to develop these skill sets.

1. Message transfer skills: message transfer skills are the skills we use the most in interpreting (whether face to face or remotely), but they are so complex that we need to develop and practice other skills to learn message transfer. Activities, such as anticipating, parroting, chunking and paraphrasing help us develop message transfer skills.
    a. Component skills: listening, analyzing and extracting the message in one language as well as converting and delivering the message in another language are all component skills. It is important to practice component skills to improve accuracy in interpreting.
    b. Memory: memory skills are needed in both consecutive and simultaneous interpreting. However, consecutive interpreting requires mental retention of information for a longer time compared to simultaneous.
    c. Note-taking: the main difference in taking notes while interpreting remotely is logistics. Remote interpreters should adapt to the workspace and decide whether to take notes by hand (whether on a notepad or whiteboard, or using a stylus and tablet) or by typing. Some factors to consider are how well and fast you type vs. how clearly you write, whether you prefer to write more symbols than words or the opposite, how strong your cybersecurity is, which note-taking materials are at hand, which software programs you may have for drawing on electronic devices, and the limitations or requirements of your work environment.
2. Assertiveness: being assertive allows us to be firm and state our limitations clearly without being timid or aggressive. Remote interpreters especially need to proactively remove obstacles to clear communication and accurate interpreting with confidence and ease. After all, we are not physically present in the room, so we cannot easily use body language in the ways that a face-to-face interpreter can. Practice assertiveness in everyday life by stating your needs confidently, calmly and with confidence using the suggestions in this chapter.
3. Session preparation: you may not always have time to prepare for the next call or session, but general preparation can help you, including:
    a. Knowing how to look up information quickly.
    b. Developing online search skills.
    c. Using keyboard shortcuts for searches.
    d. Building glossaries.
    e. Finding location-specific information.
4. Problem-solving: you may need to make decisions quickly in some cases, based on similar past situations (System 1 thinking), rather than with more time to analyze them (System 2 thinking). Plan for these problems ahead of time, however, so you can use

some System 2 thinking to be prepared to think quickly! Some of the common problems to solve in remote interpreting are:

a. Lack of context.
b. Unfamiliar information.
c. Loss of visual cues.
d. Managing language variation.
e. Multitasking.
f. Tech issues.

Work on these top four skills sets in interpreting: message transfer skills, assertiveness, session preparation and problem-solving. However, since the way to solve certain problems depends on the mode, modality and specialization or setting you perform in, you may wish to build a toolkit of skills to prioritize that are specific to your needs and identify where to improve first.

Be conscious that interpreters, especially those working remotely, need to problem-solve before, during and after the session! There is always so much more to learn.

Section 4.3 Protocols for Remote Interpreting

→ Learning objective 4.3

After completing this section, the remote interpreter will be able to explain and practice protocols specific to remote interpreting.

→ Section 4.3 Overview

Interpreters, including those who work remotely, will need to follow protocols for successful sessions.

Protocol: A Definition
Accepted or established rule or set of rules to guide procedures and behaviors in any situation.

This section addresses protocols that are common in face-to-face interpreting but will need to be adapted in remote interpreting as well as protocols that apply specifically to remote sessions.

They include:

- How interpreters and equipment need to be positioned.
- What to include in a professional introduction and how to perform it.
- Use of direct speech (first person) with some exceptions.
- How to manage the flow of the conversation by turn-taking.
- When and how to intervene or mediate.
- How to manage hold times.
- When and how to appropriately shadow communication.

Note: This section focuses on general protocols and those used primarily with AOI (including OPI), VRI and VRS. Chapter 2 of Volume 2 will discuss certain protocols that are specific only to RSI.

→ Section 4.3 Content

Protocols vs. skills

Before we discuss protocols, let's review how protocols differ from skills.

Interpreting, like all professions, requires those who practice it to always be learning ways to enhance the skills needed as well as following certain protocols to meet goals efficiently and safely.

Interpreting skills and skill sets were explored in the previous section. *Skills* refers to expertise or an ability but *protocols* are defined as accepted or established ways of doing things. For example, interpreters introduce themselves, position themselves and request clarifications or address communication breakdowns following protocols defined by professional organizations or the language services they work for. Protocols support the interpreter's ability to stay within their role and focus primarily on interpreting.

Positioning

Positioning in face-to-face interpreting

It is now considered general knowledge within the interpreting community that positioning of the interpreter when performing face-to-face sessions is important and may affect the flow of the conversation. Believe it or not, it is also important in remote interpreting...but in a different way.

In face-to-face interactions, positioning refers to choosing the appropriate place to stand or sit in relation to the participants, with the goal of promoting direct communication between or among them (Socarrás-Estrada, 2016, p. 126).

For spoken language interpreters, the physical environment, the topic or setting of the session, the number of speakers in the room and even cultural concerns may affect the decision of where to position yourself as the interpreter (NCIHC, 2003, p. 3). For sign language interpreters, the interpreter and the participant who signs will need to be able to see each other's signing spaces (Laurent Clerc National Deaf Education Center, n.d.).

Last, but not least, interpreter positioning may affect the interpreting as habitual bad posture can lead to fatigue (National Health Service, 2021).

Positioning in remote interpreting

In the case of remote interpreting, since the interpreter joins the session via a device, the importance of *device positioning* in relation to the participants lies in the ability of all individuals to hear and to be heard, or to see and to be seen (critical for signed languages).

In addition, adequate *positioning of the participants* is important in a session where everyone speaks but critically necessary in a session where anyone signs—all the more so in remote interpreting due to its limitations of visibility and audibility.

Positioning of Components in a Remote Interpreting Session*		
	For signed languages (VRI/VRS only)	**For spoken languages**
Participants	**Signers:** In front of the camera and facing it. **Non-signers:** At a short distance from the device, never blocking the camera's or the signer's view.	**VRI:** In camera view. **OPI:** Close to the speakerphone or microphone and speakers.
Device (camera or telephone)	– In front of the participant who signs, pointing at their signing space. – Area in the room with the strongest internet connection. – Facing away from bright light or windows.	**VRI** –In an area in the room with the strongest internet connection. –Ideally, where the interpreter can see all participants. –Facing away from bright light or windows. **OPI:** Device positioned close to those who will be speaking.**
Interpreter	– In front of the camera and facing it, centered in view field and including all signing space. – For signed language, with a background of a color that contrasts with the interpreter's skin tone. – Close to the microphone and speakers.**	**VRI:** In front of the camera, facing it and centered in view field. **OPI:** Close to the microphone and speakers.**

Figure 4.13: **Positioning of components in a remote interpreting session***

**All elements must be tested and adjusted during the introduction or briefing.*

***Avoid having the device so close that you may cause noise feedback or others can hear you breathing.*

Note that Figure 4.13 specifies suggestions for positioning of the different components in a remote interpreting session for the best overall participant experience.

Positioning based on configuration

In this textbook, the term *configuration* refers to how participants are located with respect to each other. For AOI, including OPI, we typically see one of two configurations—the participants are together in one location, or they are in separate locations.

For video relay service (VRS), participants are always in separate locations, since this service is essentially a telephone call with an added video component for users of signed languages.[68]

Prior to 2020, the most common configuration for VRI was to have the participants in the same location and the interpreter in another location. For example, the paramedic and the person who called 911 could be in the same ambulance. Since 2020, we have seen more varied configurations start to emerge in VRI (to the point that VRI is starting to look more like VRS). Often the participants today are in *two* different locations (with the interpreter in a third location), such as:

a. Telepsychiatry services involving an interpreter.
b. When a client calls the insurance company and there is an option to add the interpreter to the conversation.
c. In a school that obtains an interpreter via video in order to call the student's parent to schedule a meeting.

Making positioning requests

Interpreters may make repositioning requests if the current positioning of the device is not ideal or helpful for effective communication. Of course, use good customer service skills and know that sometimes it is not possible to accommodate all requests. It may be too time-consuming based on the circumstances (such as an emergency), so you will prioritize what you need in order to make the session go as smoothly as possible.

When working in AOI/OPI:

- Ask participants to position themselves close to the speakerphone (if using one).
- Ask participants to have the device located where the internet connection is strongest in the room (if using a telephone or audio-only service that depends on internet connection).

When working in VRI:

- Ask participants to have the device where the internet connection is strongest in the room.
- Ask participants to have the camera facing all of them where possible (but for signed language, at a minimum the camera should face those who sign with a clear view of the signing space).
- Ask participants to show any visual aids within the camera area when possible (such as illustrations, demonstrations on how to use equipment or physical therapy exercises).

Professional introductions

Just as in face-to-face interpreting, professional introductions are critical in remote interpreting, whether your interpreting sessions are scheduled ahead of time or not. The purpose of a professional introduction is to establish rapport, communicate how the interpreting will work and probe for more information.

---

[68] How VRS Works. Federal Communications Commission. Retrieved from: https://www.fcc.gov/consumers/guides/video-relay-services

For interpreters who accept on-demand calls, the introduction happens within the first seconds of the session. The only exception to including a professional introduction is for crises or emergency cases.

Do Not Assume!

When you make your introduction over video, do not assume that you see all the people in a room.

For remote interpreting sessions that are scheduled in advance, the introduction should happen first during a meeting before the session and also during the session itself (more information about the content of these meetings can be found throughout this book, including the second volume).

For remote interpreters, it's recommended to include your introduction even if you're certain that you've recently interpreted for a given participant. In some cases, there may be new participants who have since joined the session who may benefit from hearing your introduction. In other cases, the reminder of your procedures may still be helpful.

However, this protocol is not always standard or expected. For example, in legal remote interpreting the interpreter might be introduced to some participants ahead of time. In conference RSI, participants may simply put on headsets to hear the interpreter, who never makes introductions at all.

In service settings, however, and particularly for business interpreting and community interpreting (including medical, education, social services, refugee and mental health interpreting), the remote interpreter's introduction consistently helps to re-establish expectations about how everyone will work together remotely.

Use your best professional judgment with repeat participants and be sure to adhere to any specific requirements set out by the language services or organizations that you interpret for.

The call's setting, such as a business, healthcare facility, school or government agency, will usually guide you about what you need to include in that session's introduction. However, there are a few elements that should nearly always be included that we will shortly address.

Respect Participant Privacy

In healthcare, when you introduce yourself, *do not* read out a patient's information to the same healthcare provider that you interpreted for earlier. That provider may now be with a different patient.

For example, *do not* ask, "Is this patient Julie Xu?" or "Nurse, are you still with patient Tulaya, MRN: 1234567890?" You could be violating patient privacy!

How to perform your introduction remotely

The main objective of your introduction is to communicate who you are and your role in the session. The introduction should be brief, clear and concise: typically, it is no longer than about 30 seconds for *both* languages, though this time may vary depending on your organization's requirements for introductions or on the specialization.

Use a courteous and smooth tone with a smile to create rapport and gain trust—even if you are interpreting via telephone, listeners can hear the smile in your voice! (Of course, be careful: in sensitive, sad or tragic situations, a smile might not be appropriate.)

Assess the Mood

With time, you will learn to pick up on auditory or visual cues to "read" the room. If the mood feels somber, for example, adjust your tone of voice for your introduction accordingly.

In most cases, you introduce yourself first to participants in one language (which may include a scripted greeting specified by your language service or organization). Then introduce yourself to the other participants in the corresponding language. However, use your professional judgment about whom to address first according to the setting or specialization. For example:

1. For legal reasons, in lawyer-client meetings, address the lawyer first before speaking to the client.
    - The lawyer may be legally responsible for your conduct, including what you say.
    - The lawyer may seek to direct what you say or do.
    - The lawyer may have specific instructions for you before you interpret or introduce yourself to the client.
2. In mental health therapy, address the therapist first.
    - For example, the therapist may have specific concerns about how you introduce yourself, how you are positioned and what you will do and say—even for your introduction.
    - The therapist is responsible for creating a bond of trust with the patient (a relationship often referred to in English as the therapeutic alliance) and will not want you to say or do anything that might interfere with building it.
    - From the start, the interpreter will need to take the lead from the therapist in order, for example, to avoid having the interpreter potentially cause inadvertent harm (such as retraumatizing a patient).

Remember that your introduction is the precious time when you speak as yourself and can establish professional rapport with participants.

Best practices for the remote interpreter's introduction

There are no international standard practices for a remote interpreter's introduction and what it should include. In many cases, however, the introduction will ideally include at least the following elements (time permitting):

- Your first name, your interpreter title and/or your interpreter ID number as well as your language pair.
- State that everything in the session will be interpreted completely without adding, changing or omitting anything.[69]
- State that everything will be kept confidential by the interpreter.
- Request that participants speak to each other, not to you.

[69] This point is important to emphasize because so many participants are unaware you will do this and may think they can say things to you privately during the session.

In addition, because remote interpreting is still unfamiliar to many, when a participant indicates they are new to this modality, take advantage! Use the time to provide brief technical and logistical instructions that will help make for a smoother session.

Sample remote interpreter introduction

"Hello, my name is Sarah, interpreter ID 1234. I will be your Spanish<>English interpreter. Can you [see me and] hear me well?

- I will be interpreting everything that is said.
- Please speak to each other, not to me.
- Speak in a loud, clear tone and pause often.
- Everything I interpret will remain confidential.
- (*For community or legal interpreting, to the service provider or requester*) Is there anything I should know before we begin?
- (*After introductions with all participants have been completed*) All right, please go ahead."

> **When a Technical Problem Arises During Your Introduction**
>
> If participants answer that they cannot see you or hear you well during your introduction, you should be ready to address tech issues before moving on. See the previous section of this chapter and Chapter 3 of this volume for more information about problem-solving technical issues.

If participants indicate they are new to working with a remote interpreter and time permits, you may want to add some or all of the following:

- "I may intervene to ask for clarification or repetition, especially if there are audio [or visual] challenges."
- "I may ask you to reposition the device for optimal setup."
- "Who is participating in the session today, and what are their roles?"
- "Please remember to speak one at a time and allow me time to interpret."

If you are aware that this session involves some participants who speak the same language (for example, an English-speaking adolescent patient, English-speaking physician, and Arabic-speaking family member), give them specific guidelines during the introduction. To avoid the risk of having those who speak the same language monopolize the conversation, remind them to pause frequently in order to keep everyone informed.

Direct speech

Interpreters, including remote interpreters, are expected to interpret in direct speech (commonly referred to as "interpreting in first person"). For example, if someone says, "I don't understand why my electric bill is so high," the interpreter won't say, "They don't understand why their electric bill is high" but will interpret instead, "I don't understand why my electric bill is so high."

Why interpret in direct speech (first person)?

Let's look at examples of direct and indirect speech:

> Direct speech (first person):[70] "I have a lot of pain."
>
> Indirect speech (third person): "He says he has a lot of pain."

Although the second statement is still generally accurate, using indirect speech means the interpreter is reporting on the speech and talking *about* it—not rendering it. That indirectness leaves room to include the interpreter's sense of what the person is saying, resulting in possible additions that reflect the interpreter's conscious or unconscious "edits" of the message. This tendency becomes riskier if more content is included in—or omitted from—the message.

Let's look at another example:

> Direct speech: "Are you going to give me any medication for the pain? It still hurts a lot, but I've heard taking too many pain meds can cause constipation."
>
> Indirect speech: "She's asking if she'll be getting any meds for her pain and if those meds will cause constipation in the future."

If you simply read that second example, maybe the rendition doesn't seem too distant from the first. It may still seem roughly accurate. However, look closer and you'll see that the message and nuance the speaker expressed of still having a lot of pain is omitted. The reasoning behind the question about constipation is also omitted. The addition of the phrase "in the future" may also cause for a slightly different understanding of what is being asked.

Interpreting in direct speech can reduce confusion

Now imagine how confusing things can get when retelling a story involving more than one person:

> Direct speech: "I came into the room. You weren't there. She [your daughter] was taking some pills."
>
> Indirect speech: "She came into the room when you weren't there and she said she was taking some pills."

Doesn't it sound like mom was taking the pills when it was the daughter who did it?

Other advantages of direct speech

Accuracy isn't the only reason to interpret in direct speech. Compared to indirect speech, interpreting in direct speech:

- Is faster.
- Is easier than interpreting in indirect speech.

---

[70] Note that if one person says, "So you're in a lot of pain," and the interpreter interprets, "Ah, you're in a lot of pain," it sounds as if you're interpreting in second person! To say that you are interpreting in *direct* vs. *indirect* speech is more accurate—and less confusing—than saying that you are interpreting in first or third person.

- Promotes more direct communication among participants.
- Doesn't result in as many interpreter changes to the message, including additions or omissions.
- Has simpler sentence structures that are easier to remember and interpret.
- Is less tiring to interpret.

Referring to Yourself as "the Interpreter"

That said, interpreters—and remote interpreters in particular—may sometimes wish to refer to themselves indirectly (third person) for clarity when they intervene to ask for a repetition, request a clarification or address a communication breakdown. For example, they might say, "The interpreter needs clarification."

However, unless your language service or organization requires you to identify yourself as the interpreter this way (some do) only court interpreters are typically *obligated* to refer to themselves as "the interpreter" when they intervene. Other remote interpreters may have a bit more flexibility to intervene in other ways, for example, "Interpreter speaking. Can you repeat that for me?" or "This is the interpreter. I didn't hear what you just said." (Remember, of course, to interpret or report whatever you say or sign for any other participants.)

Unless otherwise required by your language service, use the wording that works best for you when you intervene. It should be brief and clear and flow well in the corresponding language.

For court remote interpreting, if you intervene, you are typically *required* to refer to yourself as "the interpreter." There are almost no exceptions here due to the need for clarity in the written court record.

Indirect speech

Why not interpret in indirect speech?

In addition to the confusion and inaccuracies it can cause, interpreting in indirect speech highlights the interpreter and what they say rather than the speaker. It brings other problems. For example, compared to interpreting in direct speech, interpreting in indirect speech typically:

- Is slower.
- Is less direct.
- Can be difficult to interpret (it usually requires changing the syntax).
- Tends to lead to more complex sentence structures.
- Can cause confusion.

Exceptions

Every rule carries exceptions. Here are a few cases when a remote interpreter might need to interpret in indirect speech:

- A participant is getting confused:
  - Perhaps this person is a child, elderly or has mental disabilities or delays and gets confused by the use of direct speech.

- The participant is confused due to substance abuse.
- A participant is confused due to unfamiliarity with video or audio conferencing.

- An emergency situation prompts you to summarize.[71]
- Multiple participants, such as family members, are communicating in the session. Face-to-face interpreters may use a gesture to indicate who said what, but it may be more effective for a remote interpreter to switch to indirect speech.
- The content is so horrific (for example, torture, rape or murder) that you feel the need to detach yourself briefly for self-care. ***This is a controversial recommendation for legal interpreting. Do not switch to indirect speech in legal interpreting. Also, always switch back to direct speech as soon as possible.***

Interpreting in direct speech gives the speakers responsibility for their communication and helps to take you "out of the picture." It focuses you on the message content and not what you think about the message. Interpreting in direct speech is also less intrusive.

Remember too that it is often easy to tell untrained interpreters from trained ones, because most untrained interpreters tend to interpret routinely using indirect speech. Interpreting in direct speech is one hallmark of professionalism.

Turn-taking

What "turn-taking" means

Turn-taking is a term of art (a technical term) that refers to maintaining a flow of communication that allows you to interpret accurately everything that is being stated by all participants. You may find this term more common in Europe and certain parts of the world while in the U.S. you may often hear the term, "managing the flow." The concept remains the same: no matter which mode you interpret in, one participant speaks or signs at a time. Additionally, in consecutive interpreting, participants pause for you at adequate intervals for you to interpret accurately between utterances.

If, however, people speak or sign too quickly without pausing often enough for you to interpret (for consecutive mode), or if they speak or sign at the same time, you will need to take control to address that problem.

The need to take control is the same in face-to-face and remote interpreting. Managing the flow, however, can be a greater challenge in remote interpreting.

Turn-taking management challenges in remote interpreting

All interpreters must manage turn-taking and flow in order to maintain accuracy. Yet it can be difficult for many interpreters to interrupt a speaker, especially an authority figure, such as a police officer, doctor, teacher or lawyer.

---

[71] **Note:** Summarization is a "last resort" coping strategy. It was discussed in Section 4.1. Remember to disclose performing it (as soon as you are able).

Learning to professionally, and confidently, interrupt someone so you can avoid summarizing is a critical part of remote interpreting. It is one reason why your assertiveness skills are so important.

Interpreters who have gone from face-to-face to remote interpreting may find they need to intervene assertively more often, especially if participants are in the same physical location. Even over video, the use of physical body language by the interpreter to interrupt is less reliably visible over a screen than face to face.

Also, be prepared for emotional situations that can make managing turn-taking even more challenging, for example, someone who is crying and extremely upset, shouting in anger, participants speaking over one another and so forth.

Other—often bigger—challenges

Turn-taking management becomes even more challenging when you interpret remotely for a larger group of people—and you are the only one located remotely. For example:

- You may have difficulties hearing and understanding the speakers due to background noise.
- Some of the attendees may be interrupting each other, expressing frustration or talking over each other.
- As a result, you may feel overwhelmed and you may not be able to do your job accurately.

This is where your assertiveness skills come in. Intervene to suggest solutions to reduce the challenges. For example, ask participants to speak one at a time.

The problem of the one-sentence interpreter

If you interpret primarily in consecutive mode, you will need to hone your memory and note-taking skills even more in remote interpreting than face-to-face interpreting because interrupting participants is both harder to do and more disruptive to the flow. Building these skills will take practice and time. It is essential, however.

Memory and note-taking will allow you to interpret accurately without having to interrupt speakers midthought. You don't want to be the "one-sentence interpreter!" This famous "one-sentence interpreter" is the one who does not wait for a pause in the conversation and interrupts the participant after every sentence in order to interpret, perhaps fearing they will forget what was just stated.

When to ask for pauses

Try not to ask for pauses unless and until:

- At least one full idea has been expressed.
- Your memory capacity is full.
- More than one participant is speaking/signing at once.
- Participants who use the same language are conversing without allowing time for interpretation.
- A linguistic or cultural barrier arises.

When you request pauses, be clear, brief and professional. You may even phrase your request as a reminder referring back to the professional introduction.

> **Using Gestures to Request Pauses in Remote Interpreting**
>
> Many face-to-face interpreters use a gesture to indicate the need for a pause ("T" for time out, palm raised for "stop") or possibly a culturally appropriate tap when the person communicating is a signer. Video interpreters may still employ the gestures but may find they are less effective than other strategies depending on how much visual attention the interpreter is being given. When interpreting remotely, you may need to manage the flow by verbally interrupting the participants.
>
> Signed language remote interpreters rely on participants who are physically present to tap on a signer's shoulder or get into the signer's field of vision to gain their attention. The signer's attention can now be redirected by waving or pointing at the remote interpreter's screen.

Other turn-taking management techniques

While remote interpreters cannot easily employ gestures to gain pauses, they can try other strategies:

- Take more frequent notes (to avoid requesting a pause).
- Jump in at a natural pause or when the speaker takes a breath.
- Match the tone and pace of the original speaker.
    - Take advantage if they are using a calm, steady rhythm, and remember not to rush your own interpretation.
- Ask participants, during your introduction, to speak loudly and clearly.
- Ask participants, during your introduction, to speak or sign one at a time.
- Politely request repositioning the device if needed so that you can hear and see more clearly.

Intervention

The act of speaking in your own voice to address a communication concern is often called mediation (or intervention, especially in U.S. healthcare interpreting).

When intervening in remote interpreting, consistently identify yourself as the interpreter in both languages. While many novice interpreters struggle with this protocol, it really does help to avoid confusion and make clear who is asking for the clarification.

To be *transparent,* make sure that everyone in the session knows what is happening by following these steps for strategic mediation (discussed in detail in Chapter 7 of this volume):

1. Interpret what was just said or signed.
2. Identify yourself as the interpreter and inform that participant what you are about to tell the other participant.
3. Identify yourself as the interpreter and mediate briefly with the other participant.
4. Wait for the other participant to respond and continue interpreting.

How to intervene in remote interpreting is one of the topics included in Chapter 7 of this volume.

Hold time

Most interpreters who have worked in face-to-face settings can tell you there are moments of downtime in which they are simply waiting for one or all participants to arrive.

To remain impartial, the interpreter in these cases, at least in the U.S., are often advised to step out of the room whenever one of the participants does so in order to avoid being alone with the other participant.

Remotely, there are these moments of downtime too. However, the remote interpreter has to hold the line. In other words—the remote interpreter *has* to be "alone" with one participant (often a service user).

Just as in face-to-face interpreting, remote interpreters should not really remain alone with participants and certainly will ideally not engage in side conversations. Some language services may instruct their interpreters to mute themselves and pause their video while waiting for someone to return. Others might have the interpreter request that the device be removed from the room while waiting for a participant as a way to "step out of the room."

As far as how long to wait, many language services that offer on-demand interpreting have guidelines for a maximum time frame to wait when no interpreting is taking place, partly in order not to overcharge the customers for downtime with no interpreting.

In addition, as interpreters, we are valuable resources! Rather than hold indefinitely, we want to make ourselves available to others who may need our services. Whatever the wait time is, and even if your organization has none and you need to establish one yourself, be transparent with participants. Let them know beforehand the maximum time you are able to hold.

However, be flexible if the situation is sensitive: in some cases, you might need to hold longer than you normally would. Remember, ask yourself if it would do more harm than good to disconnect.

Some language services may have interpreters accept both OPI and VRI calls to meet demand for that language. This allows the remote interpreter to cover more sessions and language services to have that language available to more users. In other cases, signed language interpreters may be interpreting on both VRI and VRS platforms.

If either of these is your case or situation, remember to follow the specific instructions about hold time provided by your language service or organization, if any. Most important of all, if you are using *two* platforms to interpret—perhaps you work for two different organizations as a contractor—focus on the one you are serving at the moment and be sure to be officially unavailable in the other one.

Shadow interpreting

Why shadow interpreting is needed

As interpreters, at times we encounter situations in which participants can communicate well enough without needing us to interpret most of the time. Participants may communicate in a shared language; however, they wish (or are required) to have an interpreter on standby in case communication breaks down.

For example, let's say that a Burmese-speaking father attends his son's parent-teacher conference. However, he knows enough English to communicate with the teacher for most of the meeting—but then gets confused by some technical terms in education.

Alternatively, a participant could insist on having someone else interpret, typically a family member or friend, and you are requested to oversee the individual's interpreting.

But what is shadow interpreting?

To perform shadow interpreting means you allow the participants to communicate either directly in one language or through another interpreter while you remain engaged and ready to jump in to interpret as soon as you're needed or requested.

Shadow interpreting is performed in both face-to-face and remote interpreting—and sometimes both. (That is, sometimes the untrained interpreter is in a face-to-face session while the shadow interpreter works remotely.)

How to be a shadow interpreter

When performing shadow interpreting, make sure to remain transparent by informing all participants what you will be doing, even if it feels obvious to you. Possible shadow interpreting scripts could be:

> "This is the interpreter speaking. I see you are communicating effectively in [English] so I will stand by ready to interpret again as needed."
>
> "Interpreter speaking. I will remain on standby as needed and ready to assist with interpretation."

And remember: no daydreaming. *It's important that you remain engaged in the conversation*, since at any time one participant may run into difficulties or tell you, "Interpreter, how do you say [this]?"

Shadow interpreting may not be permissible

When Shadow Interpreting May Not Be an Option: Two Examples

Depending on the specialization, organization or situational requirements, participants may not be allowed to bring their own interpreters.

It is also not appropriate to shadow interpret when participants share a language if there is another participant in the room who does not understand that language. For example, when an adolescent patient converses directly with the medical provider in English while the father who only speaks Ilocano is present, interpret everything for the father.

Shadow interpreting is *only* appropriate when all parties are communicating clearly and accurately and with the shared agreement that the interpreter can stand by until needed. Not all specializations and scenarios allow shadow interpreting. In some cases, a doctor, attorney or other professional might insist on having the interpreter interpret every part of the session.

When shadow interpreting breaks down

Whenever you decide to shadow, be on the lookout for cues of confusion or misunderstanding, such as a person who starts having trouble finding the words or if answers don't match questions. If you are in doubt, politely intervene to advise all participants that you will resume interpreting in order to ensure accurate communication.

A Warning About Shadow Interpreting

Shadow interpreting can become tricky when participants are overly confident of their own language skills—for example, a lawyer who took high school Spanish and thinks they remember "enough" to speak to their Spanish-speaking client.

While it is never comfortable to bring attention to someone's lack of language proficiency, the risks are too great if the interpreter does not intervene. When in doubt, go ahead and interpret.

→ Section 4.3 Review

This section reviewed seven key interpreting protocols and how they are carried out in remote interpreting:

- Positioning: it is important in remote interpreting to manage the position of both the remote interpreter and the device. Ask for repositioning to enhance the interpretation as needed!
- Professional introduction: briefly explain who you are, your role and your basic requests to all participants before the session.
- Direct speech: using direct speech when you interpret is one hallmark of a professional interpreter. Referring to yourself indirectly (third person) as the interpreter, however, may be the best approach for clarity when you intervene in remote interpreting.
- Turn-taking: management: hone your memory and note-taking skills to allow for the most natural flow of communication.
- Intervention: intervene assertively when needed to maintain accuracy. For example, ask participants to slow down, pause more often or speak one at a time.
- Hold time: be clear and transparent with all participants about how long you can wait and stick to it; be more flexible with sensitive situations.
- Shadow interpreting: participants may communicate in a shared language without your help. However, you need to remain engaged and ready to start interpreting when needed.

You may be asking yourself why these protocols exist and whether following them really makes a difference. As a remote interpreter, you may find it slightly more challenging to establish that personal connection and rapport with the participants that perhaps comes with ease when walking confidently into a face-to-face session. You may be worried about feeling too "robotic" and not "human" enough when following protocols as a remote interpreter. Luckily, with the tips and tricks found in this book and practice, it will all feel natural.

Having interpreter protocols in place helps to set consistent expectations for all participants and reinforces that you are a professional. Following them not only helps your colleagues and the field in general, but you also will likely find greater cooperation from participants when you've set a consistent and professional tone through your use of protocols.

→ Chapter Activities

Activity 4.1 (a): Consecutive role play

Classroom instructions

In small groups, interpret the following role play in consecutive mode according to guidance from your instructor.

Instructions for self-study

1. Record the following role play, either by asking family or friends to play *both* the two roles of the nutritionist and the patient in the *language of the nutritionist or* by reading out and recording both the roles yourself. (Yes, the exercise will still be helpful if you record it yourself!)

Note: If you have a study partner, don't record the role play: instead, let your partner read out both roles to you.

2. Prepare to record yourself interpreting. Test your device.
3. Play the recording—*or have your partner read the two roles for you*—and pause the recording or your partner's reading as needed to interpret, but try to pause as rarely as possible. Record your performance.
4. Review the recording and note down three aspects of your performance that you thought were strong and three that needed improving. If you have a partner, discuss them with your partner.
5. If you have a partner, reverse the exercise so that your partner can play the interpreter.

Three strong aspects of your performance

Three aspects of your performance that you would like to improve

Can you identify *why* and *how* you need to improve?

Note: This role play addresses an appointment with a nutritionist. Both the nutritionist and the adolescent patient speak the same language; the mother does not. As the interpreter, you will interpret for the mother.

NUTRITIONIST: How's everything been going? How's school?

PATIENT: It's OK.

NUTRITIONIST: Have you been getting more movement like we talked about? Your mom told me this semester you have PE[72] in school.

PATIENT: Yeah...

NUTRITIONIST: Do you have PE every day?

PATIENT: Yes.

NUTRITIONIST: Yes and how long?

PATIENT: (*mumbling—hard to hear*) Forty minutes. Well, it's thirty-five to thirty minutes when we do any exercise outside, or forty minutes of sports.

NUTRITIONIST: Do you like PE?

PATIENT: Not really. We don't do anything fun.

NUTRITIONIST: How has your diabetes been?

PATIENT: The usual.

NUTRITIONIST: Have you been comfortable with the new vegetarian plan?

PATIENT: Yeah, but all my mom really cares about is my weight, she's always complaining. And I *do* eat fruit and vegetables, I *do* try hard, but she doesn't believe me, she keeps saying she loves me but she won't leave me alone about it.

NUTRITIONIST: Well, obviously we all want you to be happy and healthy, and that's what matters. I think the reason your mom worries isn't because of how you look on the outside, it's because

[72] PE refers to physical education classes in school systems in English-speaking countries.

of what all that weight does on the inside. When there's too much fat and wobbly stuff—and we all have it a little—but if we get too much of it, we get problems on the inside like with the heart, the liver, the intestines, because all those things on the inside of you get bigger and it gets harder to move and to exercise and to breathe and so on.

PATIENT: Well, my dad says things like, "You're not built for speed, you're built for comfort." And when they tell me things like that, I just want to eat more.

NUTRITIONIST: I'm not asking you about this vegetarian plan because I think you don't look good. I think your parents are just worried what will happen in five or ten years if you get high blood pressure or high cholesterol and triglycerides. And I know these words don't mean anything to you, but they are things that will affect you, and parents worry about all that.

PATIENT: I wish they'd worry more about whether I'm happy or not. I do like meat. I miss meat. I want to eat more hamburgers, like a regular kid.

NUTRITIONIST: I know it's tough to be a kid with diabetes, but we want you to live a long, long life and be healthy. And I know right now it bothers you, but yes, it's going to be hard to live a normal life with diabetes if you don't watch carefully. I know you're young and you may not care right now, but there's some great research that says if you can just stick to the vegetarian plan, it can really help you manage your diabetes and your weight and lower your risk of heart disease when you get older. But you have to make those changes for real. Can you commit to working with your parents to find new vegetarian dishes that taste really, really good to you? And get more movement in PE?

PATIENT: Well. My mom is starting to figure out a few vegetarian recipes that aren't half bad. And my dad is grilling portobello mushrooms and fake chicken and things. They're trying.

NUTRITIONIST: You're old enough to try too, and you're the one who knows what tastes good to you. Help them experiment. Look up cool recipes online with ingredients that taste good to you. It's amazing what you can find. Try it out. You can do this!

After interpreting, write down your answers to the following questions. If you have classmates, discuss your answers:

a. What was easy and what was difficult about interpreting this script?

Focus the discussion on having to keep up and interpret everything despite the two speakers sharing a common language. Did pauses come less naturally due to both speakers using English?

b. Were you able to interpret everything?

Be honest. Consider rereading the script to confirm this. Students may realize they left something out upon hearing it again.

c. What strategy would you, or did you, use to be as accurate as possible?

You will find many strategies for accuracy throughout this chapter and the book.

d. Were there any words or phrases you didn't understand?

There are strategies to address unknown words, and this chapter and others in this book will address them. Don't worry. You're not expected to know everything!

e. Was there a word that you don't know the equivalent of in your other language? Or that has no equivalent in your other language?

There are helpful strategies to address unknown words or words without equivalents that were covered in this chapter.

Activity 4.1 (b): Parroting

Classroom instructions

1. Your instructor will read the following text out loud to the group.
2. Close this book.
3. Repeat what your instructor says, in the same language, *while* your instructor is reading the text.

Instructions for self-study

1. Have a friend or family member record the following text at a rate that is neither fast nor slow, or if that is not possible, record it yourself.
2. Alternatively, if you have a study partner, let that person read the text out loud to you in any language.
3. Play back the recording or listen to your partner.
4. As you listen, repeat what you hear *in the same language,* and do so *while* you are listening.
5. After completing the exercise, decide which kinds of recordings from the internet, television or radio (spoken or signed at reasonable speeds) that you might like to practice parroting and write down at least three examples.

> "I'm a medical interpreter working primarily onsite, and as an independent contractor, I work with several local agencies. And just like with virtually all other jobs, mine has also been affected by COVID-19. My schedule has always been unpredictable, and along with last-minute requests, cancellations and patient no-shows were nothing unusual. However, starting in mid-March [of 2020], just as the first stay-at-home order was issued in my state, there were nothing but cancellations and no-shows. Then the appointments stopped coming. Although one agency was still sending me requests, they were mostly at the local hospital where all the COVID-19 patients were being taken at the time. Every time I received a request, part of me wanted to take that job—after all, I still needed to make a living and this might be the only job I'd get that day. I also worried that if nobody was going out there to interpret, patients would be left without adequate language access. On the other hand, I was wondering whether that one-hour fee was worth the risk I was taking going to the hospital when much was still unknown about the virus and universal mask wearing wasn't yet adopted."

Three examples of recordings (from the internet, television or radio) that I will record and practice parroting:

1.______________________________

____

2.______________________________

____

3.______________________________

____

Activity 4.2 (a): Paraphrasing

Classroom instructions

1. The instructor will say the following list of words out loud while the class members call out equivalents (at the same time, *in the same language*) by paraphrasing each word.

2. It does not matter if the instructor can hear all the answers.

3. The instructor might wish to write down some of the answers on a flipchart or a screen projection to discuss.

Instructions for self-study

1. If possible, have someone read out the list of words below while you paraphrase them.

2. If that is not possible, record them.

3. As you listen to the recording or your partner, pause after each word and speak or sign as many possible equivalents as you can in the same language as quickly as possible.

- Candy
- Hill
- Store
- Car
- Party
- Fun
- Danger
- Storm
- Delicious
- Wide

- Quickly
- Difficult
- Leader
- Pain
- Successful

Activity 4.2 (b): Being assertive

How would you handle the following scenarios in remote interpreting if simultaneous is *not* an option?

1. You are interpreting for a government agency and a mother about a paternity test to determine child support, and a friend is accompanying the mother. The two start having a fast side conversation unrelated to the session, and you are unable to keep up. What can you say or do as the interpreter?
2. You are interpreting for a parent-teacher conference where the mother and father, who are divorced, are both present. The mother and father start arguing about how to address some of the teacher's concerns with their child. They ignore your attempts to ask them to take turns speaking. What can you say or do as the interpreter?
3. You are interpreting for an emergency room patient who is severely injured. The patient speaks quickly, stating what happened to them. Multiple doctors in the room are talking over one another while tending to the patient's injuries and asking you what the patient is saying. What can you say or do as the interpreter?
4. You are interpreting for a fifth-grade student with special needs, the mother and four school representatives. The mother has brought other children. The student and younger siblings are quite noisy, making it difficult for you to hear everything. In addition, the school staff and mother talk over one another. What can you say or do as the interpreter?

Note: Remember that remote interpreters in some situations will need to firmly remind speakers to speak one at a time or else they cannot interpret accurately. Sometimes you may have to interrupt participants in order to start interpreting. As a last resort, including emergency situations, interpreters may have to summarize. In all cases, you can be assertive as long as you remain calm and professional.

Activity 4.2 (c): Practice being assertive

Instructions

1. Practice being assertive by reading the situation below and the example of one possible assertive response and then, *without* rereading the response or looking at it, write out your own script for how to handle the same situation as a remote interpreter. (You can reread the situation but, if so, be sure to cover up the script beneath it.)

2. Now write a second, *different* script for how to handle the same situation, again without looking at the sample response below.
3. Reread both your scripts, compare them to the example below, and adjust them both until you are happy with your own two scripts.
4. Now say or sign all three of the assertive scripts, adjusting any of them or all of them until all three feel comfortable for you to speak or sign.
5. Next, record yourself reading all of them out loud or signing them.
6. Review the recording. Pay attention to your tone, confidence and assertiveness. Again, make adjustments to the scripts as needed.
7. Now practice all three of them again but this time without looking at the scripts.
8. When you feel confident speaking or signing them without reading the scripts, record yourself again.
9. Write down how you feel about your recordings and what you can do to appear and sound more assertive (if needed).

   You are interpreting for a customer service interaction for a bill dispute. The representative needs to place the caller on hold and instructs you, the interpreter, to explain why the charges can't be removed in the meantime:

Assertive approach, Example 1: "This is the interpreter speaking. If you can go ahead and speak directly to the caller, I would be happy to interpret for you. Otherwise, I'll stand by until you're back on the line. I'll inform the caller what was just said. Thank you."

Assertive approach, Example 2: ______________________________

____

____

____

Assertive approach, Example 3: ______________________________

____

____

____

____

How do you feel about your recordings of these three scripts?

What could you do to appear or sound more assertive (if needed)?

Activity 4.2 (d): Plan which skills to work on

Instructions

Using Figure 4.14, rank each interpreting skill area from 1 to 9 in order of importance for you (1 being most important, 9 being least important). Then list your plan of how you will work on improving that skill area in the space provided.

I need to work on...	Priority ranking (1-9)	I will work on it by...
Memory skills		
Note-taking		
Assertiveness		
Ability to pick up on context		
Information search		
Handling location-specific information		
Improving knowledge of language variation		
Coping with loss of visual cues		
Addressing tech issues		

Figure 4.14: **Rank interpreting skills**

Note: Once you develop one skill area, it will become more automatic and easier to do alongside other tasks.

Activity 4.2 (e): Practice your consecutive interpreting skills

Classroom instructions

1. Repeat the role play in Activity 4.1 (a) according to the directions of your instructor but this time practice the skill sets you reviewed in Section 4.2.

2. Interpret the role play consecutively: do not switch to simultaneous. Find the pauses and rely on your memory and note-taking skills to interpret accurately.

3. After completing the role play, answer the questions following the instructions.

Instructions for self-study

1. Unless you have a partner (or two) to read the two parts of the role play in Activity 4.1 (a) out loud, use the same recording that you made for that role play.

2. Interpret the role play, and record your interpreting of the role play, just as you did before, with these changes:

   a. Do not pause the recording, or your partner, to interpret until each speaker (the nutritionist or the patient) has finished the whole segment.

b. If that is not possible, practice the scripts discussed in Section 4.2 for intervening assertively.

c. Consciously practice the skills discussed in Section 4.2 of this chapter while you interpret, with a particular focus on using memory skills and note-taking to extend your ability to interpret longer segments.

3. After completing the role play, review the recording and answer the following questions.

Questions

- Were you able to wait for each speaker to finish and still interpret accurately (without switching to simultaneous)? YES______ NO ______
- If there were any omissions, changes or additions, what can you work on to improve accuracy?

  a. Ask for more pauses. YES______ NO ______

  b. Request clarification of unknown terms. YES______ NO ______

  c. Develop stronger note-taking skills. YES______ NO ______

  d. Develop short-term memory skills. YES______ NO ______

  e. Other YES______ NO ______

  If "y: ," specify which skills you may need to develop.

- Did you assertively intervene as needed? YES______ NO ______
- If there were any challenges, what did/would you say?

Practice your assertive script asking for pauses and repeat the role play to see how it helps your interpretation.

Activity 4.2 (f): Practice your consecutive and simultaneous interpreting skills

Instructions

1. Listen to the following audio clips of speakers of different varieties of English talking about making desserts.

2. On your first listen, note down any words or phrases that you do not understand.

3. Find the meaning of those words or phrases and listen again until you fully comprehend the message.

4. Once you understand the message, listen to the clips one more time and interpret each one first consecutively, and then simultaneously, into your non-English language, using the skills discussed in this chapter.

https://www.youtube.com/watch?v=LqYc0HDZjZI

https://www.youtube.com/watch?v=WevyYEmCDp8

https://www.youtube.com/watch?v=GMt6uoBWbQw

https://www.youtube.com/watch?v=dYLRjOqe5gI

Activity 4.3 (a): Write your remote interpreter introduction

Classroom instructions

1. Write your remote interpreter introduction in both or all your working languages (or record it if you are a sign language interpreter).
2. Divide into pairs and take turns acting the script out, with a partner.
3. Ask others to give you feedback on these areas: voice quality, confidence, ease, tone, professionalism, clear voice, good diction, easy-to-understand language and lack of grammatical errors.

Instructions for self-study

1. Write your remote interpreter introduction in both or all your working languages (or rehearse the signs if you are a sign language interpreter).
2. Act out the introduction in your working languages while you record it.
3. Review your recording and evaluate your introduction in each language by focusing on these areas: voice quality, confidence, ease, tone, professionalism, clear voice, good diction, easy-to-understand language and lack of grammatical errors.

Activity 4.3 (b): What to say when you manage turn-taking

Instructions

Read the following scenario and answer the question that follows it.

Credit Card Fraud

The Williams family is on vacation in another country. Unfortunately, they had an emergency and need to pay for medical services up front. As they are trying to pay, their credit card gets declined twice. Due to the crisis of the emergency, feeling vulnerable and not understanding the local language, the father is nervous and upset. He tries to call the bank using a local telephone number but has no luck until the fourth time. He is finally able to talk to a bank representative through an interpreter:

> **Father:** I'm calling because I need to know why my credit card has been declined twice. I am in the middle of an emergency. I need to use it. I checked and made sure we had enough money available before traveling!

Bank representative: Good afternoon, sir, we notice that your charges exceed the credit limit in your credit card. Did you not charge your credit card for a total of three thousand dollars last night from Idaho?

Father: *No*! This is crazy! It took me forever to get a hold of the bank. I can barely hear you. My daughter is in the emergency room of a foreign country. We don't understand a word of what the hospital staff are saying. They will not treat her if they can't have a deposit of two thousand dollars…and you are telling me I *have no* money available on my credit card?!...And how could I have made those charges from Idaho? I'm not even in the U.S.! I'm telling you, this is an *emergency*! I need that money NOW!

Let's assume that simultaneous mode is not an option for this case because you are interpreting OPI or VRI (or, in sign language, that father is signing too quickly and in too small a space for you to see clearly at that speed). Choose from **one** of the following scripts to intervene:

1. "Sir, this is the interpreter. I cannot keep up with everything you're saying when you speak [sign] so much. Please remember to pause."
2. "Sir, this is the interpreter. To allow me to interpret everything you're stating, can you please start over and remember to pause?"
3. "Sir, this is the interpreter. I've had this situation too and I understand how difficult it is. Please, calm down. We'll get this taken care of!"
4. "Sir, this is the interpreter. I will summarize what you're saying because the rep doesn't need all those details. Please stick to only answering the question. Thank you."

Chapter Conclusion and Review

This chapter focused on three key areas: interpreting modes, skills and protocols as they apply to remote interpreting. In brief:

Section 4.1 reviewed the two main interpreting modes, consecutive and simultaneous, and in which circumstances each is used in remote interpreting. It also reviewed the mode of sight translation, which is seldom used in remote interpreting, and the coping strategy of summarization.

Section 4.2 discussed how interpreting skills apply in remote interpreting. Message transfer skills are important in any mode, modality and specialization of interpreting. The logistics of note-taking in remote interpreting are different than in face-to-face. Problem-solving and assertiveness come in handy in any remote interpretation. Many common problems that arise in remote interpreting can be more easily addressed once you develop skills to perform multiple tasks at the same time. Assertiveness gives you the ability to be firm and state things confidently in a calm way. You also reviewed suggestions on how to build a toolkit to evaluate your needs and identify the path to take when it comes to solving problems in remote interpreting.

Section 4.3 explored seven protocols and how they are carried out in remote interpreting. These are positioning (of all participants and remote interpreting devices), professional introductions (here you give some "rules" to all participants), direct speech (use first person for most situations), turn-taking (allow for natural pauses in the conversation but intervene if there are no natural pauses), intervention (stepping out of interpreting), hold time (follow your organization's guidelines but be flexible in sensitive situations), and shadow interpreting (be ready with scripts to allow participants to communicate without your interpreting but stay engaged to interpret when needed). When applied consistently, participants will likely cooperate and earn a greater respect for the interpreting profession and its professionals.

Chapter 5

Danielle Meder, RID-NIC

Remote Interpreter Evaluation

Learning Objectives

After completing this chapter, the remote interpreter will be able to:

Learning Objective 5.1: Describe a performance evaluation tool and list reasons for using it.

Learning Objective 5.2: Evaluate their performance when starting and closing sessions.

Learning Objective 5.3: Evaluate how they manage technology and engage in the session.

Learning Objective 5.4: Evaluate their ability to engage in practices that support communicative autonomy.

Learning Objective 5.5: Evaluate how they engage proactively with participants during the session.

Learning Objective 5.6: Evaluate their accuracy during the session.

Learning Objective 5.7: Evaluate how they convey the meaning and style of the source message.

Learning Objective 5.8: Evaluate how effectively they work across all three interpreting modes—consecutive, simultaneous and sight translation—and their note-taking strategies.

Learning Objective 5.9: Evaluate how effectively they use, research and verify context-appropriate terminology.

Learning Objective 5.10: Discuss how to use The Remote Interpreter Evaluation Tool with other interpreters.

Introduction

So far in this textbook, you've learned valuable strategies, tools and techniques to help you understand and perform effective remote interpreting. As a practicing professional, however, you also need to evaluate your own performance. While you have engaged in exercises that involved assessing your performance informally, this chapter will show you how to evaluate yourself rigorously.

Remote interpreting can feel lonely. Whether you work from home, a call center or another secure location, your only engagement with other interpreters may be when you work as a team.

This isolation means you may find it difficult to get feedback on your work. In some cases, your performance might be evaluated as part of a quality assurance (QA) program for a language service (see Chapter 8 of this volume). Yet even if you have the support of a QA program that gives you monitoring and coaching, it's still important to make self-evaluation part of your routine practice.

While self-evaluation is wonderful for your own growth as an interpreter, it's equally important for the profession. When interpreters regularly evaluate their performance and use their evaluation as a tool to improve their performance, the quality of their work improves. In addition, quality interpreting supports communicative autonomy.

Evaluating yourself can feel daunting, yes—but we promise it's worth it. The evaluation tool we will introduce in this chapter can also be used to help interpreters evaluate each other, as peers, or to assist supervisors and QA staff who evaluate interpreters.

As you've read earlier, when you work remotely your client list can be local, national or even global. As a result, your peer network can be global too. Self-evaluation is necessary. It's a professional obligation. When you partner with *other* interpreters and help each *other* improve, everyone succeeds.

When you're a remote interpreter, this partner support can happen no matter where you live or work. This chapter will walk you through how to systematically evaluate the quality of your interpreting. It will also delve into the ever-important soft skills. Soft skills are not your interpreting skills in any direct way, but they are skills that help you interact well with other people and your work, including communication and problem-solving skills, flexibility, a strong work ethic, reliability, interpersonal skills, teamwork, time management and more.

This chapter will clearly explain how you can use the evaluation tool we've developed for remote interpreters. It will also show you how to use it with your peers.

Section 5.1 The Remote Interpreter Evaluation Tool

→ Learning objective 5.1

After completing this section, the remote interpreter will be able to describe a performance evaluation tool and list reasons for using it.

→ Section 5.1 Overview

This chapter introduces The Remote Interpreter Evaluation Tool. This tool is a guide to help you assess your interpreting performance or the performance of other interpreters. Please refer closely to pages 261-262 as you work through this chapter.

If you have an electronic copy of this book, you can display The Remote Interpreter Evaluation Tool on another screen as you read.

The evaluation tool is just that: a tool. You can look it up after every time you interpret. It is a valuable resource. Whether or not you keep a print a copy, *make sure to keep the two pages of the tool somewhere easy to find so that you can refer to them easily and often.*

→ Section 5.1 Content

Reflective practice and the remote interpreter

Reflective practice is a term used to refer to self-evaluation that anyone in a profession performs as a way of improving and enhancing one's performance. Certainly interpreters need to engage in it regularly.

How reflective practice works

For interpreters, perhaps the most important aspects of reflective practice to learn are:

- Observe your own performance as an interpreter *while* you interpret and especially *after* you interpret.
  - Ideally, when appropriate, record your interpretation and review the recording.
- Observe your peers and colleagues as they interpret.
- Give them targeted feedback for skill development.
- Receive feedback from supervisors (if you have any), colleagues and peers with an open mind.

Why you need to engage in reflective practice

Simply interpreting for a long time does not guarantee you will improve. Without reflective practice, simply interpreting can also reinforce your mistakes and weaknesses. However, when you engage in a thoughtful and intentional practice of self-evaluation and skill development, your interpreting will improve.

Reflective practice can advance your improvements and shorten the time it takes to acquire professional skills and expertise.

How interpreters can evaluate their performance effectively.

Trying to assess your interpreting performance is a challenge. The process is usually subjective because you may not really know how to *measure* your performance.

For interpreter evaluation to be truly effective, it's important to have a set of benchmarks and criteria to help you assess your performance (or the performance of another interpreter).

By having a defined set of criteria, you can consistently track your areas of growth and success and also identify any trends you may notice, especially as your performance improves over time.

The tool introduced in this chapter offers you a *structured* way to assess yourself. It includes two general areas of competency, each with four standards. Each set of standards has benchmarks to assess your performance, and three levels of performance with rating criteria to help you rate yourself as objectively as you can.

Does that sound complicated? It really isn't. Let's look at how to use this tool.

Introducing The Remote Interpreter Evaluation Tool

Limitations of the tool in a specific session

Before we start reviewing the evaluation tool, here is an important point to remember. No two interpreted sessions are the same, and not every interpreted session will present an opportunity to use all your skills and protocols.

However, the evaluation tool includes areas of self-evaluation for as many sessions as possible.

As you learn how to use this tool, don't worry if parts of it don't apply to you often. There will be at least one session where a less commonly used skill or protocol is used, and you'll want to have a way to evaluate your performance for those cases too.

The Remote Interpreter Evaluation Tool: Designed for you

Historically, most evaluation and self-evaluation tools for interpreters were designed to evaluate their performance in face-to-face interpreting. In addition, remote interpreting companies with QA programs typically do not publicly share their tools for evaluating remote interpreters and what they evaluate may differ from one company to another.

This tool is our gift to you. The Remote Interpreter Evaluation Tool *was designed specifically to evaluate the performance of* ***remote*** *interpreters.* You can use it yourself and share it with your peers. You can evaluate the performance of other interpreters and let them use it to evaluate you.

The Remote Interpreter Evaluation Tool is made up of two broad performance areas that we call competencies. Each of these two competencies has four standards. Each standard has two to three benchmarks that describe the range of skills to assess.

Each skill set being assessed is called a standard because you will be measuring your performance against that standard. A standard in this context is simply a performance standard: in other words, a level of skill attainment. Each standard in this tool addresses the *quality* and *effectiveness* of your performance. (A standard in this context it is *not* a standard of practice, which supports your code of ethics.)

Take a look at our visual representation of the eight standards and their benchmarks. On the next two pages, you will find Parts 1 and 2 of the evaluation tool. The first page displays Part 1: General Performance Skills. The second page displays Part 2: Message Transfer Performance Skills.

The Remote Interpreter Evaluation Tool

Part 1: General Performance Skills

Standard 1: Starting and Closing the Session

1.1: Adopts a professional tone and engaged demeanor.
1.2: Provides a complete introduction and closing.

Standard 4: Interactions with Participants

4.1: Instructs participants how to best work with interpreters.
4.2: When intervening, uses professional and culturally appropriate language.

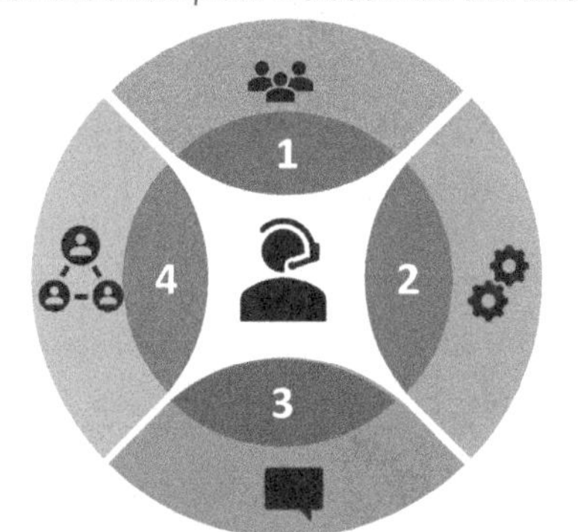

Standard 2: Managing the Session

2.1: Remains professional and calm, using appropriate strategies to manage challenges.
2.2: Stays engaged and focused throughout the session.
2.3: Works in a secure environment throughout the session.

Standard 3: Supporting Communicative Autonomy

3.1: Engages in ethical decision-making that supports communicative autonomy.
3.2: Remains transparent and impartial and redirects participants to speak to each other.
3.3: Intervenes effectively and appropriately to support clear communication.

Figure 5.1: Part 1: General performance skills

The Remote Interpreter Evaluation Tool

Part 2: Message Transfer Performance Skills

Standard 5: Accuracy

5.1: Conveys the content, tone and spirit of the source message.
5.2: Avoids omitting, adding to or changing the message.

Standard 8: Terminology

8.1: Uses correct and context-appropriate terminology.
8.2: Researches or verifies the meaning of specialized terms as needed.

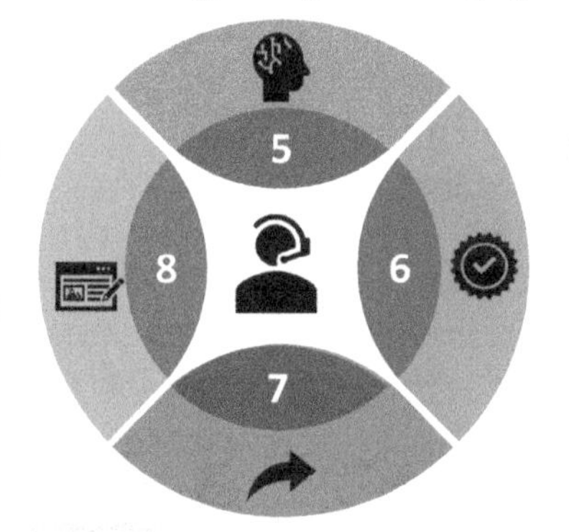

Standard 6: Completeness

6.1: Maintains the language register and style.
6.2: Transparently asks for clarifications, or requests repetitions, as needed.
6.3: Corrects mistakes of interpretation.

Standard 7: Modes

7.4: Selects the appropriate mode, switching as needed.
7.5: Takes notes, when needed, to support accuracy.
7.6: Sight translates if and when appropriate to do so, justifying decisions.

Figure 5.2: **Part 2: Message transfer performance skills**

Look at the structure of the tool

In the following sections, you will read about the standards and benchmarks of The Remote Interpreter Evaluation Tool. For now, examine the structure.

As you can see, all eight standards support the ultimate goal of communicative autonomy so that everyone in the session has the opportunity to engage in direct communication with sufficient understanding to make effective decisions.

In other words, *both parts of this tool evaluate the degree to which the interpreter enables and supports communicative autonomy.*

Also, note that none of the eight standards is more important than any other. They are all interdependent, and all of them contribute to effective communication.

The eight standards

The first four standards in Part 1 of the tool focus on soft skills and how effectively you engage them during a session. The next four standards in Part 2 focus on the linguistic choices you make to support what many interpreting specialists call message transfer skills. Message transfer skills are simply the skills that allow you to interpret accurately and effectively from one language to another while taking social, emotional and cultural contexts into account.

Part 1 of The Remote Interpreter Evaluation Tool

It's important to note that Part 1 of the tool is *language neutral.* The reason for this is that the soft skills assessed in Part 1 do not depend on any particular language.

As a result, anyone can easily evaluate you with Part 1 of this tool, even if they don't fluently speak any of your working languages.

What are soft skills?

Soft skills are interpersonal and social skills, attitudes and abilities that help you perform well and interact positively with others in a typical work environment.

These skills are powerfully important for interpreters—and for remote interpreters in particular, because remote interpreters lack the physical presence that helps to convey those skills. That is one critical reason that soft skills are part of this evaluation tool.

Many of the complaints that language services receive about their remote interpreters, even those with adequate interpreting skills, are caused by the interpreter's poor soft skills. For example, the interpreter may be accurate, but if an interpreter appears to be rude, disengaged, or annoyed, they will make a poor impression anyway.

Soft skills vs. hard skills

The kinds of performance that some call "hard skills" are the ones you learn to perform a particular job well. For interpreters, that usually means performing accurate and complete interpreting that meet the needs of a particular session and the communication styles of the participants.

In contrast, soft skills will help you interact well in almost any workplace.

The importance of soft skills

Soft skills matter because soft skills help you interact well with other people and the job. For example, if your speech style is abrupt, in over the phone interpreting (OPI) people might perceive you as rude even if you feel you are just interpreting. They can't see your face or assess your demeanor.

In video remote interpreting (VRI), if you are bending down to look at your notes, participants might feel you are disengaged and potentially distracted by something unrelated.

That's why soft skills are often part of quality assurance programs in language services. If you work for a large language company, they may monitor you not just to evaluate your interpreting skills; they also make sure you have the kinds of soft skills that make people want to work with you—to avoid getting customer complaints.

For example, almost everyone appreciates working with interpreters who are polite, patient and responsive. These are examples of important soft skills. Other soft skills that people greatly value in remote interpreters include flexibility, a strong work ethic, reliability, interpersonal skills, teamwork and the ability to think quickly and problem-solve.

Your ability to stay calm and focused when the technology breaks down and convey a sense that you are fully engaged at all times are other examples of soft skills. Well-developed soft skills can positively affect your reputation, future work opportunities, and the reputation of interpreters and the organizations they work for.

The four standards of Part 1

Let's look at the four standards in Part 1 of the tool. These address the skills that expert specialists in the field have selected for your general performance skills (including soft skills) because these standards have proven to be critically important for success in remote interpreting. While no one tool can evaluate *all* aspects of your performance, this tool focuses on the most common elements of your work.

Part 2 of The Remote Interpreter Evaluation Tool

Part 2 of the tool requires you (or anyone else who is using the tool to assess you) to be able to evaluate the *accuracy* of your performance. As a result, the tool addresses many of the linguistic and cultural dynamics of the session. While Part 1 of the tool is language neutral, this second part is not; therefore, if you work with a peer on Part 2, it's important they have the same language pair as you.

The four standards in Part 2 address your interpreting skills in the narrow sense, that is, your ability to interpret accurately and completely, taking the social and cultural contexts into account. Many specialists refer to these skills as your message transfer skills.

The goal of Part 2 is to evaluate how accurately you convey the message from one language to another. For example, did you convey the tone, spirit and intent of the source message? Did you interpret *everything* in that message? Are you maintaining the linguistic register? Do you know which mode to use? Can you look up an unfamiliar term online at top speed or verify it with the participant who used it? These are examples of your message transfer skills.

The Remote Interpreter Evaluation Tool rating scale

How to rate your performance (or another interpreter's)

It's not enough to have the tool. You need to know how to use it.

Once you have a recording of your performance, or the recording of another interpreter, the question is how you will use this tool to rate the recording of a specific performance.

The rating scale

This tool has adopted a simple, clear rating scale. The Remote Interpreter Evaluation Tool uses a three-tiered rating scale. It is loosely based on the Interagency Language Roundtable (ILR) scale for proficiency in interpreting, translation, language and competence in intercultural communication.

The original tool was created in the 1950s by the U.S. government Foreign Service Institute and only rated language on a six-point scale. By 1985, it was revised by the ILR to include more skills and descriptions on a five-point scale and became known as the ILR Scale. To simplify it for you, our tool has an adapted version of that rating system that is based on *three* points. The goal here is to make it as easy as possible for you to use the evaluation tool.

The three levels of the rating scale

The Remote Interpreter Evaluation Tool has a three-tiered rating scale. The three tiers are:

1. ***Minimal performance***
2. ***Limited working performance***
3. ***Professional performance***

How do you use it? Give yourself (or another interpreter) one, two or three points as follows:

Minimal performance:	1 point
Limited working performance:	2 points
Professional performance:	3 points

What the three levels means

To use the tool effectively, you also need to understand what each level means so that you know how many points to give yourself (or give to another interpreter) when you perform an evaluation.

Here are the guidelines:

Minimal performance

At this level, the interpreter is unable to perform according to professional standards and best practices for remote interpreting. The interpreter may make ineffective decisions that undermine clear communication and communicative autonomy.

Limited working performance

At this level, the interpreter performs according to professional standards and best practices inconsistently and sometimes makes decisions that don't support clear communication and communicative autonomy.

Professional performance

At this level, the interpreter consistently upholds professional standards and best practices and makes effective decisions that support communicative autonomy throughout the session.

Awarding points for each level

You will be giving yourself points for each level. Of course, your goal over time is to earn three points for each benchmark.

At the back of this book is a scoring template you may use each time you evaluate yourself. It has each standard and benchmark and a space to fill out the points you've earned. By using this scoring template, you can begin to track your performance, identify trends and discover areas where you may need to develop your skills further.

What you'll notice over time for almost all the standards in the tool is that any performance that earns 1 point for a minimal performance means you are starting out and still need a great deal of practice to achieve that standard. Or it may mean that you need to refocus your efforts and consider what might be affecting your ability to score higher.

Scoring 2 points for a limited working performance is usually due to inconsistency in performance. You will need more practice.

Scoring 3 points for a professional performance means that while you can still improve, you have reached a level of professionalism that will make language services, your clients and other organizations want to work with you!

Using the scorecards

At the end of this book on pp. 627-630 and also in Figure 5.3, there are two scorecards. One scorecard is for Part 1 of the tool and the other scorecard is for Part 2 of the tool. As you evaluate and assess your performance, use the scorecards to guide you through the tool. Give yourself a score and take notes on why you earned that score.

You can make copies of this scorecard and use it to track your progress. The tool has eight standards and 20 benchmarks; that's a lot to try and memorize. However, when you use the scorecards to guide you through your evaluation, you can go through the session step by step.

One thing you might notice is there is no total score for the scorecards. This is intentional. The tool is meant to help you focus on the decisions and actions that make up an entire remote interpreting session.

It is possible to earn a 1 in one benchmark, and earn a 3 in all the others and have a strong overall score. However, for the purposes of skill development, an overall score tells the whole story of how you performed. Let the individual scores in each benchmark and standard guide you rather than the overall score.

The Remote Interpreter Evaluation Tool Part 1: General Performance Skills			
Date	**OPI or VRI**	**Score**	**Notes**
Standard			
Standard 1: Starting and Closing the Session			
Benchmark 1.1	Adopts a professional tone and engaged demeanor.		
Benchmark 1.2	Provides a complete introduction and closing.		
Standard 1 Score		–/6	
Standard 2: Managing the Session			
Benchmark 2.1	Remains professional, calm and uses appropriate strategies to manage challenges.		
Benchmark 2.2	Stays engaged and focused throughout the session.		
Benchmark 2.3	Works in a secure environment throughout the session.		
Standard 2 Score		–/9	
Standard 3: Supporting Communicative Autonomy			
Benchmark 3.1	Engages in ethical decision-making that supports communicative autonomy.		
Benchmark 3.2	Remains transparent and impartial and redirects participants to speak to each other.		
Benchmark 3.3	Intervenes effectively and appropriately to support clear communication.		
Standard 3 Score		–/9	
Standard 4: Interactions with Participants			
Benchmark 4.1	Instructs participants how to best work with interpreters.		
Benchmark 4.2	When intervening, uses professional and culturally appropriate language.		
Standard 4 Score		–/6	
Final Notes and Action Plan			

The Remote Interpreter Evaluation Tool Part 2: Message Transfer Performance Skills			
Standard	**OPI or VRI**	**Score**	**Notes**
Standard 5: Accuracy			
Benchmark 5.1	Conveys the content, tone and spirit of the source message.		
Benchmark 5.2	Avoids omitting, adding to or changing the message.		
Standard 5 Score		–/6	
Standard 6: Completeness			
Benchmark 6.1	Maintains the linguistic register and style.		
Benchmark 6.2	Transparently asks for clarifications, or requests repetitions, as needed.		
Benchmark 6.3	Corrects mistakes of interpretation.		
Standard 6 Score		–/9	
Standard 7: Modes			
Benchmark 7.1	Selects the appropriate mode, switching as needed.		
Benchmark 7.2	Takes notes, when needed, to support accuracy.		
Benchmark 7.3	Sight translates if and when appropriate to do so, justifying decisions		
Standard 7 Score		–/9	
Standard 8: Terminology			
Benchmark 8.1	Uses correct and context-appropriate terminology.		
Benchmark 8.2	Researches or verifies the meaning of specialized terms as needed.		
Standard 8 Score		–/6	
Final Notes and Action Plan			

Figure 5.3: **The Remote Interpreter Evaluation Tool scorecards**

→ Section 5.1 Review

Interpreting is a practice profession. In other words, interpreting is not just about knowing: it's about knowing and *doing*.

As a result, there will always be areas of your professional practice that need improvement. Sometimes you will acquire a new skill set (like learning to interpret remotely) or a particular skill you already have may need refreshing (such as note-taking).

Routinely using a self-evaluation tool will help you assess your performance more objectively and consistently. That way you can spot areas of your performance that need improvement. You will also be able to track your skill development and improvement over time.

Most interpreter evaluation tools were designed for face-to-face interpreting. The Remote Interpreter Evaluation Tool was designed for *you*—the remote interpreter—to evaluate your own performance and that of your peers. It has two areas of competency that it assesses: general performance skills and message transfer performance skills. Each of the two areas have four standards with two to three benchmarks and rating criteria.

The tool is easy to use and can be used by experienced or novice interpreters. The following sections will review the tool and each of its eight standards. You will explore questions to ask yourself as you reflect on your work and the impact your decisions have on all participants.

Section 5.2 Standard 1: Evaluate How You Start and Close the Session

→ Learning objective 5.2

After completing this section, the remote interpreter will be able to evaluate their performance when starting and closing sessions.

→ Section 5.2 Overview

When we interpret remotely, we often only have a few moments at the beginning of a session to introduce ourselves and demonstrate our professionalism and then a few seconds to close the session smoothly.

Even if you have the opportunity to meet with event organizers, service providers or other stakeholders ahead of the session, in most cases the participants will base their impressions of you on how you perform during the session itself.

Though this first standard only has two benchmarks, it is an area that can really help advance how interpreters are seen and respected by participants.

→ Section 5.2 Content

Starting and closing the session

Standard 1: Starting and Closing the Session

- Adopts a professional tone and engaged demeanor.
- Provides a complete introduction and closing.

Standard 1: Starting and Closing the Session **Provides complete and fully engaged introductions and signoffs.**
Benchmark 1.1 **Adopts a professional tone and engaged demeanor.**
Criteria 1. Sounds or appears uninterested, distant, annoyed or irritated to one or all participants: 1 point 2. Sounds or appears professional and engaged only at the start of the session: 2 points 3. Sounds or appears professional and engaged at the start of the session and ends the session professionally and personably with all participants: 3 points
Benchmark 1.2 **Provides a complete introduction and closing.**
Criteria 1. Omits appropriate key elements of the introduction (such as name, language and the disclosure that everything will be interpreted): 1 point 2. Gives incomplete introduction, provides introduction to only one participant and/or closes the session with only one participant: 2 points 3. Provides a complete introduction and complete closing to all participants: 3 points

How to measure your performance for Standard 1

Standard 1 addresses how well you provide *complete* introductions and how you sign off with *full engagement.*

The two benchmarks to measure your performance for this standard include your tone of voice and engagement as well as how well and fully you introduce yourself and complete each session.

Tone of voice and engagement

Whether you are on camera (VRI, VRS or RSI) or audio only (OPI/AOI), most participants can tell if you are engaged and professional.

As silly as it may sound, *practice your introduction.* Record yourself performing it. How does it sound? (Or look, for signing?) Practice with the camera on too. How do you appear—confident, smooth and at ease? Do you sound, feel and look *professional*?

The emphasis on tone is an important element to keep in mind. You want to show participants that you are truly present for them and attentive to their communication needs. This level of engagement can be demonstrated through your professionalism, tone, body language and the ways you communicate at the start and close of the session.

In the case of this standard, earning a score below 3 for this benchmark is typically due to inconsistently demonstrating professionalism and engagement at the start or close of the session.

Complete introduction and closing

If you're new to remote interpreting, or even if you just need reminders, sticky notes in a visible place can be useful. Starting and closing sessions can be easily scripted (many language services give you such scripts or you may have your own for your direct clients).

For sessions with specific needs, you can add additional information to your introduction. Your sticky note for a typical session might say:

- Name
- Language
- Identification number (if relevant)
- Will interpret everything
- Intro for ALL participants

You could have these points on your note to remind yourself that *every* time you introduce yourself, you need to include *all* this information, even if certain sessions require you to add other points or introduce yourself differently.

Earning a score below 3 for this benchmark is typically due to an incomplete introduction, an incomplete closing—or both.

→ Section 5.2 Review

Standard 1 of The Remote Interpreter Evaluation Tool helps you evaluate how well you start and close the session. This first standard—beginning and ending your session—is the easiest to perform well every time you work remotely. How you start the session and set it up for success and how you close the session can leave a lasting impression with all participants.

Benchmark 1.1 is used to help you assess your tone and how engaged you appear throughout the session. Benchmark 1.2 helps you examine if you provided a complete introduction and an appropriate closing to the session.

If you are warm, alert and attentive and include all the appropriate elements of your introduction and closing, participants will sense the level of caring and personal attention you give to everything you say and do.

Participants often remember how you begin and end the session. Your level of engagement helps to advance respect for interpreters in general as well as yourself. It also highlights the importance of the professional work that interpreters do to support communicative autonomy.

Section 5.3 Standard 2: Evaluate How You Manage the Session

→ Learning objective 5.3

After completing this section, the remote interpreter will be able to evaluate how they manage technology and engage in the session.

→ Section 5.3 Overview

Remote interpreting requires a certain set of skills and protocols. One of the key skills is managing technology—and remaining calm while doing so.

As this textbook mentions often, remote interpreters may have to provide technical support during a remote session. While doing so may not be the official role of the interpreter, participants often turn to the interpreter to help troubleshoot the technology challenges they face.

Beyond technology management, an interpreter's engagement throughout the session is important. An unengaged interpreter puts communicative autonomy at risk by not allowing everyone to fully express themselves and to have control over what they say. The unengaged interpreter also damages the reputation of interpreters and undermines respect for them.

→ Section 5.3 Content

Managing the session

Standard 2: Managing the Session

- Remains professional, calm and uses appropriate strategies to manage challenges.
- Stays engaged and focused throughout the session.
- Works in a secure environment throughout the session.

Standard 2: Managing the Session **Maintains professional demeanor and focus.**
Benchmark 2.1 **Remains professional, calm and uses appropriate strategies to manage challenges.**
Criteria 1. Becomes agitated and visibly frustrated by difficult elements or dynamics and cannot remain impartial: 1 point 2. Uses strategies to manage the session but struggles to maintain professional composure or impartiality: 2 points 3. Responds to difficult elements or dynamics calmly and impartially, with professionalism: 3 points
Benchmark 2.2 **Stays engaged and focused throughout the session.**
Criteria 1. Participants need to ask the interpreter to interpret and/or interpreter appears distracted: 1 point 2. Interpreter is occasionally prompted by participants to interpret or appears occasionally distracted: 2 points 3. Interpreter is focused on the call and participants at all times; no prompting occurs: 3 points

Benchmark 2.3 **Works in a secure environment throughout the session.**
Criteria 1. Participants can hear background noise, activity or other unprofessional sounds. If on video, visual distractions and intrusions are visible. Confidentiality and security are compromised: 1 point 2. Occasional background noise and/or unprofessional visual elements are detected: 2 points 3. Participants cannot hear background noise, activity or other unprofessional elements. If on video, the environment appears professional, secure and free of distractions: 3 points

When sessions become difficult

This section of the evaluation tool focuses on how you respond when you face challenges during the session. The difficulties could have many different root causes, from technology to rude behavior from participants. However, how you respond is in your control.

Below is a list of just some of the ways a session can become difficult.

- Technology complications
  - Audio cuts in and out.
  - Video is choppy.
- Participant behavior
  - One or more participants interrupt often, making it difficult to interpret.
  - Participants often talk at the same time.
  - A participant mistakenly places blame on the interpreter for misunderstandings when another participant doesn't respond as expected.
- Session content
  - Discussions have high stakes (e.g., divorce, trauma, a fatal diagnosis).
  - Session is emotionally charged.
  - Session includes many unfamiliar terms.

Ultimately, what will help you perform at a level 3 professional performance is to remain calm and impartial.

Remaining professional and calm

"Stay calm" sounds easy. But it can be difficult to do when everyone around you is upset.

At times, interpreters can let their own frustrations show. If you let your agitation or frustration become visible, you undermine communicative autonomy. For example, if a participant feels the interpreter is upset, they may decide not to disclose difficult information and limit what they share. Or a participant might become angry with the interpreter, resulting in the interpreter becoming a part of the session.

When the technology breaks down, being familiar with the platform will help you navigate the challenges. While you may not be able to solve the problem, you can help defuse the tension by remaining calm, suggesting troubleshooting strategies and offering alternative solutions. Such solutions may involve calling in another interpreter, rejoining the session or reaching out to the information technology (IT) department of a language service. Sometimes one of the participants is from an organization that has its own dedicated IT department that may be able to assist.

Depending on the session and how it was requested, there may be other options. It is always best to have some suggestions available and share them calmly when you need to do so.

Some language services may offer you a guide or checklist for troubleshooting technical problems on their platform. If so, be sure to study it carefully and become comfortable with the latest solutions they suggest. Having solutions for common problems in mind will help you stay calm.

Remember, even when sessions become difficult or stressful it is critical for you to stay calm, follow your protocols and remain impartial.

Techniques for remaining calm

A few ways to stay calm are:

- Take a deep breath before you respond.
- Say, "This is the interpreter speaking," every time you intervene to emphasize your role and make clear who is speaking.
- Calmly remind participants that they need to speak one at a time so that you can interpret accurately.
- Remind yourself that any tension between participants is not your responsibility.

During the session you will need to keep your composure, but when the session is complete, use the self-care strategies discussed in Chapter 9 of Volume 2 to help you process your emotions.

After the session

Interpreters are in a unique position. They are necessary to help communication happen, but they are not a part of the communication.

For example, a session is often difficult because of content that challenges your ability to remain impartial and calm (such as someone being treated in a demeaning way, discussion of a suicide attempt or a report of child abuse). After the session closes, or your workday ends, be sure to reflect on how you responded during that session and assess what you can do differently next time.

Sometimes the solution is not accepting certain types of assignments. Other times it may mean having a trusted colleague available after a challenging session to help you debrief.

Staying engaged and focused in a secure environment

Remaining engaged and focused during the entire session and working in a secure environment are critical to show that you respect participants and protect their privacy. What does it look like when you don't honor these requirements? What message does your disengagement or lack of a secure environment send to the participants?

If you're working in a call center as a video remote interpreter, your focus may be pulled to your colleague or friend who walks by. You may look at them as they walk by. You might smile at them or wave. It's a nice gesture to your colleague but it is disrespectful to the people on your screen, and they now know you aren't focused exclusively on them.

You may also glance down at your phone for a brief moment to check a notification that just came on the screen. While your eye gaze may look down for just a moment, *it is obvious to the participants*. If you wear eyeglasses, the reflection of your phone may show up in your glasses and make the distraction even more offensive to the video participants. If you're using a dictionary on your smartphone, letting the participants know you're looking up a term will reassure them that you aren't distracted by something unrelated to the session.

Be sure to remain transparent when you use additional tools to support your interpreting, for example, if you perform note-taking on a tablet or laptop.

The critical importance of a secure environment

Working in a secure environment during the entire session helps promote trust that everything said will be kept confidential. It also demonstrates your professionalism and helps build trust for other interpreters and the profession.

In many cases, and in many countries, a secure environment is also a *legal* obligation, especially in healthcare, legal and social services interpreting.

Below are some ways that interpreters have not had secure environments while working:

- Children are crying in the background.
- The interpreter is doing household chores while working.
- The interpreter is driving while interpreting.
- The interpreter is talking to other people in the room.
- Participants can hear street noises.
- A cat walks across the interpreter's desk and is seen on camera.
- Dogs are heard barking.

You may be shocked, but all these scenarios have happened.

Potential consequences of working in an environment that is not secure

Whether you work in a call center, a home office or any other office, what happens off-screen and within earshot of your microphone can damage the rapport and trust that participants have with you—and with all interpreters in the future.

In addition, you may put both you and the organization you work for at risk of a lawsuit for a legal violation of participant privacy.

Every time you sit down to work, make sure you are in a secure environment where distractions, other people (including colleagues), pets and outside activity won't distract you or interfere with the session.

→ Section 5.3 Review

Standard 2 of The Remote Interpreter Evaluation Tool addresses how well the interpreter manages a session.

This tool has three benchmarks. Benchmark 2.1 is used to assess the degree to which the interpreter remains calm and professional when working on strategies to manage challenges. Benchmark 2.2 addresses how well the interpreter stays engaged and focused throughout the session. Benchmark 2.3 emphasizes the importance of working in a secure environment during the whole session.

To manage the session well, you will need to remain calm and professional at all times—even when technology *fails—and there will be moments when it fails*. You will also need to stay focused and engaged throughout the session and make sure that you work in a secure environment.

Remember: your performance reflects your professionalism and helps teach participants what to expect from interpreters. Trust and rapport take time to build, but failing to stay focused, engaged and calm during difficult sessions can destroy that trust and rapport quickly—and sometimes permanently.

Section 5.4 Standard 3: Evaluate How You Support Communicative Autonomy

→ Learning objective 5.4

After completing this section, the remote interpreter will be able to evaluate their ability to engage in practices that support communicative autonomy.

→ Section 5.4 Overview

This next standard could be considered the essence of what you do as an interpreter. This is the area of your performance where you demonstrate your ability to apply ethical principles, support communicative autonomy and intervene during a session, as needed, to address a communication breakdown.

This standard helps you go beyond observing the words you interpret. You can evaluate your role and presence in the session and how they may affect the communicative autonomy of all participants. It is in this standard where interpreters can closely evaluate when and how they choose to address communication breakdowns and whether or not their strategies are efficient.

→ Section 5.4 Content

Communicative autonomy

By now you've read the words *communicative autonomy* many times throughout the textbook. Let's revisit the definition.

Communicative autonomy, a term created by Sofia García-Beyaert (García-Beyaert, 2015, p. 363), refers to the idea that all participants, regardless of their language, are able to be in control of, and responsible for, their own communication.

In other words, participants are able to communicate what they wish, understand everything that is stated clearly and are free to make independent decisions based on their accurate understanding of what is said.

While the term communicative autonomy is currently used to address interpreting and the role of the interpreter in general, as a concept it applies to all of us. Regardless of how anyone identifies, or what groups they affiliate with, people want to be able to say what they want, when they want and how they want. The presence of an interpreter shouldn't hinder that.

We all want to be able to freely express ourselves. We also want to clearly understand those we engage with. In many cases, when people don't speak the same language, and don't work with interpreters, communicative autonomy isn't possible.

Your decisions and how you carry them out as a remote interpreter can either support or hinder communicative autonomy.

How this tool supports communicative autonomy

The first benchmark for this standard—Benchmark 3.1—evaluates how you apply ethical guidelines and requirements to your work and how effectively you support communicative autonomy.

If you look at the description of a performance that earns a score of 1 for minimal performance, you'll notice it includes decisions and behavior that do *not* support:

- *Ethical decision-making.*
- *The ethical tenet of impartiality.*
- The role of the interpreter.
- Communicative autonomy.

Scoring a minimal performance for this benchmark typically shows the behavior of an untrained interpreter.

Interpreters who perform well and attain a score of 3 for professional performance for this benchmark usually do so because their application of ethical principles is effective and efficient during the entire session. This level of performance supports clear communication.

Standard 3: Supporting Communicative Autonomy

- Engages in ethical decision-making that supports communicative autonomy.
- Remains transparent and impartial and redirects participants to speak to each other.
- Intervenes effectively and appropriately to support clear communication.

Standard 3: Supporting Communicative Autonomy **Engages in practices that enable clear and responsive communication.**
Benchmark 3.1 **Engages in ethical decision-making that supports communicative autonomy.**
Criteria 1. Disregards ethical practices, has side conversations, does not remain impartial, oversteps the role of the interpreter, does not intervene effectively and makes choices that undermine communicative autonomy: 1 point 2. May uphold ethical principles and intervene effectively but does so inconsistently: 2 points 3. Consistently applies ethical principles, remains accurate and effectively uses strategic mediation skills to address communication breakdowns: 3 points
Benchmark 3.2 **Remains transparent and impartial and redirects participants to speak to each other.**
Criteria 1. Does not remain transparent or encourage direct communication: 1 point 2. Inconsistently maintains transparency and inconsistently redirects participants: 2 points 3. Appropriately uses direct and indirect speech (interprets in first person, may intervene in third person), remains impartial, professionally redirects participants to address each other: 3 points
Benchmark 3.3 **Intervenes effectively and appropriately to support clear communication.**
Criteria 1. Doesn't intervene when necessary; intervenes with an abrupt or unprofessional tone; doesn't call attention to cultural differences that may affect communication: 1 point 2. Fails to consistently address communication breakdowns or does so awkwardly. Calls attention to cultural differences but in an inefficient or overbearing way: 2 points 3. Effectively manages the flow of communication and consistently and professionally intervenes when necessary to ensure clear communication. Draws attention to cultural differences that may affect communication while respecting the autonomy of participants and only to inform or educate: 3 points

Standard 3: A challenging performance standard

It is for this third standard that you are likely to notice the most opportunity for growth.

Those of us who evaluate the performance of remote interpreters notice that often Standards 1 and 3 in this tool need the most attention. You may know *what* you need to do, but *how* you do it is the question here.

For example, looking at Benchmark 3.3, when you intervene to address a potential cultural misunderstanding, do you do so in a way that is respectful and efficient—while also avoiding stereotyping any participants or stepping outside your role?

Strategic mediation is discussed in Chapter 7 of this volume: it involves any act or utterance of the interpreter that addresses a communication breakdown. That breakdown could be caused by environmental, linguistic, cultural, institutional or other factors.

Standard 3 and strategic mediation

The goal of strategic mediation is to restore communicative autonomy. Strategic mediation is transparent, brief and targeted. It does not violate ethical norms or the interpreter's role.

Anytime the interpreter intervenes in the session to perform strategic mediation should involve the least amount of intrusion to the flow of communication. Intervening briefly and effectively as needed also supports ethical conduct.

Avoiding disruption is critical for interpreters in general. It is even more important in remote interpreting, where a small disruption can often cause a serious problem. Intervening is necessary: it is part of what interpreters do to support communicative autonomy. This standard helps determine if the intervention strategies were efficient and appropriate to the session.

Example of level 3 professional performance

For example, imagine interpreting for an Italian-speaking parent at a parent-teacher conference about an elementary school student. The family is new to the U.S. education system and is not familiar with the term *progress report*. The family seems confused by what is being described, but the teacher doesn't notice their confusion.

Interpreters who have worked hard at refining their strategic mediation skills (again, see Chapter 7 of this volume) are able to intervene transparently, efficiently, respectfully and within the role of the interpreter. For example, the interpreter may say,

> "This is the interpreter speaking. Teacher, you may wish to ask the parent if they are familiar with the term 'progress report.'"

Strategic mediation performed in this way reflects an interpreter with professional skills as assessed by the rating scale. This approach is efficient and respectful of the parent and the teacher while allowing you to stay in the role of the interpreter.

Example of level 1 minimal performance

Yet what could happen here, like if someone scores a level 1 minimal performance?

> "This is the interpreter, the parent is from a small village in their country and has no idea what a progress report is. Give me a moment to explain it."

The interpreter intervened and made sure to be clear that it was the interpreter speaking, which is important. However, the interpreter also made assumptions about the parent and stepped out of their role by offering to explain the concept to the family. That is the teacher's job—*not* the interpreter's.

The result will likely be a side conversation that excludes the teacher, isn't transparent and could involve the interpreter giving confusing and inaccurate information. It also can set a precedent with the parent and the teacher that interpreters will step in and potentially take over communication and explain concepts rather than drawing attention to potential misunderstandings.

How to perform Standard 3 well

Spending careful time on what to say and how to say it when you intervene will significantly help you for Standard 3.

To perform strategic mediation, you will need to develop scripts and rehearse a plan for how to address different types of communication breakdowns. See Chapter 7 of this volume for many examples of scripts that address different types of breakdowns.

There is no one perfect way to perform strategic mediation. However, keep in mind that you want what you say and do whenever you intervene to be efficient, respectful and within your role as an impartial interpreter.

Remember too that intervening is part of the job—a critical part. In a remote environment, you may need to be assertive when you intervene (especially if everyone is talking at the same time). Being calm and assertive consistently will help set you up for success.

Finally, transparency and encouraging people to speak to one another is a part of this overall standard. Consistently identifying yourself and appropriately redirecting participants to speak to one another if they try to talk to you instead can easily help you perform at level 3 professional performance.

Try putting up a sticky note on your screen with the words, "This in the interpreter speaking" as a reminder to identify yourself each and every time you intervene—to *all* participants.

→ Section 5.4 Review

Standard 3 of The Remote Interpreter Evaluation Tool helps you evaluate how you either supported or hindered the communicative autonomy of participants.

Before you evaluate the three different benchmarks in this standard, remember that the root of each decision you make should be how to support the communicative autonomy of all participants. Each choice you make will either support or hinder communicative autonomy.

Interpreters do more than facilitate communication. Interpreters make choices that support everyone's ability to express themselves completely and understand what others are expressing. Without complete communicative autonomy, participants are missing out on the opportunity for authentic communication.

Benchmark 3.1 is used to assess how the interpreter engages in ethical decision-making. In Benchmark 3.2, the interpreter evaluates how transparent they are and if they appropriately redirect participants when speaking. It is in Benchmark 3.3 that the interpreter's intervention strategies are assessed, including how efficient and clear they are.

This standard captures the heart of what interpreters do. Interpreters make dozens of decisions a minute, and each decision either supports or hinders communicative autonomy. An interpreter's work is incredibly important, and this standard helps gauge the impact of the interpreter's choices.

Section 5.5 Standard 4: Evaluate Your Interactions with Participants

→ Learning objective 5.5

After completing this section, the remote interpreter will be able to evaluate how they engage proactively with participants during the session.

→ Section 5.5 Overview

Anytime there is a moment to educate participants on how to work with an interpreter, take that opportunity. There may not be a lot of time or even any time to do so during the session itself. Your interactions can help correct misunderstandings and give new perspectives about the work that interpreters do.

Every participant that you educate may work more effectively with other interpreters and other participants because of you.

Standard 4 addresses how you educate participants if you have a chance to do so. It includes two benchmarks to assess how or when you give guidance and how effective it is.

This standard also evaluates the language you use when you intervene. Remember, soft skills play an important role. Whenever you intervene, how you communicate can be as important as what you say.

→ Section 5.5 Content

Standard 1 in this tool evaluates how you engage with participants at the start and the close of a session. Standard 4 assesses how you engage with participants when you guide them on how to work with an interpreter. This standard also considers the word choices you make when using direct and indirect speech.

Why Standard 4 is necessary

Yes, of course, in an ideal world, the organization that provided the remote interpreting service would also provide client education to guide users of their service how to work effectively with interpreters.

The reality is different, as nearly all interpreters know. *You* may often have to guide participants who don't know how to work with remote interpreters in order to ensure that the session goes smoothly.

Standard 4: Interactions with Participants

- Instructs participants how to best work with interpreters.
- When intervening, uses professional and culturally appropriate language.

Standard 4: Interactions with Participants **Engages proactively and smoothly with participants during the session.**
Benchmark 4.1 **Instructs participants how to best work with interpreters.**
Criteria 1. Does not provide participant guidance when necessary, or that guidance is incorrect or incomplete: 1 point 2. Provides incomplete or inconsistent participant guidance: 2 points 3. Effectively and professionally advises participants as needed: 3 points
Benchmark 4.2 **When intervening, uses professional and culturally appropriate language.**
Criteria 1. When intervening, uses culturally inappropriate or adversarial language or tone: 1 point 2. When intervening, inconsistently uses professional and culturally appropriate language: 2 points 3. When intervening, consistently addresses participants with professional and culturally appropriate language: 3 points

Explain your role

Without a doubt, there will be sessions where you have to intervene and explain the role of an interpreter and how to work with you smoothly during the session.

It can be frustrating to have to tell participants how to work with an interpreter or to correct someone's idea of what interpreters do. Try to remember that this may be your 100th session as a remote interpreter but the first time that one (or all) the participants in that session have ever worked with a remote interpreter.

For example, imagine you're in a healthcare video session and the healthcare provider is pointing the camera at the patient's feet instead of their face. The patient is there for an appointment, fully clothed, and sitting at the desk beside the provider. The camera should be pointed at the patient so that you can see their facial expressions and body language.

If you don't see the patient, you can politely ask the provider to move the camera. For example, you might say:

> "This is the interpreter speaking. Can you please move the device so that the camera is pointing at the patient? This will allow the patient and me [or: the patient and interpreter] to see each other and support complete and accurate interpretation. Thank you."

Assuming the interpreter interprets this statement for the patient, it is professional. It clearly states what you need and briefly guides the participants on how to work effectively with interpreters.

But what if the interpreter made the request this way?

> "I can't see the patient. You need to move the camera."

In this case, the interpreter didn't explain why there is a need to move the camera and did not make the request in a professional, transparent way.

As with the three previous standards, being consistent and efficient when you intervene and remaining confident and professional as you do will help your performance go from a minimal performance to a professional performance on the rating scale.

→ Section 5.5 Review

Standard 4 of this self-evaluation tool helps you assess the language you use when you educate participants on how to best work with interpreters. Again, as important as *what* you say is, it's also important *how* you say it. What may seem obvious to you as an interpreter is not always obvious to the participants. Remember too that their session with you may be the first session, or at least the first in a long time, that requires an interpreter. If you have to ask them to speak up or reposition the camera and you do so with an impatient tone or rude attitude, you're passively teaching participants that interpreters are impatient or rude.

There also may be opportunities to educate participants on how to work with you that may involve different practices than the interpreters they worked with previously. As a remote interpreter, you are demonstrating best practices. What an interpreter did before you may not have been ideal, and now it is up to you to help adjust a participant's behavior and expectations.

Standard 4 gives you the opportunity to evaluate your word choices and approach as you intervene and educate. You may not have the opportunity often to do so, but almost all sessions will require you to intervene, and each time you do is a valuable opportunity to represent not only yourself but also the profession.

Section 5.6 Standard 5: Evaluate How You Maintain Accuracy

→ Learning objective 5.6

After completing this section, the remote interpreter will be able to evaluate their accuracy during the session.

→ Section 5.6 Overview

So far, all the standards in the first performance area have addressed your soft skills and general performance: how you manage a session and how you demonstrate professionalism.

Next, we will look at the *accuracy* of what you interpret. All of these standards work together to support communicative autonomy and all are equally valuable. You can be the most accurate interpreter, for example, but if you start and close sessions with abruptness and rudeness, you risk losing work and damaging respect for the profession.

To be sure, accuracy in interpreting is not everything. But without it, you are not interpreting.

This standard will help you evaluate your interpreting accuracy, including where you may be making additions to the message, or omitting or changing parts of it, and how well you maintain the linguistic register.

→ Section 5.6 Content

Accuracy for interpreters is so important that it is addressed in virtually all codes of ethics and standards of practice for interpreters (see Chapter 6 in this volume). Consider how accuracy, tone and the ability to maintain the spirit of the message affects communicative autonomy and the ability to build a relationship among participants.

If your interpretation isn't accurate and you alter the tone or spirit of the message, the relationship between participants may be different than they intended. Communicative autonomy is about everyone being able to say what they want, when they want and how they want. If your accuracy upholds their communicative autonomy, then rapport, connection and trust can happen. This would also include adversarial relationships.

Imagine a customer service agent who is speaking rudely and impatiently. Your accuracy will communicate to the customer that the employee is rude and impatient. If you don't uphold the spirit of the message, then the customer may not be able to express their dissatisfaction about being treated so poorly.

Accuracy, along with all the other standards, leads back to whether or not your choices support or hinder everyone's communicative autonomy.

Standard 5: Accuracy

- Conveys the content, tone and spirit of the source message.
- Avoids omitting, adding to or changing the message.

Standard 5: Accuracy **Interprets accurately and completely without changing the message.**
Benchmark 5.1 **Conveys the content, tone and spirit of the source message.**
Criteria 1. Interprets in a monotone or too literally, or otherwise fails to convey the intent, content and effect of the source message: 1 point 2. Generally conveys the intent, content and effect but at times fails to capture the spirit or meaning of the message: 2 points 3. Captures and conveys in both tone and diction (choice of words or signs) the rich complexity of the message in a contextually accurate way. 3 points
Benchmark 5.2 **Avoids omitting, adding to or changing the message.**
Criteria 1. Introduces several additions or omissions, loses cultural meanings and distorts the source message: 1 point 2. Makes minimal additions or omissions but has some difficulty conveying cultural meanings or nuances: 2 points 3. Maintains cultural meaning, adds and omits nothing and interprets idiomatic phrases accurately: 3 points

How to evaluate your accuracy

Accuracy may seem like the clearest standard of the entire tool. However, when you *evaluate* yourself for accuracy, it can be hard to be objective. You won't really remember how accurate you were in a given performance.

As a result, recording yourself in a practice session and reviewing that recording will be critical to determine your accuracy. Our memory of our performance can play tricks on us. You might not realize just how accurate your interpreting really is. Each standard and benchmark of the self-evaluation tool is important and recording yourself is one of the best ways to be as unbiased as possible without depending on your memory of a past performance.

The power of tone

One of the common complaints that participants share about interpreters is their tone. For example, someone might say, "It was an emotionally intense session, and the interpreter sounded bored as if this wasn't serious or intense."

Accuracy for interpreting includes conveying emotion, even if that emotion isn't as intense as the participant's. If someone is infuriated, upset or bursts into tears, at a minimum the interpreter should sound, in each case, angry, somewhat distressed or sad. Conveying emotion shouldn't sound like mocking the speakers. Emotion is an important element of communication and deserves your attention and appropriate representation.

Contextual accuracy

Your choice of words is also important. Words are words. Meaning is meaning. Interpreters aim to be contextually accurate and do not simply report the literal interpretation of words. This is why you need to hear one or more sentences before you can interpret.

If you interpret only the words, *you are not interpreting*, and the risk of misinterpreting because you didn't wait to grasp the entire concept can be serious. Your job is to interpret the *meaning*, which involves first listening closely and understanding the message before you find words in the target language to convey the accurate meaning.

Yes, this is all hard work! It involves a high level of skill to attain a level 3 professional performance score.

→ Section 5.6 Review

When people ask what one of the most important responsibilities of being an interpreter is, more often than not the interpreter will say, "To be accurate." As Standard 5 and its benchmarks show, there are several components to being accurate. They include staying faithful to the message and not adding to or omitting details of the source message or otherwise changing its meaning. Being accurate also involves faithfully conveying the emotional tone of the message.

Accuracy is another way that you support communicative autonomy and help participants to build and develop authentic rapport. Even when people are being rude to one another, your faithfulness to the spirit of that message is important. Your job as an interpreter, especially in your accurate renditions, enables participants to choose how they want to respond and engage as they communicate. Let this standard guide you to thoroughly evaluate your performance and learn from it.

Section 5.7 Standard 6: Evaluate How You Convey Completeness

→ Learning objective 5.7

After completing this section, the remote interpreter will be able to evaluate how they convey the meaning and style of the source message.

→ Section 5.7 Overview

Most interpreters agree that they should request a clarification of anything unclear to them. But many interpreters argue that they should be able to change register if they see a need to do so—usually by making any formal language "simpler" in order to help a participant understand the meaning more easily. Doing so hinders communicative autonomy of all participants.

Remember, it is your responsibility to maintain register. As Chapter 6 of this volume will make clear, many codes of ethics and standards of practice for interpreters around the world specifically agree that the interpreter's accuracy and completeness include maintaining the style and register of the source message.

That said, if the style and register, when interpreted accurately, appear incomprehensible, the interpreter can then request a clarification and interpret the clarification. It's your responsibility to ask for clarification when you don't understand or, in many cases, if communication breaks down when meaning is lost. It is expected that you will need to ask for clarifications as a part of the job, at least in most specializations and modalities of remote interpreting.[73]

Understanding and practicing all these elements are critical for attaining a level 3 professional performance score for Standard 6.

→ Section 5.7 Content

Sometimes the hardest part in life is admitting when you are wrong or made a mistake. Yet this standard asks you to do just that. Maintaining register and style while also being transparent when asking for clarification may seem obvious and necessary to do the job well. But what if you make a mistake—if you are inaccurate and you realize it?

Still, communicative autonomy is to be supported at all times, even when you make a mistake.

Remember, mistakes will happen. Communication can be complicated, and you are not perfect. Interpreting is a skill that is always being developed. Learning from your mistakes is a part of that process. Hiding your mistakes or ignoring them only hurts the communicative autonomy of the participants and potentially the respect that participants have for the profession.

It's not easy to admit when you make a mistake, but it's necessary, and this standard gives you the chance to assess how you handled it when you made a mistake.

[73] RSI and conference interpreting, in particular, are typical exceptions to this expectation—but in such cases, you may have printed speeches and slides sent to you in advance or other documents to help you prepare for the session.

Standard 6: Completeness

- Maintains the linguistic register and style.
- Transparently asks for clarifications, or requests repetitions, as needed.
- Corrects mistakes of interpretation.

Standard 6: Completeness **Conveys the meaning and style of the whole message.**
Benchmark 6.1 **Maintains the linguistic register and style.**
Criteria 1. Register and style do not match the source message; repeated hesitations and fillers are added: 1 point 2. Inconsistently matches the register; maintains some of the participants' style; occasionally hesitates or adds fillers: 2 points 3. Conveys the participants' style, including humor or strong emotion as appropriate, without adding hesitations or fillers: 3 points
Benchmark 6.2 **Transparently asks for clarifications, or requests repetitions, as needed.**
Criteria 1. Does not ask for clarification or repetition when information is not understood or heard: 1 point 2. Intervenes inefficiently or inconsistently to request important clarification: 2 points 3. Transparently asks for clarifications, or requests repetitions, as needed: 3 points
Benchmark 6.3 **Corrects mistakes of interpretation.**
Criteria 1. Ignores or is unaware of own mistakes; does not ask for clarification or repetition when information is not understood or heard: 1 point 2. Recognizes mistakes but handles them inefficiently: 2 points 3. Corrects own mistakes in an efficient manner with minimal disruption: 3 points

Requesting clarification

It is impossible to interpret accurately what you do not understand. You aren't expected to be a subject matter expert on every topic in the world. A doctor went to years of medical school to become qualified to care for patients. You may be a medical interpreter with a strong foundation in medical terminology, but you are not a doctor. Asking for clarification will be a necessary part of the job.

Some interpreters will say, "Oh, I don't understand the meaning of that medical term, but it's just the same term in Spanish, so I know exactly how to interpret it." As the medical reviewer for our textbooks reports (as a former doctor and practicing hospital interpreter), that approach is medically dangerous.

Terms may sound similar across languages but still have different meanings. Those differences can be critically important. When terms sound similar but mean quite different things across languages, they are commonly referred to as "false friends."

Consider this example in Italian and English.

In English, the word, "preservative" means something that helps prevent or stop rotting or decaying, especially when talking about food.

In Italian, a similar sounding word, "preservativo," means condom—a barrier form of contraception.

Imagine not asking for clarification and misinterpreting this "false friend." Doing so could lead to significant misunderstanding and undermine the trust the participants have in interpreters.

If you do not know what a term or phrase means—ask before you interpret it.

In short, it is important to request clarification of unfamiliar terms or phrases. It is just as important to have the skills to intervene quickly, transparently and effectively when you do ask.

Correcting your mistakes

Of all the standards in Part 2 of this tool, one that might challenge you the most is the third benchmark for this standard: correcting your own mistakes.

Remember, you will make mistakes. You are going to misinterpret, mishear or omit something. That's normal. You will make many mistakes during your career as an interpreter. What you do when you realize you have made a mistake is what will define your performance.

Why interpreters often fail to correct their mistakes

You may be tempted to cover the error up or quickly correct the mistake as though one of the participants corrected it (and you are simply interpreting their correction). Or you may feel as if the mistake is not worth correcting because it may make you look like a poor interpreter and you hope it will get cleared up later. Since you are probably the only person in the session who knows both languages, how will they ever know?

When you make one of those choices, you risk losing the trust of the participants. You can also damage the trust that people have in the interpreting profession.

It's still a risk to you personally as well, because even though the participants may not be fluent in one another's language, they may *understand* more than they can communicate. They sometimes know that you made a mistake and didn't correct it. While tone and attitude are chief complaints from participants about interpreters, inaccuracies and covering up mistakes are also often reported.

As with the case of the "false friends" just mentioned, this kind of complaint could be shared: "The interpreter kept mentioning birth control when we were talking about managing how many foods the patient eats with preservatives." How confusing for everyone.

The consequences of failing to report a correction

All mistakes are important to correct. Accuracy, no matter what the session is about, is critical.

To help illustrate just how serious a mistake can be for participants, consider the following scenario.

> *A Deaf patient is in the emergency room for a mental health crisis. He is struggling with depression and anxiety and is experiencing severe migraines.*
>
> *A video remote interpreter is called. A provider comes into the room and begins asking the patient routine questions. The Deaf patient describes his stress as a result of losing his job*

and he believes that the stress is causing his migraines. He's not sure how he will pay his bills and how he can afford to support his family. He just wants to talk to someone and get medication to address the migraines.

The provider asks the following question: "Do you have any weapons at home?" The interpreter interprets the question.

The Deaf person responds by signing, "No, but at this rate, just shoot me now, the stress is too much." This is a colloquial phrase that does not literally mean "Shoot me now." However, the interpreter interprets the statement as, "No, but if I had a gun, I'd shoot myself, I'm so stressed."

This interpretation is inaccurate. It doesn't honor the colloquial way the phrase was used. The provider is alarmed and decides that the patient needs to be admitted for observation and a psychiatric evaluation because he believes the patient is a risk to themselves or others.

The interpreter realizes that their interpretation of the phrase is causing an involuntary hold on the patient. Rather than correcting the mistake, the interpreter ignores it and continues to interpret.

The Deaf patient is upset because they came to the hospital for help and didn't expect to be held at the hospital. The Deaf patient asks, "Why am I being admitted? I need help but I don't want to be forced to stay here."

The provider responds, "It's for your safety." The provider says he will be back soon and the VRI service is turned off as the provider leaves the room.

The interpreter has no way to follow up to undo the harm caused by their inaccurate interpretation. The Deaf patient is left confused and no longer free.

The interpreter may never know what happens next. But the damage this interpreter has done by being inaccurate and consciously deciding not to correct that mistake had extremely serious consequences.

→ Section 5.7 Review

Standard 6 of The Remote Interpreter Evaluation Tool lays out benchmarks for assessing how completely and faithfully the interpreter conveyed the message.

Correcting mistakes to maintain accuracy is critically important and requires interpreters to be transparent. That means admitting when you've made a mistake, which can be difficult to do. Once you've identified the mistake, correcting it efficiently and getting back to interpreting is the priority. Take note of those mistakes too. You may see a pattern form that you can address after your session.

Interpreters who respect the communicative autonomy of all participants will not shy away from admitting to mistakes but rather see that as a part of the process. Mistakes can lead to growth when we are honest and also help to avoid negative outcomes.

Section 5.8 Standard 7: Evaluate How You Work Across Modes

→ Learning objective 5.8

After completing this section, the remote interpreter will be able to evaluate how effectively they work across all three interpreting modes—consecutive, simultaneous and sight translation—and their note-taking strategies.

→ Section 5.8 Overview

As you've learned, every session is different. This means that the mode of interpretation and note-taking strategies will be different too. Switching modes (where the platforms permit) can help you interpret more effectively. Sight translation may even play a part in remote interpreting.

This standard focuses on how you make choices about the modes you use that best support everyone's communicative autonomy.

→ Section 5.8 Content

Modes

Standard 7: Modes

- Selects the appropriate mode, switching as needed.
- Takes notes, when needed, to support accuracy.
- Sight translates if and when appropriate to do so, justifying decisions.

Standard 7: Modes **Works effectively across modes.**
Benchmark 7.1 **Selects the appropriate mode, switching as needed.**
Criteria 1. Does not switch mode, even when it would be effective, or inappropriately interchanges direct and indirect speech (first and third person), without transparency. Significantly disrupts the flow of communication. Tries to provide simultaneous interpreting when the remote platform is not adequate for simultaneous: 1 point 2. Inconsistently uses the appropriate mode of interpretation. When switching between first and third person as needed, does so with inconsistent transparency. Switching between modes is done with some unnecessary disruption: 2 points 3. Uses the most effective mode to support communicative autonomy. When switching between first and third person or from one mode to another as needed can efficiently explain the reason for the switch without disruption to the flow of communication. Interpreter switches to simultaneous mode only as appropriate and when remote platform allows for it: 3 points
Benchmark 7.2 **Takes notes, when needed, to support accuracy.**
Criteria 1. Uses disruptive or ineffective note-taking strategies or fails to take notes when needed to compensate for lack of concentration and undeveloped short-term memory skills: 1 point 2. Uses effective note-taking strategies but at times appears distracted by note-taking or too dependent on notes: 2 points 3. Uses effective note-taking strategies that are not distracting and that extend memory to support accuracy; is not overly dependent on notes: 3 points

Benchmark 7.3 **Sight translates if and when appropriate to do so, justifying decisions.**
Criteria 1. Sight translates documents that require professional translation instead or refuses to sight translate appropriate documents without providing a reason or other solutions to meet the need: 1 point 2. Generally sight translates only when appropriate but, when providing reasons why sight translation cannot be effectively performed, does not provide relevant and credible justification: 2 points 3. Sight translates only when appropriate, avoiding legal forms where feasible, and if sight translation is inappropriate, efficiently and calmly offers relevant, credible justification: 3 points

Switching modes

One of the greatest parts of being an interpreter is all the professional skills and strategies you have at your disposal to do the job.

One important skill set is mode switching. Managing when and how you select and change modes will make you more effective at your job as an interpreter. The choices can be trickier on a remote platform for many reasons, including the limitations of a particular platform, but they are no less important.

For modes, it is important to carefully evaluate your choices and the impact each mode can have on the session.

Performing simultaneous on the wrong platform

Let's look at an example. You may face a situation where people are talking for long stretches of time, making it harder for you to interpret consecutively. Instead of asking a participant to pause, you try to interpret simultaneously for the remainder of the session.

However, if the remote platform you're working on is not designed for simultaneous interpreting, the session will sound like two people in two different languages talking over each other, to the person you are interpreting for—and even for you. How will anyone hear and understand you well?

Additionally, the risk of you not interpreting accurately is at high risk because of all the competing voices and noise.

Switching from direct to indirect speech (from first to third person)

There are sessions where you will have to switch from direct to indirect speech. Perhaps a patient is speaking incoherently, and in that case, trying to interpret in direct speech (first person) won't make any sense. You decide to switch to indirect speech (third person) and interpret but also narrate or summarize some of what you are hearing. These can be effective and necessary choices (though risky for accuracy).

You are in effect switching out of standard modes into narration or summarizing, which are not recognized as modes. Yet doing so may be justified in emergencies and other out-of-control situations.

When interpreting in indirect speech (third person) is inappropriate

However, interpreting in indirect speech when it's not appropriate can be distracting and disruptive.

For example, if there are multiple female participants and you say, "She says..." instead of interpreting in direct speech, the risk for confusion increases and a participant may respond with, "*Who* is saying that?" The interpreter is now causing confusion. Confusion undermines communicative autonomy.

Note-taking

This standard's third benchmark allows you to evaluate your note-taking strategies, which support consecutive interpreting.

Note-taking can also be used by a team interpreter while their partner interprets. The notes can be used to assist the interpreting partner if unfamiliar terms arise or the partner needs prompting.

For a remote interpreter, note-taking can be discreet and nonintrusive. However, note-taking is a skill that takes time to develop. It's unique to you, your preferences and whatever style or type of note-taking supports you best. (See Chapter 4 of this volume for how to perform note-taking in remote interpreting.)

Risks of taking notes on video

In remote video interpreting, be careful how you take notes.

Where are your eyes looking? You are probably looking down at your notes. Where is the top of your head pointed? You'd be surprised how many interpreters on a video call will have their head turned down to look at their notes. Then participants are looking at the top of the interpreter's head!

Instead, let your eyes glance down while you turn your head *slightly* down. This angle allows your face to be seen by the participants and you won't look distracted by your notes.

Avoid dependency on notes

Sometimes when a session is full of specialized terminology, or there are complicated topics being discussed, you may become too dependent on your notes.

Notes are meant to support you, but they are not something you should heavily depend on. If you are too dependent on them, they can prevent effective interpreting.

If your performance for this benchmark reflects minimal performance, you will need to spend more time developing your note-taking skills. Note-taking skills take time to develop, and practicing them when you're new to note-taking is expected and necessary.

Handling requests for sight translation

Finally, this standard also gives you a benchmark (7.3) to help evaluate how you respond when you're asked to sight translate.

How often are interpreters called translators? Too often! The skills needed to be a translator are different from an interpreter. Yet sight translation involves oral or signed translation in real time, crossing a line between interpreting and translation. It is a task that falls on interpreters, not translators.

There are times where sight translating a document is appropriate, even in remote interpreting.

Sight translation is usually easier and more appropriate when an interpreter is onsite and able to hold the document in their hands. In a remote environment, especially when a document is held up to a camera, it can be extremely difficult to provide accurate and effective sight translation.

As a result, most often you might have to decline a request to sight translate. Benchmark 7.3 helps you evaluate how you respond when you are asked to sight translate—because in many if not most cases, you will probably have to decline.

It is acceptable to say "no" when you are asked to sight translate. Consider how you respond to such requests. Do you communicate in a professional and respectful manner? Do you suggest alternatives? Do you provide clear reasons for declining?

Sight translation can be performed remotely in some cases, but it is up to you to determine if you have the necessary skills to do so, if the conditions permit you to perform it adequately and if the text itself is appropriate to sight translate online. Most often, sight translation will probably not be appropriate in a remote session.

When you must decline to perform it, *how* you decline is important.

→ Section 5.8 Review

Standard 7 of The Remote Interpreter Evaluation Tool addresses your effectiveness with respect to modes of interpreting and the note-taking skills that support your interpreting.

This standard should prompt you to ask yourself "Why?" with regard to which modes you use, including sight translation, and whether to interpret in direct or indirect speech (first or third person) or take notes. Why do you make these choices, and which choice is the most effective for certain situations?

Similarly, when you choose *not* to sight translate, can you answer the question "Why?" And as you consider your note-taking strategies, and whether or not you decided to take notes, did you ask yourself, "Why did I?" or "Why didn't I?" Or "Why did I choose to type my notes instead of doing them on a notepad or whiteboard?" Or even "Why did I depend on notes so much?" The answers to these questions will guide you as you seek resources to support your skill development.

As you focus your efforts, you will improve your performance for this standard.

Section 5.9 Standard 8: Evaluate How You Research and Verify Terminology

Learning objective 5.9

After completing this section, the remote interpreter will be able evaluate how effectively they use, research and verify context-appropriate terminology.

Section 5.9 Overview

Specialized terminology exists in every area of your work. Some terms may be highly technical (such as medical terms) while other terminology may be more "everyday" vocabulary yet specific to the environment of the session (such as the patient who is reporting their symptoms).

It is the responsibility of the interpreter to develop glossaries and become familiar with both general and specialized terminology in all working languages.

Section 5.9 Content

Terminology

Standard 8: Terminology

- Uses correct and context-appropriate terminology.
- Researches or verifies the meaning of specialized terms as needed.

Standard 8: Terminology Uses, researches and verifies terms correctly and appropriately.
Benchmark 8.1 **Uses correct and context-appropriate terminology.**
Criteria 1. Makes several mistakes or a major mistake in use of terminology that affect the accuracy of the message: 1 point 2. Makes a few minor mistakes of terminology that do not seriously affect the accuracy of the message: 2 points 3. Uses correct and context-appropriate terminology in both languages with minimal errors: 3 points
Benchmark 8.2 **Researches or verifies the meaning of specialized terms as needed.**
Criteria 1. Does not research, or ask the participant to explain, an unfamiliar term: 1 point 2. Asks for clarification but without transparency, leading to confusion, or uses inefficient or distracting research skills to look up an unfamiliar term: 2 points 3. Asks the participant to explain an unfamiliar term with complete transparency or engages in efficient, speedy research of the term, as appropriate: 3 points

The importance of correct terminology

Self-awareness of your limitations in terminology is vital. Mistakes of terminology can damage the session, cost you work and lead to outcomes that are potentially serious.

You will need to regularly assess how well you use terms correctly. When you use this standard and its benchmarks, you may have to research to be sure your knowledge of both general and specialized terms is accurate.

General vs. specialized terminology

Sometimes it's the unexpected everyday term (such as "debit card," "ATM machine" or "credit score" in business interpreting in the U.S.) that can cause problems for interpreters during the session.

More often, technical terminology—such as APR (annual percentage rate) vs. APY (annual percentage yield)—can lead to even greater challenges for interpreters.

Specialized terminology can be a larger obstacle in remote interpreting than in face-to-face interpreting for several reasons. For example, remote interpreters often go from call to call across a wide array of specializations, each with its own highly specialized terms.

As you already know it's perfectly acceptable and expected to ask for clarification of an unfamiliar term or concept, whether in remote or face-to-face interpreting. You may be an excellent interpreter with a specialty in the automotive field, but you aren't expected to be a subject matter expert. Yet if you regularly interpret in this area, you will have an increased knowledge base of the specialized terminology in the automotive field compared to an interpreter who never works in that specialty at all.

How Standard 8 helps you assess your performance

This standard helps you evaluate how you manage interpreting terminology, especially highly specialized terminology. It also has you evaluate whether you used the specialized terminology correctly. Being able to use terms accurately, in context and in the same register, demonstrates your level of experience, knowledge and expertise.

Imagine you're in a remote audio-only session interpreting for a supply chain manager of an auto repair store. The manager is calling a distributor in Germany and wants to place an order for an auto part you've never heard of before. You already have a well-developed glossary of specialized automotive terminology, but this term is new for you.

You will need to ask the supply chain manager to define the term they are using. How would you ask?

Consider saying, "This is the interpreter speaking, I'm not familiar with that term. Could you please describe it in another way?" This way of asking sounds professional. It does not make you sound incompetent or unqualified.

Imagine, instead, if you asked this way: "This is the interpreter, what does that mean?" or even worse: "What did you say?" In that case, you risk disrupting trust in your abilities—and it may even be unclear from the way you asked who needed the clarification.

Taking ownership of what you don't know, asking for what you need and doing so in a professional, courteous and efficient manner not only makes you shine but also helps to build respect for the profession.

Polish your research skills

Chapter 4 of this volume (Section 4.2) discussed the importance of being able to research unfamiliar terms online quickly and the techniques for doing so. Please review that section.

The ability to research both general and specialized terms that are new to you, whether outside a session or during it, is a critical skill.

→ Section 5.9 Review

Standard 8 of The Remote Interpreter Evaluation Tool addresses how you manage unfamiliar terminology during the session. Using specialized terminology correctly and having well-developed research skills certainly supports communicative autonomy.

Remember, you don't have to know everything. When a term in a specialized environment comes up, do you request clarification in a professional, efficient way? Are you polite and respectful? Do you acknowledge that you don't know the term? The answer to all these questions should simply be, "Yes."

As surely as you will make mistakes, you will come across terms you don't know or understand. It is how you handle this situation that will demonstrate your professionalism and skill, including your ability to research terms.

You can hold yourself and your peers to a high standard while also being gentle with yourself. As a practicing interpreter, you know that no interpretation will ever be perfect, which simply means there is always room for improvement and progress. Paying attention to all aspects of your work and being intentional in your skill development will only make you more valuable to the specialty markets you work in.

Section 5.10 How to Use This Tool to Evaluate Interpreters

→ Learning objective 5.10

After completing this section, the interpreter will be able discuss how to use The Remote Interpreter Evaluation Tool with other interpreters.

→ Section 5.10 Overview

Remote interpreting can be lonely. If you are self-employed, or you work for a language service from home, you may not have many opportunities to give or receive feedback.

Yet self-evaluation and reflective practice are a key part of your work. Walking through this evaluation tool on your own will help you—but using it to peer evaluate other interpreters can be incredibly valuable as well.

In addition, if you are tasked with evaluating other remote interpreters, this tool will be an invaluable aid. It gives you specific standards and benchmarks that will guide the evaluation process and provide you and the other interpreter with tangible results and goals.

→ Section 5.10 Content

Giving and receiving feedback

Building a peer network of interpreters whom you can help and who will help you grow as an interpreter is invaluable. Yet giving feedback is more effective if you have formal criteria that help you talk about each other's work.

While this tool helps you perform a more effective self-evaluation and it can be used on your own, it is also a helpful tool to use with peers and colleagues. It provides specific criteria to evaluate each other's performance.

The tool also gives you a guide to talk about your work in meaningful ways. The fact that it has two parts, each with four standards and two or three benchmarks for each standard, helps you and the interpreter you are working with focus the conversation on specific aspects of your performance. You can make note of each other's current ratings and track your progress over time and your future goals.

How to give feedback

Most people, when they give feedback, tend to say what interpreters did well, what they did wrong, and what they should have done differently.

However, when you give feedback it can be far more effective (and powerful) not to *tell* the interpreter what they did but instead to ask them *questions*.

By asking questions, you can guide the interpreter to moments of self-realization. When, as the interpreter, you can think through yourself what happened and what you could have done differently, you may experience opportunities for growth and self-revelation.

Through this process of answering questions about your own performance and discussing your responses, there is greater potential for the lessons you learn to lead to real change in your work and improvement in your performance.

Questions to ask

Below are four initial questions that you and your practice partners can use to get started:

- What went well in that session?
- What would you have done differently in that session?
- Which standards do you feel you performed well in that session, and can you explain why?
- Which standards or benchmarks do you feel you could have performed differently in that session, and can you explain why?

Notice that the words "right" and "wrong" don't appear in these statements. If we talk about the work from the perspective of right and wrong, we oversimplify the work of interpreters. We also risk internalizing the feedback and becoming resistant to it.

In reality, the same behavior or decision by the interpreter can be right or wrong, depending on the circumstances. Instead of talking about right or wrong, think about which behaviors and decisions by the interpreter are *appropriate* to the context and situation. Remember, all decisions we make while interpreting support or hinder communicative autonomy.

Follow-up questions

As the interpreter (that you are evaluating) answers your questions above, consider follow-up questions, such as:

- Can you tell me what was going through your mind as ____ was happening?
- What impact do you think your decision had on the overall experience of the participants?
- Which decisions did you make that supported communicative autonomy, and can you explain why?
- Which decisions did you make that hindered communicative autonomy, and can you explain why?
- Can you think of other strategies or choices you can use next time to have a different outcome?
- Is there anything you can share with the participants or the organization to support the next session (whether with you or another interpreter)?

Questions that avoid defensive responses

Notice that none of the questions above start with "Why did you...?" When we start asking "why" questions, the person responding may feel defensive.

If another interpreter wants to hear your feedback on a session or role play practice, or if you have anything you'd like to talk about, one way to start sharing is by saying,

- "I noticed during the session you did/didn't do_____. Can you tell me your decision-making process behind that choice?"

- "During the session, do you remember when ____ happened? If so, can you tell me what was going through your mind?"

Why it is important to be cautious how you phrase questions

It may seem odd to be so careful how you phrase questions about an interpreter's performance. These may seem like passive ways of asking someone to explore their decision-making or examine a particular behavior pattern you noticed. It may even seem extreme to be so cautious with how you ask a question.

The reality is that we are all human. If we respond defensively, we shut out what we are hearing. We don't look at ourselves too closely. When you ask an interpreter about their performance, you don't want them to shut down and stop reflecting on their work.

How to dive deeper

During the conversation, you may reach a point when the other interpreter doesn't know what could have been done differently. They may say,

> "I don't know what I could have done differently. I don't know what I should have done."

When you reach this point, then you can start to provide your own input and experience.

For example, you could answer,

> "OK, if you're not sure what you could have done differently, have you considered ________?"

Again, it's a question. "Have you considered…" is more inviting than "You should do this…" By saying, "Have you considered…" you're able to share your suggestion while also giving the interpreter a chance to consider your suggestion and comment on it. This way the interpreter is also less likely to feel attacked, put down or told what to do—as if you were a smarter, better interpreter.

The problem with telling instead of asking

By telling an interpreter what they *should* do, you may make the interpreter feel like they have to accept and use your feedback even if they don't agree. Perhaps they don't feel comfortable with it. Yet they may have reasons not to openly question your suggestions or advice.

Feedback ideally will not be "top down." Instead, it will be a conversation between peers, sharing experiences that both of you can learn and grow from.

There are many questions you can ask, and you'll learn over time which questions help support a meaningful dialogue and thoughtful reflection. You can also ask yourself these same questions during your own reflective practice.

→ Section 5.10 Review

Reflective practice by interpreters is an absolute necessity. When you use The Remote Interpreter Evaluation Tool with other interpreters, it becomes invaluable for their professional development.

This section showed you how to use the tool to help other interpreters reflect on their performance. By evaluating each other, you strengthen your abilities to see your performance with fresh eyes, both immediately and over time.

Getting feedback from peers can feel scary at first (just as getting it from a supervisor or quality assurance program manager can). Yet peer feedback doesn't have to be negative or critical.

Avoid trying to evaluate other interpreters quickly. Both self-evaluation and peer evaluation need time. Be patient with yourself and patient with others. No interpreter is perfect, and there are always areas of improvement, no matter how long you've been practicing.

The goal is to use this tool and this opportunity for evaluation to learn and grow. Interpreting is difficult and rewarding work. It demands thoughtful professional development.

Finally, even if you aren't an interpreter with years of experience, you can still help your peers and they can help you. The feedback model you explored here isn't rooted in your knowing all the answers. It's based on asking other interpreters questions and talking about the work.

Through conversation, consulting the evaluation tool and using other resources in the field, you'll find there is always room to grow and evolve, no matter how many years you've been interpreting.

→ Chapter Activities

Activity 5.1: Reviewing The Remote Interpreter Evaluation Tool

You have been introduced to the self-evaluation tool and have seen the eight different standards and their benchmarks. As a remote interpreter, or even someone new to remote interpreting, you probably have a sense of where you perform well and where you need to focus your practice. Review both parts of the tool and complete the following statements:

1. In Part 1 of the tool, I feel my performance is strongest in Standard ____________ because ________________________________.
2. In Part 1 of the tool, I feel my performance needs additional practice in Standard ____________ because ________________________________.
3. In Part 2 of the tool, I feel my performance is strongest in Standard ____________ because ________________________________.
4. In Part 2 of the tool, I feel my performance needs additional practice in Standard ____________ because ________________________________.

Remember to be honest in your responses without being overly critical. This activity is to help you get started in evaluating yourself. Also, your responses may change after you learn more about the tool and practice using it. Interpreting is about improving and refining your skills, which happens when you self-evaluate.

Activity 5.2: Evaluating Standard 1

All the standards and benchmark criteria in The Remote Interpreter Evaluation Tool will prompt you to do the same thing: self-evaluate where you currently are in your existing remote interpreting practice for that standard. If you are new to remote interpreting, then you can reflect on your face-to-face interpreting skills. These reflections are meant to help you become comfortable evaluating your performance and challenge you to be honest with yourself without being overly critical.

On a separate sheet of paper or on your electronic device, write down the following statements. After you've written the statements, reflect on your most recent interpreting session, where you have the clearest memory, and respond.

Standard 1: Starting and Closing the Session

Benchmark 1.1

- My performance is (fill in your score) ____ because:

Benchmark 1.2

- My performance is (fill in your score) ____ because:

Here is an example

Standard 1: Starting and Closing the Session

- Benchmark 1.1 My performance is 2 because I was tired and didn't sound completely engaged during the introduction.

Benchmark 1.2

- My performance is 3 because I introduced myself and my language pair and ended the session courteously with all participants.

Note: The length of your answers is entirely up to you. Some benchmarks may be easier to answer in a short sentence while others need more reflection. This is your self-evaluation tool and the more thorough your response, the more insight you may gain into your performance.

Once you have written your responses, ask yourself, "What do I need to improve or maintain my performance?" These reflections and notes will guide your skill development plan after you evaluate each standard and benchmark.

Activity 5.3: Evaluating Standard 2

Continuing with the sheet of paper or electronic notes you used in the last activity, write down and respond to the same statements for Standard 2: Managing the Session.

Standard 2: Managing the Session

Benchmark 2.1

- My performance is ____ because:

Benchmark 2.2

- My performance is ____ because:

Benchmark 2.3

- My performance is ____ because:

Once you have written your responses, ask yourself, "What do I need to improve or maintain my performance?" These reflections and notes will guide your skill development plan after you evaluate each standard and benchmark.

Activity 5.4: Evaluating Standard 3

Continuing with the sheet of paper or electronic notes you used in the last activity, write down and respond to the same statements for Standard 3: Supporting Communicative Autonomy.

Standard 3: Supporting Communicative Autonomy

Benchmark 3.1

- My performance is ____ because:

Benchmark 3.2

- My performance is ____ because:

Benchmark 3.3

- My performance is _____ because:

Once you have written your responses, ask yourself, "What do I need to improve or maintain my performance?" These reflections and notes will guide your skill development plan after you evaluate each standard and benchmark.

Activity 5.5: Evaluating Standard 4

Continuing with the sheet of paper or electronic notes you used in the last activity, write down and respond to the same statements for Standard 4: Interactions with Participants.

Standard 4: Interactions with Participants

Benchmark 4.1

- My performance is ____ because:

Benchmark 4.2

- My performance is ____ because:

Once you have written your responses, ask yourself, "What do I need to improve or maintain my performance?" These reflections and notes will guide your skill development plan after you evaluate each standard and benchmark.

Activity 5.6: Evaluating Standard 5

Continuing with the sheet of paper or electronic notes you used in the last activity, write down and respond to the same statements for Standard 5: Accuracy.

Standard 5: Accuracy

Benchmark 5.1

- My performance is ____ because:

Benchmark 5.2

- My performance is ____ because:

Once you have written your responses, ask yourself, "What do I need to improve or maintain my performance?" These reflections and notes will guide your skill development plan after you evaluate each standard and benchmark.

Activity 5.7: Evaluating Standard 6

Continuing with the sheet of paper or electronic notes you used in the last activity, write down and respond to the same statements for Standard 6: Completeness.

Standard 6: Completeness

Benchmark 6.1

- My performance is ____ because:

Benchmark 6.2

- My performance is ____ because:

Benchmark 6.3

- My performance is ____ because:

Once you have written your responses, ask yourself, "What do I need to improve or maintain my performance?" These reflections and notes will guide your skill development plan after you evaluate each standard and benchmark.

Activity 5.8: Evaluating Standard 7

Continuing with the sheet of paper or electronic notes you used in the last activity, write down and respond to the same statements for Standard 7: Modes.

Standard 7: Modes

Benchmark 7.1

- My performance is ____ because:

Benchmark 7.2

- My performance is ____ because:

Benchmark 7.3

- My performance is ____ because:

Once you have written your responses, ask yourself, "What do I need to improve or maintain my performance?" These reflections and notes will guide your skill development plan after you evaluate each standard and benchmark.

Activity 5.9: Evaluation Standard 8

Continuing with the sheet of paper or electronic notes you used in the last activity, write down and respond to the same statements for Standard 8: Terminology.

Standard 8: Terminology

Benchmark 8.1

- My performance is ____ because:

Benchmark 8.2

- My performance is ____ because:

Once you have written your responses, ask yourself, "What do I need to improve or maintain my performance?" These reflections and notes will guide your skill development plan after you evaluate each standard and benchmark.

Activity 5.10 (a): Feedback

Receiving feedback and giving feedback can feel personal and, at times, overwhelming. For some interpreters, this may be a reason to not ask for feedback, give feedback or look closely at their work. One way to overcome those concerns or barriers is to write them down and respond to them through a positive lens.

Instructions

On a sheet of paper or an electronic device, which can be the same as the one from your previous self-evaluation activities, write down reasons that you may be afraid, nervous, anxious or reluctant to conduct self-evaluation or peer support.

For example:

- I'm afraid to closely evaluate my performance, because maybe there are too many things to work on, and I won't know where to start.
- If someone asks for my support but what I offer isn't what they need, I'll feel useless.
- I'm a brand new remote interpreter. Everything I do is going to need work.

Write down these thoughts. You'll address them in the next activity.

Activity 5.10 (b): Positive perspective

Instructions

Now that you've identified what might stop you from self-evaluating or providing feedback to another interpreter, let's respond with a positive perspective.

For example:

- My concern
    - I'm afraid to closely evaluate my performance because maybe there are too many things to work on, and I won't know where to start.
- My response
    - The self-evaluation tool gives me many ways to look at my work more closely. Once I identify where I need to focus my practice, I will pick the benchmarks that I can easily improve on and work on those ones first. If there are others that I need support with, I'll reach out to my trusted peers to ask for support.
- My concern
    - If someone asks for my support but what I offer isn't what they need, I'll feel useless.
- My response
    - We can all learn from each other. What I offer may not be what they need in this moment, but perhaps it will resonate later. Giving feedback isn't about solving the problem right now but working through it together and making progress step by step.
- My concern
    - I'm a brand new remote interpreter. Everything I do is going to need work.
- My response
    - I'm a new interpreter with fresh perspective. There are skills I already have that come easily and I won't ignore those. All interpreters have skills to work on; it's about progress not perfection.

Reframing your doubts, insecurities or hesitations into positive and affirming language can help you overcome unpleasant feelings about evaluation. Once you've addressed them, you will find it easier and more comfortable to engage in self-evaluation and peer support.

Chapter Conclusion and Review

The Remote Interpreter Evaluation Tool is a tool for reflective practice: it is meant to guide you during your professional performance and your intentional practice. It requires a plan to observe yourself over time and see if you are improving, and in which areas you are improving more quickly than in others.

If you only reflect on your work and don't put a *plan* in place to improve, then it will be difficult to see progress. Participants' communicative autonomy depends on interpreters' commitment to professionalism and progress. Using this tool gives you a roadmap to excellence.

The different levels of performance assessed using the tool also help you evaluate yourself beyond a "good job" or "bad job." Every interpreter has experiences where their skills and decisions reflected minimal working performance. Use those experiences and lessons to improve. Evaluating yourself honestly is the only way to authentically improve and ultimately positively affect the profession.

Reviewing your performance in a methodical and intentional way will certainly make you a better interpreter. There will be sessions where your performance was solid. There will also be sessions where your performance suffered. Knowing why you performed the way you did is valuable. While you may not be asked often, if someone did ask, "What are you currently working on in your professional development?" this tool will help you answer that question.

While the tool accounts for many decisions you make while interpreting, there are likely other areas you may need to add based on where and what you interpret. Feel free to add those to what you evaluate and determine the different levels of performance. Remember to be thoughtful about what minimal, limited working and professional performances look like for additional benchmarks or standards.

Finally, as you use The Remote Interpreter Evaluation Tool and work with peers, remember to be patient with yourself. Progress takes time. While being patient you can ask yourself tough questions and push yourself to perform better. Track your progress. Reach out to your network peers in your language pairs and outside your language pairs for support and to give support. Remote interpreting may be isolating at times, but this tool is a great way to build relationships and advance quality individually and as a profession.

Chapter 6

Marjory A. Bancroft, MA (Sections 6.1.-6.4)
Danielle Meder, NIC (Section 6.5)

A Guide to Ethics in Remote Interpreting

Learning Objectives

After completing this chapter, the remote interpreter will be able to:

Learning Objective 6.1: Define codes of ethics, standards of practice, international standards and best practices.

Learning Objective 6.2: Discuss eight similarities shared among codes of ethics for interpreters.

Learning Objective 6.3: Describe three key differences among codes of ethics for interpreters.

Learning Objective 6.4: Apply codes of ethics and standards for interpreters across specializations or national borders.

Learning Objective 6.5: Identify similarities among codes of ethics for sign language interpreters and explain how to apply them to remote interpreting.

Introduction

Code of Ethics and Standards of Practice

Community interpreters should be trained by the relevant authority using their services... to adhere to the Code of Ethics and Standards of Practice relevant to their sector and geographical area. Community interpreters should make every possible effort to become informed about the code of ethics and standards applicable, and of the entity to which ethical violations can be reported.

—International Organization for Standardization (ISO), 2014, 3.5, p. 6

Interpreters around the world have a clear responsibility to understand and adhere to professional ethical requirements. Such an expectation seems straightforward.

But is it? Perhaps interpreters who work face-to-face in one geographic area can manage this. For remote interpreters, adhering to appropriate ethical requirements is far from simple.

The citation from the International Organization for Standardization (ISO) appears in one of the five international standards for interpreter services developed by ISO and discussed in Section 6.1. It clearly outlines the expectation that interpreters around the world will be trained to and comply with the appropriate professional ethics.

In reality, it has long been a challenge to provide clear, consistent training on ethics and ethical decision-making for remote interpreters.

Face-to-face interpreters typically work in a single geographic region. Even if they work across interpreting specializations, they might need to follow only one or two codes of ethics. Such codes might be national or regional. They might apply to all interpreting specializations or only one.

Imagine, however, that you're a remote interpreter in the Dominican Republic. You work in a call center. You interpret between Spanish and English by telephone and video for a U.S. language company. You interpret primarily for hospitals but also for banks and insurance companies, government social service agencies, schools and occasionally courts. You take calls from clients in the U.S., Canada and sometimes Mexico.

Now, which code or codes of professional ethics and which standards will you follow? Will you have different codes and standards to follow depending on the assignment and the country the participants are based in?

Let's step back a moment. Perhaps you're not sure about the difference between ethics and standards. Maybe you're aware of codes of ethics for healthcare interpreters in the United States, but you don't know which codes of ethics or standards for interpreters are available for interpreting specializations in Canada and Mexico, or even if professional ethics or standards exist there.

Here is the new reality: Whether by telephone or video, the remote interpreter often works across geographical and legal boundaries as well as specializations. No single code of ethics can guide most remote interpreters. How then, should remote interpreters develop ethical practices and helpful strategies to comply with every code of ethics that might be relevant to their work?

Here we run into a problem. There are no established best practices to guide remote interpreters to adhere to professional interpreter ethics across specializations and national borders.

In order to solve this problem, the author of this section examined 240 codes of ethics, standards of practice and ethical guidelines for interpreters and translators from around the world to determine the most accepted ethical practices for interpreters.

These 240 documents in 23 languages come from 53 countries and territories in Africa, Asia, Europe, Latin America, the Middle East and North America. Some documents address the whole world, others a continent or region (such as the Middle East). These codes of ethics and standards documents apply to general, community, conference, court (or legal), medical interpreting and translation. Some target only spoken languages or signed languages,[74] while others address both.[75]

Countries with codes of ethics for interpreters and/or translators[76]				
Argentina	Ecuador	Italy	Slovakia	Territories
Australia	Egypt	Japan	South Africa	Hong Kong
Austria	England	Kenya	Spain	Northern Ireland
Belgium	Estonia	Mexico	Sweden	Northern Mariana Islands
Bosnia/Herzegovina	Finland	Netherlands	Switzerland	Saipan[77]
Brazil	France	New Zealand	Türkiye	Translation only
Bulgaria	Germany	Norway	United Kingdom[78]	Korea
Canada	Guatemala	Peru	United States	Lithuania
Chile	Hungary	Philippines	Wales	Moldova
Colombia	Indonesia	Poland		Uruguay
Czech Republic	Ireland	Portugal		
Denmark	Israel	Scotland		

Table 6.1: Countries/territories with codes of ethics or ethical guidelines reviewed for this chapter

[74] A few sign language codes also addressed other communication professionals, such as lipspeakers, electronic or manual notetaker and speech to text reporters. Some mentioned cued, tactile and oral languages.

[75] Most of the documents reviewed are intended either for interpreters or for interpreters and translators. However, 29 of them addressed translators alone. They were reviewed as a comparison and proved highly similar in scope and content to the others.

[76] This list represents only countries with codes of ethics and similar documents identified and reviewed by the author of this section. Documents that were not written or available in English, French or Spanish were reviewed in Google Translate. Due to their overall similarity in terms of structure, content and intent, Google Translate proved adequate for this review, if at times amusing.

[77] Saipan is part of a U.S. commonwealth known as the Northern Mariana Islands.

[78] Separate codes of ethics exist for the UK, Ireland, Northern Ireland, Scotland and Wales, covering public service/community, legal and sign language interpreting.

The data from this international review of ethics offers groundbreaking guidance for remote interpreters. It shows that there is global agreement on many core ethical principles. It specifies key aspects of professional conduct for interpreters around the world, no matter where they are located and whether they perform face-to-face or remote interpreting—or both.

This chapter will first provide you with a clear understanding of the differences between ethics, standards of practice, international standards and best practices. Then, it will familiarize you with the most widely accepted ethical principles for interpreters around the world. Finally, it will show you how to make ethical decision-making across national borders and specializations in remote interpreting, even when there may not be a specific code of ethics that your region requires you to follow.

No matter where you work as a remote interpreter, or which country the participants of the session are located in, whether you are a spoken or sign language interpreter, or what kind of remote interpreting you perform, you'll need to be aware of and follow the appropriate ethical requirements and guidelines for your work. This chapter will help you do so.

Section 6.1 Defining Ethics and Standards

→ Learning objective 6.1

After completing this section, the remote interpreter will be able to define codes of ethics, standards of practice, international standards and best practices.

→ Section 6.1 Overview

The remote interpreter is a language professional. Most professionals are expected to follow not only legal requirements but also ethics and standards.

This section outlines what codes of ethics are, other names for them, and how they are similar to, or different from, related documents, such as standards of practice, international standards and best practice guidelines.

The section concludes with guidance on where to identify a particular code, or codes, of ethics that remote interpreters may need to know about and apply in their daily work.

→ Section 6.1 Content

What are ethics and standards?

> *A Code of Ethics is an essential document that regulates relationships between professional interpreters and consumers of interpreting services. Codes of ethics and conduct are important in the training, evaluation and monitoring of professionals. They express agreed norms against which ethical decision-making and professional conduct can be benchmarked.*
>
> —Sign Language Interpreters Association of New Zealand (SLIANZ), 2012, p. 1[79]

First, let's examine:

- What codes of ethics are.
- What standards of practice are.
- The differences between ethics, codes of conduct, standards and best practices.
- What the remote interpreter needs to know about ethics and standards.

Confusion about ethics

Many interpreters around the world do not understand the differences between codes of ethics and standards of practice for interpreters, far less the differences among codes of ethics, codes of conduct and codes of practice.

That confusion is not the fault of interpreters. The names for these documents are confusing. The great majority of the 240 documents reviewed for this chapter were titled codes of ethics. But some were called, instead, a code of conduct, a code of practice, a code of honor or a code of professional responsibility. Only a few (about 15 percent) had another name in their title instead of, or in addition to, the term code of ethics, such as standards, guidelines or best practices.

Such names are understood in different ways by different stakeholders. Are all these documents really, in effect, codes of ethics?

To add to potential confusion, there are industry standards, international standards and general best practices for interpreters. What are all these documents? How do they differ and why do they matter for remote interpreters?

Defining code of ethics and code of conduct

Let's start by defining a code of ethics, which in most countries is typically understood to be:

> *A set of directives that specifies the requirements or expectations intended to guide the conduct of practitioners of a profession.*
>
> —Bancroft et al., 2015, p. vii

---

[79] Sign Language Interpreters Association of New Zealand (SLIANZ), *Code of Ethics and Conduct.* Retrieved from: https://slianz.org.nz/wp-content/uploads/2018/10/SLIANZ-Code-of-Ethics-2012.pdf

In other words, a code of ethics, conduct or practice for interpreters typically specifies the strictest requirements laid down for those who work in a certain country (or region) or who practice a certain specialization—or, in the case of sign language, a specific signed language. (See Section 6.5 for information specific to codes of ethics for sign language interpreters.)

A reasonably standard definition for a code of conduct is "a set of rules that members of an organization or people with a particular job or position must follow."[80]

Codes of ethics and conduct are strict documents, but they are not as rigid as laws. While you might lose your certification, your membership in an association or even your right to practice as an interpreter for violating a code of ethics for interpreters, you will not go to prison!

Ethics guide you. With the exception of some codes of ethics for court interpreters, they are not usually legally binding.

Other names for codes of ethics and codes of conduct

The vast majority of documents examined for this chapter were labeled a code of ethics. However, similar documents (in terms of their content, structure, tone and specific elements) had other names. Some names were variations on code of ethics, such as:

- Code of professional ethics
- Code of ethics and professional responsibility/responsibilities
- Code of ethics and good practice
- Code of ethics and professional practice
- Code of practice and professional ethics

Other titles included the word ethics but not code, for example, professional standards and ethics.

Still other names do not include the word ethics at all yet appeared otherwise the same as any typical code of ethics for interpreters. Some of these names are:

- Code of conduct (or code of professional conduct)
- Code of practice (or code of professional practice)
- Code of honor
- Code of professional responsibility

After code of ethics, the most common name of documents examined for this chapter is code of conduct.

Codes of ethics and codes of conduct serve a similar purpose

This chapter does not address the broader and much more complex, philosophical discussion of what ethics are. Rather, it focuses on how ethics are *applied* in the interpreting profession through codes of ethics and conduct, interpreter decision-making and ethical practice.

---

[80] Cambridge Dictionary. Retrieved from: https://dictionary.cambridge.org/us/dictionary/english/code-of-conduct

Codes of ethics and conduct for interpreters are typically a list of *requirements*. Most documents counsel interpreters to "do this and not that"—for example, interpret everything and maintain confidentiality; do not take sides or show discriminatory behavior.

The key point here is that *codes of ethics* and *codes of conduct* for interpreters (and almost any other documents labeled a code) broadly and with few exceptions are created and used for essentially similar purposes. They both target interpreter behavior: Not interpreters' ethical beliefs but the potential consequences of their practice—what they do to behave ethically.

As a result, this chapter will treat codes of ethics, codes of conduct and other codes for interpreters for practical purposes as the same type of document and will refer to them all as codes of ethics.

Remote interpreters need to familiarize themselves with the ethics document that provides guidance for interpreter ethical conduct for their region and specialization, regardless of whether it is titled a code of ethics, code of conduct or any of the other names listed previously.

The purpose of codes of ethics

An important question for interpreters is why these codes exist: What is their purpose? Here are a few answers:

> *This code of ethics of the l'Association québécoise des interprètes en langues des signes (AQILS) was drafted with the objective of ensuring the standardization and quality of sign language interpretation services in Quebec. It is also a tool which aims to inform the public, Deaf and hearing, of the duties and professional responsibilities that they are entitled to expect from the interpreters they hire or who work in a context where they are involved.*[81]
>
> —AQILS, 2016, p. 1
>
> *Ethics go beyond morals (right and wrong) to the reasons for the decisions or actions that an individual makes. In healthcare, when we say that someone is ethical, we mean that this person has analyzed his or her reasons for a decision or an action, and that the action is aligned with the ultimate goal of supporting the patient's health and well-being and the patient/provider relationship.*
>
> —California Standards for Healthcare Interpreters (CHIA), 2002, p. 32
>
> *A code of ethics is a guideline of principles designed to help professionals conduct business with integrity and honesty. A code of ethics document may outline the mission and values of a business or organization, how professionals are expected to address problems, the ethical principles based on the organization's core values, and the standards to which the professional is bound.*
>
> —Translingua[82]

[81] Translation by Google Translate except the name of the association. Retrieved from: https://aqils.ca/documents/code_deontologie_aqils.pdf

[82] *Language Interpreting Code of Ethics.* A two-page code of ethics issued by a U.S. language company, available at https://www.translingua-translations.com/language-interpreting-code-of-ethics/

Who develops codes of ethics?

Codes of ethics are most often published by professional associations. For example, a professional association for general, medical, court, conference or community interpreters (in any country or in a region, state or province) may issue a code of ethics. That code might be international, such as the code of ethics of the International Association of Conference Interpreters (AIIC) or the International Federation of Translators (FIT).

Alternatively, a code of ethics might address all interpreters in a particular country or region, such as the Australian Institute of Interpreters and Translators (AUSIT) code of ethics, which applies to interpreters in Australia.[83] A code might also address the interpreters who work in a particular region or specialization, such as the Arab Professional Translators Society's *Code of Ethics* (APTS, n.d.) or the Associazione Italiana Traduttori e Interpreti Giudiziari legal interpreters' *Codice Deontologico* (code of ethics—AssITIG, 2012).

Codes of ethics or codes of conduct for interpreters may also be issued by:

- International organizations (such as the United Nations Mechanism for International Criminal Tribunals)
- International or regional government bodies or agencies
- Courts
- School districts
- Language services (both language companies and nonprofit services)
- Nonprofit associations (such as refugee resettlement and social services agencies)

As Section 6.5 of this chapter makes clear, associations for interpreters of signed languages typically issue codes that address all interpreting specializations.

Professional associations (general)	International associations or groups[84]	Courts and legal interpreter associations[85]	Sign language associations	Language services
Argentina	AIIC	Austria	Australia	Canada
Australia	APTS	Canada	Austria	Egypt
Austria	ATA	France	Canada	New Zealand
Belgium	EU/EC	Germany	Czech Republic	Singapore
Brazil	EULITA	Italy	Estonia	Spain
Bulgaria	FIT EUROPE	Netherlands	France	Russia
Canada	IAPTI	Slovenia	Germany	UK (Wales)
Chile	IMIA	UK	Ireland	U.S.

[83] Some codes of ethics for interpreters are even specific to certain cities.

[84] Acronym and initialism abbreviations are found in Table 6.3.

[85] Court interpreter codes of ethics may be issued by either courts at federal, state or provincial levels and/or interpreter associations (typically associations of legal interpreters and translators).

Colombia	UN MICT	U.S.	Italy	
Czech Republic	UNHCR		Japan	
Denmark	WASLI		Kenya	
Ecuador			Mexico	
Egypt			Netherlands	
Estonia			New Zealand	
Finland			Norway	
France			Philippines	
Germany			Spain	
Guatemala			Switzerland	
Hong Kong			UK	
Hungary			U.S.	
Indonesia				
Ireland				
Israel				
Italy				
Japan				
Kenya				
Mexico				
Netherlands				
New Zealand				
Norway				
Peru				
Philippines				
Poland				
Portugal				
Romania				
Saipan				
Slovenia				
South Africa				
Spain				
Türkiye				
UK				

Table 6.2: **Overview of organizations that publish interpreter codes of ethics or ethical guidelines**

Examples of international professional associations or groups with codes of ethics for interpreters
AIIC: International Association of Conference Interpreters
APTS: Arab Professional Translators Society
ATA: American Translators Association
EU/EC: European Union/European Commission (Directorate-General for Interpretation)
EULITA: European Legal Interpreters and Translators Association
FIT EUROPE: International Federation of Translators: Europe
IAPTI: International Association of Professional Translators and Interpreters
IMIA: International Medical Interpreters Association
UN MICT: United Nations Mechanism for International Criminal Tribunals
UNHCR: United Nations High Commissioner for Refugees
WASLI: World Association of Sign Language Interpreters

Table 6.3: **International professional associations or groups that publish interpreter codes of ethics based on the sample reviewed for this chapter**

Standards of practice

If you see the word code in the title of a document that lays down requirements for interpreters, that document can usually be considered a code of ethics (or equivalent). But what if the document is labeled as a set of standards? What are *standards* for interpreters? Are they the same as standards of practice?

The word standards is broad and can mean many different things, ranging from a level of quality to a benchmark for measuring achievement.

Standards of practice, however, are sometimes published together with codes of ethics for interpreters. Here is one definition for standards of practice:

> *A set of formal guidelines that offer practitioners of a profession clear strategies and courses of action to support professional conduct.*
>
> —Bancroft et al., 2015, p. xii

In other words, while ethics tend to tell interpreters *what* to do, standards of practice generally guide the interpreter on *how* to do the work: That is, how to behave professionally in a situation that requires the interpreter to make decisions about their own conduct and behavior.

Names for standards

There is no "standard" name for interpreting standards. Unless the document holds both ethics and standards in its title (such as "Standards of Practice and Ethics" or "Code of Ethics and Standards of Practice"), look for some other sort of name in the title to show you it is a standards document.

Here are examples of titles for documents that include helpful standards for interpreters:

- Standards
  - Standards of interpretation
  - Standards of practice
  - Standard practice
  - Professional standards
  - Standards for educational interpreters and transliterators

Ethics vs. standards

What are the differences between ethics and standards?

As noted, codes of ethics in general tend to be stricter than standards. Codes of ethics lay down general requirements that often amount to: "Do this. Don't do that."

For example, a code of ethics may declare that interpreters should provide complete, accurate interpretation, maintain strict confidentiality and remain impartial, avoiding conflicts of interest or siding with one party. Some even require interpreters not to compete unfairly with other interpreters.

However, in real life simple rules for interpreters often don't work well. A wealth of research literature (especially about interpreting in signed languages) addresses this reality in the field (e.g., Dean & Pollard, 2011).

Let's look at how two different professional associations have addressed these differences.

The Healthcare Interpretation Network (HIN) *National Standard Guide for Community Interpreting Services* (Canada) combines its ethics and standards into a single document. Each ethical principle is defined and stated as an objective; it is accompanied by several specific standards of practice to help guide the interpreter in applying the ethical principle in day-to-day interpreting.

For example, the ethical principle of accuracy and fidelity is defined as: "Interpreters strive to render all messages in their entirety accurately, as faithfully as possible and to the best of their ability without addition, distortion, omission or embellishment of the meaning" (HIN, 2010, p. 13).

The document provides seven specific standards of practice to help guide the interpreter to *practice* accuracy and fidelity.

Here is how the document is structured:

Standard of Practice

Accuracy and Fidelity

Objective: Preservation of the meaning of the message.

1. The interpreter renders all utterances and written communication faithfully using the same grammatical person as the speaker or writer. The rendition should sound natural in the target language and there should be no distortion of the original message through additions, omissions, or explanation. The idiom, register, style and tone of the speaker is preserved.
2. The interpreter advises all parties that everything said in the encounter will be interpreted. If any party requests that the interpreter refrain from interpreting all utterances, the interpreter is obliged to inform all other parties of the request and seek direction.
3. The interpreter retains English words mixed into the other language, as well as culturally bound terms which have no direct equivalent in English, or which may have more than one meaning. Whenever possible, the interpreter will attempt a translation of that word to provide the listener with an idea of what the word means.
4. The interpreter asks for repetition, rephrasing, or explanation, if anything is unclear. Upon recognizing that the interpreter has misunderstood the communication, he/she identifies the misunderstanding and requests direction from the parties involved.
5. The interpreter ensures that the meaning of gestures, body language, and tone of voice is not lost, by replicating what has been seen or heard by the interpreter.
6. The interpreter uses a mode of interpreting appropriate for the setting. In most interview situations, spoken-language interpreting is done in consecutive mode.
7. The interpreter performs summary interpretation (i.e. some of the elements of the communication are not interpreted) only with the knowledge and consent of all parties.

Ethical Principle

Interpreters strive to render all messages in their entirety accurately, as faithfully as possible and to the best of their ability without addition, distortion, omission or embellishment of the meaning.

Figure 6.1: **HIN, 2010, p. 13**

In contrast, the U.S. National Council on Interpreting in Health Care (NCIHC) published a national code of ethics and a national standards of practice in separate documents (NCIHC, 2004 and 2005).

The code of ethics provides a detailed exploration of each ethical principle as well as a detailed discussion of the values underlying each one.

The NCIHC standards of practice document is structured similarly to the HIN document, providing the ethical principle, its objective and definition, and several corresponding standards of practice for guidance.

STANDARDS OF PRACTICE

ACCURACY

OBJECTIVE:

To enable other parties to know precisely what each speaker has said.

Related ethical principle:

Interpreters strive to render the message accurately, conveying the content and spirit of the original message, taking into consideration the cultural context.

1. **The interpreter renders all messages accurately and completely, without adding, omitting, or substituting.**

   For example, an interpreter repeats all that is said, even if it seems redundant, irrelevant, or rude.

2. **The interpreter replicates the register, style, and tone of the speaker.**

   For example, unless there is no equivalent in the patient's language, an interpreter does not substitute simpler explanations for medical terms a provider uses, but may ask the speaker to re-express themselves in language more easily understood by the other party.

3. **The interpreter advises parties that everything said will be interpreted.**

   For example, an interpreter may explain the interpreting process to a provider by saying "everything you say will be repeated to the patient."

4. **The interpreter manages the flow of communication.**

   For example, an interpreter may ask a speaker to pause or slow down.

5. **The interpreter corrects errors in interpretation.**

   For example, an interpreter who has omitted an important word corrects the mistake as soon as possible.

6. **The interpreter maintains transparency.**

   For example, when asking for clarification, an interpreter says to all parties, "I, the interpreter, did not understand, so I am going to ask for an explanation."

Figure 6.2: **NCIHC, 2005, p. 5**

You can explore the two NCIHC documents in more detail by going online and using the following links.[86] Take a look at both of them. What differences do you notice?

Code of Ethics for Interpreters in Health Care
https://www.ncihc.org/assets/z2021Images/NCIHC%20National%20Code%20of%20Ethics.pdf

National Standards of Practice for Interpreters in Health Care
https://www.ncihc.org/assets/z2021Images/NCIHC%20National%20Standards%20of%20Practice.pdf

[86] If these two links expire, simply do an online search on the titles and add NCIHC to your search to find the two documents.

Standards in action

Standards of practice can help interpreters by providing guidelines that show how to apply ethical requirements or directives to challenging situations.

> *Ethical practice and decision-making are not simply "rule-based." ...The [goal is to] help guide interpreters to apply the intent of the Code of Ethics, to make decisions that have the least harmful impacts, and to ensure consistency of behaviour across the profession...*
>
> *[These standards give] guidance to interpreters on how to apply the intent of the Code of Ethics. To ensure consistency across the profession, the points below set out the kind of conduct that is generally expected of interpreters...*
>
> *Above all, interpreters should use their professional judgment to conduct themselves in ways that have the least harmful impacts, and that align with the aims of the Code of Ethics.*
>
> —SLIANZ, 2012, pp. 2, 6

For example, someone says something to the remote interpreter privately that this participant clearly does *not* expect the interpreter to interpret. It could be a private question, a request for advice, a curse word or an insult about one of the participants, for example. Almost any code of ethics for interpreters requires accuracy and completeness—in other words, you should interpret everything.

Really? *Everything*? Even if interpreting something could offend, anger or hurt one participant or cause trouble?

Some standards offer specific, helpful guidelines on this issue. For example, the U.S. *A National Code of Ethics for Interpreters in Health Care* states only that:

> *The interpreter strives to render the message accurately, conveying the content and spirit of the original message, taking into consideration its cultural context.*
>
> —NCIHC, 2004, p. 3

But the U.S. *National Standards of Practice for Interpreters in Health Care* is more specific. It states:

> *The interpreter renders all messages accurately and completely, without adding, omitting, or substituting.*[87]
>
> *For example, an interpreter repeats all that is said, even if it seems redundant, irrelevant, or rude.*
>
> —NCIHC, 2005, p. 5

In other words—yes, interpreters need to interpret the "bad words," including insults about another participant. Interpreting harsh language may feel awkward or rude. It can also raise your fears that a participant might think you're insulting them when you are simply interpreting. But when codes of ethics and standards for interpreters around the world address this point, they tend to agree that the interpreter needs to interpret not only requests for guidance or advice but also even

[87] The content of this particular sentence can be found in countless codes, standards and guidelines for interpreters.

coarse, rude or obscene language. (Think about this. If someone spoke insultingly about you in your presence, wouldn't you want to know?)

In fact, in some court interpreting standards, the interpreter may receive more detailed guidance, including the need to interpret hesitations, filler words (such as *uh* or *mmmm)* or repetitions (*yes, yes, yes, yes, yes!*).

Table 6.4 provides a helpful summary of how interpreter codes of ethics and standards of practices are most commonly structured around the world. These commonalities are important to you, the remote interpreter. Regardless of where you are based, they provide a shared ethical framework for you to follow when you interpret.

Codes of ethics and standards of practice for interpreters Common characteristics and goals			
Codes of ethics		Standards of practice	
Characteristics	Goals	Characteristics	Goals
Are often prescriptive and rule-based.	Standardize interpreter conduct.	Are generally descriptive, not prescriptive.	Show how to do the work well.
Share a common goal of influencing conduct.	Set expectations.	Tend to focus on professional practice.	Reinforce ethical directives.
May focus on "right vs. wrong" behavior.	Uphold the profession.	Are far less common than codes of ethics.	Standardize conduct (in more detail than codes).
Are widely similar around the world.	Maintain professional standards.	Are often called standards, practices or guidelines.	Specify expectations.
Tend to be called a code.[88]	Preserve privacy.	Are typically longer than codes of ethics.	Clarify ethical directives with examples, guidance.
Are of varying lengths.	Convey full message.	Are mostly, like codes, published by professional groups.	Show how to apply ethics.
Are mostly published by professional groups.	Provide a faithful rendering.	Often based on a specific code to amplify it.	Support critical thinking.
Are typically issued by interpreter associations.	Support each other.	Have variable structures, lengths and formats.	Build trust in the profession.
May comes from some courts.	Engage in honest business practices.	Include a wide variety of content (more than codes).	Build decision-making skills.
May be issued by language services or government bodies.	Respect all participants.	Are typically more detailed than codes.	Support professionalization.
Tend to be somewhat strict, rigid and binding (on members).	Respect colleagues.	Are sometimes included in codes of ethics documents.	Provide clarity and perspective on ethical requirements.

Table 6.4: **Comparison of common characteristics and goals of ethics and standards for interpreters**

International standards

In addition to ethics and standards of practice, there are international standards. These are not the same as standards of practice. Instead, they are developed by international standardization organizations across industries and professions.

88 For example, code of ethics, code of conduct, code of professional responsibility, code of practice, code of honor, etc.

International standards help to support the *quality and safety of products, services and systems*. They also create more consistency among national or regional standards.

International standards exist for almost everything from milk and light bulbs to railroad ties and interpreting booths. The goal of standardizing professional behavior, however, is an important one as well. At this time, at least two international standards organizations have published standards for interpreting: ISO and ASTM International.

ISO

The International Organization for Standardization (ISO) is considered by many to be the leading organization for international standards. It was established in 1947. ISO has so far published five international standards for interpreting:[89]

- Community interpreting: ISO 13611:2014. *Interpreting—Guidelines for Community Interpreting.* (ISO, 2014).
- General interpreting: ISO 18841: 2018 *Interpreting Services: General Requirements and Recommendations.* (ISO, 2018).
- Legal interpreting: ISO 20228: 2019. *Interpreting Services—Legal Interpreting—Requirements.* (ISO, 2019a).
- Healthcare interpreting: ISO 21998:2020. *Interpreting Services—Healthcare Interpreting—Requirements and Recommendations.* (ISO, 2020).
- Conference interpreting: ISO 23155:2022. *Interpreting Services—Conference Interpreting—Requirements and Recommendations.* (ISO, 2022a).

In addition, ISO has developed several standards for simultaneous interpreting equipment and booths. In 2022, it published its first standard for remote interpreting platforms:

- Simultaneous interpreting: ISO 24019:2022. *Simultaneous Interpreting Delivery Platforms—Requirements and Recommendations.* (ISO, 2022b).

ISO will continue to develop or update its international standards for interpreting.

ASTM International

The American Society for Testing and Materials was formed in Pennsylvania in 1898 and rebranded as ASTM International in 2001. Its focus, outreach and recognition are international. With participation from individuals around the world, it publishes more than 12,000 standards each year that are developed by experts in more than 140 countries. ASTM International has so far published and kept updating one international standard that addresses all interpreting specializations: ASTM F2089-15, *Standard Practice for Language Interpreting*, updated in 2023.

Why international standards matter

It is important to understand that international standards are intended to guide organizations and service providers as well as interpreter associations and entities. *They do not specifically address*

[89] To be clear each "standard" is a publication that contains many "standards."

individual interpreters (although a freelance interpreter is, by definition, an interpreting service provider).

All international standards are voluntary: No interpreter "must" obey them, and no company, agency or organization "must" enforce them.

However, some organizations (including language services) go through a formal process to become ISO- or ASTM-certified. As a result, international standards are slowly having an impact, perhaps more on language services than interpreters, by standardizing expectations for professional interpreting around the world. Perhaps, one day, requiring these certifications will become the standard in the language service industry, as it has in the automotive industry, for example.

Defining best practices

Best practices are simply statements about the expectations held by interpreting professions in any country for the work and conduct of practicing interpreters. Such documents can be formal or informal. They may or may not provide specific guidance about how to support codes of ethics.

Names for best practice documents

If best practices are codified into formal documents, they tend over time to become codes of ethics, codes of conduct or standards of practice. If they are less formal, they are often referred to as best practices, guidelines or by other names. They are often simply informal standards.

Such documents have many names that often include the words practice or guide in the titles, such as the following:

- Practices
  - Best practices
  - Good practices
- Guide
  - Guidelines [for educational interpreting, in these four examples]
    - Guidelines for educational interpreters
    - Guidelines of professional conduct for educational interpreters
    - Guidelines for school interpreters
    - Professional guidelines for interpreting in educational settings
  - Guide to ethics
  - A study guide on the code of ethics
- Considerations
  - Ethical considerations for educational interpreters

Who publishes best practices?

Almost any individual or organization can publish formal or informal best practice documents, such as interpreter associations, government agencies, language services, educational institutions and even individual interpreters.

Best practices can be disseminated through conference presentations, papers and articles, and documents or online guidelines issued by institutions that employ or engage interpreters. Guidance on best practices appears on the websites of some language companies, school districts and other organizations. One of the main goals of this textbook was, in fact, to gather and present best practices for remote interpreters based on the authors' experience and expertise.

Comparison of ethics, standards and best practices for interpreters				
Type of document	**Code of ethics**	**Standards of practice**	**International standards**	**Best practices**
Alternative names	Code of conduct, code of professional responsibility, code of practice, code of honor, etc.	Professional standards, standards for interpreters/ interpreting, etc.	International guidelines, international practices, international requirements.	Good practices, guide, guidelines, guidelines of professional conduct, guide to ethics, study guide, etc.
Goal of document	Establish acceptable conduct for interpreters. Promote legitimacy for the profession.	Support ethical practice in the field.	Support quality and consistency of practice. Reduce variation at national and international level.	Help interpreters to improve and professionalize their practice.
Who issues it	Primarily professional associations, government bodies, courts, schools and language services.	Same organizations that develop codes of ethics.	International standardization groups, such as ISO and ASTM.	Almost any organization or individual that supports quality interpreting.
Format	Introduction with list of directives (tenets, principles or canons) directing interpreters to "Do this, not that."	Introduction with list or detailed guidance on practices that will support ethical conduct. May specifically address a list of ethical directives or tenets.	Introduction, definition of scope of document, glossary, list of requirements or recommendations for good practice, references, possibly an appendix.	No established format.
Length	From a few sentences to dozens of pages.	Several pages to dozens of pages.	Several pages (more than a dozen) but varying in length.	No established length.
Tone	Strict. Language of "shall" or "should." Prescriptive.	Less strict than ethics. "How to do" rather than "what to do."	Prescriptive for requirements; somewhat less prescriptive for recommendations but still strict.	Encouraging; generally somewhat positive in tone.

Table 6.5: **An informal comparison of documents that guide the conduct of interpreters**

Note: This table, of necessity, given that it addresses 240 documents, overgeneralizes its findings to illustrate trends.

Why you should follow a code of ethics

Codes of ethics are often strict. If you work as an employee or contractor for an organization that provides or specifies a code of ethics to follow, you are expected to follow those ethical directives. If you do not follow the directives, consequences or penalties might result. For example, a professional association might expel an interpreter who violates its code of ethics and specify procedures to do so in the document itself.

In addition, if you do not follow a relevant code of ethics, you might:

- Disrupt a session.
- Create confusion or misunderstanding.
- Cause communication to break down.
- Put the session's intended outcomes at risk.
- Cause significant—even legal—trouble or disruptions for the organization you interpret for.
- Create an expectation that other remote interpreters will also behave in nonprofessional, unethical ways.
- Lose professional status. For example, depending on the country, specialization or organization you interpret for, after violating professional ethics you might:
    - Lose your contract.
    - Lose your job.
    - Lose your membership in a professional association.
    - Lose your certification.
    - Lose your license to interpret.

Interpreters who work remotely for a language company and violate that company's code of ethics might lose their job or future contracts with that company. Interpreters who violate ethical behavior can even be charged with crimes in some cases. In Florida, in April 2022, an Afghan interpreter was arrested for fraudulently assisting 100 or more people to get their driver's licenses.[90]

Several codes of ethics specify the specific penalties for violating the code and processes for sanctioning interpreters.

In short, codes of ethics typically offer the strictest set of directives for interpreters while other documents, such as standards, guidance or best practices, are essentially professional guidelines.

Remote interpreters are more likely than onsite interpreters to be required to adhere to codes of ethics and conduct provided by language services rather than those developed by professional associations precisely because of the wide variety of settings and types of sessions they interpret for. Language services often blend ethics, standards and best practices into a single code of conduct or guidance document with which interpreters are expected to comply.

90 Retrieved from: https://www.news4jax.com/news/local/2022/04/16/jacksonville-tax-collector-employee-arrested-after-supplying-100-fake-drivers-licenses/

If, however, national association or government ethics apply to the interpreting they do, they will often be required to be familiar with and follow that code of ethics whenever they are in a session where it applies. As language services increasingly provide remote interpreting across national borders, their interpreters may be required to follow more than one code of ethics.

How can I find a code of ethics to follow?

Now that you know what a code of ethics is, what standards are and the differences between them, the question for you is *which* code or codes should you follow as a remote interpreter? Section 6.4 will discuss the answer to this question in detail. For now, here are a few important points to note.

1. The answer to this simple question of what code to follow is complicated, but if you work for any organization with its own general code of ethics for interpreters, you will be expected to follow that code.
2. If the session you are interpreting for requires you to be certified or qualified for a specific interpreting specialization or geographical area, *the code of ethics that applies to your specialization or geographic area should take precedence over a general agency code of conduct.* (It could be an international, national, regional or local code of ethics.)[91]
3. Next, if you are a member of a professional association, *also follow the code for that association.*

If you need to follow more than one code of ethics but there is a conflict between or among them:

- Consult your employer or the association or group you are interpreting for to determine how best to manage the conflict.
- Remember, if you disagree with the code of ethics of a language service or organization you interpret for, while you can raise the matter beforehand, if you agree to the work, you are agreeing as per your contract to abide by that organization's requirements. You always have the choice not to take on the work.

Where you can look for codes of ethics

Look for codes of ethics online or through your professional association. A few codes are translated into English; most are in the national language or one of the official national languages of the country where that code is published. To see a list of the countries with codes of ethics or ethical guidelines for interpreters reviewed for this chapter, see Section 6.4, which will also help you search for a code of ethics that applies to you.

The good news is that new codes of ethics for interpreters are being created every year. You can search online for a code for your country, region or specialization.

---

[91] If, however, a language service tries to enforce its own code of ethics, and that code diverges significantly from standard codes of ethics for interpreters or the code that applies to a certification, consider bringing any contradictions to the organization's attention. For example (a true example), if a language service instructs you to identify yourself as the interpreter *only* when you intervene with the participant who speaks the dominant language, that request is a violation of transparency and accuracy. Most professional interpreter associations around the world would not accept an ethical requirement that violates transparency and accuracy.

→ Section 6.1 Review

This section defined interpreter ethics, standards of practice, international standards and best practices. It specified that codes of ethics are created to standardize the professional conduct and activities of interpreters. Interpreter codes of ethics are also called codes of conduct, codes of practice and codes of honor (among other names), yet all these documents are essentially similar. They share the common goal of setting out directives or requirements for the professional practice of interpreters.

Codes of ethics for interpreters can be found in dozens of countries around the world. Violating the requirements or directives in a code of ethics could lead interpreters to lose their certification, contracts or license to work. They might be expelled from their professional interpreting association.

Standards of practice are usually guidelines that help interpreters to apply codes of ethics. Some of the differences between ethics and standards include:

- Ethics usually describe what to do (or not to do). Standards (and best practice documents) typically show interpreters how to conduct their work.
- Ethics tend to be stricter and more prescriptive, while standards and best practices tend to offer more flexible guidelines.
- Ethics help interpreters make decisions about "right or wrong" behavior but they can often be too strict when interpreters face challenges.
- Standards help interpreters make decisions about how to get the job done.

International standards, in contrast, are guidelines or requirements developed by an international standards organization to support quality and overcome differences among national or regional standards. They tend to address best practices for interpreting services rather than the behavior of individual interpreters.

Best practices for interpreters are widely accepted descriptions of preferred interpreter conduct and behavior. Some are formal publications while many are less formal. Best practice documents and other guidelines are intended to support decision-making by interpreters.

Section 6.2 Eight Similarities Shared Among Codes of Ethics

→ Learning objective 6.2

After completing this section, the remote interpreter will be able to discuss eight similarities shared among codes of ethics for interpreters.

→ Section 6.2 Overview

Expectations for interpreter conduct can vary. However, over the past 30 years an astonishing agreement has developed around the world about the role and accepted conduct of the interpreter.

As a result, despite some differences, most codes of ethics for interpreters in any specialization or country agree on certain basic principles. This section will focus on eight common directives[92] or tenets, found in most codes of ethics for interpreters around the world.

The eight most common principles the codes of ethics and ethical guidelines reviewed for this chapter are:

- Confidentiality (protecting privacy, maintaining secrecy)
- Accuracy (faithfulness and interpreting the whole message)
- Impartiality (taking no sides and avoiding conflict of interest)
- Professionalism (professional conduct)
- Professional development (engaging in continuing education)
- Role boundaries (defining scope of practice and professional boundaries)
- Solidarity (professional relationships that support the profession itself)
- Respect (for all participants)

The first five principles are so common they are found in almost all the 240 documents reviewed for this chapter. Because these five are nearly universal, it becomes deeply important for interpreters to adhere to them when working remotely.

This section will examine each of these eight principles to help guide the practice of remote interpreters no matter where they work or for whom they interpret.

→ Section 6.2 Content

Confidentiality

> *Interpreters/Translators keep any information learned during provision of interpretation services confidential.*
>
> —Hong Kong Community Services Centre for Harmony and Enhancement of Ethnic Minority Residents (HKCS CHEER), n.d., p. 1
>
> *All members of the Institute shall undertake...to maintain a relationship of trust with their clients/employers and to treat all information that comes to their attention in the course of their work as confidential.*
>
> —South African Translators' Institute (SATI), n.d., p. 1

[92] There is no standard term for directives such as "maintain confidentiality" or "render the message accurately and completely." Such statements are variously referred to as principles, requirements, tenets or (for court interpreting codes of ethics) canons.

Confidentiality appears to be a requirement in *all* codes of ethics and standards of practice for interpreters around the world. (Certainly, it is required in all 240 documents examined for this chapter.)

Confidentiality requirements typically specify that the interpreter may not share information learned during the assignment. Above all, the interpreter should *not disclose details that could identify participants.*

Legal requirements for interpreter confidentiality

The legal requirements surrounding interpreter confidentiality are usually strict. As a result, the first requirement for any remote interpreter is to study the privacy laws related to confidentiality in the country—and potentially the state, province or district—where the session takes place.

The second requirement is to find out if confidentiality requirements differ by specialization. For example, courts and healthcare systems may have broadly similar requirements about confidentiality and privacy of information, yet their guidance for *how* to follow these requirements may differ significantly.

(For example, in the U.S., interpreters in healthcare are required to work on devices and with data that are all securely encrypted in order to store private health information, including interpreter invoices and receipts. Interpreters must also take special training in healthcare privacy laws and understand 18 different types of personal identifier information in order to protect it. They are required stay up to date with any changes in healthcare legislation that affect privacy—and much more.)

In many countries today, including the U.S., legal privacy requirements tend to be especially strict in healthcare and legal interpreting. They are often encoded in specific legislation. (See Volume 1, Chapter 9, Language Access Laws and Language Policies, for details.)

If you interpret for a country such as the U.S. with legal privacy requirements, *learn and follow them strictly.* **The interpreter who violates any requirement related to privacy and confidentiality might not only be violating the law of that country or region: The interpreter might also expose the language service or organization that has engaged the interpreter—and any organization for which the interpreter is interpreting—to a potential lawsuit, legal penalty or criminal case.**

Examples of how to adhere to confidentiality requirements

Here are a few excellent examples of how to honor confidentiality. They will serve you well in any country.

Interpreters are not typically permitted to share detailed information about a session. When they share their work experiences, it is particularly important *not* to divulge any of the following information:

- Name, age, gender or other personal information about a participant.
- Day of the week, time of day and time of year the session occurred.
- Location.

- The participants involved—even the number of participants.
- Any particularities of the situation.

> *Maintain the confidentiality of the information contained in the translated/interpreted material, as long as the client considers the information confidential.*[93]
>
> —Himpunan Penerjemah Indonesia (HPI), 2013

> *Strict confidentiality is necessary because sharing even minimal information [can be] sufficient to identify the parties involved.*
>
> —BDG, 2020, Switzerland[94]

Figure 6.3: How to maintain confidentiality

Maintaining confidentiality can have different meanings. The single most common directive or requirement related to confidentiality in at least 26 codes of ethics reviewed is that *the interpreter should derive no personal gain or benefit from the confidential knowledge learned during the assignment.*

The second most common point to note is that confidentiality may, in fact, be broken if the interpreter is required by law to disclose certain information. For example, you may be expected to inform authorities if a person makes an explicit threat to harm themselves or others. However, if you receive a legal document, such as a subpoena, that requires you to testify in court about a session for which you interpreted, check with a lawyer first. You might or might not be required to testify and break confidentiality.

Helpful guidance on confidentiality

Try to observe the following:

- Maintain confidentiality beyond the assignment—you may be required to do so indefinitely.

[93] Adapted slightly from a Google Translate translation.

[94] Adapted from a Google Translate translation.

- Securely destroy (by shredding, if possible) any notes you take, or any other data related to the assignment.
- Protect the privacy of any documents involved.
  - For example, is your computer secure?
  - Are paper records related to your sessions locked up or destroyed?

However, for training purposes, professional development, supporting your colleagues and your own self-care and emotional well-being, several codes permit the interpreter to share *general* information from assignments. For example, as long as you do not reveal identifying details about anyone you interpret for, you could:

- Share broad aspects of an incident during a training program or conference workshop, for helpful discussion.
- Consult a colleague or supervisor for guidance about an ethical issue.
- Describe the session in broad, *general* terms to a family member or friend (for example, "I interpreted for end of life today and it was *incredibly* distressing") to reduce stress following the session or workday.

Keep in mind that there is nothing confidential about your feelings. If you need to, share your feelings about a session!

Accuracy

Almost all codes of ethics for interpreters include the ethical tenet of accuracy. Accuracy, for interpreters, typically means interpreting the message—the *whole* message—faithfully into the other language while remaining true to its spirit.

> *Every interpretation shall be faithful to and render exactly the message of the source text. A faithful interpretation should not be confused with a literal interpretation. The fidelity of an interpretation includes an adaptation to make the form, the tone, and the deeper meaning of the source text felt in the target language and culture.*
>
> —AVLIC/CASLI,[95] n.d., 2.2, p. 3
>
> *As a translator, interpreter and/or editor, a bridge for ideas from one language to another and one culture to another, I commit myself to high standards of performance, ethical behavior, and business practices.*
>
> *1. I will endeavor to translate and/or interpret the original message faithfully. I recognize that ideally such a level of excellence requires:*
>
> *a. mastery of the target language, at a level equivalent to that of an educated native speaker;*
>
> *b. up to date knowledge of the topic and relevant terminology in both source and target languages;*
>
> *c. access to information resources and auxiliary tools and familiarity with appropriate professional tools;*
>
> *d. ongoing efforts to improve, broaden and strengthen my skills and knowledge.*
>
> —Israel Translators Association (ITA), n.d., p. 1

Many codes say the interpreter should not add to, change or omit any part of the message.

[95] The former Association of Visual Language Interpreters of Canada is now the Canadian Association of Sign Language Interpreters.

A number of codes (especially for signed language) mention that you should ask about the preferred language. Perhaps you are not the ideal interpreter for that call or encounter. For example, if you are a Spanish interpreter, but one participant speaks an Indigenous language and is not fluent in Spanish, consider requesting an interpreter for the Indigenous language. If you are a signed language interpreter who sees the need for a certified Deaf interpreter, ask to work with one, if that is possible.

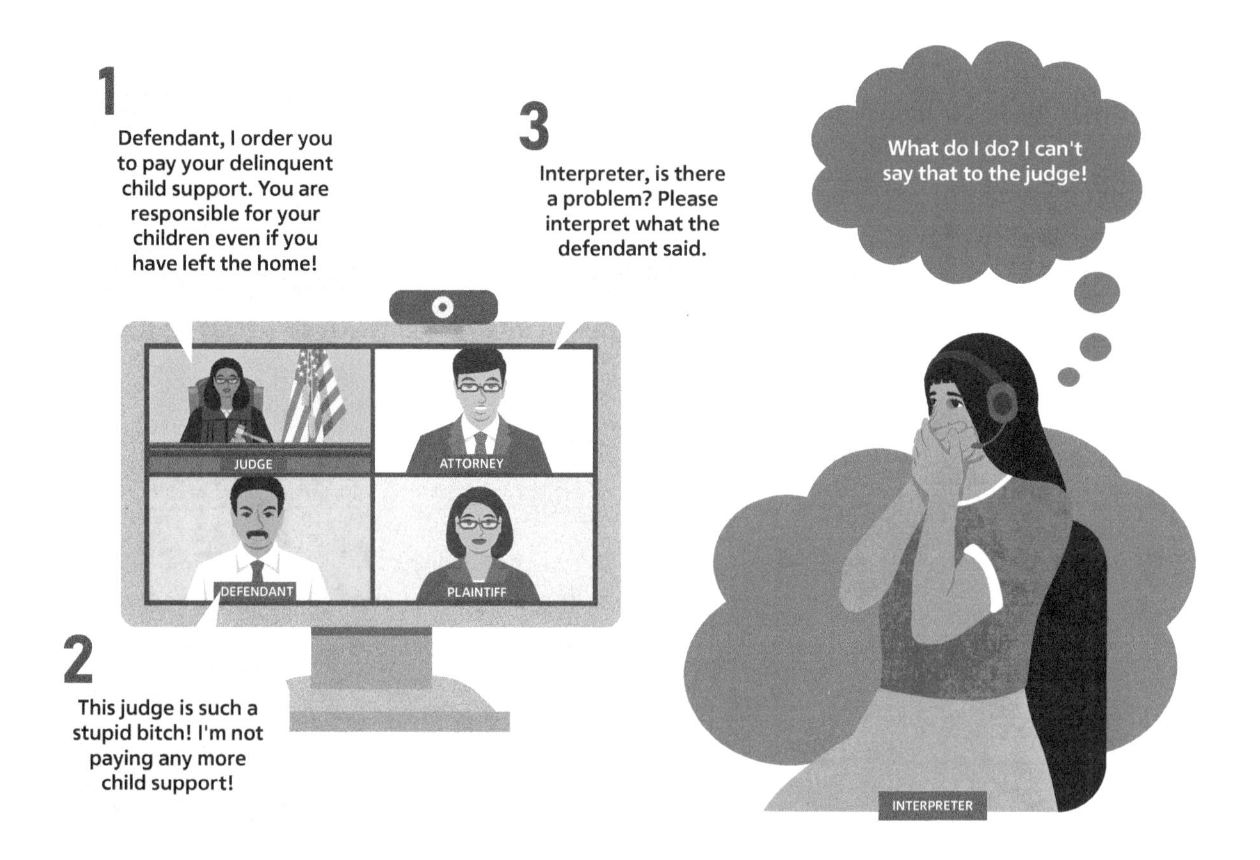

Figure 6.4: **Maintain accurate interpreting**

To support accuracy:

- Respect the intention behind the message.
- Interpret rude, uncomfortable, obscene or embarrassing language.
- Interpret tone, voice and emotions.
- Manage turn-taking to help ensure accuracy.
- Correct any interpreting errors as soon as possible.
- Maintain the register (level of language, from formal to informal).
- Interpret in an equivalent style of speech.
- Capture cultural aspects of the message.
- Convey speech errors, repetitions, fillers and hesitations, if this is required.

Avoid:

- Adding, changing, omitting or embellishing any part of the source message.
- Softening or strengthening the language of the source message.

Caution!

Avoid mimicking a speaker's intense emotions, dramatic gestures or speech impediments. For example, if the participant is shouting, raise your vocal intensity but do not shout or raise your voice too much.

If the person stutters, that stuttering is usually obvious across languages and—with some exceptions—may not need to be interpreted.

Imitating an emotional participant might offend, embarrass or distress the participants, escalate an alarming situation or cause other problems. If someone is crying or shouting, interpret with a sad or angry tone—but do not weep or shout!

Consider the following recommendations that arise in some—not most—codes of ethics.

- Should you interpret (or report) side comments?
  - Yes! At least if you hear and understand them.
  - Report the side comments you understand; inform participants about what you don't understand or can't interpret.
- Will you use the same grammatical person as the speaker? (E.g., direct or indirect speech/ first or third person.)
  - Usually, yes. If the teacher says, "I enjoy having your daughter in class," you interpret, "I enjoy having your daughter in class" (not, "She says she enjoys having…")
  - Exceptions can include emergencies, out-of-control speakers, patients with dementia or someone intoxicated or on drugs.
    - Example: A paramedic speaking to a confused child says, "I need to look into your eyes with this flashlight." The interpreter interprets, "The paramedic needs to look into your eyes with the flashlight."
- Do you need to advise all participants that you will respect confidentiality, and *everything* will be interpreted?
  - Ideally, yes.
  - Perhaps not in emergencies, out-of-control situations, regular (e.g., weekly) encounters, etc.
  - Even so, try hard to make clear you will interpret *everything* stated.

Caution!

Court interpreters should probably not interpret recordings live in court. If you are ordered to do so, state for the record that you cannot ensure accuracy in your interpretation. The same recommendation can apply to requests for you to sight translate certain documents in or out of court.

Impartiality

Almost all codes of ethics and standards or guidelines for interpreters discuss impartiality. As a general rule, being impartial (or neutral, a term found in some documents) implies that the interpreter will set aside personal feelings, take no sides, avoid conflict of interest and interpret without bias (to the extent possible).

> *[Interpreters] will refrain from altering a message for political, religious, moral, or philosophical reasons, or any other biased or subjective consideration.*
>
> *—AVLIC/CASLI, n.d., 4.2.1*
>
> *Refrain from interjecting personal opinions, beliefs or biases into the patient/provider exchange even when interpreters disagree with the message, or perceive it as wrong, untruthful, or immoral.*
>
> *—CHIA, 2002*

Keep in mind that we are all human and all biased. What is required of interpreters is not that we stop being biased, because that is impossible. Instead, we try to become *aware* of our biases enough to set them aside and—to the extent humanly possible—*act* without bias when we interpret.

In short, we try not to let our biases color or alter the meaning of the message or affect our conduct.

Examples of how to adhere to impartiality requirements

The single most common way to adhere to impartiality, specifically noted in more than two dozen codes of ethics, is that the interpreter ***should not***:

- Share opinions.
- Give advice.
- Attempt to influence any participant.

> **Caution!**
>
> Avoid sharing your opinions or advice *even if you are asked to do so.*

Equally common in codes of ethics is the strict guidance to avoid, or at least declare, any conflict of interest if the interpreter (for example):

- Knows one of the participants.
- Is related to one of the participants.
- Could benefit in any way from the encounter.

Figure 6.5: **Avoid conflicts of interest**

Some documents specify how the interpreter should declare or work out a solution for conflict-of-interest situations. In some cases, after declaring the conflict and intending to withdraw, the interpreter may be permitted to remain and interpret if both parties agree *and* the interpreter feels that interpreting impartially is possible. Some documents even allow the interpreter to do so if there is a close or family relationship with one participant—probably because in smaller language communities, it is difficult to avoid having an interpreter who knows no one in that community.

Caution!

A few codes require the interpreter to avoid interpreting for family and friends if possible (implicitly or explicitly allowing special-case exceptions) while other codes specifically state the interpreter *should not* interpret for family or friends (allowing no exceptions). In all cases, the interpreter needs to declare the conflict.

It is especially common for interpreters of signed languages or less common languages that they may know many people in their local language community who show up at interpreted sessions. While this problem is less common for remote interpreting than for face-to-face interpreting, it also arises in remote interpreting. Be prepared!

Caution!

Even if all parties agree to let an interpreter stay and interpret despite a conflict of interest, there may come a moment in the conversation where a participant realizes they are not comfortable sharing certain details with someone they know. In such cases, the interpreter should be extremely sensitive to the need to recuse themselves and withdraw even after deciding to stay.

Other common ways to adhere to impartiality include:

- Allowing no personal interests, biases or beliefs to interfere with or influence the interpretation.
- Avoiding body language, gestures, tones of voice or facial expressions that could reveal personal feelings or value judgments.
- Showing no preference or bias.
- Withholding comments that are political or pejorative comments about participants.
- Withdrawing if impartiality becomes unachievable (a point was noted in a number of documents).

Caution!

You may enjoy humor—but while acting as an interpreter, avoid making jokes.

The risks of speaking up

Many remote interpreters say things like, "No, I'm interpreting *exactly* what she's saying," (without reporting this comment in the other language) or "Sorry about that," or "You need to answer the doctor's question." Be aware that any time you intervene, you risk violating impartiality. Intervene as little as possible.

Professionalism

Professionalism as a principle or requirement can be found in virtually every code of ethics for interpreters and also in standards and guidelines. Indeed, one major purpose of such documents is to help assure consistent, reliable, professional behavior from interpreters.

A member's conduct shall be characterized by objectivity, moderation and dignity.

—Order of Certified Translators, Terminologists and Interpreters of Quebec (OTTIAQ), 2020, Division II.7

Every member shall...

2. *Refrain from any conduct which may harm the interests of APTS and/or its members.*
3. *Accept jobs for which he/she is qualified and able to timely complete, adhering to a proper level of quality.*
4. *Provide true and accurate information when representing his/her educational qualifications and experience.*
5. *Comply with best practices and responsibly, faithfully and accurately perform all translation and interpreting professional activities.*

—APTS, n.d.

To act in a professional way, follow your ethics.

Examples of how to adhere to requirements for professionalism

For remote interpreters who work on demand jumping from call to call, how do you maintain professional conduct? Here are some clear, specific answers.

Integrity and competence

Codes of ethics agree that interpreters should be honest and trustworthy. They should show integrity. More than 50 codes of ethics discussing interpreter professionalism[96] specify that professional integrity includes *interpreting only for assignments that meet the interpreter's level of competence.*

In other words, interpreters should decline all assignments for which they are not qualified. Think it through. Are you competent to interpret a particular session?

But, you may be thinking, sometimes the consequences of an interpreter declining to interpret might mean that vital services, such as medical care, can't be provided. In this case, some codes specify if there is no other viable option, interpreters can declare their limitations, receive input from participants and proceed, if truly needed.

If, for example, the situation is urgent, a language you work in is rare, or someone strongly prefers you to stay and interpret—consider staying. Perhaps you really *are* the best interpreter available.

A good practice is to discuss this type of scenario with others ahead of time to determine your best course of action for sessions that exceed your skills or qualifications.

Accurately represent your credentials

Another common professional concern in codes of ethics is to accurately represent your credentials. If you are not certified, *do not claim that you are.* Many interpreters receive complaints for claiming that they are certified when they simply hold certificates for training or testing.

Figure 6.6: Certification vs. certificate

[96] An extremely high number for any ethical requirement—more than 20 percent of the documents examined for this chapter.

Assure appropriate working conditions

Nearly two dozen of the codes of ethics examined specify that the interpreter should decline or withdraw from sessions if working conditions are inadequate. To avoid this problem, whenever possible:

- Assure good sound and your physical comfort before the session.
- For signed languages, make sure that you have clear sight lines and visibility.
- Inform parties if problematic conditions arise (e.g., loudspeakers in the background making announcements or a breakdown in sound quality).
- Make sure you have a team member if needed, and plan for team members to switch (for example, every 15 minutes or half an hour).
- For team interpreting during remote simultaneous interpreting, either work in a colocated physical hub or be sure to set up a virtual booth before the session.
- Avoid assignments that are too long or do not allow for adequate breaks.
- Get working documents in advance.
- Request a briefing session where needed.
- Address dialect and terminology issues before beginning.

Dress

For video interpreting, clothing should be both professional and appropriate for the assignment, which typically means no T-shirts, big jewelry, flashy tops or overly casual clothing. Some organizations may require wearing a uniform.

For sign language interpreting, professional dress is not enough. Many codes mention wearing appropriate colors and clothing, adapting one's appearance to the assignment, dressing neutrally, being well-groomed and so on.

A poor first visual impression on video can be hard to erase. (See Volume 1, Chapter 8, Professionalism in Remote Interpreting, for more guidance about professionalism for remote interpreters.)

Obey the law

Several codes specify that the interpreter should comply with prevailing laws, local regulations and other legal requirements. Some even mention tax laws or social security. A code from the Netherlands (NSV, 2021) made obeying laws the first tenet of its interpreter code of ethics. Other codes mention the requirement to obey association bylaws or contract terms. A few advise or require the interpreter to decline the assignment if it appears to violate the law or human rights.

> *The interpreter applies this code of ethics and any other code to which he is accountable through his affiliation. If certain articles conflict, the interpreter must make a fair decision according to his ethical and professional judgment.*
>
> —Quebec Association of Sign Language Interpreters (AQILS), 2016, 6.4, p. 4[97]

[97] Translation by Google Translate.

Accountability

Several codes of ethics state that interpreters are accountable for their performance and their decisions. Take responsibility for your own actions and mistakes.

Other elements of professionalism

Here are other ways to show your professionalism.

- Be timely.
    - Don't just show up for the remote session punctually: Make sure that you have followed the set-up protocols in Volume 1, Chapter 3, Set Yourself Up to Perform Remote Interpreting, and you are *ready* to interpret.
- Avoid harm.
    - At least six codes explicitly mention the need to avoid harm.
- Honor the dignity of the profession and the association.
    - Avoid speaking poorly of colleagues.
    - Invoice promptly and accurately.
- Where relevant, communicate with your interpreting team in advance. Collaborate.
- Resolve disputes in good faith.
- Do not attest that any participant "understood" your interpretation. (Instead, you may affirm that you interpreted accurately and completely to the best of your ability.)
- Maintain composure in emotionally charged situations.
- Seek professional qualifications, such as certification.
- Charge fair rates on contracts.
    - Do not undercharge or overcharge.
    - Refuse unfair contracts or contract terms.
    - Treat your subcontractors fairly.
- Advertise ethically.
    - Do not compete with others inappropriately.
    - Avoid unfair competition, underbidding and other unprofessional practices.

Finally, some documents require the interpreter to sign and date their code of ethics!

Professional development

At least a quarter of the codes of ethics examined for this chapter address or require professional development, that is, continuing education for interpreters.

> *You should adopt a reflective practice approach to developing your practice and pursue relevant educational opportunities.*
>
> —National Registers of Communication Professionals with Deaf and Deafblind (NRCPD), 2015, 4.2
>
> *Participating in professional development helps to develop and maintain a critical perspective on one's professional competence and practice.*
>
> —SLIANZ, 2012, p. 5
>
> *A member should take advantage of relevant opportunities to enhance and develop the talent that is the key to ensuring that [they] can offer work of the highest quality by undertaking continuing professional development activities. [The interpreter] should pay attention to improve and upgrade [their] language skills, general knowledge, and any other skills and knowledge relevant to his work.*
>
> —Association of Welsh Translators and Interpreters (CCC Cyf), 2014, p. 3[98]

The goal of professional development is not only to assure an individual interpreter's competence and skills but also to uphold the entire profession and help promote consistent expectations for the professional performance and conduct of interpreters.

Examples of how to adhere to requirements for professional development

Professional development for interpreters can include the following:

- Attend conferences, forums and professional association events.
- Engage in training, especially advanced training, and higher education, including workshops, seminars.
- Obtain formal qualifications and credentials.
- Maintain both or all working languages at a highly proficient level.
- Study terminology, including technical terms.
- Practice, refine and enhance skills.
- Stay up to date with standards in the field.
- Follow proceedings in your specialization (e.g., live, televised or recorded court events for legal interpreters).
- Read specialized literature, practice theory and publications by associations.
- Share knowledge and exchange experiences with colleagues.
- Keep abreast of current best practices and literature.
- Engage in peer review and feedback or collegial consultation on specific areas of skills development.
- Mentor or get mentored.
- Stay abreast of new technologies, current issues, laws, policies, rules and regulations that affect the interpreting profession or specialization.

98 Translation by Google Translate.

Figure 6.7: Interpreter professional development

Ideally, the interpreter is a self-directed learner. Fortunately, professional associations often offer opportunities for professional development in support of this requirement. The Italian Association of Sign Language Interpreter's code even *requires* the interpreter to inform the association of all dates, proposals, programs and other events relevant to other members (ANIMU, n.d., p. 5).

To maintain credentials, such as certification, formal continuing education with specified numbers of credits or hours of completion is usually required.

Summary

The five principles or tenets discussed so far—confidentiality, accuracy, impartiality, professionalism and professional development—are the five most commonly found in codes of ethics for interpreters. They appear in nearly all the documents examined. That trend has not changed in decades.

The next three principles or tenets are also common: role boundaries, solidarity and respect.

Role boundaries

Role boundaries for interpreters are *professional* boundaries.

> *The interpreter is not authorized to give explanations about the culture or cultural habits of the user and may refuse to interpret if the professional requires this information from him / her.*
>
> —Univerbal, 2016[99]
>
> *The interpreter must limit [their] role to a communication agent, even if, in other moments, contexts, outside the work situation, [they have] interpersonal relationships of another type with the [D]eaf user.*
>
> —ANIMU, n.d., p. 4[100]

For role boundaries, the idea is not to be cold or wooden (for example, by speaking in a monotone voice or with a disengaged manner). Through your demeanor, posture, tone and other behavior you can convey professional warmth, attentiveness and respect while you interpret, yet still respect role boundaries.

The goal behind respecting role boundaries is that you will maintain an appropriate distance in your role. Try not to engage in social chatting beyond professional courtesy and respect. Avoid performing more than one job at a time when you interpret. For example, if a service provider leaves you alone on the call for a short period to go and find a consent document, and the patient asks your opinion about the medical information they have just received, you would politely decline to do so. If you chose to answer, you would be stepping into the job or role of the provider.

> **Examples of Role Boundary Ethical Directives**
>
> *Sign language interpreter focuses strictly only on professional work. An interpreter does not agree to perform non-translation tasks in a translation situation (such as making coffee, giving explanations to a [D]eaf person, drawing up documents, inviting someone to bring something, etc.) even if he or she is asked or required to do so.*
>
> —Estonian Sign Language (EVK), 2018, 6.6, p. 3[101]
>
> *Prior to the initial court appearance, the court [interpreter] shall:*
>
> - advise the . . . Deaf or Hard of Hearing person to direct all questions to counsel or to the court; and
> - advise the . . . Deaf or Hard of Hearing person that the interpreter cannot engage in independent dialogue, discussions or conversations with the . . . Deaf or Hard of Hearing person.
>
> —New York State Unified Court System (NYSUCS), 2020, p. 9

In general, interpreters will restrict their professional activities to interpreting. Bilingual employees who interpret will ideally refrain from engaging in other duties while interpreting.

[99] Translation by Google Translate. Univerbal is a community interpreting language service, a coalition of nongovernmental organizations led by migrants, making this code of ethics both an unusual and especially interesting one.

[100] Translation by Google Translate.

[101] Translation by Google Translate.

Examples of how to adhere to requirements for role boundaries

To avoid acting outside your role boundaries:

- Avoid taking on other roles, such as providing advocacy, guidance or advice.
- Clarify your role as needed.
- If you are a bilingual employee who interprets, clarify that while interpreting you will abide by ethical requirements for interpreters.
- Support the communicative autonomy and decision-making of all participants.
- Try to be unobtrusive.
- Clarify if you need to take on another role (and must cease interpreting).

Remember that you are not a participant in the conversation. You are the interpreter.

Solidarity

Solidarity or professional relationships as an ethical duty or requirement appears in about one in six of the documents examined for this chapter. Many codes do not use the term solidarity and speak only of professional relationships,[102] often in terms such as collegiality, cordiality, support, assistance and support for colleagues, respect for colleagues and mentoring and supporting the professional development of fellow interpreters.

> *Strengthen ties with national and international associations that share objectives similar to those of ACTTI.*
>
> —Colombian Association of Translators, Terminologists and Interpreters (ACTTI), 2020[103]
>
> *Members avoid behaviors such as lying, harassment, slander, humiliation, insult, mobbing (intimidation) in their professional relations.*
>
> —Turkish Conference Interpreters Association (TKTD), 2016[104]

Professional relationships, including professional solidarity, are a critical way to support the interpreting profession. Remote interpreters often work in isolation, even more than face-to-face interpreters. They need to engage in professional relationships.

Examples of how to adhere to requirements for professional relationships and solidarity

To demonstrate solidarity with your colleagues who are also remote interpreters can be a challenge, but here are some things you can do.

---

[102] The Australian Institute of Interpreters and Translators (AUSIT, 2018) treats professional solidarity and professional relationships as two separate requirements. The National Accreditation Authority for Translators and Interpreters (NAATI, 2013), in its detailed standards, which support the previous and current AUSIT code of ethics, does the same.

[103] Translation by Google Translate.

[104] Translation by Google Translate.

- Support newer colleagues and mentor others.
- Avoid criticizing others or your professional association.
- Uphold the profession and its dignity.
- Resolve disputes collaboratively and amicably.
- Conduct yourself with courtesy, fairness, respect and professionalism with colleagues.

By supporting colleagues, you also help set expectations for those who work with interpreters. When you decide to take action, think before and after if your action is helpful for the next interpreter.

The requirement to avoid making negative comments about one's colleagues is specified surprisingly often in codes of ethics. Some codes also support joining and supporting professional associations and giving tactful feedback to colleagues. A few mention the need to report an interpreter who breaches the code if the problem cannot be resolved between colleagues.

Respect

More than one in six of documents examined for this chapter included the word respect (or a comparable term) as a tenet, directive, ethical principle or ethical requirement.

> *The interpreter treats all parties with respect.*
>
> —NCIHC, 2004, p. 3
>
> *Respect the dignity of users.*
>
> —Federación Española de Intérpretes de Lengua de Signos y Guías-Intérpretes (FILSE) n.d., p. 2[105]
>
> *Tact, diplomacy and kindness are fundamental skills for the profession of interpreter. They allow a relationship of mutual respect with the [D]eaf.*
>
> —ANIMU, n.d., p. 4, Italy[106]

In many other codes, the word respect (or respectful) is at least included in the text. Other related terms include:

- Courtesy
- Nondiscrimination
- Dignity
- Cultural sensitivity
- Equal treatment

Several documents specify the need to respect client or consumer autonomy for users of community services (all codes from Europe, Canada and the U.S.). One cited the need to alert healthcare providers when the concept of patient autonomy conflicts with the patient's cultural beliefs (CHIA, 2002, pp. 27-28).

---

[105] Translation by Google Translate.

[106] Translation by Google Translate.

Figure 6.8: **Maintain respect for all participants**

Examples of how to adhere to requirements for respect

Here are some ways that codes and other documents recommend to show respect:

- Uphold the dignity of participants.
- Maintain a culturally and situationally appropriate tone of voice.
- Use culturally appropriate ways to address participants.
- Show kindness, tact and diplomacy.
- Display a caring, attentive, discreet and impartial attitude.
- Refrain from judging an individual's questions, concerns and needs.
- Do not assume; always check with the participants.
- Practice transparency, including when you intervene.
- Show respect for *all* participants.

The last point is important because some interpreters may consciously or unconsciously display more deference and respect toward some participants than others, especially if the latter come from disadvantaged, low-income or rural backgrounds, or from a cultural or ethnic social group perceived to be in opposition to the interpreter's. Equal respect for all is a critically important precept for interpreters.

Nondiscrimination

A surprising number of documents[107] (especially for signed language interpreting) specified that interpreters should avoid discriminating against individuals. While only some of the elements of the following list might be mentioned in a specific code, in general, interpreters are expected to act respectfully and independently of a participant's:

- Race
- Color
- Nationality
- Gender (including gender reassignment)
- Nationality[108]
- Ethnicity
- Religion
- Cultural beliefs
- Disability
- Sexual orientation
- Age
- Marriage or partnership status
- Reputation
- Intellectual status
- Pregnancy
- Social (socioeconomic) status
- Political viewpoint
- Personal practices
- Mindset
- Any other factor or element

With all this in mind, interpreters are expected to provide services that respect the right to self-determination and autonomy of all participants. How interpreters behave and address participants, their body language and even their dress can all convey—or fail to convey—respect.

Caution!

Interpreters should not dress themselves in a manner that shows disrespect to the other participants of the interaction.

—Hebenstreit, G., Marics, A. & Hlavac, J., 2022, p. 78

[107] The directive to avoid discriminating was noted in at least 14 of the documents examined but may also have appeared in others.

[108] And perhaps by extension, tribal status.

To conclude, remember this

Some language services have their own code of ethics for interpreters. If you find that something in their code contradicts, or doesn't fit well, with the eight ethical directives or principles reviewed in this section, feel free to discuss that contradiction with the organization. Get their guidance. Share your own. Then decide if you feel ethically comfortable interpreting for that organization.

Also remember that if you hold a certification or are specialized in medical, legal or any other interpreting specialization, you may be required to adhere to a specific code of ethics that supersedes codes created by agencies. For example, a certified community interpreter in Canada should adhere to the *National Standard Guide for Community Interpreting Services* (HIN, 2010).

→ Section 6.2 Review

Around the world, many interpreters struggle to adhere to their ethical requirements. Remote interpreters face the additional burden of working across specializations, regions and even national borders, often navigating dozens of calls in a single day (or night). It can be difficult to remember which code of ethics to follow and harder still to jump from call to call and be certain what to do.

Fortunately, as this section showed, by following eight ethical directives that appear in nearly all codes of ethics for interpreters around the world, and knowing how to apply them to their work, remote interpreters can be reasonably confident they are conducting themselves professionally. The eight directives, or tenets, discussed in this section are:

- Confidentiality
- Accuracy
- Impartiality
- Professionalism
- Professional development
- Role boundaries
- Solidarity
- Respect

The first five of these are virtually universal. As a remote interpreter, follow them all and learn how to apply them in your work. You will not only professionalize your own behavior but also help to set standard expectations for remote interpreters around the world.

Section 6.3 Three Areas of Ethical Controversy for Interpreters

→ Learning objective 6.3

After completing this section, the remote interpreter will be able to describe three key differences among codes of ethics for interpreters.

→ Section 6.3 Overview

Certain ethical tenets or directives in codes of ethics for interpreters differ from country to country or among specializations. Some unique or infrequent tenets are not especially controversial.

For example, international ethics for conference interpreting state that interpreters shall request a briefing session whenever appropriate and that working documents and texts to be read out loud at a conference be sent to interpreters in advance (AIIC, 2018, p. 3). This is an unusual point for a code of ethics, but not a controversial one.

However, three areas of application for ethical principles appearing in a number of codes of ethics are highly controversial. There is little international agreement about them. The three are:

1. Communication breakdowns.
2. Cultural mediation.

   Whether or not interpreters should act as cultural mediators if a cultural misunderstanding arises during the session.

3. Advocacy.

   Whether or not interpreters are responsible for protecting the safety, well-being, human dignity and human rights of participants.

This section examines these three areas in detail because they involve important and common decisions you will have to make. As a remote interpreter, you will face these types of ethical challenges often—and perhaps daily—on the job. You may need to discuss them with the organizations you interpret for, to plan how to address them. Conversely, they may have established protocols for how and when interpreters should intervene (and what to say when they do) that you will be expected to follow. Such protocols can differ from one organization to another.

→ Section 6.3 Content

The previous section focused on what most codes of ethics for interpreters agree on. This section examines three broad areas of disagreement and risk. The goal is to provide you with guidance about which types of ethical situations should be approached with great caution in remote interpreting and help you plan how to address them.

These three areas of disagreement are central to your decision-making in both face-to-face and remote interpreting. For example, is the interpreter present *only* to interpret? Or should you also facilitate communication and "fix" communication breakdowns? Is the interpreter obliged to manage cultural misunderstandings and try to resolve them? Does the interpreter have the obligation to intervene in cases of harm and actual or potential discrimination toward any participants in the session?

These three areas of disagreement in the field involve controversies that date back to the birth of the profession. Above all, they address the still unresolved question of the role of the interpreter.

The role of the interpreter

This textbook, as discussed elsewhere, takes the position that the role of the interpreter is to enable and support communicative autonomy, that is, the capacity of all participants in an encounter to be responsible for, and in control of, their own communication.

In other words, the interpreter is present to allow participants to communicate in their own true voice and, through their accurate understanding of the shared communication, have full agency in the encounter as if all participants shared a common language.

Most of us want, and arguably need, communicative autonomy when we interact with services, institutions and individuals. But for those who do not share a common language, interpreters are *essential* to make communicative autonomy possible.

Yet to this day there is no universally accepted understanding of the interpreter's role, either across or within national borders or across different specializations. For example, a code of ethics for medical or community interpreters can often appear less rigid or strict than one for legal interpreters. A U.S. document states:

> *The healthcare interpreter role encompasses all the values, ethical principles duties, tasks, and behaviors established in the NCIHC Code of Ethics and the NCIHC Standards of Practice. Therefore, when healthcare interpreters engage in an act of advocacy, they are not stepping outside the healthcare interpreter role.*
>
> —NCIHC, 2021, p. 11

In contrast, legal interpreters are typically not permitted to engage in advocacy. For example, *Professional Standards and Ethics for California Court Interpreters* explicitly states: "You are not to be an advocate for non-English speakers" (Judicial Council of California, 2013, p. 20).

First, let's examine these three areas of controversy. Then the next section will help show how to navigate these challenges.

Addressing communication breakdowns

> *Should a serious communication problem arise between the interpreter and one party the interpreter should bring this to the attention of the other party.*
>
> —Irish Translators and Interpreters (ITIA), 2009, p. 3

The practical need to address communication breakdowns is an urgent requirement to support communicative autonomy and clear, direct communication between or among participants. But what do we mean by communication breakdown?

What is a communication breakdown?

A communication breakdown is a situation where the interpreter and the participants, or the participants themselves, no longer understand each other well. Such situations can occur in virtually any session.

There are two main types of communication breakdowns:

- The interpreter cannot understand the message.
- The participants cannot understand the message.

Both these situations can, of course, occur at the same time.

The reasons for a lack of understanding by the interpreter or the participants can be environmental (for example, background noise or an audio or video equipment failure) or situational (almost any other cause). Let's break these two categories down a little more.

Environmental communication breakdowns

Remote interpreters routinely encounter situations where they have problems hearing or understanding parts of messages. Here are a few typical examples that occur in remote interpreting:

For the interpreter, participants or both

- Background noise interferes with understanding.
  - Other speakers may be conversing in the background.
  - Street noises, construction, etc., outside may be loud.
- Audio breaks down (sound is too loud, quiet, or fails completely).
  - Interpreter or participants may or may not have control over their audio feed.
- Video pixilates or the screen goes dark or too bright.
  - Again, interpreter or participants may or may not control video quality.

Situational communication breakdowns

The interpreter

- Misses part of the message.
  - Perhaps someone spoke too quietly, too loudly, unclearly or quickly.
  - In such cases, the interpreter will request a repetition if possible.
- Needs clarification
  - The interpreter has not understood part or all of a message.
  - The interpreter will ask a participant to clarify it.

- Has to manage turn-taking
  - Participants may speak too long, too fast or at the same time.
  - Interpreter will need to ask participants to pause, slow down or speak one at a time.
- Faces a cultural misunderstanding.
  - The participants may not be aware a cultural misunderstanding is taking place.
  - The interpreter may notice and understand a cultural barrier but feel uncertain what to do about it.
  - The idea that the interpreter should address this common problem (and if so, how) is highly controversial.

Participants

- One or more participants clearly (in the interpreter's observation) does not understand what is stated.
  - Often, only the interpreter notes this problem.
  - Whether or not the interpreter should address this common situation is highly controversial.
- One or more participants (in the interpreter's observation) experiences a cultural misunderstanding.
  - Again, often only the interpreter notes this problem.
  - Whether or not the interpreter should address this common situation is highly controversial.

Cultural misunderstandings are so complex that they are addressed separately below, even though they are in essence a form of communication breakdown.

Not all of these situations are controversial. Broadly speaking, in those cases where the *interpreter's* understanding breaks down, there is broad agreement worldwide and across specializations that the interpreter *should* intervene to address it.

Cases where participants *fail to understand a message or conversation are the controversial cases.*

Common types of communication breakdowns			
Environmental		Situational	
Interpreters	Participants	Interpreters	Participants
Background noise interferes with understanding.		Misses part of message.	Lacks understanding.
Audio breaks down (too loud, quiet, or silent).		Needs clarification.	Needs clarification.
Video breaks down (pixilates; screen too dark or too bright, etc.).		Must manage turn-taking.	Grows confused.
		Perceives a cultural misunderstanding.	Has a cultural misunderstanding.
			Faces someone antagonizing, angry or discriminatory.
			Faces a systemic barrier to communication, such as discrimination, racism or economic exclusion.

Table 6.6: Examples of common types of communication breakdowns involving interpreters or participants

Green: Widely ethically accepted that the interpreter should intervene.
Yellow: Some codes of ethics would suggest the interpreter should intervene.
Red: Not generally accepted that the interpreter should intervene.

What codes of ethics say about communication breakdowns

The need to address communication breakdowns is often mentioned or addressed in codes of ethics for interpreters. Certain documents acknowledge, implicitly or explicitly, that it is *acceptable* and even *necessary* for interpreters to address the conditions needed to ensure accuracy. For example, the interpreter should:

- Ask for equipment to be moved to improve sound quality.
- Request repetitions or clarifications of anything the interpreter couldn't hear or see adequately.
- Request clarification of terms or concepts whenever needed (except in specific, narrow cases such as U.S. asylum hearings).

After all, you cannot accurately interpret what you do not understand.

What About Court Interpreting?

Many court interpreters hesitate to intervene, including remote interpreters, except to request clarification of terms they do not understand, even if they cannot hear or see well.

If you do not understand part of a message, request a change in the environmental conditions as needed (for example, you could ask someone to move the audio equipment closer to a speaker). You may also request a repetition or ask for clarifications. Some codes of ethics discuss these points. A Polish association (TEPIS, 2019) clearly states that the interpreter has the right to ask a participant (such as a lawyer) to explain or specify the meaning of legal or other specialized terms.

At least seven documents examined specifically mention that requesting clarification is either permitted or required, even in court interpreting. These codes are in agreement that interpreters cannot interpret accurately what they cannot hear (or see, for signing) or understand.

Several codes of ethics around the world specifically authorize interpreters to interrupt the session in order to point out impediments to performance, such as poor sound quality, two or more people speaking at once or degrading visual quality. Some codes of ethics suggest that requesting clarification is permitted, others state it is *required.* For example, "Interpreters shall seek clarification when needed" (Center for Interpretation and Translation Studies, University of Hawaii, n.d., p. 1). If you do not understand something—intervene and request a clarification!

Should you ask permission before intervening?

In general, if you intervene because you, the interpreter, cannot understand the message, you do not need to ask permission. You are simply doing your job.

However, one document, a set of ethical guidelines for interpreters in asylum procedures, also specifies that "Where necessary, interpreters seek the agreement of the interviewer or the applicant when requesting clarification" (Hebenstreit, Marics & Hlavac, 2022 p. 78). This might also be advisable in specific situations such as therapy, attorney-client interviews and certain court cases.

Intervening to address participant misunderstandings: The controversy

The difficulty comes when the interpreter perceives—either with full or partial certainty—that one or more of the *participants* does not understand. Many interpreter associations feel that intervening for such a reason goes beyond the interpreter's role and constitutes an unprofessional intrusion. Others feel the opposite: In other words, interpreters *should* intervene to help clarify participant misunderstanding.

Here are examples. Certain codes of ethics state that interpreters either should or should *not* intervene during a communication breakdown in order to:

- Check for understanding.
- Ask one participant to check for understanding.
- Request clarification of what might be causing the misunderstanding.
- Explain what the interpreter thinks has caused the misunderstanding.
- *Request* cultural clarification.
- *Provide* cultural clarification.

One code of ethics states that when acting as the interpreter, one must not intervene, even when requested to do so, though perhaps the intent here is to avoid the interpreter getting involved in the discussion (ARILS, 1998, p. 1). Legal interpreting is a special case. A small number of codes of ethics specifically limit intervening by the interpreter in legal settings.

> *Upon recognizing that a communication may have been misunderstood, interpreters may bring the possible misunderstanding to the attention of the provider, who will decide how to resolve it. (Not to be done in legal proceedings.)*
>
> —Center for Interpretation and Translation Studies, University of Hawaii (n.d., p. 1)

Few codes specify what the interpreter should do when facing a breakdown in communication among participants. One Polish code of ethics (despite primarily addressing legal interpreting) specifies that the interpreter should "notify" the legal services provider if there has been an incomplete understanding or if there is a need to supplement the interpretation statement with information or comments necessary to understand the content and intention of the interpreted statement (TEPIS, 2019, p. 28).

Identify yourself as the interpreter

If you intervene for any reason, be sure to identify yourself as the interpreter. (See Volume 1, Chapter 7, Addressing Communication Breakdowns, for details.) One code specifically states that the interpreter should say, "I, the interpreter, need clarification" (SLIANZ, 2012, Accuracy, p. 1). U.S. courts typically require the interpreter to refer to themselves only as "the interpreter" (for example, "The interpreter requests a repetition") to avoid confusion in the written record for the case. The same is true in Poland (TEPIS, 2019).

Referring to yourself as "the interpreter" even in nonlegal interpreting can, for remote interpreters, help to provide clarity and efficiency. But if you work with a language service, make sure that you use any specific wording the service requests or requires interpreters to state whenever they intervene.

Cultural mediation

> *The sign language interpreter has a moral obligation to try to overcome cultural differences in the translation and, if necessary, to signal the risk of misunderstanding, while avoiding distorting the source text.*
>
> —EVK, 2018, 7.2, p. 3[109]

[109] Adapted slightly from a Google Translate translation.

What is cultural mediation?

The second big area of ethical controversy involves cultural misunderstandings. Around the world, there is no agreement among codes of ethics about whether or not the interpreter should try to manage cultural misunderstandings, a specific type of communication breakdown rooted in cultural differences. There is also no wide agreement on what cultural mediation is, although the term itself is widely used around the world.

What is cultural mediation? For purposes of this textbook, it is defined as any act or utterance of the interpreter intended to address or clarify a cultural misunderstanding.

As with other types of communication breakdowns, the controversy is not about what to do if the *interpreter* faces a cultural misunderstanding. In that case, the interpreter will request clarification. It is helpful (and efficient, especially in remote interpreting) to ground such questions by requesting clarification of a cultural term or practice that is causing you confusion.

The controversy among codes of ethics, and more broadly among interpreter associations and groups, is what to do if the interpreter perceives a cultural misunderstanding among participants that they cannot address or resolve without the interpreter's assistance.

Interpreting cultural phrases vs. intervening

The idea of taking cultural differences into account affects how you interpret a statement and whether you decide to intervene. Perhaps, with effective interpreting, you won't need to intervene at all. For example, if you interpret a cultural expression such as "The sky is clouding," as "This is a difficult time for the country," and thus convey its actual meaning, then you have provided an interpretation that is as culturally accurate as you know how to make it. You don't have to ask the participant to explain it.

If, however, you are unfamiliar with the cultural or metaphorical meaning of the phrase "The sky is clouding," then you would need to intervene to request a clarification.

Cultural communication breakdowns: An example

But when should you intervene over cultural issues? What does a *cultural* communication breakdown mean? Volume 1, Chapter 7, Addressing Communication Breakdowns, addresses that question in more detail. For now, let's look at an example where you might need to intervene.

You are interpreting for a dispute between a public housing program and a family who was denied services. At the beginning of the meeting, you realize there is confusion about the family's surnames and their cultural naming practices, although you interpreted everything correctly. The mediator conducting the interview has not captured the family's legal names correctly on official paperwork. You worry that this mistake could lead to legal harm for the family. However, if you intervene, you will have to address a misunderstanding about a specific cultural practice. How will you proceed?

In general, to avoid undermining communicative autonomy, or violating the requirement to be impartial or causing other problems for the participants or yourself, simply *interpret* and avoid interrupting the session unless:

- Communication breaks down completely.
- Someone is at risk of harm.
- The desired outcome of the session (whether legal, medical, etc.) is at risk.

If someone is at risk, or the outcome is, you could say, for example, "The interpreter wishes to point out a potential misunderstanding about the family's legal name. You may wish to verify their name." (You don't need to use the word cultural.)

The interpreter would then tell the family members, "The interpreter just informed the mediator of a potential misunderstanding about your legal name and suggested they verify it with you."

Requesting vs. providing cultural clarification

The interpreter may perceive a cultural misunderstanding. The interpreter may even—perhaps accurately—understand the reasons for it.

But if the breakdown in communication is quite serious, is there international agreement that the interpreter should take action to *address* the cultural misunderstanding?

If you say "yes," here is another question for you. Is the correct, accepted action by the interpreter to point out the existence of a culturally based misunderstanding—to request clarification for it—or to provide the interpreter's own cultural explanation?

First, to illustrate what we mean, let's look at these three general common strategies for addressing cultural misunderstandings.

Three approaches to cultural mediation			
The interpreter...	***Points out* the misunderstanding**	***Requests* a cultural clarification**	***Provides* a cultural explanation**
Action	The interpreter explains nothing but points out the basis of the communication breakdown.	The interpreter asks for clarification without explaining anything.	The interpreter explains the cultural issue.
Statement	The interpreter suggests what might be *causing* the misunderstanding, e.g., a cultural term, concept, belief, perspective or practice.	The interpreter requests that one person *clarify* or *explain* a cultural term, concept, belief, perspective or practice.	The interpreter provides an *explanation* for a cultural term, concept, belief, perspective or practice.
Medical example	*The interpreter suspects there may be a misunderstanding about what "epidural" means.*	*The interpreter suggests the doctor ask the patient what they think "epidural" means and its effects.*	*The interpreter wishes to point out that in the patient's country, people confuse epidurals with spinal blocks and don't want to have them.*
Legal example	*The interpreter wishes to note a possible misunderstanding about the legal meaning of "wife."*	*The interpreter suggests the lawyer ask the client if the term "wife" refers to his legally wedded spouse.*	*The interpreter says, "This confusion is caused by your client calling that woman his wife when it's just because she has a child with him, out of respect for her, not because they're legally married."*

Table 6.7: How interpreters address cultural misunderstandings: Three common approaches

History of the problem

Historically, conference interpreting and court interpreting were the first two specializations of interpreting to be established worldwide. Neither encouraged interpreters to engage in cultural explanations. However, community interpreting existed for decades *before* it professionalized, particularly in four service areas: medical, social services, educational and refugee interpreting. In all four, cultural misunderstandings arose constantly. There was often a general expectation that the interpreter would be from the same culture as the patient or participant (or at least knowledgeable about that culture) and would take care of any cultural misunderstandings.

Historically, in parts of Europe, such as Switzerland and Belgium, and in the U.S. in the 1990s, medical interpreters were trained to do almost anything to help out patients when cultural misunderstandings caused confusion. Over time, in Europe, a second profession emerged of intercultural mediators who are formally tasked not only with interpreting but also with addressing cultural issues (García-Beyaert, 2015, pp. 371-379).

For a long time, the practice of explaining or managing cultural misunderstandings was enshrined in some publications, for example, in various editions of medical interpreting training manuals in the U.S. published in the 1990s and 2000s.

The interpreter as cultural expert?

> *Interpreters will engage in patient advocacy and in the intercultural mediation role of explaining cultural differences/practices to health care providers and patients only when appropriate and necessary for communication purposes, using professional judgment.*
>
> —IMIA, 2006, p. 1

A historical problem has been that participants and others have looked at interpreters as "cultural experts." Interpreters felt this responsibility and acted on it. The problem is that while interpreters may have some degree of knowledge about different cultures, no interpreter is a cultural expert on any specific individual.

For example, the interpreter may be aware that the communication breakdown between a welfare case worker and an immigrant woman could be because, in the woman's culture of origin, women often have to ask their husband's permission to work outside the home. However, that doesn't mean the interpreter knows for certain what is true for this individual woman.

A shift away from the interpreter as "cultural expert"

By the end of the 2000s, the pendulum in countries began to swing away from the ideal of the interpreter as "cultural expert." Today, the idea that the interpreter is *not* a cultural expert has become far more widely accepted. For example, Canadian national standards for community interpreters (HIN, 2010) and many standards for court interpreters do not allow interpreters to intervene to explain cultural misunderstandings. Their professional culture suggests that interpreters who do so risk violating strict role boundaries and impartiality.

Canada's national code of ethics and standards of practice for community interpreting services provides historical background and states clearly that their ethics and standards:

> *differ (significantly) in the expectations for interpreter role boundaries (and the interpreter's responsibility to intervene as needed to remove barriers to communication)... [These standards] do not endorse cultural brokering and advocacy...*
>
> *Historically interpreters [in Canada] were identified as "cultural interpreters" with a role to bridge "cultural misunderstandings" between service providers and non/limited English speakers. Determining how and when an interpreter should intervene created conflicts for all parties for a variety of reasons. Although cultural differences can exist between individuals who do not share a common language, cultural differences can also exist between individuals who do share a common language. Given the complexity of factors that impact and influence an individual's culture, acting as a "cultural broker/bridge" goes beyond the scope of an interpreter's duty... Expecting an interpreter to perform that function, in and of itself, contravenes the ethical principle and standard of practice to remain impartial, and furthermore begs the question of the demonstrated competence of the interpreter to perform that function... the role of the interpreter focus[es] on the delivery of messages between individuals who do not share a common language rather than "cultural differences/nuance" of the speakers.*
>
> —HIN, 2010, p. 12

Indeed, in Canada today even community interpreters are widely expected to restrict intervening to requesting clarification, quite the opposite of expectations in the U.S. for medical interpreting—but in keeping with much of U.S. legal interpreting! Given these conflicting approaches to cultural mediation, what is the remote interpreter to do?

Codes of ethics and cultural clarification

A U.S. Medical Perspective

First and foremost, interpreters have to work at understanding the cultural basis of the way they themselves make sense of the world. How we see the world influences the meaning we give to experiences—what we understand and what we remember. By developing awareness of their own culturally based understandings and biases, interpreters are better able to focus on the meaning of the messages expressed by others and refrain from unwittingly interjecting their own perspectives or biases. This ethical principle actually assists interpreters in fulfilling their obligations under another ethical principle, that of impartiality.

Secondarily, this principle also acknowledges that there are many cultures that interpreters may encounter in the course of performing their duties. Does this mean that interpreters have to know everything about the patient's culture? Or the provider's culture? Or the culture of biomedicine? Obviously, this is impossible. No single interpreter, or provider for that matter, is expected to know the particular cultural beliefs and values that may apply in any given situation. Culture is an abstraction that is mediated in each individual by their unique circumstances and experiences, such as their personality; family values and beliefs; class, gender, education and other personal characteristics; and level of acculturation into another culture. Culture, therefore, is manifested in each individual in a different way.

The ethical obligation of interpreters is to possess enough understanding of culture and cultural practices and beliefs to be able to facilitate communication across cultural differences, seeking to minimize, and, if possible, avoid, potential misunderstanding and miscommunication based on cultural assumptions and/or stereotyping. Under certain conditions, such as clashing cultural beliefs or practices, a lack of linguistic equivalency, or the inability of parties to articulate the differences in their own words, the interpreter should assist (with the explicit consent of all parties to this intervention) by sharing cultural information or helping develop an explanation that can be understood by all.

—NCIHC, 2004, p. 18

At least four codes of ethics specify that the interpreter is *expected* or *required* to engage in cultural clarification if a cultural misunderstanding arises. For example,

> *The Interpreter/Translator when working with the patient...makes every effort to understand and communicate to others the context (social, cultural) in which the patient is operating, particularly as it may affect the patient's medical needs and status.*
>
> —American Medical Interpreters and Translators Association (AMITAS), n.d., p. 1

At least six other codes of ethics *permit* cultural clarification. Other documents suggest that the interpreter use personal judgment in such cases. Still others state or imply that *providing* cultural explanations is acceptable.

A strong recommendation for remote interpreters

Limitations on the Interpreter's Role in Cultural Mediation

[The interpreter's] role in such situations is not to "give the answer" but rather to help both provider and patient to investigate the intercultural interface that may be creating the communication problem. Interpreters must keep in mind that no matter how much "factual" information they have about the beliefs, values, norms, and customs of a particular culture, they have no way of knowing where the individual facing them in that specific situation stands along a continuum from close adherence to the norms of a culture to acculturation into a new culture.

—MMIA/IMIA, 1995, pp. 15-16

This textbook takes the position that requesting clarification—whether for the interpreter or for participants—supports communicative autonomy. However, allowing the interpreter to provide cultural explanations, as opposed to requesting a cultural clarification, may, and probably does, undermine or destroy communicative autonomy.

In addition, most professional language services today prefer remote interpreters to restrict their interventions to clarification whenever feasible. While cultural clarification (that is, requesting one or more of the *participants* to clarify or explain a cultural issue) may be acceptable, cultural *explanations* from the interpreter are perceived by many language services as high risk and to be discouraged, with the possible exception of extreme cases or emergencies.

In short, you are likely to be on safe ground if, faced with a cultural misunderstanding, you simply request clarification of a cultural term, concept or practice that you then *interpret* without adding your own opinions or beliefs about it. Let's look at an example.

Keep your cultural clarifications simple!

Let's say that you interpret for a patient who is clearly (to you) confused by informed consent—but doesn't say so. You could tell the provider, "The interpreter requests that you explain informed consent." (Adding to the patient, "The interpreter has just requested that the nurse explain the term informed consent.") The underlying cultural issue might be that from your perspective, the patient seems to have no familiarity with the informed consent *process* and needs more guidance to understand its legal, logistical and medical significance. However, by requesting a clarification of the *term,* you are staying more clearly within your interpreter's role.

If it is not possible to request clarification of a specific term, you may—or may not—be authorized to request clarification of a concept. For example, you could state to a lawyer, and then immediately report such a statement to the client: "The interpreter senses a breakdown in communication about how to collect victim compensation funds. You may wish to check for understanding."

A conscientious lawyer will want to be certain that a client fully understands their lawyer.

Requesting cultural clarification of a cultural practice is trickier still, but if you can bring it down to a term or phrase—for example, "The interpreter suggests you ask the teacher about the purpose of back-to-school night"—you are probably on safe ground.

Cultural clarification in conference interpreting

For conference interpreting, there is no standard practice for intervening to alert speakers of potential cultural problems. Formal ethics documents typically do not cover mechanisms for handling cultural misunderstandings in conference interpreting. Instead, strategies are most commonly taught through best practices and common scenarios.

For example, during simultaneous interpreting, when it is clear that a statement may cause cultural confusion, such as a joke or a specific cultural reference to a widely known television show, the interpreter may add a brief contextual explanation or use a more general term (for example, "a television comedy called..." instead of simply the name of the country-specific television show).

To give another example, during long consecutive interpreting, conference interpreters are trained to maintain the equivalent degree of intentional ambiguity expressed by two diplomats in delicate negotiations.

A great deal more can be said about how conference interpreters handle these kinds of situations, but such strategies lie outside the scope of this book. For more information about remote conference interpreting, see Volume 2, Chapter 3, Conference Interpreting.

Advocacy and protecting human rights

> *Interpreters respect and advocate fundamental human rights of all persons... Interpreters make sincere efforts to enable [D]eaf people to participate independently in all social activities and situations by fully applying their professional skills and knowledge.*
>
> —Japanese Association of Sign Language Interpreters (JASLI), 1997, p. 1

The third big area of ethical controversy for interpreters is advocacy. Around the world, codes of ethics for interpreters of signed languages seem more likely than codes for spoken language interpreters to specifically suggest that the interpreter has a duty to protect the human rights of Deaf participants. However, even some codes of ethics for spoken language interpreters (e.g., NCIHC, 2004) discuss advocacy.

In certain cases, the concepts surrounding human rights and the interpreter's duty to consider protecting them are included in sections of the documents that detail the underlying values that frame a particular code of ethics or code of conduct, for example:

> *SLIANZ also acknowledges that its purpose of upholding ethical, high quality interpreting practice accords with the objective of the United Nations Convention on the Rights of People with Disabilities…to promote Deaf people's equitable access in society.*
>
> —SLIANZ, 2012, p. 2

> *Recognition of the communication rights of America's women, men, and children who are [D]eaf is the foundation of the tenets, principles, and behaviors set forth in this Code of Professional Conduct.*
>
> —National Association of the Deaf and Registry of Interpreters for the Deaf (NAD-RID), 2005, p. 1

In some contexts, rather than taking action, you are expected to refrain from interpreting. An example from a U.S. professional association for both spoken and sign language interpreters in New England (in the U.S.) prohibits interpreting for the abuse of prisoners. Interpreters are required to:

> *Adhere in all respects to the NETA "Resolution Condemning the Cooperation of Interpreters and Translators in Physical and Mental Abuse and Torture of Military Prisoners and Detainees, and in Interrogations of Prisoners," adopted January 21, 2007; specifically:*
>
> *a) To refrain from any knowing participation in, cooperation with, or failure to report, the mental or physical abuse, sexual degradation, cruel treatment, or torture of prisoners or detainees.*
>
> *b) To work only in lawful settings governed by a system of rights and due process in accordance with jurisdictional national and international law.*
>
> *c) To support the rights of interpreters and translators to be protected from retribution for refusing to participate or cooperate in abuse or torture, or deprivation of rights in military or other settings anywhere.*[110]
>
> —New England Translators Association (NETA), 2007, p. 1

Advocacy

Advocacy in interpreting has two meanings: One kind of advocacy refers to speaking up on behalf of the profession itself. This kind is widely accepted and encouraged by the same professional associations that issue codes of ethics. The other kind of advocacy refers to speaking up on behalf of a participant within an interpreting session, which is frowned on or prohibited in certain specializations in spoken language interpreting but somewhat more broadly accepted in signed language interpreting.

---

[110] The American Translators Association (ATA) also took a stand in 2006 against allowing its members to interpret or translate for cases of torture, abuse or human degradation. See page 11: https://www.ata-chronicle.online/wp-content/uploads/2006-November-December.pdf

Advocacy for the *profession* is almost universally encouraged and expected of interpreters; it is even enshrined in some codes of ethics, where advocacy can appear as a duty, for example, the duty to join and support professional associations.

Advocacy for participants is quite different. It can be defined as "Taking action or speaking up on behalf of a [participant] whose safety, health, well-being or human dignity is at risk, with the purpose of preventing harm (Bancroft et al., 2015, p. vii). Here is a widely known definition in medical interpreting from the code of ethics of the U.S. National Council on Interpreting in Health Care (NCIHC):

> *When the patient's health, well-being, or dignity is at risk, the interpreter may be justified in acting as an advocate. Advocacy is understood as an action taken on behalf of an individual that goes beyond facilitating communication, with the intention of supporting good health outcomes. Advocacy must only be undertaken after careful and thoughtful analysis of the situation and if other less intrusive actions have not resolved the problem.*
>
> —NCIHC, 2004, p. 3

In its standards of practice, NCIHC states: "The interpreter may speak out to protect an individual from serious harm" (NCIHC, 2005, p. 10).

Historically, U.S. medical interpreting has, since its beginnings in the 1990s, tended to permit interpreters (with limitations) to engage in advocacy, though only if truly needed and in narrow circumstances (NCIHC, 2004 and 2005; IMIA, 1995; and AMITAS, n.d.) due to the risks, including the risk of violating ethical requirements. For example:

> *In general, advocacy means that a third party (in this case, the interpreter) speaks for or pleads the cause of another party, thereby departing from an impartial role.*
>
> —NCIHC, 2005, p. 11

For a more recent NCIHC perspective on advocacy, containing perhaps the most thoughtful, in-depth perspectives on this topic currently available to interpreters, see *Interpreter Advocacy in Healthcare Encounters: A Closer Look* (NCIHC, 2021).

Advocacy in interpreting: Views from the world

Advocacy is a highly controversial topic for interpreters. *Inform yourself about expectations on advocacy with any organization you interpret for.* In addition, be mindful that expectations around the world may differ by specialization as well as by language service.

In the U.S., for example, advocacy *may* be permitted by the medical interpreting profession—but perhaps not by specific U.S. hospitals, states or language companies. However, advocacy in legal interpreting is generally considered to be prohibited in the U.S.

Advocacy in signed and spoken language interpreting

> *Deaf people form a cultural and linguistic minority in Germany. You have the right to full and equal participation in all areas of society. Interpreters and translators (D / Ü) who commit themselves to these professional and honorary regulations recognize this right and advocate its implementation as part of their work. In doing so, they respect the Basic Law of the Federal Republic of Germany, the UN Convention on the Rights of Persons with Disabilities and the General Equal Treatment Act.*
>
> —Federal Association of German Sign Language Interpreters (BGSD), 2018, p. 1

As a general trend, interpreters for signed languages in some countries or settings may be expected to engage in advocacy to support or protect the legal and human rights of participants who are Deaf or Hard of Hearing.

However, expectations about advocacy for sign language interpreters may differ greatly depending not only on the country and specialization (e.g., legal vs. educational interpreting) but also the region you interpret for. Once again, inform yourself with your professional association and any organizations that engage or hire you as well as consulting other remote interpreters.

Spoken language interpreters, on the other hand, in most countries of the world and in nearly all specializations, are typically expected *not* to engage in advocacy to protect participants because such advocacy can be seen as a violation of the interpreter's role, impartiality and the communicative autonomy of the participants.

> **Caution!**
>
> In some countries, interpreters may be expected to defend and protect participants from discrimination, whether by individuals or a service system, possibly during or outside the session (for example, in U.S. healthcare interpreting: NCIHC, 2004; NCIHC, 2021).
>
> In remote interpreting, be careful. It is easy to cross role boundaries. Some American Sign Language (ASL) interpreters in the U.S. have been reported because they tried to protect a participant who is Deaf but sacrificed privacy or confidentiality. The consequences of breaking privacy laws can be severe.

Advocacy: Permitted or forbidden

At least two documents noted by the author of this section specifically prohibit or do not endorse advocacy:

> *Unlike [U.S. medical interpreting standards], the LITP [Language Interpreting Training Programs] Standards of Practice do not endorse cultural brokering and advocacy.*
>
> —HIN, 2010, p. 12

> *Interpreters do not, in the course of their interpreting duties, engage in other tasks such as advocacy, guidance or advice.*
>
> —SLIANZ, 2012, p. 5

In some cases, the permission to engage in advocacy is implicit, not explicit. For example, the idea that interpreters should "strive to ensure that all persons have access to the resources, services, and opportunities required for health care" (AMITAS, n.d., p. 9). In rare cases, actual permission to engage in advocacy may appear:

> *A Community interpreter may knowingly waive impartiality only if the welfare or dignity, life or health of one of the participants in the conversation is significantly endangered. In this case, he may exceptionally intervene for the endangered party in the conversation, but he must first obtain his explicit permission.*
>
> —Stridon Slovenian Translatological Society et al. (SSTD/DPT/ZZTZSZJ/ZKTS), 2021[111]

In U.S. medical interpreting, many in the field have long stated that healthcare interpreters should, in certain cases, engage in patient advocacy (IMIA, 1995; NCIHC, 2004; NCIHC, 2021). Not all U.S. hospitals or U.S. remote interpreting services agree.

What should the remote interpreter do about advocacy?

Be aware that as a remote interpreter you will need to look for guidance on the specific issues of what to do if someone during a session experiences potential harm and you wish to speak up. Give specific examples when you seek guidance. If you are overly general or vague, for example, a remote interpreting service that specializes in signed languages might expect you to take action on behalf of the human rights of Deaf participants whom you interpret for. But if you clarify that you are asking about whether or not to let a family know their child has a legal right to certain types of services and extension of exam times at school, even though a teacher at the school has just told the family incorrectly they do not have those rights, you might get a more specific answer from the language service you interpret for.

In another example, a language service that you perform medical and legal interpreting for might expect you *never* to engage in advocacy or any other action on behalf of a participant's human rights. But if you ask what to do if you know from another session the patient is taking medications that should be stopped prior to surgery but hasn't mentioned those particular medications during a preoperative consultation—or someone's life is at risk—perhaps the language service will allow you to engage in advocacy at certain times.

Do not assume anything. If you know discrimination against certain participants is a concern for you as an interpreter, ask the organizations that you interpret for—and also read their guiding documents carefully—to find out what their expectation is regarding interpreters' protecting human rights, the human dignity of participants, relationships of power and concerns about equity.

Finally, matters of personal conscience may sometimes impel interpreters to step out of their role and engage in advocacy, even if doing so creates a situation of risk for themselves, the participants, the outcomes of the session or the interpreter's continued work with an organization.

---

[111] Translation by Google Translate.

→ Section 6.3 Review

This section examined three controversial directives found in codes of ethics for interpreters around the world. Whether interpreters should address communication breakdowns, perform cultural mediation or engage in advocacy to prevent harm and protect human rights. It also provided remote interpreters with some practical guidance about how to address these three areas of controversy.

Remote interpreters who encounter these concerns will need to exercise great caution on the job. There is no widespread agreement, either within or across national borders or interpreting specializations about how to address these three areas.

This section offered guidance, examples and specific points that remote interpreters may need to consider for decision-making. It also advised them to discuss these three areas of controversy with the organizations they interpret for.

Section 6.4 Applying Ethics in Remote Interpreting

→ Learning objective 6.4

After completing this section, the remote interpreter will be able to apply codes of ethics and standards for interpreters across specializations or national borders.

→ Section 6.4 Overview

This chapter has introduced you to codes of ethics and standards of practice for interpreters, including eight common ethical practices and three controversial areas of ethical practice that could potentially complicate your ethical decisions.

The purpose of this section is to help you make effective decisions to support your ethical conduct as a remote interpreter.

→ Section 6.4 Content

Ethical decision-making is a challenge for all interpreters. For remote interpreters, making ethical decisions can be even more demanding because no single code of ethics will easily apply to all your sessions. In addition, you may transfer quickly from one call to the next. Perhaps you perform conference interpreting all day, or perhaps the calls are for healthcare or educational interpreting. Perhaps they are a mix of business, healthcare, educational, refugee, court, emergency and mental health interpreting. Perhaps, as is becoming increasingly common, you may interpret sessions that take place in multiple countries on a single day or during the course of the week.

Think about this a moment. One minute you interpret for a family whose house is on fire. In the next call, you interpret for an insurance dispute. The call after that is for a parent-teacher meeting. Then you interpret nearly an hour for a sexual assault survivor who recounts her rape, in graphic detail, to a therapist. Then it's on to a town meeting (a meeting of local politicians and citizens). Through all these calls, you will be confronted with decision after decision. For example:

- What should I do when the lawyer asks in the middle of the call, "Interpreter, is this just a cultural issue, or do you think my client has a mental health problem?"
- How do I handle culturally rich idioms, humor and slang?
- One participant is shutting down completely—you know why—but the other participant clearly doesn't know why and is getting frustrated.

You may not have adequate breaks between calls to recover from interpreting fatigue, never mind decision-making fatigue. You may work for multiple organizations, each with their own expectations for your behavior (and perhaps their own ethical guidelines). Some of their expectations may contradict others.

This section focuses on steps you can take to assure that you are complying with general ethical requirements while also making decisions that make you feel good about yourself, your work and your human dignity as well as the human dignity of participants. We'll keep it practical.

Here are the points this section will address:

- Review a partial list of codes of ethics from around the world.
- Identify the code or codes of ethics you need to work with.
- List common ethical concerns that you know could arise in your work. Add to that list as needed.
- Consider the eight safe areas of ethical practice.
- Consider the three controversial areas of practice.
- Consult the organizations or language services you work with on specific questions.
- Consult interpreters, mentors, interpreter service coordinators and other colleagues.
- Make System 2 decisions about your ethical conduct.
- Log critical incidents.

Countries with codes of ethics for interpreters

Interpreter codes of ethics around the world			
U.S. and Canada	**Australia and New Zealand**	**Europe**	**Other parts of the world**
General interpreting • ATA code used in U.S. and abroad. • Canada has national and provincial ethics (seven provinces) covering general and especially conference, court and community/healthcare interpreting.	*General interpreting* • Australia national ethics and standards. • New Zealand national code.	*General interpreting* • FIT Europe code covers Europe. • Codes in Austria, Belgium, Bulgaria, Czech Republic, Denmark, Finland, France, Germany, Ireland, Poland, Romania (three), Russia, Slovakia, Spain (two) and Catalunya, Switzerland (two), Wales, UK.	*General interpreting* • Africa: South Africa. • Asia: China, Indonesia, Saipan (code proposed), Singapore. • Middle East: general code for Arabic, one for Israel, two for Egypt. • Latin America: e.g., Argentina, Brazil, Chile, Colombia, Ecuador, Guatemala.
Conference interpreting • TAALS code applies. • AIIC code in use.	*Conference interpreting* • General ethics and standards apply to conference interpreting. • AIIC members follow AIIC code too.	*Conference interpreting* • AIIC code dominant. • European Commission code. • National codes: e.g., France, Germany, Italy, Spain, Türkiye.	*Conference interpreting* • AIIC used in many countries. • China: one language service code in China. • Latin America: TAALS code and national codes, e.g., Argentina, Brazil, Mexico, Peru.
Court interpreting • U.S.: national (federal) U.S. code. • Most U.S. states have similar codes. • Canada: 1998 Supreme Court standards, immigration court national standards and codes in Ontario, BC.	*Court interpreting* • Australia: national code of conduct. • Code for Queensland (nearly one-quarter of the continent). • New Zealand: national ethical/code of conduct "guidelines."	*Court interpreting* • United Nations criminal courts. • EULITA code for all Europe. • Court codes for several countries also—Finland, France, Germany, Italy, Netherlands, Spain, UK.	*Court interpreting* • Most countries across Asia do not have codes for court interpreting.
Community interpreting • Canada national code (HIN). • U.S. national codes and a state code for healthcare; a national code for educational (another pending).	*Community interpreting* • Follow general code of ethics: not specific to community interpreting.	*Community interpreting* • Codes in Belgium, France, Ireland, UK. • Almost none in others.	*Community interpreting* • Few codes noted for community interpreting. • Asia: Hong Kong. • Latin America: Mexico (for indigenous languages).
Sign language interpreting • U.S. and Canada national (general) codes; some U.S. state codes. • A few national, regional, local U.S. codes for educational interpreting.	*Sign language interpreting* • Australia national code. • New Zealand national code for sign language.	*Sign language interpreting* • Codes in several countries: Austria, Czech Republic, Estonia, Italy, Norway, Spain, Switzerland (French, German), UK.	*Sign language interpreting* • Africa: South Africa, Kenya. • Asia: Japan, Philippines, Taiwan. • Latin America: e.g., Argentina, Brazil, Mexico. • Middle East: no codes found.

Table 6.8: **Examples of codes of ethics for interpreters from around the world**[112]

112 **Note:** This table represents only those codes of ethics reviewed by the author of this section and does not purport to be exhaustive.

Where will you find a code of ethics for interpreters that addresses your country, region or specializations of interpreting? Or should you perhaps follow several codes?

Table 6.8 provides examples of codes of ethics from around the world. Many other codes may exist. Internet sites for these documents are not included because such links frequently expire after publication. Instead, to find these codes, perform an online search with the name of organization and country or region and the term "code of ethics" (inside the quote marks). In addition, see the bibliography at the end of Volume 1 for examples of codes of ethics by title.

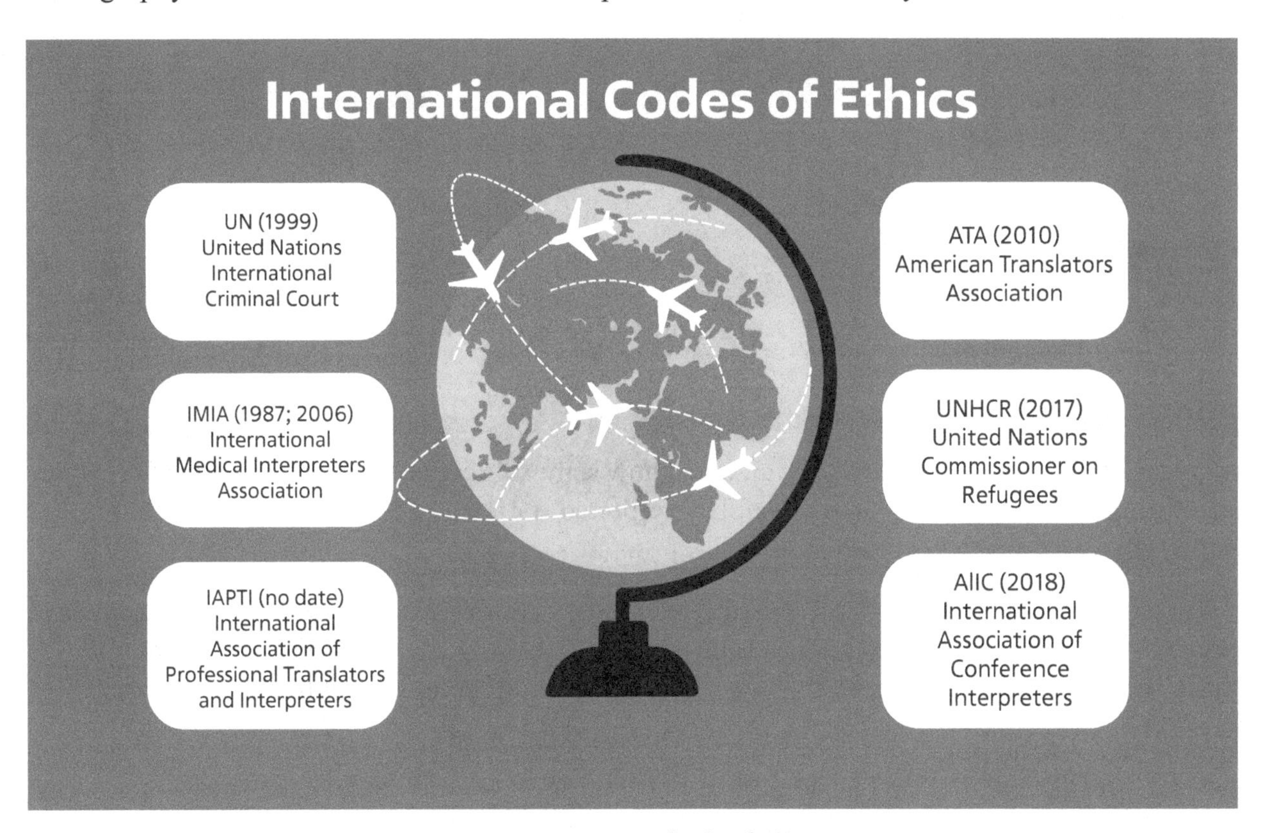

Figure 6.9: International codes of ethics

Note that many countries across Europe and the Americas have state, provincial or local codes of ethics for interpreters. Some of these documents are decades old. Some were published recently. In an encouraging trend in the past few years, a significant number of new or revised codes of ethics for interpreters have been published.

Identify the code(s) of ethics you need to work with

Now that you've reviewed some of the codes of ethics from around the world, your next task will be to make a decision about which code or codes of ethics to work with. To do so:

- Look at the information in Table 6.8 to determine which types of codes of ethics may be available to you by region, country and specialization.
- Try to identify, in particular, any codes that address the specializations you plan to interpret in, whether internationally or in your own country or region.

- Ask other interpreters you know which codes and standards they follow.
- Consult the organizations or language services you work for to learn if they recommend specific codes of ethics or standards for their remote interpreters and if they also have written ethical guidelines.

Keep your final selection in a place where you can easily consult these documents.

Once you have made your selection, study the documents carefully. Then reread them as needed to refresh your memory.

Why to Reread Your Codes of Ethics Often

Reread any codes of ethics you work with at least once a year, even after you know them well. Apply the content to some of the challenging interpreting situations you face. You will be surprised how much coming back to the same code of ethics with fresh eyes and more experience can help you evaluate what to do in the future.

As you reread these documents each year, you may also note how your perspective on their content changes and evolves along with your work and life experience!

List the ethical concerns you know could arise

If you are a practicing interpreter, you already know some of the easy and difficult ethical decisions you face. For example, you have probably interpreted for someone who didn't seem (to you) to understand what was being said but didn't say so.

As a large body of research[113] and our own life experiences make clear, we tend to make better decisions when we have time to think about them quietly. The decisions that remote interpreters make spontaneously—and incredibly quickly—while interpreting are not nearly as effective.

Ethical decisions are among the hardest decisions interpreters will ever make in our work. Therefore, list any ethical situations or decisions you encounter in your work and decide how you can best handle them (continue reading this section for guidance). Add to that list often. This will prepare you and help you remain calm and composed when you encounter variations on these situations in your work.

Develop a plan for handling ethical challenges

Do you know how you would handle an ethical challenge? Let's take the example of confidentiality. If you interpret in a less common language, even remote interpreters might end up interpreting more than once for the same person—and that means you know and perhaps remember information from other encounters. A real-life example might involve knowing that a patient has an allergy, to latex, say—but then forgets to mention it when a provider in a different session asks if the patient has any allergies.

[113] See Volume 1, Chapter 4, Essential Protocols and Skills, and Chapter 7, Addressing Communication Breakdowns, for more details about research on System 1 (fast, reflexive) thinking and System 2 (slow, reflective) thinking that shows we make more effective decisions when we have time to reflect on them.

What do you do?

- Simply interpret?
- Suggest the patient might wish to reconsider their answer?
- Tell the healthcare provider about the allergy?
- After the session, report the allergy to the organization that engaged you to interpret?

Here is a model for how to handle such challenges.

Figure 6.10: **Ethical decision-making model chart**

Consider the eight safe areas of practice

Before we illustrate how you might work with this ethical decision-making model chart, keep in mind that Section 6.2 of this chapter described eight common directives, or ethical principles, that constitute areas of agreement among codes of ethics around the world. Consult that section. Then examine your list of ethical concerns to identify:

- Which of your ethical challenges fall into one or more of these eight areas?
- How can you reasonably and effectively make decisions using the chart in Figure 6.10?

To guide you in applying the chart, see Table 6.9 (a) and (b): Guidance on how to use the ethical decision-making chart. These real-life examples may be helpful.

Consider the three controversial areas of practice

The previous section explored three controversial areas of ethical practice—addressing communication breakdowns, cultural mediation and advocacy, including protecting human rights. There is no one answer that everyone can agree on about how to approach these areas. Depending on your specialization, country and who you interpret for, these areas will involve consulting extensively and in depth with the organizations you work for, colleagues, peers, interpreting associations you belong to and any interpreter forums, support groups and collaborative organizations (including online and social media networks) you belong to or participate in. Conferences may also be helpful. Where should you start?

Addressing common ethical challenges in remote interpreting: Part 1				
Ethical tenet	**Confidentiality**	**Accuracy**	**Impartiality**	**Professionalism**
Challenge	A patient, asked about allergies, says "none." You already know the patient has an allergy to latex.	A participant tells you, "Don't interpret what I just said."	You arrive at a video call. It is your niece of 16. She is pregnant.	In a legal interview for a person seeking refugee status, you realize you do not speak the dialect well.
Question 1 to ask yourself: **Is there a legal requirement or serious, imminent risk to safety?**				
Answer	No.	No.	Yes. If you stay, she might not disclose certain information.	Yes. Inaccuracy could jeopardize the case.
Question 2 to ask yourself: **Do I have a clear sense of the ethically appropriate decision?**				
Answer	Yes? Proceed. E.g., simply interpret now and report later.	Yes. You interpret what was just said. Then the participant shouts at you and says you should never interpret again!	Yes. Even though they are asking me to stay (because they trust me) I know I should not stay. I will withdraw.	Yes. You will need to withdraw.
Question 3 to ask yourself: **Who, when and how can I consult or report to about this concern (while respecting privacy)?**				
Answer **Note:** Do not mention any identifying details unless the person you talk to is permitted to know them.	Consult colleagues, perhaps a mentor too. But also file a critical incident report to determine what to do now, given the future risk.	Consider consulting a colleague and mentor. But also report this critical incident to your supervisor, if possible in writing right after the call.	Report the incident to a supervisor. Even though you acted correctly, the organization you interpret for will normally need you to report.	Report the incident to a supervisor. Even though you acted correctly, the organization you interpret for will typically need you to report.

Table 6.9 (a): **Guidance on how to use the ethical decision-making chart, part 1**

Addressing common ethical challenges in remote interpreting: Part 2				
Ethical tenet	**Professional development**	**Role boundaries**	**Solidarity**	**Respect**
Challenge	You learn at a conference that you shouldn't interpret in court due to lack of qualifications.	A participant asks you to explain a term the other participant used.	Another remote interpreter appears and claims this is their video call, not yours.	One participant says something profoundly derogatory and racist to the other participant.
Question 1 to ask yourself	**Is there a legal requirement or serious, imminent risk to safety?**			
Answer	No (unless you continue to perform court interpreting).	No.	Not usually.	No.
Question 2 to ask yourself	**Do I have a clear sense of the ethically appropriate decision?**			
Answer	Yes. Take no more court assignments until you have adequate training and qualifications to perform it.	Yes. Report what was said and ask the other participant to clarify the term.	Perhaps not. Some decisions will depend on the specific situation and organizations involved. Usually preferable to withdraw and report.	Yes. Interpret it. If necessary, withdraw from the session.
Question 3 to ask yourself	**Who, when and how can I consult or report to about this concern (while respecting privacy)?**			
Answer	I might ask colleagues about the best way to obtain adequate training, skills and qualifications because I want to perform court interpreting again in the future.	I might consult the organizations I interpret for or other interpreters about what to say.	I need to consult with the organization that sent me to know their policy in future about how to address this specific problem.	I might need to report the incident as a critical incident to the organization I interpret for. I might need to seek support from colleagues.

Table 6.9 (b): **Guidance on how to use the ethical decision-making chart, part 2**

Consult interpreters, mentors, interpreter service coordinators and other colleagues

The organizations you interpret for might—or might not—have helpful guidance. Who does have such guidance? First, your fellow interpreters! The most seasoned interpreters have usually confronted so many ethical decisions that they have much to share and are often happy to share it.

It is particularly important to seek out interpreters who have interpreted remotely for years because their input will be specific to the ethical challenges of remote interpreting. While some challenges are the same as for face-to-face interpreting, others (as noted throughout this book) are specific to remote sessions.

After that, without giving any identifying details about participants, consider consulting a forum, group or organization for interpreters, including conferences, unless the question is time sensitive. If questions that arise are urgent, gather the best solutions you can, write them down and approach the organization you interpret for. Specifically, in language services, interpreter service coordinators are often a source of valuable guidance and support. Even colleagues who are not interpreters but work closely with interpreters and hear their stories—such as interpreter managers or supervisors—can be incredibly helpful for certain questions.[114]

That said, if you approach language service and other organizational staff with potential solutions gathered from experienced remote interpreters, the guidance you receive from such staff members will likely be far more helpful. Also, you will look more professional with your wise suggestions!

Make System 2 decisions about your ethical conduct

In Chapter 7, Addressing Communication Breakdowns, you will explore differences between System 1 thinking (when you have to make decisions quickly while you interpret) and System 2 thinking (the slower, more deliberate kind of thinking we can engage in when we have time to reflect and plan ahead).

To engage in System 2 thinking, take out your list of ethical decisions that you commonly face, collect advice you have been seeking from interpreters, mentors and other colleagues as well as language services or other organizations you interpret for, and write down what you plan to do when you face the ethical challenges you have listed, whether common challenges or less common ones.

Now refer to the codes of ethics and standards you have selected as being most relevant for your work. See if they offer any specific guidance. If so, note it down beside the relevant ethical challenge.

To help you, see Activity 6.4, Apply your ethical knowledge, at the end of this chapter. It can help you structure your responses.

This planning work will help you with the types of incidents or challenges that you have listed. *It will also help you think quickly and effectively to make decisions about other ethical challenges you have never encountered.* You will remain calmer as well. Your decisions will be more likely to conform both to ethical requirements and to standards or best practices.

The reason is that simply engaging in ethical decision-making in a calm, rational and non-emotional way makes the decision-making process almost second nature. It prepares your mind for new encounters in real life. It sharpens and hones your thinking.

You will find this planning time well spent, especially in the remote environment, where such decisions play out at top speed and where you face, potentially, so many different kinds of calls in rapid succession over several hours.

[114] In an ideal world, all these supervisors, interpreter service coordinators and quality assurance staff interpreters would themselves be former or current interpreters—but that is still not always the case.

Consult the language services or organizations you work with about specific questions

Once you have identified your ethical questions or concerns and consulted with peers and colleagues—fellow remote interpreters—your next step is to determine how to approach the organizations or language services you work for. When you do, be specific. For example, you could state:

Example 1

> I often find that families I interpret for at school have no idea what a report card is, but the teacher doesn't usually notice the problem. *Here are some things I have considered or tried doing. [Give examples.] How would you like me to handle this kind of issue?*

Example 2

> Many of the participants I work with seem unaware when the client or patient doesn't understand them but, for cultural or other reasons, doesn't ask questions—but then asks *me* questions during or near the end of the session. *Here are some things I have considered or tried doing. [Give examples.] How would you like me to handle this kind of issue?*

Example 3

> Many of the speakers I interpret for in RSI have poor audio (no headset or microphone), which interferes with my ability to be accurate. *[Give examples.] Do you prefer to address this problem, or should I? If I should do so, here are some things I have considered or tried doing [Give examples.]*

Example 4

> When I interpret VRI for [my signed language], sometimes the pixelation of the video undermines my ability to interpret faithfully. *Here are some things I have considered or tried doing. [Give examples.] How do you prefer I act if the situation clearly suggests it would be better to call in an onsite (face-to-face) interpreter instead?*

Log critical incidents

Sometimes things go wrong. You make the best decisions you can. Sometimes they work well; sometimes they lead to problems.

Make a written formal record (a log) of any critical incident that arises *immediately* after the call—or at least as soon as possible, while your memory is still fresh.

Ethical challenges and critical incidents are normal in face-to-face interpreting. They are just as *common* in remote interpreting. If a participant yells at you for interpreting a remark they thought they made to you privately, or says that you misinterpreted something when you were accurate, or suggests you have done something else wrong—here's what to do.

- First, don't panic. Stay calm.
- Conduct yourself as professionally as possible until the session closes.
- Take a break as soon as possible and document everything you can remember.

- Report the incident to the appropriate person in the organization you interpreted for right away, and include your written log or notes when possible.
- Add that incident to your list of ethical challenges. A critical incident almost by definition will involve an ethical challenge (or several).
- Engage in self-care as soon as you can. (See Volume 2, Chapter 9, Self-care for Remote Interpreters.)
- Consult with colleagues, if possible, to solicit their input when you are emotionally ready.
- Put in potential solutions or suggestions to yourself on your list about how to handle a similar situation in the future.
- Congratulate yourself for acting professionally. This is hard work!

→ Section 6.4 Review

This section explored how remote interpreters who work across specializations or national borders can engage in effective ethical decision-making. The following recommendations appeared:

- Identify the code or codes of ethics you need to work with.
    - Consult the codes and standards mentioned in this chapter (and any in the bibliography at the end of this volume) to help you determine if your country has a relevant code of ethics.
    - If no code specific to your region is available, consider those that are broader in scope or general enough (such as international ones) to address your work.
    - Try to find codes that address the specializations you interpret in.
    - Ask other interpreters you know which codes and standards they follow.
    - Consider using international codes or other relevant (broad) codes or standards for your region or specialization.
    - Consult the organizations or language services you work for to learn if they have their own code of ethics or if they recommend specific codes of ethics or standards for their remote interpreters.
- List the common ethical concerns you know could arise in your work.
    - Focus on ethical challenges that arise often.
    - Add to that list as needed.
- Consider the eight shared directives or principles for ethical practice.
    - Consult your list of ethical challenges.
    - Consult the codes of ethics you have selected.
    - Where you cannot see answers to your ethical questions, identify which of the eight directives commonly found in codes of ethics might apply.

  - Use the guidance in Section 6.2 and this section to help you determine a helpful course of action for the ethical challenges you listed. As needed, consult with peers, senior remote interpreters, interpreter service coordinators and other staff.
- Consider the three controversial areas of practice.
  - If your selected codes of ethics do not address controversial issues that arise in your own work, or the eight most commonly shared directives addressed in Section 6.2, look at Section 6.3 to see if the guidance there will help you.
- Consult interpreters, mentors, interpreter service coordinators and other colleagues.
  - If questions remain, consult colleagues for their answers, especially seasoned remote interpreters.
- Consult the organizations or language services you work with on specific questions.
  - For any questions you find difficult to resolve, consult these organizations.
  - Make your questions specific. "Here is a common situation I face [in detail]. How would you like me to respond?"
- Make System 2 decisions about your ethical conduct.
  - Review all the guidance you have collected and received.
  - In a quiet setting, write down what you plan to do when you face similar ethical challenges in future.
- Log critical incidents.
  - If something goes wrong, usually ethical decisions are involved.
  - Document every critical incident the moment you can after it happens.
  - Report the critical incident to the appropriate person.
  - Consult colleagues and your code or codes of ethics and standards; then make a plan for how to handle similar situations in the future.
- Keep your final selection in a place where you can easily consult these documents.

Section 6.5 Codes of Ethics for Sign Language Interpreters

→ Learning objective 6.5

After completing this section, the remote interpreter will be able to identify similarities among codes of ethics for sign language interpreters and explain how to apply them to remote interpreting.

→ Section 6.5 Overview

Many different sign language interpreters have their own code of ethics that are applicable in the interpreter's general practice. This section will guide you through the similarities among different signed language interpreter codes of ethics.

As remote interpreters, your clients can be global. However, in the case of signed language interpreters, the codes of ethics you follow may be of the signed language you interpret and not only the country you're interpreting in.

This section will explore how signed language interpreters apply their code of ethics everywhere they work, no matter the subject or environment.

→ Section 6.5 Content

Recognizing signed languages as official languages

Sign language isn't universal. There are over 300 different signed languages around the world. In some cases, the signed language is named after the country where it is used. For example, Brazilian Sign Language is used in Brazil and Japanese Sign Language is used in Japan.

However, many signed languages are named after the spoken language equivalent and not tied to a specific country. For example, French Sign Language (LSF/LSQ) is used in France as well as in Canada.

However, it's important to know that there are many countries where a signed language is still not recognized as an official language. Even though a signed language may be used by thousands of people in a country or region, the government may not recognize it as an official language. The World Federation of the Deaf speaks to the importance of signed languages being recognized and says,

> *We recognise national sign languages as the key to the inclusion of [D]eaf people in society. National sign languages are full, complex natural languages with the same linguistic properties as spoken languages, including phonetic, phonemic, syllabic, morphological, syntactic, discourse, and pragmatic levels of organisation. They are the [native language] and the natural languages of [D]eaf children. They are the vector of the inclusion of [D]eaf children both in [D]eaf communities and in society, fostering the building of their own identities and communities.*[115]

It wasn't until May 19, 2021, that Italy formally recognized Italian Sign Language (LIS) as an official language. Deaf Italians struggled for many years to gain recognition because the government didn't classify Italian Sign Language (LIS) as a *minority language*; a classification that offers support and protection. Additionally, there has been strong division across the country regarding the best language to educate Deaf children; this division negatively affected language policy planning.[116]

---

[115] *WFD Charter on Sign Language Rights for All.* Sec 2.2. Retrieved from: http://wfdeaf.org/charter/

[116] Carlo Geraci. (2012). Language Policy and Planning: The Case of Italian Sign Language. *Sign Language Studies*, 12(4), pp. 494–518. Retrieved from: http://www.jstor.org/stable/26190877

How does having a signed language nationally recognized affect interpreters of these signed languages? First, when a country recognizes a signed language of the Deaf community, then language access and services to the Deaf community are potentially more protected and supported. Government recognition gives additional support, potential funding, and opportunity for more robust training and standards and formation of professional interpreting associations.

It's important to note that not every country with a signed language has a professional interpreting organization. Therefore, there may not be a code of ethics that includes every signed language, country or interpreting community.

Countries with codes of ethics for sign language interpreters[117]			
Argentina	Estonia	Mexico	Spain
Australia	France	Netherlands	Switzerland
Austria	Germany	New Zealand	Taiwan
Brazil	Italy	Norway	UK
Canada	Japan	Philippines	U.S.
Czech Republic	Kenya	South Africa	

Table 6.10: Examples of countries with codes of ethics that address sign language interpreters (but not spoken language interpreters)

World Association of Sign Language interpreters

Sign language isn't universal. However, there is a world association that works to support the advancement of sign language interpreters around the globe.

The concept for an international association started in 1975 in Washington, DC. In 2003, the World Association of Sign Language Interpreters (WASLI) was formally established.

A part of WASLI's mission is to, "Encourage the establishment of national associations of sign language interpreters in countries that do not have them."[118]

WASLI works to support the creation of national associations and a part of that process is the creation of a national code of ethics for interpreters of signed languages in each country. WASLI does not have its own code of ethics; however, on its website, WASLI has collected codes of ethics for sign language interpreters from around the world.

WASLI partners with the World Federation of the Deaf (WFD) to provide accreditation for International Sign language interpreters. There isn't a universal sign language, but there is an International Sign language. WASLI defines International Sign language and its uses as:

> *International Sign (IS) is a contact variety of sign language used in a variety of different contexts, particularly at international meetings such as the World Federation of the Deaf (WFD) congress, events such as the Deaflympics, in video clips produced by Deaf people and*

[117] This list does not include all countries with codes of ethics that address both spoken and sign language interpreters in the same document.

[118] Retrieved from: https://wasli.org/about/mission-objectives

> *watched by other Deaf people from around the world, and informally when travelling and socialising. It can be seen as a pidgin form of sign language, which is not as conventionalised or complex as natural sign languages and has a limited lexicon.*[119]

WFD-WASLI has its own code of conduct for accredited International Sign language interpreters (WFD-WASLI, 2018).[120] It is not to be confused with an international code of conduct for signed language interpreters around the world.

Codes of ethics and similarities across signed languages

In spoken language interpreting, codes of ethics often address specific specializations, such as healthcare or legal interpreting (depending on the country). They are language neutral. However, most signed language interpreters adhere to a code of ethics published by their professional association that addresses a particular signed language.

Additionally, codes of ethics for sign language interpreters, with some exceptions, are not usually tied to specific specializations or settings but apply to the interpreter's general practice.

For example, in the United States, American Sign Language (ASL) interpreters, once they are certified by the Registry of Interpreters for the Deaf (RID), are governed by the Code of Professional Conduct (CPC) as written by RID.

The CPC is meant to be applicable for all specializations and in all settings for ASL interpreters. This also means it is the code of ethics that ASL interpreters follow and it applies wherever they work, *even when outside of the United States.*

A similar situation exists for British Sign Language (BSL) interpreters. Their professional interpreter organization identifies BSL as the language that UK sign language interpreters use to be a part of the national register.

Why does this point matter? Imagine that an ASL interpreter takes an assignment in London for an American Deaf student who is attending a summer study abroad program. The ASL interpreter will adhere to the code of professional conduct from RID in the U.S. because that is where the interpreter has professional affiliation. Even though there is a code of ethics for interpreters in the UK, their code of ethics is for BSL interpreters and not ASL interpreters. The same would apply to a VRI interpreter who is interpreting ASL for a Deaf visitor to London.

There are several codes of ethics around the world for sign language interpreters. While each was created by a professional association of sign language interpreters, they share strong similarities. Table 6.11 highlights some of the codes of ethics in the world and their similarities.

---

119 International Sign Definition. Retrieved from: https://wasli.org/international-sign-definition#:~:text=International%20Sign%20(IS)%20is%20a,Deaf%20people%20from%20around%20the

120 See https://wfdeaf.org/wp-content/uploads/2018/12/WFD-WASLI-Code-of-Conduct-18012018-Final.pdf#:~:text=This%20WFD-WASLI%20Code%20of%20Professional%20Conduct%20%28hereinafter%20called,bound%20to%20respect%20in%20their%20work%20as%20interpreters.

Common ethical directives in codes of ethics for sign language interpreters						
	Professional conduct	Confidentiality	Competence[121]	Accuracy	Impartiality	Professional develop-ment
Registry of Interpreters for the Deaf–ASL	✓	✓	✓	✓	✓	✓
Philippine Association of Interpreter for Deaf Empowerment	✓	✓	✓	✓	✓	✓
National Registers of the Communication Professionals with Deaf and Deafblind (BSL; UK)	✓	✓	✓	✓	✓	✓
Federación Española de Intérpretes de Lengua de Signos y Guías-Intérpretes (Spain)	✓	✓	✓	✓	✓	✓
Kenyan Sign Language Interpreters Association	✓	✓	✓	✓	✓	✓
Canadian Association of Sign Language Interpreters	✓	✓	✓	✓	✓	✓

Table 6.11: A comparison of common ethical directives across sign language interpreter codes of ethics

This list is only a sample of the existing codes of ethics for sign language interpreters. Whatever sign language you interpret, determine if there is a professional sign language interpreter association for that language and also determine if there is a code of ethics that applies to you.

However, what do you do if there isn't a professional interpreting association where you live and there isn't a professional code of ethics for you? One option is to look at the ethical tenets listed in the codes of other organizations, including those (such as Finland for community interpreting or the U.S. NCIHC code for medical interpreting) that address both spoken and sign language interpreters. Adopt them as your own until a professional code of ethics is created for your signed language. While this approach isn't ideal, as discussed in Sections 6.3 and 6.4, adopting this approach can help guide your practice and conduct as a signed language interpreter.

121 "Competence" in this context refers to the requirement that interpreters accept only those assignments for which they are fully competent, skilled and qualified and which are within their scope of practice.

After all, as revealed in Table 6.11, there is widespread agreement on basic ethical principles among codes of ethics for interpreters of signed languages, just as there is for spoken language interpreters or codes that address both.

Sign language interpreters' codes of ethics and video remote interpreting

As this chapter makes clear, many codes of ethics are similar in their values, tenets (principles or directives) and the practices they support or require.

However, for BSL and ASL interpreters, a sign language interpreter doesn't give up their code of ethics and adopt the codes of ethics of another professional association just because their client is in another country. Your professional association's ethics follow you, no matter where you interpret.

What happens when you are a remote sign language interpreter for a client in another country? The answer is simple: Follow the codes of ethics of your professional sign language interpreting association.

It may be obvious, but it is worth stating that sign language interpreters are able to work remotely only via video. The sign language interpreter must be visible to the Deaf participant. If the session is one where the Deaf participants won't be able to comment, then the sign language interpreter may not be able to see the Deaf participant. Situations such as news conferences or political speeches don't typically make the Deaf person visible to the interpreter.

Codes of ethics for signed language interpreters don't often specify remote interpreting because the codes of ethics may have been written before remote interpreting was common or available. However, many of these codes require interpreters to interpret accurately and faithfully. If the video quality of the session is interfering with the interpreter's ability to interpret accurately and faithfully, then the interpreter must call attention to that problem and use the skills learned through this volume to determine next steps.

However, if you interpret for a session where there will be two-way communication, then the interpreter and the Deaf participant must be able to see each other, and the video quality and connection is of utmost importance.

Additionally, video remote interpreting is not suitable for all Deaf people in all situations. For example, a face-to-face interpreter may be the best option for the following:

- Deaf/Blind participants.
- Children.
- Highly emotional/stressful healthcare sessions.
- Deaf people with intellectual disabilities.

Remember that signed languages are three-dimensional language. VRI is seen in two dimensions. Video can "flatten" signing and affects communication for many individuals who are Deaf or Hard-of-Hearing. Body language, facial expressions, and the three-dimensional nature of signed language is limited by a flat screen.

Some Deaf people may lose their full communicative autonomy via video and need an onsite (face-to-face) interpreter. Each Deaf participant and session are different. Sign language interpreters will have to evaluate each session on a case-by-case basis to determine if VRI is adequate for that session. Otherwise, the session's outcomes might be at risk.

→ Section 6.5 Review

All interpreter codes of ethics require interpreters to act professionally while maintaining confidentiality. Virtually all of them require accuracy and faithfulness to the message, whether the sessions are face-to-face or conducted remotely.

Sign language interpreters, like spoken language interpreters, can use their association's code of ethics to guide them on how to handle remote sessions. A key difference, however, is that many codes of ethics for signed languages are specific to that language, not to interpreters who work across all languages in that specialization or geographical area.

As a result, whether you interpret in one country or several countries, follow the code of ethics *specific to the signed language you interpret for* and not the code of ethics in the geographical region where the participants may be located.

Finally, be aware that VRI "flattens" sign language and may not be adequate for all Deaf participants or situations. If you are unable to do so, consider reporting that the working conditions are inadequate for accurate interpreting to avoid compromising outcomes for that session.

→ Chapter Activities

Activity 6.1 (a): Define code of ethics

Instructions

1. Read the definitions (a-h) below.
2. Decide which definition best fits code of ethics for interpreters.
3. Write your selection into the blank lines below. Check the answer key at the back of this book to see if it agrees with your answer.
    a. A list of rules for interpreters.
    b. Guidelines for interpreters.
    c. Best practices for interpreters.
    d. Industry standards for interpreters.
    e. A list of requirements for interpreters issued by a professional association.
    f. A list of recommendations and best practices for interpreters published by an official group.

g. A set of directives that specifies the requirements or expectations intended to guide the conduct of members of a profession.

h. A set of national rules telling interpreters what to do when they face ethical challenges.

Activity 6.1 (b): Match the definitions

Instructions

1. In the blank column to the right (labeled Document number), write the *number* (1 through 5) for the appropriate document type (shown in color) beside each *definition* (a-d) in the table below.
2. Note that one definition matches *two* terms. So in one box, you will need to add *two* numbers.

Definitions	Document number
a. A standard developed and published by an international standardization organization.	
b. A set of formal guidelines that offer practitioners of a profession clear strategies and courses of action to support professional conduct.	
c. Protocols, procedures and guidelines that are recognized by a profession as being effective and recommended.	
d. A set of directives that specifies the requirements or expectations intended to guide the conduct of practitioners of a profession.	

Document types

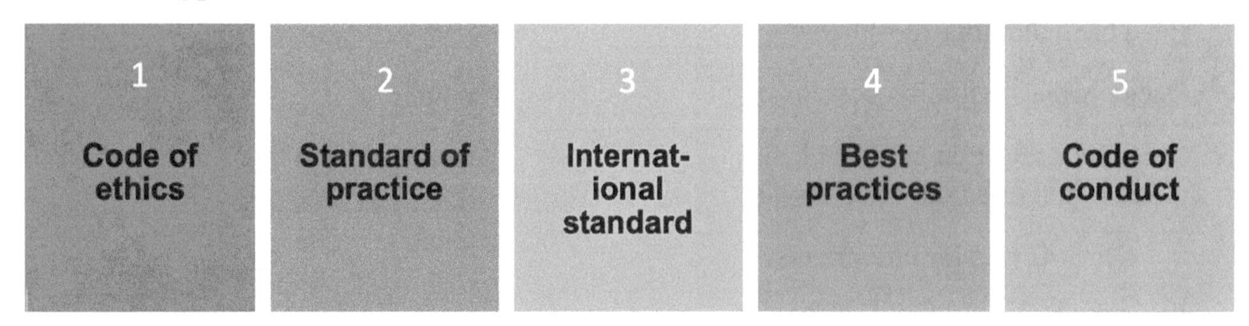

Activity 6.1 (c): Following a code of ethics

Classroom instructions

1. Using the examples in Activity 6.1 (b), conduct an online search and find and save or print at least one code of ethics or code of conduct that is relevant to your country and/or at least one of your interpreting specializations or the language services you work for.

2. Divide into small groups based on who might work with a particular code or work most often with that code (compare to other codes).
3. Discuss how that particular code applies to the work of the members of that group.
4. Identify in that code at least three tenets or principles that most or all in the group already follow (such as confidentiality).
5. Identify the tenet or principle that most or all in the group would find the *most difficult* to follow as a *remote* interpreter (such as professional solidarity). State why, in writing.
6. Identify the tenet or principle that the group found most *helpful* for remote interpreters. State why, in writing.
7. Discuss your findings with other small groups.

Instructions for self-study

1. Using the examples in Activity 6.1 (b) or examples of your own, conduct an online search and find and save or print at least one code of ethics or code of conduct that is relevant to your country or one of your interpreting specializations.
2. Identify in that code of ethics at least three tenets or principles that you already follow (such as confidentiality).
3. Identify the tenet or principle that you would find the *most difficult* to follow as a *remote interpreter* (such as professional solidarity). State why, in writing.
4. Identify the tenet or principle that you found most helpful. State why, in writing.
5. If possible, discuss your findings with another remote interpreter and see if the two of you agree or disagree and discuss why.

Activity 6.2: Compare code of ethics

Classroom instructions

1. In Section 6.2, you studied eight important common directives or principles shared by many codes of ethics (confidentiality, accuracy, impartiality, professionalism, professional development, role boundaries, solidarity, and respect). Compare them to the principles or directives in the code (or codes) of ethics you identified in Activity 6.1 (a).
2. Write down any of the eight directives or principles that you can find in your own code or codes of ethics.
3. Write down any directives or principles in your own code or codes of ethics that are different from the eight directives.
4. Answer the following questions, labeled a through f.
5. Discuss your answers with your small group.

Questions

a. Why do you think certain points in your code or codes of ethics are similar to those in Table 6.4 (for spoken language interpreters) or Table 6.11 (for sign language interpreters)?

b. How do you explain why certain points are different?

c. How do these similarities and differences apply to your work as a remote interpreter?

d. Do you disagree with any of the eight common points in codes of ethics around the world?

e. What changes will you make to your work as an interpreter as a result of studying this section?

f. Identify and write down any tenet or principle you would choose to add to the code or codes of ethics that you currently work with.

Instructions for self-study

1. Follow all the classroom instructions.
2. Find a fellow interpreter or other colleague who is concerned with interpreter ethics and conduct.
3. Discuss your answers to the questions with that interpreter or colleague.

Activity 6.3 (a): Reading quiz

Instructions

1. Read Section 6.3 carefully.
2. Answer the true-false and multiple-choice questions below. Check the answer key at the back of this book to see if your answers are correct.

Self-test on three areas of disagreement in codes of ethics for interpreters
True or false

1. Countries and associations around the world generally agree that interpreters should avoid trying to explain cultural misunderstandings.
2. Most legal service providers and courts do not permit interpreters to engage in advocacy on the job.
3. Addressing a serious communication breakdown might be necessary for the remote interpreter to support communicative autonomy.
4. The potential disruption when an interpreter intervenes to address misunderstandings is much less serious in remote interpreting than in face-to-face interpreting.
5. Remote interpreters are not *generally* expected to support human rights.
6. Interrupting a session can easily lead to confusion and also to side conversations, even in remote interpreting.
7. All interpreter codes of ethics encourage the interpreter to intervene as needed whenever a misunderstanding arises.
8. When intervening in court, interpreters may be required to identify themselves as "the interpreter" (e.g., "The interpreter requests a clarification of the term…") in order to avoid misunderstandings in the court record.
9. Ten interpreting codes of ethics examined for this program permit or require that the interpreter request cultural clarifications.

10. This textbook suggests that permitting the interpreter to provide cultural explanations risks undermining or destroying communicative autonomy.
11. Advocacy in interpreting means speaking up only on behalf of participants.
12. In some countries, codes of ethics may require or strongly recommend that interpreters protect participants from discrimination.

Multiple choice

Mark any and all answers that are correct. Check the answer key at the back of this book to see if your answers are correct.

13. To address a communication breakdown, the following strategies by the remote interpreter will normally be acceptable:
    a. Request a repetition.
    b. Ask for equipment, such as a speaker telephone or video screen, to be moved to make the audio or video easier for the interpreter to hear and see.
    c. Request a change in participant positioning to enhance sight lines and clear visual information.
    d. Explain the cultural background of a participant.
    e. Where possible and appropriate, request a relay interpreter (such as a certified Deaf interpreter or an Indigenous language interpreter), to facilitate clear understanding.
    f. Ask participants to speak one at a time.
14. Although communication breakdowns are often difficult and delicate to address, the interpreter can consider trying to:
    a. Suggest that one participant rephrase or restate the confusing information.
    b. Request (rather than provide) a clarification.
    c. Recommend that a participant explain or specify the meaning of technical or specialized terms.
    d. Point out, rather than explain, the basis of a possible misunderstanding (e.g., "The interpreter is concerned that the term informed consent might be causing some confusion.").
    e. Suggest a participant ask a question that might resolve the misunderstanding (e.g., "The interpreter suggests you ask the applicant what he means by spouse.").
15. If the interpreter notes that a participant seems not to understand the other participants, and the potential consequences are serious, the interpreter may reasonably:
    a. Check for participant understanding.
    b. Restate the information in a way that is easier for the other participant to understand.
    c. Ask the participant to verify the other participant's understanding.
    d. Request a clarification or restatement by the participant of the confusing information.

16. In the event of a cultural misunderstanding, even in legal interpreting many or most interpreters around the world would be permitted to:
    a. *Request* cultural clarification.
    b. *Provide* cultural clarification.
    c. *Explain* a cultural misunderstanding.
    d. *Describe* a participant's cultural beliefs.
17. Most codes of ethics or professional associations would permit the interpreter to engage in advocacy;
    a. During the session.
    b. Outside the session, on behalf of a participant.
    c. Outside the session, on behalf of the profession.
    d. Never (either for participants or for the profession).
18. Advocacy on behalf of a participant may be defined as:
    a. Telling people your honest opinion of a situation.
    b. Giving guidance or advice when something goes wrong.
    c. Taking action, or speaking up, on behalf of a participant in order to prevent or reduce harm.
    d. Supporting the profession of interpreting.
19. To avoid violating the ethical requirement to remain impartial, it is best to simply interpret and avoid interrupting the call unless:
    a. You sense that there is perhaps the possibility of a misunderstanding.
    b. Communication breaks down completely.
    c. Someone's safety or well-being is at serious risk.
    d. You disagree strongly with what is being said or signed

Activity 6.3 (b): Guidance on cultural mediation—fill in the blanks

Instructions

1. For this two-part exercise, use the terms listed below each part to fill in the blank spaces of those paragraphs.
2. Each term may be used only once.
3. Check the answer key at the back of this book to see if your answers are correct.

Part 1 Cultural mediation

Cultural mediation is a term used ______________ to refer to any act or ______________ of the interpreter that is intended to address a cultural ________________. Cultural mediation is also known by other terms such as ________________, cultural interpreting or ______________________. The remote interpreter will need to learn the expectations that surround cultural mediation in both the country where the participants need interpreting and often in particular _______________ of interpreting (such as court vs. ____________ interpreting).

For some countries such as Canada and the UK, even for community (including medical) interpreting you may not be permitted to ____________ cultural mediation. In others, you may be able to perform cultural mediation in community settings but not in ______________.

courts | community | misunderstanding | internationally | utterance
cultural clarification | specializations | culture brokering | perform

Part 2 Example of cultural mediation

Let's look at one example: the United States. Expectations in the U.S. about cultural mediation are more ____________. While in ____________ interpreting the general attitude among interpreters is not to perform cultural mediation, the actual ____________ varies. In general, it is permitted in U.S. courts to clarify certain cultural misunderstandings that are either ____________ based or that reference common cultural practices. However, performing such cultural clarification is difficult without ____________ legal training, and most ____________ interpreters should not attempt it without such training.

In community, including healthcare, interpreting, U.S. national ethics and standards (NCIHC, 2004 and 2005) lay down a ____________ but permitted avenue for interpreters to clarify cultural misunderstandings—not by explaining them, but by ____________ one or all participants to offer their own cultural ____________.

narrow | linguistically | complex | explanations | remote
legal | inviting | advanced | practice

Activity 6.4: Apply your ethical knowledge

Instructions

Part 1: Select relevant codes of ethics

- Take out a sheet of paper or open a blank document file on your computer or device.
- Identify three or more codes of ethics you will need to work with.
- Write down their titles, the organizations that published the codes and where to find them.
- To accomplish this:
  - Consult the codes and standards mentioned in this chapter and also any mentioned in the bibliography at the end of this book to help you determine if your country has a relevant code of ethics.
  - If no code specific to your country is available, consider those that are international in scope and general enough to address your work.
  - Try to find codes that address the specializations you interpret in.
  - *Write down the titles of the codes you select and keep copies of each one.*
  - Ask other interpreters you know which codes and standards they follow.

- If you cannot find codes of ethics for your own country or specializations, write down the name of relevant international codes or other relevant (broad) codes or standards for your region or specialization.
- Consult the organizations or language services you work for to learn if they have their own code of ethics or if they recommend specific codes of ethics or standards for their remote interpreters.

Part 2: Identify common ethical concerns

- List at least six common ethical concerns or challenges that could arise often in your work (such as finding yourself in a call that is too difficult for you or for which you are not qualified) and write them down.
    - Try to focus on ethical challenges that will come up most often.
    - Make your examples clear and specific.
    - Base them, if possible, on your past experiences.
    - After completing the exercise, keep this list and add to it as needed.

Part 3: Identify solutions to ethical challenges

- Consider the eight accepted areas of ethical practice: confidentiality, accuracy, impartiality, professionalism, professional development, role boundaries, solidarity, respect).
    - Consult your list of six ethical challenges.
    - Consult the codes of ethics you have selected.
    - Look for guidance especially in the sections for these eight commonly accepted areas of ethical practice.
    - Use the guidance in Sections 6.2 and 6.4 to help you determine a helpful course of action for the ethical challenges you listed.
    - As needed, consult with peers, senior remote interpreters, interpreter service coordinators and other staff.
    - Write the solutions down with clear, specific details on how to conduct yourself when you deal with each of the six challenges.

Part 4: Look for ethical guidance

- Share your proposed solutions to the six ethical challenges with colleagues and peers.
- Also consult appropriate staff (such as quality assurance) at the organizations or language services you work with on specific questions.
    - Ask for their honest reactions to your proposed solutions.
    - If you could not find solutions in each case, ask for their guidance.
    - Make your questions specific, for example: "Here is a common situation I face [in detail]. How would you like me to respond?"

Part 5: Make System 2 decisions

- Make System 2 decisions about your ethical conduct.
  - Review all the guidance you have collected and received from documents, your own written solutions to the six ethical challenges and feedback from colleagues and peers.
  - In a quiet setting, write down what you plan to do when you face similar ethical challenges in the future in remote interpreting sessions.

Part 6: Log (and study) critical incidents

- Set up a file to log critical incidents, making sure to observe legal and ethical requirements related to privacy and confidentiality and to secure the written or typed information.
  - Document every critical incident the moment you can after it happens.
  - Report the critical incident to the appropriate person.
  - Study each critical incident. Note that if something goes wrong during a session, usually ethical decisions are involved.
  - Consult colleagues about the critical incident and also your codes of ethics and standards, for guidance; then make a plan about how to handle similar situations in the future.
  - Keep your final plans in a place where you can easily find and consult them.

Activity 6.5: Compare two codes of ethics for sign language interpreters

Instructions

As a remote sign language interpreter, you may work for Deaf people who are communicating with others outside of the country you reside in. While the codes of ethics may be similar, some of the specific ethical requirements may differ from one code to another.

1. Consider the countries listed in Table 6.10 and select a few codes of ethics for sign language interpreters to explore.
2. Compare the code of ethics for at least one other country to the codes of ethics in your country.
3. What is similar? What is different? Write down at least three similarities and three differences between the codes of ethics for your country and those of the other country.
4. Now, imagine you are working at an international conference with a sign language interpreter from the country whose code you just studied. Are there any differences or similarities in ethical expectations and requirements that you would want to discuss in advance? Would the differences have any impact on how you work together?

Note that while this scenario may not be a common one, it's a helpful exercise to identify what is similar or different in codes of ethics for sign language interpreters and the potential impact of those similarities and differences on your work.

Chapter Conclusion and Review

Remote interpreters jump in and out of multiple geographic regions and service settings on a daily basis. Unlike onsite interpreters, who can more easily identify which code of ethics apply to their workplaces and areas of specialization, remote interpreters have, until now, been left on their own to sort out which ethical requirements and guidelines apply to their work. This chapter provides that missing framework.

Based on a comprehensive review of over 200 ethics documents from around the world, the chapter began by providing clear definitions for ethics, standards of practice and international standards and best practices. Each plays a distinct role in standardizing and professionalizing the work interpreters do. For instance, codes of ethics propose strict guidelines that advise an interpreter what to do, while standards of practice offer strategies for how to do it.

Next, the chapter identified eight core ethical principles within the documents reviewed that have widespread global agreement. They represent, in a way, a universal code of ethics shared by most interpreting specializations and countries around the world and include confidentiality, accuracy, impartiality, professionalism, professional development, role boundaries, solidarity and respect. Areas of ethical practice where there is less agreement, but which are still addressed globally, include the decision of when to intervene, mediate or, potentially, advocate on behalf of a participant.

This framework is followed by guidance for interpreters working across specializations or within multiple countries on how to choose the most appropriate ethics and standards to follow for any given encounter. Interpreters can take a systematic approach to narrow options. For example, if no there is no code of ethics specific to the region they are working, interpreters may consult relevant international standards or speak with other interpreters about the codes and standards they follow.

Finally, the chapter investigated codes of ethics that apply to sign language interpreters and discussed how they are applied remotely. Core principles such as professionalism and confidentiality are as vital in sign language interpreting as they are in spoken. One key distinction is that many codes of ethics for signed languages are specific to that language, not to any specialization or region of the world.

There will never be one single code of ethics or guideline to best practices that interpreters can turn to when interpreting. Interpreters work in all settings and nations. Instead, interpreters need to know how to make ethical decision-making across national borders and specializations in remote interpreting, even when there may not be a specific regional code of ethics they are required to follow.

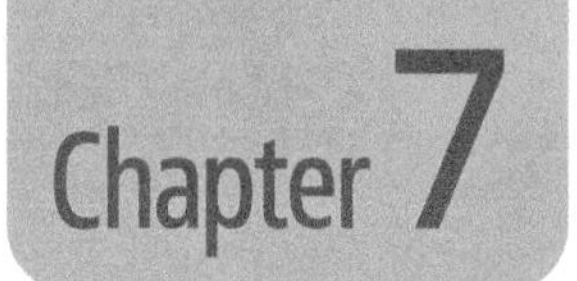

Chapter 7

Tatiana González-Cestari, PhD, CHI-Spanish
Sarah Stockler-Rex, MA, CHI-Spanish
Contributing Authors: Lyana Mansour, CHI-Arabic
Monika McCartney, CoreCHI

Addressing Communication Breakdowns

Learning Objectives

After completing this chapter, the remote interpreter will be able to:

Learning Objective 7.1: Engage in self-examination in order to identify and address communication breakdowns in remote interpreting.

Learning Objective 7.2: List reasons to address a communication breakdown and strategies to manage it.

Learning Objective 7.3: Develop scripts to address communication barriers.

Learning Objective 7.4: Perform strategic mediation in OPI, VRI and VRS.

Learning Objective 7.5: Decide if, when and how to address cultural misunderstandings.

Special Note—Use of the Terms Intervention and Strategic Mediation in This Textbook

Interpreters often have to interrupt their work of interpreting. Other textbooks by this publisher define intervening as "the act of interrupting the interpreted session to address a problem or concern [related to the session]. The term strategic mediation refers to any act or utterance of the interpreter that goes beyond interpreting and is intended to remove a barrier to communication or service delivery" (Bancroft et al., 2016, p. 131).

However, many in the field—especially in the U.S.—use these two terms synonymously (that is, more or less in the same way). There is also no consistent international term that addresses the interpreter's act of interrupting a session.

Given the audience for this textbook, the two terms in question are used interchangeably.

Introduction

Communication in interpreting often breaks down. In remote interpreting, as you saw in Chapter 3, technical issues often cause the breakdown. This chapter addresses what to do when communication itself breaks down.

Let's say the interpreter is interpreting accurately, but the participants clearly don't understand each other. Should the interpreter simply continue interpreting? Or try to fix the problem? Or take some other action? These are huge questions. The rest of the field, in all its specializations, grapples with it on a daily basis. They are *real* problems.

These problems create hard decisions for interpreters—and perhaps even harder ones for remote interpreters. Technology, logistics, time constraints and situational limitations and complexities add to the tough decision-making.

In addition, as you saw in the previous chapter, national ethics and standards for interpreters (where they exist) may contradict each other on whether or how interpreters should address communication breakdowns. After all, these issues go to the heart of questions about the interpreter's role that date back to the birth of the profession. To this day, there is no international agreement on the role of the interpreter.

As previous chapters have made clear, the authors collectively agree that the role of the interpreter is to enable and support *communicative autonomy,* that is, the concept that all participants in a session are responsible for, and in control of, their own communication. In other words, everyone in the session can freely communicate with each other and make appropriate decisions without interference.

If the participants in question do not share a common language, however, and they require an interpreter, to the extent that the interpreter *enables and supports communicative autonomy*, the interpreter is (in the perspective of the authors) staying within the interpreter's role.

In that context, the interpreter *will* need to address communication breakdowns that interfere with or undermine communicative autonomy.

As if all those issues were not complex enough, professional cultures and language service policies can contradict each other—and potentially confuse the interpreter. Interpreting remotely often make the challenges so much greater.

Don't give up. These challenges can mostly be overcome.

This chapter will give you practical strategies to make decisions about whether or not to address a communication breakdown—and how to do so effectively. The chapter will discuss aspects of bias, common barriers to communication, scripts for what to say when we intervene to overcome a barrier, how to use the Strategic Mediation Model and effective strategies for addressing cultural barriers in remote interpreting.[122]

---

[122] **Note:** The version of the Strategic Mediation Model used in this textbook is an updated 2022 version with four steps instead of five.

Section 7.1 Aspects of Bias

→ Learning objective 7.1

After completing this section, the interpreter will be able to engage in self-examination in order to identify and address communication breakdowns in remote interpreting.

→ Section 7.1. Overview

Remote interpreting is really no different from face-to-face interpreting when you consider that in either scenario, interpreters are doing one of two things at any time during the interpreted session: they are either interpreting or intervening.

Interpreters generally intervene to address some barrier to interpreting, for example, to state that they are unable to hear or understand one of the participants, or to request clarification of a term.

Interpreting should be the core of the work you do. You intervene *only if necessary*. Any delays, distractions or interruptions during the session can lead to many problems. For example, if the interpreter interrupts a session for any reason, that interruption can often lead to side conversations, distracting the participants from their original thoughts, or encouraging a participant to build a relationship of trust with the interpreter instead of the other participant.

Yet you also know that sometimes you will *have* to intervene or there will be no effective communication.

Let's focus for a moment on what would influence your decision to intervene. In addition to common and obvious reasons for intervening, such as the need to request clarification or repetition, some reasons for intervening and your decision-making process about if and how to intervene are influenced by *unconscious* processes in your mind.

In this section, we will examine our unconscious thoughts, how they influence our decisions (including whether or not to intervene), and what to say and how to act if we do intervene.

→ Section 7.1 Content

What is implicit bias?

One of the most important research projects in the world on implicit bias, Project Implicit, is an international collaborative founded in 1998. Here is how it defines implicit bias:

> *Implicit bias is an automatic reaction we have towards other people. These attitudes and stereotypes can negatively impact our understanding, actions, and decision-making.*[123]

Why issues of bias matter for (remote) interpreters

> *I once worked for a nonprofit where all the bilingual staff interpreted for healthcare and social services. Sometimes on the phone. Our receptionist was from Mexico, and she interpreted too.*

123 Retrieved from: https://www.projectimplicit.net

> *The receptionist was fired. When I asked why, it turned out she had behaved in a very discriminatory way—toward other Mexicans! I was told she was biased because she was a middle-class, educated, white Mexican, and our Mexican clients were mostly a very different level of education and background from her. She looked down on them.*
>
> *I have to say, that really shocked me! I had never really thought of Mexicans as having bias toward other Mexicans, but now it makes sense to me. We all have biases!*
>
> —A U.S. interpreter

As interpreters, we often struggle with our own conscious and unconscious biases. For example, if a participant insults another participants, many of us feel angry. That is because most interpreters who work in community (including medical, educational, social services, refugee, humanitarian, disaster response and mental health interpreting) tend to have a bias toward equity, respect for all parties and nondiscrimination.

(These issues are so important that respect for all participants and nondiscrimination can be found in a number of codes of ethics, especially those for sign language interpreters, as you saw in Chapter 6.)

We may also encounter the biases of the participants when we interpret. Those biases can impact us too. These biases, like our own, can be either conscious or unconscious and may affect our decision to intervene or simply keep interpreting.

Bias

Bias is a personal attitude or perspective that is not impartial and tends to prefer one viewpoint or one social group to another.

Bias is often unconscious. Whether it is conscious or unconscious, bias may lead to prejudice and acts of discrimination against an individual or group.

—Bancroft et al., 2015, p. 197

Becoming aware of our own biases

Becoming aware of our own biases and those of participants in a remote session can be critical to help us make effective decisions that support the intended outcomes of the session—for example, decisions about whether or not—and how—to intervene if communication breaks down. Let's look at an example:

> A video remote interpreter was needed for a student during a classroom review. The other students in the class were being disrespectful, not allowing the interpreter time to interpret, and making fun of the English language learner (ELL).
>
> The educators were also not cooperating with the interpreter and made her job harder by interrupting often and not repeating when repetition was requested. Whether the educators realized it consciously or not, they were prioritizing the native English-speaking learners' needs over those of the ELL. Having been in similar situations in her own schooling, the

> interpreter started analyzing the situation to see if intervening was necessary to better manage the session and flow of the conversation.
>
> Before the interpreter was able to take any action, the ELL student spoke up in broken English. She yelled for everyone to stop talking so that she could hear the interpretation. She asked her classmates to think about being in her place, and for her teachers to be patient because she was also trying to learn.

In this example, the student took control of the situation for herself and defended her right to learn the lesson. Because of that choice, the interpreter did not have to take action.

Let's now imagine that the ELL student hadn't spoken up. Let us also imagine that the interpreter is either a sign language interpreter and child of a Deaf adult (CODA) or a spoken language interpreter who grew up interpreting for parents in healthcare, education and social services because they didn't speak the language of service.

In that case, the interpreter might have decided to intervene. Personal bias would likely have been a factor. The interpreter may have questioned herself: should she intervene, or would she be projecting her own past personal hurt and family experiences onto the situation?

Interpreting for groups

Another factor that greatly affects communication in remote interpreting is the group setting. During a video remote interpreting (VRI) session, you may have to manage turn-taking of the participants and may need to do so more often and more assertively compared to face-to-face interpreting. You *will* have to intervene if participants speak too fast, speak at the same time or move too far from a speakerphone for over the phone interpreting (OPI).

Many remote interpreters interpret for far more sessions and participants in a day than when they work face to face. This is because travel time is not a factor in remote interpreting, and you may also interpret for many participants outside of your local communities. This potential for performing far more interpreted sessions in a day for a wider variety of participants could lead to more opportunity for bias to affect the interpreter's decision-making.

Whether the biases are those of the interpreters or the participants, those biases will affect the session in a variety of ways that influence the interpreter's decisions to intervene or not to intervene—and what to say when they do.

The risks of intervening

An example of interpreter bias

Each time an interpreter intervenes during the session, this act involves risk. For example, by intervening the interpreter can take up valuable time, distract the speakers, draw too much attention on the interpreter or cause other problems or delays. Other common risks include the interpreter giving incorrect information (often by providing information the interpreter thinks might be helpful), irritating the participants or even offending someone.

Let's look at another example. Matt, a video remote interpreter, interprets in healthcare, and the patients for whom he interprets often get confused with the question "Do you have an advance directive?" Let's see how Matt handles this situation:

> **Nurse:** Do you have an advance directive?
>
> **Interpreter:** (*Interprets this statement then immediately intervenes, speaking first to the nurse.*) Interpreter speaking. I need to clarify. (*to patient*) Interpreter speaking. An advance directive is a document stating your wishes regarding your healthcare in cases where you cannot make those decisions.
>
> **Patient:** Yes, I know what it is. I have one.

We see here that Matt quickly intervened before he truly knew there was a breakdown in communication. He *assumed* that the patient did not understand what "advance directive" means simply because he interprets for so many patients who have no idea what an advance directive is. Yet this patient understood the term perfectly.

Matt also chose to *define* what an advance directive is, which is actually the role of the provider. If Matt was completely sure there was a communication breakdown caused by his awareness that the patient clearly had no idea what an advance directive is while the healthcare provider was failing to notice the problem, Matt could simply have asked the provider to clarify the term (for example, by saying "Interpreter requests a clarification of 'advance directive'" and reporting this request to the patient).

While the consequences of Matt's action don't seem too severe, the patient may now be offended at Matt's assumption of their level of understanding. These interventions could also create unrealistic expectations from participants about the role of the interpreter as they may think that the interpreter's role is to explain unfamiliar terms.

Note too that Matt's bias leads him to overgeneralize. He assumes, based on past experience, that patients he interprets for have a low level of education, health literacy and knowledge of terms such as advance directive.

When in doubt, stay out!

The lesson here is a simple one. Whether you interpret remotely or face to face, whenever a potential communication barrier occurs, let your first instinct be *to wait and see if the problem resolves itself.*

After all, you can almost always intervene later if needed. And if you do, you will be more certain by that time that you need to do so. You are not, by then, reacting instinctively or based on bias but on a more objective view of the needs of the situation and not your personal feelings.

Waiting before you make a decision to intervene to be more certain that intervening is really necessary also supports communicative autonomy and clear communication.

When in doubt, stay out!

How to problem-solve?

System 1 thinking vs. System 2 thinking: Fast and slow

As mentioned in the previous chapter, you will face many situations that require you to take action. When we face decisions, we generally engage in two different types of thinking, often referred to as "System 1" and "System 2" thinking (Kahneman, 2011).

> **System 1 thinking**
>
> Your mind has to make decisions automatically and unconsciously. You use System 1 thinking in situations that require you to "think on your feet"—in other words, to make quick or "snap" decisions. You are reacting.
>
> **System 2 thinking**
>
> You have more time, ideally in a peaceful setting, which allows your mind to be more analytical, deliberate and rational. In other words, you have more time to think. You are reflecting, not acting or reacting.

Why interpreters need to engage in System 2 thinking

An overwhelming body of research shows that all of us (not only interpreters) tend to make far more effective and beneficial decisions when we engage in System 2 rather than System 1 thinking (Kahneman, 2011).

The trick, then, is for interpreters to plan how to handle common communication breakdowns by planning for them *outside* the session and then deciding if, when and why to intervene to address these breakdowns or simply keep interpreting.

While the languages and specializations you interpret in—and whether or not you interpret remotely—will all affect *which* challenges you will face most often, the reality is that all interpreters face a range of common communication-breakdown challenges.

By planning how to address these challenges *outside* the session, it becomes easier to engage in System 2 thinking and examine our reasons for intervening or not intervening. We can therefore identify our own biases that may affect those decisions.

It is incredibly hard to make the best decisions in a given session if we haven't reflected on it outside the session. However, if we plan how to handle an array of challenges well outside the session, the decision-making process itself becomes automated to a degree.

In other words, if you plan well outside the session (System 2 thinking) you will be able to respond more effectively even when you face a new challenge because your System 1 thinking will be sharpened by all the previous System 2 thinking you have engaged in.

The rest of this chapter will help you do exactly that by providing helpful scenarios, activities and scripts to get you thinking deeply about what action to take—or not to take—when communication breaks down. Then the decisions you face in your sessions will hopefully be easier to handle, even without thinking too much or for too long.

As you acquire skills, some decisions that once required slow deliberation may now become automated (System 1 thinking).

System 1 and System 2 Thinking for Interpreters

System 1 thinking: Fast, reflexive—*reactive*

System 2 thinking: Slow, reflective—*proactive*

Plan outside the session for what to do about common communication problems you encounter. Slower System 2 thinking will help you create new habits when you interpret—helpful habits that support communicative autonomy.

→ Section 7.1 Review

We all have biases because we are human. However, as interpreters, we have to consider how these biases may affect our decisions and behavior.

Ideally, whether you interpret face to face or remotely, your first instinct will be to interpret unless the communication breaks down to a point that you feel something *must* be done to support communicative autonomy or clear communication. This section helped interpreters examine and question the interpreter's motives for wanting to address communication barriers too quickly. It also addressed the idea that decisions we make about typical or common challenges *outside* the session, allowing us to plan ahead for common communication challenges, help interpreters to engage in slower System 2 thinking (which is proactive) that results in better decisions than those we make quickly during the session in System 1 thinking (which is reactive).

It is a reality of remote interpreting that you can take on more interpreting sessions in a day than you ever could engage in face to face during the same time due to not having to travel from site to site. As a result of having more sessions, you may encounter a much wider variety of participants, situations and communication problems compared to most face-to-face interpreting. For these reasons, you may also find yourself more often in circumstances where your own implicit biases affect the session.

A good guideline is "When in doubt, stay out!" First, examine your motives for *wanting* to be reactive. Use System 2 thinking to make proactive decisions outside the session about if, when and why to address a communication barrier when it arises.

Section 7.2: Common Barriers to Communication in Remote Interpreting

→ Learning objective 7.2

After completing this section, the remote interpreter will be able to list reasons to address a communication breakdown and strategies to manage it.

→ Section 7.2 Overview

In this section, you will explore situations and techniques to assess communication breakdowns in remote interpreting and develop strategies to resolve them. Together with the information in the following section, you will also get a clear overview of best practices for doing so.

The focus in this section, as in much of the book, will be on remote interpreters based in the United States or who interpret remotely for sessions taking place there. However, the suggestions offered here may also be helpful for remote interpreters around the world. Be aware, however, that your country, your professional associations or the language services or other organizations you work for may have requirements that limit what you can do when communication breaks down. Inform yourself.

(See Chapter 6 of this volume for details about how ethical requirements related to managing communication breakdowns can vary by country or code of ethics.)

Communication barriers arise in many situations in all modalities of interpreting and in all types of remote interpreting, whether OPI, VRI, video relay service (VRS) and remote simultaneous interpreting (RSI). This chapter focuses primarily on OPI and VRI, with some comments about VRS. See Volume 2, Chapter 2, for a deeper discussion of communication challenges in RSI.

The first point to keep in mind about a communication barrier, whether it comes up in face-to-face or remote interpreting, is that ideally your first response will be to continue interpreting to let the participants resolve their communication problems. The exception would be if something is stated that *you* don't understand—in which case you need to request clarification—or if there is an environmental or technical problem, such as too much background noise or poor audio or video quality—in which case you need to intervene to address that problem.

However, in other situations, and if and when permitted, the interpreter can choose to step in and help resolve communication breakdowns. The goal of taking action is to remove the communication barrier and redirect participants to the original discussion without undermining communicative autonomy—that is, the capacity of all participants to be responsible for, and in control of, their own communication.

→ Section 7.2 Content

We will begin with a real-world example of a communication breakdown, discussed in Rickford & King, 2016, p. 952.

In a courtroom in the Northern Territory of Australia, an Aboriginal witness was being cross-examined. Though the witness spoke English, an interpreter was assigned to stand by in case interpreting services would be needed at any point.

The witness referred to the night in question and mentioned "a half-moon shining." The cross-examining counsel jumped on this, knowing there was no "half-moon" that night. Fortunately, the Aboriginal English interpreter knew that in this participant's Aboriginal variety "half" can mean "small part" or, in this case, a crescent moon.

The witness was asked to draw the moon he saw that night and indeed drew a crescent moon. The interpreter intervened to alert the court and was able to address this communication breakdown. This small phrase would have had a major impact if misunderstood and the interpreter's intervention allowed the participant to validate his testimony.

Even though the interpreter's intervention was justifiable in this example, because it focused on the *linguistic* aspect of the communication breakdown, taking this kind of action is not always advisable or appropriate.

Anytime that an interpreter on the job says or does anything beyond interpreting, that act poses a risk for the participants and the outcomes. It also creates potential legal exposure and liability for the language service or organization and the interpreter.

These risks are not small. They should not be taken lightly.

What is your role? According to the authors of this book, your role is to support communicative autonomy so that all participants can manage their own communication effectively and make informed decisions. How do you do so? You facilitate communication among speakers who do not share a common language to put them on the same footing as if they did share the same language. How will you do so if communication breaks down? This chapter offers effective solutions that support—and do not undermine—communicative autonomy.

In general, the techniques and strategies provided throughout this chapter are in accord with and support nearly all codes of ethics and standards of practice for interpreters around the world, in most specializations.[124]

To be ready to address communication barriers, you will need to do some work before the interpreted session.

- Examine potentially acceptable reasons to address a communication barrier.
- Prepare scripts for what to say if and when you decide to do so.
- Have a plan for how to address common communication barriers quickly and effectively, without getting "stuck" or confused.
- Develop specific techniques for redirecting misunderstandings without getting directly involved, providing information or explaining cultural or other issues yourself.

Having a plan based on the steps above and knowledge gained from this chapter, you will be able to quickly address communication barriers as they arise and manage them remotely, even in OPI, perhaps the most challenging area of remote interpreting in these cases because you lack visual cues. You will:

[124] Controversial exceptions may include military and humanitarian—conflict zone—interpreting and some types of business interpreting (and even, in certain instances, high-level diplomatic interpreting). Such exceptions will tend to occur in specializations or extreme situations where the interpreter is not following a code of ethics because either no relevant code exists or the interpreter is engaged in a specific mission that overrides both interpreter ethics and the interpreter's traditional role of enabling communicative autonomy. If a mission is paramount, and the interpreter's job is to support that mission, then no impartiality is possible, and accuracy may also be compromised. Without accuracy and impartiality, no true communicative autonomy is achievable.

1. Identify the problem.

   Is there a genuine communication barrier here? What is it? How serious is the breakdown or misunderstanding? What could happen if you simply continue interpreting without addressing it?

2. Analyze the problem.

   Why do you want to do something besides interpret? Think about why you feel it is your responsibility to fix the communication barrier. (Keep in mind the previous section about assessing your own bias.)

3. Decide and act.

   Should you intervene? What are the benefits and risks of doing so? Do the potential benefits outweigh the potential risks? Once you can answer those questions, take action—either continue interpreting or intervene to address the breakdown.

Throughout this chapter, we provide real-life examples of communication barriers in remote interpreting and their potential effect on the outcome of the session if they are not addressed or if the interpreter addresses them inadequately (or inappropriately).

We will also review examples of the consequences of intervening when there is no real barrier.

Be Careful

Different types of communication barriers may need different solutions depending on the interpreter's specialization.

For example, legal or courtroom interpreters may not be able to address communication barriers in the same way a medical or community interpreter might do so, if at all. For more information on legal remote interpreting, see Volume 2, Chapter 5.

Why address common communication barriers in remote interpreting?

Communication barriers arise often in remote interpreting. Interpreters can overstep their roles and intervene too often.

It is also possible for interpreters to not intervene enough or not at the right moment, causing frustration for participants.

Yet interpreters are often the only ones present who understand all of what is being said. Interpreters are also often aware of contextual clues and other aspects of communication that go well beyond the words and color their meaning. Keep in mind that, as you saw in Chapter 6, quite a number of codes of ethics specify that the interpreter is responsible for accuracy, which includes conveying the intention, tone and spirit of the message.

In short, we have the responsibility to make sure that everyone involved receives the meaning of the message, which goes well beyond the literal meaning of the words.

When in doubt, stay out!

That said, be careful. As this chapter keeps repeating, your first instinct should be to keep interpreting and *not* intervene right away, even when you face a real communication barrier. Wait first to see if the problem resolves itself. Intervene only when there is a powerful reason to do so.

While that advice is generally true for face-to-face interpreting, it is even more important in remote interpreting. Intervening is harder to perform well remotely and the consequences of managing it poorly can be even more problematic than in face-to-face interpreting.

If you intervene

If you do intervene, remember to follow your code of ethics.

In addition, remember that interpreters are not mind readers or cultural experts. *We will need to avoid making assumptions during our sessions.* We have to constantly monitor each situation and verify if there really is a communication barrier.

If there is a communication breakdown, and you decide to intervene, try to guide the participants to find their own resolution as much as possible.

In short, "When in doubt, stay out!" until you are sure you need to intervene, that is, you feel sure that the consequences of *not* intervening could be significant or serious. And whenever you do intervene, help the participants resolve the barrier: do not try to "fix" it yourself.

How to address communication barriers in remote interpreting

Common reasons to address communication barriers

When there are communication breakdowns in remote interpreting that the participants cannot solve alone, we may cautiously step in to guide them. Below are some of the common reasons to address communication barriers.

There are of course many other situations that may cause such barriers. This section will provide strategies on how to navigate the most common cases that come up and the next section will include sample scripts to help guide you when you intervene.

Barrier: The interpreter has not heard, or cannot remember, everything that was just said.

We are humans, and sometimes we miss parts of a message. In remote interpreting, not hearing or seeing the whole message or statement is an even more common problem than in face-to-face interpreting.

Potential causes
Here are some examples of how this problem can arise:

- You heard or saw the message, but soon after you don't remember the whole message.
- Technology problems or the positioning of equipment or the participants may affect your ability to take in the whole message (see Chapters 3 and 4 of this volume for more about technology and positioning).

Practical solutions
Here are a few potential solutions:

- Be polite but assertive (see Chapter 4, Section 4.2, of this volume) and ask for repetition when it's needed.
- If the statement is long, try to ask the speaker to repeat only the part you can't remember, such as, "The interpreter noted you said that the patient needs physical therapy, medications and something else. What was the third treatment?"
- If technology problems cause you to miss part of the message, share that: "Interpreter speaking. The audio cut out for a moment. Will you please repeat what you said?"

Unfortunately (and be prepared for this), some participants may refuse to repeat themselves. But never guess at the message or skip over what you missed. *Be firm that you need a repetition* because you are professionally and ethically required to interpret everything the participants state.

Don't Apologize

Don't apologize when you request a repetition.

Interpreters often say, "I'm sorry," when they ask someone to repeat themselves. There is no need to do so. You are doing your work. Make these requests without apologies; you will also sound more professional and confident.

Barrier: The interpreter does not understand what was said.

Even when you hear and see everything clearly, there are times you simply don't know or don't understand a particular message.

Potential causes
For example:

- A participant uses a term that is unfamiliar to you.
- You're interpreting for a participant with a certain accent that is new to you or challenging to understand.

Practical solutions
Here are potential solutions:

- Ask for clarification.
    - Asking for clarification refers to the act of intervening to *request* information from one of the participants.
    - Usually, a clarification helps the interpreter understand what was just said or signed.
- Look up the term and confirm its meaning.
    - See more about how to handle unfamiliar information by developing online search skills (discussed in Chapter 4, Section 4.2, of this volume).

- Rephrase or describe the meaning of a term if there is no equivalent in the other language.
  - Do not leave terms in their original language unless you plan to *immediately* request a clarification of that term (and let everyone know the term).
  - *Do not guess or invent your own words.*
- Note down any terms you struggled with; then study them later.

Barrier: A participant seems to not understand what was said.

On some occasions, you understand and interpret the message, but a participant shows many consistent signs that they do not understand, and the other participants do not appear to notice this confusion or lack of understanding.

Possible causes

For example:

- A participant may show confusion in their body language (VRI). For example, through downcast or glazed eyes, a complete lack of facial expressivity or a frozen or intimidated facial expression.
- A participant may show confusion in their tone of voice (OPI and VRI). For example, they may sound hesitant, have a flat (monotone) voice or respond in quiet syllables, not confident sentences.
- A participant may fall nearly silent and barely respond while the other participant simply keeps talking and does not ask questions to verify understanding.

Practical solutions

You may need to intervene to:

- *Prompt a participant* to check for understanding.
- Suggest to all participants that you sense a break in communication about (e.g., a particular term, concept, process or procedure).
- Suggest to all participants that you are uncertain that what you are interpreting about a certain topic is clear.

Take this action only if, after you have interpreted for a time, it is clear that:

a. The confusion has not been resolved.
b. It is unlikely to resolve itself.
c. Communicative autonomy and the desired outcomes of the session are compromised.

Barrier: Communication is not flowing well or clearly due to cultural differences.

Possible causes

The general perception of cultural differences is narrow. People often speak casually about how "American culture" is so different from "Latinx" (or English, Nigerian or Chinese) culture. They speak as if all Americans and all Latinx were culturally the same.

In reality, each and every culture has its own subcultures—subcultures influenced by individual culture. Cultures vary within countries, regions, cities, neighborhoods, families and individuals. Culture is also influenced by people's abilities, disabilities, privileges, socioeconomic statuses, languages and so much more. These are all variables that make each of us *culturally unique*.

All these cultural differences interact inside us and in our communication with others. They may therefore affect communication during a session. These cultural variables can include age, racial and religious differences, family values and dynamics, education levels, understanding of the legal, educational and medical systems and so on.

We have included this barrier in this list since it is a common communication barrier in remote interpreting. However, due to its complexity, we have devoted a whole section to it later in this chapter. Go to Section 7.5 for specific examples and potential solutions to address breakdowns in communication stemming from cultural differences.

Barrier: Communication is not effective due to language differences or language mismatches.

Possible causes

Often, callers who place a request for interpreters assume that interpreters and participants understand each other merely because their languages seem similar.

For example:

- The interpreter may have to clarify that a Russian-speaking individual cannot effectively communicate with a Polish-speaking interpreter.
- The interpreter may have to clarify that a person from Guatemala doesn't necessarily need "Guatemalan Spanish," but a Mam interpreter.

Let's look at an example that illustrates why it is so important to work with an interpreter for the correct language, even if the languages are closely related:

> Maria receives a call for a medical Spanish interpreter. She realizes early in the session that the patient is a Portuguese speaker, but the patient pleads with Maria to stay on the line. Maria does not inform the provider of the language difference but requests clarification if she feels unsure of what the patient said.
>
> At one point, the provider asks the patient what is wrong. The following happens:
>
> **Patient:** *Estou embaraçada.*
>
> **Interpreter:** I'm pregnant.
>
> **Provider:** For how long?
>
> **Interpreter:** *¿Por cuánto tiempo?*
>
> **Patient:** *Por um tiempo.*
>
> **Interpreter:** For some time.
>
> **Provider:** Let's do an ultrasound.

Maria's misunderstanding of the Portuguese word "*embaraçada*," meaning "embarrassed," for the Spanish "*embarazada*" or "pregnant," led to a major communication error, which resulted in the patient undergoing an unnecessary ultrasound. The patient also did not receive care for her actual concern.

Why does this happen?

Why was Spanish requested to begin with? The provider may have assumed the patient was a Spanish speaker based on her name or appearance. Or perhaps, the patient requested it, assuming that she would not be able to receive interpreting services in Portuguese since it is less common in the U.S. than Spanish is.

Why should you address this problem?

Requests for interpreters for an incorrect language are a common occurrence. We see them every day in remote interpreting!

In many cases, these requests are also easily to remedy: where possible, confirm the language with your client ahead of time, or work with your language service or organization to address situations like these.

Table 7.1 lists some real-life examples of linguistic misconceptions that can lead to serious communication breakdowns if they are not addressed.

Language requested	Language needed
Polish	Russian
Asian	Mandarin
English	American Sign Language
Muslim	Arabic
African	Swahili
Arabic	Somali
Guatemalan Spanish	Mam
Portuguese	Spanish
Mexican	Spanish
Oaxacan	Mixteco

Table 7.1: Language requested in remote interpreting versus language needed

In the Arabic/Somali mix-up in Table 7.1, Arabic was requested solely based on the individual's appearance. This is not uncommon. Arabic VRI interpreters report being connected to speakers of Bengali and Hindi based on the participants' dress (use of a head scarf, for example).

Requests for specific varieties of a language are sometimes legitimate due to past experiences of communication breakdowns, so don't assume that requests like "Guatemalan Spanish" are incorrect—they may truly need a Spanish interpreter from Guatemala to address certain slang terms or communication styles.

The examples above, taken from real remote interpreting scenarios, help you realize that *you* may have to support meaningful language access even before the session starts. Remember: communicative autonomy will break down if the wrong language is requested unless you address the problem. And again, in remote interpreting this problem occurs incredibly often.

You cannot solve every problem in remote interpreting. But identifying the correct languages needed and working together with participants and organizations to resolve linguistic problems is crucial.

Remember too that you are ethically and professionally obligated to be accurate. Except in extreme cases or emergencies, work only in languages you are qualified to interpret.

Practical solutions

Here are potential solutions:

- Whenever possible, clearly announce your language pair as part of your introduction.[125]
- Step back in your mind to examine the situation carefully and make logical, thoughtful decisions based on the participants' best interests, the intended outcomes of the session and how high the stakes could be if there are interpreter errors.
  - Note that many mistakes that remote interpreters make are caused by quick (sometimes emotional) reactions or decisions and the interpreter's unexamined assumptions, for example, that they can manage to interpret Portuguese for a quick encounter even though they are not qualified in that language.
- Be clear and transparent about the language differences *immediately*.
- If possible, instead of interpreting, offer and secure an interpreter for the correct language. (This will of course be far easier to manage if you interpret for a language service with many interpreters available.)

Barrier: The interpreter does not speak the same language variation as the participant.

Possible causes

The earlier case with Maria was a little more straightforward since the interpreter and the participant spoke two different languages (Spanish and Portuguese). But what about cases where the participant and interpreter speak the same language but each is from different geographic locations that have many different regional variations? In other words, they speak "the same language" but in reality cannot understand each other.

For example:

- The participant speaks Moroccan Arabic and the interpreter speaks Iraqi Arabic. A highly educated Moroccan Arabic speaker and the interpreter *might* then be able to switch to Modern Standard Arabic (MSA) but that solution absolutely will not work in all cases.

A similar example would be Brazilian Portuguese and Azorean Portuguese.

---

125 Stating your language may be important in your introduction in face-to-face interpreting—but it is critical in remote interpreting, where incorrect language requests are extremely common and the interpreter may potentially encounter far more of them.

Let's give you more granular examples. Take the word "dehen/دهن" in Arabic. In Iraqi Arabic, this word means oil. In Palestinian Arabic, however, it means lotion. Variations like these could have a huge impact on the session, depending on the context.

Therefore, if you feel you can interpret the session for the most part understandably and accurately, but you are aware of the difference, request clarifications whenever possible to ensure accuracy. Please see Chapter 4, Section 4.2, of this volume for more information about problem-solving when you face language variation.

Practical solutions

- Verify a language match before or at the beginning of the session when possible.
  - For certain specializations or situations (such as lawyer-client interviews, psychiatric evaluations, police interrogations or therapy), you may want to request permission to ask a participant questions as part of this verification. In either case, be sure to interpret your questions and the participant's answers for the other participants.
- Be transparent with all participants when you verify a language match and request clarification.
  - Remember: even a minor language mismatch is a potentially serious barrier to communication.
- Don't assume that the participant *won't* understand you. Verify.
  - For example, a growing number of Arabic speakers today can converse fairly comfortably with Arabic speakers from across the Middle East and North Africa.
- Interpret if you feel your linguistic skills can manage the language variation.
  - Nevertheless, constantly monitor and assess the session for communication breakdowns.
- Request clarification as often as needed to ensure accuracy and adequate understanding while you interpret.
- Withdraw if your interruptions become so frequent that they halt the flow.
  - In such cases, if possible request another interpreter to ensure accuracy and avoid undermining communicative autonomy.

Note that a major benefit of on-demand remote interpreting is the ability to find a replacement interpreter relatively easily and quickly compared to face-to-face sessions. For example, if you work for a large language service, securing a replacement can often be done with the click of a button.

Language Preferences

Due to the level of demand and availability of interpreters for certain languages, speakers of these languages often resort to requesting an interpreter for a language other than their primary one.

For example, K'iche' or Mam speakers may request a Spanish interpreter, knowing from past experience they will not have an interpreter for their own language. Similarly, Maay speakers may request a Somali interpreter and Chaldean speakers might ask for an Arabic interpreter.

If you sense a possible communication breakdown due to a language mismatch, verify what language the participant prefers.

Barrier: A participant with limited proficiency tries to communicate directly in the other's language.

Possible causes

Here is a common problem: many service providers truly believe they speak enough of a language to communicate directly in that language. Most interpreters have witnessed the mess that can result! This true story is one example.

> A young male medical provider comes into the room of an older Polish female patient. The provider wants to make small talk and tries to joke with the patient. He tells the video interpreter, "I know a little bit of Polish, my friend growing up knew Polish." He turns to the patient and says, "Hi! I'm going to be quick; I don't want to be a *boli* in your *dupa*."
>
> The patient's demeanor immediately changes, and she becomes tense and short in her answers. The provider, unaware that he had been rude toward the patient, is confused as to why the patient suddenly seems cold.

What went wrong in this situation?

Obviously the provider was not fully fluent in Polish and didn't know how older people are typically treated in Polish culture. Typically, younger Polish people, especially strangers, will show great respect to older people. The provider was trying to be informal by casually saying "I won't be a pain in your ass," changing some of the English words to the Polish ones he knew.

But the translation of his English phrase came out as something completely different: "I won't be an ulcer on your ass." This was offensive language.

Other possible causes

Other examples of one participant trying to make conversation in the other participant's language may not involve profanity or vulgar and offensive words. Instead, they may involve words that just don't make sense. Sometimes the person trying out the other person's language incorrectly conjugates a verb or simply mispronounces words and sounds ignorant or senseless. These mistakes can be confusing and even risky, no matter who uses them.

Practical solutions

- Let direct communication happen if participants limit the exchange of communication to simple greetings, for example.
- Be ready to graciously guide participants not to use the other participant's language if they are not fully proficient.
    - Your goal is to ensure that you can interpret accurately and support communicative autonomy.
- See the next section (7.4) for specific scripts to address this barrier.

Natural Language Contact

Be careful not to confuse situations like the Polish/English example with instances of natural language contact. When multiple languages are in contact, words will naturally be borrowed from one to another and mix in everyday life (such as Moroccan Arabic speakers using French and Spanish words and Spanish speakers using English words).

Interpreters intervene when there are barriers to communication. They are not there to control language use.

Barrier: A participant uses high-register terminology, which is not understood.

Possible causes

One common problem in remote interpreting, just as in face-to-face interpreting, is the participant who speaks in highly educated or technical language that other participants (and perhaps the interpreter) do not understand.

Some examples of words with more than one register would be:

- Sweat (lower register) vs. perspiration (higher register).
- Throw up (lower register) vs. vomit (higher register).
- Students (lower register) vs. pupils (higher register, and typically used only for primary/elementary-school levels).

Practical solutions

- Have reliable resources ready for quick searches.
- Request clarification from the participant if you're unable to find the high-register equivalent for a term or phrase they use.
- Ask the participant to simplify their language, but only after exhausting the first two recommendations.
- Note down any new or unfamiliar terms you encounter and study them after the session.

You may also need to ask a participant to simplify their language if you perceive or strongly sense that the person receiving the message is confused and does not understand. Make it clear you are making the request so that you can interpret in a way that is understood (for example, "The interpreter requests you to rephrase" or "Interpreter speaking. Could you please explain (the term/concept/process/etc.) in other words so that I can interpret it more clearly?").

In other words, do not imply that one participant does not understand the other. (You might assume so, and you might be right; but do not say so.)

Barrier: Participants are not taking turns to speak or sign, or are not pausing when needed.

Possible causes

In Volume 1, Chapter 4, we discussed turn-taking. Turn-taking, which involves managing the flow of communication, is a big part of how the interpreter manages the session. Doing so ensures that all participants are heard and understood. When turns are taken out of order, or someone speaks far too long for you to interpret accurately, this problem creates a communication breakdown that you as the interpreter need to address.

Figure 7.1: **Conversation flow roundabout**

Ideally, the conversation should flow like a traffic circle or roundabout. You pull up and wait when you see someone else in the roundabout, and you know it's not your turn. You wait until the other vehicle has passed you before you enter the circle. You may turn right behind the car in front of you, only a little behind them (like the lag in simultaneous interpreting) or you may wait for them to clear the intersection completely (as in consecutive interpreting).

In either scenario, sometimes the flow is disrupted. If that happens too often—you may need to add a traffic light! (The interpreter's intervention.)

Figure 7.2: **Conversation flow disruption**

Practical solutions

Reestablishing the order of turns is especially important in sessions that involve two or more users of one language and another participant who cannot communicate or participate without the interpreter. For example, a minor who speaks fluent English needs no interpreter in an English-speaking country but may accompany a Burmese-speaking family (that does need an interpreter) to a court hearing, medical appointment or parent-teacher conference.

Here are potential solutions:

- Interpret everything even if turns are taken out of order, so that nothing is omitted. (In other words, a teacher speaks, the English-speaking child speaks, and then you interpret both what the teacher and the child said to each other for the Burmese-speaking parent.)
- Reestablish the proper flow. For example, if you are an English<>French interpreter, a language pattern for the session should be English-French, French-English, English-French and so on.

Figure 7.3: **Proper language flow**

- Be assertive and remind everyone to speak or sign one at a time.
    - It is common for those who share a language to converse with each other without pausing and forget that you are there and that you need to interpret for the other participant.
- Make sure participants speak or sign at a manageable pace and allow you time to interpret.
    - You may need to ask the participant to slow down or pause more often.
    - Again, because they are communicating to each other in the same language, they may forget that you and the other participant are there.

Barrier: A technical problem impacts the session.

Possible causes

Even with all the technical information you learned in Chapters 2 and 3 of this volume, one of the biggest challenges in remote interpreting is unexpected technical problems. Be prepared!

Technical issues include, for example:

- Disruptions to the video or audio feeds.
- Disruptions to the internet or telephone connectivity.
- Service disruption problems.
- Loss of battery power.

All of these problems could be intermittent or even cause your session to abruptly end. They can occur from the interpreter side or from the participant side.

In certain settings, network connectivity may be weaker or hampered by the surroundings. For example, Wi-Fi signals may be disrupted in the imaging and radiation departments of medical facilities, in older buildings, in basements built with thick and sturdy materials or in modern metal structures.

Practical solutions

- Ask participants to move the device or change locations (perhaps moving to an area closer to an internet access point) to improve video and audio quality.
- Pause the video to improve the audio quality *if no other troubleshooting tactics have been successful* (when applicable and for spoken language interpreters only).
- Follow your client or language service's guidelines about how to handle this type of situation if nothing helps improve the connection.
- Secure another on-demand remote interpreter to take over the call if your platform and your language service or organization allows it.
- Transfer a VRI call over to OPI, where network bandwidth requirements are less demanding (if permitted and feasible).
- Be transparent and let participants know what issues you are experiencing, if you are able to communicate with them in any way.
    - Also, let participants know if help is on the way or if they need to contact their information technology (IT) department (if they have one available).

Barrier: A participant shows cognitive limitations.

This last example of a communication barrier is not as common as the others above—but it can have a much greater impact on your session.

Possible causes

If a participant is young in age (for example, under the age of eight), has dementia or developmental delays or suffers from mental illness, they may not understand you are their interpreter, what an interpreter does, or how remote interpreting works.

For example:

- Young children may get confused when you use direct speech (first person) while interpreting.
- Some elderly participants may have difficulties understanding VRI ("I don't want to watch TV!", some say).
- Some participants may be confused due to other cognitive limitations, such as suffering from the effects of a stroke or having a mental health condition.

Practical solutions

- Switch to indirect speech with young children when speaking with them.
  - For example, "Your teacher would like you to..."
- Turn off your video (if possible).
  - For spoken language interpreters, this simulates a telephone interaction, which may be more accepted or familiar to the confused person.
  - Be transparent with all other participants by explaining why you removed your video.
  - Emphasize that you turned off video for clear communication.
  - Do not discuss an impairment or cognitive limitation.
- Work with the other participants for more context to help you remain accurate and interpret clearly and effectively.
- Stop interpreting if meaningful communication is not occurring.
  - Withdrawing from the encounter and directing the participants to secure another remote interpreter can sometimes help with this type of communication breakdown.
  - However, withdrawing this way should not be your first option.
- Recommend a face-to-face interpreter when it seems to be the best solution.
- For signed language, consider recommending a certified Deaf interpreter, if appropriate.

→ Section 7.2 Review

As interpreters, we try to address communication breakdowns only if doing so is needed. (When in doubt, stay out!) However, in remote interpreting, for OPI, VRI and VRS we also have to consider that we may not have as many opportunities to address communication breakdowns as in face-to-face interpreting. For example, the session may end sooner than expected (due to technical issues, intentional or accidental disconnection from one participant, the brevity of certain types of calls and so forth). If you're providing services on demand, you may not interact with the same participants again.

The reasons mentioned in this section for intervening during a remote session are all important but they do not address every potential reason. Here is a review of those reasons discussed in this chapter:

1. A technical problem interferes with clear communication.
2. The interpreter has not heard or cannot remember everything that was just said.
3. The interpreter does not understand what was said.
4. A participant appears to not understand what was said.[126]
5. Communication is not effective due to language differences or language mismatches (when the interpreter does not speak the same language or the same language variation as the participant).
6. A participant with limited proficiency tries to communicate directly in the other's language.
7. A participant uses high-register terminology, which the interpreter observes is not understood by the other participants.
8. Participants are not taking turns to speak or sign or are not pausing as needed.
9. Communication is not flowing smoothly due to cultural misunderstandings.[127]
10. A participant shows cognitive limitations (for example, due to substance use, dementia or mental illness; also participants who are either extremely young or especially old might have certain types of cognitive limitations).

Potential solutions reviewed in this section are summarized below:

1. Remain calm and have a plan for handling technical challenges and breakdowns (see Chapter 3 of this volume).
2. Request repetition if you missed information, whether due to not hearing or a technical problem.
3. Request clarification when you did not understand what was just said or signed.
4. Request that the participants verify understanding when there are cues of misunderstanding.
5. Alert participants to language differences (language variation between a participant and the interpreter) and language mismatches (when the interpreter is called on to interpret for a language the interpreter is not proficient in). If you are requested to remain despite strong regional language variations, constantly assess for communication barriers. Address these throughout the session. If the communication barrier disrupts the flow, you may need to assist in locating a more qualified interpreter for that participant.
6. Be ready to graciously guide participants not to use the other participant's language if they are not fully proficient in it to ensure accurate interpretation.

126 This reason for intervening is not universally accepted. However, as discussed here and elsewhere in this textbook, in the U.S. and some other countries there is growing acceptance that in certain specializations in particular, communicative autonomy requires understanding among participants and therefore the interpreter may request clarification (particularly clarification of terms, phrases, concepts or processes) not only for the interpreter's understanding but also, as needed, to help assure understanding by participants.

127 Again, as discussed in the chapter, not all countries and specializations accept this reason for intervening whereas the authors of this textbook state that communicative autonomy requires carefully considering cultural misunderstandings as a potential reason for intervening. Clearly, however, any decision to intervene due to an apparent cultural misunderstanding poses great challenges. See Section 7.5 of this chapter for details.

7. Have reliable resources ready for quick searches of unknown or high-register terms. If needed, request clarification, and, after the session, study the new or unfamiliar terms you encountered. You may request that a participant simplify their language as a last resort.
8. Intervene to manage turn-taking so that everyone is understood. Participants may speak too long or out of turn, or speak over one another. Be ready to manage the flow of communication for accuracy.
9. If accepted under your ethical requirements (see Chapter 6 of this volume), be ready to alert participants to the possibility of cultural differences. Navigating cultural differences will be explored further in Section 7.5 of this chapter.
10. Intervene to clarify your role when participants don't understand that you are the interpreter (or how remote interpreters work) due to cognitive limitations.

In all cases, be transparent by informing both or all participants what is happening each time you intervene.

As an interpreter, it is up to you to pick up on cues given by all participants to support communicative autonomy and to use your best judgment to decide if you need to intervene. Interpreters need to use quick critical thinking skills to be able to make decisions instantly by weighing the benefits of intervention against the possible consequences of a communication breakdown.

Section 7.3 Scripts to Intervene to Overcome a Barrier

→ Learning objective 7.3

After completing this section, the remote interpreter will be able to develop scripts to address communication barriers.

→ Section 7.3 Overview

Interpreting is based on communication between participants. The interpreter's role is to enable and support communicative autonomy so that participants not only understand each other but can also make informed decisions based on their understanding.

When this communication is disrupted or breaks down, it is incredibly beneficial for interpreters to have scripts prepared for common communication barriers. Having a plan like this will reduce the interpreter's stress and powerfully enhance their skills and response time when they face unexpected challenges.

Many face-to-face interpreters rely on having "mental scripts" for common scenarios that arise. One benefit of remote interpreting is the ability to have easier and faster access to your scripts (for example, on your computer screen). In this section, we will cover script suggestions that address a variety of common communication barriers in remote interpreting.

→ Section 7.3 Content

A new OPI interpreter is interpreting for a medical exam. During the session, a technical glitch allows another call to ring in during the session. Instead of intervening to notify the participants of the issue of dealing with two calls at the same time, the interpreter panics and adds to the end of his interpreted statement to the doctor, "I'm sorry, doctor, there's something ringing in my ears." This leads the doctor to assume that "ringing in the ears" is one of the patient's symptoms.

Almost anything can happen in remote interpreting! Though situations like this one can be unsettling, having a script prepared allows you to stay calm rather than panic. Keep reading to learn how to develop scripts.

Scripts for intervening

What is a script?

A script is a written version of what you plan to say. One example is an intervention script, which is the written version of what you plan to say in both languages when you pause interpreting and intervene to address a communication barrier.

Why have scripts?

As a general rule, it is a good idea to plan what you will say ahead of time when you need to intervene. Otherwise, you may:

- Freeze and feel as if your mind has gone blank.
- Get nervous.
- Begin to panic.
- Speak too long to one participant.
- Forget to speak to the other participant (losing transparency).
- Engage in a side conversation.

If you prepare, memorize and practice scripts for intervening ahead of time, you will find it much easier to:

- Be brief, clear and to the point.
- Identify what has caused the miscommunication.
- Avoid getting emotionally involved.
- Remain professional and polished.
- Feel confident and in control.

Considerations for writing scripts

A. Length

Remember to keep your scripts short. In remote interpreting, participants often expect that the session will move quickly and efficiently. Short scripts help interpreters accomplish this goal. They can also help avoid frustrating the participants.

Short scripts also help prevent you from getting into side conversations or getting questions from participants ("What are you telling her?"). Most important, with short scripts you avoid changing the flow of the conversation; if done well, participants will still control their own communication.

B. Transparency

Transparency is a requirement for all interpreters. It does not only apply to what you interpret but also applies to what you say when you intervene.

In other words, when you intervene as the interpreter, *whatever you say to one participant needs to be stated for the other participant*. This is true transparency. *Everything* will be interpreted, including what the interpreter says when intervening.

Similar scripting in two different languages

If your specialization and the context of the session allow you to use the same script in both working languages, do so. This will help maintain transparency. This is not always easy to do because scripts need to be clear and unoffensive to all involved.

For example, you might say to the prospective clients in an international business meeting: "This is the interpreter speaking. I need to remind the sales executives to speak one at a time" and then tell the executives, "This is the interpreter speaking. I need to remind you to speak one at a time."

You could also say: "Interpreter speaking. I will clarify an unknown term with the client"[128] to an insurance agent and "Interpreter speaking. Can you please clarify what you mean with (unknown term)?" to the client.

C. Avoid unconscious bias in your scripts

The interpreter, Sofia, is interpreting a video session for a counselor and a potential victim of domestic abuse. Sofia senses a communication breakdown and says to the counselor: "Could you explain what domestic violence is? She really doesn't get it. It's her culture. She thinks this is how men behave." She then informs the client, "I just asked the therapist to explain something that wasn't clear."

While it may not be apparent to the participants, or even to Sofia herself, the differences in what she says to the counselor and the potential victim may hold unconscious bias. These scripts do not fully maintain transparency. (If you can think of sessions during which you were not transparent, you may want to ask yourself *why* you spoke differently to each participant.)

---

128 In some perspectives, the interpreter would state in both languages the specific term that needs clarification (keeping the term itself in the source language) but not everyone in the field agrees that stating the term itself to all participants is required for transparency.

Sometimes differences in the way that you address participants have to do with your own comfort levels and how familiar one person feels to you compared to the other. For example, if you and one participant are from the same country, perhaps you feel more comfortable with them and their worldview.

Or perhaps you have experience from other professional roles working side by side each day with certain participants you interpret for and you feel more strongly connected to them than to the other participants.

These differences can also be partly driven by a shared native language. Which participant you feel more comfortable with can also change throughout the session.

Mediation and Respect

Whenever you intervene—and whatever you say—try hard to show equal respect for all participants.

Be careful too: as you begin to perform strategic mediation with one party, imagine how what you want to say will sound when you interpret it for the other party.

Every time you intervene, say only what you would want everyone present to know.

Writing basic scripts for intervening

The value—and limitations—of a few basic scripts

Writing your own scripts is your key to intervening effectively. If you write even a few, you will then be able to adapt them to a variety of situations.

(Note that some large language services might even have a few scripts prepared that you will need to use when you intervene, but they will inform you if so.)

When you interpret remotely, the scripts you use will not be the ones in this textbook. You will need to write your own, because they need to sound and feel natural. They need to be in your own voice.

Unless you interpret for an organization that requires you to use "frozen" (unchangeable) scripts, write your own script for the most common situations you will intervene for using the kind of language that sounds like you.

Make the language natural, not stiff. Write scripts that sound friendly and polite. How you write your scripts can even help you build rapport and trust—which is hard to do when you interpret remotely.

Helpful tips for writing scripts

1. List the most common communication barriers you encounter.
2. Write short, targeted scripts for intervening in both (or all) your working languages.
3. Practice saying or signing your scripts.
4. Pay attention to clear pronunciation.
5. If the scripts feel long, shorten them.

6. If possible, practice them with a trusted colleague or friend.
7. If they flow naturally, write or type them out for easy reference.
8. Memorize them.
9. Practice role plays (preferably on a remote platform, if possible), with a colleague, and use your scripts again and again in the role plays.
10. See which scripts work well for you—and which ones don't.
11. As you gain experience, keep adapting and writing new scripts as needed.

The importance of appropriate scripting

Here is an example of an untrained interpreter trying to intervene with the doctor and patient. Because the patient seems confused, the interpreter wants to make sure the discharge instructions were clear.

> **Interpreter:** (*to doctor*) Doctor, could you explain the discharge instructions to her a bit more clearly? She doesn't understand the kind of language you use because the medical terminology is confusing her, and I don't think she's literate in her own language.
>
> **Interpreter:** (*to patient*) I just asked the doctor to explain a bit more.

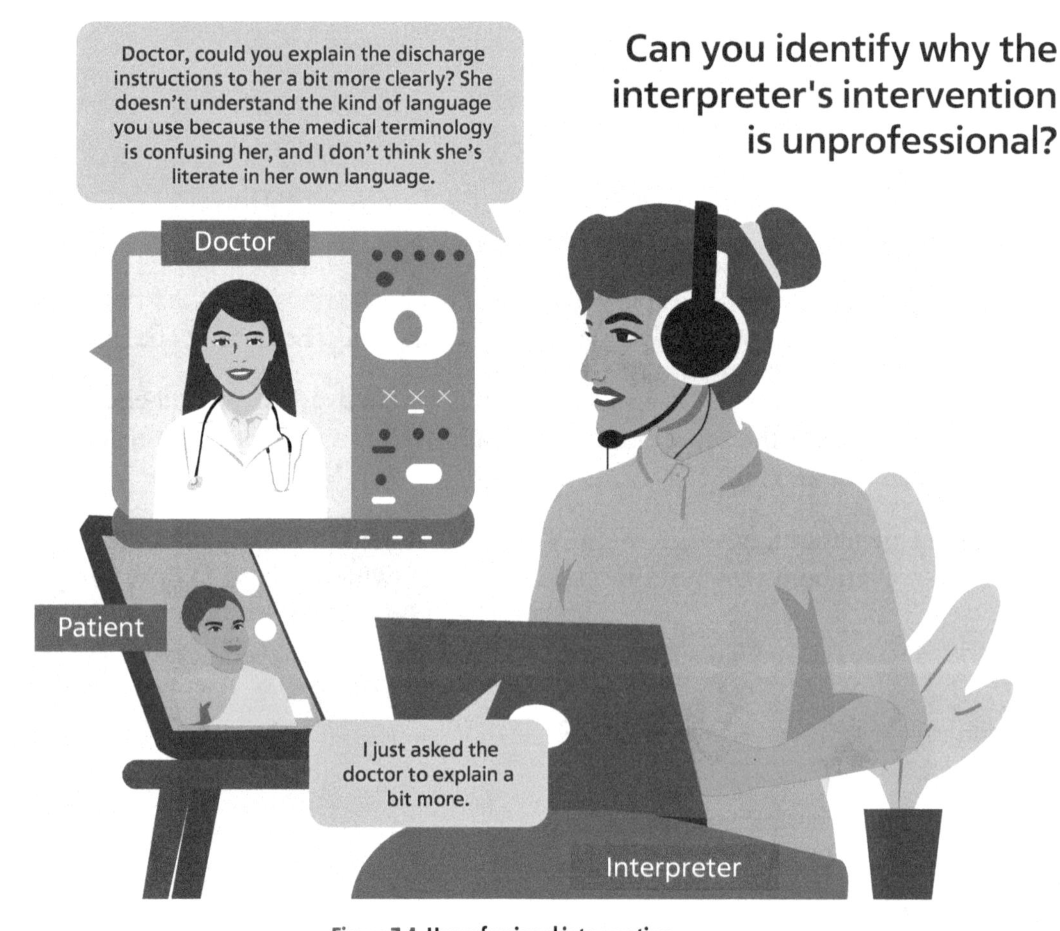

Figure 7.4: Unprofessional intervention

Not only was the interpreter *not* transparent but she also:

- Assumed that the patient didn't understand her.
- Assume that the patient wasn't literate.
- Spoke in a paternalistic that could have offended the patient.
- Forgot that often participants *understand* another language more than they can speak it.

It is important to avoid assuming that participants cannot understand the other language.

The correct way to address this situation is to not assume that the patient (or any participant) does not understand something but instead to take action to support communicative autonomy and clear communication.

For example, the interpreter could say this.

> **Interpreter:** (*to the doctor*) The interpreter is concerned that what I interpreted about the discharge instructions isn't clear.
>
> **Interpreter:** (*to the patient*) The interpreter just informed the doctor that I'm concerned what I interpreted about the discharge instructions wasn't clear.

Do you see the difference? This time the interpreter was transparent. She also:

- Introduced herself as the interpreter.
- Didn't assume that the patient failed to understand the instructions.
- Didn't blame the doctor for not communicating clearly.
- Didn't blame the patient for failing to understand.
- Didn't blame herself for not interpreting well.

Sample scripts

Table 7.2 lists some sample scripts for situations described in the previous section. Remote interpreters can use these scripts to intervene as needed. However, check with your language service or clients first, because they may have internal policies or guidelines for what they want you to say (or not say) when you intervene. They may also have specific scripts that they want you to use.

Remember to keep your own scripts short and to the point. Always introduce yourself as the interpreter, and use the same scripts, as much as possible, with ***all*** participants, for transparency, clarity and consistency. Doing so will also make it easier for you to intervene efficiently.

This means you will write your scripts as identically as possible in *both* (or all) your working languages. Of course, in reality the scripts will differ slightly from language to language and situation to situation.

For example, sometimes, for cultural reasons, precisely how your script addresses one party in one language might change for languages that have certain kinds of tonal variations or cultural titles of respect that vary by age or social status and for which no precise equivalents exist in the other language.

Also, you may say something to one participant, such as a request for clarification (for example, "Excuse me, the interpreter requests that you explain what 'constructive termination' means") but to the other party you would *report* what you just said (for example, "The interpreter just asked the lawyer to explain what 'constructive termination' means.").

In short, make your two scripts as close to identical as possible—but within reason. See Table 7.2 for further examples.

Situation	Sample Scripts[129] (Remember to be transparent and have a script in both or all languages.)
Requesting repetition	(The interpreter didn't hear all of the last message.) (After interpreting what you've understood.) (to the participant you just interpreted for) *The interpreter will request repetition for the last part that was stated.* (to the other participant) *Could you please repeat what you said after "the final report"?* (If a participant refuses to repeat, address the other participant.) *The interpreter requested repetition, but the speaker said, "Never mind."*
Requesting clarification	(to the participant you just interpreted for) *The agent used a term the interpreter is not familiar with. I will ask the agent to clarify what it means.* (to the agent) *As the interpreter, I'm not familiar with the term "face amount." Could you please clarify what it means?*
Cultural differences	(to the loan officer) *As the interpreter, I sense two different approaches to how loan financing is handled. Could you please ask the loan applicant to explain their understanding?* (to the loan applicant) *As the interpreter, I sense two different approaches to how loan financing is handled. I just suggested that the loan officer ask you to explain your understanding.*
Language differences and language mismatches	(If participant speaks another language as their primary language and needs another interpreter.) (to the service provider) *Interpreter speaking. I need to verify the client's primary language.*

129 Adapt any terms to your own context. These are only examples and should be adjusted for your specialization, the context and type of session and the organization or language service you work for. Remember that you may be asked to use scripts provided by clients or the language service.

	(to the servicer user) This is the interpreter speaking. I need to ask if your primary language is [X] or a different language. (after verifying) *The interpreter verified the client's primary language is Italian, not Spanish. I will connect you with an Italian interpreter to assist further.*[130] (wrong language requested) *Interpreter speaking. The client speaks Russian, and I was requested for Polish; however, I can transfer you to a Russian interpreter momentarily.*
Regional language variations	(Be transparent with the participant if there's a dialect difference.) (to the participant to whom you are disclosing the dialect difference) *There is a difference in dialects. The interpreter may need to request clarification often to ensure accuracy.* (to the participant with whom you have a difference in dialects) *There is a difference in our dialects. The interpreter may need to request clarification often to ensure accuracy.* (Withdrawing due to dialect differences.) (to the participant with whom you have a difference in dialects) *Due to the differences in our dialects, the interpreter cannot communicate effectively and accurately. I will connect you with one of my colleagues who can assist you further.* (to the other participant) *Due to the differences in our dialects, the interpreter cannot communicate effectively and accurately. I will connect you with one of my colleagues who can assist you further.*
Participant knowing some of the other language	(If communication is flowing smoothly.) (in one working language) *The interpreter can follow the communication and step in if needed.* (in the other working language) *The interpreter can follow the communication and step in if needed.* (If interpreter notices communication is not flowing.) (to English speaker attempting to speak Arabic) *This is the interpreter. It will help for accurate interpretation if I can interpret between Arabic and English. Please only speak in English and I will interpret into Arabic.* (to Arabic speaker) *This is the interpreter. I advise that it will help for accurate interpretation if I can interpret between Arabic and English and for the other participant to please only speak in English and I will interpret into Arabic for you.*

130 Of course, if you are not interpreting for a language service or another organization that has an interpreter of that language readily available, you will need quite a different script.

Unknown terminology	(to participant who used unknown term) *This is the interpreter speaking. Would you please spell the name of the medicine so I can find the equivalent in Thai?* (to the other participant) *This is the interpreter speaking. I asked for spelling of the name of the medicine so I can find the equivalent in Thai.* (No equivalent exists.) (to participant who used the term with no equivalent) *This is the interpreter speaking. There is no equivalent in my language for this concept. Would you please explain it?* (to the other participant) *This is the interpreter speaking. I explained there is no equivalent for a concept mentioned and asked to please explain it.* (Meaning unknown for acronym/initialism.) (to the participant who used the initialism) *Interpreter speaking. What does CPCU mean?* (to the other participant) *Interpreter speaking. I asked for the meaning of an English initialism.*
Challenges with high register	(to participant using high register) *Excuse me, as the interpreter I'm concerned that what I'm interpreting isn't clear.* (to the other participant) *Excuse me, as the interpreter I let the other participant know that I'm concerned that what I'm interpreting isn't clear.* (to participant using high register) *The interpreter asks you to explain this information so that I can interpret it more clearly* (to the other participant) *The interpreter asked the other participant to explain this information so that I can interpret it more clearly* (to participant using high register) *The interpreter suggests you use simpler language so that I can interpret what you say accurately and clearly.* (to the other participant) *The interpreter suggested the other participant use simpler language so that I can interpret what they say accurately and clearly.*

Turn-taking/ flow control	(to the participant who is not pausing enough) *This is the interpreter speaking. I would like to remind you to pause more often so I can interpret accurately.* (to the other participant) *This is the interpreter speaking. I reminded the other participant to pause more often so I can interpret accurately.* (Participants are speaking over one another.) (in one working language) *This is the interpreter speaking. Please speak one at a time so I am able to interpret accurately.* (in the other working language) *This is the interpreter speaking. Please speak one at a time so I am able to interpret accurately.* (When two or more participants speak the same language and at least one needs an interpreter.) (in one working language) *This is the interpreter. Please allow me time to interpret so I can keep the family informed.* (in the other working language) *This is the interpreter. Please allow me time to interpret so I can keep the family informed.*
Technical issues	(for video spoken language interpreters) (in one working language) *The interpreter will remove the video to see if the connection improves.* (in the other working language) *The interpreter will remove the video to see if the connection improves.* (to one participant) *Interpreter speaking. We seem to be having connection issues. Can you please reposition the device to see if that improves the sound?* (to the other participant) *Interpreter speaking. We seem to be having connection issues. I requested we reposition the device to see if that improves the sound.* (If technical issues cannot be resolved.) (to one participant) *Please contact the IT customer support line and call us back once they've resolved your issue. Thank you.* (to the other participant) *I let them know to please contact the IT customer support line and call us back once they've resolved the issue. Thank you.*

Participant cognitive limitations (for example, extremely young or old participants, dementia, substance use or mental illness)	(If participant does not understand video modality.) (in one working language) *The interpreter will remove the video.* (in the other working language) *The interpreter will remove the video.* (If limitations cannot be overcome.) (in one working language) *The interpreter will withdraw from this session. I suggest working with a face-to-face interpreter (or certified Deaf interpreter) for this case.* (in the other working language) *The interpreter will withdraw from this session. I suggest working with a face-to-face interpreter (or certified Deaf interpreter) for this case.*

Table 7.2: **Sample scripting for intervening to address communication breakdowns.**

Don't Worry If Your Scripts Feel Awkward—Try Again!

If your script doesn't work on the first try, don't give up. You may have to try rewriting a script several times before it feels natural and smooth. Adjust your wording each time to make your script brief and clear and to help it flow.

Take note of any changes to your scripts *in writing*: you are not likely to remember the changes if you don't write them down.

→ Section 7.3 Review

Have scripts ready for whenever you need to intervene. It is incredibly valuable to have intervention scripts, both for face-to-face and remote interpreting. They need to be short, simple and accessible. They should feel smooth and easy for you to say in all your working languages. Preparing scripts in advance that you can adapt as needed helps you automatically train yourself to use similar scripting in both languages and maintain transparency. Scripts that are general enough can easily be applied to many different types of communication breakdowns.

Having scripts ready is especially important in remote interpreting because you will need them even more often, given that you can interpret many more sessions a day remotely than in person.

Also, unlike face-to-face interpreting, in remote interpreting you cannot simply intervene with a gesture or body language. (You could certainly try, but it probably won't work!) Because you can't typically use gestures to intervene, a remote interpreter can sound extremely awkward and unprofessional if they are not prepared with scripting and stumble through an intervention.

Having intervention scripts prepares you so that you don't "freeze," get nervous, sound awkward or say something inappropriate. Remember:

- Prepare scripts for the most common communication breakdowns you encounter.
- Write scripts in your own voice, so that they feel natural for you.
- Practice saying them in front of a mirror, by recording yourself, or saying or signing them to a friend or colleague.
- Plan how you will access your scripts during sessions.
- Adapt your basic set of scripts to each new situation.

If your organization requires you to use their intervention scripts, use them. In all other cases, having your own set of scripts will help you sound polished and professional. It will also build your confidence and show participants how competent and skilled you are.

Section 7.4 How to Use the Strategic Mediation Model

→ Learning objective 7.4

After completing this section, the remote interpreter will be able to perform strategic mediation in OPI, VRI and VRS.

→ Section 7.4 Overview

This section will discuss the Strategic Mediation Model and adapt it for remote interpreting. In interpreting, *mediation* is a term of art. It refers to "any act or utterance of the interpreter that goes beyond interpreting and is intended to remove a barrier to communication or facilitate a [participant's] access to the service" (Bancroft et al., 2015, p. x).

If your specialization allows using this model whenever you intervene, it will help you to ensure accuracy and understanding and support communicative autonomy.

Performing strategic mediation in remote sessions may be more challenging than when you interpret face to face. However, with ongoing practice it becomes natural. And once strategic mediation becomes a habit, it liberates you! Each time you intervene to address a communication breakdown, performing strategic mediation frees up your concentration from worrying about *how* to intervene so that you can focus on quick effective solutions—and get back to interpreting.

→ Section 7.4 Content

Mediating in remote interpreting

Strategic mediation is a vital tool in virtually all interpreting specializations and modalities, including remote interpreting. Yet the techniques to perform it vary from specialization to specialization.

In the case of remote interpreting, one major difference has to do with whether you have the context you need to make the decision to perform mediation because you are not physically present. Also, you may need to address technology problems and breakdowns, unlike face-to-face sessions.

How do I mediate?

The authors of the Strategic Mediation Model (Bancroft et al., 2015, pp. 237-244) proposed the following five steps for mediating in face-to-face interactions:

1. Interpret what was just said or signed.
2. Identify yourself as the interpreter.
3. Mediate briefly.
4. Report your mediation to the other party.
5. Resume interpreting.

However, for remote interpreting, use this new adaptation of the model, which was updated by Sarah Stockler-Rex and Tatiana González-Cestari in 2022 and has four steps instead of five:

1. Interpret what was just said or signed.
2. Identify yourself as the interpreter and inform that participant what you will tell the other participant.
3. Identify yourself as the interpreter and mediate briefly with the other participant.
4. Wait for a response and continue interpreting.

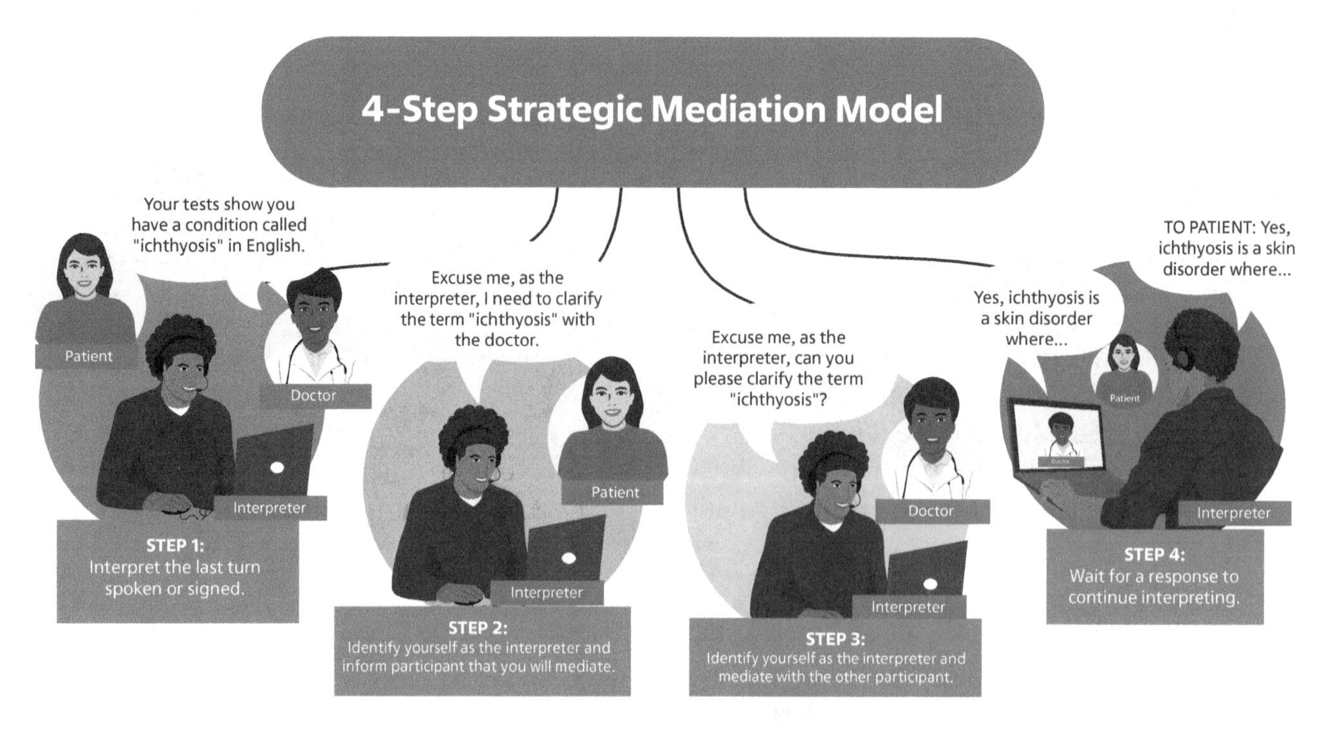

Figure 7.5: **Flow chart with adapted Strategic Mediation Model**

Know that some of these steps in the Strategic Mediation Model may merge or happen simultaneously when working from a signed<>spoken language pair. A signed<>signed language pair can still typically follow the steps above.

The reason for these modifications to the Strategic Mediation Model is based on stricter adherence to the turn-taking pattern to put greater emphasis on transparency. Transparency helps maintain rapport and trust by keeping all participants informed of what is happening at all times.

Depending on the interpreter's specialization, steps 2 and 3 may need to be switched. For example, some specific instances require you to mediate with a judge, lawyer or mental health provider first. In these cases, complete step 3 and then step 2.

In this example, the interpreter starts with Step 3 and mediates directly with the judge first, and then completes Step 2 by reporting the mediation to the defendant.

Figure 7.6: **Adapted Strategic Mediation Model, step 3 before step 2**

In face-to-face interpreting, you have a physical presence that allows you to clearly indicate that you're about to perform mediation with a simple gesture, making eye contact or by leaning closer to participants. In remote interpreting, any deviation from the turn-taking order may seem like a side conversation. You will need different strategies.

Let's go through each of the four steps of the Strategic Mediation Model.

The Strategic Mediation Model

1. *Interpret what was just said or signed.*

This step is a crucial point to remember, because if you do forget to interpret what came before you intervene (which happens often), you will not be accurate.

Following this step is also liberating. That is, by interpreting what was said or signed *before* performing the other steps in the mediation process, you don't have to rely on your memory or notes to go back and interpret the message *after* you have mediated.

In some cases, you may need to skip this step because nothing was heard or understood for you to interpret. However, be sure not to skip it by mistake. With practice, you will integrate this step into your protocol in no time.

2. *Identify yourself as the interpreter and inform that participant what you are about to tell the other participant.*

Transparency in remote interpreting is even more critical than in face-to-face interpreting because the interpreter cannot rely on their own body language (such as leaning forward) and gestures or physical presence to convey certain cues.

For this reason, you will *report* that you need to engage in mediation before actually *performing* it. These two actions are grouped into one step to remind you that they are supposed to happen one right after the other in the same language.

As mentioned earlier, only perform step 3 before step 2 if your specialization or circumstance specifically requires you to address one particular party before the other.

Another part of transparency in this step is showing that you are speaking up *as* the interpreter. In community interpreting, you can do so in first or third person:

> (direct speech/first person): As the interpreter, could I ask you to clarify…
> (indirect speech/third person): The interpreter requests clarification of…

If you work in legal, especially court interpreting, you will need to develop the habit of referring to yourself as the interpreter (in third person) each time you intervene.

The mistake that interpreters typically make is to ask one participant questions and not follow intervention protocols with transparency so that everyone knows exactly what is taking place.

> "Excuse Me, as the Interpreter..."
>
> You may wish to start performing strategic mediation with the brief phrase, "Excuse me."
>
> In many or most languages, saying "Excuse me" (or the equivalent phrase) gets attention. It signals a break in the conversation.
>
> If you don't include some special phrase to signal a break in interpreting, be sure that your tone indicates it. Otherwise, due to the distance caused by remote interpreting, it's easy for participants to miss the interpreter's intervention.

3. *Identify yourself as the interpreter and mediate briefly with the other participant.*

Here is another two-action step that starts with being transparent, only now you will do so with the other participant: the one who said or did something that made you decide to intervene. The reasons to be transparent are the same as for step 2.

This step ends with the mediation. Here is where your intervention scripts will be so useful. Reread Section 7.3. And remember, each time you intervene, to be brief and focused.

4. *Wait for a response and continue interpreting.*

Once you have received information from the participant in step 3, go back to interpreting by simply interpreting whatever speech or signing comes next. That way, you continue the turn-taking pattern, and the conversation can resume naturally.

The beauty and strength of this process is that you have avoided a side conversation with the person you just spoke to.

Let's read the following example that illustrates the adapted Strategic Mediation Model.

> Hang was interpreting for a property sale agreement between a Realtor and a first-time homebuyer when the audio cut out. Below is how Hang used mediation to resolve the communication problem.
>
> **Realtor:** The seller will be charged with the costs of a title report, title search and title guaranty policy in the amount of the purchase price.
>
> **Hang:** (*in Vietnamese*) The seller will be charged with the costs of a title report, title search... Now the interpreter needs to request that the last part be repeated.
>
> **Hang:** Excuse me, Realtor, interpreter speaking—the audio cut out. I heard the seller will be charged with the costs of a title report, title search—and what was the rest?
>
> **Realtor:** And title guaranty policy in the amount of the purchase price.
>
> **Hang:** (*in Vietnamese*) And title guaranty policy in the amount of the purchase price.

Practice the steps

Have your scripts ready

Start practicing the four steps in the remote interpreting Strategic Mediation Model with scripts. Here are a few examples:

- "The interpreter asks you to clarify..."
- "As the interpreter, could I request a clarification of..."
- "Excuse me, the interpreter requests you to explain..."

Find an opening script that works for you. Practice, practice, practice this type of phrasing in both or all your working languages until it becomes automatic! Be patient, it will happen.

Remember: the exact phrasing doesn't matter. Let it sound natural in both languages. Just be brief, clear and to the point—and transparent.

What can happen if you don't follow the four steps

The following example illustrates the huge importance of following these four steps for strategic mediation when you interpret remotely:

> *A landlord was speaking with his tenant over the phone through an interpreter when suddenly he heard a heated argument between the interpreter and the tenant. The interpreter abruptly dropped off the call, leaving only the landlord and the tenant. The landlord could only assume that the interpreter had hung up based on what he heard.*
>
> *In reality, the interpreter was requesting clarification from the tenant, when the call dropped due to a technical issue. Though the clarification wasn't actually heated, it was perceived that way by the landlord.*
>
> *If the interpreter had followed the order of the four steps in the adapted Strategic Mediation Model by first informing the other participant of the need to request clarification, the landlord would have understood clearly what was happening.*

A remote interpreter may have less control of, or less visibility in, the physical environment of the participants than a face-to-face interpreter. Because of this, aim to keep all participants fully informed just in case someone suddenly leaves the call, for any reason.

If you don't follow the four steps, certain things can go wrong, including losing the participants' trust. You might even receive a complaint about your interpreting. Some things may not go wrong initially after you intervene, but they could require a lot more explaining from you, which undermines communicative autonomy, gets you into a side conversation and takes *time*...

Time is precious in remote interpreting. Don't waste it. Follow the four steps above for strategic mediation.

→ Section 7.4 Review

The primary job of interpreters is to interpret. They intervene only if communication breaks down. Intervening, however, poses many risks and can undermine communicative autonomy. By using the four steps of the adapted Strategic Mediation Model discussed in this section and practicing scripts for intervening, you will be able to perform quick, efficient mediation while maintaining a good flow of communication.

For effective mediation, follow the four steps listed for the adapted Strategic Mediation Model.

1. Interpret what was just said or signed.
2. Identify yourself as the interpreter and inform that participant what you will tell the other participant.
3. Identify yourself as the interpreter and mediate briefly with the other participant.
4. Wait for a response and continue interpreting.

Whether these steps overlap or not will depend on your language pair or interpreting mode. The important point is to be *brief and targeted* and *return to interpreting* as soon as you are able. This efficiency will help maintain rapport and transparency. It will also support communicative autonomy.

Section 7.5 Effective Strategies to Address Cultural Barriers

→ Learning objective 7.5

After completing this section, the remote interpreter will be able to decide if, when and how to address cultural misunderstandings.

→ Section 7.5 Overview

As interpreters, we are in a unique position because we have knowledge of the cultures in which we live and from which we come and those we interpret for. We also aim to become professionally familiar with relevant cultural contexts when we interpret. We may be the only person in the session with a combined knowledge of many of the cultures involved in a given session.

All this knowledge is essential to help guide you when you address communication breakdowns, especially if cultural misunderstandings happen.. Yet you also need to be careful not to try to *fix* cultural problems. Just as with any other communication breakdown, you will intervene *only if needed—and permitted.*

Cultural mediation is an important component of interpreting. In many countries with strict rules about cultural mediation, such as the UK, the interpreter's role is strictly to interpret. Other countries, such as Canada and Belgium, were not at first highly structured in their rules or ethical obligations surrounding cultural mediation in the early years (e.g., 1960s to 1990s) and allowed interpreters some considerable liberty to address cultural issues; however, their approach to these issues evolved considerably over the years and led to a repudiation of "cultural mediation" as the work of the interpreter (e.g., HIN, 2010; Agentschap, 2015; Cox, 2015; Verrept & Coune, 2016).

Australia's code of ethics does not address interventions due to cultural misunderstandings but cautions interpreters against taking on other roles such as "advocacy, guidance or advice" (AUSIT, 2012, p. 6). A code of professional conduct from the UK states: "[Interpreters] shall not interrupt, pause or intervene except...to alert the parties to a possible missed cultural reference or inference" (NRPSI, 2016, 5.12).

For this section, we will be focusing on cultural mediation between these extremes, which is the situation in the United States (for nonlegal interpreters), where interpreters are permitted some latitude to address cultural misunderstandings. Even court interpreters may be permitted to request or provide clarification of culturally bound terms and address cultural-based communication breakdowns in certain contexts, particularly if they can ground the misunderstanding in a language-specific context (Framer et al., 2010).

In this curriculum, interpreters are encouraged to address communication breakdowns to support communicative autonomy. Often simply transparently requesting a clarification of a confusing term or concept when a miscommunication arises will eliminate the need for cultural mediation.

Keep in mind that what you are permitted to say or do to address cultural misunderstandings may vary depending on the specialization and the country for which you interpret.

→ Section 7.5 Content

Interpreters, culture and meaning

As interpreters, we tend to have a highly sensitive "cultural communication radar." This sensitivity is an understandable response because languages are influenced by culture and vice versa.

Interpreters do not interpret words: they interpret meaning. If meaning isn't inherent in the words alone, where does it lie? Meaning is shaped by the social context that imbues the message. Without culture, there is no meaning in a message. (This reality is likely one of the reasons that there is no reliable, completely accurate machine translation or interpreting program to date.)

However, it is important to understand that interpreters don't always need to react to when there are cultural differences. And when we do need to react because communication has broken down, the less intrusive we are, the better.

One difference we have noticed in remote interpreting compared to face-to-face interpreting is that face-to-face interpreters have more control over when they leave the interpreting area or room (versus a machine that is disconnected, turned off or moved out of a room by someone other than the interpreter). Face-to-face interpreters may also be called back more often to be able to interpret for participants at a follow-up session.

However, remote interpreters may have to respond more quickly to communication breakdowns before they lose the call and the opportunity to verify that all participants have the same understanding. Remember, due to the nature of remote interpreting, you will be exposed to a greater variety of cultural backgrounds and, potentially, more cultural misunderstandings than in face-to-face interpreting. Read on!

Potential cultural misunderstandings

Strategic mediation has to be brief and efficient to avoid disrupting your session. Cultural breakdowns can be caused by being unfamiliar with or unaware of another person's culture and cultural traditions. Sometimes people will learn specific facts about a culture and project those onto similar cultures.

Interpreters do this too. For example, if the interpreter comes from a particular country where people often defer to professionals and assume that such professionals (including doctors, lawyers, professors and accountants) will make all the decisions, the interpreter may then assume that everyone from that country will defer their decisions to professionals in the same way, which simply isn't true.

Some people also assume that a norm in their culture is the norm everywhere, such as the idea that patients should never be told they are going to die or that everyone wants democracy.

But these are assumptions. Assumptions, in interpreting, are dangerous. Interpreters constantly need to question their own assumptions.

Let's look at the following cases.

Case 1

> A homeowner is convinced she will not receive at-home plumbing repair services during Roman Catholic Holy Week. The plumber does not understand why and continues to reassure the homeowner that her repairs will be completed in a timely manner.
>
> After some confusing exchanges back and forth, the remote interpreter intervenes to prompt the homeowner to share why she is concerned there will be a delay in services. The homeowner then explains that in her country, such services are not available during Holy Week.
>
> The interpreter's instinct to ask for clarification ended up resolving the communication barrier without the need for the interpreter to provide any cultural explanations.

Here, both the homeowner and the plumber did not consider the possibility that there may be a difference in service availability in the other person's country. Because the interpreter had knowledge of the culture in both countries, she had insight as to how the cultural misunderstanding developed. She helped guide the participants to mediating the issue themselves and resolving the situation.

Prior to initiating any cultural mediation, make sure that your mediation is not strictly based on your own personal biases or assumptions. If you have a feeling that there is a cultural issue but are not completely sure, request clarification first to remove any doubts.

Case 2

> A male video healthcare interpreter was called to interpret for a female patient in the postpartum department after she gave birth to her baby. The interpreter was uncomfortable with the subject matter and jumped to the conclusion that the patient was also uncomfortable with his presence. The interpreter intervened and let the provider know that the patient seemed to be uncomfortable with the male interpreter and that he would be happy to transfer the call to a female interpreter instead. However, when the interpreter checked with the patient, the patient declined and said that there was no problem having the male interpreter continue with the session.

In this example, the interpreter himself was uncomfortable with the nature of the call and therefore assumed the patient was uncomfortable as well. Deep down, he may have assumed this so he could use it as a reason to withdraw from the uncomfortable situation. He quickly tried mediation before inviting the provider to confirm that the patient was indeed uncomfortable with a male interpreter. The interpreter might have used the patient's discomfort to hide his own but was incorrect in his assumption.

As remote interpreters (and interpreters in general), we will need to adapt to interpreting for sessions that are outside our cultural norms. We also cannot allow our personal biases to interfere with our interpreting.

When to address cultural misunderstandings

Consider taking no action

The examples above show that some cases don't require mediation at all, while others do require mediation but in the form of a simple request for clarification (as opposed to a cultural mediation).

When to perform cultural mediation? The answer might be "never."

Cultural mediation in interpreting "refers to the act of addressing a cultural misunderstanding while acting as an interpreter, during or outside the session" (Bancroft et al., 2016, p. 162). However, this term, like other terms such as culture brokering and cultural interpreting, has been used in so many ways, in so many countries, that there is no consistent usage that clarifies *how* the cultural misunderstanding is being addressed.

Many people think that cultural mediation means having the interpreter explain cultural issues to one or both parties, fix cultural problems or otherwise get involved in a session. As a result, many interpreters, language services, interpreting associations, government agencies and other organizations around the world firmly believe that interpreters should not engage in cultural mediation at all.

How to make a decision about when to address cultural misunderstandings

First, find out if any organization you interpret for has a policy that forbids interpreters to engage in cultural mediation.

However, even if that is the case, it does not mean you cannot take action if communication breaks down due to cultural misunderstandings. (How to do so will be discussed shortly.) But do not take such action right away. Act only if the cultural misunderstanding is *affecting the dialogue* in a way that puts the desired outcomes in jeopardy. Otherwise don't address it.

Remember, "When in doubt, stay out!" You can always monitor the situation and intervene later. Try to wait until you are sure that mediation of some kind is needed.

When to intervene

However, don't wait too long—especially in remote calls—because you may lose the opportunity during the call. Most likely, you will *not* have the chance to interact with the same participants after the session is over.

In short, the answer to "when" to address a cultural misunderstanding is when you sense strongly that something bad will happen if you simply continue to interpret and take no action. If the consequences of *not* intervening exceed the risks of intervening, you may have no choice.

After all, your job is to interpret in a way that supports communicative autonomy, whether for cultural misunderstandings or any other reasons that undermine clear communication. Around the world, disagreements on this point will continue to swirl. Make your own decisions—and act on them.

The question is: how can you take action that will respect most codes of ethics and professional requirements and expectations around the world? Doing so is a challenge. Let's examine it.

How to perform cultural mediation

Many, many people and organizations around the world do not want you to perform cultural mediation at all. Partly because that is because too many interpreters have used "cultural mediation" as an umbrella for sharing their own cultural opinions rather than taking a professional course of action.

Therefore, let's start here. Keep in mind the following key points when you consider performing cultural mediation.

- You are not a cultural expert. The only cultural "expert" on a participant's culture is that participant.
- Before you act, try to identify clearly what the cultural misunderstanding is.
- If you intervene, point out what you think has caused the misunderstanding—*do not explain it.*
- Let the participants explain any cultural issues to each other.

Practical solutions for cultural misunderstandings

If you determine that cultural mediation *is* needed, how exactly do you perform it?

To perform effective cultural mediation, follow the four steps of the adapted Strategic Mediation Model discussed in Section 7.4 while integrating the cultural implications listed here. First, review the four steps of the model and the additions a, b and c below.

A model for cultural mediation in remote interpreting

Performing Cultural Mediation With the Adapted Strategic Mediation Model

1.	Interpret what was just said or signed.
2.	Identify yourself as the interpreter and inform that participant what you are about to tell the other participant.
3.	Identify yourself as the interpreter and mediate briefly with the other participant. a. Identify the basis of the cultural misunderstanding briefly and clearly (e.g., mention a term, concept, process or possible assumption that appears to be causing confusion). b. *Avoid speaking about any person or their beliefs.* c. Avoid overgeneralizing or stereotyping.
4.	Wait for the other participant to respond and continue interpreting.

If you are an interpreter for court or legal settings, keep in mind that your mediation may be more limited (see Chapter 5 of Volume 2).

Apply the steps

Let's look at how these steps apply to a real-life example:

> A Polish-speaking patient visits the doctor who asks what medications he is using.
>
> **Patient**: (*in Polish*) I use Amol.
>
> **Doctor:** What is that?
>
> **Patient:** (*in Polish*) It's Amol. Everyone knows what Amol is!
>
> The interpreter identifies that the word Amol, which is common in the country of Poland, is causing a cultural misunderstanding. Rather than explaining it himself, he will invite the participant to explain the term to the doctor.

The interpreter follows the steps as outlined below:

1. **Interpret:** The interpreter interprets the patient's statement.
2. **Identify and report:** "This is the interpreter speaking. The interpreter will ask the patient to explain what Amol is and what it is used for since it is not commonly known in the U.S."
3. **Identify and mediate:** "This is the interpreter speaking. Amol is not commonly known in the U.S. Can you explain what it is and what it's used for?"
4. **Continue interpreting:** The interpreter interprets the patient's explanation of Amol.

While cultural examples like these seem simple to the interpreter, who may have the urge simply to explain the term, following this model takes little time, promotes communicative autonomy and sets realistic expectations for the interpreter's role.

Following the model consistently helps to create helpful habits for performing cultural mediation. Habits, especially in the fast-paced environment of remote interpreting, can make complex tasks feel simple, easy and even reflexive. Cultivate them. Habits based on protocols like this one also help to reduce interpreter stress.

When cultural mediation does not go smoothly

In this case, the interpreter knows what "Amol" is, but that won't be the case for every cultural misunderstanding. Let's see how this situation could have worked out a little differently.

Patient: (*in Polish*) I use Amol.

Doctor: What is that?

Patient: (*in Polish to the interpreter*) Tell him what Amol is, surely you know!

Although the interpreter interprets the last statement, the doctor doesn't ask what Amol is and the patient does not offer any further explanation. At this point, it appears that the only way forward is for the interpreter to offer a brief explanation, which he has confirmed with a reliable online source (in this particular case, doing so is permissible for U.S. medical interpreting; however, the interpreter's authorization to provide this information will depend on the specific situation and the interpreter's specialization, organization or association requirements, country and code of ethics, among other factors).

Interpreter: "Amol is an all-purpose, topical herbal tonic."

The interpreter interprets this same explanation to both parties and asks them to verify the information among themselves, then resumes interpreting.

However, if a similar scenario happens in court or other legal interpreting, even in the U.S., or in medical interpreting in Canada, for example (where cultural mediation is not permitted according to national standards for community interpreting, see HIN, 2010), the interpreter would need another strategy.

In other words, if the participant in this case does not want to explain what Amol is, you can make an effort to get the participant to do so. For example:

> **Interpreter:** (*to lawyer*) The interpreter will ask the client to clarify what Amol is.
>
> **Lawyer:** Go ahead.
>
> **Interpreter:** (*to client*) The interpreter requests you to explain what Amol is. The lawyer approves this request.

By adding the authority of the lawyer to your request, you may find it easier to get the participant to provide the explanation instead of supplying it yourself.

Also, please note, if you do encounter these challenging situations and decide to provide cultural clarification yourself, emphasize that *you may be wrong*. Because that is simply true. The participants may think that you are an expert. You know you are not (we hope). Make that point clear.

Sample cultural mediation scripts

Intervening can be hard without a script. Performing cultural mediation without one is even harder.

Scripts can be simple yet save you a lot of time. Cultural misunderstandings are often the most challenging cases. You might struggle with them. You might have no idea what to say because the situation is so complex. It feels hard.

Table 7.2 in Section 7.3 included one example of a script for cultural mediation. Here are two more:

> Mediation script: *The interpreter is concerned about possible confusion concerning a traditional form of massage. You may wish to ask the patient about it.*
>
> Alternative version: *The interpreter senses a possible misunderstanding about traditional healers and the kind of massage they perform. You may wish to explore this issue with the patient.*

Exceptions to cultural mediation

Of course, in an ideal world, every situation would allow enough time to address cultural misunderstandings according to the adapted Strategic Mediation Model. However, in real life, and especially in remote interpreting, time is often short.

Urgent situations

Imagine you are interpreting for a conference, and suddenly the fire alarm goes off. Though you have interpreted the notice to evacuate, you see the participants you're interpreting for are taking much longer than others to leave. You suspect this is because fire drills are not common in the participants' culture.

In this case, you may intervene to emphasize the urgency of the situation without culturally mediating since there is simply no time to follow the four steps of the adapted model.

Here are some examples of time-sensitive situations that may not allow for the four-step Strategic Mediation Model process:

- Trauma situations
- Emergencies
- Domestic violence
- Natural disasters
- Other out-of-control situations (involving, for example, substance abuse, mental health concerns, dementia, several people speaking excitedly at once, etc.)

Depending how you choose to address these scenarios, you may cross into advocacy. Be careful before you do, and refer to Section 6.3 in Chapter 6 of this volume for more about the risks and benefits of advocacy.

Interpersonal dynamics

Another practice that varies widely across cultures is how parents speak to their children while disciplining them. In many cultures, some phrases, when literally interpreted, may sound much more severe and threatening in the language. In the source language, phrases like "I will kill you," "I'll hang you," "I'll slaughter you," can actually sound quite playful and friendly.

You may even decide not to interpret a lullaby that has some of these "brutal" lyrics, but rather point to their cultural significance. Please note, however, that these are particularly risky examples because child abuse can occur in any culture, and the interpreter cannot make assumptions about particular cases. The goal, instead, would be to alert the provider to ask the parent what "I'll hang you" means (and not for the interpreter to volunteer the information that such phrases are "playful").

Insults across languages

It is also common to encounter emotionally charged situations that involve insults that differ from culture to culture, in which case you may need to carefully choose your interpretation while accurately transferring the message. For example, the word *nègre* in French could be translated into English as black, Negro—or using a highly offensive slur that American specialists in the field would question whether an interpreter should say at all (and most U.S. language services would probably not wish their interpreters to say).

Everything we interpret depends on context—but that context can be complicated.[131]

These situations of course happen in face-to-face settings as well. The main difference as a remote interpreter will be how often you face such challenges, the amount of time at your disposal to perform appropriate mediation and the (typical) lack of rapport with participants.

131 See for example https://www.npr.org/templates/story/story.php?storyId=130970738

When cultural mediation is not appropriate

The above situations are difficult enough when interpreting face to face, so you can imagine the added layer of complexity when you interpret remotely. Below are other types of situations that limit the interpreter even further due to being remote:

- A participant is actively moving or turning away from the device.
- The interpreter is left alone with a participant and an emergency arises.

How the interpreter handles situations like these will depend on other factors. If the participant leaves, the interpreter can inform others as quickly as possible what's happening. But what if everyone else leaves too, perhaps to follow the person who left? The interpreter could be left alone or hung up on abruptly.

Be prepared

You will have to be ready to think *quickly* when you face a possible cultural misunderstanding. Afterward, some sessions may also require documentation, escalation or other actions. Your decisions about a cultural misunderstanding and how you manage it could get close attention.

In cases of an emergency when the interpreter is the only witness, such as a violent act, or if a participant is left alone and collapses, there may be a point of contact to escalate to or an emergency service number to call (whether in the organization you are interpreting for or perhaps the language service that engaged you). The authors have even heard stories of remote interpreters calling out for help until someone near the participants hears the interpreter and comes to assist!

No one wants to be caught in these situations unprepared. Ask your clients or language service if there is a policy or protocol in place for how the interpreter should manage or navigate emergencies.

Benefits of interpreting remotely as they relate to cultural dynamics

Though some cultural misunderstandings are made more difficult to address when interpreting remotely, the opposite is also true. Some situations become simpler or easier to address in remote interpreting, for example:

- Requests for an interpreter of a specific gender can sometimes be more easily accommodated and even integrated into the technology on the requestor's end.
- Concerns related to the interpreter's ethnic group or conflict zone sensitivities may not arise if the interpreter interprets solely for OPI (since participants cannot make judgments based on the interpreter's appearance). However, if these concerns still come up, a request for a different interpreter can often be facilitated more swiftly and smoothly than in face-to-face interpreting.
- Certain participants may have more concerns related to confidentiality and privacy within their community for cultural reasons. Working with a remote interpreter is often more anonymous and feels more private (Gany et al., 2007).

→ Section 7.5 Review

This section shows how the adapted Strategic Mediation Model can help address cultural misunderstandings in remote interpreting, in a way that is appropriate for most specializations and many countries around the world. Use it as follows:

Performing Cultural Mediation With the Adapted Strategic Mediation Model

1. Interpret what was just said or signed.
2. Identify yourself as the interpreter and inform that participant what you are about to tell the other participant.
3. Identify yourself as the interpreter and mediate briefly with the other participant.
   a. Identify the basis of the cultural misunderstanding briefly and clearly (e.g., mention a term, concept, process or possible assumption that appears to be causing confusion).
   b. *Avoid speaking about any person or their beliefs.*
   c. Avoid overgeneralizing or stereotyping.
4. Wait for the other participant to respond and continue interpreting.

The goal is to phrase the basis of the misunderstanding in a single term or phrase that encapsulates the cause of the communication breakdown (such as a cultural term or phrase, object, remedy, belief or custom) and invite one participant to explain it to the other *as if it were a linguistic clarification.*

The moment cultural mediation goes beyond cultural-linguistic clarification, the risks rise quickly. Therefore, in some countries, for some language or community services as well as in U.S. court interpreting, cultural mediation may *not* be permitted. Inform yourself.

That said, if you perform the mediation carefully as if you are requesting a *linguistic clarification* or a term, statement or concept, this approach might be permissible even in countries like Canada where national standards prohibit community interpreters from performing culture brokering or cultural mediation. Requests for linguistic clarification are generally widely accepted in interpreting.

In an emergency, provide the minimum cultural information necessary to redirect the participants but make clear that you could be mistaken about the information you are providing since there's no time to verify that information.

If there is no urgency, but the cultural misunderstanding is serious and complex, take time to decide if it's safe or appropriate to intervene by monitoring the situation while you interpret. Then if you do intervene, again, provide the *minimum* information necessary for them to grasp the cause of the communication breakdown and urge them to explore it directly with each other.

The techniques proposed in this section are risky in any area of interpreting (and especially remote interpreting). However, sometimes the risks of *not* intervening are greater still. Reflect before you act. Proceed with care!

→ Chapter Activities

Activity 7.1 (a): How implicit bias affects interpreting

Instructions

1. Complete an online test on implicit bias by Project Implicit.[132] Choose any test. After you complete the test, answer these questions, in writing, then discuss them with your class or with another interpreter or other colleague.
   a. What surprised me about this test and my results?
   b. What do these results suggest about my possible biases as an interpreter?
   c. What could I do to become more aware of unconscious biases that could affect how I make decisions when I interpret?
2. Identify a time when you made a wrong assumption about someone when interpreting. What were the consequences?

Activity 7.1 (b): Bias and communication barriers

Instructions

1. Come up with a list of five potential communication barriers for your working languages and the cultural groups you interpret for. You may want to consider settings you will interpret in often. (For example, which aspects of the education system you interpret in are different from the education system of the families you interpret for?)
2. Add these potential communication barriers to Table 7.3 and for each one give:
   a. An example of taking action based on an interpreter's misunderstanding based on bias (e.g., preconceived ideas).
   b. An example of how to address that same communication barrier with less bias.

Potential Communication Barrier	Acting With Bias	Addressing the Barrier With Less Bias
Example 1: The patient I interpret for doesn't have much education; they do not understand high-register terms.	You assume, before knowing or confirming if it is true, that patients are uneducated and that is why they need an interpreter. As a result, this potential communication "barrier" may not exist, and your assumption may be related to bias.	After interpreting accurately while maintaining the high register, the patient shows signs of confusion and is repeatedly saying "I don't understand," "What is that?"
Example 2: The lawyer I interpret for may be confused by the poor, confusing grammar and disjointed language of the refugee client; the language is almost impossible to interpret accurately and anyway, the lawyer will not understand it.	You assume, because the lawyer is educated, that you need to "clean up" the client's story and make it coherent, grammatically correct and easy to follow instead of just interpreting it or intervening to clarify why you find it difficult to interpret.	The problem may be one of mental health, crisis or trauma, not poor education. But when the client goes to court, the court interpreter will not "clean up" the client's language—therefore, although it is difficult to render accurately, the interpreter should match the speaker's communication style and grammar as accurately as possible. Not doing so could have serious consequences in court.

Table 7.3: Potential communication barriers and biases

132 Go to https://www.projectimplicit.net

Activity 7.1 (c): When cultural mediation is needed

Instructions

Read the following scenario and answer the questions that follow it.

Scenario

> A video remote interpreter was asked to interpret for an Arabic-speaking patient in postpartum after she gave birth. The social worker started out by explaining the process of obtaining the newborn's birth certificate and asked the mother to answer a few questions to fill out the application.
>
> The mother responded by requesting that the social worker return at a time when her husband could be present, so that he could provide answers for the application.
>
> After the social worker agreed to return later and left the room, the interpreter was requested to remain on the line to interpret for the nurse. The nurse explained that she needed to assess the patient's pain level and whether she had any symptoms postdelivery. The patient answered the nurse's questions, once again, by requesting that the nurse return when her husband was present as she could not provide answers on her own.
>
> The patient's response provoked the interpreter to intervene, believing that this was a good opportunity for cultural mediation. The interpreter stated to the nurse that this is a typical response from an Arab wife, as the husband is often the one in control and the sole decision-maker in all situations.

Questions

1. Was this a situation that called for cultural mediation? Why or why not? (Note that your answer to this question may depend in part on which codes of ethics you follow and potentially also whether or not that code addresses healthcare or community interpreting.)
2. If so, did you find the interpreter's statements professional and appropriate? Why or why not?

Activity 7.2 (a): All those questions again!

Instructions

1. Read the following brief scenario and choose the best answer.

2. Discuss your answers with the class or with another interpreter or colleague.

A paralegal asks a client multiple questions before the lawyer arrives. The lawyer then starts to ask the same questions. As the interpreter, you:

a. Summarize the client's responses that were given to the paralegal to save the lawyer and client time.
b. Continue interpreting the lawyer's questions even though they are the same as the paralegal's.

c. Answer each question on the client's behalf since you already know their answers.

d. Ask the client if they would want you to answer for them because you have already interpreted their previous answers.

Activity 7.2 (b): Should you intervene?

Instructions

1. Identify which of these scenarios requires the interpreter to intervene.
2. In the second column, state whether yes, no or maybe you think the interpreter should intervene.
3. In the third column, state your explanation of why the interpreter should intervene or not intervene.

Scenario	Yes, No, Maybe	Explanation
You are interpreting remotely for a lawyer and a client. Communication is flowing well, but when asked for a phone number, the client suddenly switches to the language of the lawyer.		
A patient refuses to answer the doctor's questions.		
A school social worker meets with a child's parents to discuss the child's performance at school. She asks if the parents know what ADHD[133] is.		
As an audio interpreter, you notice the internet connection with the bank manager is so poor it prevents you from clear understanding.		
A police officer at a police station needs help communicating with an intoxicated individual who was just brought in for questioning.		
In VRI, a social worker is interviewing a client, and the client's answers do not match the questions. For example, when the social worker asks who lives in the household, the client answers that she likes to wake up early in the morning. You interpret everything as stated and the social worker turns to you and says, "Interpreter, that's not what I asked her."		

133 Attention deficit hyperactivity disorder.

Activity 7.2 (c): Manage the flow

Instructions

Read the scenario below and answer the question that follows it.

You interpret for a parent-teacher conference on a video remote platform, which only allows consecutive interpreting. The mother and father, who are divorced, are both present.

The mother and father start arguing about how to address some of the teacher's concerns with their child.

You make various attempts to intervene to ask them to take turns speaking. They ignore your requests. After a few minutes, the teacher says, "OK, interpreter, what did they say?"

As the interpreter, what would you do now?

Activity 7.3 (a): Write your scripts

Instructions

1. Using Table 7.3, develop a script for each situation in your other working languages.
2. Practice delivering the scripts in both or all your working languages.
3. Record yourself delivering the scripts.
4. Review the recording to make sure you delivered the same information in both languages for each script and note how natural (or unnatural) the scripts sound to you.
5. Adapt each script, in writing, to make the scripts sound more like "you." In other words, rewrite the scripts to reflect your own voice.
6. Record yourself delivering the new scripts.
7. Keep adjusting the scripts and recording yourself until you feel the scripts are ready to try out in a live remote interpreted call or session.

Activity 7.3 (b): Write scripts for Alee

Instructions

Part 1

1. Read the following story.

2. List what the interpreter, Alee, did or did not do well and state why in writing.

Alee is interpreting remotely when a customer service representative uses a word that can have two different meanings. Alee realizes she needs to request clarification to accurately render the message. She immediately asks for clarification from the customer service representative. When she starts interpreting what the customer service representative said, the client asks, "What did he say?"

Alee interprets that question. The customer service person says, "Are you asking what I said?"

Alee interprets that question. The customer then adds, "You two were talking and I don't know what you were saying. I don't want to miss anything about the instructions I need to follow...I wish I could understand what you are saying. It's so frustrating."

Part 2

Now develop intervention scripts (at least two) in your working languages for the clarification request and write them in a way that might eliminate or reduce some of the problems Alee encountered.

Activity 7.3 (c): Finish these scripts

Instructions

Refer to the sample scripts in Table 7.2 in Section 7.3 to guide you in completing the unfinished scripts in this activity. Remember that you are the remote interpreter in these scripts.

1. A patient is in a clinic to sign consent forms for her upcoming surgical procedure. Request a clarification for the underlined term.

Nurse: You will be undergoing your spinal tap procedure next week. Do you have any questions about it?

Interpreter: (*to the patient in one language*) This is the interpreter speaking. ____________

____

____.

Interpreter: (*to the nurse in the other language*) This is the interpreter speaking. ____________

____

____.

2. A client is present at a bank appointment, accompanied by two relatives, to complete opening a mortgage loan.

Mortgage officer: Unfortunately, we will not be moving forward with the closing today because you are a permanent resident and not a U.S. citizen.

The officer's remark is interpreted and prompts the client and both family members to become furious. They start speaking loudly all at the same time at the mortgage officer.

Interpreter: (*to mortgage officer*) ______________________________________

____

____.

Interpreter: (*to client and family members*) ______________________________

____

____.

3. An elderly individual is in court to dispute a speeding ticket. When he notices you on the video monitor, his demeanor changes and he becomes agitated.

Defendant: Who is this? Why is she on the monitor? I know her, she's a spy. She works for the government. I'm not talking to her. Turn her off.

You interpret the defendant's statements and try to move forward with the session, but it becomes clear the defendant will not cooperate or respond to you. You see you will need to withdraw so that the court and defendant can resume the session with a different interpreter.

Interpreter: (*to court*) ____

____

____.

Interpreter: (*to defendant*) ____

____

____.

Activity 7.3 (d): Script, record and evaluate your intervention

Instructions

1. Read the scenario and write scripts in both languages to address the communication breakdown.
2. Record yourself saying (or signing) these scripts in both working languages.
3. Review your recording.
4. Answer the self-evaluation questions about your performance.

A sanitation employee meets with a restaurant owner to explain the county's requirements for recycling and uses the word "commingled." You suspect that this term means recycling metal, paper and plastic items together but you are not certain.

Script

Interpreter: (*to the sanitation employee*) _________________________________

____

____.

Interpreter: (*to the restaurant owner*) ______________________________

____

____

Self-evaluation questions

1. Did I use a professional tone with an engaging attitude? __________
2. Did I remain professional and calm? __________
3. Was I transparent with both parties? __________
4. Was my delivery:
   a. Fast or slow? ____________________
   b. Smooth or awkward? ____________________
   c. Convincing or unconvincing? ____________________
   d. Different in each language or similar in both? ____________________
5. Was my tone:
   a. Respectful or abrupt? ____________________
   a. Kind or impatient? ____________________
   b. Different when speaking to one person vs. the other person? If so, describe the differences you noticed: ______________________________
6. Having listened to my recording and answered the questions, what would I say now for the same situation that might sound more natural and appropriate? Write a new script for this situation, in both languages. Try to imagine what you would want to say in a similar situation.

____

____

____

Activity 7.4 (a): Write the four steps

Instructions

1. Read the following scenario.

A transnational pharmaceutical company is working on becoming internationally certified in certain processes. For the certification process, a Swahili-speaking coordinator is communicating with a Norwegian-speaking coordinator through an over the phone interpreter.

As the participants are setting up some deadlines and follow-up meeting times, the interpreter notices that neither of them is taking into consideration the different time zones where they are located. The interpreter monitors the situation. Realizing that participants will end the call soon and did not account for the time differences, the interpreter decides to intervene (knowing this confusion will also affect when the interpreter logs in to interpret the next session).

2. Now imagine that *you* are the interpreter, and you will also be the interpreter for the participants' next session.

3. You decide to intervene. Write down the four steps of the adapted Strategic Mediation Model and add what you would specifically say to participants when following steps 1, 2 and 3.

1. Interpret ______________________________.
2. Identify ______________________________.
   Interpreter: (*to Swahili coordinator*)

____

____

____

____

____

____

3. Identify______________________________.
   Interpreter: (*to Norwegian coordinator*)

____

____

____

____

____

4. Wait ______________________________.

Activity 7.4 (b): Assess the mediations

Instructions

1. Read the following interpreted interactions.
2. After doing so:
   a. Review the four-step adapted Strategic Mediation Model and identify any steps the interpreter in each scenario did *not* perform.
   b. Write down anything the interpreter may have done *incorrectly*.

Interaction 1

The interpreter is interpreting remotely for an individual coming into the Department of Motor Vehicles (DMV).

DMV representative: All right, everything you need is filled out for your driver's license renewal. But since you're telling me you've changed your last name since you just got married, you'll need to get back out of line and go fill out the green form.

Interpreter: (*to customer*) OK, you have everything you need filled out for your driver's license renewal. But since you're saying you've changed your last name since your recent wedding...

Interpreter: (*to DMV representative*) Did you say, "a green sheet: for the appointment"?

Write down any of the four steps of the adapted Strategic Mediation Model that the interpreter did *not* perform.

____

Write down anything the interpreter may have done *incorrectly.*

____

____

Interaction 2

The interpreter is interpreting a telephone conversation between a bank help-line representative and a customer. The customer sent a check by mail to pay their monthly apartment rent, but the check was lost in transit.

Bank representative: Thank you for calling National Bank. My name is Cathy. How may I help you?

Customer: Hello. Yes, I need to cancel a check. It's check number eight nine seven four three. I sent it to pay my rent on the first of the month, and it got lost in the mail!

Bank representative: OK, no problem. I can stop the check. In order to proceed, I'll need you to consent to our transaction discontinuation procedure. By consenting, you agree to our one-time fee of twenty dollars. You also acknowledge that if the original recipient were to attempt to cash the check, you also may be charged a fee. Do you want to continue?

Customer: What? No, I just want to stop the check.

Bank representative: (*Sighs loudly in frustration.*) Interpreter, clearly you're not saying everything right. Tell her what I said again.

Interpreter: *(to bank representative*) Ma'am, I just said everything exactly as you said it, but I don't think she understands.

Write down any of the four steps of the adapted Strategic Mediation Model that the interpreter did *not* perform.

Write down anything the interpreter may have done *incorrectly.*

Interaction 3

A young English-speaking woman booked a trip for her family of five to an all-inclusive resort in another country. She has just called the travel agency. Since the travel agency is based in the destination country, she needs an interpreter to speak with them.

Travel agent: Hello, thank you for calling Best Trips Ever Bookings. My name is Tomas. How may I help you?

Customer: Hi. Yes, my name is Sharon Brodie. I booked the all-inclusive resorts package for this week. We're actually on the trip now...but we have a situation. We were at the hotel restaurant and bar, and we got charged a huge tab for alcohol. But we didn't have any drinks! I've tried settling this with the hotel directly, but they won't listen. I know whose bill it is. It was the couple next to us that night. They were pissed!

Travel agent: OK, ma'am, I'd be happy to help you sort this out. I do see your booking here. But help me to understand. Was the couple's anger directed at your family specifically?

Customer: What? They weren't angry. We didn't even talk to them.

(*The interpreter interprets everything but realizes they interpreted the term "pissed" with the term's American meaning of angry, but the customer is from the UK. In the UK, the term "pissed" means drunk or inebriated.*)

Interpreter: (*to travel agent*) The interpreter would like to request clarification from the customer.

Interpreter: (*to customer*) The interpreter would like to request clarification of the term "pissed." Did you mean they were angry or that they were drunk?

Customer: (*laughs*) No, no! They weren't angry. Far from it. They were happily drunk. They were smashed, wasted, sozzled!

Write down any of the four steps of the adapted Strategic Mediation Model that the interpreter did *not* perform.

Write down anything the interpreter may have done *incorrectly.*

Activity 7.4 (c): Write scripts, mediate and self-evaluate

Instructions

1. Imagine you are the interpreter for each scenario in Activity 7.3 (b).
2. Write out the script *you* would use for each scenario.
3. Make sure it includes all steps of the remote interpreting Strategic Mediation Model.
4. Practice performing the scripts while recording yourself.
5. Review the recordings and evaluate them based on the questions below.

Script in both languages for Interaction 1

Script in both languages for Interaction 2

Script in both languages for Interaction 3

Self-evaluation questions

1. Did I use a professional tone with an engaging attitude? ______
2. Did I remain professional and calm? ______
3. Was I transparent with both parties? ______
4. Was my delivery:
   a. Fast or slow? ______________________
   b. Smooth or awkward? ______________________
   c. Convincing or unconvincing? ______________________
   d. Different in each language or similar in both? ______________________
5. Was my tone:
   a. Respectful or abrupt? ______________________
   b. Kind or impatient? ______________________
   c. Different when speaking to one person vs. the other person? If so, describe the differences you noticed: ______________________

____

____

6. Having listened to my recording and answered the questions, what would I say now for the same situation that might sound more natural and appropriate? Write a new script for this situation, in both languages. Try to imagine what you would want to say in a similar situation.

____

____

____

____

____

____

Activity 7.5 (a): Healthcare: blood transfusion

Instructions

1. Read the following scenario.
2. Answer the multiple-choice question that follows it.

You take a video call for the emergency department. The patient is a 10-year-old boy brought in by his mother. The boy has been in an accident and needs a blood transfusion.

Doctor: I know it's difficult seeing your son like this, ma'am. But I do believe he's going to be all right. When you arrived, you told the nurse you're OK with your son receiving a blood transfusion if it's necessary to save his life.

Mother: Yes.

Doctor: OK. I do recommend we give him blood. I have the consent form here for you to sign so we can go ahead and start the procedure.

Mother: My husband is on his way. He can sign the consent.

Doctor: Time is of the essence. It will be better if you can sign now so we can start setting everything up. You can always call your husband as soon as you sign to let him know what's going on.

Mother: No, no, I prefer we wait for him. He'll be here pretty soon. I don't want to sign anything without him here.

Doctor: OK. Just so you know, as the boy's mother, you do have the right to sign the consent without your husband present.

Mother: I know he would want us to wait for him. I can't sign without him here, and I prefer he signs the consent.

As the interpreter, you decide to…(choose one option below)

a. Interpret the conversation and allow the participants to sort out the decision.
b. Point out that there may be a cultural difference regarding blood transfusions in the patient's religion.
c. Point out that there may be a cultural difference in how family medical decisions are made and invite the participants to explore that idea.
d. Emphasize the time-sensitive nature of the procedure in your interpretation since you see the mother doesn't understand the urgency.
e. Take another action.

Activity 7.5 (b): Cultural misunderstandings

List possible cultural misunderstandings that may arise between the participants that you know you are likely to interpret for. For example, in Orthodox Jewish culture, work should not be done on the Sabbath, which may cause misunderstandings with certain participants.

____

____

____

____

____

____

Activity 7.5 (c): Addressing cultural misunderstandings

You are interpreting a meeting between a Somali student's parents and the school principal (head teacher). The school has many Somali students. The parents express frustration that the school will remain open during Eid al-Fitr, an important holiday in the Islamic calendar. The principal does not understand what the issue is. The school is closed on many other holidays, but you understand this is an important holiday in the Somali community. The student has already had a lot of unexplained absences in the school year, and the principal is denying the parents' request to take their child out of school for three or four more days.

What would you say to the participants in this case? Answer yes, no, or maybe if it is appropriate to use the scripts below and briefly explain your answer. *Assume that all scripts would be relayed in both languages.*

Script for addressing cultural misunderstandings with participants	Yes, No, Maybe	Explanation
1. (*to the principal*): "Eid al-Fitr is a major religious holiday in the Somali community. You should approve the parents' request."		
2. (*to the principal*): "This is the interpreter. Please ask about the student's unexplained absences. There may be a cultural misunderstanding."		
3. (*to the parents*): "Muslim holidays are not acknowledged here. This request will not be approved no matter what you say."		
4. (*to the principal*): "The interpreter would like to point out a possible cultural misunderstanding related to the importance of this holiday in the family's community. You may wish to ask the parents about it."		
5. (*to the principal*): "The interpreter would like to explain that Eid al-Fitr is a major holiday in the Somali community. You may wish to discuss its importance with the parents."		

Chapter Conclusion and Review

This chapter addressed communication breakdowns in remotely interpreted sessions.

Section 7.1 examined the motives interpreters may have when they intervene to address communication barriers. Remember, "When in doubt, stay out!" First, examine your motives for *wanting* to interrupt the session. Where possible, use System 2 slow, reflective thinking outside the session to make decisions about if, when and why to address a communication barrier when it arises.

Section 7.2 discussed common communication barriers that you may face in remote interpreting and ways to address them. The list of common barriers and their solutions was not exhaustive, but it gave you practice in using critical thinking skills to weigh the pros and cons of intervening. No matter what type of barrier you face, make sure the way you address it promotes the communicative autonomy of all participants.

Section 7.3 helped you develop scripts to address communication barriers if your specialization allows. Scripts need to be short, simple and easy to access during remote sessions. Scripts should be as similar as possible in all working languages in order to maintain complete transparency.

Section 7.4 reviewed the Strategic Mediation Model and introduced four revised steps that are helpful for both remote and face-to-face interpreting. It's critical that you inform the other participants when you are about to mediate before performing mediation in order to maintain transparency in a remote session.

Section 7.5 guided you in deciding if, when and how to address cultural misunderstandings. Even if you are permitted to perform cultural mediation by your country, any professional associations you join and your specializations, addressing cultural misunderstandings can be tricky and risky. Remember, you are not necessarily *the* cultural expert for any participant. Where it is permissible, use the adapted Strategic Mediation Model to direct participants to explore a possible cultural misunderstanding themselves and go back to interpreting as soon as possible.

Tatiana González-Cestari, PhD, CHI-Spanish
Sarah Stockler-Rex, MA, CHI-Spanish
Contributing Author: Analía C. Lang, CHI-Spanish

Professionalism in Remote Interpreting

Learning Objectives

After completing this chapter, the remote interpreter will be able to:

Learning Objective 8.1: List and describe the key components of professional conduct.

Learning Objective 8.2: Explain typical requirements and expectations for interpreters employed by a language service or other organization.

Learning Objective 8.3: Explain the typical requirements and expectations for self-employed interpreters.

Learning Objective 8.4: Develop a continuing education plan.

Introduction

There has been a widespread misconception that remote interpreting tends to be less professional than face-to-face interpreting because interpreters are not physically present in the same location as participants.

Yet remote interpreters exhibit great professionalism and integrity. The misperception is currently shifting, especially since the onset of the COVID-19 pandemic.

Professionalism involves more than simply following a set of best practices or a code of conduct; professionalism starts from within. It is the passion and conviction that we must give our best to any task, role or responsibility that we have taken on. More than that, it is a personal belief that anything we set out to do we will carry out with the utmost integrity and our best effort.

As we address professionalism in remote interpreting, keep in mind that your professional performance will represent the interpreting profession as a whole and also your work as a remote interpreter. Whether you are self-employed or employed by a language service, or by any other organization, this chapter will provide you with a clear understanding of the requirements and expectations for your professional conduct in remote interpreting.

Section 8.1 Professional Conduct

→ **Learning objective 8.1**

After completing this section, the remote interpreter will be able to list and describe the key components of professional conduct.

→ Section 8.1 Overview

Professionalism encompasses several important aspects of behavior in any type of business. Perhaps the most common term for one's behavior at work is "professional conduct." In general, professional conduct involves ethics, morals and standards of behavior in the context of performing a job, whether you are an employee or a contractor.

Throughout this section, we will define what professional conduct means when interpreting remotely and which kind of actions and behaviors are necessary in order to provide excellent service and convey the highest level of professionalism.

→ Section 8.1 Content

Professional conduct

Professional conduct is the sum of the actions that interpreters take while interpreting to ensure a smooth, successful session and all the ways in which interpreters engage with colleagues, clients and the public. Yes, a foundational part of professional conduct is having the skills required to transfer messages accurately and completely, but that is just the beginning!

Professional conduct encompasses professional etiquette, interpreting protocols (covered in Chapter 4 of this volume) and adherence to ethics (addressed in Chapter 6 of this volume). When all the elements of professional conduct are combined with strong interpreting skills, the interpreter can fully support communicative autonomy (see Chapter 5 of this volume) and will also be an excellent ambassador for the profession.

You may think that as a remote interpreter, you have to focus only on how you conduct yourself during your sessions. After all, we don't face many of the challenges that our face-to-face colleagues do, such as being presented with gifts, asked for a ride home, or having participants' eyes on us when we arrive, wait for, and exit our appointments.

However, there is still more to professional conduct than the session itself. All the following are examples of professional conduct for remote interpreters.

- How you interact with colleagues and clients in speech, or signs, and writing.
- How promptly you "arrive" for your sessions.
- How you conduct yourself at professional events (even if they are virtual).
- How knowledgeable and skilled you are in using technology.

Professional etiquette

"Professional etiquette" is similar to terms like "common sense." You know the concept is important, but there is usually no clear definition for it.

Professional etiquette depends on the environment, the culture and the role you perform. There are no official manuals that define it comprehensively for every profession, far less for every person or circumstance.

Nonetheless, interpreters are ambassadors not only for language services or other organizations they interpret for but also for the interpreting profession itself. They also convey aspects of each participant's culture to other participants and are ambassadors of their own cultures. Who would want to poorly represent any of these stakeholders?

One university defines professional etiquette as "An unwritten code of conduct regarding the interactions among the members in a business setting. When proper professional etiquette is used, all involved can feel more comfortable, and things tend to flow more smoothly."[134]

Professional Etiquette vs. Customer Service

In some respects, professional etiquette may overlap with what is often called "customer service." Salesforce, one of the largest technology companies in the world, specializes in customer relations management solutions. It defines customer service as "The support you offer your customers—both before and after they buy and use your products or services—that helps them have an easy and enjoyable experience with you."

The Salesforce website emphasizes how important it is to have excellent customer service if you want to retain your customers and grow your business[135]—which interpreters ideally will want to do (especially contract interpreters).

Displaying professional etiquette and developing strong customer service skills will enhance the career of virtually any interpreter.

Professional etiquette and customer service are important in all modalities of interpreting. However, it is especially important that remote interpreters give extra emphasis to applying them. When interpreting remotely, it is difficult to build rapport with participants since you are not physically present. Furthermore, the first time you meet them might also be the last time. You have little time in remote interpreting to build rapport.

Soft skills

All aspects of your professional etiquette are important. Many of them you surely know well and were addressed earlier in this volume (for example, how to dress, introduce yourself and appear professional on video). However, one often-overlooked concept to keep in mind for your professional conduct is your soft skills.

Soft skills are the nontechnical skills that you use when engaging and communicating with other people. Your tone and your willingness to learn, your open-mindedness, integrity, ethics, dependability and ability to express empathy are all part of your soft skills.

---

134 Retrieved from: https://www.rgmcet.edu.in/assets/img/departments/CIVIL/materials/R15/3-2/PESS/unit-2.pdf

135 Retrieved from: https://www.salesforce.com/products/service-cloud/what-is-customer-service/

Think of soft skills as the way you convey yourself in communication with others. Even silence is communication. For example, failing to respond promptly to a work email or voicemail sends a powerful message—but not one you would wish to convey!

Soft skills are difficult, since they cannot be taught and learned in the same way that other skills can. Knowledge alone is not enough; there has to be a desire to employ soft skills (Dewey, 1933). Pay close attention to others' cues in your daily interactions and try to think how you would perceive your own actions, words and behaviors, if you were them. Soft skills are especially important in initial meetings and interviews.

People with soft skills learn to think flexibly. They take into consideration how their attitudes and emotions may block or enhance personal (and professional) progress. They make decisions with others and the whole situation in mind. Soft skills are crucial to a person's success in life. They are critically important in remote interpreting and in most other professions. You can go far with hard skills, but your opportunities will grow exponentially with soft skills.

What does professional etiquette mean for a remote interpreter?

A. Dress code

Interpreters on video may be asked to follow a dress code, which may include specifications with the participants' visual experience in mind. For example, patterns and bright or neon colors may create a strobe effect on a screen and may therefore be discouraged. Just as in face-to-face sessions, remote interpreters should be well-groomed and have a clean appearance.

Professional Etiquette and Professional Dress

Keep in mind that "professional dress" does not mean "Western clothing." As you saw in Chapter 3, it might be perfectly appropriate to wear traditional clothing while you interpret. Simply check with the language services or other organizations that you interpret for, as they may help guide you in ways to wear traditional clothing on camera that still adhere to the organization's dress code (if any).

In addition, it is recommended that sign language interpreters wear solid colors that contrast with their skin tone but if any nail polish is used, it should be close in color to their skin tone. Be cautious of wearing any large, loose, or flashy, shiny jewelry that may cause visual disruption. Interpreters may be required to avoid hair colors that appear unnatural or distracting on camera, depending on the language service. In sign language interpreting it is ideal to be as visually unobtrusive as possible (NAD-RID, 2005).

Do OPI Interpreters Have a Dress Code?

If you perform OPI from a home office, you probably have no dress code—unless you also perform VRI or VRS and have to be prepared for both audio only and video calls.

OPI interpreters who work in a call center or office will of course need to comply with the clothing etiquette guidelines of their organization.

B. Body language

Interpreters should use their body language to display engagement during an interpreted session in a way that demonstrates appropriate customer service and professionalism. While it may seem that this section applies only to video interpreters, body language may come through in your voice too.

Sit up straight to project your voice well and maintain clear voice quality. Avoid reacting physically with eye-rolling or other negative facial expressions or bodily responses, because these acts could influence your tone of voice even in OPI. Though participants may not see you, moving around and fidgeting could also be audible through your microphone and cause distraction. See examples in Figures 8.1 through 8.7 for both inappropriate and appropriate body language.

Inappropriate body language

Here are a few images of inappropriate body language for remote interpreters. (These images are provided courtesy of Martti by UpHealth as part of its "dos and don'ts of camera presence" training module.)

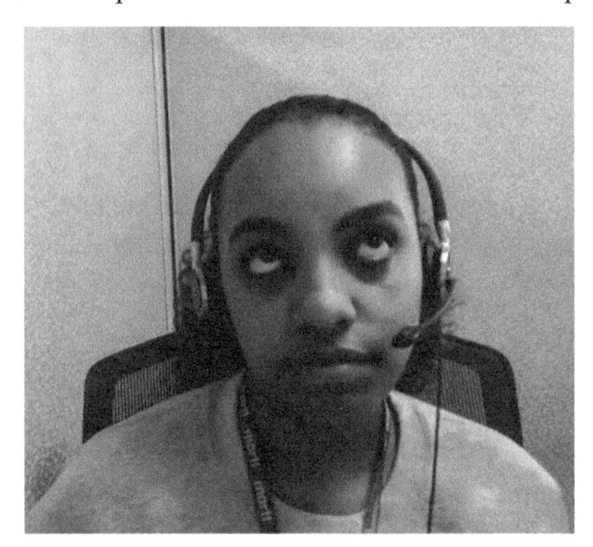

Figure 8.1: **The eye-rolling interpreter**

Rolling one's eyes is a sign of serious rudeness.

Figures 8.2 and 8.3: **The overly relaxed interpreter**

The interpreter's posture is far too informal, leaning back and then leaning to one side in positions that are not only unprofessional but also potentially rude, disrespectful or offensive to participants.

Figure 8.4: **The interpreter who drinks on camera**

Here the interpreter is showing her water cup on camera. We need to hydrate from time to time, but it's recommended to turn off the video while doing so (if your organization or language service permits it), or at least take sips of water discreetly from a container with neutral colors that is not bright or distracting.

Figure 8.5: **The frustrated interpreter**

The interpreter is rubbing his temples in obvious frustration, which can annoy, distract or perhaps even anger participants.

Appropriate body language

Here are a few images of appropriate body language in video interpreting.

Figure 8.6: **The alert, engaged interpreter**

Interpreter is sitting up straight, smiling and looking at the camera. All of these elements help her to appear engaged and fully present. Her warmth is visible and welcoming yet not distracting.

Figure 8.7: **The neutral yet engaged interpreter**

This interpreter has the body-language elements mentioned above with a more neutral expression. Sometimes it is important to recognize and react to the mood in the session.

In face-to-face sessions, the spoken language interpreter often averts direct eye contact to promote direct communication among participants. In video interpreting, however, avoiding a direct gaze can be perceived as disengagement or distraction.

Video interpreters ideally will look directly at the camera to show engagement and professionalism. There may be exceptions. For example, for cultural reasons or for sensitive topics (certain types of medical appointments, for example) you might sometimes need to avert your gaze.

C. Camera presence (video calls only)

Camera presence in remote interpreting is the key to projecting a professional image and building rapport. While face-to-face interactions include the interpreter's entire physical presence, a video interpreter will need to make a good impression with a limited field of view.

Camera presence involves everything that is in the camera view, from interpreters to their close surroundings. For a pleasant customer service experience, try the following:

- Remain centered on camera.
- Let the camera view stay clear of hallways (especially in a call center), ceilings or floors.
- Sit up straight, not slouching, leaning back or resting on your side.
- Maintain a clear workspace, with no visible clutter on camera. No other items will be visible such as tablets, laptops, or telephones.
- Follow the appropriate dress code.
- Smile (when appropriate) and make eye contact. Place the video window right below the camera to facilitate eye contact.

See examples in Figures 8.8 through 8.11 for inappropriate camera presence.

Inappropriate camera presence

Figure 8.8: **Missing in action**

The interpreter is looking down to take notes, and her backpack and other items are visible on screen. In video interpreting, you should glance up and make eye contact to show engagement even while taking notes.

Figure 8.9: **The dangerously distracted interpreter**

The interpreter is texting someone and distracted by his telephone. Doing so may even be a policy violation for some language services.

Figure 8.10: **The poorly positioned interpreter**

The camera view shows an area above the cubicle wall, and a window is visible. The interpreter is not centered in the frame.

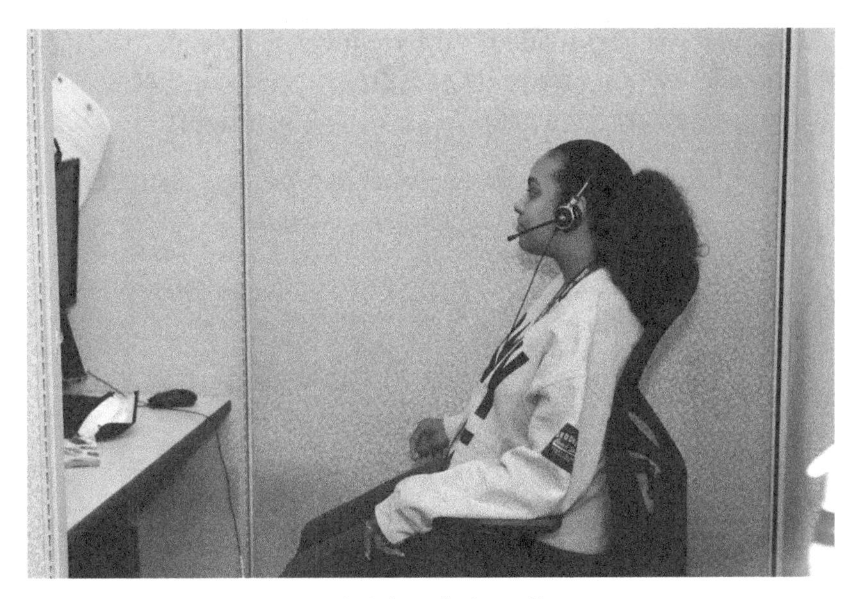

Figure 8.11: The informally dressed interpreter

The interpreter is dressed too casually for work, in a sweatshirt with large letters.

As you can see in the photos, you wouldn't want to make these kinds of impressions on camera. Be careful not to appear disheveled or unprepared. Be mindful of your behaviors, as some are unconscious: you don't want to be the interpreter who's called out for biting their nails on screen or resting their head on their hands!

D. Backdrop or background (video calls only)

Figure 8.12: The interpreter's backdrop

Try to have a background that is not distracting for the participants and the interpreter. (And yes, video interpreters should check themselves periodically while on camera.) Your background is important in all video interpreting and even more important for sign language interpreters.

An appropriate background can be provided in different ways: for example, a professional office/ home office wall; a cubicle wall; a retractable backdrop (a green or blue screen, for example) or a backdrop mounted over the back of a chair.

Solid color backdrops or backgrounds are preferred as they are less distracting and provide better video image quality (e.g., the color blue for signed languages).

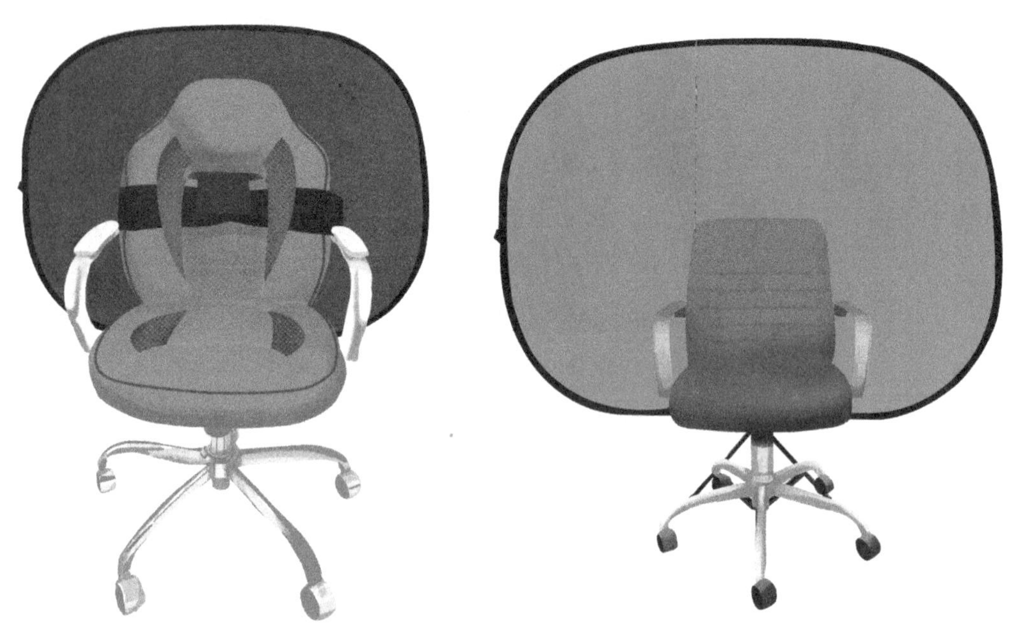

Figure 8.13: **Chair mounted backdrop**

Figure 8.14: **Collapsible backdrop**

Figure 8.15: **Backdrop with stand**

Virtual backgrounds such as those available on teleconferencing platforms are popular now. There are many choices. Ask your client or your language service if an electronic background is an acceptable choice for you.

Virtual backgrounds may not be a good option for sign language interpreters, however, as some signs may be obscured.

Figure 8.16: **Example of a language service virtual background**

E. Call readiness

Be ready! Remote interpreters are expected to work in a quiet, private environment and have the telephone or video device connected with the headset on. They should be ready to begin *before* the start of the session.

Have everything ready that you may need during your call or shift. Set it all up before beginning your work for the day: any needed materials for note-taking, your water, online resources that need to be accessed and so on. Be ready to perform.

Try not to do what this interpreter did at the beginning of the call.

Figure 8.17: **The unprepared interpreter**

The interpreter answered the call before he was ready to begin and the client can see him putting his headset on.

Yes, the participants were already trying to communicate with the interpreter, and everybody could see this action.

F. Tone of voice and positive scripting

Any time you speak up as the interpreter—for example, to request a repetition or a clarification—and you use your *own* words, not repeating or rendering a message, your tone of voice should be pleasant and courteous. The times when you choose to speak out as an interpreter may include your professional introduction, clarifications, addressing misunderstandings, audio issues or technical difficulties or call closings (that is, what you say when you leave a call). Remember to mute your microphone or move away from it whenever you sneeze or cough.

How to phrase your own interventions and responses

Your tone and choice of words can greatly affect how others perceive you and respond to your requests or comments. In Table 8.1, there are some phrases to use and some to avoid when you are speaking for yourself (Griffin, 2013):

Words and Phrases to Use	Words and Phrases to Avoid
A pleasure to help	Complain/complaint
Accept	Don't talk to me like that.
Accommodate	Give it a shot.
Action	I can't do much.
Apologize[136]	I can't help you with that.
Appreciate	I disagree.
Approve	I don't know.
Assist	I'm hanging up.
Expedite	It may take a long time.
Focus, grant	It's against our policy.
Grateful for your patience/understanding	It's not my area/problem.
Help/helpful	Nobody has told me that before.
No problem	Slow down!
Patience	That can't be.
Quickly	That's not the way it's done.
Recognize	There's nothing I can do about that.
Support	This has never happened before.
Thank you	We're getting nowhere.
Welcome	Will do what I can.
Will gladly assist you	You don't understand.
Work together	You have to call back.
	You must be doing something wrong.
	You're not being clear.

Table 8.1: Words and phrases to use and to avoid

[136] **Note:** *Only apologize if you have made a mistake.* You do not need to apologize for requesting repetitions, clarifications or having someone move a piece of equipment (for example), because such requests are part of your work. Over-apologizing can appear unprofessional.

Examples of how to respond politely

What might these interactions look like, and when will you need to use these phrases? Let's consider some examples.

Doctor: It took forever to get an interpreter today!

> *Don't* say, "There's nothing I can do about wait times."
>
> *Do* say, "Thank you for your patience. I'm ready to start interpreting."

Teacher: We can't hear you, interpreter!

> *Don't* say, "I'm speaking as loud as I can. I can't do anything about that."
>
> *Do* say, "The interpreter will continue to speak as loudly and clearly as possible. Are you able to move the device any closer or raise the volume?"

Bank customer: That's not the question I asked. You're not interpreting what I'm asking.

> *Don't* say, "Yes, I am! You must not be asking it right; I'm just saying what you're saying."
>
> *Do* say, "As the interpreter, I am interpreting everything as it's said. Would you like me to repeat your question?"

G. Responding to participants' requests for assistance

As an interpreter who works remotely, you will not be asked to give a patient a ride, the way face-to-face interpreters often get personal requests for assistance. Nor will you be asked to hold someone's hand while a nurse places an IV, or transport someone down a hallway or accompany them to their next appointment.

However, you may still receive requests from participants that fall outside your role.

Remote interpreters adhere to the codes of ethics and professional standards as face-to-face interpreters do (as you saw in Chapter 6 of this volume). Even though codes of ethics vary both within and across specializations and national borders, many codes mention that interpreters should only act within the role or scope of the interpreter and not step into other professional roles.

Despite participants' best intentions, however, remote interpreters are often asked to do things or share information and otherwise act outside their role.

What will participants ask you?

Participants may ask the remote interpreter many types of questions. Such questions could arise because a participant joined the session midway through, or they want to know the interpreter's opinion or simply because they know the interpreter has worked with certain participants before.

Below are some common examples of questions asked by participants after the session.

- What happened? (E.g., what the outcome was: a particular diagnosis, mediation agreement, educational plan.)
- Were other appointments or services scheduled?
- How did the interaction go?
- Did (another participant) arrive on time, behave professionally, etc.?
- Do you have information about (another participant)?

What should you say?

You *may* disclose how long the session lasted. Other than the duration, direct the participants to communicate directly with each other about the session. There may be certain cases where information must be shared outside of a session. Keep reading!

How to maintain privacy and confidentiality

Privacy vs. confidentiality

Privacy and confidentiality are highly sensitive matters in all interpreting specializations. Privacy refers to an individual's right to control access to their personal information. It also includes their ability to control how other people see them or obtain information about them.

Violations of privacy can involve circumstances such as participants being photographed or recorded without consent, being asked personal questions in a public setting, being seen without clothing, being observed while conducting personal behavior or disclosing information about abortions, health status, illegal drug use, and so on.

Confidentiality refers to how private information provided by individuals will be protected. For more information on privacy and confidentiality in codes of ethics for interpreters, see Chapter 6 of this volume. For information on privacy laws in remote interpreting, see Chapter 9 of this volume.

The type of information shared during an interpreted session can range from matters of national security or end-of-life situations to scheduling a home cleaning service or asking about breakfast at a hotel. Even if the session is for simple matters that don't sound as if they need to be kept confidential, many times information shared during the interpretation could identify a participant.

For this reason, interpreters have specific protocols for keeping information private and confidential. If that information becomes public, it can bring harmful consequences to participants and interpreters, including legal ones.

Who says so?

It is not only best practice or the right thing to do to keep confidential information private, but there are also laws in many countries about confidentiality. Here are some examples (also discussed in Chapter 9 of this volume).

- The Health Insurance Portability and Accountability Act (HIPAA) and the Children's Online Privacy Protection Act (COPPA) in the U.S.

- The Personal Information Protection and Electronic Documents Act (PIPEDA) in Canada
- The General Data Protection Regulation (GDPR) in the European Union
- The Australian Privacy Principles (APPs)
- The Brazilian Internet Act
- Decree 1377 in Colombia
- The French Data Protection Act
- The Information Technology Act in India
- The Italian Personal Data Protection Code
- The Personal Information Protection Commission in Japan
- The Data Protection Law in Morocco
- The Electronic Communications and Transactions (ECT) Act in South Africa

Violating privacy may cause harm

Not abiding by the regulations of your location, the location of the service and all participants, and those laws, requirements or policies that are specific to the service or to the interpreting specialization may cause *harm* and have legal consequences.

Violations of privacy may even lead to termination of your employment or contract.

Interpreting remotely means you may answer a call from almost anywhere in the world on a given day. Treat privacy and confidentiality as universal norms, since it is highly unlikely that you'll know every single local privacy law for every location for which you interpret.

Maintaining privacy and confidentiality may look slightly different across specializations or national borders. For example, legal interpreters will have to keep lawyer-client privilege in mind. (See more in Chapter 5 of Volume 2.) Faith-based interpreters who interpret a confession with a Catholic priest are required to abide by the same confidentiality the priest does: tell no one, no matter the content.[137]

What about your own privacy?

We can all agree that it's important for interpreters to know about privacy and confidentiality and the best practices surrounding them in order to protect the participants and avoid ethical violations.

However, as a remote interpreter you also have a duty to protect yourself. What would you do if a participant tried to take a photo of you during a video interpreting session? What if you find out that a participant is discreetly using a recording device? These are all important questions to ask the language service or any organization that you interpret for, as well as yourself, so that you can have a plan in place to address situations like these.

---

[137] Code of Canon Law. The Minister of the Sacrament of Penance. Can. 983. Retrieved from: http://www.vatican.va/archive/cod-iuris-canonici/eng/documents/cic_lib4-cann959-997_en.html

If you've never considered these questions before, know that in some countries you have rights as an interpreter when it comes to having your interpretation recorded.[138] Some interpreters may even have terms in their contracts about recordings. Being recorded while interpreting is a tricky topic to navigate. There are pros and cons to being recorded.

Pros and cons of being recorded

Being recorded for quality monitoring and coaching purposes may be part of your contract with a language service (these recordings are private, internal to the language service itself) and can be an incredibly beneficial experience for you. Seeing and hearing your own performance can make you a better interpreter!

In some legal interpreting situations, recordings are not optional. In order to be given the assignment, you must agree to being recorded. Since many interpreters identify possible errors in their interpretation after the session, having a recording means that a third party can view, confirm and correct any errors as necessary.

Think of the way a sporting event is recorded so that plays can be reviewed by referees before a decision is deemed final. Imagine how much more crucial such a review is when dealing, for example, with legal, medical or business outcomes. The ability to review a recording ensures fair outcomes for situations that could otherwise significantly alter the course of a participant's life.

Some interpreters don't wish to be recorded for the same reason that many doctors do not wish to be recorded: the recording can be used against them (even though they have done nothing wrong).

With the rapid and increased shift to remote interpreting, recording now has other implications for interpreters. For example, a remote presentation is held online and you interpret the content. The presentation recording goes on to gain millions of views and even generate revenue for the company. You did your interpretation once, and you were paid once. Is this situation fair to the interpreter? Is an interpretation rendered in real-time appropriate for recording and distribution after the session, or is another service, such as translation and subsequent voiceover, more suitable?

These questions and related ones are prevalent in the international debate about the recording of remote interpreters.

As you can see, there is no simple answer to the question of how to handle recordings. Many factors will affect your decision about whether to permit such recordings. You may even decide to increase your rates if a recording is to take place. Do your research, consult with colleagues and check with your professional association for guidance in your country and specializations.

---

[138] For example, see Gio Lester. (2012). Recording, Consent and Copyrights: What We Need to Know. Retrieved from: https://najit.org/recording-consent-and-copyrights-what-we-need-to-know/

Other aspects of maintaining privacy and confidentiality in remote interpreting

H. Handling notes

The main goal of any interpretation is to render the message accurately and completely. Most interpreters rely on note-taking to meet this goal. However, note-taking opens up the possibility of revealing information from each session if anyone were to gain access to these notes.

Depending on your language service's or the organization's or client's guidelines on note-taking and note handling, notes may be taken on paper and destroyed immediately after the session (using shredders or a disposal service that only designated people have access to) on a secure computer or on whiteboards where it is simple to erase information as soon as the session ends.

If you work from home, clarify the requirements for note handling and destruction. Remember, even if you think that no one else could possibly read your notes, they must still be properly disposed of!

Examples of Privacy Violations

The interpreters in these stories had no ill intentions. However, their anecdotes illustrate the importance of shredding all private information before leaving the workplace or private area in the office.

1. At the end of a long day filled with interpreted sessions, Natasha, a work-from-home remote interpreter, decided to take her notes with her to a café to study some unknown terms she had noted down. While she had good intentions, she should have transferred the terms to a separate notebook and never kept the personal information of participants. To make matters worse, she left these notes in her car while she ran another errand. Unfortunately, someone broke into her car, stealing the notes, among other items.
2. Pierre works as a video remote interpreter in a call center. He knows he cannot take notes home. However, at the end of his shift, rather than using the shredder at the call center exit, he stores his notes in his wire mesh locker in a common area. Not only is he violating the language service's policy on note destruction, but also this kind of locker allows the notes to be accessible and visible to others who should not have access to them. Even though Pierre did not take the notes outside the building, the language service terminated his employment due to this privacy violation.

I. Data collection

In many instances, interpreters collect information to keep track of the session: for example, when it happened and who was involved. This information is typically requested to ensure accurate billing and tracking of services used.

In remote interpreting, most of this information may be shared through the internet. As much as we try to protect our online information, we know that someone may be malicious and skilled enough to hack into a system and obtain that information.

Of course, there are many ways to have layers of security to prevent anyone outside an organization accessing the information that reduce the risk of exposure. Moreover, not every country enforces regulations about handling private and confidential information the same way.

Protect your privacy too

In addition to protecting information related to participants, remote interpreters should also protect information about themselves or the organization they work for. It may be fine to share the name of the state or province where you live, especially if you are licensed in that area (see licensure information in Chapter 9 of this volume) but refrain from sharing more details.

If you work for a language service, you may also be asked not to share your schedule or staffing information (for example, how many people work with you). If you're not sure what you should or shouldn't share, ask the language service or organization you work with so that you know how to respond to questions you receive from participants or others.

Breaking confidentiality

When can an interpreter disclose private and confidential information?

If for any important reason you are asked, by anyone, to share your experience from an interpreted session, follow your organization's guidelines (and the law!) to reduce the risks of liability and of sharing that information.

If you are an independent contractor, you may consider reaching out to a professional network for guidance if you need it, including a professional association. That guidance can be valuable. For example, it is best practice to never put any private health information in an unencrypted email.

Below are some examples of cases when you might be asked to disclose private and confidential information:

- Acute, life-threatening situations
- A debrief session
- When you change shifts (for example, during labor and delivery of a baby) and another interpreter comes on the call and needs briefing
- Team interpreting (again, your partner may need briefing)
- Customer complaints or grievances
- Quality assurance
- To testify in court (for example, after receiving a subpoena)

How should an interpreter share the information?

If you *must* share confidential information about a session, doing so in person and in a private, protected environment is ideal. In remote interpreting, in-person communication may be in call centers. When you work from a home office, then a telephone call, videoconference or protected digital communications (for example, end-to-end encrypted email through a secure email provider or system) are the best options.

Important Information on Breaking Confidentiality

Only share participants' identifiers (information that could identify them) in private, ideally during a live meeting, and *only* if doing so is absolutely necessary and legally permissible or required and you are speaking with persons *authorized to know that private information.*

If you are in doubt, you may need to consult a lawyer. Protect yourself.

Important ways to protect yourself

There's more to privacy than meets the eye

As part of the service that interpreters provide, we tend to focus on protecting information that does not belong to us; however, it is also important to protect our own privacy and that of the organizations we work for.

Consider what to do in circumstances like the following. What will you say if someone tries to take a photo of you during an interpreted session? Or if someone is discreetly using a device to record the session? Or if someone is simply trying to find out your work hours?

If you ask remote interpreters these questions, their answers (and comfort levels with those situations) vary from person to person. We advise you to research the situation by making inquiries both where you live and where you work about what is permissible and not permissible and how best to protect your privacy. Then create some scripts to use if these situations arise.

For example, video interpreters in healthcare situations may alert the provider that a patient is recording them. The provider, who may also not wish to be recorded, will likely stop them. Some spoken language interpreters also report pausing their video if photos or recordings are being taken against their wishes.

If you do develop scripts to manage these increasingly common situations and concerns, consult with the language services or other organizations that you work with to make sure they are aware of and approve what you say in situations such as these. Increasingly, they are becoming aware of the problem and may have policies to support you and perhaps even scripts for how to manage them.

A True Story

An interpreter we will call Mara interpreted a remote session for a participant who liked her interpreting. He asked Mara where she was located to see if she was local to his area because he wanted to continue to have her interpret for him.

Though Mara gave the correct response—that she could not disclose this information, or give him details about her location—the participant was able to look up her location online. He found an address for the call center. He then went there in person to talk to Mara!

Fortunately, the language service had security measures in place and was able to resolve the situation.

→ Section 8.1 Review

In this section, we showed how remote interpreters can conduct themselves professionally, for example:

- Clothing etiquette: Dress for success, keeping in mind both participants' visual considerations (for video interpreting) and organizational policies.
- Body language: Be careful of reacting physically. Maintain good posture and an appropriate facial expression. Even if you're not on video, remember that your body language can be perceptible in your tone of voice.
- Camera presence (video calls only): Display engagement through eye contact, posture and attentiveness.
- Backdrop or background (video calls only): Avoid distracting backdrops or backgrounds, bright colors or visible objects. Make sure that your video quality is adequate.
- Call readiness: Arrive on time and well prepared with all the technology and resources that you need to begin a session.
- Tone of voice and positive scripting: Smile and be courteous when speaking up as the interpreter to intervene and remember to be assertive and calm (not hesitant or apologetic). When interpreting, match the tone of the speakers.
- Responding to participants' requests for assistance: Abide by the regulations of your location, the location of the service and the communicative autonomy of all participants.
- Handling notes: Destroy any notes right after the session, even if you think no one can read them.
- Data collection: Collect required data in a way that does not reveal any participant's protected information.

Section 8.2 Working for a Language Service

→ Learning objective 8.2

After completing this section, the remote interpreter will be able to explain typical requirements and expectations for interpreters employed by a language service or other organization.

→ Section 8.2 Overview

This section lays out some of the most important general expectations and requirements for remote interpreters who work for a language service, whether it is a for-profit or nonprofit language service.[139] It is especially applicable for interpreters employed by language company call centers. However, most if not all the information in this section can also be helpful for staff interpreters at schools, hospitals, government agencies and other organizations that employ dedicated interpreters (or those acting as full-time interpreters and translators).

In all cases, the *quality* of the service is essential. The interpreting profession is unique in that those who use interpreting services depend completely on the knowledge and skills of the interpreter. They don't typically know the other language. Complete trust in the service is vital for all participants.

Consequently, any language service of a certain size will probably have a quality assurance program in place. While some of the requirements listed in this section vary according to the modality and specialization and type of organization, many requirements are broad and general—and all are important.

→ Section 8.2 Content

Working for a language service

Remote interpreters who are employed by a language service or another organization have rules to abide by and expectations to meet, both on and off their calls. These professional requirements are established in part so that anyone who purchases or uses interpreter services can expect consistent quality and a positive customer experience.

In order to create this consistency and also operate efficiently, language services have layers of employee support. Interpreters may have leads (colleagues who provide leadership and help a particular team of interpreters work effectively),[140] supervisors, managers or others who oversee the performance of interpreters. Management staff can monitor job performance and oversee other employee behavior, such as interaction with colleagues and professional communication in the workplace. We will discuss these areas in more detail throughout this section.

Do you know if you want a career as a staff interpreter at a language service (or another organization)? Or do you prefer to work as a freelance (contract) interpreter?[141] There are a few points you may want to consider when you make that decision.

First, read Sections 8.2 and 8.3!

Before we begin, *even if you already know that you want to work as an independent contractor*, we urge you to read this section carefully, along with the next section (which addresses professional requirement for contract remote interpreters).

---

139 Many nonprofit language services exist, including community language banks; refugee interpreter services; services run by nonprofits that serve immigrants; nonprofit hospitals with their own interpreter services; and remote interpreting nonprofit networks shared across organizations, among others.

140 "Lead" is a U.S. term that refers to an employee who works with other employees in a group with the goal of helping the group to perform their work efficiently and effectively. Leads, or lead workers, may also interact with supervisors and management to discuss their team, organize meetings and otherwise act in a quasi-managerial capacity for a team of workers.

141 The terms "freelance interpreter" and "contract interpreter" are used interchangeably in this textbook. They mean essentially the same thing: a self-employed interpreter who works for multiple language services or other organizations.

And even if you already know that you want to work as a full-time employee of a language service or any other organization, read the next section too.

The reason to read both sections 8.2 and 8.3 of this chapter with care is that being employed by a language service or another organization and directly contracting with one as a freelance interpreter involve quite a number of similarities yet many important differences. Keep in mind too that any organization may work with both self-employed interpreters as well as staff interpreters, so you will need to read the next section to understand the work opportunities available for remote interpreters.

What kind of organization do you want to work for?

The first thing to be aware of if you are considering a career as a staff interpreter at a language service or any larger organization is that language services and other large organizations typically lay out their expectations and requirements based on their own organizational goals. Many of them aim for high interpreter performance and customer satisfaction. They may also have genuine concerns for the well-being of their employees.

Some organizations are deeply concerned with language access—that is, the goal of supporting equity by providing language assistance to those who do not speak the language of service in order to make meaningful access to community (and other) services possible for them.

Other organizations may be more concerned with profits. Inform yourself by doing research about them. If you can, talk to employees who already work there. This will be time well spent and help you make decisions that are right for you. You can align your work with your own values.

Applying for work at an organization that provides language services

What to expect when you apply to work as a remote interpreter

> **Note:** The content on the next few pages is based primarily on U.S. language services. However, increasingly the authors are seeing similar conditions, processes and requirements developing in language services in other countries.

Remote interpreters may work in OPI, in video interpreting (VRI, VRS or RSI) or both. Those who work for a language service typically work either from a home office or a call center.

Organizations that provide language services can be based anywhere in the world. So can their interpreters. It is becoming more common for remote interpreters in call centers to interpret for participants and services located both across whole countries and even in other countries. This trend will likely continue to spread rapidly over the years to come.

Remote interpreters who apply to work for an organization providing language services might be required to fulfill any of the following as employees:

- Take and pass a language proficiency test and/or an interpreting skills test for all their working languages, or provide successful test results prior to hire.*
- Provide proof of past professional training* (or the organization might provide training—or additional training—after hire).

- Obtain any required licensures or professional certifications prior to hire,* or agree to do so within a certain timeframe once hired. (For more information on how to build on our portfolio of credentials, see Chapter 10 of this volume.)
- Adhere to an established code of ethics, demonstrate basic interpreting skills, perform standard protocols and meet general qualifications required by the interpreting profession of the interpreter's country or specialization.*

*Self-employed interpreters may be asked to meet the same requirements prior to signing a contract with an organization that provides language services.

Legal considerations

Dishonesty doesn't pay

Part of professionalism is operating with honest practice. As you saw in Chapter 6 of this volume, the majority of codes of ethics around the world for interpreters *require* ethical, honest conduct.

Below is a real-life example of why it doesn't pay to be a dishonest interpreter.

> *An interpreter that we'll call John Doe interprets as an over-the-phone interpreter from home. Lately, he hasn't been getting as many calls. Because of this, his pay has decreased. John concludes an interpreted session one day but realizes he can stay on the line a few extra minutes and get paid for them. He does this a little from time to time to increase his pay. He thinks,* What harm could this really do? It's only a few minutes here and there. No one will even know the difference!

These minutes add up and can have a huge impact on any organization. Today, in remote interpreting, everything can be tracked electronically and automatically. Even when you think you can get away with doing certain things, *connection times, both from the remote interpreter side and the participants' side, are tracked in the platforms.*

In short, the language service discovered what John was doing—and he lost his job for it. The company even had the option to pursue legal action against him. Though we often think language services and other organizations have less control over self-employed interpreters, a similar result could occur had John been a contract interpreter with the company. A violation of this type is grounds for contract termination or other consequences.

Everyone makes mistakes, of course, so if you realize there are any errors in the number of actual minutes of interpretation you reported, or any other possible errors, simply alert the organization you work for as soon as possible. One mistake is not a pattern. Honesty about mistakes is noticed and generally valued.

Knowing anything that might have gone wrong *helps* organizations that provide language services. They can then plan what to do about the problem. If something happened to you, it has probably happened with other remote interpreters.

Giving away interpretations for free

As mentioned earlier, interpreters are sometimes asked to collect information from participants to ensure accurate billing and tracking of services. Asking for names, locations and other pieces of data can get monotonous, but these questions may be *extremely important*.

There have been cases where everything went right with the interpretation—the video and audio were perfect, and the interpreter felt good about their performance—but at the end of the month, the language service could not invoice for that session because the interpreter failed to document the required information. If the language service can't invoice for the session, that means it is forced to give away the interpreting at no charge.

While most interpreters are caring people who want to help their communities, too many of these unbilled sessions hurt the organization and, in the end, the interpreter.

Investments: a two-way street

Many organizations invest money, time and effort into developing and supporting their employees. They may sponsor professional development for interpreters, including paying for their participation in conferences, workshops, trainings and mentoring programs. A language service, a hospital, or a school may also pay for the interpreter's certifications and licenses and purchase books and other resources for them.

You are more likely to get free professional development as an employed interpreter than as a self-employed interpreter for legal and cost reasons, among others.

It is generous of organizations to invest in their staff, but they also need a return on their investment. After all, if they pay a lot of money and a few months later you leave to go work for a different language service or organization, they lose that investment.

In order to have the resources to sponsor these events and benefits, language services and other organizations need to make sure the programs are sustainable. This is the reason why you may sign agreements that involve a way to "return" that investment, perhaps in the form of a commitment to work for a minimum number of months or to create training materials to share the knowledge you acquired.

Working across multiple countries, states or provinces

Even though you may not think that you need to pay attention to legal matters as an employee, or that laws in other areas or countries don't apply to you, that certainly is not the case in remote interpreting! Find ways to keep up with laws and regulations that affect your work and your benefits as an employee. They will potentially depend not only on the city, the state or province and the country in which you reside but also the ones you serve. (See Chapter 9 of this volume for details.)

The organization you work for has to do its part as an employer. That is, the organization must be up to date with any legal aspects of the service offered, including specific implications of having employees in many locations who interpret for sessions located in other countries and legal jurisdictions.

One legal aspect that may relate to location of the business is liability insurance and coverage. In many instances, employees are likely to have liability insurance covered by the company, but each country, state or province may have different specifications or types of coverage.

Terms and conditions

You've likely seen the phrase "terms and conditions" when you click a little checkbox online, which states that "you have read and agree to" everything in an online contract.

If you work as a remote interpreter for an organization, especially a larger one, you will probably have to review a document about the requirements for your behavior whether you work as an employee or a contractor. *Make sure you read it.* Read it with care, be sure you understand it and decide if you are comfortable making these commitments. Don't be shy about asking questions about anything you don't understand.

This legal document may be defined as the terms, rules and guidelines for acceptable behavior the interpreter must respect and follow on the job. These guidelines could vary according to the nature of the business and legal requirements for the organization, which will depend on its location. But when you sign this document, you are making a *legal* commitment. If you violate any of the terms in the document, you could potentially lose your job or contract.

These employee or contractor agreements usually include many different requirements. However, one that is usually emphasized for remote interpreters is the importance of privacy.

a. Privacy at a call center

Organizations that provide language services typically have requirements to protect the participants' and the interpreter's privacy. When working at a call center, for example, the organization could require the remote interpreter to not have any electronic devices near them, such as cell phones, tablets, personal computers.

Organizations may provide shredders for call center employees to dispose of any written information, specifically including notes you may take during the call. Interpreters are increasingly required to dispose of any participant information, including their notes, before they leave the work area.

The call center may be separated from the rest of the office to provide a quiet, private area for the interpreter and participants to communicate. Additionally, the building must be secure with limited access only to those individuals who will abide by the privacy requirements.

Yes, in call centers the interpreters may be working quite close to each other. But they are provided with noise-cancelling headsets or headphones to eliminate hearing, or being heard by, other interpreters.

b. Privacy in your home office

The same requirements apply if you work for an organization from your home. Meeting those requirements, however, requires a higher level of trust from the organization. Your employment contract might list these requirements to ensure you are legally bound by them.

Other factors to consider

Here are a few other factors to consider if you decide if you want to work (or continue working) for a language service or another organization.

- Work schedules: You may have to adhere to a specific work schedule as an employee.
- Breaks and meals: Legal requirements for breaks and meals vary depending on the country, state or employment status. Check with your employer.
- Answer time requirements: Interpreters may have required answer times for their calls in order to serve participants in a timely manner.
- Session-time protocols: How long you spend on a given session, also referred to in many call center environments as "handle time," will depend on the organization. Check with your employer about what protocols to follow on handle times for long interpreted sessions to avoid fatigue.[142]
- Quality expectations and requirements: These expectations and requirements may be depend on your employer. They are so important for employed (and self-employed) interpreters that the subsection below addresses them in detail.

Quality assurance expectations and requirements

What is quality assurance (QA)?

Quality assurance is a systematic process implemented by an organization in order to ensure that the service provided meets quality standards. QA processes support interpreters through routine call monitoring and coaching to improve their performance and help build their confidence. A robust QA program truly distinguishes a professional, established language service from an amateur or emerging one.

Why QA programs are important

When a well-rounded QA program is in place, those who receive interpreting services can also be confident that they are experiencing quality services from interpreters. QA programs for remote interpreters have been developing in a serious way, gradually, since the 1990s.

For larger language services in particular, and often even in midsize services, QA has become sophisticated and driven by key performance indicator (KPI) data that can be quantified.

As an interpreter, you can learn a great deal from a solid QA program. What you learn will truly help you improve your performance and skills.

Does the idea of being monitored for your performance make you feel a little scared? We'll talk about that. But first, take comfort in the idea that as a QA best practice, those people who monitor you have been remote interpreters. They know and understand what you do.

How QA works

Let's look at how QA works in practice. This is where QA for face-to-face and remote interpreting is completely different! Technology not only allows remote interpreting to happen; but it also provides opportunities to monitor and evaluate your calls *regularly*. That situation may be quite different from most face-to-face interpreting, where you may rarely get feedback or support.

[142] Such protocols may be similar or identical for self-employed interpreters who contract with the same language service.

In addition, depending on the organization, your calls could be recorded for further review. Areas that QA programs will assess and score for remote interpreters cover many aspects of the interpreter's performance, often including professional etiquette, interpreting skills, ethical conduct and adherence to protocols.

QA scorecards for any profession are designed to be objective. Evaluators observing calls need to have a standardized tool to measure performance, which will ensure that performance is being assessed in the same way among evaluators and from interpreter to interpreter. Additionally, QA departments regularly hold calibration sessions to continually validate that the scorecard is being applied in the same way by the whole team. The data generated is then analyzed (as key performance indicators) and compared to benchmarks for data-driven decisions.

What the QA program will assess

Here is a list of aspects of your performance a typical remote interpreting QA program might assess.

a. Adherence to interpreter ethics and best practices (including accuracy and completeness)
b. Message conversion and delivery
    - Culturally appropriate forms of address
    - Proper grammar and syntax
    - No delays or long hesitations in transferring the message
c. Adherence to interpreter protocols
    - Professional introduction
    - Briefing instructions
    - Use of direct speech, unless indirect speech is appropriate
    - Maintaining transparency when intervening
    - Use of appropriate interpretation mode
d. Addressing communication breakdowns
e. Customer service
    - Courteous tone of voice during direct interactions
    - Offering assistance as needed
    - Appropriate problem-solving and issue escalation[143]
f. Adherence to organizational policies or other regulations
g. Call closings
    - Confirm no additional assistance is needed from you
    - Close the call with both parties in a manner appropriate to the context

143 To escalate a customer service concern, after the call—or in an extreme case, during the call—consult or report the situation to the appropriate supervisor, who would either advise you what to say or would speak directly to the participants.

For video interpreters, QA monitoring may also address the interpreter's on-screen presentation, which may include:

- Clothing etiquette
- Body language
- Camera presence (discussed in Chapters 3 and 4 of this volume)
- Appropriate background/backdrop
- Camera angle
- Appearing on camera, unless there is a valid reason to disable video

Do Not Disable Your Video

Here is an example of what a QA program might capture and discuss with you after a call.

If a call comes in as a video call, this is the modality that was requested and paid for by the participants. Sometimes an interpreter will disable video for a valid reason (for example, a poor internet connection at the participant end might make it impossible to continue interpreting on video) or for a reason that is not valid (e.g., to eat something, or because someone is entering the interpreter's space who has no authority to be there).

It is important not to disable your video unless you have a valid reason to do so and have communicated this reason with all participants. Document the reasons as soon as possible so that you do not forget them! As needed, report them after the call.

QA and quality improvement programs provide both a method of detection and prevention. QA departments may work with training teams. When QA staff notice trends in certain challenges for their interpreters, these are the topics they also end up coaching interpreters on most often. They can also pass this information along to the training team to develop continuing education for those areas of challenge.

In addition to routine monitoring of interpretations, QA may partner with another team to address customer concerns as well. In other words, if a participant states that you struggled with specific terminology on a call (for example, oncology terms or insurance vocabulary), QA follows up and provides resources to improve your knowledge of that topic.

Benefits of quality monitoring

Quality monitoring is the ongoing evaluation of performance that includes call monitoring, scoring, coaching, feedback and reporting. The QA team can review your interpreted sessions in various ways. Some organizations may have call recordings, others monitor you in real time, and you may not even know you are being monitored at the moment!

Benefits to quality monitoring include:

- Immediate feedback on your performance, including your strengths and areas of improvement.
- An opportunity for you and the QA team to discuss unusual or difficult situations, why they occurred and how they can be remedied.
- Motivation to perform to the best of one's ability, which may include achieving higher monitoring scores.

- Fulfillment of ongoing monitoring requirements agreed on with clients in their efforts to comply with industry standards.
- Visibility to areas of improvement for interpreters.
- Trends in common challenges that face remote interpreters, which can lead to helpful training and continuing education.
- Proactively implemented performance improvement or corrective action measures as needed. (In other words, the QA team will guide you on what you can do to improve to address specific concerns.)
- A mentoring relationship that leads to the ability and habit to self-reflect on your interpreting performance. (See Chapter 5 of this volume for detailed information on self-evaluation.)
- High quality interpretation and customer service.

Implementing feedback

Don't be afraid of feedback. It is essential for growth! When done well, it helps you continually develop the skills you need to excel.

Receiving feedback benefits you by pointing out your areas of strength and their positive impact in the interpreted session. Likewise, addressing your weaknesses alerts you to opportunities for change. Feedback keeps the job challenging, interesting and adventurous.

Your QA department may provide feedback in multiple forms, such as live coaching sessions, written reports or a combination of both.

But receiving feedback is only part of the process. The other part falls on you: accepting and implementing that feedback.

As we discussed in Chapter 5 of this volume, accepting feedback on your performance can feel uncomfortable at first. Yet *accepting* feedback without becoming defensive or self-protective is an important first step that will allow you to better *implement* feedback.

For example, let's say you're a new interpreter, and you have trouble following the protocols for transparency. You're coached on it, but you think, *Oh, transparency is a waste of time. I mean, both sides don't need to hear* everything*, and QA is being too picky for pointing it out.* You have not accepted this feedback; therefore, it will be difficult for you to implement it.

However, if you listen to feedback with an open mind, you may change your perspective. After you hear a QA representative share the experience that they were once accused of a side conversation due to not remaining transparent when they interpreted in the past, you can see why it's important to follow the protocol each and every time.

Just as when you receive feedback from a peer in more informal settings, it's important to:

a. Be open and receptive.

b. Listen.

c. Reflect.

d. Engage!

Ongoing feedback on your performance as an interpreter is *invaluable*. Reading Chapter 5 of this volume carefully will allow you to get the most out of the QA feedback. And remember: it's all right to ask questions!

Check in with QA or those who supervise you regularly. Actively seek personalized feedback on your areas of strength and weakness. Be sure to be proactive in seeking help and do not shy away from feedback; on the contrary, embrace it! When quality monitoring is a formalized process, you can also dispute any disagreements to ensure you are getting a fair and consistent evaluation.

→ Section 8.2 Review

This section reviewed many aspects of working as an employee for an organization. Among those that you need to remember are:

- When you apply to work for an organization that provides language services, have documents ready that attest to your language and interpreting skills, if you have them. If you don't have them, testing may be provided by the organization.
- Keep in mind that your well-being and the organization's best interests should be aligned.
- Be aware of key legal and professional requirements or expectations for working as an employee, for example:
  - Be ethical and honest.
  - Honor contractual obligations to remain employed with an organization for a specified period of time. (Many organizations invest in their employees' professional growth and development, and that investment may lead to these requirements.)
  - Pay attention to different laws and regulations when working for organizations that provide services across multiple countries, states or provinces, including any insurance liability implications.
  - Study and make certain you agree with key terms and conditions in your contract (including privacy requirements). Read them thoroughly and understand every aspect of a contract to avoid future misunderstandings or confusion.
- You may have to agree to specified work hours. Also, check with your employer about what is expected from you about breaks and mealtimes as well as answer and handle times for calls.
- It is now common to have quality assurance processes for employed interpreters to ensure that the service meets quality standards. QA processes help improve your performance and build your confidence through monitoring and coaching. Be open to feedback and ready to implement it, no matter how experienced you are.

Section 8.3 Self-employed Interpreters

→ Learning objective 8.3

After completing this section, the remote interpreter will be able to explain the typical requirements and expectations for self-employed interpreters.

→ Section 8.3 Overview

Most people would agree that a self-employed person is an individual who makes a living working for themselves. (If you are self-employed, you are your own manager!) This definition could differ depending on your area or country of residence, so it is important to become familiar with the specific laws and regulations that apply to you.

In this section, we cover the general professional, legal and logistic expectations for self-employed remote interpreters. Keep in mind that most of the information in this section would apply in the U.S. and many other countries, but be sure to do careful research about your own legal jurisdiction.

This textbook does not provide legal advice. Nonetheless, it offers important general guidance and areas to consider as you decide whether or not to work (or continue working) as a self-employed remote interpreter.

This section outlines the basics of what you need to know about working as an independent contractor. It discusses what language services and other organizations or clients will expect of you. You will explore topics such as ethics, quality assurance, professional development and continuing education through the lens of self-employment. By the end of this section, you will have a clearer understanding of what it means to be a contract (freelance) remote interpreter.

→ Section 8.3 Content

Self-employed? You are a business!

Working for yourself can be exciting and demanding at the same time. Even though you are technically your own manager, there will always be someone you're accountable to for your performance.

As a self-employed or freelance remote interpreter, you might report to either an organization that provides language services or a direct client. A *direct client* is your own client. It could be an individual or organization (such as a motor vehicle agency, a school, a lawyer's office, a therapist in private practice, a bank, an insurance company or a health department). You contract directly with that entity. In other words, you are not engaged by a language service: you have your own contract with that person or organization.

It is important to understand that if you are a self-employed interpreter, *you are a language service provider*. You are a business!

As a result, you will certainly need to understand and develop contracts. Seek legal guidance before you start and throughout your freelance career. Also look for resources online, including your professional association. For example, the American Translators Association (ATA) offers a direct client outreach kit, and even an article about that kit.[144] ATA also hosts what appears to be the largest annual international conference for interpreters and translators.[145] Interpreter conferences are a wonderful way to learn how other remote interpreters work with direct clients.

As a freelance interpreter, work hard to develop an excellent understanding of any organization that engages you to provide remote interpreting. Learn how they work. Remember that you are an organization, engaging with another one. Be mindful that although you work remotely, you still represent any organization that you contract with.

Professionalism, for all interpreters, is of the *utmost* importance. As Chapter 6 of this volume showed you, professionalism appears as an ethical requirement in nearly every code of ethics for interpreters around the world!

Running a business

Let us repeat: as a self-employed interpreter, *you are a language service provider.*

In this capacity, you provide your services directly to another individual or business as your own business entity. This legal concept exists in probably most countries around the world.

That is why you should consult with a lawyer and ideally an accountant when you first set yourself up as an independent contractor, so that they can advise you on the legal and accounting requirements for your business *both in the legal jurisdiction where you reside and those localities where you provide services* (in other states or provinces, or even other countries).

What to plan for

The following are critical aspects to consider and plan for.

a. Legal requirements for contract interpreters

Find out the legal requirements of your state/province or municipality in order to set yourself up and function as a business—whether you rent office space or work from home. For example:

- Find out if you need to register a business. If so, do it promptly.
- Do you need a trade name (a name for your business)? Are special business taxes involved? Investigate.
- Identify your business structure.
    - For example, are you a sole proprietorship? A partnership? Some type of limited liability company?

144 Client Outreach Kit. ATA. Retrieved from: https://www.atanet.org/career-education/client-outreach-kit/ and https://www.atanet.org/wp-content/uploads/2020/10/4407_14_cash_zampaulo.pdf

145 See https://www.atanet.org/ata-events/annual-conference/

- Get licenses and permits, if needed.
    - For example, are you allowed to set up a business in your home freely, or will you need a permit to do so?
- Will you engage contract interpreters to work with you as subcontractors, for example, as your team interpreters? If so, you are potentially obligated to require special forms for your subcontractors to sign.
    - For example, in the U.S., your subcontractors would have to fill out a W-9 form for you each year, and then after the end of the year you (or your accountant) would issue them special legal forms (for example, a 1099 form for every subcontractor, which you then send to the federal and state government to specify what you paid each subcontractor, assuming you paid them more than a certain threshold).
- Make sure you understand the difference between engaging contractors and hiring employees.
    - For example, in the U.S. under federal and state language laws, you can't *require* that an interpreter show up at a particular date and time to work with you—but you might be able to set up a contractual offer where the interpreter can *agree* to do so. (But this is not legal advice! *Always* consult a lawyer in your jurisdiction to guide you on legal issues.)
    - If you hire employees, another huge set of legal requirements typically comes into play that you might not want to deal with, so be careful to understand the difference between engaging other interpreters as subcontractors versus employees. If you are ever audited on these issues, the penalties and legal costs could be steep.
- Learn about self-employment income taxes *and plan accordingly*.
    - For example, you might have to pay estimated taxes quarterly, not all in one annual sum, and could face penalties if you fail to do so.

b. Business type

The legal requirements for setting up a business vary depending on the country and local jurisdiction, although many general requirements for freelancers are somewhat similar.

But *if you need to register a business,* it is important to understand the legal ramifications of each business type and its legal status. We repeat this point so many times because it is hugely important for your future: consult with a lawyer before making any decisions. (In some countries, there may be business services that help you set up your business for a reasonable fee.)

c. Recordkeeping

As a self-employed remote interpreter, you will need to develop a reliable system to note down information about the session in order to invoice it accurately later (and also if any critical incidents should arise).

This information that you will note down is *not* a violation of privacy: it has nothing to do with the individuals you interpret for but the session itself: organization, location, contact person (if appropriate), date, time, duration—whatever information the organization requires you to note down, and also the information that you need for your own legal records.

Document, document, document! Keep a log of each interpreted encounter, especially its date, time and duration, and whether anything unexpected happened. Keep records of communication, especially of decisions made and confirmations.

Having this documentation is essential if any problems arise. For example, a participant may complain that the interpreter hung up on them, and you can refer to your documentation that the call dropped.

d. Bookkeeping

Here are some important bookkeeping items to consider.

- Confirm how pay rates will be handled.
  - Will your client pay you by the minute? Hour? Per assignment? Per half-day or day?
  - Are they willing to pay more if your interpretation is recorded and replayed in the future?
  - If so, is that extra fee for their use of the recording specified in your contract?
- Learn whether you need to submit invoices to be paid and when you will be paid.
  - Typically, a contractor gets paid by the job, but most self-employed remote interpreters (unless they are conference interpreters) are paid by the minute or hour.
  - You might then need to invoice monthly for all work performed.
- Even if your language service or participant is keeping track of your billable time and pay, you should keep your own records.
- Know your tax laws.
  - In the U.S., for example, you are usually responsible for your own tax payments, including quarterly estimated self-employment taxes (where applicable). The estimations are adjusted each year at tax time and you will either pay what you owe or receive a refund if you overpaid estimated taxes.
- Keep records of all trainings, credentials or any other documents you have acquired for your résumé.

e. Liability insurance

As we have discussed so far, running a business is a major undertaking. Being *self*-employed means just that: *you* run the show. It is imperative to protect yourself as a business owner. For example, in the U.S., having liability insurance is essential.

Check to see what is available to you in your country, state, province and city. Talk to other people and see how it has worked for them to be self-employed in your profession, since most likely that experience is not the same for each industry.

Inform yourself as much as possible and don't base your decision solely on one source. In some countries, there can be many different types of liability insurance coverages. For example, in the U.S., interpreters often have general liability insurance but also errors and omission insurance, which is now so common that some insurers even refer to it as "interpreter professional liability insurance."[146]

Know that any contractor is likely to have some liability. You need to cover yourself in the event of an error—whether it actually occurred or someone incorrectly accuses you of an error.

Additionally, liability insurance typically does not prevent a company from suing a contractor, even if that company's insurance covered the costs of being sued over mistakes you made. Do your research and find a policy that's right for you.

f. Ethical practice

Regardless of the modality you practice in this profession, there will be a code of ethics to abide by. (See Chapter 6 of this volume to learn which codes you should be looking for.)

Professionalism, in one form or another, will almost certainly be in the code of ethics you are expected to adhere to. In the U.S., the principle of professionalism from the *National Standards of Practice for Interpreters in Health Care* of the National Council on Interpreting in Health Care (NCIHC) has as its main objective "To uphold the public's trust in the interpreting profession" and states that "Interpreters at all times act in a professional and ethical manner." Though this tenet was intended for healthcare interpreters, many other codes of ethics include similar statements, and they generally apply to all interpreters.

In addition to abiding by your code of ethics while interpreting, you will also practice as an ethical business. For example:

- Identify your general principles that would lead to fair business practices.
  - Write a business vision and mission statement if you wish. (Look up those terms online if they are unfamiliar to you.)
  - Draft a policy document to state your own business practices.
  - If you have a website, post these documents.
- Write out specific statements that will assist you in making ethical day-to-day decisions.
  - For example, examine your code of ethics and make decisions about what do to in common difficult situations you know you will encounter often.
- Allow that ethical challenges or dilemmas do not always have a perfect solution.
  - Make the best decisions you can make in the moment.
  - Take responsibility for your decisions.
  - Stay calm and courteous if things go wrong. (And always document everything after the session.)

---

146 See, for example, Interpreter Insurance. Trusted Choice. Retrieved from: https://www.trustedchoice.com/n/54/interpreter-insurance/.

Remember; one's reputation is everything. As U.S. Founding Father and inventor Benjamin Franklin[147] said, "It takes many good deeds to build a good reputation, and only one bad one to lose it."

Quality assurance expectations

As a self-employed remote interpreter, you may work for one or several language services (in addition to or instead of other organizations). If the language service is of any significant size, it may have a quality assurance program with the same kind of monitoring and expectations as quality assurance programs for employees, discussed in the previous section.

The quality monitoring could be done by the language service you contract with or by a third party engaged by the language service—or even a vendor engaged by another organization, for example, a hospital. For more details on QA and what to expect, see the previous section.

Be proactive: plan for success

The following list will get you started, whether you work as an employee or you are self-employed. Make an inventory of what you have, what you need and how you are going to get there. As French author Antoine de Saint-Exupéry wrote in *The Little Prince,* "A goal without a plan is just a wish."

Tips for success

Have or develop:

- A résumé and short biography of your experience.
- Business cards (digital or physical depending on your needs).
- A portfolio of credentials. (See Chapter 10 of this volume.)
- An appropriate email address (not "fangirl99@hotmail.com").
- A telephone number.
- A *professional* voicemail message.
- If possible, a website or social media presence.
    - A website confers credibility and allows you to truly market yourself effectively and show off the reasons you are highly qualified.
    - It also provides an easy way for potential direct clients to contact you.
    - LinkedIn, Facebook, Twitter and Instagram are examples of large-scale social media used extensively by professionals to help brand themselves.
- A branding statement.
    - Research online to learn more about branding statements.[148]

---

[147] Franklin was also a famous statesman, author, publisher, scientist, diplomat, printer, philosopher and polymath.

[148] You might also wish to subscribe to a U.S. podcast called "Brand the Interpreter" at https://www.brandtheinterpreter.com

- Keep your branding statement brief and let it show "who you are" and what makes you and your interpreting services special.
- Use the branding statement in all your promotional (marketing) materials, including your business card, on your website (if you have one) and when you speak to potential direct clients.
- Use it on your social media pages and in professional networking sites.
- Consider adding it below your email signature.

- Marketing materials.
  - Decide if you want online brochures or fliers, customized invoices and other materials. (Most remote interpreters might not need print materials except when attending conferences and face-to-face client meetings.)
    - Consider engaging a professional graphic designer: they are well worth the expense.
  - Post your marketing materials on your website and social media.
  - If you are asked for a quote or a proposal, you may wish to include promotional materials.
- Clear guidelines of communication and expectations with language services or direct clients.
  - Develop a one-page PDF document that you can send out with your quotes, proposals or contracts stating your policies.
  - Educate your clients! Let them know how your services work and what to expect.

For details on how to create a portfolio of credentials, see Chapter 10 of this volume.

→ Section 8.3 Review

Being successful in any profession doesn't happen overnight. Success can be especially challenging when you have to market yourself aggressively and the competition is high. The more prepared you are in every aspect of the business—for interpreting is a commercial enterprise, not just a profession—the more likely you are to succeed.

The theme of this section is that the self-employed interpreter is a *business.* This section provided helpful tips on how to successfully run your business. It addressed many aspects of the work, from planning out your legal status to bookkeeping, insurance coverage and marketing yourself to establish a business presence. It also addressed quality assurance processes, which self-employed interpreters may be subject to just like employed remote interpreters.

As you can see, it takes organizational skills as well as motivation to successfully be your own manager and operate a sound business. But with the tips and guidelines provided here, you can rest assured that you're headed in the right direction!

Self-employed remote interpreters are expected to practice ethical conduct and show professionalism at all times despite the challenges of working across whole countries or even international borders. Ethical conduct and professionalism are key to the success of any interpreter.

Section 8.4 Continuing Education Plan

→ Learning objective 8.4

After completing this section, the remote interpreter will be able to develop a continuing education plan.

→ Section 8.4 Overview

Learning is a lifelong activity. How do you continue your education as a remote interpreter? This section will help you do so.

Professional development and continuing education go together. They are paramount in remote interpreting, regardless of your level of expertise. New interpreters and veterans alike need to constantly develop their knowledge and skills. Why?

- The interpreting profession does not stand still. It is a fast-evolving field that practitioners need to stay caught up on to remain relevant.
- Remote interpreting, in particular, has evolved at incredible speed since the onset of the COVID-19 pandemic.
- Your language learning is never done.
- Technology changes on a constant basis. So do remote interpreting platforms.
- Being more knowledgeable and comfortable with a range of topics increases the likelihood of having smooth, successful sessions—especially because remote interpreters can encounter so many topics and sessions.
- Skills-based training allows you to hone and perfect your craft.

Having a high level of confidence is essential in this modality as the exact content of the session can be unknown ahead of time, and many remote interpreters quickly transfer from call to call and topic to topic. Added to this comes the additional stress of technical challenges coupled with the lack of human contact.

Nevertheless, this sense of dynamism fosters an incentive for remote interpreters to work hard, succeed and exceed expectations from both participants and organizations.

This section explores the kinds of professional development and continuing education available for remote interpreters, a growing amount of which is available online.

→ Section 8.4 Content

Completing an interpreter training program is just the beginning of your journey. If you are employed full-time by a language service or another organization, perhaps a path for your professional growth is already set in place. For example, a language service might have plans for you to pursue certification or require you to complete a certain number of continuing education hours every year.

Self-employed remote interpreters are on their own. They will have to plan and implement their own continuing education. This may also be the case for many employees if their organization does not directly support their professional development.

Time management, organizational skills and discipline are critical elements for success, as you saw earlier in this chapter. Now think about additional factors such as recordkeeping, managing training deadlines and updating your résumé with your latest training and education. All these elements will come into play in your continuing education plan as a remote interpreter.

Professional development and continuing education

> **Professional Development**
>
> Professional development is a requirement in nearly any profession. It addresses your ability to keep learning and improving through practice, study and continuing education.
>
> —García-Beyaert, 2015, p. 433

Professional development

More than at any other time in history, education is at our fingertips! Think about it: we can now learn anything from all types of electronic devices, such as computers, laptops, tablets and even our telephones. There is no need to leave home in order to invest in our professional growth.

Before we explore opportunities for professional development and continuing education, let's define these terms. *Professional development* simply means the process of increasing your knowledge and improving your skills at a certain job or task through practice, study and continuing education.

Continuing education

Continuing education involves the actual activities that contribute to improving your capabilities. For example, you could attend a conference workshop, take an online course or register for a practice certification exam.

In short, continuing education is part of your professional development. It is often measured in units. In the U.S., interpreters often receive "continuing education units" for taking a course or attending a webinar, whereas interpreters in Australia get "professional development points."

How continuing education works

The number of units or points (whichever term is used) that you receive for your continuing education typically depends on the number of *hours* involved. The professional association or certifying body chooses to award a specific number of units or points for each particular program or workshop—but the organization that offers the programs, courses, workshops or webinars must first *apply* for those units or points. Otherwise the interpreter may not receive credit for taking the continuing education.

Perhaps the credit does not matter to you: the education does. But if you are certified or licensed (see Chapter 10 of this volume for details), or have some other important credential, you will probably need to obtain a certain number of continuing education credits to keep your credentials.

Inform yourself before taking continuing education to find out (a) which kinds of credits you need to either maintain your certifications or other credentials (if you have any), or to show your employer or other organization that you are in compliance with professional requirements and expectations; (b) how many credits you will receive for completing the continuing education in question; (c) what kind of proof you will receive afterward.

For example, in the U.S. and in some other countries, you would typically get a *certificate* after completing a continuing education program. That certificate would specify the number of credits you receive.

Why professional development matters

For remote interpreters, professional development is essential because you deal with a vast array of situations, content and terminology in your work. For instance, a remote interpreter in court might interpret for topics such as traffic tickets, driving under the influence, divorces and murders in just a few hours. Often there is no warning of what interpreting scenario you will encounter next, especially if your interpreted sessions are on-demand rather than scheduled ahead of time.

What is available for your professional growth?

Embarking on this journey of learning is exciting. There are plenty of opportunities for growth in the interpreting industry, and it is important to look for reputable training and educational organizations. Let's look at exactly how to do that. First, let's consider what is already available.

How to choose continuing education

Here are some of the pros and cons of different types of continuing education opportunities.

Face-to-face training (short courses and conference sessions) and education programs (at colleges and universities)

Training typically refers to short programs that focus on skills and knowledge. Sometimes training can involve professional job guidance, coaching or preparation.

Education usually refers to more formal instruction at schools, colleges and universities.

Similarly, in interpreting, *training* typically refers to short courses offered outside academic institutions, while *education* most often refers to programs offered by academic institutions of higher education: colleges and universities.

The term *continuing education* in general often refers to short, one-time workshops or presentations, whether they are provided face to face (onsite) or online. Continuing education typically does not often refer to degree programs at colleges and universities.

If you take a course, a certificate program or a degree at a university or college, that education is usually considered *preparation* for your career. Continuing education is more likely to take place in the context of training *after* you begin work. In addition to short courses, you can attend conferences, webinars, symposia and other opportunities for professional development.

Face-to-face vs. online training and continuing education

Face-to-face training and education programs

Pros of face-to-face programs

Remote interpreters might work in an office space, a call center or from home. Attending a face-to-face program, whether a shorter or longer one, benefits the interpreter by providing in-person contact with an instructor to address questions or concerns. Additionally, interacting with classmates makes learning easier and more enjoyable for many people. Those who work in front of a computer often enjoy human contact and a break from technology.

The ability to interact in real time, practice interpreting face to face with other interpreters, watch others interpret in a classroom and receive immediate feedback from peers and instructors is hard, though not impossible, to fully replicate in online programs and online practice.

Being physically present allows for many complex layers of interaction, and the same degree of professional growth is not always possible through online learning, whether it is "live" online (for example, a synchronous program where you interact with the instructor and other participants in real time) or "self-paced" online learning (an asynchronous program where you study on your own, on your computer).

Cons of face-to-face programs

When training is provided face-to-face, participants must be physically present—all in the same location at the same time. You need a room that is big enough and equipped with everything needed for training, which can be costly. There may be a limited number of seats and space in the classroom, which will also limit the number of people who can attend. Many times, sign-ups must be done on a first-come, first-served basis.

Parking may also be an issue, not to mention logistics of transportation depending on the remote interpreter's situation. For some interpreters, face-to-face training might not really be an option. For example, interpreters in rural areas, or certain countries, report that they have almost no options to attend training and cannot afford to travel great distances to attend it.

Face-to-face training may also be far more expensive, both because of the costs of providing the program and the participant cost of traveling to attend it. Finally, if the program lasts more than one day, there may be additional costs involved for the interpreter, such as hotels and food.

Online training and education programs

Pros of online programs

Online training and education for interpreters has become far more widespread today, and it is especially widespread in Australia, Canada, Europe, New Zealand and the U.S. Since the onset of the COVID-19 pandemic, online training opportunities for interpreters have become more and more common, especially for those interpreters who are reasonably fluent in English.

Often, any interpreter in any country can attend such training, although it can be difficult to manage time differences for "live" online training programs. (Self-paced training programs can be taken at any time, so time differences do not matter.)

Easy access to information and lower cost has made online training a good option for many people. In particular, there is now a high demand for self-paced (asynchronous) programs. Whether it is a short or longer program, remote interpreters can take the class on their own time and in the comfort of their home.

Besides, a self-paced class means exactly that: you can study at your own pace. You might also be able to interact with other classmates and the instructor at a different time, for example, in a discussion forum. This type of continuing education is especially helpful in accommodating students from several time zones.

Some forms of live or self-paced continuing education are not training but presentations, such as webinars. Webinars are not training: they are one-way presentations of information, typically without much interaction. They rarely involve skills-based practice and training. Interpreting is a practice profession, so webinars may be a useful addition to professional development, but they are no substitute for interactive workshops and skills-based training with role plays and other opportunities for interpreting practice, followed by feedback about your performance.

Although not interactive, webinars are however often available after the live sessions as recordings, which again makes learning easier and more accessible than face-to-face classes.

Finally online training and presentations may be less expensive than face-to-face continuing education, depending on the course and institution offering the classes, and because no travel is involved.

Cons of online programs

Regardless of the duration of the training/programs, or whether they are live or self-paced, online training and education will be less personal. The same level of human interaction and dynamics of face-to-face training are simply not present for self-paced training, and less present—or different—for live online training.

In addition, both for live online training but especially with self-paced programs, it is far easier to get distracted when you are not there in a class in person. For self-paced training in particular, it's easy to make excuses to postpone it.

Online training in general and self-paced online training in particular requires a high degree of self-motivation and self-discipline. Otherwise, you might not fully benefit from the training.

How Much Does Interpreter Training Cost?

University programs are the ideal form of interpreter long-term education but, of course, they are expensive (unless you live in a country that makes higher education free or low cost). In general, conference interpreters, and in some countries sign language interpreters, will take courses at colleges and universities prior to launching their careers. Most other interpreters around the world take training programs to enter the field.

The question most interpreters these days want to know for continuing education is: *How much does the training cost? And which training should I take?*

The answers to these questions will vary greatly depending on each individual program, whether you take it in person or online. But online training makes it far easier to find out the cost of training! Do your research carefully. Balance affordability with quality. Look to see if experts have developed the programs and if you can get a free sample course or a video about the programs to assess the quality of the instruction. Be careful when you decide which program will work best for you. For cost, content and quality, you will have to do the research!

Skills training vs. knowledge acquisition

Skills training

Interpreting is a practice profession. You can't learn to do it simply by reading about it or watching webinars.

"Skills training" (or skills-based training) refers to programs that equip you with a range of skills that you need to do a certain job well, typically by offering courses in modules or sections that students can progress through.

Examples of skills training for interpreters are note-taking, fingerspelling, memory skills and guidance and practice for improving your performance in the three modes: consecutive, simultaneous and sight translation. These are skills you will always need to improve.

Skills-based activities—even in self-paced online courses—could include role plays, self-recording exercises (audio and/or video) with self-assessment or assessment by instructors, practice in note-taking, memory skills activities, anticipation or paraphrasing exercises and much more.

Sometimes testing after a skills-based program can involve having you interpret a live or recorded role play. Then a trainer, instructor, coach or evaluator would study the recording and award you a grade based on your performance.

Knowledge acquisition

Knowledge acquisition is the process of learning information about a certain subject. Typically you do so by reading, listening or watching—for example, reading a manual, listening to an audio file or watching a webinar.

In order to assess whether or not you learned that knowledge, someone has to test you. An evaluation of the knowledge you acquired could be a short quiz, a multiple-choice test or a long exam, depending on the length of the course you take and its requirements for successful completion.

Why you need both skills training and knowledge acquisition

Both skills training and knowledge acquisition are essential; you can't do without one simply because you excel in the other. The knowledge or the theoretical part is crucial to learn, remember and integrate. Then the skills you acquire must be practiced, practiced and practiced some more before you become truly competent.

Even after you develop strong skills, they must be constantly honed. There is always room for growth.

How to assess your continuing education needs

Be honest with yourself. This honesty is something we will ideally all practice in every aspect of our lives. For interpreting, it will help us to see which areas of our practice we need to work on. These are the first steps to learning.

For you, the process starts by assessing your continuing education needs.

It is your time to start thinking as a remote interpreter. If you don't believe you can think that way, don't worry. Find help. Table 8.2 shows a way to assess your continuing education needs. It's a great place to start. Answer the questions in that table and start tracing your path of growth.

What Continuing Education Do You Need?		
After finishing basic training as a remote interpreter, ask yourself...	**If your answer is...**	**We recommend...**
Do I know or have an idea which specialization I am going to work in?	Yes	Go to the next question.
	No	You need to start defining that path in order to know where to start or simply choose any.
Is this a specialization I have practiced in the past?	Yes	Start by making a list of topics you have already identified as areas of growth. (If you have not interpreted in that specialization or topic for a while, you may at least have an idea where to start.) Now answer the next question.*
	No	See Volume 2 for chapters about specializations in remote interpreting. You can also reach out to other interpreters or check locally for professional associations specific to that field.*
Have I practiced in this specialization as an interpreter or in another job position (where I also interpreted)?	Yes, as an interpreter	See "Yes" recommendation in the question above.
	Yes, in another job (e.g., teacher, medical assistant, social worker)	Start by looking for trainings that focus on interpreting in that field or specialization.
	No	Study the field in question. For example, for medical interpreting, you could take a college class in medical terminology, study online videos on anatomy and physiology, purchase textbooks or training manuals on medical interpreting or view live or recorded webinars on common medical topics. Be sure to research the field itself, not only interpreting within that field.
Do I hold a certification that requires continuing education credits?	Yes	Research which types of credits your certifying body accepts. There may be a certain number of hours per year that have to be fulfilled by a certain type of training. Meet your requirements with topics that interest you but will challenge you to learn something new and apply to your daily work.
	No	Research the certifications available to you and consider whether they could be beneficial.

*If you have or are planning to apply for a certification or license, your continuing education plan will likely be guided by that organization's requirements.

Table 8.2: Assessing your continuing education needs

Search online and ask the organization you work for or any professional group you have joined what recommendations they may have. Look for training opportunities in the corresponding topics that you have identified in Table 8.2 and find out whether the programs are held in person or online (and if online, whether they are live or self-paced), whether they are free, low-cost or paid and whether they are short programs or multisession courses.

Choosing a reputable training

There are many interpreter trainings available to you for continuing education and professional development. To ensure you're choosing reputable trainings, look for opportunities offered by organizations with a strong presence in the industry, professional recognition and a history of recognized success.

You may also want to check for reviews on specific areas of professional development that matter to you most. Listen to feedback and recommendations from trusted interpreters in your modality and specialization.

Reflective practice

Self-evaluation, evaluation by your peers and reflective practice in general are a *critical* part of your professional development! Please reread Chapter 5 of this volume and refer to it often.

Professional associations

One of the most important ways you can ever improve as an interpreter is to join a professional association. Depending on where you live, there may be one (general) professional association of interpreters—or many.

In the U.S., for example, there is a national association for interpreters and translators in general (American Translators Association, which has many international members) and also various national, regional and local associations for general, sign language, medical and court interpreters.

Most professional associations are nonprofit membership associations. They exist to support both the profession and their members. Almost all of them vigorously support ethical practice and a large percentage of them draft their own code of ethics for their member interpreters. (See Chapter 6 of this volume.)

Professional associations for interpreters often seek to educate the public about the work of interpreters.

Typically, professional associations charge an annual membership fee that supports the cost of their activities and member benefits, which often include annual conferences, workshops, papers and guidance. Their activities are often fun as well as beneficial to attend—and you often make good friends there.

Here are few other benefits for member of professional associations.

- Online membership database: By listing yourself online in a public database of association members (if there is one), with information about your skills, credentials and specializations, you and many practicing interpreters can get work. Often language services and other organizations look online in these databases for specific types of interpreters—including remote interpreters. This can be a wonderful way to find work.
- Continuing education: Most associations offer conferences. A number of them also provide face-to-face or online courses, workshops and webinars.
- Publications and other information: Many associations publish white papers on specific topics or standards, guides, best practices, booklets or other helpful publications.
- Networking: An annual conference is usually an association's highlight event of the year for networking. Even smaller local events hosted by the association can provide opportunities to connect to others in your field—or find work with organizations.
- Mentoring: If you are lucky, your association may have a mentoring program and pair you with a volunteer veteran interpreter who can guide you down the path of professional remote interpreting.
- Insurance: Insurance for interpreters can be a challenge to find. Your association may have done that research for you and even secured a discount policy for its members.
- Companionship: Interpreters can often feel solitary in their work. Remote interpreting may seriously increase that sense of isolation. To attend a conference, engage with other interpreters in the chat feature of a webinar, make friends across the country and remain in contact with them—these are just some of the social and professional advantages of joining an association.
- Supporting the profession: Last but *not* least: every interpreter who joins a professional association *supports the profession as a whole.* "Strength in unity" is more than a slogan. It is a reality.

Professional organizations are usually, but not always, legally structured as a membership category of nonprofit association. (The legal requirements for such organizations will vary from country to country.) As such, they may be comprised of a board of directors, committees and sometimes subcommittees.

Generally, the individuals on these boards and committees are leaders from around the country who work in different areas of interpreting, depending on the specialization of that association.

In some cases, the members are not only interpreters. Other members might be interpreter service coordinators, trainers, translators, clinicians, policymakers, researchers, advocates and others. Participating in events and conversations with these members will only serve to enrich your professional development.

Here are some examples of these associations.

- International Association of Conference Interpreters (AIIC)
- American Translators Association (ATA), which has many international members

- International Medical Interpreters Association (IMIA)
- World Association of Sign Language Interpreters (WASLI)
- International Federation of Translators (FIT), which includes interpreters
- International Association of Professional Translators and Interpreters (IAPTI)
- Arab Professional Translators Society (APTS), which includes interpreters
- European Legal Interpreters and Translators Association (EULITA)
- The American Association of Language Specialists (TAALS), an international association
- Registry of Interpreters for the Deaf (RID)

In addition to the examples listed here, there are countless national, regional and local professional associations around the world. Finding an association near you is perhaps the best place to start, at least if one is available. If not, you will probably find a national or regional association.

Conferences and other events by professional associations

Professional associations often organize events that can support multiple aspects of your career. There are many of these events around the world. Some are hosted in the U.S. and many in other countries. Search online to find events in your area or specialization.

To give you an idea of one country that offers various types of annual events for interpreters, here are some examples from the U.S.

- ATA (American Translators Association) Annual Conference
- CHIA (California Healthcare Interpreting Association) Annual Conference
- NAJIT (National Association of Judiciary Interpreters and Translators) Annual Conference
- NCIHC (National Council on Interpreting in Health Care) Annual Membership Meeting
- NETA (New England Translators Association) Annual Conference
- RID (Registry of Interpreters for the Deaf) National and Regional Conferences
- TAHIT (Texas Association of Healthcare Interpreters and Translators) Annual Educational Symposium

In addition to the fairly large events listed above, there are *many* annual conferences for small associations in the U.S. that are attended by 50-200 interpreters.

Online conferences and events

Due to the need to shelter in place beginning in 2020, many interpreter conferences went completely virtual. While in-person conferences have made their return, many of them now offer the opportunity to attend either in person or online.

Attending an online conference, even if just for a day or one session, can be a good choice for interpreters who may not be able to pay for travel and lodging.

→ Section 8.4 Review

What is the most important message that the authors want you to remember from this section—and live by—as a remote interpreter? That learning and growing ought to be ongoing processes for the rest of your career!

The reasons are simple: interpreting in general is a practice profession that evolves constantly, and remote interpreting as both a profession and a career is evolving by the moment.

Not only does each specialization change often (for example, medical interpreters need to pay attention to new medical procedures, diseases and treatments) but also remote interpreting technology, platforms and certain protocols are evolving too. Some of these changes are swift.

You can always learn more by reading books or checking out online resources, but there are many more efficient (and fun) ways to enhance your professional development. Seek continuing education opportunities that apply to your field and come from known and reliable sources.

You have the option of taking training, online or in person, in a synchronous or asynchronous way (that is, live or self-paced—and potentially recorded). You could enroll in short training sessions or longer courses. Ideally you could take advantage of programs in universities, but those opportunities—and their cost—vary from country to country.

To enhance your skills and increase knowledge, identify what best fits your own needs for professional growth but be flexible as well by trying multiple approaches. No single type of training can cover all needs and learning styles.

Get involved with professional associations and attend their events. Associations help both you and the profession to grow.

Finally, assess your continuing education needs and create a plan based on the needs you identified. Reassess and review your plan often. That way, your professional development plan will be up to date.

→ Chapter Activities

Activity 8.1 (a): Unprofessional conduct

Instructions

1. Read the following scenario.
2. Answer the questions below the scenario.

A video interpreter answers the call leaning to one side, with their face slightly cut off. The interpreter is gathering pen and paper for notes as they answer. There is background noise of people talking. The interpreter is wearing exercise clothes in neon colors with stripes.

The interpreter is positioned in front of an open window (with their back to it). The interpreter greets the callers by saying, "Hello? Can you hear me?"

Once the interpreter sees the first caller and recognizes this person from a previous session, the interpreter says, "Oh, good! I still have my notes from your call from yesterday!" and holds them up to the screen. Both callers, though appearing to be uncomfortable, continue with the session. One participant gives a long explanation for the reason of the call. The interpreter gives an incomplete summarization and uses indirect speech (third person).

1. On the lines below, list 10 aspects of this interpreter's conduct that were unprofessional. Be specific.
2. In each case, describe what you would do differently.

Activity 8.1 (b): What may the interpreter say?

Instructions

1. Read the following script.
2. If you are in a classroom, act out the script in groups of three with an interpreter who does not read (or see) the script.
3. Now imagine that for the rest of the encounter, the survivor describes her rape in graphic detail. You are the interpreter.

4. Next, imagine you are the interpreter going home to talk about your day to a partner or spouse, a family member or a roommate.
5. Look at the list of statements (in quotes) listed below "What May the Interpreter Say"; then rewrite each statement under the one of the three appropriate categories in the blank lines below each category label.

Advocate: Hi, my name is Jean Smith. The sexual assault crisis center sent me here.

Survivor: My name is Maria. Why are you here?

Advocate: I'm here because I am an advocate. As soon as the police bring anyone here for a sexual assault exam, our center sends out an advocate to support you and be here for you because we know this can be a scary experience and we don't want you to feel alone. You seem a bit nervous and upset—has anyone upset you?

Survivor: The police brought me here. I didn't ask for any exam or an advocate. The hospital and police keep asking me for my address.

Advocate: I know, and please understand that everyone wants you to feel safe here. The hospital needs that information, like your address, so you won't get charged for the exam. The police need it to investigate your case. Would you feel safe sharing your address so they can take care of all that and then you don't have to worry about the cost?

Survivor: (*sighing*) My address is 11234 Castle Creek Road, Austin, Texas.

Advocate: Miss Maria, what is your Social Security number? It's just for the hospital, not the police, and the hospital absolutely will not share it. That is strictly your confidential information.

Survivor: All right. It's 314-55-4141.

Advocate: Thank you. I'll go get the nurse for you. And would you like some blankets? And then I can go and get you some snacks too. Would you prefer apple juice or orange juice? And can I get you a sandwich, granola bars, raisins, nuts or a candy bar?

What May the Interpreter Say?

Take the following statements and insert each statement (by rewriting it) into the blank lines of *one* of the three sections below, in the category you find most appropriate.

- "I had a sad call today about sexual assault."
- "Didn't you have a Jean Smith in your social work program? I interpreted for her today! I don't think she recognized me on the video."
- "I interpreted for someone who lives a block away from us today! Can you believe that? She lives at 11234. I think it's the yellow house."
- "So, I had this session today, for a 'Maria.' It took me a second, but I realized this Maria is a famous singer back home in our country. The other people had no idea who she was."
- "I had a rough session today, but I'm thankful I was able to help by interpreting for the survivor."

- "You're not going to believe what happened today! Someone I interpreted for today was a mom from the kids' school. I almost didn't recognize her in the video and I almost never see people I know. I can't mention details, but I don't want our kids hanging around those kids anymore."
- "I had one session today that really struck a chord with me. The survivor of sexual assault had the same name as one of my cousins, who went through something similar."
- "Even though I can't share details about it, I had a really tough interpreting session today. Let's watch something funny on TV tonight."
- (*Interpreter's partner*) "Do you need this telephone number you have written down on this piece of paper?" (*Interpreter*) "Oh, wait! That's not a telephone number. That's a social security number I wrote down from my notes!"

1. What the interpreter *may* say (legally and ethically).

2. What the interpreter may legally say but probably shouldn't (to protect and respect the survivor's privacy and out of caution).

3. What the interpreter *must not say* for legal and other reasons.

Activity 8.3 (a): Pros and cons

Instructions

List the possible pros and cons for the following:

1. Working as an employee for a language service or other organization.
2. Being self-employed but contracting with a language service or other organizations.
3. Being self-employed with direct clients.

Note: answers will vary. Some examples of these pros and cons could be:

- Possible qualification for benefits such as a retirement plan, dental benefits or life insurance.
- More predictable pay versus fluctuating income.
- More predictable schedules versus more flexible schedules.
- Possible compensation for continuing education (for example, training, participation in conference).
- Providing services to multiple language services or types of clients, or in multiple specializations.

Activity 8.3 (b): Employee or self-employed

Instructions

1. Review the list of remote interpreting expectations and requirements for interpreters below.
2. Decide for each one whether that statement pertains to being *employee*, *self-employed*, or *both.*
3. Write one of those terms (the most relevant one) in the blank line that follows each statement.
    - Start your shift on time. ______
    - Ensure technical support is available. ______
    - Have adequate hardware/computer. ______
    - Have headsets. ______
    - Abide by scheduled breaks/mealtimes. ______
    - Monitor your own performance/self-assessment. ______
    - Engage in professional development. ______
    - Ensure the fulfillment of CEUs. ______
    - Complete qualifying training. ______
    - Obtain certification, if applicable. ______
    - Abide by state/governmental policies and regulations. ______
    - Pass a language proficiency test. ______
    - Follow clothing etiquette. ______
    - Have supplies available, such as paper, pen, pencil, shredder. ______
    - Make sure internet connectivity is reliable and adequate. ______
    - Abide by code of ethics and standards of practice. ______

- Carry out established protocols. ______
- Apply hard and soft skills. ______
- Provide a noise-free environment. ______
- Uphold professional conduct. ______
- Engage in self-care and support personal wellness. ______
- Understand and take advantage of fringe benefits (for example, retirement plan, paid time off, insurance). ______
- Watch for camera presence. ______
- Assure adequate furniture, lighting, backdrop, etc. ______

Activity 8.4: Plan for continuing education

Instructions

1. Complete the continuing education self-assessment tool in Table 8.2 of Section 8.4.
2. Create a list of potential continuing education topics that will help you grow as a remote interpreter.
3. Investigate conferences, trainings and other continuing education for those topics that you could afford and find time to attend.
4. In the blank lines below, create a personalized continuing education plan to be completed in the next year based on those topics and your availability. Include at least three to six events or programs you will attend, such as an online training, a conference, a webinar.
5. Be specific and for each event or program give the name, the dates you will attend or complete it and the name of the organization hosting or providing it.

Chapter Conclusion and Review

Section 8.1 reviewed professional conduct and how that applies to remote interpreters during and outside their interpreted sessions. For example, it is critically important to be ready for when calls come in; watch the tone of voice you use when you intervene and speak up as the interpreter. Be sure to pay great attention to the importance of privacy and confidentiality.

Sections 8.2 and 8.3 reviewed many aspects of working as an employed or as a self-employed remote interpreter, respectively. Many elements and considerations of being employed or self-employed overlap. For example, you may be subject to quality assurance monitoring regardless of your employment status. There are also many important differences, such as the way in which training can be required or given to you, the benefits may be available to employees but not contractors, and how, if you are self-employed, you are a business.

Section 8.4 emphasized that learning and growing never stops for professionals. Continuing education for interpreters is available in many forms that make it easier for remote interpreters to attend, including self-paced or live online training, and in-person or virtual conferences and other events. Professional associations offer continuing education opportunities as one of the main benefits of membership. Today, more than ever, opportunities abound for continuing one's education as a remote interpreter.

Chapter 9

Danielle Meder, RID-NIC

Language Access Laws and Language Policies

Learning Objectives

After completing this chapter, the remote interpreter will be able to:

Learning Objective 9.1: Discuss language access laws and their impact on access to community, medical and legal services.

Learning Objective 9.2: List some of the most critical U.S. federal language access laws and assess their impact on access to services and on remote interpreting as a profession.

Learning Objective 9.3: Assess and compare language access laws around the world.

Learning Objective 9.4: Describe data privacy requirements and how they affect the interpreter's decision-making.

Introduction

Language access laws are created by local, state or federal governments to support access to public services for people who need language assistance, including service providers and service users.

It is important for remote interpreters who interpret for nearly any kind of service provision to be aware of the relevant laws that protect a person's right to communicate in the language they feel most comfortable in. Without equitable and quality language assistance, no meaningful access to services is possible.

In addition, language access laws have helped to shape the interpreting profession in certain countries, including the U.S., South Africa and Australia, among others. Such laws support the communicative autonomy of all participants, allowing them to express what they wish to communicate and to make appropriate decisions.

As this textbook has made clear, the authors consider the role of communicative autonomy foundational for any interpreting that supports access to services. In addition, for remote interpreters in particular, language laws and language policies across state lines and national borders may affect how you work.

This chapter will examine various laws around the world that mandate language access. We will also explore privacy and compliance laws that affect your work as a remote interpreter. It's not expected that you will know all of the language and privacy laws in every country, but it is helpful to have a general understanding of how these laws are similar to or different from one another, especially in the countries where, or for which, you work.

Fortunately, there are many similarities among language laws and policies in countries such as Australia, Canada, the UK and the U.S., as well as some western Asian and European countries and South Africa.

Remote interpreting opens up the world to you. It gives you countless opportunities to provide your services across state and national borders. Upholding the laws of the country or region where your services are being provided, including language access regulations, supports respect for the profession. This chapter will discuss some of the world's key language laws and privacy requirements.

Although this chapter reviews some of the laws that are most critical to language access, it's important that you continue to do your own research and consult with the laws of the country or countries you're working in—and for—to be sure you're compliant.

Laws change, and new laws are written frequently. It's critical that you become or remain well connected to your national and local interpreting communities so that you can stay informed about changes in language access laws.

Section 9.1 The Impact of Language Access Laws

→ Learning objective 9.1

After completing this section, the remote interpreter will be able to discuss language access laws and their impact on access to community, medical and legal services.

→ Section 9.1 Overview

Interpreters are critical to ensuring that those who do not share a common language can either access or provide access to community, legal and medical services. When a qualified interpreter is needed and provided, all participants' communicative autonomy is supported in that session.

Depending on the location of the service and the country, language laws may require interpreting services to be provided. While these laws don't speak about communicative autonomy directly, their application helps everyone exercise their communicative autonomy. In this way all participants can both understand and communicate at every stage of the session and also make informed decisions based on that communication.

→ Section 9.1 Content

Language access laws and interpreting

What are language access laws?

A language access law can be defined as "Legislation that requires or stipulates that the impact of discrimination in access to public services be reduced through the provision of competent language assistance" (Bancroft et al., 2015, p. ix). It is important to note that language access laws are most common in the U.S. but also exist in several other countries, as discussed later in this chapter.

While it should be obvious that language assistance is needed if the participants in a service or legal process don't share the same language, certain laws are enacted to assure that language assistance is provided, including interpreters, and to hold service providers responsible if they do not provide language assistance when it is needed.

Language access laws are meant to protect individuals from discrimination and from being denied a service (or experiencing an inferior service) based on language differences. Currently, most often that right to language assistance is protected in environments where a person's life may drastically change if they don't have language assistance—for example, in court or a hospital.

Increasingly, however, in some countries such as the U.S., the right to language assistance is also protected in other publicly funded services, such as schools, social services, transportation, housing agencies and even motor vehicle departments.

Unfortunately, there are many cases where a qualified interpreter was not provided in court or healthcare and someone died or was wrongly convicted. These situations can often lead to the passage (enactment) of language access laws. These laws help prevent future incidents of discrimination rooted in language differences and may specify that a publicly funded entity is responsible if an incident occurs.

The most common language access laws in the U.S. require language assistance to ensure equal access to federally funded services—and, in many cases, state or municipally funded services—including healthcare, legal services, social services, housing, transportation and education.

Limitations of language access laws

The U.S. Court Interpreters Act of 1978 (Public Law 95-539)[149] stipulated that interpreters be provided in both criminal and civil cases in U.S. federal courts. In state and local courts, however, the situation is not as clear. There is some agreement that interpreters must be provided for state criminal and asylum cases (Abel, 2009, p. 8) but not necessarily for civil cases, depending on the state. (See, for example, Abel, 2009, and U.S. Department of Justice, Civil Rights Division, 2016.)

There are many other countries with similar laws or standards for any person needing an interpreter or language access in a legal proceeding. For example, Canada, Australia, Albania, South Africa and Slovakia are a few of the countries that have laws or articles in their constitutions requiring interpreters in certain, if not all, court proceedings.

For other services around the world, it can be even more difficult to assure that language access is provided, even when laws exist to prevent discrimination based on language or national origin in the provision of public services.

Sadly, when it is determined an interpreter is needed, the quality and training requirements of the interpreter are often not mentioned or they are described briefly and vaguely.

There are also times where a law may be in place that requires an interpreter, but the client seeking the service has not requested an interpreter and will rely on an unqualified language assistant (such as a family member or friend) or attempt to communicate with gestures. Such cases, unfortunately, are common even in countries with language access laws intended to prevent such incidents.

Not having a qualified interpreter undermines communicative autonomy for those who need the service, creates barriers to accessing services effectively and can jeopardize the life, safety, rights, health, autonomy, human dignity and future of participants.

How language access laws affect you

When service users bring their own interpreter

As a remote interpreter, you may often work with service users who choose to provide interpreters when they aren't legally obligated to do so. For example, a patient might say they prefer their grown daughter to interpret, or a parent might bring their brother or a friend to interpret for a school meeting.

---

[149] This landmark law, which had a significant impact on the development of interpreting as a profession in the U.S., can be found at https://www.congress.gov/95/statute/STATUTE-92/STATUTE-92-Pg2040.pdf

These environments are an excellent opportunity to reinforce the choice to bring in a professional, qualified interpreter. Your professional performance highlights the value of interpreters. It helps reinforce the concept of interpreting as an essential service. It also shows how much more effective communication can be when an interpreter is provided instead of family, friends or someone who is supposedly bilingual.

Show how language access laws support your role

As challenging as it can be to make clear that your role is to enable communicative autonomy and the value of that role when you show up at an onsite meeting where someone has brought in a family member or friend to interpret, clarifying your role remotely is harder still.

Perhaps the participants expect you to stand by and interpret only as needed, which is challenging for you. If you know the prevailing language access laws and can mention them, reinforcing that you are happy to interpret because the law provides for it and that the other person is still welcome to remain as an advocate while you take the burden of professional interpreting off their shoulders, perhaps it will be easier for you to remain and do your work.

You can also cite that you are trained, tested and qualified to interpret accurately and impartially to support the rights of all present and to assure that they can make informed decisions.

Please be aware that if you work for a language service or other organization, they may have *specific scripts or policies for you to follow in such cases*. Inform yourself and respect those policies.

Who decides?

Ultimately, the decision to work with an interpreter should never be left to only one participant. Communication decisions will ideally be made by all participants, with everyone in agreement on how to best communicate.

Therefore, as an interpreter, you can help facilitate those conversations to make sure that everyone has a chance to say how they prefer to communicate.

What You Can Say When a Family Member or Friend Offers to Interpret

Be prepared for the situation where a family member or friend is brought in to interpret instead of you. For example, you could say:

> "This is the interpreter speaking, I know you'd like your family to interpret for you, but I'd like to confirm with the other participants how they would like to communicate. I'm here to support communication and can take that responsibility on so your family member can support you without trying to worry about the job of interpreting."

Or you might say:

> "This is the interpreter speaking, the school district's policy as well as laws are in place so you don't have to rely on family to interpret. I'm more than happy to interpret so everyone else can focus on helping the student."

Some people may not have the experience of having a professional interpreter and are used to providing their own. The simple act of confirming preferences and getting agreement prior to proceeding may be just enough for everyone to realize that a professional interpreter is present and ready to work.

You don't have to cite the laws directly, but knowing they exist can help influence how you intervene and what you say in situations like these.

Language access laws support the profession

When language access laws are in place, they often reinforce the stability and growth of the interpreting profession. Since interpreters are required, there is a natural increase in demand. As demand increases, so do quality standards and expectations. The U.S., for example, has seen a huge increase in both demand and quality in healthcare, court, educational and social services interpreting in the past two decades as a direct result of federal, state and local language access laws.

Quality standards also spur additional training and support the development of credentials, such as training, language testing and certification. In addition, they help advance the development of interpreting specializations.

Language access laws are wonderful for participants—and also for the interpreting profession!

→ Section 9.1 Review

This section reviewed what language access laws are and how they can support equal access to publicly funded services for those who need them but do not speak the language of service.

Language access laws can make communicative autonomy possible by stipulating that language assistance, including interpreters, be provided in order to prevent discrimination in the provision of publicly funded services. Most countries do not have such laws, but those that do have seen that they not only increase access to services but also strengthen the interpreting profession, especially community (including healthcare) and legal interpreting.

Interpreters benefit from these laws as well. Laws that mandate language assistance provide further opportunity for interpreters to demonstrate their value and professionalism.

Remote interpreters obviously provide services outside their own local communities, and even in other countries. You don't need a thorough understanding of every language law where your services are provided, but you should be familiar with them.

Section 9.2 U.S. Language Laws

→ Learning objective 9.2

After completing this section, the remote interpreter will be able to list some of the most critical U.S. federal language access laws and assess their impact on access to services and on remote interpreting as a profession.

→ Section 9.2 Overview

This textbook cannot address the language access laws of all countries that have enacted them. However, as an illustration, this section will focus on U.S. language laws because they provide an excellent case in point. (This textbook is also published in the U.S.)

In the U.S., while dozens if not scores of national, state and local language access laws exist, four critical laws that mandate language access accommodation address interpreters, and they have set the bar and the model for the other laws.

While it's not necessary to memorize the language access laws (if any) of your own country, it is important to understand how language access laws evolved and how they support language assistance. The U.S. provides a clear example.

→ Section 9.2 Content

Two key U.S. language access laws

Although language access laws in the U.S. are not perfect, they did improve access to publicly funded services in the past 15 years. These laws are valuable and as such have had a national impact, and perhaps a global influence, on equitable language access.

To help explain U.S. federal and state laws that support language access, here is a brief overview from the National Health Law Program (Youdelman, 2019).

> ***Federal Laws Requiring Language Access***
>
> ***Title VI of the Civil Rights Act of 1964 ("Title VI")****—ensures that all federal fund recipients cannot discriminate on the basis of race, color, or national origin. Title VI's implementing regulations also prohibit "disparate impact" discrimination. Through Executive Order 13166, Title VI applies to federal agencies themselves.*
>
> ***Section 1557 of the Affordable Care Act****—applies both to federal fund recipients as well as all programs and activities administered by the federal agencies and entities created under Title I of the ACA, primarily federal and state marketplaces and qualified health plans. The regulations implementing Section 1557 outline requirements for notifying clients/ patients of language services, providing oral interpreting and including taglines on significant written documents.*

***Hill-Burton Act**—hospitals that received funding under this Act have an ongoing "community service" obligation which includes non-discrimination in the delivery of services. These hospitals must post notices of this obligation in English, Spanish, and other languages spoken by ten percent or more of the households in the service area.*

***Emergency Medical Treatment and Active Labor Act**—requires screening, treatment and transfer requirements which would be challenging to meet without effective communication with a . . . patient [whose primary language is not English].*

—Youdelman, 2019, p. 5

The two U.S. federal laws that greatly affect U.S. healthcare interpreters are Title VI of the Civil Rights Act of 1964 and the Affordable Care Act of 2010. The rest of this section will give you a deeper understanding of how these two laws support and increase language access in the U.S.

Both laws have had a huge impact on medical interpreting in particular, including remote medical interpreting. The U.S. arguably has the most advanced medical and remote medical interpreting professions in the world.

Without a doubt, these two federal laws have contributed greatly to that success.

Title VI of the Civil Rights Act of 1964

What Title VI requires

The U.S. Department for Health and Human Services (HHS) summarizes Title VI by saying:

Title VI and Department of Health and Human Services regulations, 45 C.F.R. Section 80.3(b)(2), require recipients of Federal financial assistance from HHS to take reasonable steps to provide meaningful access to . . . persons [*who do not speak English as their primary language*].

—Office for Civil Rights, 2020

In the U.S., a person who does not speak English as their primary language may or may not be able to read, write or communicate in English. English is the dominant language in the U.S.

It is important to note that English is not the legally official language of the U.S., although English is the official language of more than 30 U.S. states.[150]

Organizations that must follow Title VI requirements

Next, let's identify the types of organizations and programs that tend to receive federal financial assistance. If they receive any federal funding—directly or indirectly[151]—they are required to take reasonable steps[152] to provide language assistance to prevent discrimination and ensure equal and meaningful access to public services.

150 The number varies by source. A strongly pro-English organization cites 32 U.S. state laws declaring English as the official language. Retrieved from: https://proenglish.org/official-english-map-2/

151 What directly or indirectly means in this context is discussed below.

152 What reasonable steps means will vary according to a four-factor analysis that takes into account the organization's size and resources. It is discussed later in this chapter.

Such organizations and programs include:

- Hospitals
- Healthcare facilities
- State or local health programs
- HHS grant recipients
    - For example, the Coronavirus Aid, Relief, and Economic Security Act (CARES Act) grants provided in 2020 to organizations and programs during the COVID-19 pandemic
- Universities
- Public schools
- Head Start (early intervention)[153] programs
- Courts
- Many nonprofit legal services
- Other legal services
- State and local social service programs
- State and local housing programs
- State and local transportation programs
- Any other organization, program or service that receives even a small amount of federal money

The role of federal funding

It's important to note a few things. First, if federal assistance funds first go to a state government entity, and then to a local government entity, which then gives part of that federal funding to a local nonprofit—that money still counts as federal financial assistance and Title VI will apply.

Second, if that state government, local government or nonprofit gets the federal money for one program or service, Title VI now applies to all their other programs and services that the state, local or nonprofit provides. For example, a small community-based nonprofit organization might not receive federal funding. However, if it receives a grant or other financial assistance from an organization that is receiving federal funds itself (such as a local government agency, a refugee resettlement agency or a healthcare organization) and then disbursing those federal funds, then legally the entity that receives this indirect federal financial assistance falls under Title VI requirements.

Third, this law applies specifically to those entities that serve (among others) those who do not speak English, the usual language of service in the U.S. A different law that also mandates language assistance is the Americans with Disabilities Act (ADA) of 1990. The ADA addresses individuals who are Deaf and Hard of Hearing and will be discussed later in this chapter. But in this regard, the language of Title VI and ADA, and what they require in terms of providing interpreters, is similar.

---

153 Head Start is a U.S. federal program that promotes the school readiness of children from low-income families from birth to age five by enhancing their cognitive, social and emotional development.

Fourth, Title VI stipulates that any entity receiving federal funding for any part of the services it offers is required to *take reasonable steps* to provide language access to persons who do not speak English as their primary language for all its programs and services. In other words, this law doesn't say that everyone who gets federal money has to provide interpreters. But in reality, in legal cases to date, most larger entities (especially in urban areas) or organizations with adequate resources are typically expected or required to provide interpreters when they are needed.

In many cases, larger organizations, such as hospitals, school districts and even departments of transportation, have been investigated and sometimes sued by regional U.S. Department of Health and Human Services Office for Civil Rights for violations of Title VI. These cases have resulted in significant improvements to language access, not only for the entities in question but also for many others, contributing to nationwide progress in language access.

What is meaningful access?

Title VI requires that *meaningful* language access to services must be provided. This language is broad enough that the question of *how* to provide meaningful access is often left up to individual interpretation of the law based on the communities that a service provider is engaging with.

The U.S. federal government has put in place a four-factor evaluation so that service providers can develop an effective language access plan (discussed below) to work with service users who do not speak English as their primary language. This four-factor evaluation includes:

1. The number of service users who may access the service.
2. How frequently the service user accesses the service.
3. The value and impact the service may have on the service user and their family.
4. The availability of resources (interpreters) and the cost to provide access.

This four-factor evaluation gives each service provider a chance to evaluate their community, resources and cost. However, there are cases where service providers will say the cost of providing language access is too expensive, and as a result they may not always provide quality language access.

For example, the Virginia Department of Transportation (VDOT) is a large agency that receives federal funding. If an employee or a community member and the relevant service provider need language assistance, they are required to provide it. VDOT has many resources. VDOT would not be able to accurately state, "Well, we're a small local agency, we just don't have the resources to provide interpreters."

Consider, however, a rural health department in an isolated area that sees few immigrants and refugees. Perhaps the health department has experienced many funding cuts in recent years and can't afford to engage interpreters, especially after the onset of the COVID-19 pandemic. That small, rural health department may receive a complaint from the regional U.S. Department of Health and Human Services Office for Civil Rights for not providing an interpreter. However, this health department might not be legally required to provide face-to-face interpreters for the occasional Haitian-Creole-speaking migrant farmworker or Farsi-speaking resident. They might still need to provide other reasonable accommodations that are more affordable, such as OPI services.

The availability and generally lower cost of OPI services has generally led to a far greater implementation of meaningful language access through OPI and VRS interpreters, for example, for remote and rural agencies.

The five-step plan and language access plans

Once a service provider determines that their agency needs to provide language access, there is a five-step plan to support effective language access.

1. Identify the service users who need language access.
2. Determine how to identify and use resources (translators, interpreters, captioning, etc.).
3. Train staff on how to provide language access (including how to use remote interpreting technology).
4. Inform the service users that resources are available.
5. Regularly evaluate and update the language access plan.

In the U.S., a language access plans (LAP) outlines how language access will be provided for services to individuals who do not speak English as their primary language. An LAP can include interpreting and translating as well as other effective language access activities, such as posting multilingual signage informing recipients of public services about their rights to language assistance, or distributing bilingual "I Speak" cards for each recipient stating their name and language needs in both the recipient's primary language and English.

Each federal agency that receives funding and also provides funding to any public or private organization, agency, company, or contractor is required to have a language access plan.[154]

How language assistance works

Language assistance takes many forms. Interpreters are one way to provide language access. Translated documents, captioning and bilingual support services (for example, having a Spanish-speaking employee assist with a patient history) are examples of other ways of providing language assistance.

However, in most cases, an agency that receives public funding may not rely on family and friends as interpreters unless the speaker specifically requests it and the family or friend agrees to interpret. When this happens, the agency may still request that an interpreter be present to shadow interpret (as discussed in Chapter 4), that is, to stand by and interpret as needed.

Working with a professional interpreter even when a family member or friend interprets can help assure quality language access and communicative autonomy.

Suggesting or requiring a service user to provide their own interpreter or bring in family or friends to interpret could be a potentially serious violation of Title VI—and, as we shall see shortly, of other state and local language access laws.

[154] The plans for each federal agency can be found at https://www.lep.gov/title-vi-guidance-for-recipients

When language assistance breaks down

Unfortunately, there are situations where language access is not provided, or the quality of the access is unacceptable. People who are denied meaningful language access can file a complaint with their regional Office for Civil Rights of the relevant U.S. department, for example, Department of Health and Human Services, Department of Education, Department of Justice (for the courts), Department of Housing and Urban Development, Department of Transportation and so on. Complaints should be filed within 180 days of the denial of service.

Here is a famous example of when language access was denied.

> *Thirteen-year-old Gricelda Zamora was like many children whose parents speak limited English: she served as her family's interpreter. When she developed severe abdominal pain, her parents took her to the hospital. Unfortunately, Gricelda was too sick to interpret for herself, and the hospital did not provide an interpreter. After a night of observation, her Spanish-speaking parents were told, without the aid of an interpreter, to bring her back immediately if her symptoms worsened, and otherwise to follow up with a doctor in three days. However, what her parents understood from the conversation was that they should wait three days to see the doctor. After two days, with Gricelda's condition deteriorating, they felt they could no longer wait, and rushed her back to the emergency department. Doctors discovered she had a ruptured appendix. She was airlifted to a nearby medical center in Phoenix, where she died a few hours later.*
>
> —Chen et al., 2007, p. 362

Language access laws such as Title VI may not fully prevent these life-and-death situations. However, they at least offer a way to hold service providers accountable for violations.

Americans with Disabilities Act (ADA)

How ADA defines disability

In 1990, the Americans with Disabilities Act (ADA) became law. As its name says, this law was enacted specifically to support the rights of individuals with disabilities who reside in the U.S.

The ADA was created with the Civil Rights Act of 1964 in mind. The Civil Rights Act of 1964 prohibits discrimination on the basis of race, color, religion, sex or national origin. However, all attempts to include disability were unsuccessful for many years.

As a result, the ADA was passed into law to protect people with disabilities from discrimination and exclusion from access to services in public and private areas of life. The purpose of the law is not to help people with disabilities; instead, it focuses on providing *equal opportunity* regardless of a person's disability.

Before we explore the law and how it affects language access, let's first define disability.

The ADA defines a person with a disability as someone who has:

> *A physical or mental impairment that substantially limits one or more major life activities, a person who has a history or record of such an impairment, or a person who is perceived by*

others as having such an impairment. The ADA does not specifically name all of the impairments that are covered.

—ADA, 1990

In 2008, the definition of disability was broadened and took effect in 2009. The original definition of disability had become limited by a series of cases decided by the U.S. Supreme Court. The definition has been broadened, making it easier for individuals with disabilities who are U.S. residents and undocumented immigrants to get protection under the law.

The five titles of ADA

Within the ADA, there are five titles, or areas that the law applies to.

1. Employment (Title I)

Employers must provide reasonable accommodation for applicants and employees with disabilities. Title I prohibits discrimination because of disability. This would include providing interpreting services for people who are Deaf or Hard of Hearing.

2. Public Services (Title II)

Public services, including state and local agencies, must be accessible to people with disabilities. Title II also includes public transportation and wheelchair-accessible ramps onto buses.

3. Public Accommodations (Title III)

Public accommodations, including places such as hotels, grocery stores, restaurants and shops, must be accessible to individuals with disabilities. One accommodation would include automatic opening and closing doors.

4. Telecommunications (Title IV)

Telecommunications companies that provide telephone access must have accommodation for people who are Deaf or Hard of Hearing or people with speech disabilities. This is often done through the federal government's Telecommunications Relay Services (TRS), which include captioned telephone, speech-to-speech relay, and video relay service.

5. Miscellaneous (Title V)

Title V prohibits anyone from coercing, threatening or retaliating against a person with a disability or anyone supporting a person with a disability. For example, if a person who is Deaf requests an interpreter for their medical appointment at a hospital, and the doctor decides to not treat them anymore to avoid paying for interpreters, such an act might be considered retaliation and a violation of Title V.

ADA and language access

The ADA is one of the most powerful U.S. federal laws that supports language access for individuals who are Deaf and Hard of Hearing. Remote sign language interpreters are often requested due to the ADA. It is important to note that prior to the COVID-19 pandemic, many individuals in the Deaf community preferred to work with face-to-face interpreters and would work with remote interpreters until a face-to-face interpreter was available.

After the start of the COVID-19 pandemic, face-to-face interpreters weren't as readily available, or safety precautions made it difficult to work with face-to-face interpreters. Remote interpreting is now more accepted as a result, even by participants (whether Deaf or hearing) who were wary of working with remote interpreters. When the act was signed in 1990, President George H.W. Bush said,

> *[ADA] will ensure that people with disabilities are given the basic guarantees for which they have worked so long and so hard: independence, freedom of choice, control of their lives, the opportunity to blend fully and equally into the rich mosaic of the American mainstream. Legally, it will provide our disabled community with a powerful expansion of protections and then basic civil rights.*[155]

This law, as President Bush described, also supports communicative autonomy by giving people with disabilities, including the Deaf and Hard of Hearing, the ability to be responsible for and in charge of their communication.

Affordable Care Act Section 1557

The Affordable Care Act of 2010

Title VI of the Civil Rights Act of 1964 was important for all recipients who receive federal funding and all providers who offer services. The Affordable Care Act (ACA) of 2010 is a healthcare reform law that focuses exclusively on healthcare environments. The purpose of the ACA is to help provide more affordable health insurance for many low and midlevel income individuals in the U.S.

The importance of ACA Section 1557

Within the ACA is Section 1557, a provision that requires any health programs or services that receive federal funding or programs administered under ACA to take reasonable steps to ensure meaningful access to these programs and activities by individuals. Plainly speaking, a covered healthcare entity needs to provide meaningful language access to its services for any patients, regardless of the language they use.

Much of the law echoes what is written in Title VI. However, Section 1557 goes further by specifying more clearly *what* is required to provide meaningful access.

As with all laws discussed in this book, it is important to be aware that *such laws can change at any time, and so can federal interpretation of these laws.*

Three critical requirements under Section 1557

Currently, there are three main requirements in ACA Section 1557.

1. Individuals with limited English proficiency do not have to provide their own interpreter for healthcare appointments covered under the act, and they are not expected to bring family members, friends or children to act as an interpreter (also a requirement under Title VI).

---

[155] Remarks of President George H.W. Bush at the Signing of the Americans with Disabilities Act. July 26, 1990. Retrieved from: https://www.ada.gov/ghw_bush_ada_remarks.html

2. When interpreters or translation services are provided, the patient is not charged (also a requirement under Title VI).
3. Translators and interpreters must meet minimum qualifications (mentioned but not described in Title VI). Specifically, under Section 1557 interpreters and translators are required to:
    a. Adhere to ethical principles, including confidentiality.
    b. Demonstrate language proficiency in their working languages.
    c. Practice effective, accurate and impartial interpreting, using specialized terminology as needed.

Qualifications of interpreters under Section 1557

When you review this law, you may notice that it does not require certification of interpreters or translators or identify which ethical principles they should follow. While the requirements are somewhat vague, they are still a huge step forward in the U.S. in ensuring that patients have effective language access. These laws also show that interpreters and translators are professionals who provide an essential service.

Changes to ACA

There were two major changes made to ACA Section 1557 in June 2020. In 2010, when the ACA became law, all health programs and services covered under the act were required to post nondiscrimination statements in their offices and on their websites in the top 15 languages spoken in that area (city, state or region).

This requirement changed; as of June 19, 2020, the nondiscrimination statements need to be posted in languages other than English only when necessary to ensure meaningful access. This could lead to a situation where significant numbers of patients may not know what nondiscrimination protections they have.

Finally, the original ACA Section 1557 law required any healthcare program covered under the act with over 15 employees to have a designated staff member responsible for grievances from patients when language access or discrimination had taken place. There also needed to be a plan to address and resolve the grievance in a fair and timely manner. Under the revised law from June 2020, that requirement no longer exists.

As you can see, laws change. It is important that you research not only the laws in your country and region but also any new updates that may affect language access in your country or region. They may affect how you work as a remote interpreter and how communities know or learn about their rights.

State and local language access laws

U.S. state laws

Many states in the U.S. have additional laws to protect language access. Some, such as Maryland's law (Maryland General Assembly, Statute § 10-1103),[156] are almost mirror images of Title VI except

156 Maryland General Assembly Statutes Text. Retrieved from: https://mgaleg.maryland.gov/mgawebsite/Laws/StatuteText?article=gsg§ion=10-1103

that, with some minor differences, the requirements apply to entities that receive state funding and not only federal funding.[157]

In other states, the language access laws can be quite different from federal law, or apply only to specific areas, such as healthcare, or to certain populations, such as the Deaf and Hard of Hearing.

Fortunately, one U.S. organization tracks the laws at a local, state and federal level for patients in the U.S. healthcare system. The National Health Law Program (NHeLP) has a report on all the healthcare language access laws in each state. The report is thorough and periodically updated; it was most recently updated in April 2019 (Youdelman, 2019). While these laws center on healthcare, a number of them affect other programs and services as well.

To help you understand how these state language access laws work, we will look at the laws of three states from the NHeLP report. Again, it is highly recommended that you consider where you provide remote interpreting services (both the area where you work and the area for which you interpret). Review the laws of those regions, states or provinces. You aren't expected to become an expert on language access laws, but it is important to know about them.

The NHeLP report includes information on what laws were recently changed or added, as well as the intent of recent changes. This level of detail helps you get a better understanding of a state's priorities for language access. The report also lists how many language access provisions are in place.

The goal of the report is well summarized here:

> *We hope that policymakers, advocates, interpreters, translators, and . . . individuals [who do not speak English as a primary language] will use the information in these charts to understand what laws in their own states may address their needs or provide protections. Additionally, those interested in improving effective communication and access for . . . individuals [who do not speak English as a primary language] can get ideas from other states they may want to adopt in their own state.*
>
> —Youdelman, 2019, p. 12

Iowa

In 2019, Iowa had 36 provisions to support language access in healthcare settings (Youdelman, 2019, pp. 144-150). The report states that Iowa:

> *Implemented regulations focused on reducing communication barriers for its Spanish speaking population, requiring interpreter and translation services for care facilities and early intervention services and promoting language access for adults with disabilities.*
>
> —Youdelman, 2019, p. 8

California

In 2019, California had 257 provisions to support language access in healthcare settings (Youdelman, 2019, pp. 37-88).

---

[157] For helpful details about the Maryland language access law, see https://www.peoples-law.org/node/24761

New Jersey

In 2019, New Jersey had 104 provisions to support language access in healthcare settings (Youdelman, 2019, pp. 209-221). The report states that New Jersey:

> *Implemented new regulations requiring translation services as a condition of licensure for long term care facilities, hospitals, and home health services, sterilization services, health insurance, pre-natal care and community health centers.*
>
> —Youdelman, 2019, p. 9

Remember, you don't have to be an expert in these laws or even know them all, whether in the U.S. or any other countries. You should however know where to look for them and have a general sense of what language access provisions your country has and, if relevant, know the laws for each state or province in your country where you provide remote interpreting services.

Knowing the laws that affect you as an interpreter is part of being an informed, conscientious professional.

U.S. local laws

The U.S. has a surprising number of local language access laws. While a number of them are located in California, locations across the country, such as New York City, Philadelphia and the District of Columbia (DC), among others, also have their own specific laws.

For example, in 2004, DC enacted a law for its municipal services. It is described as follows.

> *The DC Language Access Act obligates the DC government to provide equal access and participation in public services, programs, and activities for residents of the District of Columbia who cannot . . . speak, read, or write English.*
>
> *If you request a service within DC government and you cannot speak, read, write or understand English, you have the right to:*
>
> - *Request and receive interpreter services at no cost to you.*
> - *Request and receive vital documents in your language at no cost to you.*
> - *Make a complaint if denied any service at a DC government agency.*[158]

In 2018, the law was expanded (D.C. Law 22-282. Language Access for Education Amendment Act of 2018) to add public schools and public charter schools to the list of requirements in the 2004 Act.[159]

This is another example of how language access laws constantly evolve: more and more U.S. cities have enacted langua ge access laws of their own. Be sure to stay up to date with local as well as state or provincial and national laws.

---

158 Office of Human Rights. DC.gov. Retrieved from: https://ohr.dc.gov/service/know-your-rights-language-access

159 D.C. Law 22-282. Language Access for Education Amendment Act of 2018. Retrieved from: https://code.dccouncil.us/us/dc/council/laws/22-282

→ Section 9.2 Review

This section laid out some of the most critical language access laws that have impacted the United States. Most notably, Title VI of the Civil Rights Act of 1964, the Americans with Disabilities Act, and the Affordable Care Act Section 1557. There are numerous other laws but these three changed the landscape when legislating and defining equitable language access.

While interpreters are not attorneys and shouldn't provide advice or council, it is helpful to be familiar with the laws. Laws, however, are not static and can change. Regularly reviewing the national Health Law Program (NHeLP) to familiarize yourself with any relevant changes will be beneficial.

This section also outlined elements of language access plans. If you work for a facility that has a language access plan, reviewing the elements of that plan will help you learn about the other resources or strategies available to provide access.

Ultimately, being familiar with the current laws at a local and federal level as well as any relevant language access plans will equip you with the information necessary to stay compliant.

Section 9.3 Language Laws and Policies in Several Countries

→ Learning objective 9.3

After completing this section, the remote interpreter will be able to assess and compare language access laws around the world.

→ Section 9.3 Overview

As you've seen in this chapter, many federal and state laws govern language access for residents in the U.S. However, when you look outside the U.S., different policies and laws address language access, especially in countries with several official or dominant languages.

Each country determines its own language access laws and policies. Most countries have not enacted language access laws or policies, but a number of them have done so.

In 2005, *An International Perspective on Language Policies, Practices and Proficiencies* was published and it outlined and addressed language policies around the world. The editors stated:

> *It is an unfortunate fact that there are precious few language policies in place across the globe. This begs the basic question—why? [There is a] lack of priority given to linguistic diversity by many in powerful positions across the globe.*
>
> —Cunningham & Hatoss, 2005

Unfortunately, this means many countries have no language access laws or policies, or their laws may not be as robust as those in the U.S.

What this means for a remote interpreter is that your work may not be requested as often in those countries that lack such laws. You may also find a low level of understanding about the vital services that interpreters provide and potentially underdeveloped professionalism among interpreters.

The publication mentioned above is a valuable resource to learn about language policy, education and preservation for the nondominant languages spoken in multilingual countries. As language access laws are enacted and formal language policies are written and enforced, the need for remote interpreters will likely grow sharply around the world.

→ Section 9.3 Content

Let's consider language laws and policies in a few countries. If you live in any of these countries, are you familiar with these laws and policies? If your country isn't mentioned, do you know of any laws or policies that affect language access? If not, ask your colleagues.

China

Some countries have a national language and dozens of regional languages and dialects. China is an example of a country that has significant language diversity. The Law of the People's Republic of China on the Standard Spoken and Written Chinese Language became official in the People's Republic of China on October 31, 2000. It is the first national law that addresses language in China.

The law gives people the freedom to use their own spoken and written language; however, there is now an official national language. This law states that Pǔtōnghuà (standard Mandarin Chinese) is the only national language of the People's Republic of China.

The intended goal of the law, according to the national government, is to achieve language harmony across the country and foster a national identity. Across China, educational programs increase fluency in the national language while public agencies still offer services in the region's other dominant languages.

However, for someone who may have just moved to the region and doesn't speak Mandarin or another standard language spoken in that region, there are no specific laws for the right to an interpreter. Bilingual speakers may be the only way someone is able to access a service. However, as you know, bilingualism alone does not make an interpreter.

Canada

The Official Languages Act

In Canada, there are two official languages, French and English, and access to services provided by federal institutions in both languages is protected.

The Official Languages Act was enacted in 1969, but a new act was adopted in 1988, with a set of regulations about communication with and services to the public. Revised in 2005, the stated purpose of the act was to:

- Ensure respect for English and French and equality of status and equal rights and privileges as to their use in federal institutions.
- Support the development of English and French linguistic minority communities.
- Advance the equal status and use of English and French.

Language assistance to immigrants

However, unlike the case of U.S. laws, immigrants to Canada who don't speak French or English have no legal right to language assistance to access most public services.

Local immigrant community service groups might help with language access. These groups assist new immigrants, but not all may have the financial resources to provide professional language services.

Language assistance for the Deaf

For Deaf people in Canada, their right to language assistance is supported by the Canadian Human Rights Act of 1985 and the Accessible Canada Act of 2019. In addition, three provinces have their own disability laws.

Language access is protected as a need related to disability in great part due to a Supreme Court of Canada decision in 1997 (the Eldridge decision, regarding a case in British Columbia), which made clear that:

> *The failure to provide sign language interpretation where it is needed for effective communication in the delivery of health care services violates the rights of deaf people...*
>
> *The Supreme Court decision went beyond ensuring interpreters for deaf people in medical situations. It stated that governments cannot escape their constitutional obligations to provide equal access to public services. Within reasonable limits, no disabled person should be prevented access to a government service. Education, training, health care, social services, all are affected by this landmark decision.*[160]

[160] Interpreting Services Information for Deaf Community, Clients, Funders and Interpreters. Retrieved from: https://interpreter.deafandhearalberta.ca/hearing-clients/advocacy/

Language access in the courts of Canada

In Canada's legal system, language access *is* a right, but that right is not clear. As researchers at the University of Ottawa stated, "The linguistic situation [in courts and judicial proceedings] is complicated [and] difficult to explain. Access to services in the minority language with regards to justice depends at times on federal laws, and sometimes on provincial and territorial laws."[161]

Historically in Canada, the far greater concern over language access in the courts has been the right to an interpreter for the other official language (English or French, or—in Nunavut—Inuit).

That said, the first part of the Constitution Act, 1982 is the Canadian Charter of Rights and Freedoms, which includes Section 14—Right to an interpreter:

> *Provision*
>
> *14. A party or witness in any proceedings who does not understand or speak the language in which the proceedings are conducted or who is deaf has the right to the assistance of an interpreter.*

Of great interest is that the federal interpretation of this provision makes reference both to other Canadian laws *and* to "international instruments binding on Canada," specifically:

- Section 2(g) of the *Canadian Bill of Rights.*
- Section 15(1) of the *Official Languages Act.*
- Article 14(3)(f) of the *International Covenant on Civil and Political Rights.*
- International, regional and comparative law instruments that are not legally binding on Canada but include similar provisions: article 6(3)(e) of the *European Convention for the Protection of Human Rights and Fundamental Freedoms*; and article 8(2)(a) of the *American Convention on Human Rights.*

Canada's System of Justice furthermore adds that in the criminal context (which is the chief concern in Canada, as it is in the U.S., given the potential loss of life or liberty due to miscarriages of justice based on lack of meaningful language access), Section 14 of the Canadian Charter of Rights and Freedoms has a close relationship with:

- Section 7 (fundamental justice).
- Section 11(d) (fair trial).
- Sections 15 (equality rights), 25 (Aboriginal rights) and 27 (multicultural heritage).[162]

Section 27 mandates that the charter be interpreted in a manner consistent with the preservation and enhancement of the multicultural heritage of Canadians. Additionally, Canada's System of Justice says that "In so far as a multicultural heritage is necessarily a multilingual one, it follows

[161] Introduction to the Language of Courts and Proceedings. Retrieved from: https://www.uottawa.ca/clmc/legislative-framework/language-tribunals

[162] Section 14—Right to an Interpreter. Retrieved from: https://www.justice.gc.ca/eng/csj-sjc/rfc-dlc/ccrf-ccdl/check/art14.html

that a multicultural society can only be preserved and fostered if those who speak languages other than English and French are given real and substantive access to the criminal justice system."[163]

While in principle, interpreters are involved in criminal cases in Canadian courts so that all participants can have meaningful access, the reality—just as in the U.S. and in other countries that mandate language assistance in the courts—varies widely.

This legal right to an interpreter in criminal cases is nonetheless critical because life-changing decisions are often made in legal settings.

Language assistance and informed consent in healthcare

Canada's Health Care Consent Act supports patients' rights to make informed decisions when consenting to a specific healthcare treatment. Therefore, patients and their family who do not speak the language of the healthcare facility or provider are provided with interpreters, including remote interpreters, for the consent process in healthcare.

Indigenous languages in Canada

Between 1828 and 1996, Canada operated residential schools (also known as boarding schools) for Indigenous (Aboriginal) Canadians. These schools were funded by Canada's Indian Affairs department and operated by Christian churches across Canada. While the residential schools operated, more than 150,000 children were forcibly taken from their homes and raised in the residential schools. Many were physically, emotionally and sexually abused. More than 4,000 died.[164] The last schools closed in 1996.[165]

The mission of the residential schools was to remove Indigenous children from their homes and assimilate them into Canadian culture and language. Children were denied access to their ancestral language and culture and severely punished for speaking their own language.

(Note that nearly identical or similar events have played out in other countries and regions, including the U.S., Australia, New Zealand, Latin America and Asia. (See Smith, n.d.)

In 2006, the Indian Residential Schools Settlement Agreement was reached, Canada's largest class action lawsuit to date. The suit was between the Canadian government and approximately 86,000 living Indigenous people in Canada who attended the residential schools. Between 2007 and 2015, the Truth and Reconciliation Commission (TRC) traveled throughout Canada to hear the stories of survivors, create a record of the experiences and ultimately create the 94 calls to action. These calls were recommendations by the TRC to support further reconciliation between Canada and the Indigenous communities.

---

163 Section 14—Right to an Interpreter. Retrieved from: https://www.justice.gc.ca/eng/csj-sjc/rfc-dlc/ccrf-ccdl/check/art14.html

164 Ian Austin. (2022). How Thousands of Indigenous Children Vanished in Canada. Retrieved from: https://www.nytimes.com/2021/06/07/world/canada/mass-graves-residential-schools.html

165 For an overview of the residential schools, see, for example, https://indigenouspeoplesatlasofcanada.ca/article/history-of-residential-schools/

One such call to action was the preservation, protection and strengthening of Indigenous languages. As a result, on June 21, 2019, the Indigenous Languages Act became law in Canada.

Within the rules of the Indigenous Languages Act is a section titled, "Access to services in Indigenous languages." This section states that when a speaker of an Indigenous language needs access to a federal institution's activities, language access needs to be provided in their Indigenous language. Specifically, the following Section 11 of the act applies:

> ***Translation and interpretation***
> *11 A federal institution may cause*
>
> > ***(a)*** *any document under its control to be translated into an Indigenous language; or*
> >
> > ***(b)*** *interpretation services to be provided to facilitate the use of an Indigenous language in the course of the federal institution's activities.*

South Africa

Language use and policy in South Africa began with colonization by the Dutch. It evolved throughout the nation's history, including the Union of South Africa, the dominance of two languages (English and Afrikaans) during the apartheid era and the official declaration of 11 languages of equal status in 2000.

English was declared the official language of South Africa in 1822 because the British were in power and used English as a way to maintain power and control over the Indigenous peoples.

During apartheid, Afrikaans and English were the only two official languages. After apartheid ended, nine Indigenous languages were added to the constitution as official languages of South Africa.[166]

The constitution also added that the government must take steps to ensure that the nine Indigenous languages are treated equally. The language most commonly used in a municipality that is one of the eleven languages should be prioritized when it involves official or government matters.

In 1995, the Minister of Arts, Culture, Science and Technology formed the Language Plan Task Group (LANGTAG) to advise the ministry on language-related issues. The primary goal of LANGTAG was to ensure language access to society in South Africa. One way to do so was "establishing equitable language facilitation services."[167] Several committees were created to support language rights of South Africans and to support the equitable use of the 11 official languages. The National Language Policy Framework of 2003 states:

> *For the purposes of conducting meetings or performing specific tasks every effort must be made to utilise language facilitation facilities such as translation and/or interpreting...where practically possible.*

---

166 Lilly Marjorie. (2010). Language Policy and Oppression in South Africa. Retrieved from: https://www.culturalsurvival.org/publications/cultural-survival-quarterly/language-policy-and-oppression-south-africa

167 A. Idah and J.O. Onu. (2017). Multilingualism and the New Language Policy in South Africa: Innovation and Challenges. Retrieved from: https://pdfs.semanticscholar.org/bb8b/43551da6e0cea89ae6b1a3938999f74783b2.pdf

> *For* official correspondence *purposes, the language of the citizen's choice must be used.* All *oral communication must take place in the preferred official language of the target audience.*[168]

The new Language in Education Policy (LiEP) was created to facilitate communication among the languages and regions of South Africa and show equity and respect for language diversity. The LiEP works to support the home language of the student while encouraging students to learn other languages. Students who are multilingual or polyglots (they know and use several languages) are considered valuable for the future of South Africa.

There are several provisions in place to protect the student's preferred language in education (of the 11 official languages). When a student's preferred language is not available in their school, the student can request accommodation for their preferred language.

However, there is still great debate in South Africa (just as in the U.S. and Canada) over what is written into the constitution and what is practiced daily. English and Afrikaans are still the most dominant languages spoken, and the remaining nine Indigenous languages do not have the same status or use. The risk of a language dying or disappearing is higher for Indigenous languages than dominant languages because most Indigenous languages are not widely spoken or used in higher education, the workplace or generally in society. The less a language is used, the easier it is to disappear or for its speakers to be discriminated against (Skovsholm, 2000).

South Africa has evolved from the original language practices of early colonization. The policies in place to preserve, support and respect language diversity and language equity are valuable. Yet it is the implementation and adherence to the constitutional principles that make it difficult to see the policies in action in South Africa (Beukes, 2009).

The professionalization of interpreting in South Africa, as in most of the world and particularly in developing nations, is a work in progress (Pienaar & Cornelius, 2015). Yet as a nation with robust language access laws and policies, South Africa may soon see extensive opportunities for remote interpreting. As policies and their applications fall more in line, the need for remote interpreters may well grow exponentially.

Australia

Language access requirements in Australia

> *Historically, the Australian Government has seen the provision of effective communication services for adult migrants as a key to their social and economic integration. Today, new language skills, cultural competency, the ability to navigate support systems, and access to social networks are some of the issues migrants face in successfully integrating into Australian society.*
>
> —Commonwealth of Australia, 2013, p. 4

In 2013, the Australian government issued the *Multicultural Language Services Guidelines for Australian Government Agencies.* These guidelines were written because, "All Australians have the right to communicate and engage with the Australian Government, irrespective of their first language preference" (Commonwealth of Australia, 2013, p. 7).

---

[168] National Language Policy Framework. (2002). Retrieved from: https://www.gov.za/sites/default/files/gcis_document/201409/langpolicyfinal0.pdf

The guideline states that each government agency must have a Language and Communication Plan for the communities they serve (similar to the language access plans required by federal and often state or local government agencies in the U.S.). These plans must outline how government institutions and services will work with interpreters and translators among other forms of language assistance

This document of guidelines is 55 pages with dozens of scenarios to demonstrate best practices. Additionally, there are several pages that outline the role of an interpreter, interpreting modalities (remote versus face-to-face) as well as the prioritization of credentialed interpreters with National Accreditation Authority for Translators and Interpreters (NAATI), discussed below.

Additionally, these guidelines suggest that a telephone interpreter be considered as the first way to provide interpreting services if the needs and demands of the session allow for it.

The guidelines suggest working with the highest NAATI-credentialed interpreter if available. They further outline the risks of working with bilingual staff who act as interpreters when they have not been professionally trained or credentialed. Additionally, the guidelines highlight why working with a NAATI-credentialed interpreter, or others considered qualified, helps to avoid the risk of conflict of interest.

NAATI

In 2012, NAATI launched a comprehensive review of its accreditation program. The process engaged universities, businesses and thousands of practitioners. From this review, NAATI developed a new Certification System, which debuted in 2018. Key features of the new system were:

- The utilization of live role players for dialogue tasks.
- The introduction of a recertification model that requires all practitioners to demonstrate work practice and professional development every three years to maintain their credentials.
- A minimum level of formal higher education to be eligible for testing.

Assessment rubrics were also introduced, as well as specialized interpreting tests in both the legal and health domains.

In 2022, NAATI tested and certified in 60 languages, with a target of testing in 70 languages by 2025. For languages where testing is not available, "Recognised Practising" credentials are awarded. These have the same minimum training, recertification, intercultural and ethics competencies requirements but utilize work practice evidence instead of testing for demonstration of skills.

In 2022, "Recognised Practising" was offered in 140 languages. NAATI specializes in certifying interpreters using live role play dialogues as part of their entry-level professional test (Certified Provisional Interpreter). This test is comprised of two face-to-face interpreting role plays and a third role play that involves remote interpreting. All can be tested remotely. The "Certified Interpreter" credential tests face-to-face and remote interpreting with role play plus recorded consecutive monologues, simultaneous monologues and sight translations.

Australian Sign Language (Auslan) is included, and in 2022, certification was available in 14 Indigenous languages; more are being added. More than 800 people coordinate these exams. There is no comparable program in any other country in the world, far less one that incorporates and includes remote interpreting to this degree. Over 13,000 practitioners in Australia hold NAATI interpreting or translating credentials in one of almost 200 languages.

NAATI is currently exploring an enhanced live role play online testing platform to replace commercially available video conference platforms such as Microsoft Teams and Zoom. Two of the authors of this textbook are involved with that process, which may result after the publication of this book in potential opportunities for NAATI certification of interpreters who live and work outside Australia.

Australia's national Translation and Interpreting Service (TIS)

Another remarkable achievement in Australia that dates back several decades is its national Translating and Interpreting Service (TIS National).

TIS National is a government interpreting service for immigrants and their service providers, government agencies and businesses, including those that provide healthcare and community services. TIS National offers both onsite and remote interpreters in more than 160 languages.

TIS National was established more than 50 years ago. Its prototype, the Commonwealth translating service, began in 1947. In 1973, what is apparently the world's first national remote interpreting service began: Australia's free Emergency Telephone Interpreting Service, provided to immigrants who did not speak English and their service providers. In 1991, the national telephone and national onsite interpreting services combined to create TIS National.[169]

In 2022, TIS National has access to more than 2,700 interpreters in more than 150 languages and provides both on-demand and scheduled OPI. It is available 24/7 for a local call to anyone or any organization in Australia. Its goal is access and equity in language services for all Australian residents.[170]

TIS National has developed a rigorous and thorough vetting process that Australian government agencies can trust.

Western Australia and its language policies

In February 2020, the Western Australian Multicultural Policy Framework (WAMPF)[171] was implemented for the public sector. It requires agencies to create multicultural plans that will service culturally and linguistically diverse populations.

---

169 For a more detailed history of TIS National, see https://www.tisnational.gov.au/About-TIS-National/History-of-TIS-National.aspx

170 About TIS National. See https://www.tisnational.gov.au/en/About-TIS-National

171 Western Australian Multicultural Policy Framework. Retrieved from: https://www.omi.wa.gov.au/docs/librariesprovider2/default-document-library/wa-multicultural-policy-framework-poster.pdf?sfvrsn=5da06f56_3

Since this is a new policy, the first copy of an agency's multicultural plans were due in January 2021 for review and its progress must be reported annually.

On November 3, 2020, Western Australian Language Services Policy[172] went into effect. The policy states that it "ensures equitable access to Western Australian public sector services, through the provision of language services" (Department of Local Government, Sport and Cultural Industries, 2020, p. iii).

The Minister for Citizenship and Multicultural Interests stated in the Foreword of the policy, "It is the obligation of all in the public sector to understand how to make services accessible to everyone. The Western Australian Language Services Policy 2020 is a key tool to do this" (Department of Local Government, Sport and Cultural Industries, 2020, p. i).

The policy defines language services as:

- Provision of NAATI credentialed interpreters.
- Translation of documents by qualified translators.
- Provision of print materials or digital materials in languages other than English.
- Provision of bilingual/multilingual staff for language-concordant services.
- Special telephone equipment for Deaf or Hard of Hearing people.

How the policy guides meaningful language access

The 37-page policy outlines the different ways an interpreter's services can be accessed (both face-to-face and remotely) as well as providing a decision-making guide to help the hiring entity know when to request an interpreter.

The policy also provides guidelines for booking an interpreter, considerations to make when choosing an interpreter and the modality of services, how to prepare for the session, the role of an interpreter and best practices and quality assurance when working with an interpreter.

How a language policy can affect remote interpreters

For you, a remote interpreter, this kind of policy is incredibly valuable. Not only are there policies in place to require language access but also there is practical information to guide those who request interpreting services. Remember, in remote interpreting you may be faced with participants who don't know your role or how to use your services.

In Western Australia, the leaders have created simple yet important tools to support language access, specifically including remote interpreting (although the strong focus there is on OPI). This guidance offers a clear and important example for other nations to follow.

As Chapter 10 of this volume makes clear, it's important to learn the qualifications necessary to work in a particular state or country. WAMPF includes several pages describing the required

---

172 WA Language Services Policy 2020. Retrieved from: https://www.omi.wa.gov.au/resources-and-statistics/publications/publication/language-services-policy-2020

qualifications for interpreters. If you interpret remotely for Western Australia from another country, the qualifications of interpreting in Western Australia are in effect and need to be followed. Review the requirements and determine next steps to become qualified and eligible to interpret for Western Australians.

→ Section 9.3 Review

This section offered several examples of language access laws around the world. Other countries have different language policies, and many (including a number in Europe) focus more on minority and Indigenous languages than language access for immigrants and refugees. In general, language policies, laws and other legislative approaches to providing language access continue to evolve around the world.

As a remote interpreter, your client list is potentially global. As you enter new markets to interpret, be sure to spend time looking up and studying relevant language access laws. You don't have to become an expert on them. Yet having some fundamental knowledge of these laws helps you both to comply with them and to become an informed professional in the field.

Section 9.4 Data Privacy

→ Learning objective 9.4

After completing this section, the remote interpreter will be able to describe data privacy requirements and how they affect the interpreter's decision-making.

→ Section 9.4 Overview

As an interpreter, you understand the incredible privilege it is to be brought into someone's private life to interpret for them. You hear and see things only because the participants do not share a common language and your services are needed.

There are ethical requirements in place for medical interpreters and legal interpreters that speak to the confidentiality of those sessions, but there is no overarching ethical standard for *all* interpreters in the U.S. or in most other countries of the world that addresses privacy.

Yet in every country that has codes of ethics for interpreters, confidentiality is a universal requirement in those codes, whether for general interpreting, interpreting in signed languages, or interpreting for particular specializations. (See Chapter 6 of this volume for an overview of codes of ethics for interpreters.)

Even if there were a broader ethical standard for all interpreters in every country, ethical standards are not law. They are the strictest form of guidelines for interpreters. The direst possible consequences are rare and typically involve the interpreter being expelled from a professional association or, in rare cases, not being allowed to practice interpreting professionally in that country.

However, several industries and nations have laws in place to ensure privacy. Such laws lay out the legal consequences when privacy is violated by anyone who provides services in specific areas, most commonly healthcare and legal services. This section will explore these privacy laws.

→ Section 9.4 Content

Privacy laws around the world

Data privacy is not just what is entered into a computer database. Data privacy addresses *all* the personal identifiable information that interpreters learn in the course of their work about participants who receive certain services or participate in certain programs, and in some cases about the people and institutions that provide those services.

Interpreters can learn incredibly private and sensitive information about people, companies and even countries.

Many countries have privacy laws of many kinds. Here are a few examples:

- Australia: Privacy Act
- Brazil: Civil Rights Framework for the Internet
- Canada: Personal Information Protection and Electronic Documents Act (PIPEDA)
- Colombia: Data Protection Law, Decree 1377
- European Union: General Data Protection Regulation (GDPR)
- France: Data Protection Act
- India: Information Technology Act (ITA)
- Italy: Personal Data Protection Code
- Japan: Act on the Protection of Personal Information (APPI)
- Morocco: Data Protection Law
- South Africa: Electronic Communications and Transactions Act
- U.S.: Children's Online Privacy Protection Act (COPPA)
- U.S.: Health Insurance Portability and Accountability Act (HIPAA)

The following two laws are examples of widely known privacy laws that affect interpreters in the U.S. and Europe. It's important that you study the privacy laws that affect your work, in whichever country or countries you provide interpreting services. These examples will help you understand what many privacy laws require and how they can affect interpreters.

U.S. Health Insurance Portability and Accountability Act (HIPAA) of 1996

Before we start exploring HIPAA, it's useful to know the definition of three key terms: covered entity, business associates and protected health information.[173]

Covered entity: Health plans, healthcare providers and healthcare clearinghouses that electronically transmit healthcare information.

Business associates: A person or member who provides services to a covered entity that has access to protected health information. Business associates must sign a contract with the covered entity describing what information they will learn, how it will be used and how it will be protected.

Protected health information: Individually identifiable information that is collected by a covered entity or a business associate. This information could include name, date of birth, diagnosis, address, health history and even primary language (if that information is enough to be able to identify a person in a specific context).

Now that you are familiar with some key terms, it's important to understand the purpose of HIPAA. The Centers for Disease Control and Prevention (CDC) states:

> *The Health Insurance Portability and Accountability Act of 1996 (HIPAA) is a federal law that required the creation of national standards to protect sensitive patient health information from being disclosed without the patient's consent or knowledge.*
>
> —CDC, 2022

The HIPAA Privacy Rule is a critical component. The CDC states:

> *A major goal of the Privacy Rule is to make sure that individuals' health information is properly protected while allowing the flow of health information needed to provide and promote high-quality healthcare, and to protect the public's health and well-being.*
>
> —CDC, 2022

HIPAA was signed into law in August 1996; however, it wasn't until April 2003 when the HIPAA Security Rule went into effect. The HIPAA Privacy Rule and Security Rule also prompted the creation of the Enforcement Rule in 2006. The Enforcement Rule allowed investigation into covered entities when they didn't comply with the Privacy Rule.

(Yes, this information is important for interpreters. This section will show why shortly.)

Then in 2009, the Health Information Technology for Economic and Clinical Health Act (HITECH) became law. This law started the transition of paper health records to electronic health records. The transition to digital files required that covered entities maintain protected health information of their patients.

---

[173] Health Insurance Portability and Accountability Act of 1996 (HIPAA). (2022). Centers for Disease Control and Prevention. See https://www.cdc.gov/phlp/publications/topic/hipaa.html

Finally, this process led to HIPAA being applied specifically to business associates, including *interpreters and language services*. Interpreters and language services are indeed business associates, because they provide a service to a covered entity. So they *must* observe this powerful privacy law.

HIPAA implications for remote interpreting

For a remote interpreter, what does HIPAA mean? It means it is against the law to share any information you learn about a patient in the U.S. with anyone outside the patient's treatment team, even if you do so by accident.

That requirement sounds simple, right? But it is not as simple as many interpreters think to obey strict privacy laws.

For example, while there is no such thing as being HIPAA certified, you are expected to be HIPAA compliant. Complying with the HIPAA Privacy Rule and Security Rule involves having *administrative, technical and physical safeguards* for the information handled and stored.

Examples of administrative safeguards are HIPAA courses or training sessions that give interpreters an overview of privacy requirements, expectations and how to be HIPAA compliant. There are also courses online that can teach you many of the important details of HIPAA compliance. Completing a course like this as an independent contractor working in medical environments can show that you know the requirements and expectations. There are many companies that offer a HIPAA compliance course online at a low cost.

Typically, these courses open interpreters' eyes to the *complexity* of safeguarding privacy and data.

There are several technical, physical and other administrative safeguards that you or your language service can adopt and maintain to comply with HIPAA. For example, written security and privacy policies and procedures, initial and annual training on HIPAA, electronic data secured and only accessed by a limited number of authorized individuals.

As a remote medical interpreter, consider the following for HIPAA compliance:

- Are you interpreting in a private and secure environment (where no one can overhear your interpreting or see into your workspace)?
- Do you have a method for destroying your notes?
- Is your internet connection secure?
- When reading emails with assignment details (on your computer or telephone), do you have security measures in place in case your computer or telephone is stolen or hacked?
- Do you minimize exposure of protected health information by encrypting your emails that contain such information, or by deleting or not adding protected health information when you don't need to do so?
- Do you know how to respond when a patient's family member asks about the patient's medical history, situation or plans?

General Data Protection Regulation (GDPR)

The General Data Protection Regulation (GDPR) is a European Union (EU) law that protects the personal electronic data for residents of countries in the EU (GDPR.eu, n.d.). The law applies to all businesses that come into contact with any EU citizen and collect data during a business transaction.

This regulation became law in 2016. It gave businesses until 2018 to become compliant. GDPR replaced the European Data Protection Directive of 1995, which gave all EU countries the freedom to customize the law, something the GDPR does not allow. Additionally, the Data Protection Directive had become outdated and not comprehensive enough for the digital age.

In 2020, the GDPR updated how U.S. companies complied with GDPR regulations. Ultimately, GDPR became law as the global economy and the digital age made personal electronic data less private and easier to misuse.

Before discussing GDPR further, the following definitions are important to know:

- Personal data: Any information that could be used to identify a person.
- Data processing: How data get collected, stored, shared or modified.

As a remote interpreter, you have the opportunity to work for people all over the world. Whether you are located in the EU or not, you have a responsibility to protect the information of those who live in the EU.

In the GDPR, there are eight basic people's privacy rights:

1. Right of access: Citizens have a right to ask for a copy of any personal data an organization has about them and how and why it is being used.
2. Right to be informed: Citizens have a right to know how their personal data is being used.
3. Right to restrict processing: Citizens can tell a business how that business can or cannot use their data.
4. Right to data portability: Citizens have a right to access their personal data in a way that works for them.
5. Right to object: Citizens can demand that a company stop processing their personal data.
6. Right to rectification: Citizens have the right to correct their information.
7. Rights in relation to automated decision-making and profiling: Citizens have the right to stop or prevent automated processing to make decisions for them.
8. Right to erasure: Citizens have the right to demand that a company destroy all of their personal data. (Some restrictions apply.)

There are steps you can take to ensure that you are protecting EU residents' private data. (Some of them are similar to following HIPAA requirements.) You may receive private data via email or text when accepting an assignment or when you are sent preparation material. Personal data can be as simple as an email address or a telephone number that is part of the invoicing process.

If someone were to steal that personal information from you, would the thief be able to identify that person? If the answer is yes, then that data needs to be protected or the use of it minimized.

As a remote interpreter, if you provide interpreting services to an EU business or individual, you certainly have access to—and the requirement to protect—personal data.

→ Section 9.4 Review

The two privacy laws discussed in this section, HIPAA and GDPR, are two important laws about data privacy. Depending on where you live, the kind of remote interpreting work you do, whether you work as an independent contractor (freelancer) or for a language service and which countries, specializations and services you interpret for, there may be important national privacy laws or policies that you will need to be aware of and follow.

In addition, any organization you interpret for may have its own privacy requirements for interpreters.

Data privacy, personal information and security may not be the first things you think about when you consider remote interpreting work, yet they are a vital part of your interpreter toolkit.

Knowing the laws and having the right practices and security measures in place are your responsibility. It can feel overwhelming to have to know about privacy laws, but there are experts available and other interpreters can often help you. You may work alone as an interpreter, but you need a community to help you learn, grow and stay in compliance with your legal requirements.

When you're in doubt, you can always reach out to the following people/places to get guidance:

- The language service or organization that requested your services.
- Local interpreting organizations or associations.
- A trusted peer and mentor.
- Professional organizations with community forums or social media pages.

→ Chapter Activities

Activity 9.1: Talking about language access laws

After reading about language access laws and how they support communicative autonomy, can you explain how these laws might apply to your work as an interpreter?

Instructions

1. Have a device, such as smartphone, that is able to record. Set it up to record.
2. Imagine that a participant in an interpreted session tells you, "No, the patient can communicate well enough—we don't really need you here, interpreter." (You can even ask a colleague, family member or friend to ask you this question in their own words—perhaps aggressively.)

3. Record yourself answering this question.
4. Listen to your recording.
5. Answer these questions:
   a. Did you sound confident and firm but friendly and professional?
   b. Was your answer clear, brief and to the point?
   c. Did it take into account (where relevant) the service user or patient's right to language assistance and communicative autonomy?
6. If any of your answers are "No," record yourself again answering the same question as above.
7. Keep practicing, recording and listening until you feel confident you can answer this question well.

Here is a sample you can consider using. Modify as needed.

> To the participant who speaks the language of service:
>
> "This is the interpreter speaking. I understand that you believe the participant speaks English well enough and doesn't need me here to interpret. However, I want to confirm with the participant that they're comfortable not working with an interpreter before I leave the session. One moment, please."
>
> To the participant who does not speak the language of service:
>
> "This is the interpreter speaking. The provider believes you speak English well enough to communicate and you don't need an interpreter. Are you comfortable speaking in English or would you like to communicate through an interpreter?"

Activity 9.2: Compare state language access laws

Instructions

1. Go to this link: https://healthlaw.org/resource/summary-of-state-law-requirements-addressing-language-needs-in-health-care-2/ (If the link is no longer active, do an internet search to locate the NHeLP publication, *Summary of State Law Requirements Addressing Language Needs in Health Care*).
2. Once you have downloaded this report, open it and look up the laws for the U.S. state where you live. If you do not reside in the U.S., choose any state that you would like to visit or live in.
3. Answer the following questions:
   a. Number of language access provisions in this state: ____________
   b. What is the most important content of the newest regulations in this state?

____

____

c. Read all the regulations for this state. Which ones strike you as surprising or important? Which ones are new to you?

___

___

4. Now look up the laws in a U.S. state that you interpret for often or think you may interpret for often. (Again, if you do not reside in the U.S., pick any state you wish.) Answer the same questions, below, and then in addition consider any differences or similarities between the laws of these two states.

   d. Number of language access provisions in this state: ________

   e. What is the most important content of the newest regulations in this state?

___

___

   f. Read all the regulations for this state. Which ones strike you as surprising or important? Which ones are new to you?

___

___

   g. Compare the laws of these two states and note down any similarities and any differences.

___

___

___

___

Activity 9.3: Explore language access laws in different countries

Instructions

Working as a remote interpreter means you may have a global client list. Look at the countries where your clients may be located and research which language access laws may exist.

As you are researching, answer the following questions:

1. In the countries where your clients (or potential clients) are located, are there language access laws for healthcare, legal, educational, community or humanitarian settings? If so, what are their key requirements?

___

___

2. Are there any laws outlining the qualifications of interpreters? If so what are they?

   How do you meet those qualifications? If you don't, how can you meet them?

3. Can you find any initiatives or efforts to implement language access laws or policies? If so, what do you think they are intended to achieve?

Activity 9.4 (a): How to respond to a family request for patient information

Background

You have accepted a VRI assignment for a U.S. health clinic. You recognize the patient from recent interpreted sessions.

The session is for an inpatient appointment. When the call connects, the family is in the room, the patient is asleep and the provider has just stepped out of the room for a minute. The family recognizes you from the previous interpreted encounters and asks you for an update on the patient's health.

The family isn't a part of the healthcare team. You are the interpreter and not a healthcare provider. The patient has also not, to your knowledge, allowed their healthcare information to be shared with the family. For you to answer their question and share information on the patient would be a violation of HIPAA (or other privacy laws).

Instructions

1. Write down what you will say in response to the family's request for information.
2. Practice saying it.

Your answer may sound something like this. Adapt this model and rewrite it for your own language, culture and the professional context of the service.

"This is the interpreter speaking. I understand you want an update about your loved one. Once the doctor comes back, I'd be happy to interpret your questions."

Activity 9.4 (b): Develop a plan to protect privacy

Background

You have recently been contracted to provide interpreting services for a virtual conference in Italy and you live in Minnesota. (Or choose another U.S. state or another country.) You will be sent materials before the session as well as information about the participants. All this information will be shared over email, and a WhatsApp group will be created for you and the other interpreters assigned to this conference to communicate easily.

As you prepare for this conference ask yourself:

- Are you collecting only the information necessary for the job?
- Do you have consent from the person who lives in the EU to collect personal data?
- If any of the eight basic rights are exercised by the EU citizen, do you know how to respond?
- What security measures do you have in place to protect the individual's information (on your computer, telephone, cloud-based services)?
- If the data is stolen, do you have a communication plan for alerting the affected individuals?
- Does the interpreting platform that you will be using have disclosures on how it is GDPR compliant?

If the answer to any of these questions is "No," write down your plan to address those privacy concerns:

Chapter Conclusion and Review

This chapter gave you an introduction to some of the most common laws and policies in language access around the world. You also learned how important data privacy is for all of us, not only for those who rely on interpreters for communication. As this chapter made clear, language access laws and policies vary from country to country and state to state.

When you work as a remote interpreter, part of supporting communicative autonomy involves respecting the laws and policies that govern language access, privacy and security. While it's unfortunate that not every country or state has robust language access laws, those places that do provide valuable examples and models for others.

Remember, the laws and policies that govern interpreting services might not be the same as in the place where you physically work as a remote interpreter. Having a global client list may feel overwhelming. You're not expected to know all language laws, nor are you expected to speak about them as if you were a lawyer. However, being familiar and staying up to date with relevant laws and policies will help you keep informed and can have a direct impact on the services you provide.

Quality language access solutions include remote interpreting and supporting participants' ability to access public services and healthcare. When needed, they should be provided. Unfortunately, in many places that does not happen, and language access laws are necessary. Sometimes the injustice that leads to a new law is difficult to witness or learn about, but it paves the way for the communicative autonomy of all and further elevates the need for professional language access solutions.

Chapter 10

Danielle Meder, RID-NIC

Portfolios for Remote Interpreters

Learning Objectives

After completing this chapter, the remote interpreter will be able to:

Learning Objective 10.1: Discuss the importance of having an interpreter portfolio.

Learning Objective 10.2: Define and describe different types of interpreter credentials.

Learning Objective 10.3: Identify the most common specializations in remote interpreting and relevant credentials for each of them.

Learning Objective 10.4: Describe key strategies to enhance one's interpreting network and professional presence through social media.

Learning Objective 10.5: Develop a plan for finding work as a remote interpreter.

Introduction

Remote interpreters can work anywhere. Your potential clients may be in your local area or around the globe. Building a portfolio to demonstrate your skill, training and experience is an important part of working as a remote interpreter.

Showcasing your professionalism not only helps you but it also helps the organizations, and all the participants you interpret for, learn what to expect and seek from remote interpreters.

It would be easy if a common credential for remote interpreters were accepted all over the world in every language. Unfortunately, credentials, such as certification or licensure and even education or training, vary widely by location and specialization. They don't typically include all languages.

Yet all interpreters can build a portfolio to showcase their competency. Building a portfolio goes beyond simply sharing your credentials. It includes other important elements. This chapter will explore many of them in detail.

Section 10.1 Your Interpreter Portfolio

→ Learning objective 10.1

After completing this section, the remote interpreter will be able to discuss the importance of having an interpreter portfolio.

→ Section 10.1 Overview

When you read the word *portfolio*, what comes to mind? Do you perhaps think of an architect or an artist with a large dark folder full of their renderings or paintings? Or perhaps an investor who wants to show you where all their money is invested?

A portfolio can be any collection of your qualifications, credentials and experience that highlights the quality of your work. If a potential client asks to see your interpreter portfolio, what would you include in it? Where would you keep it?

Remember, you're a remote interpreter. Your portfolio doesn't have to be something that you physically give to the client. Your clients may be global, and the interpreters they work with may also work anywhere in the world. You will want to stand out as a true professional and a skilled, reliable remote interpreter. A digital portfolio can help you demonstrate your *value*.

A digital portfolio is also an excellent marketing strategy for people to learn about you. This chapter will show you how you can easily communicate to others your skills and professionalism.

→ Section 10.1 Content

What goes into a portfolio?

A portfolio is more than just a résumé. It's a collection of items that, taken together, showcase your training, qualifications, credentials, experience and make you look like the true professional you are.

Especially if you're an interpreter in a language with no certification available, your portfolio will demonstrate who you are as a remote interpreter and why clients will want to work with you.

Here are some items to include in your portfolio.

- Personal statement
- University degree, college degree and other higher education
- Interpreter-specific training
- Language proficiency scores or certificates
- Interpreting skills assessments
- Relevant certifications
- Services offered and markets served

- Industry-specific training (e.g., automotive, medical terminology, biomechanical)
- Testimonials from clients and previous employers
- Clients served (with permission)
- Link to social media platforms
- Samples of your work
- Remote interpreting modes and modalities:
  - Consecutive
  - Simultaneous
  - Over the phone interpreting (OPI)
  - Video remote interpreting (VRI)
  - Remote simultaneous interpreting (RSI)
- Remote platforms you have experience in such as:
  - Zoom
  - KUDO
  - Ablio
  - Webex

Be careful what you share

It's important to remember that one of the most critical ethical tenets of the interpreting profession is confidentiality. (See Chapter 6 and also Section 9.4 of this volume.) If you want to share that you worked for a certain client, be sure to get that client's written consent first. Once you do, reveal only what they consent to let you share. In general, plan to share as little as possible without revealing what or for whom you interpreted.

Samples of your work can be an excellent way to demonstrate your skills. However, you may need to receive consent from everyone involved to do so. If you interpret for an event or meeting that is advertised and publicly available, such as a televised COVID-19 pandemic press conference, you may usually share that work without permission, but be careful.

Your personal statement

What is a personal statement?

The first item at the top of the portfolio list above is your *personal statement.* A personal statement is a personalized biography or a clear description of your brand (discussed later in this section).

In other words, a personal statement is a short paragraph, or a few sentences, about you and your work. It could describe:

- Why you became an interpreter.
- What industries you work in.

- What services you offer.
- Your activity in the field.

Examples of personal statements

How personal statements look can vary widely. Here is an example of a personal statement.

> *My name is Natalia, and I am a Polish interpreter committed to quality and integrity in language access. In my 10-year career as a professional interpreter, I have completed dozens of hours of interpreter training and have developed a specialization in healthcare and pharmacology interpreting. I'm an active member of several national and international interpreting organizations and a mentor to new interpreters.*

If you have an interpreting company name that you use instead of your name, your company statement might look like the one that Words Across Borders has used:

> *The power of being understood. This essential need drives human communication. yet understanding takes so much more than simply finding the right words.*
>
> *Everything at Words Across Borders starts from this basic premise—you have something you need to communicate and you want to be truly understood, with all the nuances and depth of meaning preserved.*
>
> *Whether you need Spanish-English interpreting and translation, training and curriculum development, language resources for international development, or event planning and public speaking,* ***Words Across Borders*** *understands that your success depends on achieving authentic understanding through communication.*[174]

These are just two examples, but there are plenty of ways to make a personal or company statement. At the end of this chapter, you'll have an opportunity to write one.

Where should you keep your portfolio?

Digital professional networks

A digital (or social) professional network is a platform similar to social platforms, such as Facebook and Instagram; however, it focuses instead on allowing professionals to connect with one another and share news, updates, professional events and other industry information.

Examples of large digital professional networks include LinkedIn (based in the U.S. but international in scope), Dajie, Wealink and Renhe in China and India Mobile Congress (created for information technology professionals) in India.

An online professional network is an ideal place to post links to your work, share a personal statement, have clients and colleagues write reviews and market yourself. These professional networking sites also offer you a quick and easy way to create a digital portfolio. (See Section 10.4 of this chapter for more details about professional social media networks.)

---

[174] Retrieved from: https://www.wordsacrossborders.com/. Disclaimer: This statement is from the website of one of the authors of this textbook (Katharine Allen), who is not the author of this chapter.

An interpreter website

There are many free services to help you build and host your own professional website if you choose to have one. The website address can be your name or the name of your business. All the items in the list above, and more, can be posted on the website.

Many professional interpreters add a section to receive requests for quotes or even share articles or blogs they have written. For example, Katty Kauffmann, a senior conference interpreter with extensive experience in remote interpreting, has a website that highlights her extensive experience and also includes videos that feature her or that she created. (See https://kattykauffman.com/interpreting/)

To view other websites with interpreter portfolios, search for interpreter profiles on LinkedIn, ProZ.com or other interpreter marketplaces to get an idea of how professional interpreters create online portfolios.

Remember to keep your portfolio up to date. Whenever you complete a training program, receive a letter of recommendation, get an award or any other credential or have another accomplishment, be sure to include it in your portfolio.

You are a remote interpreter with a potentially global client list, so you can include any relevant credentials. In the next section, we'll explore the different kinds of credentials and what they mean.

Creating a brand as a remote interpreter

What is your brand?

Branding is a way of defining yourself and who you are as a professional. It can involve many different elements—there is no single way to brand yourself.

For example, you can share publicly, in various ways:

- Your professional vision, mission and goals.
- What makes you different from other interpreters.
- What benefits you offer that help you "stand out" from your competitors.
- Who your customers are.
- What your logo and tagline are (more on that below).
- Information about *you:* your integrity, commitment, passion, experience, specialties and more.

Why remote interpreters need to brand themselves

Creating an online presence in our current digital age is crucial for building *brand identity.* It's particularly important, however, for the remote interpreter.

Figure 10.1: **Elements of a personal brand**

After all, if someone in another state, province or country wants your services, they will probably never meet you face to face. You can't easily make a personal impression if you can't meet the person—unless you brand yourself.

Develop your brand

One way to develop a brand is to research the online presence of other successful interpreters—especially their websites and social media posts.

Another way is to be true to your brand. Live up to what you convey about yourself. Take a look at Figure 10.2, from the website of a U.S. interpreter, Mireya Pérez, who has become famous for her podcast that helps interpreters to brand themselves.

Figure 10.2: **Mireya Pérez, Brand the Interpreter, Inc.**

When you work as a remote interpreter, consider creating or revamping your *digital footprint:* that is, your online reputation. Creating a brand is about the *ideas* you represent, sharing consistent *values* and the *impressions* these leave on others when they think of you.

Where to start

To begin branding yourself, or your business, it's important to have a clear understanding of your own values and vision, so don't be afraid to sit down and expand on these topics. (See Figure 10.1: Elements of a personal brand.)

Understanding and knowing these foundational elements will help bring clarity and meaning to your work. Start thinking of yourself as a brand and begin by asking yourself questions, such as:

- What do I want to be known for?
- What subject matter do I want to be perceived as an expert in?
- What do I want potential clients to remember when they think of my brand?
- How and where can I show up consistently to share my messaging?

In essence, creating a brand is about repeating a message with enough consistency that it brands itself in the minds of others. Clarify your intention, provide powerful value and create a consistent online presence in several ways (for example, on a website, professional networking platforms and other social media) to create a personal brand that others will remember. Make a name for yourself—and honor it.

Business branding vs. branding yourself

There are many reasons you could choose to market yourself under a business name rather than your own name. If you market your services only under your own name, your branding will look different (and more personal) than if you do so under your company name.

But if you have a company, you can still include a personal statement on your website and in social media, such as a biography or paragraph that is only about yourself. In other words, you can brand yourself *and* your business. Both are important.

→ Section 10.1 Review

Portfolios for a remote interpreter are a valuable way to market your services, enhance your remote interpreting presence and increase work opportunities. A strong interpreter portfolio can help you brand yourself, enhance your career and lead you to success.

As a remote interpreter, you may lack opportunities to meet people in person and make a truly personal impression. As you can see, remote interpreters might have clients all over the world. Having an online portfolio that you can point someone toward will be useful for interpreters in general, but it is *critical* for remote interpreters to have one.

The items to include in your portfolio suggested in this section are only the beginning. Your portfolio should reflect your experience, qualifications and personality. These will grow and change over time. Your personal statement can give others a window into your interests, values and what makes you different and distinct. A portfolio is a wonderful way to shine and make your mark in a global marketplace.

Section 10.2 Interpreter Credentials

→ Learning objective 10.2

After completing this section, the remote interpreter will be able to define and describe different types of interpreter credentials.

→ Section 10.2 Overview

Interpreters have many ways to demonstrate their professionalism and experience. To understand just how varied interpreting credentials are, let's set the stage with several interpreters who have just met each other at a North American interpreting conference. All these interpreters have many years of experience. They come from all over the continent and interpret in different industries.

As the interpreters sit down at their table, they begin to introduce themselves.

Interpreter A from Canada is an accredited interpreter.

Interpreter B from Mexico is a qualified Indigenous interpreter trained by INALI.[175]

Interpreter C from Idaho in the U.S. is a licensed interpreter.

Interpreter D from Washington State in the U.S. is an authorized medical interpreter with the Washington State Department of Social and Health Services (DSHS).

Interpreter E from Florida in the U.S. is a registered court interpreter.

Interpreter F from Alabama in the U.S. is a certified medical interpreter with CCHI.[176]

These six interpreters from all over North America have quite different credentials. This situation can be confusing, not only for clients and consumers of remote interpreting services but also for interpreters.

Which credentials should *you* pursue? All these interpreters live and work in North America. Imagine trying to decide which credentials to pursue, if they are even available in your language, when you work as a remote interpreter with a potentially global client base.

Before we explore this section, let's define some important terms that are used to explain interpreter qualifications and give you clear examples of each.

→ Section 10.2 Content

Definitions

Certificate

Certificates are written attestations. In other words, they show that you have accomplished something. Often you'll get a certificate after attending a workshop, a webinar or a noncredit course. These programs may have been offered at no cost or charged a registration fee.

Certificates may demonstrate participation or completion—*but they don't mean you are certified.*

A common example of a certificate for interpreters is the one you receive after completing a foundation training program. For example, a 40-hour healthcare interpreter training course in the U.S. qualifies interpreters to apply for national medical certification. It is a gateway to enter the professions of community and medical interpreting. This certificate is therefore a critically important credential in the U.S.—but a certificate does not *certify* you as an interpreter. (Certification will be explained later in this section.)

---

175 Instituto Nacional de Lenguas Indígenas, created in 2003, is an organization responsible for defending and promoting the linguistic rights of Indigenous communities in Mexico. See https://en.wikipedia.org/wiki/Instituto_Nacional_de_Lenguas_Ind%C3%ADgenas. In 2022, the Mexican presidency announced the dissolution of INALI.

176 CCHI is a U.S. nonprofit organization founded in July 2009 to develop and administer certification programs for healthcare interpreters in the U.S. Its programs include Core Certification Healthcare Interpreter and Certified Healthcare Interpreter. See https://cchicertification.org/about-us/

University and college degrees

You will find interpreter degree programs all over the world. In the U.S., for example, students can earn an associate's degree at a two-year college in either spoken or sign language interpreting. It will be much harder to find a bachelor's or a master's degree program in interpreting or translation at a four-year university in the U.S.; there are few.

To be a recognized conference interpreter in Europe, you would probably need a master's degree in that field, and such degree programs exist in many European Union universities. But to be a community or a medical interpreter in Europe, just as in the U.S., you might struggle to find a university degree in that subject. (Spain is an interesting exception. Many universities in Spain offer degrees in community interpreting, which is known there as public service interpreting.)

Some—not many—countries in the world offer four-year or graduate degrees in interpreting or translation, including (for example) Canada, Japan, Kazakhstan, Korea, Lebanon and Mexico. Most of these degree programs focus on conference, general or sign language interpreting. Some may address court or medical interpreting.

Yet even a university degree does not mean you are a *certified* interpreter. For example, interpreters studying at Rochester Institute of Technology National Technical Institute for the Deaf (located in Rochester, New York, U.S.) can register for a bachelor's degree program in American Sign Language-English Interpretation. Students who graduate from this program will have studied interpreting skills for four years, but will not be able to say they are *certified.*

Language proficiency

Assessing language proficiency

Language proficiency is the measure of your ability to communicate in a given language. A language proficiency test evaluates your ability to speak, understand, read and/or write in that specific language.

Many agencies offer language proficiency assessments. The results are often scored based on national or international language proficiency scales. These respected scales are somewhat similar to each other. They include:

- United Nations Language Framework (UNLF)
- Common European Framework of Reference for Languages (CEFR)
- Council of Europe (COE)
- Interagency Language Roundtable (ILR)[177]
- American Council on the Teaching of Foreign Languages (ACTFL)[178]

[177] Used primarily by the U.S. federal government but developed in collaboration with the academic community and the private sector.

[178] Used by U.S. institutions of higher education, a number of language services, interpreter training organizations and other private entities in the U.S. **Note** that the ILR and the ACTFL scales are closely calibrated with each other to help support a degree of consistency across U.S. government and the U.S. private sector language proficiency testing.

- Canadian Language Benchmarks (CLB)
- Australian Foreign Service Language Proficiency Ratings

To be clear, language proficiency is considered a *necessary* but not *sufficient* qualification for interpreting. If you are not bilingual (or multilingual), you should not interpret. However, as all readers of this book are likely well aware, being bilingual does not mean one can interpret.

Language proficiency tests should be research-based and scored to a national or international language proficiency scale. The uses to which those tests are put should be rigorously externally evaluated.

In 2020, ASTM International, the leading U.S.-based organization for international standards, published a valuable guide to recognized best practices and industry standards for creating reliable, validated language proficiency tests (ASTM, 2020). This document focuses on testing of language for communicative purposes.

However, many poor quality language tests are used in the U.S. and other countries to test interpreters. Such tests provide results that may not be reliable, consistent or accurate. They can also give inflated confidence in a candidate's ability to communicate in the tested language.

Confusion about language testing

Having a quality language proficiency certificate or test result in your portfolio demonstrates your proficiency in a language. It does not show your ability to interpret. Language proficiency can be tested for oral, written, reading or comprehension skills. Interpreters should ideally be tested for oral proficiency skills at a minimum, although most interpreters also need reading and writing skills in their work.

Which language to test?

A great deal of confusion exists about language testing. One type of confusion concerns which language to test because, in many cases, due to the cost of testing, organizations will test interpreters in only one language. Often, the language that interpreters are exempted from being tested for is the language that is *not the* national or official language (e.g., English in the U.S., which is the national, but not official, language). This type of exemption is a serious mistake!

After all, if reasons of costs or logistics are going to exempt an interpreter from language testing in *one* language, *that exemption should be the language they are most proficient* in—that is to say, exempt them for testing in their *primary* (usually native) language.

In some cases, however, their dominant language is unclear, for example, if someone immigrates to another country as a young teen. It may be that either language (their original native tongue or the dominant language of their new country) is their primary language.

Only language proficiency testing in *both* languages can even determine what the interpreter's dominant or primary language is. Therefore, interpreters should be tested for language proficiency in all their working languages.

Testing heritage speakers

Heritage speakers grow up speaking another language at home. This language is not the official or dominant language of the country or region where they live and are educated.

Heritage speakers are an excellent example of the need to test interpreters in all their working languages. For example, a heritage speaker will often say that their native language is the one they grew up speaking at home with their family. However, a language test will reveal that the language that they used at school, in the larger community and later in the workplace is almost always their primary language.

Additionally, the language spoken in the home may not be reflective of the professional command necessary to interpret in the native language. Being able to communicate in any language at all levels of language is necessary. For example, if you grew up speaking Thai at home because your parents are both Thai, this does not imply that you are able to accurately interpret medical terminology, a lawyer's advice to a client, a financial qualification form or a retirement plan into Thai. You might even struggle with interpreting everyday vocabulary into Thai, such as pain symptoms (stabbing, piercing or throbbing, for example) or school matters (school patrols, lockers, gym shorts, for example).

Everyone has their own perception of how well they communicate in their primary language. Only a reliable language proficiency test reports actual proficiency. It is highly recommended, cost permitting, to assess interpreters in their primary or native (A) language as well as their secondary (B and C) languages because the results are often surprising and informative.

If cost precludes testing the interpreter in all working languages, then at a minimum the interpreter should be tested in their weaker working languages. Use a reliable screening process to determine which of the interpreter's languages is the primary or dominant versus their weaker languages.

Professional membership

As a remote interpreter you may often work alone, but you can still be a part of the larger interpreting community. Joining different interpreting organizations will help you stay connected to trends, best practices, the evolution of the profession and more.

Most often, to be a member of any interpreting organization, you don't have to be a certified interpreter or even professionally trained. Yet being a member demonstrates your commitment to professionalism and to the interpreting industry as a whole.

There are many types of interpreting organizations. Some are true membership professional organizations. Some represent interpreters (or translators and interpreters) in general, while others also support anyone who works with and supports interpreters.

Some of the associations or groups focus on general interpreting, while others are for specific specializations, such as court, medical or conference interpreting. The organization could be national, regional or local interpreters. A number of them also include translators.

Here are several membership organizations that you may want to consider joining. The list below offers only well-known examples. Depending on where you live and where you provide your remote interpreting services, you may want to consider the organizations in those countries. For a helpful list of international professional associations, see the website of Inbox Translation.[179]

A few international professional associations

- The American Association of Language Specialists (TAALS)
- International Association of Conference Interpreters (AIIC)
- International Association of Professional Translators and Interpreters (IAPTI)
- International Federation of Translators (FIT) [includes interpreters]
- World Association of Sign Language Interpreters (WASLI)

National U.S. organizations

- American Translators Association (ATA)[180]
- California Healthcare Interpreting Association (CHIA)[181]
- International Medical Interpreters Association (IMIA)[182]
- National Council on Interpreting in Health Care (NCIHC)
- Registry of Interpreters for the Deaf (RID)

Examples of professional associations in other countries

- Australian Institute of Interpreters and Translators (AUSIT)
- Canadian Translators, Terminologists and Interpreters Council (CTTIC)
- Colombian Association of Translators, Terminologists, and Interpreters (ACTTI)
- Ecuadorian Association of Translators and Interpreters (ATIEC)
- International Association for Egyptian Translators (IAFET)
- Israel Translators Association (ITA)
- Japanese Association of Sign Language Interpreters (JASLI)
- New Zealand Society of Translators and Interpreters (NZSTI)
- Polish Association of Conference Interpreters (PSTK)
- South African Translators' Institute (SATI)
- Translators Association of China (TAC)

Again, these are only a few examples.

---

179 See https://inboxtranslation.com/resources/professional-associations-translators-interpreters/#italy

180 ATA members include many interpreters.

181 Technically a regional association, CHIA has a wide national membership and attendance at events.

182 Although IMIA is an international association, its activities are primarily located in the U.S.

Accredited interpreter

At least two countries, Canada and Australia, have historically offered accreditation programs for interpreters. Australia has switched in recent years to a national certification program (discussed shortly), while Canada still accredits interpreters.

The Canadian Ontario Council on Community Interpreting (OCCI) defines accredited interpreter as:

> *An interpreter who has passed the screening criteria of a particular organization and has been awarded a certain recognition or accreditation. An accredited interpreter is NOT necessarily a Certified Interpreter a Certified Court Interpreter or a Certified Conference Interpreter.*[183]

The Canadian federal government even has guidelines about working with accredited interpreters in interviews involving immigrants and refugees.[184] However, broadly speaking, the focus in Canada is more on the certification than the accreditation of interpreters, and specifically the certification of conference, court and community interpreters.[185]

Licensed interpreter

Licensure is more than certification. It authorizes individuals to practice a profession in a given geographical region, typically after taking a federal, state or provincial exam.

State licensure requirements often require interpreters to demonstrate national certification, training and background checks. Licensure in the U.S. is most often for American Sign Language (ASL) interpreters and does not apply generally to spoken language interpreters. Two exceptions are Washington State, which both certifies and licenses medical and social services spoken language interpreters,[186] and Oregon, which in effect licenses (but does not certify) healthcare interpreters.[187]

Many states in the U.S. require ASL interpreters to hold state licensure to work, even if they do not reside in or travel to work in that state (but may perform remote interpreting in that state). Some states, such as North Carolina, specifically license interpreters to work in the state. The licensure requirement ensures that interpreters meet the state's minimum requirements to work while also holding interpreters legally accountable if they work without licensure.

Licensed interpreter trainer

Licensing *trainers* of interpreters appears to be a phenomenon unique to the U.S. Some U.S. training programs have licensed trainers to teach their material to other interpreters. In this case, licensed means "authorized by a private entity." (For example, the publisher of this textbook licenses trainers to present three of its interpreting programs.[188])

183 Retrieved from: https://www.occi.ca/occi-accreditation-framework-details

184 See https://www.canada.ca/en/immigration-refugees-citizenship/corporate/publications-manuals/operational-bulletins-manuals/interview/interpreter/program-specific-procedures.html

185 See https://www.cttic.org/certification/

186 See https://www.dshs.wa.gov/office-of-the-secretary/language-testing-and-certification-program

187 See https://hciregistry.dhsoha.state.or.us

188 At the time of publication, the publisher of this textbook, under its training department, has more than 425 licensed

Licensing is not the same as licensure (a *government* authorization to practice a profession) but rather a *commercial* license to present a specific program.

Licensing for interpreter trainers gives them permission to teach general or specialized programs based on the specific requirements set out by the licensing organization, agency or company to use their materials and information in teaching the licensed programs. Licensing in this case applies only to organizations and/or trainers, not interpreters.

Certification

Let's look at the definition of certified interpreter from the U.S. National Council on Interpreting in Health Care (NCIHC).

> *A certified interpreter is an interpreter who is certified as competent by a professional organization or government entity through rigorous testing based on appropriate and consistent criteria.*[189]

In short, certification is a *process* by which a third party—for example, a *federal* or *state government* agency, a *professional organization* or a *certifying body*—attests that someone is trained and qualified to provide or perform a particular service.

If you are a certified interpreter, your certification is a powerful credential because it offers evidence of your interpreting skills. You usually get certified by taking a test or exam—a formal assessment. The exam has to be overseen and administered by a *qualified* entity—not simply a company, a school or a language service but a *recognized certification body.*

Certification is perhaps the most significant credential you can obtain (if it is available to you) because certification lets everyone know you have certain necessary qualifications and skills to perform the work.

How do you get certified?

Most interpreter certification is voluntary (unless it is also licensure). To be certified, you must usually:

- Prove you are eligible to be an interpreter (for example, show you are older than 18, with the required experience, level of education and potentially other credentials).
- Pay the examination fee.
- Take a written test or exam of knowledge.
- Take a test of interpreting skills (consecutive, simultaneous and/or sight translation, or even translation).
- Take continuing education classes to maintain your status.

trainers for its programs in 44 U.S. states, Washington, DC, Guam, Puerto Rico and six other countries. See www.cultureandlanguage.net for details.

[189] Retrieved from: https://www.ncihc.org/faq-translators-and-interpreters

Where do you get certified?

Now you may be asking, "Where can I get certified?" There are several organizations that certify interpreters, and we will explore examples of those shortly. The certification examples that will be discussed come primarily from the U.S. because the authors are U.S.-based and because so few certification programs are available elsewhere, but programs in Canada, Australia and the UK will also be mentioned.

Why interpreter credentials are important–especially certification

The terms used to describe interpreter credentials are often confusing, but you may need to take the time to explain them to organizations that you work with to help demonstrate your own professionalism and qualifications.

In order to explain these terms clearly, you will need to examine why having and listing your credentials in a portfolio is so important. They help you to establish and maintain trust with the organizations you work for. You are not just saying, "I am a professional." With your portfolio, you are *demonstrating* your value as a professional.

However, if you are certified, you might have to explain in more detail just what certification means for an interpreter and why it matters.

Highlight your relevant qualifications–again, especially certification

You may say, "I work remotely. I'm providing interpreting services to other states or another country. Do I even need credentials? Does it matter which ones I have?"

Yes. It does matter. It's important for you to know the answer to these questions. For example, perhaps there is an abbreviation you should be putting after your name (on your business card, website, your emails and so on) that shows which certification you have.

You want your portfolio to reflect and highlight your *relevant* qualifications and how they meet the client's needs and local requirements.

Let's look at professionals in other industries for a moment. Teachers, plumbers, nurses, pilots and lawyers all must complete training, hands-on learning, and then pass an assessment to validate their knowledge, experience and effectiveness as a professional. It's likely that most people will only want trained and qualified plumbers coming to their home to fix a leak. It's also likely that most people wouldn't feel comfortable flying in an airplane with a pilot who hasn't been tested and qualified to fly the plane safely or have hand surgery performed by someone who was never licensed as a surgeon.

Training, experience and credentials (especially certification or licensure) give consumers peace of mind that only *professionals* are working in their selected industries.

Interpreting in most parts of the world isn't licensed or monitored in that way. You are a professional and offer an incredibly valuable and essential service, but you have to show that. It takes a great deal of work, training and practice to become a competent, reliable interpreter. Earning interpreter credentials demonstrates that you are not only qualified for the work but also you are acting as a member of a recognized *profession*.

The more interpreters who commit to pursuing certification or other formal credentials, the stronger the field becomes and the more interpreters will be recognized *as* professionals.

It is *your* responsibility as a remote interpreter to build your portfolio. Look at the specializations you want to interpret in, the countries or regions where your services will be provided and then determine which relevant credentials are available to you. Earn credentials that will help you demonstrate your qualifications, skill and experience and your commitment to providing high-quality services.

Should you pursue certification?

As you can see, there are many different credentials an interpreter can earn. Certification is certainly an important one and possibly the most important because it tests, and attests to, your interpreting skills.

Yet as a remote interpreter, depending on your language pair, you may not be eligible to pursue certification. You may interpret for clients in the U.S., for example, but unless you reside in the U.S., most of the certifications listed above would not be easily available to you.

You should familiarize yourself with certification and how it differs from other credentials because clients and participants may not always know what credentials you have or can obtain. They may not know that few countries offer certification for interpreters. Yet in an increasingly global and remote interpreting world, a client may ask to see your certification.

If your country or language doesn't have an available certification, you may have to educate the client about it.

Remember, credentials are not just certifications but can also be demonstrated by professional memberships and education. Certification is available to such a limited number of countries and language pairs that until there is a certification in every language, interpreters will need to use other credentials, such as training, proficiency exams, education and letters of attestation or recommendation to demonstrate their competency.

How to assess available credentials

So far this chapter has shown you examples of some of the credentials available for interpreters.

The question now is how you will determine *which* credentials to pursue.

Let us use the example of certification to highlight these choices. We will look first at the U.S. to show the different kinds of certification globally. Then we will examine three countries for details about certification or an equivalent credential: medical certification in the U.S., general spoken and sign language interpreting Australia and the UK diploma in public service (community) interpreting, because this is a credential that in many ways is equivalent to certification.

U.S. example: An overview of U.S. interpreter certification

Certain interpreter certification programs in the U.S. are national; others are state programs. Some states in the U.S. have specific certification exams for court interpreters, sign language interpreters and/or medical and social services interpreters.

As a remote interpreter outside of those states, you may not be eligible or required to take those certifications to work in that state. However, you may have to show proof of a different certification to the hiring agency if you were to perform remote interpreting work for individuals or organizations in that state.

State-certified or authorized community or medical interpreter

For example, Washington State has obligatory certification programs for interpreters who interpret for face-to-face medical and social services appointments in the state. Some certification languages have a written and an oral exam, while other languages have only a written exam available.

The state of Oregon has a mandated registry of certified and qualified healthcare interpreters. Its website states:

> *Oregon Revised Statute(ORS) 413.550 requires working with certified and qualified [Health Care Interpreters] HCIs. By law, qualified and certified HCIs have completed 60 hours of required training, demonstrated language proficiencies, applied for and received certification or qualification letters and identification numbers from the Oregon Health Authority. Interpreters who do not meet the above requirements are not approved by the Oregon Health Authority and therefore not listed on the mandated state Registry.*[190]

Federal-certified court interpreter

The U.S. federal government has a national certification exam in Spanish for interpreters in federal courts (the exam was previously offered also in Navajo and Haitian Creole). Historically the pass rate for this rigorous written and oral exam was between 4 and 5 percent.

State-certified court interpreter

Each U.S. state determines the necessary requirements to become a state-certified court interpreter. Similar requirements exist in a few other countries, such as Canada.

In the U.S., the National Center for State Courts provides resources and materials and lists the steps required to become a state-certified court interpreter in each state, but the state courts administer the exams.[191]

Nationally certified American Sign Language (ASL) interpreters

The U.S. Registry of Interpreters for the Deaf (RID) certifies ASL interpreters. It has two certification programs, including a major program to certify Deaf and Hard of Hearing interpreters.[192]

---

190 Retrieved from: https://hciregistry.dhsoha.state.or.us

191 See https://www.ncsc.org/education-and-careers/state-interpreter-certification/interpreter-certification

192 See https://rid.org/rid-certification-overview/available-certification/cdi-certification/

The primary ASL national interpreter certification (NIC) program for hearing interpreters was retired on May 18, 2022, and replaced by a new program.[193] In July 2022, a new test entered the beta period and is accepting candidates who wish to take the test.

National certification of ASL interpreters in the U.S. requires that they have a four-year university degree.

State-certified sign language interpreter

In some U.S. states, the state government has instituted requirements for the certification of ASL interpreters but not spoken language interpreters. The U.S. Registry of Interpreters for the Deaf has an online database that tracks state requirements for ASL interpreters.[194]

The most prominent state program, in Texas, is considered by a growing number of interpreters in the U.S. as equivalent to national certification due to the quality of the exam. The Texas Health and Human Services, Board for Evaluation of Interpreters (BEI) Certification Program is accepted in a number of other U.S. states.[195]

U.S. certified medical interpreter

The U.S. has two national certification programs for medical interpreters offered by the Certification Commission for Healthcare Interpreters (CCHI)[196] and The National Board of Certification for Medical Interpreters (NBCMI).[197]

Both these programs require a minimum of 40 hours of training in medical interpreting (including medical terminology), proof of language proficiency and a secondary school diploma, among other requirements. One of them (CCHI) offers full certification with an oral exam in three language pairs; the other (NBCMI) offers certification in six language pairs.

More information about these exams is mentioned below.

Questions to ask yourself when you wish to become certified

Here are some questions you should ask yourself when looking at any certification program:

- Is this a generalist certification or a certification for a specialization?
- What are the requirements to apply?
- Which language pairs are available (including spoken versus signed languages)?
- What is the test structure?
- How rigorous and respected is the test? Is it a validated or accredited exam?
- Are there different kinds of certification for that program?

---

193 As of May 2022, this was the latest information available: https://www.casli.org/2022/05/23/casli-update-may-2022/

194 See https://rid.org/advocacy-overview/state-information-and-advocacy/

195 See https://www.hhs.texas.gov/providers/assistive-services-providers/board-evaluation-interpreters-certification-program/bei-testing

196 See https://cchicertification.org

197 See https://www.certifiedmedicalinterpreters.org

The concluding part of this section will answer all these questions using the example of each of these four credentials:

- Two U.S. national medical interpreter certifications (CCHI and NBCMI)
- A U.S. state certification for social services and medical interpreters (Washington State)
- An Australian national generalist certification for interpreters (NAATI)

The discussion will then briefly address an equivalent credential in the UK that is not called certification but is as rigorous as certification (the DPSI qualification).

Certification Commission for Healthcare Interpreters (CCHI) Certification

- Is this a generalist certification or a certification for a specialization?

CCHI offers certification for the specialization of healthcare interpreting. It was established in 2010.

- What are the requirements to apply?

All candidates must meet the following requirements to be eligible for the written exam.

    - Age 18 or older
    - U.S. high school, GED or equivalent secondary diploma
    - At least 40 hours of healthcare interpreter training
    - Documented language proficiency in both or all working languages

- Which language pairs are available?

At the time of publication, CCHI offers full certification (written and oral exam) in three language pairs:

    - Spanish <> English
    - Arabic <> English
    - Mandarin <> English

- What is the test structure?

The CCHI certification process is broken up into two separate tests. The first part is a knowledge-based exam in English.[198] Candidates have two hours to complete the written exam. The exam has 100 multiple choice questions that include:

    - Professional Responsibility and Interpreter Ethics (22 percent of the score)
    - Manage the Interpreting Encounter (22 percent)
    - Healthcare Terminology (22 percent)
    - U.S. Healthcare System (15 percent)
    - Cultural Responsiveness (19 percent)

---

198 See https://cchicertification.org/certifications/preparing/corechi-description/

Candidates who pass the written exam receive the CoreCHI certification. However, if the candidate speaks Spanish, Arabic or Mandarin, they must take the oral exam to be considered fully certified. Once they pass the written and oral exam they are considered a Certified Healthcare Interpreter (for example, CHI-Spanish).

The oral exam is 60 minutes long and includes:

 - Consecutive Interpretation—four vignettes (75 percent of the score)
 - Simultaneous Interpretation—two vignettes (14 percent)
 - Sight Translation—three brief passages (9 percent)
 - Written Translation—one multiple choice question (2 percent)

- How rigorous and respected is the test? Is it a validated or accredited exam?

The CCHI process for certification has been accredited by the National Center for Credibility Assessment (NCCA) since 2012, and was reaccredited in 2019.

- Are there different kinds of certification for that program?

For candidates who seek a credential for other languages, passing the CCHI written exam confers a credential known as CoreCHI, which is awarded only to interpreters for whom no CCHI language-specific oral performance exam is available.

Core vs. performance certification

Now you may ask , "Am I *certified* if I have the CoreCHI credential but have only taken a written exam—not an oral exam?" That is a tricky question to answer and often confuses not only interpreters but also those who hire and contract with interpreters.

If you are trying to get certified as a Spanish, Arabic or Mandarin interpreter and you have taken only the written exam, then no, you are not certified by CCHI.

If you interpret in any other language and have passed the written exam, then you are technically "core certified" by CCHI. The important distinction to remember is that if you take only the written exam, you have not demonstrated your skills or ability to *interpret*.

When CCHI decided to label the CoreCHI a *certification*, this decision caused confusion in the field. A written exam does not test your interpreting abilities, skills or performance; it tests only your *knowledge* of those skills and healthcare interpreting.

Most national experts in the field have not endorsed the concept that passing a written exam should confer a credential labeled as interpreter certification because it does not test the interpreter's ability to interpret.

CoreCHI is therefore a controversial part of CCHI's certification process that is important to understand and be aware of as you select your healthcare credential. CCHI is accredited by NCCA as mentioned above, which means that its written exam has been through a thorough external validation process, making it an important credential in the field.

However, ultimately if you, as an interpreter, take only the written exam (because no oral exam is available for your language pair), you will have to decide whether or not to represent your CoreCHI as certification or a credential and whether or not to call yourself a "certified" interpreter.

The National Board of Certification for Medical Interpreters (NBCMI) Certification

- Is this a generalist certification or a certification for a specialization?

NBCMI is another U.S. national program for certifying medical interpreters. It was founded a year before CCHI in 2009.

Similarly to CCHI, NBCMI offers a national credential accepted by most language services and hospitals. NBCMI is also an independent division of International Medical Interpreters Association (www.imiaweb.org).

- What are the requirements to apply?

All candidates must meet the following requirements to be eligible for the written exam.

  - Age 18 or older
  - U.S. high school, GED or equivalent secondary diploma
  - 40 hours of healthcare interpreter training or three college credit hours in medical interpreting
  - Documented language proficiency in both or all working languages

- Which language pairs are available?

Currently, at the time of publication, NBCMI offers full certification (written and oral exam) in six languages paired with English:

  - Spanish
  - Cantonese
  - Korean
  - Mandarin
  - Russian
  - Vietnamese

- What is the test structure?

The NBCMI certification test is broken up into two parts. The first part is a knowledge-based exam in English. Candidates have 75 minutes to complete the written exam. The exam is 51 multiple choice questions that include:

  - Roles of the Medical Interpreter (8 percent)
  - Medical Interpreter Ethics (15 percent)
  - Cultural Competence (8 percent)

- Medical Terminology in Target Language (38 percent)[199]
- Medical Specialties in Working Languages (23 percent)
- Interpreter Standards of Practice (5 percent)
- Legislation and Regulations (3 percent)

Candidates who pass the written exam receive the credential of Hub-CMI. However, candidates who speak any of the six languages available for the oral exam must take the oral exam to be considered fully certified. Once they pass the written and oral exam, they are considered a Certified Medical Interpreter (CMI).

The oral exam is 45-60 minutes long and includes the following:

- Mastery of Linguistic Knowledge of English (15 percent)
- Mastery of Linguistic Knowledge of the Other Language (15 percent)
- Interpreting Knowledge and Skills (25 percent)
- Cultural Competence (10 percent)
- Medical Terminology in Working Languages (25 percent)
- Medical Specialties in Working Languages (10 percent)

- How rigorous and respected is the test? Is it a validated or accredited exam?

NBCMI in 2009 went through the same accreditation process as CCHI, using the same agency (NCCA) for external validation of its certification program. However, in 2017 NBCMI announced it would not renew that accreditation, which set off a controversial national debate about the importance of accreditation of certification exams.[200]

Not having a certification exam accredited means that NBCMI now self-determines the quality of its certification exam and how they administer, develop and rate the exam and award certification.

As a professional interpreter, you will have to evaluate each organization whose credentials you are considering and determine which credentials may be most valuable to you. If you are in the U.S. and considering CCHI or NBCMI certification, it is important to note that the NBCMI exam is still widely recognized by most if not all hospitals in the U.S. and also by language services.

- Are there different kinds of certification for that program?

For candidates who seek a credential for other languages, since 2020 passing the NBCMI written exam confers a credential known as Hub-CMI that is similar to the CoreCHI credential.

Like CoreCHI, Hub-CMI is awarded only to interpreters for whom no NBCMI language-specific performance exam is available.

---

199 Technically, this nomenclature is inaccurate. "Target language" refers to the language one interprets into at any given moment. Thus, the target language changes from moment to moment. No interpreter has a "target language."

200 See, for example, https://rpstranslations.wordpress.com/2018/04/09/should-healthcare-interpreters-in-the-u-s-be-concerned/

Am I certified with a Hub-CMI credential?

Once again you may ask, "Am I certified if I only have the Hub-CMI credential?" In terms of U.S. recognition from the profession for having certification, the answer is no.

The situation is similar to having CoreCHI. Passing the written test is a valuable credential and demonstrates knowledge of medical interpreting but doesn't necessarily demonstrate your interpreting skills.

Washington State Department of Social and Health Services (DSHS)

Overview of the certification program

Washington State established its own testing and certification program to support quality, compliance and risk management for patients and clients (whose first language is not English) of publicly funded medical and social services in the state. This state certification program has existed for approximately three decades.

DSHS does not contract interpreters directly; rather, the state outsources the contracting of interpreters. Any interpreter working with DSHS patients or clients of DSHS social services must be certified by WA DSHS.

DSHS offers its exam only to interpreters in Washington State who can take the exam onsite. Washington is the only U.S. state that offers state medical interpreting and social services certification programs.

DSHS Certification (Washington State)

- Is this a generalist certification or a certification for a specialization?

Washington State Department of Social and Health Services (DSHS) created the Language Testing and Certification program for interpreters who interpret for state public medical and social services (WA DSHS, n.d.). It offers separate certification exams for each of these two specializations.

- What are the requirements?

All candidates must meet the following requirements to be eligible for the written exam and oral exam:

  - Age 18 years or older
  - U.S. high school, GED or equivalent secondary diploma

- Which language pairs are available?

Currently, DSHS has six certified languages paired with English:

  - Cantonese
  - Korean
  - Mandarin
  - Russian

- Spanish
- Vietnamese[201]

DSHS also offers testing for screened languages.

Two categories of credentials: Certified and screened languages

Like CCHI and NBCMI, DSHS has two categories of credentials. However, unlike CCHI and NBCMI, the languages in both categories have written and oral exams available.

DSHS tests both certified and screened languages.[202] It tests for the six certified languages specified above. It also has a means of testing 124 other specified languages, "Plus any other language(s) and dialect(s) of any language not listed" (WA DSHS, p. 5).

In short, Washington State tests language proficiency in all languages, as needed.

The oral certification exam is fully developed for the six languages. There is a more limited written and oral screening testing for all other languages.

Interpreters who speak a certification-eligible language and successfully pass the written and oral exam are awarded a state credential as certified interpreters. Interpreters who successfully pass the written and oral exams for a screened language are considered *authorized* interpreters (WA DSHS, p. 10).

- What is the test structure?[203]

Certified language candidates first take a 90-minute, five-part, multiple choice, written exam. The five sections include:

- Code of ethics
- Medical terminologies
- Clinical/medical procedures
- Writing test in the English language
- Writing test in a non-English language

Screened language candidates first take a 90-minute, four-part, multiple choice, written exam. The four sections include:

- Professional code of conduct
- Medical terminologies
- Clinical/medical procedures
- Indirect writing test in the English language

---

201 See https://www.dshs.wa.gov/office-of-the-secretary/test-information

202 See https://www.dshs.wa.gov/office-of-the-secretary/test-information

203 The testing information in this section is taken from WA DSHS (n.d.).

Certified language candidates take a 30-minute oral exam with two sections:

- Sight translation
- Consecutive interpretation

Screened language candidates take a 45-minute oral exam with three sections:

- Sight translation exercise—ten sentences
- Memory retention test
- Consecutive interpretation from a target language[204] into English

Remote interpreters who live in Washington State can earn these credentials and partner with agencies that provide interpreting services to WA DSHS remotely or onsite.

- How rigorous and respected is the test? Is it a validated or accredited exam?

Opinions vary on the rigor of the DSHS certification exams. The exam does not appear to be accredited. It has apparently not undergone a process of external validation of its uses. Concerns about the age of the exam and its administration are legitimate.

However, no U.S. state has a more comprehensive or robust testing process for either medical or social services interpreters. The longevity of the program is impressive. Its contribution to the professionalization of both medical and social services interpreting in the state is significant and is a good model for other states.

Australia example: National Accreditation Authority for Translators and Interpreters (NAATI)

Overview of NAATI certification program

It is helpful to look outside the U.S. at an example of general certification for interpreters that may well be the most extensive and robust interpreter certification system in the world.

NAATI is an unusual organization. It is the national standards and certifying authority for translators and interpreters in Australia. It is also the only organization in Australia that certifies interpreters and translators.

NAATI began in 1977 as a government entity primarily to support migrants, working with the Australia Department of Immigration and Ethnic Affairs. It was incorporated as a private company in 1984.

There are several pathways for spoken and sign language interpreters as well as Deaf interpreters to earn a certification or a credential through NAATI. Originally, NAATI was an accrediting entity and not a certifying organization. However, in 2011 it underwent an extensive review of the accrediting and testing system and reemerged in 2018 with a new certification system (NAATI, 2018).

---

204 As noted earlier in this chapter, this usage is technically incorrect: "target language" refers to the language one interprets into at any given moment. Thus, the target language changes from moment to moment. No interpreter has a "target language."

NAATI credentials

At the time of publication, the number of NAATI credentials and certification programs available by level and language has increased rapidly. Currently there are twelve different interpreting credentials that interpreters can earn from NAATI. They are:

- Recognised Practising
- Certified Provisional Interpreter
- Certified Provisional Auslan Interpreter (sign language)
- Certified Provisional Deaf Interpreter
- Certified Interpreter
- Certified Auslan Interpreter (sign language)
- Certified Specialist Health Interpreter
- Certified Specialist Legal Interpreter
- Auslan Certified Specialist Health interpreter (sign language)
- Auslan Certified Specialist Legal Interpreter (sign language)
- Certified Conference Interpreter
- Auslan Certified Conference Interpreter (sign language)

The difference between Certified Provisional and Certified interpreters is that the Certified Provisional interpreter may interpret noncomplex, nonspecialized sessions. Certified interpreters are assessed as being able to interpret more complex, nonspecialized sessions.

Additionally, the Recognised Practising credential is for low-demand languages where a certification exam is not available.

Let's turn to the five questions.

National Accreditation Authority for Translators and Interpreters (NAATI) Certification

- Is this a generalist certification or a certification for a specialization?

Most NAATI certification exams are for general interpreting, but some are for healthcare, legal and conference interpreters. Sign language and Deaf interpreters can also earn certification.

- What are the requirements?

All interpreters pursuing NAATI certification must complete the following:

    - Complete formal interpreter training.
    - Pass an English proficiency assessment.
    - Submit an application with the following:
        - Photo of applicant.
        - Passport or Australian driver's license.

    - Pass the ethical competency test, which includes:
        - Three knowledge-based short answer questions.
        - Three scenario-based short answer questions.
    - Pass the intercultural competency test, which includes:
        - 20 hours of self-directed online modules.
        - Three knowledge-based short answer questions.
        - Three scenario-based short answer questions.
- Take the certification exam (discussed below).
- Which language pairs are available?

At the time of publication, NAATI is still adding certification languages. As of March 2022, it officially listed 67 languages for which some form of certification exam was available (mostly for the Certified Provisional Interpreter credential) with testing in another 10 languages in active development and scheduled for release in 2022 or 2023.[205]

Dozens of languages can earn a Certified Provisional or a Certified credential. Of the remaining languages not eligible for certification, interpreters can earn the Recognised Practising credential.

Recognised Practising interpreters don't have an assessment available that evaluates the interpreter's oral or signing skill. However, recent work experience, language proficiency and training are accepted. When a language pair has limited work opportunities, NAATI will review each application for its merits.

- What is the test structure?

Certified Provisional Interpreters must complete (online or in-person):

    - Two consecutive interpreting face-to-face dialogue tasks (10-12 minutes, delivered as a live role play)
    - One consecutive interpreting remote dialogue task (10-12 minutes)

Certified Interpreters must complete (online only)

    - Two sight translations in both directions (about 200 words)
    - Two simultaneous monologues in both directions (about 300 words)
    - Two consecutive monologues in both directions (about 300 words)
    - Pass the CPI test

- How rigorous and respected is the test? Is it a validated or accredited exam?

The NAATI certification exams are not externally validated or accredited. Historically that lack of validation became a matter of concern. It was in part the reason for the overhaul of the former accreditation system that led, in 2018, to the debut of the new certification system.

---

205 Retrieved from: https://www.naati.com.au/wp-content/uploads/2022/03/Certification-Testing-Languages_Mar22-.pdf

However, due to the integrity of the testing process, the national scope and complexity of the exam, the extensive requirements to apply and succeed, the pass rates and NAATI's long history of testing, the test appears today to be considered far more rigorous and thorough than the former system.

In addition, to the authors' best knowledge, no national certification exam for general interpreting incorporates live role plays administered in person across the nation. This is a considerable achievement.

- Are there different kinds of certification for that program?

As explained above, NAATI offers a dozen interpreting credentials, and all but one of them involve certification. However, not all language pairs can earn a Certified or Certified Provisional credential. That said, NAATI is the only credentialing entity in the world that includes such a lengthy list of language pairs and so many different certification credentials.

For those pursuing a Certified Provisional or Recognised Practising credential, all components can be completed remotely. While currently the exams are not available to all countries, NAATI may at a later date open up its testing process to interpreters who reside outside Australia. If this option becomes available, it would probably be the first national, widely recognized certification credential to be potentially available to remote interpreters in many countries.

It is worthwhile to keep checking the NAATI website (www.naati.com/au) to monitor plans for its remote testing platform.

UK example: Diploma in Public Service Interpreting (DPSI)

Although this UK diploma program is not technically a certification, DPSI is an important qualification for interpreters. It is worth mentioning in this section because this qualification is both rigorous and critically important for obtaining work in the UK as a community interpreter (known as a public service interpreter there).

The DPSI exam rivals many certification exams. The DPSI credential thus acts as a proxy for what many would call certification.

In brief, the DPSI has three exams for interpreters who work in:

- Legal settings
- Healthcare
- Public services (such as housing, social services and schools)

DPSI is considered a degree-level qualification that is recognized by law enforcement in the UK (specifically the DPSI Law credential). It allows application for full membership in the UK Chartered Institute of Linguists and registration on the National Register of Public Service Interpreters. The exam addresses skills not only in all three modes (consecutive, simultaneous and sight translation) but also in written translation from English.

The DPSI exam is currently offered in 19 languages paired with English.

→ Section 10.2 Review

Understanding interpreting credentials can be a challenge. This section explored various kinds of credentials available to remote interpreters who work across specializations and regional and national borders with a special focus on one that many consider to be the most important qualification: interpreter certification. This knowledge can help you further your career and build your portfolio.

Because remote interpreting is evolving at high speed, many remote interpreters in many countries are seeking ways to demonstrate their skills and professionalism. To do so yourself, you will need to become familiar with the different kinds of credentials available. You will also need to both understand and use the terms for these credentials correctly.

You also need to know why credentials in general and certain types of credentials in particular are critically important to advance the interpreting profession. These credentials and your ability to communicate their value will affect your opportunities to be taken seriously by people and organizations that work with interpreters.

Being able to discuss the credentials available to you and why they are important help you both look and sound like the *professional* you are.

Section 10.3 Specializations

→ Learning objective 10.3

After completing this section, the remote interpreter will be able to identify the most common specializations in remote interpreting and relevant credentials for each of them.

→ Section 10.3 Overview

This section explores the clients you typically provide interpreting for, or that you want or plan to interpret for. It helps you to ask some key questions so that you can make decisions about how much remote interpreting you'll perform and which specializations you prefer to interpret for.

→ Section 10.3 Content

Interpreter client list

You will need to look at many questions before you decide which organizations you want to interpret for. Some of these questions are for you. Some questions are for the organizations or language services you might wish to interpret for. Other questions will involve doing your own research in order to find answers.

Let's consider a number of these practical questions.

1. Assume that you decide to work for a language service specialized in remote interpreting:
    a. Will you be able to choose which kinds of calls you interpret? For example, consider whether you will or want to interpret for these specializations:
        i. Medical
        ii. Legal
        iii. Business
        iv. Educational
        v. Other subjects
    b. Has the interpreting service told you which credentials you need to take those calls?
        i. If yes, do you have these credentials already?
        ii. If no, what research do you need to do to obtain them?
2. If you choose to interpret remotely for hospitals (whether directly or through a language service):
    a. Are any of these hospitals located in another state, province or country?
        i. Does that country or region require a healthcare interpreting credential?
            1. If yes, do you have it?
            2. If no, or you don't know, what research do you need to do?
        ii. Can you get training specific to that country or region's healthcare system, healthcare privacy laws and healthcare interpreting requirements?
        iii. If you will work for the hospital through a language service, will the language service help guide you about the relevant healthcare system, privacy laws and healthcare interpreting requirements?
3. If you choose to interpret remotely for schools:
    a. Are any of them located in another state, province or country?
        i. Does interpreting for schools in that area require a credential?
            1. If yes, do you have it?
            2. If no, or you don't know, what research do you need to do?
        ii. Can you get training specific to that country or region's educational system, education privacy laws and educational interpreting requirements?
4. If you choose to interpret remotely for courts or other legal interpreting:
    a. Is any of that work located in another state, province or country?
        i. Does legal interpreting in that area require a credential?
            1. If yes, do you have it?
            2. If no, or you don't know, what research do you need to do?

ii. Can you get training specific to that country or region's legal system, laws surrounding confidentiality and lawyer-client privilege and legal interpreting requirements?

5. Do you have a language proficiency assessment on file?
   a. If not, where can you get a reliable, externally validated language proficiency test scored to a national or international scale for language proficiency?
   b. If your language doesn't have a test available, how will you demonstrate your proficiency?

As the world becomes ever more global, remote interpreting evolves and remote communications technologies advance. The list of remote interpreting specializations is bound to keep growing. Here is an opportunity for you to develop a niche as a remote interpreter specialized in certain areas.

The more you can plan your career strategically, the more likely you are to succeed in remote interpreting.

→ Section 10.3 Review

Working as a remote interpreter allows you to work easily in one or many different specializations. As you can see, there are many types of interpreting you can easily perform as a remote interpreter. The challenge is whether you wish to do so—and if you are qualified to do so.

Remember, no interpreter is best suited to work in *all* specializations or settings. Most interpreters have their own preferred specializations. Learning your limits and where you are most successful is an important part of your professional development.

When you look at the list of questions in this section and evaluate your own skills, experience, training and qualifications, you'll begin to see which specializations suit you best. You may also discover other specializations that you would like to consider working in later.

Finally, planning on which credentials to pursue for the specializations that attract you most while preparing to work in any market or location will help ensure that you are qualified and compliant for the assignments you want most.

Section 10.4 Social Media

→ Learning objective 10.4

After completing this section, the remote interpreter will be able to describe key strategies to enhance one's interpreting network and professional presence through social media.

→ Section 10.4 Overview

When you're a local interpreter working face to face, your relationships in the community are important. Your reputation and engagement within that local and professional community help you grow your network and expand your potential work opportunities.

The same is possible when you work remotely. It takes more intentional engagement in the remote world, but taking the time to create an online presence as a qualified, credentialed remote interpreter will help you to grow your reputation and client base.

One way to share your portfolio and to network with other interpreters and with industry professionals is to create a social media presence. This section helps you explore how to do so.

→ Section 10.4 Content

Interpreters and social media

Social media can be a powerful and effective way to market yourself and your remote interpreting services. For example, LinkedIn is the largest professional social media platform in the world. It brings together professionals from every sector in every corner of the world.

WeChat in China is a social network of more than one billion users and that includes both social and business connections. Dajie, Wealink and Renhe are Chinese professional networking platforms.

Your client list can be global. Your networking should be global too.

You can use online professional networks to discover other professionals, follow organizations and share your perspectives with interpreters and other colleagues about industry events.

But remember: what you share can't easily be taken back and what you share can be seen by anyone or large groups (depending on your privacy settings). Thoughtful posts and activities that reflect your professional perspectives are important to keep in mind.

Why to engage with social media

Engaging with social media can help you identify which companies you may want to follow so you can stay current with industry news and events. In addition to networking with other professionals, online professional networks are an ideal place to share your professional views, endeavors and interests. You can find and pass on articles that address language access, interpreters, interpreter training and advances in technology that affect remote interpreting.

Sharing articles with your own commentary or perspective will help your followers learn about you. Professional social media platforms build professional networks, so focus your posts and engagement on content that is relevant to your work.

Be careful about confidentiality—your own and the privacy of others. What you post, share, comment on or "like" can be seen by current and future clients, interpreters or companies. It's a powerful way for people to learn what is important to you in the field of interpreting and what your specializations and experience are.

How to use hashtags

Hashtags are short labels that begin with the symbol #. People on major social media platforms use hashtags to label their posts in a way that others can see them even if they are not following that person or company.

Common examples of hashtags for interpreters are:

- #interpreters
- #interpreting
- #1nt
- #remoteinterpreting

There are many more. As you spend more time on LinkedIn and other social media platforms, you will find many more hashtags that may be of interest. You can also use them in your own posts to help you gain more exposure.

Learn about events

Learn about training, workshops, webinars, conferences and more. One of the many advantages of being active on LinkedIn and other professional networks is that events and networking opportunities are often advertised there. Remember that even attending a webinar can give you opportunities to engage with interpreters in your own area and other countries via chat that you can connect with later on social media.

Signing up for the email distribution lists from these organizations that host such events is helpful too. You can then follow them on their own social media platforms. You can see who else might be attending these events and share your involvement or interest.

LinkedIn

Because LinkedIn is the largest professional social network in the world, and because it is international, remote interpreters may find it a particularly valuable form of social media. If you engage with no other platform, consider LinkedIn carefully.

Your LinkedIn profile

Simply having your profile on LinkedIn is a marketing tool for interpreters. If you are set up with a business name, you can also set up your own company page. Both your personal profile and company page are valuable.

If you're new to LinkedIn, it is important to start with the About section in your profile. Take it seriously. Fill it out completely. Update it regularly. Be sure to include all your relevant education and training and your work experience as a remote interpreter, including the specializations you interpret for.

Once you have completed or updated your profile, search for the organizations you are a member of or that you trust within the industry and the profession so that you can follow them.

LinkedIn groups

A LinkedIn group is a place where professionals who work in a particular industry or field and who may share common interests can gather to discuss their experiences and work and consult one another for advice. A LinkedIn group is yet another way to build your network.

You will find many professional interpreting groups on LinkedIn. Some are international. Some are national or regional. A number of them are broad and general groups, while others are specific to a topic or specialization (such as simultaneous interpreting or interpreting for a specific language pair).

Listed vs. unlisted groups

On LinkedIn, listed groups can be found in search results. If you belong to a listed group, other LinkedIn members can see that group in your profile under Interests. Unlisted groups cannot be found in search results (except by members of the same group). They are not visible in your profile.

You can only access an unlisted group if you are invited to join it or receive a direct link.

Many social media groups were originally public (meaning that anyone could sign up). Today, for privacy and to avoid spam, LinkedIn unlisted groups are private, members-only groups, which is why you can join them only by approval or invitation.

How to find LinkedIn groups

One way to find LinkedIn groups to join is to do a search at the top of your homepage. If you are active on LinkedIn and have many connections, over time you will probably get invited to join quite a number of interpreting groups.

How to network effectively in groups

Whether you join a LinkedIn group or any other group on a social media platform, you can often start by introducing yourself. Respond to other members' posts. Ask for their guidance. You may be able to send private messages to members to make a more personal connection.

Finally, hashtags are another excellent way to follow what is happening on LinkedIn.

Confidentiality, privacy and common sense

It is critically important to remember confidentiality on your personal social media platforms—for your own privacy and that of others. Be careful what you post.

If you are feeling emotional, avoid posting.

If you are asking, "Should I post this?" the answer is "Probably not." Wait until the next day and decide then. Social media, in general, has created a culture of immediacy. Professional networking means showing your best professional self. Do not allow an emotional moment to result in a post that undermines your dignity or professionalism.

Keep your professional networking *professional.*

Be careful about sharing your personal views on social media

Sharing your personal life on social media platforms that are not professional networks also carries risk. Many of us have a number of friends in both worlds: our social media and our professional platforms. Many social networks (including Facebook and WeChat) are often used socially and professionally as well.

Keep in mind that it can be difficult for others in social media to separate your personal life from your work life. Your personal views do not need to align with the subjects or topics you interpret for. However, people not familiar with interpreting may see your personal views as potential barriers to your ability to interpret impartially, especially on controversial issues such as politics and world events.

Privacy settings

If you engage on social media platforms personally (not only professionally), remember to check your privacy settings. If you want to post something only to family and friends, make sure your settings are set up for you to do exactly that.

→ Section 10.4 Review

Social media can be a powerful tool to market your services and engage and network with other interpreters and organizations. Social media can also help you stay current with industry changes, research and events.

Use social media platforms wisely. Learn how to set yourself up, keep a strong profile and establish a company page if you have a business or trade name. Engage online with other remote interpreters and the organizations that work with them. Attend events online or in person that you find on social media; then use social media platforms to connect with the people you meet there.

Social media can expand your horizons, keep you up to date and help you find future interpreting opportunities and clients.

Section 10.5 Finding Work as a Remote Interpreter

→ Learning objective 10.5

After completing this section, the remote interpreter will be able to develop a plan for finding work as a remote interpreter.

→ Section 10.5 Overview

You've done it! You've built your portfolio, identified the markets you want to work in and chosen the credentials you need to demonstrate your proficiency and skills. You've considered how to market yourself and how to network on social media.

Now it's time to find work!

→ Section 10.5 Content

As a remote interpreter, in most countries you have two basic choices about how you are legally classified to work: as a contractor or as an employee.

For example, you can work as an independent contractor for several language services and other organizations. These organizations can then send you calls or assignments. You could be paid by the minute, hour or day. You will work on contracts. You are *self-employed.*

You can also work directly for an organization that *hires* you as an interpreter, whether you are paid hourly or have a salary as a full-time staff interpreter. In either case you are an *employee*.

Self-employed vs. employed interpreters

If you're new to remote interpreting, it might feel overwhelming at first to get started. Before you start looking for work, it's important that you evaluate what is important to you. Ask yourself the following:

- Do I want a set schedule, or do I want to choose when and for whom I work?
    - If you prefer a set schedule, try to be hired directly by a language service as a staff interpreter.
    - If you want to control your own schedule and work *when* you want and for *whom* you want, set yourself up as an independent contractor—but remember that you are then legally a small business. You will need to research the legal requirements for setting up a small business. Those requirements could be local, state or provincial *and* federal.
- Do I want to be responsible for my taxes or do I want taxes to be handled by an employer?
    - If you work directly as an employee, in most countries the employer will deduct your payroll taxes.[206]
    - If you work as an independent contractor or freelancer, you are responsible for submitting your own tax payments. In the U.S., for example, contractors are expected to submit quarterly estimated tax payments.
- Do I want a regular salary with benefits?
    - If you work as an employee, you will receive regular payments (salary or hourly wages).

[206] You are still responsible for your tax obligations, which the government will probably require you to address, typically once a year at tax time. For example, if your employer did not deduct enough taxes from your salary or wages that year, you would have to pay the remaining tax obligations.

        - You may also have access to a retirement plan, a health plan or healthcare supplement plan, sick leave, vacation time and other benefits.
    - If you work as a contractor, typically you will be paid only for time worked.
        - Most contract interpreters would not have access to additional benefits, such as a retirement plan.

Find work!

There are several ways to find work and build your client list.

Study the marketplace

There are large, medium and small language service agencies in the U.S. and around the globe. Perform an internet search. Reach out to other interpreters and ask about organizations that they recommend for work.

Additionally, many websites post available jobs. Searching a keyword such as "interpreter" or "remote interpreter" can help you find these open positions.

Engage with social media

Leverage your social media connections. Ask your groups about work opportunities. Read your feed. Many social media platforms, including LinkedIn and Facebook, allow you to search for jobs.

For example, job postings on Facebook can be found on the pages for specific companies seeking interpreters but you can also go to a separate jobs page and do a search by location, industry skill and the job type. You can even do this type of searching on your telephone.

Try online job search engines

Many people find work on job search platforms. Examples in the U.S. include Indeed, CareerBuilder, Glassdoor, SimplyHired, Getwork and more.

Ask other interpreters, both your colleagues and your friends on social media, which job search platforms have worked best for them or their colleagues.

Prepare to apply for work

Before you apply to any company, do your due diligence: visit language service websites and learn about their values. Which markets do they serve? What kind of remote interpreting services do they offer and what kind of interpreters do they need?

Each language service (or other organization) is different, and so is its engagement with interpreters. It is often useful to explore reviews about the organization that have been posted online by other interpreters and clients. While the experiences of interpreters and clients are subjective, these posts can help you learn more about a company before you apply to work there.

Submit your application

Once you've narrowed down the places you'd like to apply to, you will need to submit your application and résumé. If you have an online portfolio, you can share your website so employers can learn about you and potentially see an interpreting sample.

Earlier in this chapter we talked about your personal statement. Your résumé is an excellent place to include your personal statement. It can outline why you want to be an interpreter and work with the company you're applying to.

If you're selected for an interview, here are a few things to keep in mind:

- You may have to complete a language proficiency or interpreting skills test that is conducted by the company or by a third party.
- You may have several interviews.
- Be prepared to talk about your experience in remote interpreting, if applicable, and your ease and comfort level with technology.
- Prepare your own questions so that you can learn more about the company culture, expectations and the kinds of remote interpreting services it provides.
- If you receive an offer, be prepared to negotiate, then get the final rate and terms *in writing*.

Soft skills

Part of successful interviews and relationship building are your soft skills, which are the nontechnical skills you use when you engage and communicate with other people. Your tone, willingness to learn, open-mindedness, integrity, ethics, dependability and ability to express empathy all come through when you're interviewing or talking to clients and other professionals.

Your ability to demonstrate those soft skills in interviews and when you work with clients will further set you apart as not only a professional interpreter but also someone people want to work with, now and in the future.

Any job you take should be rooted in trust and open communication. As one seasoned interpreter says, "Remember, communication is a two-way street." It's exciting when you're hired or have been contracted to provide interpreting. Being clear about pay and expectations will set you up for success.

Advice from a Remote Interpreter
Olena Hart
(freelance Ukrainian and Russian interpreter)

Based on my own experience as well as feedback from other interpreters, I suggest starting the process of looking for a job in the interpreting field with a list of must-dos.

First and foremost, divide your actions into four main categories:

1. Prescreening of the language company's market

2. Applying for a job

3. Preparing for and passing rounds of tests and interviews

4. Negotiating the job offer

Since interpreting is an emerging profession in the United States (the first OPI interpreting session took place in 1981), the job market is not flooded with companies offering interpreting services. Nevertheless, it is constantly growing, creating more job opportunities for interpreters. I suggest you start your employment-seeking journey by writing down a list of companies you would like to work at (potentially). Go to their websites to subscribe to the Careers page updates or simply check them regularly for new job postings.

I highly recommend you read reviews of current or past employees of these companies on websites like Glassdoor or Indeed. There is no such thing as too much information on your prospective employers.

2. Applying for a job

When you find an interpreting job with a reliable company, it's time to check your résumé. Make sure it's well-structured and formatted. It should also include all your interpreting certifications and relevant training. If an employer leaves you an option to attach a cover letter, have it ready, but always customize it to each job application. Good luck!

3. Preparing for and passing rounds of tests and interviews

Applying for an interpreting job entails having to pass your language proficiency tests (usually in the non-English languages you are fluent in). It's a part of the deal. Sometimes you might have as many as three or four rounds of telephone or video-recorded job interviews as well as a couple of tests before the company is ready to make a decision about whether to hire you.

Never hesitate to ask a human resource (HR) specialist or a talent acquisition specialist ALL the questions you have during the hiring process. I cannot stress enough how important it is to avoid any miscommunication. Also, don't shy away from asking HR to send you the list of benefits or specific employment conditions in writing (via email). This simple practice will protect you from fraudulent employers and scam job offers.

4. Negotiating the job offer

Congratulations! You have received a job offer. It's quite an accomplishment. Now it's time to thoroughly read the job offer and make sure there are no discrepancies from what you were previously told by the recruiter. If in doubt, ask! While the company is looking for a qualified interpreter, you are looking for a reliable company and fair treatment. Remember: it's a two-way street. If there are no issues, sign the offer, and welcome to the team!

→ Section 10.5 Review

As a remote interpreter, perhaps you work alone where you live—but your network of interpreters and clients, and the organizations you work for, can be anywhere in the world!

As you seek work, first decide about whether you want to work as a self-employed or employed interpreter. Examine the pros and cons of each option carefully. Then study the marketplace. Research your options. Consult with colleagues and your social media connections. Use your social media platforms to learn more about both job opportunities and the companies you might want to work for. Consider online job search engines.

Remember to apply only to companies whose values reflect your own. Submit a polished résumé and highlight your qualifications, experience and skills. Be prepared for a complex application, screening, interview and testing process.

Connecting to other professionals, organizations and having a place to showcase your qualifications is important to your growth as an interpreter. Be mindful of your social media engagement and use your online professional networks to advance the profile and value of interpreters.

→ Chapter Activities

Activity 10.1: Write your personal statement

Instructions

Reread the sample personal statement near the beginning of Section 10.1 and then think about what you might say. Your personal statement might go through several drafts. Write a first draft of your personal statement.

Activity 10.2: Are you certified?

Instructions

You've just learned about a number of certifications. Depending on your language pair, where you live and which specializations you work in, a certification may not be available to you.

For this exercise, imagine you are talking to someone who is unfamiliar with the interpreting profession and who says, "Cool! You're an interpreter. Are you certified?"

If you have a certification available to you but don't have it yet, what would you say? Write it down.

If you don't have a certification available to you, what would you say? Write it down.

If you are certified, why is that certificate important to you? Write it down.

Now write down, in detail, how you would describe to someone in conversation, or during a job interview, the important credentials that you *do* have. (If you have any certifications, start with certification.)

Note that practicing how to answer these questions and how to explain your credentials is critically important. Your ease in discussing your credentials, and especially certification, not only reflects your professional knowledge but it also helps to correct any misunderstandings that all language pairs or interpreting specializations have their own certification.

Activity 10.3: Self-assessing the certifications, training and credentials you will need to pursue

Instructions

1. Review the content in Section 10.3.
2. Answer each question about your existing or desired client list. (You may need to do additional research or ask questions of your current clients or language companies.)
3. Identify where you may need to obtain a certification, more training or additional qualifications and credentials to perform remote interpreting in your preferred specializations.
4. Write down which certifications, trainings or credentials you will work to obtain.

Activity 10.4: Update your social media

Introduction to this activity

If you currently don't have a social media presence, such as a LinkedIn account, this may be the time to set one up. If you already have a social media presence, now is the time to review it, update your profile and decide if you want to make any changes based on what you have read in this chapter.

This activity is one that you should consider doing regularly to make sure that what you share on social media accounts offers the best representation of your professionalism and value to the world of remote interpreting.

Instructions

1. Go to your social media platforms.
2. Find your own pages that other professionals may see and review.
3. Edit, or add, the following:
    - Updated security settings
    - Photos
    - Your personal statement
    - Training
    - Qualifications
    - Experience
    - Memberships
    - People, organizations and language services that you follow or may follow

Activity 10.5: Assessing the current job market

Whether you are looking for a job at this time, the following exercise can help you see what the current job market looks like for remote interpreters.

Go to any of the listed job search sites mentioned in Section 10.5 and look for an interpreting job. Read through the posting, open the application, and do your research on the language company.

Ask yourself, and write down:

(a) What do you notice that you like or admire about the job and the organization?

(b) What questions do you have about the job and the organization?

(c) Is there anything you found out about the organization that is concerning to you?

(d) If you were to fill out the application, do you have all the necessary documents or qualifications? Which ones do you need to obtain? How will you get them?

Note that even if you're not looking for new work opportunities, it's always beneficial to keep looking out for new trends, companies or patterns that may affect you when you do decide to find a new or additional interpreting job. Come back to this activity a couple of times a year to see what new things may have emerged.

Chapter Conclusion and Review

In this chapter you've seen a multitude of ways that you can demonstrate your skills, experience and qualifications. Whether you do so with a certificate or a credential, a social media presence or a dedicated website, your options to build your brand are plentiful.

Your brand is important for your career. Carefully crafting it to reflect your values and priorities will take time but will be worth it. As you leverage social media to build your network, be attentive to what you post. Nothing ever truly disappears on the internet, and you don't want a comment you posted when you were emotional to detract from what you really believe and support.

As you build your portfolio, practice how you will talk about the credentials you've earned and perhaps why you didn't pursue or earn a different credential. Perhaps your language pair doesn't have a certification, or the specialization doesn't have certification at all; know how to talk about your choices and the state of the profession.

Certification was covered in this chapter, though not exhaustively. New certifications or credentials may become available, or perhaps there is one you know of that was not reviewed in this chapter. Become familiar with them, pursue them if they meet your professional goals and share their value with the profession.

When it is time to pursue a work opportunity, whether as an employee, a contractor, or a combination, be thorough in the application and vetting process. While you may be interviewing for a job, you should be interviewing the agency or company to ensure that it reflects your values and is a champion of best practices in the interpreting field.

It has been said many times in this book; you're a remote interpreter, so your client list has the potential to be global. A well-developed portfolio can help you grow your brand, grow your client list and also further advance the respect of professional interpreters. Remote interpreting evolved dramatically due to the COVID-19 pandemic, and it is still evolving. Use your platforms and your passion, values and qualifications to be an ambassador for best practices. In doing so, you can set the tone for what to expect from remote interpreters, no matter where they reside and where their services are requested.

Activities Answer Key

Activity 2.1 (a): A remote interpreting technology quiz

Instructions

For each statement, write down whether you consider that statement true or false.

1. VRS technology developed after VRI technology. F
2. The cloud (cloud-based computing) made remote interpreting easier. T
3. IMS stands for interpreter manager services. F
4. AI (artificial intelligence) in interpreting will soon replace interpreters. F
5. IDP refers to interpreting delivery platform. T
6. Sign language interpreters can work on both VRI and VRS platforms. T
7. Machine interpreting isn't really interpreting because it's text-based. F

Activity 2.1 (b): The evolution of RSI

Instructions

For each of the three parts of this exercise, use the list of words at the bottom to fill in the blanks for each missing word or phrase in the text.

RSI evolution, Part 1

When did RSI launch? It started in medical services in the mid-1990s in New York City. But there was a long gap before real RSI platforms were developed after 2010. Yet even before special platforms existed, interpreters figured out the real problem. To perform simultaneous interpreting remotely, you need *more than one audio channel*!

More and more interpreters figured out how to hack consecutive interpreting video platforms by adding a second phone line. But these were the "bad old days." Then came new special RSI platforms that *combined* a video platform with the ability to provide simultaneous interpreting. How? By adding: (a) multiple audio channels; and (b) a back end for interpreters to coordinate with each other.

simultaneous, coordinate, audio, developed, remotely, RSI platforms, video

RSI evolution, Part 2

By the mid-2010s, RSI was just beginning to be performed on what we call dedicated RSI platforms. These are videoconferencing platforms that add audio channels and a back end where two remote simultaneous interpreters can take turns interpreting and communicate to say whose turn it is, or other information.

But dedicated RSI platforms are expensive. So far, mostly conference interpreters work on them. Then the pandemic hit. Overnight, community and business services, schools, courts and healthcare often wanted interpreters to interpret simultaneously on standard videoconference platforms that didn't have multiple audio channels or a back end. Community services and interpreters worked hard to create hybrid solutions.

expensive, back end, audio, simultaneously, videoconference, dedicated, multiple

RSI evolution, Part 3

What are hybrid solutions? They are newer versions of the hacks (workaround methods) that add audio channels to videoconference platforms such as Webex to perform simultaneous interpreting. Today, as a result of the COVID-19 pandemic, many services provide RSI over videoconference platforms such as Zoom, Microsoft Teams, Google Meet, GoToMeeting and Webex.

At the beginning of the pandemic, Zoom was the only one with a built-in simultaneous interpreting feature by adding audio channels. This RSI feature is still not fully developed. However, Zoom is big in RSI now—and not only for community services. A 2021 study from CSA Research showed Zoom is used 60 percent of the time for RSI, which means that many conference interpreters use it too!

interpreting, platforms, solutions, feature, channels, RSI, audio

Activity 2.2: Remote interpreting scenarios

Instructions

Match the scenario to the best remote interpreting technology by writing down, in the blank right column, the platform that best matches each scenario on the left.

OPI/VRI platform
IMS
RSI platform
Unified IDP and IMS

Scenario	Technology Platforms
A public health department holds a monthly community meeting at rotating locations. Three times a year, the meeting is held remotely. They need simultaneous interpreting in Spanish, Hmong and Russian.	RSI
A school district needs to schedule half hour parent-teacher conferences for seven schools in six languages. The meetings will all take place onsite.	IMS
A hospital needs on-demand interpreting services for weekend and evenings.	OPI/VRI
A small, rural clinic has three face-to-face Spanish-English interpreters who cover 90 percent of interpreting services requested, but it occasionally needs on-demand interpreters for emergencies and languages other than Spanish.	OPI/VRI

Activity 3.2: Compare the checklists

Instructions

1. Study both checklists in this chapter. Checklist 1 is Prepare for Remote Interpreting. Checklist 2 is Setup and Tech Check for Remote Interpreters.

2. Compare the two documents.

3. For each statement below, write #1 or #2 in the blank space to indicate which checklist that statement applies to. If the statement applies to both checklists, write #1 and #2.

    1. Use this checklist to prepare yourself for your remote interpreting career. #1
    2. Use this checklist if you are preparing for a session right now. #2
    3. Use this checklist to help you decide what computer to buy. #1
    4. Use this checklist to help assess your audio and video. #1, #2
    5. Use this checklist to remember to reboot your computer before starting. #2
    6. Use t*his* checklist to assess what kind of headset and microphone to use. #1

Activity 3.3 (a): Solve the technical difficulties

Instructions

For each technical challenge below, identify the appropriate solution.

1. Your webcam is working, but no one can see you because your image is too bright and hazy. What should you have done before the call? Choose one answer.

    c. Check how you appear and change the lighting from behind you to in front of you or on both sides before accepting calls.

2. Your webcam isn't working properly. You aren't visible. What do you do? Choose one answer.

    d. All of the above.

3. You have an audio problem: participants hear hissing sounds when you speak. What do you do? Choose one answer.

    b. Adjust your microphone so that it is just a little lower—not too close to your mouth.

4. Your webcam is working, but you're washed out and look pale. What should you have done before the call? Choose one answer.

    c. Check how you appear and change the lighting from behind you to in front of you or on both sides before accepting calls.

5. During a VRI or VRS call, participants tell you that you are pixilating and they can't see you anymore. This is a serious video problem. You know it is *your* problem because both the participants are pixelating for you too. What do you do? Choose all the answers that could apply here.

    d. None of the above.

Activity 4.3 (b): What to say when you manage turn-taking

Instructions

Read the following scenario and answer the question that follows it.

Credit Card Fraud

The Williams family is on vacation in another country. Unfortunately, they had an emergency and need to pay for medical services up front. As they are trying to pay, their credit card gets declined twice. Due to the crisis of the emergency, feeling vulnerable and not understanding the local language, the father is nervous and upset. He tries to call the bank using a local phone number but has no luck until the fourth time. He is finally able to talk to a bank representative through an interpreter:

> **Father:** I'm calling because I need to know why my credit card has been declined twice.. I am in the middle of an emergency. I need to use it. I checked and made sure we had enough availability before traveling!
>
> **Bank representative:** Good afternoon, sir, we notice that your charges exceed the credit limit in your credit card. Did you not charge your credit card for a total of three thousand dollars last night from Idaho?
>
> **Father:** *No*! This is crazy! It took me forever to get hold of the bank. I can barely hear you. My daughter is in the emergency room of a foreign country. We don't understand a word of what hospital staff are saying. They will not treat her if they can't have a deposit of two thousand dollars...and you are telling me I *have no* money available on my credit card?!...And how could I have made those charges from Idaho? I'm not even in the U.S.! I'm telling you, this is an *emergency*! I need that money NOW!

Let's assume that simultaneous mode is not an option for this case because you are interpreting OPI or VRI (or, in sign language, that father is signing too quickly and in too small a space for you to see clearly at that speed). Choose from **one** of the following scripts to intervene:

Answer key:

1. "Sir, this is the interpreter. I cannot keep up with everything you're saying when you speak [sign] so much. Please remember to pause."

   Not the best answer. While you did remind the speaker to pause, this wording may make them frustrated, or they may continue without repeating the information you missed.

2. "Sir, this is the interpreter. To allow me to interpret everything you're stating, can you please start over and remember to pause?"

   This answer is ideal. You remind the speaker to pause and they will repeat from the beginning, so everything is captured accurately. Sometimes when people repeat information in a story like this, they actually add important details the second or third time.

3. "Sir, this is the interpreter. I've had this situation too and I understand how difficult it is. Please, calm down. We'll get this taken care of!"

Not the best answer. While in customer service interactions, this may be applauded as showing empathy, the interpreter should not share personal experiences or offer to help when they are merely there to interpret.

4. "Sir, this is the interpreter. I will summarize what you're saying because the rep doesn't need all those details. Please stick to only answering the question. Thank you."

   Not the best answer. If the father continues without pausing after you've attempted to get them to pause, you may have to summarize. However, this should not be your first course of action.

Note: The best script to use will really depend on the situation. For example, the interpreter may have been able to take notes and keep up with part or all of the lengthy statement. If this is the case, you should go ahead and interpret everything you can, then intervene to get repetition for the part you need.

Activity 6.1 (a): Define code of ethics

Instructions

1. Read the definition (a-h) below.
2. Decide which definition best fits code of ethics for interpreters.
3. Write your selection into the blank lines below.
   a. A list of rules for interpreters.
   b. Guidelines for interpreters.
   c. Best practices for interpreters.
   d. Industry standards for interpreters.
   e. A list of requirements for interpreters issued by a professional association.
   f. A list of recommendations and best practices for interpreters published by an official group.
   g. A set of directives that specifies the requirements or expectations intended to guide the conduct of members of a profession.
   h. A set of national rules telling interpreters what to do when they face ethical challenges.

Activity 6.1 (b): Match the definitions

Instructions

1. In the blank column to the right (labeled Document number), write the *number* (1 through 5) for the appropriate document type (shown in color) beside each *definition* (a-d) in the table below.
2. Note that one definition matches *two* terms. So in one box, you will need to add *two* numbers.

Definitions	Document Number
a. A standard developed and published by an international standardization organization.	#3
b. A set of formal guidelines that offers practitioners of a profession clear strategies and courses of action to support professional conduct.	#2
c. Protocols, procedures and guidelines that are recognized by a profession as being effective and recommended.	#4
d. A set of directives that specifies the requirements or expectations intended to guide the conduct of practitioners of a profession.	#1, #5

Document types

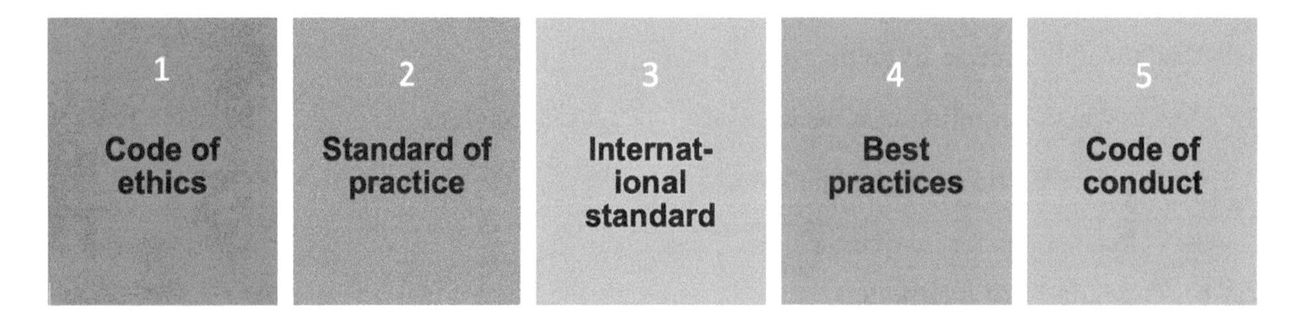

Activity 6.3 (a): Reading quiz

Instructions

1. Read Section 6.3 carefully.
2. Answer the true-false and multiple-choice questions below.

Self-test on three areas of disagreement in codes of ethics for interpreters
True or false

1. Countries and associations around the world generally agree that interpreters should avoid trying to explain cultural misunderstandings. F
2. Most legal service providers and courts do not permit interpreters to engage in advocacy on the job. T
3. Addressing a serious communication breakdown might be necessary for the remote interpreter to support communicative autonomy. T

4. The potential disruption when an interpreter intervenes to address misunderstandings is much less serious in remote interpreting than in face-to-face interpreting. F
5. Remote interpreters are not *generally* expected to support human rights. T
6. Interrupting a session can easily lead to confusion and also to side conversations, even in remote interpreting. T
7. All interpreter codes of ethics encourage the interpreter to intervene as needed whenever a misunderstanding arises. F
8. When intervening in court, interpreters may be required to identify themselves as "the interpreter" (e.g., "The interpreter requests a clarification of the term...") in order to avoid misunderstandings in the court record. T
9. Ten interpreting codes of ethics examined for this program permit or require that the interpreter request cultural clarifications. T
10. This textbook suggests that permitting the interpreter to provide cultural explanations risks undermining or destroying communicative autonomy. T
11. Advocacy in interpreting means speaking up only on behalf of service users. F
12. In some countries, codes of ethics may require or strongly recommend that interpreters protect service users from discrimination. T

Multiple choice

Mark any and all answers that are correct.

13. To address a communication breakdown, the following strategies by the remote interpreter will normally be acceptable:
    a. Request a repetition.
    b. Ask for equipment such as a speaker phone or video screen to be moved to make the audio or video easier for the interpreter to hear and see.
    c. Request a change in participant positioning to enhance sight lines and clear visual information.
14. Although communication breakdowns are often difficult and delicate to address, the interpreter can consider trying to:
    a. Suggest that one party rephrase or restate the confusing information.
    b. Request (rather than provide) a clarification.
    c. Recommend that a participant explain or specify the meaning of technical or specialized terms.

d. Point out, rather than explain, the basis of a possible misunderstanding (e.g., "The interpreter is concerned that the term 'informed consent' might be causing some confusion").

e. Suggest a participant ask a question that might resolve the misunderstanding (e.g., "The interpreter suggests you ask the applicant what he means by 'spouse'").

15. If the interpreter notes that a participant service user seems not to understand the service provider, and the potential consequences are serious, the interpreter may reasonably:

c. Ask the service provider to verify the service user's understanding.

d. Request a clarification or restatement by the provider of the confusing information.

16. In the event of a cultural misunderstanding, even in legal interpreting many or most interpreters around the world would be permitted to:

a. *Request* cultural clarification.

17. Most codes of ethics or professional associations would permit the interpreter to engage in advocacy:

c. Outside the encounter, on behalf of the profession.

18. Advocacy on behalf of service users may be defined as:

c. Taking action, or speaking up, on behalf of a participant in order to prevent or reduce harm.

19. To avoid violating the ethical requirement to remain impartial, it is best to simply interpret and avoid interrupting the call unless:

b. Communication breaks down completely.

c. Someone's safety or well-being is at serious risk.

Activity 6.3 (b): Guidance on cultural mediation—fill in the blanks

Instructions

1. For each part of this two-part exercise, use the terms below each paragraph to fill in the blank spaces of that paragraph.
2. Each term may be used only once.

Part 1 Cultural mediation

Cultural mediation is an <u>international</u> term. It usually refers to any act or <u>utterance</u> of the interpreter that is intended to address a cultural <u>misunderstanding</u>. Cultural mediation is also known by other terms, such as <u>culture brokering</u>, cultural interpreting, or <u>cultural clarification</u>.

The remote interpreter will need to learn the expectations that surround cultural mediation in both the country where the participants need interpreting and often in particular specializations of interpreting (such as court versus community interpreting).

For some countries, such as Canada and the UK, for example, even for community (including medical) interpreting you may not be permitted to perform cultural mediation. In others, you may be able to perform cultural mediation in community interpreting but not in courts.

Part 2 Example of cultural mediation

Let's look at one example: the United States. Expectations in the U.S. about cultural mediation are more complex. While in legal interpreting the general attitude among interpreters is not to perform cultural mediation, the actual practice varies. In general, it is permitted in U.S. courts to clarify certain cultural misunderstandings that are either linguistically based or that reference common cultural practices. However, performing such cultural clarification is difficult without advanced legal training, and most remote interpreters should not *attempt it without such training.*

In community, including healthcare, interpreting, U.S. national ethics and standards (NCIHC, 2004 and 2005) lay down a narrow but permitted avenue for interpreters to clarify cultural misunderstandings—not by explaining them, but by inviting one or all parties to offer their own cultural explanations.

Activity 7.2 (a): All those questions again!

Instructions

1. Read the following brief scenario and choose the best answer.
2. Discuss your answers with the class or with another interpreter or colleague.

   A paralegal asks a client multiple questions before the lawyer arrives. The lawyer then starts to ask the same questions. As the interpreter, you:

   b. Continue interpreting the lawyer's questions even though they are the same as the paralegal's.

Activity 7.2 (b): Should you intervene?

Instructions

1. Identify which of these scenarios requires the interpreter to intervene.
2. In the second column, state whether yes, no or maybe you think the interpreter should intervene.
3. In the third column, state your explanation of why the interpreter should intervene or not intervene.

Scenario	Yes, No, Maybe	Explanation
You are interpreting remotely for a lawyer and a client. Communication is flowing well, but when asked for his phone number, the client suddenly switches to the language of the lawyer.	Maybe	You may be able to shadow the communication and not necessarily intervene (for more on shadowing see Volume 1, Chapter 4). However, you may intervene to verify that the phone number was interpreted correctly.
A patient refuses to answer the doctor's questions.	No	The patient has a right to answer (or not to answer) questions as they wish. Refusing to directly answer a provider's questions is an answer. Let the doctor manage the situation.
A school social worker meets with a child's parents to discuss the child's performance at school. She asks if the parents know what ADHD[207] is.	No	The interpreter should interpret the question and not offer an explanation, allowing the parents to give an answer. The social worker will explain the condition if needed.
As an audio interpreter, you notice the internet connection with the bank manager is so poor it prevents you from clear understanding.	Yes	The interpreter should inform both participants about the issue and offer troubleshooting tips to the bank manager to resolve the technical issue or withdraw from the session.
A police officer at a police station needs help communicating with an intoxicated individual who was just brought in for questioning.	Maybe	If any parts of the individual's speech were unintelligible, a request for clarification may be needed. If communication continues to break down despite the request, remain transparent and clearly state as needed that you do not understand the individual being questioned.
In VRI, a social worker is interviewing a client, and the client's answers do not match the questions. For example, when the social worker asks who lives in the household, the client answers that she likes to wake up early in the morning. You interpret everything as stated and the social worker turns to you and says, "Interpreter, that's not what I asked her."	Yes	The interpreter was correct in interpreting what was said, even if it was seemingly irrelevant. Part of communicative autonomy is allowing participants to choose how they communicate. However, since the social worker stated "Interpreter, that's not what I asked her," you need to intervene to first interpret the social worker's statement and then clarify to both participants that you are interpreting everything as stated.

Activity 7.2 (c): Manage the flow

Instructions

Read the scenario below and answer the question that follows it.

> You interpret for a parent-teacher conference on a video remote platform which only allows consecutive interpreting. The mother and father, who are divorced, are both present.
>
> The mother and father start arguing about how to address some of the teacher's concerns with their child.

[207] Attention deficit hyperactivity disorder.

You make various attempts to intervene to ask them to take turns speaking. They ignore your requests. After a few minutes, the teacher says, "OK, interpreter, what did they say?"

As the interpreter, what would you do now?

Guidance: During the session, make sure you are transparent with all participants about your requests for pauses so that the teacher can manage the conversation when the parents argue and do not pause for you to interpret. Since the teacher didn't step in, in this scenario, take as many notes as possible during the argument; then at the first opportunity, remind the participants of the instructions you gave during your introduction or briefing, that is, they need to speak one at a time to ensure your accuracy. Ask for clarification and repetition as needed and, only as a last resort, summarize what the mother and father said. If you do so, report to all parties that you summarized, and when and why you summarized, as soon as feasible.

Activity 7.3 (c): Finish these scripts

Instructions

Refer to the sample scripts in Table 7.2 in Section 7.3 to guide you in completing the unfinished scripts in this activity. Remember that you are the remote interpreter in these scripts.

1. A patient is in a clinic to sign consent forms for her upcoming surgical procedure. Request a clarification for the underlined term.

Nurse: You will be undergoing your spinal tap procedure next week. Do you have any questions about it?

Interpreter: (*to the patient in one language*) This is the interpreter speaking. I need to clarify the term *spinal tap* with the nurse so that I can interpret it accurately.

Interpreter: (*to the nurse in the other language*) This is the interpreter speaking. The interpreter would like to request clarification: can you explain the term "spinal tap" for me so that I can interpret it accurately for the patient?

2. A client is present at a bank appointment, accompanied by two relatives, to complete opening a mortgage loan.

Mortgage officer: Unfortunately, we will not be moving forward with the closing today because you are a permanent resident and not a U.S. citizen.

The officer's remark is interpreted and prompts the client and both family members to become furious. They start speaking loudly all at the same time at the mortgage officer.

Interpreter: (*to mortgage officer*) The interpreter will ask the client and family members to speak one at a time so that I can interpret accurately.

Interpreter: (*to client and family members*) This is the interpreter speaking. I would like to remind you to please speak one at a time so that I can interpret everything accurately for the mortgage officer.

3. An elderly individual is in court to dispute a speeding ticket. When he notices you on the video monitor, his demeanor changes and he becomes agitated.

Defendant: Who is this? Why is she on the monitor? I know her, she's a spy. She works for the government. I'm not talking to her. Turn her off.

You interpret the defendant's statements and try to move forward with the session, but it becomes clear the defendant will not cooperate or respond to you. You see you will need to withdraw so that the court and defendant can resume the session with a different interpreter.

Interpreter: (*to court*) Because the defendant will not speak with the interpreter, the interpreter will remove herself from this call. You will be connected to another interpreter.[208]

Interpreter: (*to defendant, after interpreting the court's response, if any*) Because the defendant will not speak with the interpreter, the interpreter will remove herself from this call. You will be connected to another interpreter.

Activity 7.4 (b): Assess the mediations

Instructions

1. Read the following interpreted interactions.

2. After doing so:

   a. Review the four-step adapted Strategic Mediation Model and identify any steps the interpreter in each scenario did *not* perform.

   b. Write down anything the interpreter may have done *incorrectly*.

   Interaction 1

   The interpreter is interpreting remotely for an individual coming into the Department of Motor Vehicles (DMV).

   DMV representative: All right, everything you need is filled out for your driver's license renewal. But since you're telling me you've changed your last name since you just got married, you'll need to get back out of line and go fill out the green form.

   Interpreter: (*to customer*) OK, you have everything you need filled out for your driver's license renewal. But since you're saying you've changed your last name since your recent wedding...

   Interpreter: (*to DMV representative*) Did you say, "a green sheet for the appointment"?

   Write down any of the four steps of the adapted Strategic Mediation Model that the interpreter did *not* perform.

   The interpreter missed all four steps. The interpreter did not finish interpreting what was just said or signed; identify themselves as the interpreter and inform that participant what they were

208 If you do not work for a language service that can switch out interpreters, adjust this sample script as needed.

about to tell the other participant; identify themselves as the interpreter and mediate briefly with the other participant; or wait for a response (after these three steps, which were not correctly performed) and continue interpreting.

Write down anything the interpreter may have done *incorrectly.*

In addition to the four missed steps, the interpreter was not transparent with the customer that mediation was needed.

Interaction 2

The interpreter is interpreting a telephone conversation between a bank help-line representative and a customer. The customer sent a check by mail to pay their monthly apartment rent, but the check was lost in transit.

Bank representative: Thank you for calling National Bank. My name is Cathy. How may I help you?

Customer: Hello. Yes, I need to cancel a check. It's check number eight nine seven four three. I sent it to pay my rent on the first of the month, and it got lost in the mail!

Bank representative: OK, no problem. I can stop the check. In order to proceed, I'll need you to consent to our transaction discontinuation procedure. By consenting, you agree to our one-time fee of twenty dollars. You also acknowledge that if the original recipient were to attempt to cash the check, you also may be charged a fee. Do you want to continue?

Customer: What? No, I just want to stop the check.

Bank representative: (*Sighs loudly in frustration.*) Interpreter, clearly you're not saying everything right. Tell her what I said again.

Interpreter: *(to bank representative*) Ma'am, I just said everything exactly as you said it, but I don't think she understands.

Write down any of the four steps of the adapted Strategic Mediation Model that the interpreter did *not* perform.

The interpreter missed all four steps. The interpreter did not interpret what was just said or signed; identify themselves as the interpreter and inform that participant what they were about to tell the other participant; identify themselves as the interpreter and mediate briefly with the other participant; or wait for a response (after these three steps, which were not performed) and continue interpreting.

Write down anything the interpreter may have done *incorrectly.*

In addition to the four missed steps, the interpreter was not transparent with the customer that mediation was needed, added their own assumption by stating that the customer didn't understand and sounded condescending about the customer.

Interaction 3

A young English-speaking woman booked a trip for her family of five to an all-inclusive resort in another country. She has just called the travel agency. Since the travel agency is based in the destination country, she needs an interpreter to speak with them.

Travel agent: Hello, thank you for calling Best Trips Ever Bookings. My name is Tomas. How may I help you?

Customer: Hi. Yes, my name is Sharon Brodie. I booked the all-inclusive resorts package for this week. We're actually on the trip now...but we have a situation. We were at the hotel restaurant and bar, and we got charged a huge tab for alcohol. But we didn't have any drinks! I've tried settling this with the hotel directly, but they won't listen. I know whose bill it is. It was the couple next to us that night. They were pissed!

Travel agent: OK, ma'am, I'd be happy to help you sort this out. I do see your booking here. But help me to understand. Was the couple's anger directed at your family specifically?

Customer: What? They weren't angry. We didn't even talk to them.

(*The interpreter interprets everything but realizes they interpreted the term "pissed" with the term's American meaning of angry, but the customer is from the UK. In the UK, the term "pissed" means drunk or inebriated.*)

Interpreter: (*to travel agent*) The interpreter would like to request clarification from the customer.

Interpreter: (*to customer*) The interpreter would like to request clarification of the term "pissed." Did you mean they were angry or that they were drunk?

Customer: (*laughs*) No, no! They weren't angry. Far from it. They were happily drunk. They were smashed, wasted, sozzled!

Write down any of the four steps of the adapted Strategic Mediation Model that the interpreter did *not* perform.

The interpreter performed all four steps.

Write down anything the interpreter may have done *incorrectly.*

In the perspective of many people, the interpreter here has done nothing incorrectly. However, the interpreter was not fully transparent with the travel agency employee, perhaps to disguise their own mistake. The two mediations should have been mirror reflections of each other. Because of this lack of transparency, when the interpreter resumes interpreting, the travel agent may be confused due to not knowing where the misunderstanding came from.

Activity 7.5 (a): Healthcare: blood transfusion

Instructions

1. Read the following scenario.

2. Answer the multiple-choice question that follows it.

You take a video call for the emergency department. The patient is a 10-year-old boy brought in by his mother. The boy has been in an accident and needs a blood transfusion.

Doctor: I know it's difficult seeing your son like this, ma'am. But I do believe he's going to be all right. When you arrived, you told the nurse you're OK with your son receiving a blood transfusion if it's necessary to save his life.

Mother: Yes.

Doctor: OK. I do recommend we give him blood. I have the consent form here for you to sign so we can go ahead and start the procedure.

Mother: My husband is on his way. He can sign the consent.

Doctor: Time is of the essence. It will be better if you can sign now so we can start setting everything up. You can always call your husband as soon as you sign to let him know what's going on.

Mother: No, no, I prefer we wait for him. He'll be here pretty soon. I don't want to sign anything without him here.

Doctor: OK. Just so you know, as the boy's mother, you do have the right to sign the consent without your husband present.

Mother: I know he would want us to wait for him. I can't sign without him here, and I prefer he signs the consent.

As the interpreter, you decide to…(choose one option below)

a. Interpret the conversation and allow the participants to sort out the decision.

b. Point out that there may be a cultural difference regarding blood transfusions in the patient's religion.

c. Point out that there may be a cultural difference in how family medical decisions are made and invite the participants to explore that idea.

d. Emphasize the time-sensitive nature of the procedure in your interpretation since you see the mother doesn't understand the urgency.

e. Take another action.

Note: This is a complex scenario, and other answers are possible.

Activity 7.5 (c): Addressing cultural misunderstandings

You are interpreting a meeting between a Somali student's parents and the school principal (head teacher). The school has many Somali students. The parents express frustration that the school will remain open during Eid al-Fitr, an important holiday in the Islamic calendar. The principal does not understand what the issue is. The school is closed on many other holidays, but you understand this is an important holiday in the Somali community. The student has already had a lot of unexplained absences in the school year, and the principal is denying the parents' request to take their child out of school for three or four more days.

What would you say to the participants in this case? Answer yes, no or maybe if it is appropriate to use the scripts below and briefly explain your answer. *Assume that all scripts would be relayed in both languages.*

Script for Addressing Cultural Misunderstandings with Participants	Yes, No Maybe	Explanation
1. (to the principal): "Eid al-Fitr is a major religious holiday in the Somali community. You should approve the parents' request."	No	The interpreter is expressing their own opinion instead of guiding the participants to find a resolution.
2. (to the principal): "This is the interpreter. Please ask about the student's unexplained absences. There may be a cultural misunderstanding."	No	The misunderstanding likely has to do with the holiday, not the absences.
3. (to the parents): "Muslim holidays are not acknowledged here. This request will not be approved no matter what you say."	No	The interpreter is expressing their own opinion instead of guiding the participants to find a resolution.
4. (to the principal): "The interpreter would like to point out a possible cultural misunderstanding related to the importance of this holiday in the family's community. You may wish to ask the parents about it."	Yes	This is an ideal script to start with as it does not assume anything and redirects participants to discuss the issue themselves.
5. (to the principal): "The interpreter would like to explain that Eid al-Fitr is a major holiday in the Somali community. You may wish to discuss its importance with the parents."	Maybe	This script should only be used if the participants still do not realize what the cultural misunderstanding is after you use script four (or something similar). The interpreter here is clearly identifying what seems to be causing the cultural misunderstanding and guides the principal to address it with the parents.

Activity 8.1 (b): What may the interpreter say?

Instructions

1. Read the following script.
2. If you are in a classroom, act out the script in groups of three with an interpreter who does not read (or see) the script.
3. Now imagine that for the rest of the encounter, the survivor describes her rape in graphic detail. You are the interpreter.

4. Next, imagine you are the interpreter going home to talk about your day to a partner or spouse, a family member or a roommate.
5. Look at the list of statements (in quotes) listed below "What May the Interpreter Say?"; then rewrite each statement under one of the three appropriate categories in the blank lines below each category label.

Advocate: Hi, my name is Jean Smith. The sexual assault crisis center sent me here.

Survivor: My name is Maria. Why are you here?

Advocate: I'm here because I am an advocate. As soon as the police bring anyone here for a sexual assault exam, our center sends out an advocate to support you and be here for you because we know this can be a scary experience and we don't want you to feel alone. You seem a bit nervous and upset—has anyone upset you?

Survivor: The police brought me here. I didn't ask for any exam or an advocate. The hospital and police keep asking me for my address.

Advocate: I know, and please understand that everyone wants you to feel safe here. The hospital needs that information, like your address, so you won't get charged for the exam. The police need it to investigate your case. Would you feel safe sharing your address so they can take care of all that and then you don't have to worry about the cost?

Survivor: (*sighing*) My address is 11234 Castle Creek Road, Austin, Texas.

Advocate: Miss Maria, what is your Social Security number? It's just for the hospital, not the police, and the hospital absolutely will not share it. That is strictly your confidential information.

Survivor: All right. It's 314-55-4141

Advocate: Thank you, I'll go get the nurse for you. And would you like some blankets? And then I can go and get you some snacks too. Would you prefer apple juice or orange juice? And can I get you a sandwich, granola bars, raisins, nuts or a candy bar?

What May the Interpreter Say?

Take the following statements and insert each statement (by rewriting it) into the blank lines of *one* of the three sections below, in the category you find most appropriate.

- "I had a very sad call today about sexual assault."
- "Didn't you have a Jean Smith in your social work program? I interpreted for her today! I don't think she recognized me on the video."
- "I interpreted for someone who lives a block away from us today! Can you believe that? She lives at 11234. I think it's the yellow house."
- "So, I had this session today, for a 'Maria.' It took me a second, but I realized this Maria is a very famous singer back home in our country. The other people had no idea who she was."

- "I had a rough session today, but I'm thankful I was able to help by interpreting for the survivor."
- "You're not going to believe what happened today! Someone I interpreted for today was a mom from the kids' school. I almost didn't recognize her in the video and I almost never see people I know. I can't mention details, but I don't want our kids hanging around those kids anymore."
- "I had one session today that really struck a chord with me. The survivor of sexual assault had the same name as one of my cousins, who went through something similar."
- "Even though I can't share details about it, I had a really tough interpreting session today. Let's watch something funny on TV tonight."
- (*Interpreter's partner*) "Do you need this phone number you have written down on this piece of paper?" (*Interpreter*) "Oh, wait! That's not a phone number. That's a Social Security number I wrote down from my notes!"

1. What the interpreter *may* say (legally and ethically)

- "I had a very sad call today about sexual assault."
- "I had a rough session today, but I'm thankful I was able to help by interpreting for the survivor."
- "Even though I can't share details about it, I had a really tough interpreting session today. Let's watch something funny on TV tonight."

2. What the interpreter may legally say but probably shouldn't (to protect and respect the survivor's privacy and out of caution).

- "You're not going to believe what happened today! Someone I interpreted for today was a mom from the kids' school. I almost didn't recognize her in the video and I almost never see people I know. I can't mention details, but I don't want our kids hanging around those kids anymore."
- "I had one session today that really struck a chord with me. The survivor of sexual assault had the same name as one of my cousins, who went through something similar."

3. What the interpreter *must not say* for legal and other reasons.

- "Didn't you have a Jean Smith in your social work program? I interpreted for her today! I don't think she recognized me on the video."
- "I interpreted for someone who lives a block away from us today! Can you believe that? She lives at 11234. I think it's the yellow house."
- "So, I had this session today, for a 'Maria.' It took me a second, but I realized this Maria is a very famous singer back home in our country. The other people had no idea who she was."

- (*Interpreter's partner*) "Do you need this phone number you have written down on this piece of paper?" (*Interpreter*) "Oh, wait! That's not a phone number. That's a Social Security number I wrote down from my notes!"

Activity 8.3 (b): Employee or self-employed

Instructions

1. Review the list of remote interpreting expectations and requirements for interpreters below.
2. Decide for each one whether that statement pertains to being *employee*, *self-employed*, or *both*.
3. Write one of those terms (the most relevant one) in the blank line that follows each statement.

- Start your shift on time. *Both.*
- Ensure technical support is available. *Both. Interpreters employed by a language service will have access to the company's IT support for themselves. Self-employed interpreters may have to act as technical support for their clients.*
- Have adequate hardware/computer. *Both.*
- Have headsets. *Both.*
- Abide by scheduled breaks/mealtimes. *Employee.*
- Monitor your own performance/self-assessment. *Both.*
- Engage in professional development. *Both. This could be a requirement if you're an employee, however, all interpreters should pursue professional development.*
- Ensure the fulfillment of CEUs. *Both. This could be a requirement if you're an employee, however, all interpreters should pursue professional development.*
- Complete qualifying training. *Both.*
- Obtain certification, if applicable. *Both. Certification could be a requirement for both employees and self-employed interpreters. All interpreters should seek applicable certifications available to them.*
- Abide by state/governmental policies and regulations. *Both.*
- Pass a language proficiency test. *Both.*
- Follow clothing etiquette. *Both. Depending on if you appear on camera.*
- Have supplies available, such as paper, pen, pencil, shredder. *Both.*
- Make sure internet connectivity is reliable and adequate. *Both.*
- Abide by code of ethics and standards of practice. *Both.*
- Carry out established protocols. *Both.*

- Apply hard and soft skills. *Both.*
- Provide a noise-free environment. *Both.*
- Uphold professional conduct. *Both.*
- Engage in self-care and support personal wellness. *Both.*
- Understand and take advantage of fringe benefits (for example, retirement plan, paid time off, insurance). *Employee.*
- Watch for camera presence. *Both. Depending on if you appear on camera.*
- Assure adequate furniture, lighting, backdrop, etc. *Both. Depending on if you appear on camera.*

Bibliography

Abel, L. (2009). *Language Access in State Courts.* Brennan Center for Justice at New York University School of Law. Retrieved from: file:///C:/Users/jonim/Downloads/Report_LanguageAccessinStateCourts.pdf

ADA. (1990). Introduction to the Americans with Disabilities Act. Retrieved from: https://www.ada.gov/ada_intro.htm

Agentschap. (2015). *Training and Certification of Social Interpreters in Flanders.* Leen Veerraest, Agentschap Integratie en Inburgering / Kruispunt Migratie-Integratie. Retrieved from: https://ec.europa.eu/education/knowledge-centre-interpretation/sites/default/files/soctolkenvertalen_eng_def.pdf

Akhulkova, Y., Hickey, S., & Hynes, R. (2022). *Nimdzi Language Technology Atlas: The Definitive Guide to the Language Technology Landscape.* Nimdzi Insights. Retrieved from: https://www.nimdzi.com/language-technology-atlas/?output=pdf

Allen, K. (2015). Note-taking for Consecutive Interpreting. In M.A. Bancroft (Ed.). *The Community Interpreter®: An International Textbook.* Culture & Language Press, pp. 174-189.

Amato, A., Spinolo, N., & González Rodríguez, M.J. (Eds.). (2015). *Handbook of Remote Interpreting. SHIFT in Orality Erasmus+ Project.*

ASTM International. (2020). ASTM F2889-11(2020). *Standard Practice for Assessing Language Proficiency.* American Society for Testing and Materials International.

AUSIT. (2012). AUSIT *Code of Ethics and Code of Conduct*. Australian Institute of Interpreters and Translators. Retrieved from: https://ausit.org/wp-content/uploads/2020/02/Code_Of_Ethics_Full.pdf

Bancroft, M.A. (2005). *The Interpreter's World Tour: An Environmental Scan of Standards of Practice for Interpreters.* California Endowment.

Bancroft, M.A., García-Beyaert, S., Allen, K., Carriero-Contreras, G., & Socarrás-Estrada, D. (2015). In M.A. Bancroft (Ed.). *The Community Interpreter®: An International Textbook.* Culture & Language Press.

Bancroft, M.A., García-Beyaert, S., Allen, K., Carriero-Contreras, G., & Socarrás-Estrada, D. (2016). In M.A. Bancroft (Ed.). *The Medical Interpreter: A Foundation Textbook for Medical Interpreting.* Culture & Language Press.

Beukes, A-M. (2009). Translation in South Africa: The Politics of Transmission. *Southern African Linguistics and Applied Language Studies, 24*(1), pp. 1-6.

Braun, S. (2015). Remote Interpreting. In H. Mikkelson, & R. Jourdenais (Eds.). *Routledge Handbook of Interpreting.*

Braun, S., & Taylor, J.L. (Eds.). (2012). *Videoconference and Remote Interpreting in Criminal Proceedings.* Intersentia.

Burruss, C.C., Bjornsen, E., & Gallagher, K.M. (2021). Examining Potential User Experience Trade-Offs Between Common Computer Display Configurations. *Human Factors: The Journal of the Human Factors and Ergonomics Society.* Retrieved from: https://journals.sagepub.com/doi/10.1177/00187208211018344

Canadian Charter of Rights and Freedoms. (1982). Section 14—Right to an Interpreter. Retrieved from: https://www.justice.gc.ca/eng/csj-sjc/rfc-dlc/ccrf-ccdl/check/art14.html

CDC. (2022). Health Insurance Portability and Accountability Act of 1996 (HIPAA). Centers for Disease Control and Prevention. Retrieved from: https://www.cdc.gov/phlp/publications/topic/hipaa.html#:~:text=Health%20Insurance%20Portability%20and%20Accountability%20Act%20of%201996%20(HIPAA),-On%20This%20Page&text=The%20Health%20Insurance%-20Portability%20and,the%20patient's%20consent%20or%20knowledge

Chen, A.H., Youdelman, M.K., & Brooks, J. (2007). The Legal Framework for Language Access in Healthcare Settings: Title VI and Beyond. *Journal of General Internal Medicine, 22*(S2), pp. 362–367. Retrieved from: https://doi.org/10.1007/s11606-007-0366-2

Chen, S. (2017). The Construct of Cognitive Load in Interpreting and Its Measurement. *Perspectives, 25*(4), pp. 640-657.

Commonwealth of Australia. (2013). *Multicultural Language Services Guidelines for Australian Government Agencies.* Retrieved from: https://www.dss.gov.au/sites/default/files/files/foi_disclosure_log/12-12-13/multicultural-lang-services-guidelines.docx

Cox, A. (2015). Do You Get the Message? Defining the Interpreter's Role in Medical Interpreting in Belgium. *Monographs in Translation and Interpreting—Special Issue,* pp. 161-184.

Cunningham, D., & Hatoss, A. (2005). *An International Perspective on Language Policies, Practices and Proficiencies.* Retrieved from: https://eprints.usq.edu.au/3042/1/Cunningham_Hatoss.pdf

Dawson, H., Hernandez, A., & Shain, C. (Eds.). (2022). *Language Files: Materials for an Introduction to Language and Linguistics.* (13th ed.). The Ohio State University Press.

Dean, R.K., & Pollard Jr., R.Q. (2011). Context-based Ethical Reasoning in Interpreting. *The Interpreter and Translator Trainer, 5*(1), pp. 155-182. Retrieved from: http://intrpr.info/library/dean-pollard-context-based-ethical-reasoning-in-interpreting.pdf

Dean, R.K., & Pollard Jr., R.Q. (2022). Improving Interpreters' Normative Ethics Discourse by Imparting Principled-Reasoning Through Case Analysis. *Interpreting and Society: An Interdisciplinary Journal, 2*(1), pp. 1-18. Retrieved from: https://journals.sagepub.com/doi/10.1177/27523810211068449

Department of Local Government, Sport and Cultural Industries. (2020). *Western Australian Language Services Policy 2020.* Western Australia: Office of Multicultural Interests Retrieved from: https://www.omi.wa.gov.au/docs/librariesprovider2/language-services-policy-2020/wa-language-services-policy-guide_2020_edited2.pdf?sfvrsn=51165610_4

Dewey, J. (1933). *How We Think: A Restatement of the Relation of Reflective Thinking to the Educative Process*. D.C. Heath & Company.

Downie, J. (2019). *Interpreters vs. Machines: Can Interpreters Survive in an AI-Dominated World?* Routledge.

Flerov, C. (2013, updated 2020). On Comintern and Hush-a-Phone: Early History of Simultaneous Interpretation Equipment. aiic.net. Retrieved from: https://aiic.org/document/893/AIICWebzine_2013_Issue63_5_FLEROV_On_Comintern_and_Hush-a-Phone_Early_history_of_simultaneous_interpretation_equipment_EN.pdf

Framer, I., Bancroft, M.A., Feurle, L., & Bruggeman, J. (2010). *The Language of Justice: Interpreting for Legal Services.* Culture & Language Press.

Gaiba, F. (1998). *The Origins of Simultaneous Interpretation: The Nuremberg Trial.* University of Ottawa Press.

Gallagher, K.M., Cameron, L., De Carvalho, D., & Boulé, M. (2021). Does Using Multiple Computer Monitors for Office Tasks Affect User Experience? A Systematic Review. *Human Factors, 63*(1), pp. 433-449.

Gany, F., Leng, J., Shapiro, E., Abramson, D., Motola, I., Shield, D.C., & Changrani, J. (2007). Patient Satisfaction with Different Interpreting Methods: A Randomized Controlled Trial. *Journal of General Internal Medicine, 22*(2), pp. 312-318.

García-Beyaert, S. (2015). The Role of the Community Interpreter. In M.A. Bancroft (Ed.). *The Community Interpreter®: An International Textbook.* Culture & Language Press, pp. 359-442.

García-Beyaert, S., Bancroft, M.A., Allen, K., Carriero-Contreras, G., & Socarrás-Estrada, D. (2015). *Ethics and Standards for the Community Interpreter®: An International Training Tool.* Culture & Language Press.

GDPR.eu. (2019). GDPR Compliance. General Data Protection Regulation. Retrieved from: https://gdpr.eu/

Goldsmith, J., & Bowman, N. (2021). *The Interpreter's Guide to Audio and Video.* Techforward.

Griffin, J. (2013). *How to Say It: Creating Complete Customer Satisfaction: Winning Words, Phrases, and Strategies to Build Lasting Relationships in Sales and Service*. Prentice Hall Press.

Hale. S. (2007). *Community Interpreting.* Palgrave Macmillan.

Hickey, S. (2021). The 2021 Nimdzi Interpreting Index. Nimzdi Insights. Retrieved from: https://www.nimdzi.com/interpreting-index-top-interpreting-companies/#Remote-interpreting-is-here-to-stay

HIN. (2010). *National Standard Guide for Community Interpreting Services*. Healthcare Interpretation Network. Retrieved from: https://docslib.org/doc/13359189/national-standard-guide-for-community-interpreting-services-published-by-the-healthcare-interpretation-network-hin-toronto-canada

Hornberger, J.C., Gibson Jr., C.D., Wood, W., Dequeldre, C., Corso, I., Palla, B., & Bloch, D.A. (1996). Eliminating Language Barriers for Non-English-Speaking Patients. *Medical Care, 34*(8), pp. 845-856.

ISO. (2014). Interpreting—Guidelines for Community Interpreting. 13611:2014. International Organization for Standardization.

ISO. (2018). Interpreting Services: General Requirements and Recommendations. 18841:2018. International Organization for Standardization.

ISO. (2019a). Interpreting Services—Legal Interpreting—Requirements. 20228:2019. International Organization for Standardization.

ISO. (2019b). Translation, Interpreting and Related Technology—Vocabulary. 20539:2019. International Organization for Standardization.

ISO. (2020). Interpreting Services—Healthcare Interpreting—Requirements and Recommendations. 21998:2020. International Organization for Standardization.

ISO. (2022a). Interpreting Services—Conference Interpreting—Requirements and Recommendations. 23155:2022. International Organization for Standardization.

ISO. (2022). Simultaneous Interpreting Delivery Platforms—Requirements and Recommendations. 24019:2022. International Organization for Standardization.

JCCD. (2022b). *Recommended National Standards for Working with Interpreters in Courts and Tribunals.* (2nd ed.). Judicial Council on Cultural Diversity. Retrieved from: https://www.naati.com.au/wp-content/uploads/2022/04/JCDD-Recommended-National-Standards-for-Working-with-Interpreters-in-Courts-and-Tribunals-second-edition.pdf

John, A., Poonamjeet, L., Peter, M., & Musa, N. (2015). Demographic Patterns of Acoustic Shock Syndrome as Seen in a Large Call Centre. *Occupational Medicine & Health Affairs, 3*(4), pp. 1-2. Retrieved from: https://pdfs.semanticscholar.org/1c9d/ad5d22b16f2c92e79bacef9c631c2e95fbd0.pdf?_ga=2.110675778.676031370.1665495845-1062426509.1646692000

Johnson, K. (2020). Google Translate Launches Transcribe for Android in Eight Languages. Retrieved from: https://venturebeat.com/ai/google-translate-launches-transcribe-for-android-in-8-languages/

Kahneman, D. (2011). *Thinking, Fast and Slow*. Farrar, Straus and Giroux.

Kelly, N. (2008). *Telephone Interpreting: A Comprehensive Guide to the Profession.* Trafford Publishing.

Kimbrough, K. (2021). What Will the World of Work Look Like in 2022? Expect Employees to Remain in the Driver's Seat, Demanding More Out of Work. Retrieved from: https://www.linkedin.com/pulse/what-world-work-look-like-2022-expect-employees-remain-kimbrough

Kimbrough, K. (2022). The Great Reshuffle in 2022: Top Trends to Watch. Retrieved from: https://www.linkedin.com/pulse/great-reshuffle-2022-top-trends-watch-karin-kimbrough

Laurent Clerc National Deaf Education Center. (n.d.). Interpretation and Translation. Retrieved from: https://gallaudet.edu/interpretation-and-translation/

Locatis, C., Williamson, D., Sterrett, J., Detzler, I., & Ackerman, M. (2011). Video Medical Interpretation over 3G Cellular Networks: A Feasibility Study. *Telemedicine and e-Health, 17*(10), pp. 809–813.

McFerren, D. (2015). Acoustic Shock. *Canadian Audiologist, 2*(2). Retrieved from: https://canadianaudiologist.ca/acoustic-shock/

Mikkelson, H. (1999). Relay Interpreting: A Solution for Languages of Limited Diffusion? *The Translator, 5*(2). Retrieved from: https://acebo.myshopify.com/pages/relay-interpreting-a-solution-for-languages-of-limited-diffusion

Mikkelson, H., & Jourdenais, R. (Eds.). (2015). *Routledge Handbook of Interpreting.* Routledge.

Moore, G.E. (1965). The Future of Integrated Electronics. Retrieved from: https://archive.computerhistory.org/resources/access/text/2017/03/102770836-05-01-acc.pdf Originally published as Cramming More Components onto Integrated Circuits. *Electronics, 38*(8), pp. 114-133. Retrieved from: https://www.computerhistory.org/collections/catalog/102770836

NAATI. (2018). *One Year in Transition: Annual Report 2017/18.* National Accreditation Authority for Translators and Interpreters. Retrieved from: https://www.naati.com.au/wp-content/uploads/2020/10/Annual-Report-2017-2018.pdf

NAD-RID. (2005). *NAD-RID Code of Professional Conduct.* National Association of the Deaf (NAD) and Registry of Interpreters for the Deaf (RID). Retrieved from: https://acrobat.adobe.com/link/track?uri=urn%3Aaaid%3Ascds%3AUS%3A154885ef-2f50-3664-ba5e-f9654c395ddf&viewer%21megaVerb=group-discover

NAJIT. (2020). *Team Interpreting in Court-Related Proceedings.* Position Paper. [U.S.] National Association of Judiciary Interpreters and Translators. Retrieved from: https://najit.org/wp-content/uploads/2016/09/Team-Interpreting-5.2020.pdf

National Health Service. (2021). Self-help Tips to Fight Tiredness. Retrieved from: https://www.nhs.uk/live-well/sleep-and-tiredness/self-help-tips-to-fight-fatigue/

NCIHC. (2003). *Guide to Interpreter Positioning in Health Care Settings.* The National Council on Interpreting in Health Care Working Papers Series. Retrieved from: https://www.ncihc.org/assets/documents/workingpapers/NCIHC%20Working%20Paper%20-%20Guide%20to%20Interpreter%20Positioning%20in%20Health%20Care%20Settings.pdf

NCIHC. (2004). *A National Code of Ethics for Interpreters in Health Care.* The National Council on Interpreting in Health Care. Retrieved from: https://www.ncihc.org/assets/documents/publications/NCIHC%20National%20Code%20of%20Ethics.pdf

NCIHC. (2009). *Sight Translation and Written Translation: Guidelines for Healthcare Interpreters.* The National Council on Interpreting in Health Care. Retrieved from: https://www.ncihc.org/assets/documents/publications/Translation_Guidelines_for_Interpreters_FINAL042709.pdf

Noreña, A.J., Fournier, P., Londero, A., Ponsot, D., & Charpentier, N. (2018). An Integrative Model Accounting for the Symptom Cluster Triggered After an Acoustic Shock. *Trends in Hearing, 22*. Retrieved from: https://journals.sagepub.com/doi/full/10.1177/2331216518801725

NRPSI. (2016). Code of Professional Conduct. National Register of Public Service Interpreters. Retrieved from: https://www.nrpsi.org.uk/for-clients-of-interpreters/code-of-professional-conduct.html

Office for Civil Rights. (2020). Guidance to Federal Financial Assistance Recipients Regarding Title VI and the Prohibition Against National Origin Discrimination Affecting Limited English Proficient Persons—Summary. U.S. Department of Health and Human Services. Retrieved from: https://www.hhs.gov/civil-rights/for-providers/laws-regulations-guidance/guidance-federal-financial-assistance-title-vi/index.html

Pielmeier, H., & O'Mara, P. (2020). The State of the Linguist Supply Chain. CSA Research. Retrieved from: https://docslib.org/doc/9191165/the-state-of-the-linguist-supply-chain-translators-and-interpreters-in-2020-by-h%C3%A9l%C3%A8ne-pielmeier-and-paul-o-mara-january-2020

Pienaar, M., & Cornelius, E. (2015). Contemporary Perceptions of Interpreting in South Africa. *Nordic Journal of African Studies, 24*(2), pp. 186-206. Retrieved from: https://www.researchgate.net/publication/297714810_Contemporary_Perceptions_of_Interpreting_in_South_Africa

Pöchhacker, F. (2016). *Introducing Interpreting Studies* (2nd ed.). Routledge.

Pöchhacker, F., & Kelly, N. (2015). Telephone Interpreting. *Routledge Encyclopedia of Interpreting Studies*. Routledge.

Rickford, J., & King, S. (2016). Language and Linguistics on Trial: Hearing Rachel Jeantel (and Other Vernacular Speakers) in the Courtroom and Beyond. *Language, 92*(4), pp. 948-988. Retrieved from: http://johnrickford.com/portals/45/documents/papers/Rickford_and_King_2016_Language_and_Linguistics_on_Trial-Hearing_Rachel_Jeantel_and_Other_Vernacular_Speakers_in_the_Courtroom_and_Beyond.pdf

Roziner, I., & Shlesinger, M. (2010). Much Ado About Something Remote: Stress and Performance in Remote Interpreting. *Interpreting, 12*(2), pp. 214-247.

Seeber, K.G. (2022). When Less Is Not More: Sound Quality in Remote Interpreting. UN Today. Retrieved from: https://untoday.org/when-less-is-not-more-sound-quality-in-remote-interpreting/

Shlesinger, M. (2010). Relay Interpreting. *Handbook of Translation Studies.* Volume 1. John Benjamins Publishing Company, pp. 276–278.

Skovsholm, K. (2000). South Africa's System of Official Languages. *Verfassung Und Recht in Übersee / Law and Politics in Africa, Asia and Latin America, 33*(1), pp. 5–25.

Smith, A. (n.d.). *Indigenous Peoples and Boarding Schools: A Comparative Study.* Secretariat of the United Nations Permanent Forum on Indigenous Issues. Retrieved from: https://www.un.org/esa/socdev/unpfii/documents/E_C_19_2009_crp1.pdf

Socarrás-Estrada, D. (2016). Interpreting Protocols and Skills. In M.A. Bancroft (Ed.). *The Medical® Interpreter: A Foundation Textbook for Medical Interpreting.* Culture & Language Press, pp. 83-127.

Stockler-Rex, S., & González-Cestari, T. (2020) Volume V: Behind the Scenes of Video Remote Interpreting. Retrieved from: https://www.cloudbreak.us/2020/10/23/behind_the_scenes_vri/

Tay, S.W., Ryan, P., & Ryan, C.A. (2016). Systems 1 and 2 Thinking Processes and Cognitive Reflection Testing in Medical Students. *Canadian Medical Education Journal, 7*(2): e97–e103.

U.S. Department of Justice, Civil Rights Division. (2016). *Language Access in State Courts.* Retrieved from: https://www.justice.gov/crt/file/892036/download#:~:text=State%20courts%20can%20provide%20language%20access%20in%20many,hearing%20information%20spoken%20in%20one%20language%20and%20orally

University of Pittsburgh, Institutional Review Board. (2014). *Privacy Versus Confidentiality.* Retrieved from: https://www.hrpo.pitt.edu/sites/default/files/privacy_vs_conf_4.1.2014.pdf

Verrept, H., & Coune, I. (2016). *Guide for Intercultural Mediation in Health Care.* FPS Health, Safety of the Food Chain and Environment. Retrieved from: https://www.health.belgium.be/sites/default/files/uploads/fields/fpshealth_theme_file/2017_11_14_guide_english_0.pdf

WA DSHS. (n.d.). *Professional Language Certification Examination Manual.* State of Washington Department of Social and Health Services. Retrieved from: https://www.dshs.wa.gov/sites/default/files/ltc/documents/ExamManualWebVersion.pdf

Whiteside, F. (2019). Why American Sign Language Interpreters Are Bilingual, Bicultural, and Bimodal. Cloudbreak Health. Retrieved from: https://www.cloudbreak.us/2019/10/21/asl-interpreters/

Youdelman, M. (2019). Summary of State Law Requirements Addressing Language Needs in Health Care. National Health Law Program. Retrieved from: https://healthlaw.org/resource/summary-of-state-law-requirements-addressing-language-needs-in-health-care-2/

Zhu, X., & Aryadoust, V. (2022). A Synthetic Review of Cognitive Load in Distance Interpreting: Toward an Explanatory Model. *Frontiers in Psychology, 13*:899718. Retrieved from: https://www.frontiersin.org/articles/10.3389/fpsyg.2022.899718/full

Bibliography: Codes of ethics

Note: The following entries reflect only codes of ethics cited in Chapter 6. Titles of the documents listed here and/or the organizations that published them are provided in English only in cases where the relevant organizations provided English translations.

ACTTI. (2020). *Código de ética de la ACTTI*. Associación colombiana de traductores, terminológos e intérpretes (Colombian Association of Translators, Terminologists and Interpreters).

AFILS. (2016). *Code déontologique*. Association française des interprètes et traducteurs en langues des signes (French Association of Interpreters and Sign Language Translators).

AIIC. (2018). *Code of Professional Ethics.* Association Internationale des Interprètes de Conférence (International Association of Conference Interpreters).

AIT. (2009). *Code of Ethics.* Association of Interpreters and Translators.

AITI. (2013). *Code of Professional Ethics and Conduct.* Associazone Italiana Traduttori e Interpreti.

AMITAS. (n.d.). *AMITAS Code of Ethics for Medical Interpreters and Translators.* American Medical Interpreters and Translators Association.

ANIMU. (n.d.). *Codice Deontologico per gli interpreti L.I.S.* Associazione nazionale interpreti di lingua dei segni italiana (Italian Association of Sign Language Interpreters).

APTS. (n.d.). *Code of Ethics*. Arab Professional Translators Society.

AQILS. (2016). *Code de déontologie des interprétes de l'Aquils.* Association québécoise des interprètes en langue des signes (Quebec Association of Sign Language Interpreters).

ARILS. (1998). *Code de déontologie.* Association Romande des Interprètes en Langues de Signes (Romand Association of Sign Language Interpreters).

ASLI. (n.d.). Codice deontological per gli interpreti L.I.S. Associazione Nazionale Interpreti di Lingua dei Segni Italiana (Italian National Association of Sign Langauge Interpreters).

AssITIG. (2012), *Codice deontologico e responsabilità professionali.* Associazione Italiana Traduttori e Interpreti Giudiziari.

Assointerpreti. (2015). *Codice deontologico.* Assointerpreti.

ASTM International. (2020). ASTM F2889-11(2020). *Standard Practice for Assessing Language Proficiency.* American Society for Testing and Materials International.

ASTTI. (1999). *Code de déontologie de l'Association suisse des traducteurs, terminologues et interprètes*. L'Association suisse des traducteurs, terminologues et interprètes.

ATA. (2010). *Code of Ethics and Professional Practice.* American Translators Association.

ATIM. (1997). *Code of Ethics.* Association of Translators, Terminologists and Interpreters of Manitoba.

AUSIT. (2013). *Code of Ethics for Translating and Interpreting Professionals.* Australian Institute of Interpreters and Translators.

AVLIC/CASLI. (n.d.). *Code of Ethics and Guidelines for Professional Conduct.* Association of Visual Language Interpreters of Canada/Canada Association of Sign Language Interpreters.

BDG. (2020). *Ehrenkodex der GebärdensprachdolmetscherInnen.* Berufsverbandes der GebärdensprachdolmetscherInnen Deutschschweiz (Professional Association of Sign Language Interpreters in German-speaking Switzerland).

BDU. (2014). *Befus- und Ehrenordnung.* Bundesverband der Dolmetcsher und Übersetzer e.V.

BGSD. (2018). *Berufs- und Ehrenordnung der Dolmetscher/-innen und Übersetzer/-innen des BGSD.* Bundesverband der Geberärdensprachdolmetscherinnen Deutschlands e.V (Federal Association of German Sign Language Interpreters).

CCC Cyf. (2014). *Cod Ymddygiad Proffesiynol.* Cymdeithas Cyfieithwyr Cymru (Association of Welsh Translators and Interpreters).

Center for Interpretation and Translation Studies, University of Hawaii. (n.d.). *Interpreter Code of Ethics.*

CHIA. (2002). *California Standards for Healthcare Interpreters: Ethical Principles, Protocols and Guidance on Roles and Intervention.* California Healthcare Interpreting Association.

CIP. (2018). *Court Interpreter Handbook.* Ministry of Attorney General, British Columbia, Court Services Branch Court Interpreting Program.

CONADIS. (2020). *Código de Conducta Profesional para los Intérpretes de la Lengua de Señas Mexicana.* Consejo Nacional para el Desarollo y la Inclusión de las Personas con Discapacidad.

CTE. (1999). *Déontologie du traducteur-interprète assermenté.* Chambre des Experts-Traducteurs et Traducteurs Jurés de l'Est.

CTPSF. (1992). *Códiga de Ética.* Colegio de traductores de la provincial de Santa Fe.

DPTS. (2014). *Code of Ethics of the Court Interpreter Section of the Association of Translators and Interpreters of Slovenia.* Association of Translators and Interpreters of Slovenia.

EU/EC. (n.d.). *Professional Ethics and Standards* [for conference interpreters]. European Union/European Commission.

EULITA. (2013). *Code of Professional Ethics.* European Legal Interpreters and Translators Association.

EVK. (2018). Viipekeeletõlgi kutse-eetika nõuded. Eesti Viipekeeletõlkide Kutseühing. Estonian Sign Language.

FILSE. (n.d.). *Código deontológico.* Federación Española de Intérpretes de Lengua de Signos y Guías-Intérpretes. Spain.

FIT Europe. (n.d.). *Code of Professional Practice*. International Federation of Translators: Europe.

Hebenstreit, G., Marics, A., & Hlavac, J. (2022). Professional Ethics and Professional Conduct. In UNHCR Austria (Ed.). *Handbook for Interpreters in Asylum Procedures*, United Nations High Commission on Refugees, Austria, pp. 74-88.

HIN. (2007). *National Standard Guide for Community Interpreter Services.* Healthcare Interpreting Network.

HIN. (2010). *National Standard Guide for Community Interpreting Services,* 2nd ed. Healthcare Interpretation Network.

HKCS. (n.d.). *Code of Ethics of CHEER's Interpreters/Translators.* Hong Kong Community Services Centre for Harmony and Enhancement of Ethnic Minority Residents.

HPI. (2013). *Kode Etik Profesi Penerjemah.* Himpunan Penerjemah Indonesia (Association of Indonesian Translators).

IAPTI. (n.d.). *Code of Ethics.* International Association of Professional Translators and Interpreters.

IMIA. (2006). *Code of Ethics for Medical Interpreters*. International Medical Interpreters Association.

ISO. (2014). Interpreting—Guidelines for Community Interpreting. 13611:2014. International Organization for Standardization.

ISO. (2018). Interpreting Services: General Requirements and Recommendations. 18841:2018. International Organization for Standardization.

ISO. (2019). Interpreting Services—Legal Interpreting—Requirements. 20228:2019. International Organization for Standardization.

ISO. (2020). Interpreting Services—Healthcare Interpreting—Requirements and Recommendations. 21998:2020. International Organization for Standardization.

ISO. (2022). Interpreting Services—Conference Interpreting—Requirements and Recommendations. 23155:2022. International Organization for Standardization.

ISO. (2022). Simultaneous Interpreting Delivery Platforms—Requirements and Recommendations. 24019:2022. International Organization for Standardization.

ITA. (n.d.) *Code of Ethics: ITA—Code of Professional Conduct and Business Practices.*

ITIA. (2009). *Code of Ethics for Community Interpreters.* Irish Translators and Interpreters Association.

JASLI. (1997). *Code of Ethics for Certified Interpreters*. Japanese Association of Sign Language Interpreters.

JTP. (2014). *Etický kodex tlumočníků a překladatelů.* Jednota tlumočníků a překladatelů.

Judicial Council of California. (2013). *Professional Standards and Ethics for California Court Interpreters.*

MFTE. (2015). *Etikai kódex.* Magyar Fordítók és Tolmácsok Egyesülete.

MMIA/IMIA. (1995). *Medical Interpreting Standards of Practice.* Massachusetts Medical Interpreting Association/International Medical Interpreting Association.

NAATI. (2013). *Ethics of Interpreting and Translating: A Guide to Obtaining NAATI Credentials.* National Accreditation Authority for Translators and Interpreters.

NAD-RID. (2005). *NAD-RID Code of Professional Conduct.* National Association of the Deaf (NAD) and Registry of Interpreters for the Deaf (RID).

NCIHC. (2004). *A National Code of Ethics for Interpreters in Health Care.* National Council on Interpreting in Health Care.

NCIHC. (2005). *National Standards of Practice for Interpreters in Health Care.* National Council on Interpreting in Health Care.

NCIHC. (2021). *A Deeper Delve into Interpreter Advocacy to Prevent Harm in the Healthcare Encounter.* National Council on Interpreting in Health Care.

NCIHC. (2021). *Interpreter Advocacy in Healthcare Encounters: A Closer Look.* National Council on Interpreting in Health Care.

NETA. (2007). *Code of Professional Ethics.* New England Translators Association.

NRCPD. (2015). *Code of Conduct.* National Registers of Communication Professionals with Deaf and Deafblind. A revised code will come into effect on 1 November 2023.

NSV. (2021). *Beroepscode Schrijftolk.* Nederlandse Schrijftolk Vereniging.

NYSUCS. (2020). *Court Interpreter Manual and Code of Ethics.* New York State Unified Court System.

OTTIAQ. (2020). *Code of Ethics of the Order of Certified Translators, Terminologists and Interpreters of Quebec.*

Queensland Courts. (2022). Guideline: Working with Interpreters in Queensland Courts and Tribunals.

RID. (2005). *NAD-RID Code of Professional Conduct.* Registry of Interpreters for the Deaf

SATI. (n.d.) *SATI Code of Ethics.*

SIGV. (2003). *Erecode.* Vereniging van gerectstolken en juridisch vertalers [court and legal translators and interpreters].

SLIANZ. (2012). *Code of Ethics and Conduct.* Sign Language Interpreters of New Zealand.

SSTD/DPT/ZZTZSZJ/ZKTS. (2021). *Sprejeti slovenski standardi prakse in etični kodeks skupnostnih tolmačev.* Stridon Slovensko translatološko društvo, Društvo prevajalcev in tolmačev, Zavod Združenje tolmačev za slovenski znakovni jezik in Združenje konferenčnih tolmačev Slovenije (Stridon Slovenian Translatological Society, Association of Translators and Interpreters, Institute of Slovenian Sign Language Interpreters and Association of Conference Interpreters of Slovenia).

STP. (1993). *Karta Tłumacza Polskiego.* Association of Polish Translators and Interpreters, *Karta Tłumacza Polskiego.*

TEPIS. (2019). *Kodeks Zawodowy Tlumacza Przysieglego.* Polski Towarzystwo Tlumaczy Przyieglych. Polskie Towarzystwo Tlumaczy Prsysieglychi i Specjalistycznych.

TKTD. (2016). *Etik Kurul Yönetmeligi.* Türkiye Konferans Tercümanian Dernegi (Turkish Conference Interpreters Association).

Tolkvorbundet. (2017). *Tolkeprofesjonens yrkesetiske retningslinjer.* Tolkvorbundet.

Translingua. (n.d.). *Language Interpreting Code of Ethics.*

UN. (1999). *The Code of Ethics for Interpreters and Translators Employed by the International Criminal Tribunal for the Former Yugoslavia.* International Criminal Tribunal for the Former Yugoslavia.

UN MICT. United Nations Mechanism for International Criminal Tribunals.

UNHCR. United Nations High Commissioner for Refugees.

Univerbal. (2016). *Code de déontologie de déontologie de* [sic] *interprète.*

WASLI. World Association of Sign Language Interpreters.

WFD-WASLI. (2018). *WFD-WASLI International Sign Interpreters Code of Conduct.* World Federation of the Deaf-World Association of Sign Language Interpreters.

ZZTZSZJ. (2021). *Etični kodeks skupnostnih tolmače.* Zavod Zdruzenje tolmacev za slovenski znakovni jezik

The Remote Interpreter Evaluation Tool

Part 1: General Performance Skills

Standard 1: Starting and Closing the Session

1.1: Adopts a professional tone and engaged demeanor.
1.2: Provides a complete introduction and closing.

Standard 4: Interactions with Participants

4.1: Instructs participants how to best work with interpreters.
4.2: When intervening, uses professional and culturally appropriate language.

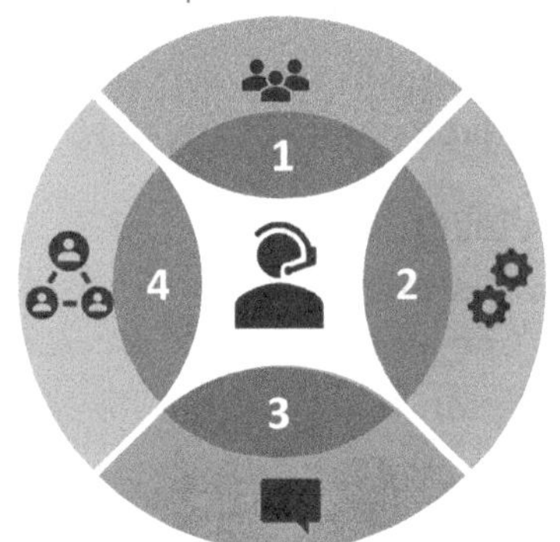

Standard 2: Managing the Session

2.1: Remains professional and calm, using appropriate strategies to manage challenges.
2.2: Stays engaged and focused throughout the session.
2.3: Works in a secure environment throughout the session.

Standard 3: Supporting Communicative Autonomy

3.1: Engages in ethical decision-making that supports communicative autonomy.
3.2: Remains transparent and impartial and redirects participants to speak to each other.
3.3: Intervenes effectively and appropriately to support clear communication.

Figure 5.1: **Part 1: General performance skills**

The Remote Interpreter Evaluation Tool

Part 2: Message Transfer Performance Skills

Standard 5: Accuracy

5.1: Conveys the content, tone and spirit of the source message.
5.2: Avoids omitting, adding to or changing the message.

Standard 8: Terminology

8.1: Uses correct and context-appropriate terminology.
8.2: Researches or verifies the meaning of specialized terms as needed.

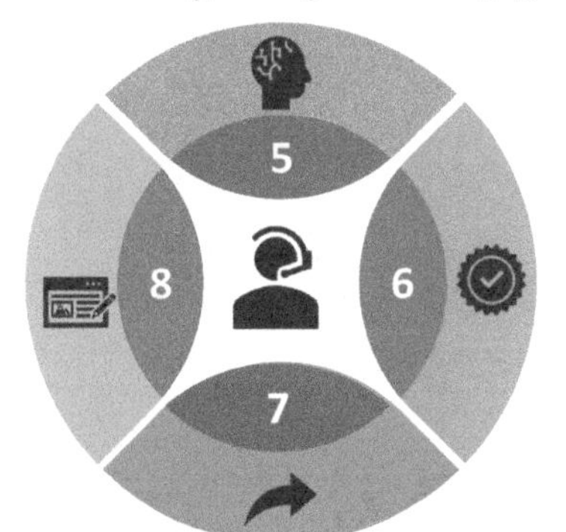

Standard 6: Completeness

6.1: Maintains the language register and style.
6.2: Transparently asks for clarifications, or requests repetitions, as needed.
6.3: Corrects mistakes of interpretation.

Standard 7: Modes

7.4: Selects the appropriate mode, switching as needed.
7.5: Takes notes, when needed, to support accuracy.
7.6: Sight translates if and when appropriate to do so, justifying decisions.

Figure 5.2: **Part 2: Message transfer performance skills**

The Remote Interpreter Self-evaluation Tool Scorecards

Parts 1 and 2

Using the Scorecards

The scorecards for Parts 1 and 2 are meant to help you track your performance. This template allows you to fill in your score, take notes and build a history of your self-evaluation sessions. This is only a template, and you may find ways to adapt it or expand on it to help you track your progress. Feel free to make copies to have handy while assessing your performance.

There is a place to fill in the date, select the modality, as well as the sector. The sector, such as education, business, healthcare, etc., is important. Perhaps one of the benchmarks is easier to perform well in based on the sector for which you are interpreting. Those details can help you further refine your skill development plan.

Use the notes column to explain your score or to remind yourself where you performed well or where you need additional support. At the end of the scorecard, there is space to fill in your final notes and action plan after completing the entire self-evaluation.

The Remote Interpreter Evaluation Tool Scorecard
Part 1: General Performance Skills

Date	OPI or VRI/Specialization	Score	Notes
Standard			
Standard 1: Starting and Closing the Session			
Benchmark 1.1	Adopts a professional tone and engaged demeanor.		
Benchmark 1.2	Provides a complete introduction and closing.		
Standard 1 Score		–/6	
Standard 2: Managing the Session			
Benchmark 2.1	Remains professional, calm and uses appropriate strategies to manage challenges.		
Benchmark 2.2	Stays engaged and focused throughout the session.		
Benchmark 2.3	Works in a secure environment throughout the session.		
Standard 2 Score		–/9	
Standard 3: Supporting Communicative Autonomy			
Benchmark 3.1	Engages in ethical decision-making that supports communicative autonomy.		
Benchmark 3.2	Remains transparent and impartial and redirects participants to speak to each other.		
Benchmark 3.3	Intervenes effectively and appropriately to support clear communication.		
Standard 3 Score		–/9	
Standard 4: Interactions with Participants			
Benchmark 4.1	Instructs participants how to best work with interpreters.		
Benchmark 4.2	When intervening, uses professional and culturally appropriate language.		
Standard 4 Score		–/6	
Final Notes and Action Plan			

The Remote Interpreter Evaluation Tool Scorecard Part 2: Message Transfer Performance Skills			
Standard	**OPI or VRI**	**Score**	**Notes**
Standard 5: Accuracy			
Benchmark 5.1	Conveys the content, tone and spirit of the source message.		
Benchmark 5.2	Avoids omitting, adding to or changing the message.		
Standard 5 Score		–/6	
Standard 6: Completeness			
Benchmark 6.1	Maintains the linguistic register and style.		
Benchmark 6.2	Transparently asks for clarifications, or requests repetitions, as needed.		
Benchmark 6.3	Corrects mistakes of interpretation.		
Standard 6 Score		–/9	
Standard 7: Modes			
Benchmark 7.1	Selects the appropriate mode, switching as needed.		
Benchmark 7.2	Takes notes, when needed, to support accuracy.		
Benchmark 7.3	Sight translates if and when appropriate to do so, justifying decisions.		
Standard 7 Score		–/9	
Standard 8: Terminology			
Benchmark 8.1	Uses correct and context-appropriate terminology.		
Benchmark 8.2	Researches or verifies the meaning of specialized terms as needed		
Standard 8 Score		–/6	
Final Notes and Action Plan